The American Directory *of* Writer's Guidelines

What Editors Want, What Editors Buy

Compiled and Edited
by
John C. Mutchler

Fresno, California

Copyright © 1997 by John C. Mutchler
All Rights Reserved

Published by
Quill Driver Books/Word Dancer Press, Inc.
950 N. Van Ness
P.O. Box 4638
Fresno, California 93744-4638

Printed in The United States of America
FIRST EDITION

Quill Driver Books/Word Dancer Press books may be purchased at special prices for educational, fund-raising, business or promotional use. Please contact:

Special Markets
Quill Driver Books\Word Dancer Press, Inc.
P.O. Box 4638
Fresno, CA 93744-4638
1-800-497-4909

To order an additional copy of this book
please call 1-800-497-4909

ISBN 1-884956-00-9

The American directory of writer's guidelines : what editors want, what editors buy / compiled and edited by John C. Mutchler.

p. cm.

Includes index.

ISBN 1-884956-00-9 (trade paper)

1. Authorship--Handbooks, manuals, etc. 2. Journalism--Authorship--Handbooks, manuals, etc. I. Mutchler, John C., 1945-

.

PN147.A479 1997
070.5'02573--DC21

97-4266
CIP

For Susan,
and
for Rachel and Sarah,
the essence of our love.

Contents

Section One: Periodicals

Section Two: Book Publishers

Acknowledgments

MANY HANDS HELPED ME build this book. Some of the hands involved were patient, hard-working hands. My wife, Susan, became an expert at stuffing and stamping envelopes and at doing whatever had to be done to keep the project moving. My publisher, Steve Mettee, showed continuous patience, as well as good humor, while teaching this author some tricks of the trade.

Two of the hands were mentoring hands in the truest sense. Donald R. Gordon, himself a well-published gentleman, helped me immensely in his role as my instructor for a writing course I was immersed in at the time the idea for this book came to be in me (Long Ridge Writer's Group). D.R. gives best what would-be writers need most: honest critique and words of encouragement backed by the knowledgeable tone of his experience.

Most of the hand prints on the book belong to the many publishers, editors, editors-in-chief, managing editors, editorial directors, editorial assistants and assistant editors, among others, who consented to have their work included as part of my work. It has only been since I started work on this book that I finally achieved a broad understanding of what you are all about. The insight into your collective world has been fascinating.

My hands applaud you all. Thank you.

Introduction

DEAR FELLOW WRITER,

For many years I helped write and produce sales literature, promotional material and product user documentation for corporations such as Litton Industries, Inc. and Johnson Controls, Inc.

I wish I had been fortunate enough during that time to have had clear-cut writer's guidelines to help ensure the first draft of the copy I produced was as close as possible to what it had to be in final form. Many hours of hard work (read *rewrites*) could have been saved, had that been the case.

You might say I learned the hard way that writing without guidelines is a time-consuming and not very rewarding pursuit.

About a year ago I decided to try my hand at writing again and became determined to use what I had learned during those early corporate days to help myself and other writers become better marketers. I decided to create a book to help writers better understand what they had to do to market their work effectively. I knew the key to such a book would be writer's guidelines, not in distilled form, but the real thing.

This book is the result. It is filled with the "real thing." It can help you produce more marketable pieces by guiding your efforts as well as providing you with thousands of fresh ideas on what to write about.

Hundreds of editors from a diverse collection of periodical and book-publishing houses have generously contributed their writer's guidelines for this directory.

Editors create guidelines to explain where they are coming from editorially speaking; to explain *exactly* what they expect to receive from writers. Simply put, these expectations can be boiled down to two things: professionalism in the business end of things, including queries and manuscript format, and—most important—good writing, properly slanted toward the interests of those who read their publications or purchase the books they produce.

Collectively, these guidelines represent a thorough primer on how to become a more successful writer *and* marketer. Study them to discover what editors want, what editors buy.

Such a set of "buyer expectations" is standard fare in most industries. Almost every day, in the course of working at my current day job as business development manager for a small but successful web printing press automation company, I am confronted with the equivalent of writer's guidelines—known as product specifications in the printing equipment industry. Potential buyers of our products and services tell us what they need (or want), and we set out to create the best possible product configuration that will satisfy their requirements. I never argue with these prospects or consider their "demands" unfair. I don't waste their time or mine by trying to offer them something that misses the mark by a wide margin. If we decide that we want to do business with these people, we simply conform to their expectations to the extent possible, sell them on our ability to deliver as promised, and then try our best to deliver a bit more than what we actually promised.

I try to do the same with my writing. I think of the guidelines in this book as "the buyer's expectations." Then I try to meet or exceed these expectations. I encourage you to do so, too, and sincerely hope you'll benefit from perusing them as much as I have.

Best wishes for your writing and marketing success.

John Mutchler

P.S. If you would like to make a comment or suggestion about how this book could be improved, e-mail me at jmutchler@worldnet.att.net

How to Use This Book

• Publications and publishing houses are arranged alphabetically by name: periodicals in Section One and book publishers in Section Two. Contact information for submissions is shown at the end of each set of guidelines.

• At the back are two indexes. The Topic Index is a list of areas of interest such as agriculture, science fiction or woodworking. Names of the publishers interested in seeing material on or relating to these subjects and the page number where the particular publisher's guidelines may be found are listed along with the subject. The General Index provides an alphabetical list of the various publications and publishing houses as well as other items.

When you already have an idea:

If you have a certain subject you wish to write about, consult the Topic Index. Periodical publishers are *italicized*, book publishers are set in roman type. If you know the name of the publisher or periodical you are looking for, look in the General Index.

To develop new ideas:

Brainstorm for article, short story and book ideas by browsing both the guidelines themselves and the Topic Index. Doing so should be enough to shake loose some wonderfully creative thoughts from even the most horribly blocked minds in the writing universe.

Keep track of your submissions:

Photocopy the Submission Tracking Sheet on pages 528 and 529 to track and jot notes about your submissions.

A couple of notes:

The guideline contributors selected the topics under which they are listed from a list supplied to them and added their own subjects when appropriate. The guidelines have been left much as they came in but were edited to avoid repeating *basic* manuscript preparation and submission requirements. You'll find this information in Marketing Your Work Professionally on page 2 and Standard Manuscript Format, page 6. Some publishers have special requirements, so be sure to check individual guidelines carefully before submitting.

Marketing Your Work Professionally

A HIGH-PROFILE MAGAZINE MAY RECEIVE HUNDREDS of submissions each month, yet publish fewer than twenty articles or stories per issue. Likewise, many book publishers receive hundreds of submissions each year, but—without regard for the quality of the submissions—can only publish a small percentage of what comes in.

For argument's sake, and because it'll be pretty close to the truth in many instances, let's say a publisher's acceptance-to-rejection ratio represents a one-in-fifty chance of any individual submission being published. While these are good odds compared with those offered by any of the various state lotteries, one-in-fifty still represents a highly competitive market.

How can you shave these odds? By making certain your submission fits what the editor needs and that your writing, including grammar, spelling and punctuation—along with its physical presentation in the form of your query letter, proposal or manuscript—adheres to professional standards.

A good place to start on this professional course is by studying a publisher's writer's guidelines. It's here, at least in the better-written guidelines, that you'll find exactly what an editor needs in content, word count, tone, focus, voice and the other elements that go into making up a successful submission.

And, although most editors prefer to see query letters or book proposals instead of complete manuscripts, photocopies of art or photographs instead of originals, and are pleased with a standard manuscript format as shown on page 6, if a publisher does have special requirements for submissions, the place to find these requirements is in the publisher's quidelines. Guidelines offer a wealth of information, and the smart—the professional—writer checks them out before submitting.

Making it past the first cut

The stack of unsolicited submissions—in publishing jargon called the "slush pile"—is so tall on the desks of many editors that they have developed methods similar to ones used by individuals in other industries who must deal with a heavy volume of incoming mail.

For example, if a personnel manager advertises to fill a vacancy, she may receive dozens of resumes in response. She may approach the task of evaluating the resumes by sorting them into two piles, those which exhibit a professional appearance and those that do not. This is a "first cut," and the sloppiest of the resumes will not survive it. She assumes those who submitted sloppy resumes will, if hired, do a sloppy job. And it's a good bet she's right.

Editors are not unlike our make-believe personnel manager. Here are some things you can do to assure your submission makes it past the first cut:

• Use 20- to 24-pound, good quality, letter-sized white paper for manuscripts and book proposals. Query letters and cover letters may be on your letterhead. If you use fanfold computer paper, separate the pages and tear off the line holes.

• Type or print on only one side of a page.

• Avoid difficult-to-read copy. Editors prefer clean, dark type. Anything hard to read has a good chance of rejection. Photocopies should be top quality. Handwritten copy is almost always the kiss of death. Check individual guidelines to see if dot-matrix submissions are accepted.

• Unless a publisher's guidelines call for something different, follow a standard manuscript format such as the one shown on page 6 including:

  • Double-space all manuscripts and book proposals (cover letters and query letters are single-spaced.)
  • Allow generous page margins, at least one inch left and right, and one and one-half inches top and bottom. Type the title about one-third of the way down from the top of the first page.
  • Indent paragraphs and leave the right side unjustified.
  • Do not hyphenate words at the end of a line.
  • Include your name, address and daytime telephone number (including area code) on all letters and on the first page of all manuscripts.
  • Include a slug line consisting of your last name, a key word taken from the title of the piece, and the page number at the top of the second and subsequent pages of a manuscript.

• Include an SASE (self-addressed, stamped envelope). Most editors won't acknowledge receipt of or reply to—and some report they don't even read—an unsolicited submission unless it is accompanied by an SASE. This can be a large envelope for the return of all the material you submitted or a business-sized envelope for return of your cover or query letter and perhaps one or two sheets from the publisher. If you do not wish any part of the material you submitted returned to you, you may mark the outside of your submission "recycle if rejected" and include a self-addressed, stamped postcard, with the details of the submission written on it, for an editor to use in acknowledging your submission. If you submit to a foreign publisher, include International Reply Coupons for the return postage. Never include metered postage, coins, currency, checks, or stamps in lieu of affixing the correct postage.

Other things you can do

Focus your submissions to the right publishers. Don't send book proposals on woodcarving to publishers of political commentaries or an article on vegetarian cooking to business magazines. Look through the guidelines for publishers who have a history of publishing material similar to what you plan to submit, then familiarize yourself with exactly what they publish. This is particularly true with periodicals. Obtain and read at least the last four or five issues.

Consider submitting to the less glamourous markets. The large, highly-visible publishers are inundated with submissions and may choose authors with name recognition over others. Search for smaller publishers that specialize in the topic you're writing about or those that don't yet have vast distribution. After you have a few articles or stories published and/or a book or two under your belt, the heavily sought-after publishers are likely to be more receptive to your proposals.

Always submit your highest quality work. This means that you will have double-checked spelling and grammar. It also means that you will have checked your facts. Many editors rely on writers to check facts, quotations, citations, and the spelling of names and foreign words.

How long shall I wait?

Most editors don't have time to spend on the phone with authors calling to see if the editor has read a query letter or book proposal. If five or six weeks have gone by and you haven't heard anything, it's OK to drop the editor a self-addressed, stamped postcard with a note asking about the status of your submission. If you still don't hear anything, the editor is a louse and you should simply move on.

Query letters

Nonfiction editors often want to see query letters instead of book proposals or complete manuscripts. A query letter is simply a one-page, single-spaced letter, addressed to a specific editor by name, asking if he or she would be interested in seeing an article or book proposal.

Query letters need to come right to the point. Begin with a sentence that will capture the attention of the editor, then, in four or five paragraphs, outline what you are proposing and why you are qualified to write it. Since this letter runs the chance of being the only example of your writing the editor is going to see, it needs to be your best. This is no place for extra words or thoughts. Write your query letters crisply and succinctly.

Book proposals

With novels, a writer without a successful track record will nearly always need to submit a finished manuscript, but nonfiction books are often presented and sold to editors—even by first time book authors—before they are written. This is done with an outline called a book proposal. A typical book proposal, about ten to thirty double-spaced pages, consists of an overview that includes a summary of the book, where and to whom the book will sell, an approximation of how many words it will have, what illustrations, if any, will be included, why the author is qualified to write the book and all other pertinent information that may convince the editor to commit to the project. It also includes a table of contents and one or two sample chapters.

Precise instructions for writing a book proposal are contained in *The Portable Writers' Conference* workshop by agent-author Michael Larsen titled "Sell Your Book Before You Write It." *The Portable Writers' Conference* is available at libraries or bookstores.

Electronic submissions

Because it saves re-keyboarding, many publishers now want computer files of a manuscript accepted for publication as well as hard copy. Unfortunately, with all the different word processors and other software programs available, there are many non-interchangeable formats for these files. However, most current software programs can save a text file in a variety of formats, one of which will probably be acceptable to the publisher.

Consult the publisher's guidelines or check with them about which formats are acceptable. If you find you need to convert your files to a format your software can't handle, DataViz, Inc. (55 Corporate Drive Trumbull, CT 06011, 1-800-733-0030) makes a useful utility called Conversions Plus which not only converts format to format for most popular software programs, but will do so across the Macintosh and PC platforms.

Standard Manuscript Format

There is no single correct physical format for a manuscript, but following common format conventions, as shown here, is a good way to say to an editor: "I am a professional." Always use letter-sized, white paper. Always be sure the print is dark and legible. Paper clip sheets together or use a manuscript box; never staple. Be sure to check individual guidelines for special requirements.

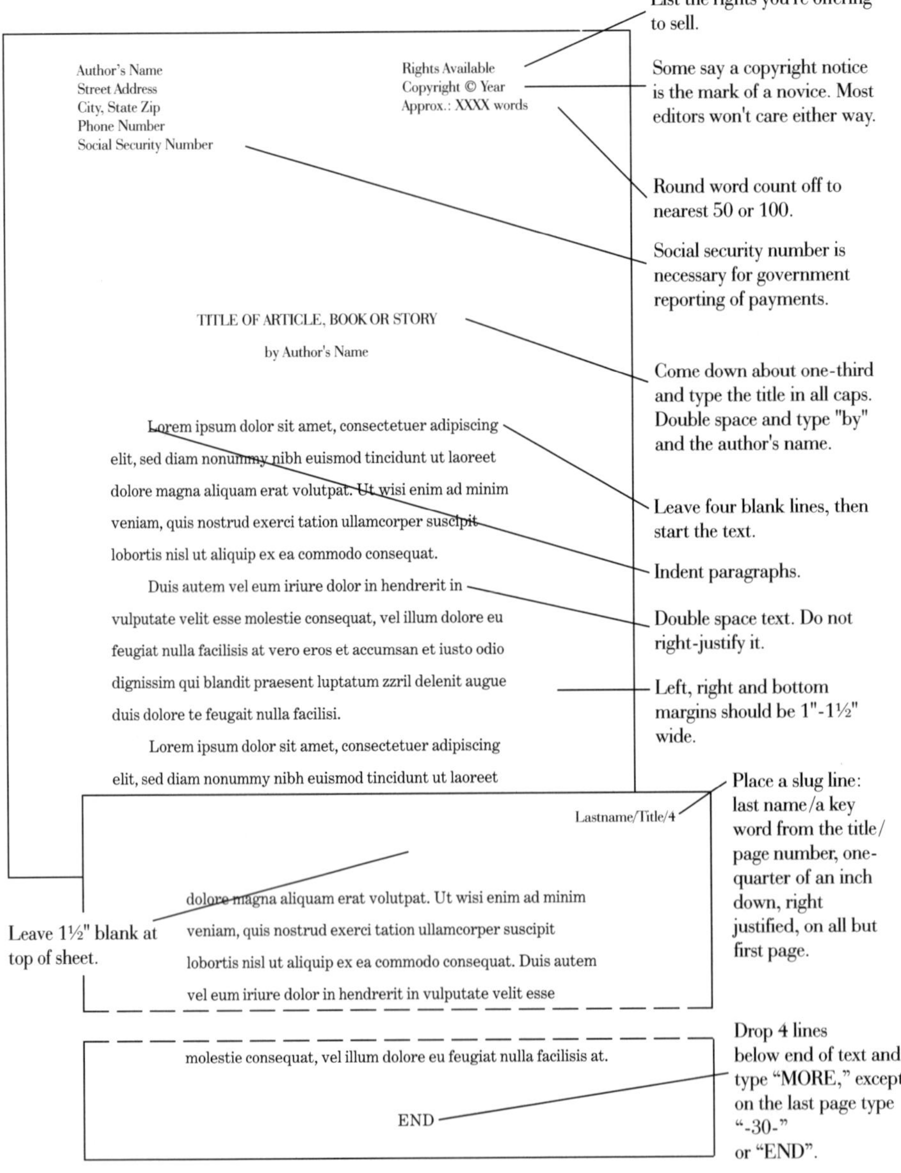
List the rights you're offering to sell.
Author's Name
Street Address
City, State Zip
Phone Number
Social Security Number
Rights Available
Copyright © Year
Approx.: XXXX words
Some say a copyright notice is the mark of a novice. Most editors won't care either way.
Round word count off to nearest 50 or 100.
Social security number is necessary for government reporting of payments.
TITLE OF ARTICLE, BOOK OR STORY
by Author's Name
Come down about one-third and type the title in all caps. Double space and type "by" and the author's name.
Lorem ipsum dolor sit amet, consectetuer adipiscing elit, sed diam nonummy nibh euismod tincidunt ut laoreet dolore magna aliquam erat volutpat. Ut wisi enim ad minim veniam, quis nostrud exerci tation ullamcorper suscipit lobortis nisl ut aliquip ex ea commodo consequat.
Duis autem vel eum iriure dolor in hendrerit in vulputate velit esse molestie consequat, vel illum dolore eu feugiat nulla facilisis at vero eros et accumsan et iusto odio dignissim qui blandit praesent luptatum zzril delenit augue duis dolore te feugait nulla facilisi.
Lorem ipsum dolor sit amet, consectetuer adipiscing elit, sed diam nonummy nibh euismod tincidunt ut laoreet
Leave four blank lines, then start the text.
Indent paragraphs.
Double space text. Do not right-justify it.
Left, right and bottom margins should be 1"-1½" wide.
Lastname/Title/4
Place a slug line: last name/a key word from the title/page number, one-quarter of an inch down, right justified, on all but first page.
dolore magna aliquam erat volutpat. Ut wisi enim ad minim veniam, quis nostrud exerci tation ullamcorper suscipit lobortis nisl ut aliquip ex ea commodo consequat. Duis autem vel eum iriure dolor in hendrerit in vulputate velit esse
Leave 1½" blank at top of sheet.
molestie consequat, vel illum dolore eu feugiat nulla facilisis at.
END
Drop 4 lines below end of text and type "MORE," except on the last page type "-30-" or "END".

Section One
Periodicals

Ad Astra

Ad Astra is the bimonthly magazine of the National Space Society, a nonprofit organization dedicated to promoting space exploration and the establishment of spacefaring civilization. The magazine is circulated to more than 26,000 members of our grassroots organization and to members of Congress and key personnel at the White House and NASA.

Approximately 50% of the articles in *Ad Astra* are submitted by freelance writers and we are always looking for new sources and fresh ideas. The articles are generally nontechnical and cover a wide range of space-related topics.

Feature articles should be between 2,000 - 3,500 words and focus on any issue concerning space or space exploration. Articles with an emphasis on our future in space are of greater relevance to *Ad Astra* than historical accounts. Please query our editorial office prior to submitting any feature article. Unsolicited manuscripts will not be returned. *Ad Astra* pays $150 - $250 for feature articles.

Several single page departments are also open to freelance writers. Most of these articles are donated, though in some cases *Ad Astra* will pay up to $75. These submissions are limited to 750 words and include reviews, editorials and pieces oriented towards education.

All writers should follow the guidelines of the *Associated Press Stylebook*. We prefer submissions on a 3-½" Mac Word, Word for Windows or WordPerfect disk. Disks should include author's name, address and phone number. We can also accept articles transferred by modem in the above formats or in ASCII format. When necessary, we will accept typewritten articles.

We are always looking for exciting and space-related original art. We prefer to receive 35mm slides, 4"x5" transparencies or prints of all artwork or photography. Black and white submissions should be prints of originals. *Please label each piece of artwork with the artist's name, address and phone number for crediting purposes*.

Contact Information:
Submissions
National Space Society
922 Pennsylvania Avenue, SE
Washington, DC 20003-2140
(202) 543-1900 • FAX: (202) 546-4189

Adventure West

America's Guide to Discovering the West

ALL SUBMISSIONS WILL BE PAID UPON PUBLICATION

All stories submitted to the editor will be considered for possible publication. We will respond to written queries or manuscripts within six to eight weeks. We do not accept phone queries. If your query is selected for publication, you will be notified by the assigning editor. Please include your social security number for our records. Submissions must be, whenever possible, accompanied with a 3.5-inch, double-sided disk for use on a Macintosh computer. First North American serial rights to publish stories shall remain with *Adventure West* for a period of six months.

PAYMENT

Articles will be paid in full within 30 days of publication. *Adventure West* will not be held responsible for expenses such as long distance phone calls, mileage, photo developing costs, photocopying or postage. Express mail charges are not reimbursable unless specifically requested by the assigning editor.

Specific fees are listed in department descriptions that follow.

KILL FEES

A 15% kill fee may be paid when a contracted article is not received in a form acceptable to the assigning editor. If a story is contracted but must be rescheduled for a future issue rather than the one for which it was written, the author may either receive a partial payment with the balance of payment received upon future publication or may have the article returned for submission to other publications.

PHOTOGRAPHY RATES 1996

Photographs must be itemized on a separate submission sheet which should include your name, address, telephone number and social security number. This will be used as your receipt. If you do not include an itemized breakdown of the slides you sent, we cannot be responsible for claims of lost slides.

Up to ¼ page	$50
1/3 page	$65
½ page	$75
2/3 page	$100
Full page	$125
1 & 1/3 page	$150
1 & ½ page	$175
1 & 2/3 page	$200
2 full pages	$225
Cover*	$350

All photographs will be returned after the publication is printed; photographs not selected for use will be returned as soon as possible after an initial selection has been made.

*Inset cover photos will be paid at 300% of an interior shot of the same size.

ADVENTURE WEST EDITORIAL CRITERIA

The reader must be able to take action from the text . . . otherwise the story doesn't belong in the magazine. *Adventure West* magazine profiles the people and places in the West that embody the sense of adventure and mystique found only in the West. Our goal is to deliver to our readers those adventures that go beyond the norm. Our stories contain elements of risk and excitement that will inspire our readers to experience adventures for themselves and will provide them with enough information to do them. We go where most readers have not gone, show them what they have not seen and tell them how to actively pursue their goals.

GENERAL GUIDELINES

1. Stories must take place in the 13 western states: Alaska, Arizona, California, Colorado, Hawaii, Idaho, Montana, Nevada, New Mexico, Oregon, Utah, Washington and Wyoming, plus western Canada (British Columbia, Yukon and Alberta) and western Mexico.
2. Stories must challenge or provoke the reader; they must make the reader want to experience it.
3. When possible, they should demonstrate environmental awareness and respect.
4. Stories must be factual and entertaining; always include humor when appropriate.
5. They should include both the positive and negative aspects about each place or experience.

Adventure West articles must also include the following elements:

1. EXCITEMENT - Our readers are risk-takers; therefore, risk must be included in our stories. The risk might be physical or psychological, but it must cause the adrenaline to flow, the emotions to soar. Readers must feel they are with you, or perhaps be thankful they're not.

2. CONTEXT - People are not only interested in traveling to new and exciting places, they are interested in learning about those places as well. Writers should strive to place their stories, and the locations in which they take place, within a cultural, historic or natural-scientific context. Readers should appreciate the value and significance of the stories and their locations.

3. ORIGINALITY - Adventures should be unusual, offbeat and creative. If the story is about an activity, then is there a different way of doing it? If it is about a place that is well-known, then is there something that is often overlooked, an activity not usually done?

4. INFORMATION - Maps, sidebars and side-trip information are key ingredients in our magazine; therefore, we encourage writers to research their topics thoroughly and include helpful tips.

5. A POINT - Stories must have narrative drive (a plot, a challenge to overcome or a build-up to a climax, discovery or insight that will make the reader want to continue). We will not consider simple chronicles of "what I did on my summer vacation" or passive, third- (or second-) person accounts of what activities await the reader in a given region. This information should be blended into the writer's own story.

ADVENTURES OF A LIFETIME

(2,500-3,000 words, including sidebar; provide a map) Pays approximately $725-$875.

Features adventure stories about experiences you will never forget and that may have changed the course of your life. These types of adventures may last from one week to several months and require some degree of expertise. The places may be harder to get to than normal destinations: remote, wild and definitely risky.

LITTLE ADVENTURES

(1,500-2,000 words, including sidebar; provide a map) Pays approximately $425-$575.

These trips require less time, from one day to several days, but still offer a high degree of excitement. It is an adventure only the more open-minded and dedicated would consider.

QUICK GETAWAYS

(1,000-1,500 words, including sidebar; provide a map) Pays approximately $275-$425.

North Americans are foregoing long summer vacations and are taking more frequent, two- to four-day vacations throughout the year. Quick Getaways features the short excursion with comprehensive information about where to stay and what to do in a particular area.

PERSONALITY PROFILE

"Whether rich and famous, or obscure but worthy."

(1,200-1,500 words, including sidebar) Pays approximately $350-$425.

Features people whose lives embody the spirit of adventure. It is not enough to have done something adventurous in life - one's life must be adventurous. This candidate should be a role model.

DISCOVERIES/WESTERN FOOD ADVENTURES

(500-800 words, including sidebar) Pays approximately $150-$240.

Discoveries profiles those hideaways that every adventurer longs to discover, a place that locals know about - a secluded resort, a forgotten canyon, a deserted stretch of beach, a restaurant or recipe. They are places our readers can count on enjoying and Western restaurants or recipes they may not find elsewhere and are sure to enjoy.

LIFE IN THE WEST

(1,250-1,500 words) Pays approximately $375-$425.

This section is an opportunity for readers and writers to send in their stories - preferably humorous - about experiences in getting lost, taking the wrong turn or becoming involved in something that was unpredictable.

THEN AND NOW

(1,000-1,600 words, including sidebar) Pays approximately $300-$480.

This section addresses an historic or cultural aspect of some place in the West. The point is to contrast what a place once was to what it is today.

THINK ABOUT IT

(1,000 words) Pays approximately $300.

This is an editorial section in which we present a balanced, objective, well-researched and intelligent essay about an interesting or controversial subject concerning the outdoors and/or the American West. This is not a political soapbox, rather a forum for provoking thought, debate and understanding.

A TOUCH OF THE OLD WEST

(600 words) Pays approximately $150.

This last page of the magazine is dedicated to the Old West. Historic characters places and traditions are highlighted. A photo or photos must accompany the piece.

ADVENTURE SHOWCASE

(Pay minimum $50.) Readers are asked to submit photographs that capture a specific activity in the West. Each issue, the topic is determined by the department editor. Final photos are selected and featured along with descriptive editorial. The deadline for photo submissions is printed in the magazine.

Contact Information:
Photography/Adventures of a Lifetime: Brian Beffort, Editor
Personalities/Little Adventures: Michael Oliver, Associate Editor
Discoveries/History: Kristina Schreck, Managing Editor
P.O. Box 3210
Incline Village, NV 89451-9423
(702) 832-1641 • FAX: (702) 832-1640

Air & Space Smithsonian

AIR&SPACE/Smithsonian is a general interest magazine about flight. Its purpose is to enlighten and to entertain. Its goal is to show readers, both the knowledgeable and the novice, facets of the enterprise of flight that they are unlikely to encounter elsewhere. The emphasis is on the human rather than the technological, on the ideas behind events, rather than a simple recounting of details

Writing should be clear, accurate, and engaging. It should be free of technical and insider jargon, and generous with explanation and background.

The first step every aspiring contributor should take is to study recent issues of the magazine. If back issues are unavailable at your public library, you may obtain a sample copy by sending a check or money order for $3.50 (includes postage) payable to AIR&SPACE/ Smithsonian. Our address is below; please be sure to include yours.

The next step is to submit a one-page proposal introducing the article you envision. Describe the approach, the sources, and the possibilities for illustration, as well as your credentials. Editors read proposals especially to evaluate writing skill and imaginativeness of approach. Clips should accompany the proposal.

For first time contributors, writing a department - a short piece that often has a personal point of view - offers the best chance for acceptance. Payment for departments is usually between $500 and $1,000, except for Soundings and Reviews, which generally pays $150 to $300. Departments include:

Above & Beyond: a first person narrative of an adventure in air or space. Many have been written by pilots and astronauts. An "I was there" flavor is essential. (1,500 words)

Flights & Fancy: a whimsical, brief reflection that should leave the reader chuckling quietly. This department offers the opportunity for a range of tones, from nostalgic to mischievous to satiric. (800-1,000 words)

Soundings: short news items reporting oddball or amusing events, efforts, or situations; also, the stories behind the news. Soundings need to be fairly current. (300-1,000 words)

Reviews & Previews: a description and critique of a soon-to-be-released book, video, movie, or slide set. Reviewers should have specific experience or knowledge that enables them to give informed evaluations. Quotations from the text must be accompanied by page numbers. (200-1,000 words)

Collections: a tour of a museum, domestic or international, that displays air- or space-related artifacts. Off-the-beaten-path collections are preferred to well-known ones. The piece should evoke both a sense of place and the subculture of flight the facility represents. (800 words)

From the Field: a first person account of an experiment or program in aviation or spaceflight. Should reflect on the broader implications - cultural, historical, sociological - of the work observed. (1,500 words)

Oldies and Oddities: a bit of funky, little-known history; generally records the rise and fall of a design or idea that was ingenious but doomed. Descriptions of the personalities behind the brainstorms are especially encouraged. (1,500 words)

Feature articles: These require substantial research and reporting and average 2,500 words. Fees vary widely, depending on the type of treatment proposed but are generally between $1000 and $2,500. In the event that an article is not accepted for publication, a kill fee is negotiated. Payment for First North American Serial Rights is made upon acceptance.

Contact Information:

Feature proposals: Linda Shiner, Senior Editor
Short matter, news: Pat Trenner, Departments Editor
901 D Street, SW
Washington, DC 20024
(202) 287-3733 • FAX: (202) 287-3163

Air Force Times

(Please refer to Times News Service)

Alfred Hitchcock Mystery Magazine

Thank you for your request for these Writer's Guidelines. Finding new authors is a great pleasure for all of us here, and we look forward to reading the fiction you send us. Since we do read all submissions, there is no need to query first; please send the entire story. You don't need an agent.

Content: Because this is a mystery magazine, the stories we buy must fall into that genre in some sense or another. We are interested in nearly every kind of mystery, however: stories of detection of the classic kind, police procedurals, private eye tales, suspense, courtroom dramas, stories of espionage, and so on. We ask only that the story be about a crime (or the threat or fear of one). We sometimes accept ghost stories or supernatural tales, but those also should involve a crime.

You might find it useful to read one or more issues of *AHMM*; that should give you an idea of the kind of fiction we buy. For a sample copy, send a check made out to *AHMM* for $4.00 to Meghan Germinder at the address below.

Style: We prefer that stories not be longer than 14,000 words; most of the stories in the magazine are considerably shorter than that. They should, of course, be well written. We are looking for stories that have not been previously published elsewhere, and among them for those that are fresh, well-told, and absorbing. They should be entirely fiction, please do not send us stories based on actual crimes, for instance, or other true events.

Manuscript preparation: Manuscripts should have your name and address at the top of the first page. The title of the story as well as the byline you want to use should be on the first page of the story also. (We prefer that there not be a separate title page.) If you use a word processor, please do not justify the right-hand margin. Every page of the story should be numbered, preferably in the upper right-hand corner. If you number the pages by hand, be sure before you start that no page has been omitted. Underline words to indicate italics.

Indent for each paragraph. Do not leave 1-line spaces between paragraphs. The number of lines per page should be uniform, or mostly so.

Stories should be mailed to us flat, with the pages bound together by a paper clip only —not stapled or enclosed in a binder. A cover letter isn't necessary. If you have sent us a photocopy and do not want it back, please advise us of that and enclose a smaller SASE for our response.

Revisions: Revised versions of a story should be submitted only on our request, as a rule. At the very least, tell us in a cover letter that the story has been submitted before but has been revised, and explain how.

NOTE: Stories submitted to *AHMM* are not also considered by or for *Ellery Queen's Mystery* magazine, though we share the same address. Submissions to *EQMM* must be made separately.

We do not accept multiple submissions.

Contact Information:
Submissions Editor
1270 Avenue of The Americas - 10th Floor
New York, NY 10020
(212) 698-1313

Aloha
The Magazine of Hawai'i and the Pacific

ALOHA, The Magazine of Hawai'i is a bimonthly regional magazine of international interest. The majority of this publication's audience is outside the state of Hawai'i, although most readers have been to the Islands at least once. Even given this fact, the magazine is directed primarily to residents of Hawai'i in the belief that presenting material to an immediate critical audience will result in a true and accurate presentation that can be appreciated by everyone.

EDITORIAL CONTENT

ALOHA offers a wide variety of subject matter, all of which is Hawai'i-related. Categories generally covered in each issue and open to freelance writers are the arts, business, people, sports, destinations, food, interiors, history, Hawaiiana, fiction and poetry. All material with historical background must be thoroughly researched with a bibliography provided. Words in the Hawaiian language must be accurately spelled and correctly used. Dialect is not generally appreciated. Neither do we want vivid word pictures of romantic sunsets and swaying palms. Fiction depicting a tourist's adventures in Waikiki is not what we're looking for. As a general statement, we welcome material reflecting the true Hawaiian experience.

LENGTH

Depending on the depth of the story material, manuscripts can run to 4,000 words, with 2,000 to 3,000 being the average length.

PROCEDURE

We prefer to receive queries on all proposed submissions, with the exception of fiction and poetry. Both queries and completed manuscripts should be mailed to Cheryl Chee Tsutsumi, Editorial Director, at the address below. Upon acceptance, a letter confirming the assignment will be mailed.

MANUSCRIPTS

The University of Chicago's *Manual of Style* is our accepted book of style. Hawaiian language words are not italicized, although all other non-English words are. Where the word "Island" is used to replace the word "Hawaiian," it is capitalized. Do not hyphenate words at the end of a typed line. We appreciate receiving a copy on a disc, in Macintosh Microsoft Word format.

RATES

Payment for stories ranges between $150 and $400. Payment for poetry is $30. Payment is made within 30 days after publication. ALOHA purchases first North American serial rights and requires a signed contract, including the writer's social security number and General Excise Tax number, before payment can be made. If accepted for publication, the original manuscript will not be returned.

PHOTOGRAPHY GUIDELINES

ALOHA features one photo essay in each issue "Beautiful Hawai'i," which is a collection of photographs illustrating that theme. A second photo essay by a sole photographer on a specific theme is featured on occasion. Queries are essential for the sole photographer essay. Decisions concerning photography for Beautiful Hawai'i are made during the first week of every other month, beginning January 10. Transparencies must be properly captioned and submitted in clear plastic-slide sheets. All photographs are returned after use.

SIZE

Minimum size for black-and-white prints is 5"x7", with 8"xl0" preferred. Minimum size for transparencies is 35mm. Color prints are rarely used.

All prints must bear the photographer's name, address and brief caption information. Even though caption sheets might accompany photographs, key location words on the photographs are very helpful. Caution: do not use paper clips to attach photo information as they may damage the slides.

RATES

ALOHA buys one-time rights to most photos used. Standard rates are:

- $25 each for black-and-white photographs.
- $75 each for color photos used inside the magazine (less than full page).
- $100 each for photos used as a full-page.
- $125 each for photos used as a double-page spread.
- $250 for photographs selected for an ALOHA cover, Model releases are required for identifiable people in a cover shot.
- Assignments: Some assignment work is available on a flat fee basis.

ALOHA assumes liability for loss or damage of up to $500 for each original transparency accepted (maximum of $5,000). Liability for duplicate transparencies is limited to the cost of replacement.

SAMPLE COPIES

One sample copy of ALOHA is available at $2.95 plus $3.20 postage.

Contact Information:
P.O. Box 3260
Honolulu, HI 96801
(808) 593-1191 • FAX: (808) 593-1327

American Astrology

THE EDITORS are always happy to review original, unpublished articles relating to astrology. We are interested in features that cover all facets of astrology, but we are especially interested in the following topics, listed in current order of preference:

1) Profiles of current newsmakers or celebrities, as long as they are based on complete and verifiable birth data.

2) "How-to" articles that teach the elementary level student more about astrology.

3) "Case history" articles that show astrology at work in individual lives, illustrating this through the use of transits, progressions, return charts, etc.

4) Theoretical or research pieces, written so they are accessible to a nontechnical audience.

5) Humorous, tongue-in-cheek pieces illustrating astrological principles or satirizing astrological foibles.

6) General articles about the Sun, Moon or planets in signs or houses.

Rules for submission: Be sure to list your Social Security number in your cover letter or on the first page of your manuscript. Note: Submissions sent on computer disk without an accompanying manuscript will not be read, as dealing with the many different possible disk and word-processor formats makes for too many difficulties at this stage of the process.

If a word processor or computer is used: Please enclose a note about what computer and word processing program you're using, as we may be able to use your files in the editing process.

Data and sources: Make sure to include data sources and complete birth data for every chart used, even if the data itself is not to be published. In your article itself, be as explicit as possible about your sources. For example, don't just say your data is from "Jane Doe," but mention in what book or article (and in what issue of which magazine), or in what other source, she states this data. And what was her source? If she doesn't give it, mention that; if she does, let us know what it is. On your charts, mark the house system used, as well as the latitude and longitude and the sidereal time, as these will be useful in recalculating and checking your work.

Acknowledgment: We make an effort to acknowledge all submissions with a letter of acceptance or rejection within 30 days from the date we receive it, though on occasion it might take longer. Allowing time for the manuscript to reach us and our letter to reach you, this means that you should allow at least six weeks for us to look at your manuscript and give you an answer.

We look forward to seeing your articles. Good luck with your writing!

Contact Information:
Kenneth Irving, Co-Editor
Lee Chapman, Co-Editor
P.O. Box 140713
Staten Island, NY 10314-0713
E-mail: AAEDITORS@aol.com (No e-mail submissions, please.)

American Brewer

American Brewer is a business magazine for the micro and pub brewing industry. This trade magazine is a must for anyone interested in building a brewpub. It covers everything from styles and varieties of beers to personalities who have shaped the industry. Articles should be informative and fun to read!

Contact Information:
Bill Owen, Publisher/Brewmaster
Box 510
Hayward, CA 94543-0510
(510) 538-9500 • FAX: (510) 538-7644
Web site: www.ambrew.com

American Careers

Publication Information

American Careers magazine is published three times during the school year for middle school, junior high school, high school and vocational-technical school students. Each issue contains up-to-date information on emerging careers, self-assessment questionnaires, how-to articles and other stories designed to promote career awareness, exploration and education.

Assignment Procedures

1. Many of our stories are provided at no charge by authors in business, education and

government. Career Communications, Inc., sometimes makes work-for-hire assignments or buys all rights.

2. We assign stories by phone or letter detailing the story idea and focus, possible contacts, deadline, etc. We may ask you to include photographs, or suggest sources for photographs or other art to illustrate your article.

3. A signed contract must be on file before any payment is made.

4. We accept late copy only if you consult with us first. Writers who do not meet deadlines may not receive future assignments.

5. You may submit story ideas. Please query in writing.

Payment Rate

1. Payment rate varies with assignment.

2. Payment is made within 30 days of receipt of assigned work.

3. Reasonable expenses, approved in advance and documented, will be reimbursed within 30 days.

Copy Requirements

1. We request a hard copy of your manuscript along with a Macintosh-compatible diskette (Quark, Microsoft Word or WordPerfect programs preferred). If you use another word processing program, submit in text format.

2. Use a head and page number on each page.

4. When possible we would appreciate photographs complementing your article, particularly photos of specific people addressed in your story.

5. Submit permission slips or release forms from all people photographed and all photographers. Also submit a list of all resources and a list of all the names, addresses and phone numbers of your interviewees with each article.

6. Also submit one sentence of biographical information with your story.

Style

1. Reading Level/Story Length. Articles should be written at a seventh-grade reading level, or they will be returned for rewrite. Articles in *American Careers* usually run from 300 - 750 words. Some topics may require additional space for impact and clarity. These topics are discussed on an individual basis. Sometimes we run half-page or single-page items on topics such as recent career news or people who have been successful climbing the career ladder.

2. Style. Use the *Associated Press Stylebook* as a guide for style.

3. Names. First reference to students should include complete name, age (where relevant), class (e.g., freshman), school attended, location (city and state) and major (if possible). First reference to teachers and other adults should include complete name, position, school or company and location. Use first names in subsequent references to students. Use last names in subsequent references to teachers and other adults.

4. Focus. Stories should exhibit a balanced national focus, unless the assignment covers only one region or school.

5. Other Style Matters. Style matters particular to *American Careers* will be handled in editing. Career Communications, Inc., reserves the right to edit and revise all materials for publication.

Deadline and Issue Dates

Copy	*Deadline*	*Issue date*
Fall Issue	June 15	Sept. 15
Winter Issue	Oct. 15	Jan. 15
Spring Issue	Jan. 15	April 15

Contact Information:
Career Information: Mary Pitchford, Editor
6701 West 64th Street
Overland Park, KS 66202
(913) 362-7788 • FAX: (913) 362-4864

American Health

Dear Friend,

AMERICAN HEALTH is always looking for stories that are new, authoritative, and helpful to readers. We cover both the scientific and lifestyle aspects of health, nutrition and fitness. In each issue we run several feature articles of 1,000 to 3,000 words as well as 20 to 30 shorter news items of 100 to 350 words each.

Ideas for feature articles are largely generated by editors at the magazine although we are open to proposals from experienced journalists.

The best way to help us decide about a story suggestion is with a written query. You should submit ideas in a few paragraphs, offering the best possible sample of your writing style and approach to the material as well as describing the value of the story and its basic facts. You may include a resume and a clip or two.

We also read completed manuscripts sent to us on speculation.

We look forward to hearing from you.

Contact Information:
Editorial
American Health Magazine
28 West 23rd Street
New York, NY 10010
(212) 366-8900

American Medical News

American Medical News is the nation's most widely circulated newspaper focusing on socioeconomic issues in medicine. Published weekly by the American Medical Association, *AMN* covers the full spectrum of non-clinical news affecting physicians' practices. Our primary readers are about 320,000 physicians, most of whom receive the publication free as part of their AMA membership. Readers also include administrators of health-care organizations, government health-care policy makers and others with a professional interest in physicians and the U.S. health-care system.

AMN contracts with a relatively small group of freelance writers for news and feature articles that focus on policy development, legislation, regulation, economic trends, and physician-impact coverage in the categories that follow. We also seek articles about innovative efforts by individuals or groups to improve health-system functioning or physician practice in these areas.

Population health & related trends

- Health promotion and disease prevention: tobacco, alcohol and drug use; family and community violence; maternal and child health, including immunization; clinical preventive services
- Infectious diseases: AIDS; tuberculosis
- Treatment issues: health of targeted groups, including minorities, women, children, adolescents, elderly and disabled; access to care for homeless, medically indigent and rural residents; organ transplantation
- Health protection: environmental and occupational health; accident prevention; food and drug safety
- Impact of health care market trends and policy developments on patients and population health
- How doctors are helping to implement public health goals
- Physician health, well-being and job satisfaction
- Physician-patient relationships
- Consumerism and patients' rights

Professional issues

- Medical education and training, including undergraduate, graduate and continuing medical education, specialty training, certification, credentialing and physician supply issues
- Medical-legal matters, including professional liability, antitrust, fraud, abuse and related questions
- Quality assurance, including licensure, discipline, professional regulation, peer review, outcomes measurement and practice standards
- Professional and clinical ethics
- Technology, medical informatics, the pharmaceutical industry and related biomedical research
- The institution of organized medicine

Health system structure and finance

- Developments in public policy and the private marketplace that affect the structure of the health care industry and determine the conditions, quality and financial rewards of the practice of medicine
- Physician services financing issues, including Medicare, Medicaid, other government payers, Blue Cross and Blue Shield, commercial insurers and managed care; physician pay
- Physician relations with health care delivery systems, including HMOs, PPOs, group practices, hospitals and integrated hospital/physician networks
- Workforce issues: supply of physicians, the mix between specialists and generalists, relations between physicians and other health professions
- Federal and state health system reform efforts

Business

- Practice management, including general small-business issues (i.e. taxes, employment policies, salary and benefits), small-business issues unique to medical practices (i.e. CPT coding, relations with other physicians and third-party payers), contracting with insurers, strategic planning, raising capital, integrating new technology in practice settings, forming partnerships and managing groups

Please submit written queries of about one typewritten page, containing a detailed account of what you intend to cover and beginning with a lead you consider suitable for a finished article. Alternatively, you may submit the story to us on speculation. Send queries to the appropriate topic editor at:

Contact Information:
Barbara Bolsen, Editor
515 North State Street
Chicago, IL 60610
(312) 464-4429

The American Scholar

Articles

The *Scholar* is a quarterly journal published by Phi Beta Kappa for general circulation. Our intent is to have articles by scholars and experts but written in nontechnical language for an intelligent audience. The material that appears in the magazine covers a wide range of subject matter in the arts, sciences, current affairs, history, and literature. We prefer articles between 3,500 and 4,000 words, and we pay up to $500. To be accepted for publication, a manuscript must receive the affirmative votes of the editor and at least two members of the editorial board.

Poetry

Poems for submission to the *Scholar* should be typewritten, and each sheet of paper should bear the name and address of the author and the name of the poem. We have no special requirements of length, form, or content for original poetry. A look at several recent issues of the *Scholar* should give a good idea of the kind of poetry we publish and the way poems look on our pages. We suggest, too, that, from the author's point of view, it is probably most effective if not more than three or four poems are submitted at any one time. We pay $5 for each accepted poem.

We do not have arrangements for sending sample copies of the *Scholar* to prospective contributors. It would be possible, of course, for you to purchase the latest issue for the regular price of $6.95. If you do not care to purchase a copy, your library would probably have copies you could see.

Contact Information:
Essays: Jean Stipicenic, Managing Editor
Book Reviews, Poems: Sandra Costich, Associate Editor
1811 Q Street, NW
Washington, D.C. 20009
(202) 265-3808

American Technology
The Best American Products and Services for Export

American Technology is a business publication designed to promote exports of American products to Vietnam. American Technology is distributed in Vietnam and will be read by Vietnamese buyers in search of products to buy from America.

Vietnam has been experiencing fast economic growth. As Vietnam continues modernizing and investing in key infrastructure projects, the demand for advanced technology, products and services has increased rapidly. We want to showcase the best American technology, products and services.

The objective behind *American Technology* is simple: Vietnamese purchasers have a strong preference for American products but they have no access to information on American companies. Directories, books, periodicals and reference manuals are rare in Vietnam. We will fill this void by putting a copy of American Technology on every Vietnamese decision maker's desk.

We are looking for editorial contributions from all industries. We hope your company may be able to send us a public relations/media package in order to offer our readers expert knowledge on their industry. The more information you can provide us, the more likely it will be published. This would include a company overview, as well as photos, and specific product information.

For more information on *American Technology*, check our Web page at http://www.well.com/www/gdisf/amtech.html

Contact Information:
Ms. Lisa Spivey, Editor/Publisher
Global Directions, Inc.
116 Maiden Lane, 2nd Floor
San Francisco, CA 94108
E-mail: gdisf@aol.com

American Visions

American Visions is the only magazine of its kind, in that it presents the elegant, sophisticated side of African-American culture in a pop-scholarly fashion. Its scope includes the arts, history, literature, cuisine, genealogy and travel—all filtered through the prism of the African-American experience. Though we frequently include a historical perspective on a topic, we are not a scholarly publication. The magazine is reportorial, current and objective rather than academic or polemical.

Our main features run 6 to 8 double-spaced, typewritten pages; department stories run 4 to 6 double-spaced, typewritten pages. Length is ultimately determined by subject matter and illustration possibilities.

If you have not written for us before:

1) Query us with a suggestion of no more than one page, or submit a manuscript on speculation.

2) Send us your resume and three samples of your writing; and

3) Include your telephone number in correspondence.

We suggest that you familiarize yourself with the magazine before querying.

American Visions does not accept fiction or poetry.

Please include a self-addressed, stamped envelope and allow 2 to 3 months for review. Do not send material that you wish to have returned.

DEPARTMENTS

Arts Scene

A potpourri of articles on current events in the realms of theater, film, television, dance, music, visual arts, literature and more.

Books/Recent & Relevant

Reviews of recent releases and their social relevance, as well as profiles of writers and suggested reading lists./Capsule book reviews.

Calendar

A vibrant section listing major cultural events of interest to the black community.

Cuisine

A column devoted to defining an African-American cuisine, sometimes discussing specific foods, sometimes offering profiles of black chefs or restaurateurs, nearly always including a recipe or two.

Film

Articles on the film industry, ranging from profiles of actors, producers, directors and technicians to reviews of theatrical releases.

Genealogy

Essays that encourage readers to explore their ancestry by recommending ideas and strategies, and by relating the adventures of others.

Music Notes/Earworthy

Interviews with musicians, as well as essays on the genres and literature of black music./ Capsule reviews of newly released recordings.

***Technology/Software Titles**

Essays that explore the ways in which computer technology and trends in the industry are affecting African-Americans./Capsule reviews of software titles aimed at the African-American market.

Travel

A historical and pleasure guide to areas of interest to African Americans.

*Future addition.

Contact Information:
Joanne Harris, Editor
1156 15th Street NW, Suite 615
Washington, DC 20005
(202) 496-9593 • FAX: (202) 496-9851

American Woman MotorScene
Sharing The Spirit Of Adventure

AMERICAN WOMAN MOTORSCENE Magazine is a monthly national automotive and recreational motorsports publication geared toward working and family women of all ages and descriptions who are purchasing the 79 million vehicles each year, a $65 billion market. Features include but are not limited to: automotive interests, motorcycling; and four-wheeling. We accept unlimited manuscripts per year. Payment is always on publication, with an average six-month holding period. The AMERICAN WOMAN MOTORSCENE is typically career and/or family oriented, independent, and adventurous. She demands literate, entertaining and useful information from a magazine. Below are some specific suggestions to follow before submitting your manuscript:

Articles or evaluations on vehicles should be written in an educational as well as entertaining format. AWM educates women on vehicle knowledge in a language she understands and can learn from.

Personality Profiles:

These interview-format articles focus on women who are taking a stand by breaking the traditional rules regarding womanhood. She is active in the industry as either a professional making her way to the top or a motorsport adventuress who ultimately serves as a positive role-model to other women that "they can do it, too." One of her many interesting qualities is her love and knowledge of the growing and exciting world of today's American woman motorscene. Please use quotes and humor whenever possible. We like to hear about women who've challenged and overcome hardships, beat the odds, etc. Be sure to include other hobbies and sports she's involved in and add details about her career and family.

Touring and/or Traveling:

Submit articles describing rides/events of special interest. Touring articles must be accompanied by decent, clear black & white glossy photos.* Also, submit particularly female-friendly restaurants, hotels, campgrounds, etc.

Columns:

Commentaries are always welcome. Humor is best. Tell us your views about your respective automotive, motorcycle or motorsport experience, about non-enthusiasts, about anything that relates. Views on women adventurers need an unusual slant to be valuable and interesting. Bimbo stories not welcome. Please try to avoid "my first motorcycle/car stories" unless they are particularly humorous.

Feature articles should be approximately 1,500 words. Columns should be approximately 750 words.

Submissions should be typewritten (dot matrix O.K.), using a 55 character width. They should be submitted on 3-inch disk for MACINTOSH whenever possible. Typed articles reduces fee.

Payment fluctuates between $25 and $100, depending on quality, not length. Special features will be negotiated with the publisher.

Illustrations/ Cartoons:

We are always looking for talented illustrators and cartoonists. Please send your samples for consideration.

Thank you for your interest in AMERICAN WOMAN MOTORSCENE magazine, sharing your spirit of adventure.

*Photo submissions: Only high quality photos will be accepted. Photos must be B&W 5"x7" or 8"x10". We prefer glossy without borders. For color, we prefer either Kodachrome or Fujichrome transparencies. Color prints must be accompanied by negatives/slides.

Contact Information:

B.J. Killeen, Editor
1510 11th Street, Suite 201B
Santa Monica, CA 90402
(310) 260-0192 • FAX: (310) 260-0175

American Woodworker
A Rodale Press, Inc. Publication

AMERICAN WOODWORKER motivates, entertains, and challenges woodworking enthusiasts with accessible, in-depth information that will help them improve their skills.

Our writers are all woodworkers—amateur and pros—who want to share what they know with other craftsmen.

WHAT TO WRITE ABOUT

The best place to look for article ideas is in your own workshop. Maybe you've developed a new technique or designed a clever jig. Maybe you've figured out a better way of doing something. Perhaps you've designed a project that other woodworkers would like to build. Maybe you want to reach others about a skill you're especially good at or share what you've learned about design, finishing, shop layout, etc.

Technique Articles

We're always in need of instructional articles that teach woodworking skills such as joinery, sharpening, safety, machine techniques, machine maintenance, veneering, carving, turning, wood drying, etc. We're especially interested in articles that teach the basic principles of furniture design and construction.

Projects

We're interested in good-looking, well-built original woodworking projects and period reproductions. Projects may range in difficulty from the very simple to the very challenging, from toys to tools to highboys. We'll consider any style of furniture, from period designs to ultramodern.

Our readers want to know how you built your project. What tools, techniques, and materials did you use, and why? What jigs or fixtures did you use in the process? Do you have any anecdotes or historical background on the project that would interest other woodworkers?

HOW TO GET STARTED

1. Get your hands on a recent issue of AMERICAN WOODWORKER and read it. Get a feel for the magazine; the types of articles; the style of writing; and the way that text, drawings, and photos work together and make instructions clear. Find an article that's similar to the article you want to write, and use it as a model when you write.

2. Write us a letter. Describe your article idea or project and be sure to include photos and drawings, if appropriate, to give us a clear idea of what you've got in mind. While you're at it, tell us about yourself. What kind of woodworker are you? What sort of things do you make? Do you have any writing experience? Do you have any drafting or photography skills?

After receiving your letter, we will contact you by mail or by phone within a month and let you know if we can use your idea. If we're interested in your project or article, we'll assign an editor to work with you and you'll receive further instructions. If we can't use your idea, we'll return your materials.

While we will consider unsolicited manuscripts, you stand a much better chance of being published if you send us a query letter first.

WHAT TO SEND ALONG

When you submit an article, be sure to include the following:

- A manuscript with your name, address, daytime telephone number, and Social Security number. Computer disks are also acceptable in either MS-DOS or Apple format. Please indicate word-processing format and version (e.g., WordPerfect 3.2).
- Drawings or sketches that explain processes, jigs and/or construction details with dimensions.
- Color slides of the finished project (if applicable) and/or key steps in the process you're describing. (See PHOTOGRAPHS.)
- Sources for any unusual hardware, tools, finishing materials, etc. mentioned in your article.

PHOTOGRAPHS

Photos for publication must be color slides (transparencies) in 35mm or larger format. Color prints or black-and-white prints are acceptable with a query letter.

If you know how to use a 35mm camera, we encourage you to try taking your own photographs.

For indoor shots without professional flash equipment, we recommend Kodak Ektachrome 160T tungsten slide film. Light your work with two or three 150-watt incandescent lights. Eliminate all daylight, fluorescent light, and flash when using tungsten film.

For outdoor daylight photography, use Ektachrome or Fujichrome slide film. If for some reason you can't supply publishable photos, we can arrange to have a photographer visit your workshop.

DRAWINGS

We don't expect you to draw like Michelangelo. What we're looking for are drawings or sketches that are clear enough to provide our illustrators with the information needed to produce final art. Just do the best you can to illustrate the important points of your article (jigs, tool setups, etc.) or the construction details of your project.

DEPARTMENTS

If you're interested in writing for AMERICAN WOODWORKER Departments, here's what you need to know:

Letters to the Editor—Reader letters on topics of interest to woodworkers. We do not pay for letters to the Editor.

Offcuts—Woodworking news items and anecdotal pieces with a woodworking theme. A maximum of 1,000 words. Minimum payment $50.

Q & A—Woodworking experts answer questions from our readers. This service is free to our readers and we do not pay for questions.

Tech Tips—Woodworkers share their original tips and tricks for doing a job better, faster and easier. We pay $50 for each item we publish and $200 for the best tip of the issue. Submissions must include a short description along with a photo (color prints are OK) or sketch for our illustrator to work from. Sorry, "Tech Tip" submissions cannot be returned.

Gallery—Photos of current work in wood. Submissions must include a description of the piece and a publishable-quality color slide in 35mm format or larger. Enclose a self-addressed envelope for return of slides. We pay $35 for each photo we publish.

Shop Solutions—Versatile jigs, fixtures, or shop accessories that can be explained in one drawing and up to 250 words. If we publish your "Shop Solution," you'll win a valuable prize. (See most recent issue for details.)

PAYMENTS AND RIGHTS

AMERICAN WOODWORKER pays upon publication unless special arrangements have been made in advance. Our standard rate for new authors is $150 per published magazine page. We buy the right to publish the article in AMERICAN WOODWORKER magazine and the option to republish the article in all other media for an additional payment for each use. Freelance photo and illustration rates upon request.

Thanks for your interest in AMERICAN WOODWORKER.

AMERICAN WOODWORKER is a how-to magazine for the woodworking enthusiast, whether amateur or professional. It provides readers with useful, accurate woodworking information in a style that's informal, entertaining, and easy to understand.

AMERICAN WOODWORKER is a reader-written magazine. The articles are written by amateur and professional woodworkers who want to share what they know. You don't need to be an accomplished woodworker to be published in AMERICAN WOODWORKER. Our editors are woodworkers, and they can help you put your ideas into words.

If you'd like to write for AMERICAN WOODWORKER, these guidelines will help you get started. Photographers and illustrators will also find the guidelines helpful.

Davis Sloan, Editor and Publisher

Contact Information:
Proposals: Ellis Walentine, Executive Editor
33 East Minor Street
Emmaus, PA 18098
(610) 967-8315 • FAX: (610) 967-8956

America's Civil War

(Please refer to Cowles History Group)

Américas
Organization of American States

Américas Magazine and the OAS

Américas is a bimonthly publication of the Organization of American States issued in separate English and Spanish editions. Apolitical in content, it seeks to advance mutual understanding among the peoples of the Western Hemisphere. It is a general interest magazine focusing on OAS member nations and relies on freelance contributions from all parts of the Hemisphere.

Type of Articles Desired

The articles in each issue cover a wide variety of topics including culture, history, literature, visual arts (pre-Columbian, colonial, modern), performing arts, architecture, science, destinations, the environment and economics. Articles should not report on events as news, but rather focus on their broader implications. Highly technical articles and articles of limited interest are not used.

Américas is especially interested in articles that portray contemporary developments in the hemisphere. OAS member countries include: Antigua and Barbuda, Argentina, Barbados, Belize, Bolivia, Brazil, Canada, Chile, Colombia, Commonwealth of Dominica, Commonwealth of the Bahamas, Costa Rica, Cuba, the Dominican Republic, Ecuador, El Salvador, Grenada, Guatemala, Guyana, Haiti, Honduras, Jamaica, Mexico, Nicaragua, Panamá, Paraguay, Peru, St. Kitts and Nevis, Saint Lucia, Saint Vincent and the Grenadines, Suriname, Trinidad and Tobago, the United States, Uruguay and Venezuela.

Readers of *Américas* are of diverse cultural backgrounds - writers should keep in mind that what is common knowledge in one country is not necessarily so in others.

Note: U.S. topics usually should have some Latin American or Caribbean tie-in.

Submitting Manuscripts

Query first with a 3 to 4 paragraph summary of your proposed story.

Upon editors' favorable response, articles may be submitted in English, Spanish or Portuguese. *Américas* provides translations. Manuscripts must be unpublished and should be approximately 8 to 12 typewritten pages (3,000 words maximum).

Quotations that have been translated must be accompanied by the text in the original language, and the source must be noted. *Américas* does not use footnotes, so explanatory material should be incorporated into the text. To facilitate translation, *Américas* requests that authors provide titles of published works in the original language and of any published translations; names of places, buildings, private and government organizations in the original language; and Latin names of flora and fauna, along with their local names.

All articles are received only on speculation, and decisions on publication are made by the editors. *Américas* accepts no responsibility for unsolicited manuscripts. The editors reserve the right to edit articles for style and length.

If a manuscript is accepted, a modest honorarium will be paid upon publication, necessarily limited by *Américas* character of nonprofit enterprise. Checks are issued in U.S. dollars for authors residing in or possessing bank accounts in the United States, or in the national currencies of the countries where authors live abroad.

If available, professional quality color transparencies or 8"x10" black and white prints should accompany the text. If graphics are not available, suggestions for possible sources of photos or other illustrations would be appreciated. Preference will be given to manuscripts accompanied by excellent illustrations. Payment for the use of graphic materials is made separately from the article payment and also upon publication. Photographs and other illustrative material are returned after publication when requested.

Authors should provide brief biographical paragraph to serve as the basis for an author's note.

Contact Information:

Rebecca Medrano, Managing Editor
19th Street and Constitution Avenue, NW, Suite 300
Washington, DC 20006
(202) 458-6214

Analog
Science Fiction and Fact

Analog will consider material submitted by any writer, and consider it solely on the basis of merit. We are definitely eager to find and develop new, capable writers.

We have no hard-and-fast editorial guidelines, because science fiction is such a broad field that I don't want to inhibit a new writer's thinking by imposing Thou Shalt Nots. Besides, a really good story can make an editor swallow his preconceived taboos.

Basically, we publish science fiction stories. That is, stories in which some aspect of future science or technology is so integral to the plot that, if that aspect were removed, the story would collapse. Try to picture Mary Shelley's Frankenstein without the science and you'll see what I mean. No story!

The science can be physical, sociological, psychological. The technology can be anything from electronic engineering to biogenetic engineering. But the stories must be strong and realistic, with believable people (who needn't be human) doing believable things-no matter how fantastic the background might be.

Author's name and address should be on the first page of a manuscript. Indent paragraphs but do not leave extra space between them. Please do not put manuscripts in binders or folders.

Analog pays 6-8 cents per word for short stories up to 7,500 words, $450-600 for stories between 7,500 and 10,000 words, and 5-6 cents per word for longer material. We prefer lengths between 2,000 and 7,000 words for shorts, 10,000-20,000 for novelettes, and 40,000-80,000 for serials.

Please query first on serials only. A complete manuscript is strongly preferred for all shorter lengths.

The entire contents of each issue is copyrighted at the time of publication. Payment is on acceptance.

Fact articles for *Analog* should be about 4,000 words in length and should deal with subjects of not only current but future interest - i.e., with topics at the present frontiers of research whose likely future developments have implications of wide interest. Illustrations should be provided by the author in camera-ready form.

In writing for *Analog* readers, it is essential to keep in mind that they are, in general, very intelligent and technically knowledgeable, but represent a wide diversity of backgrounds. Thus specialized jargon and mathematical detail should be kept to a necessary minimum. Also, our readers are reading this magazine largely for entertainment, and a suitable style for our articles is considerably more informal than that in many professional journals.

[Fact] Articles are paid for at the rate of 5.75 cents per word.

Good luck!

Contact Information:
Stanley Schmidt, Editor
1270 Avenue of The Amricas - 10th Floor
New York, NY 10020
(212)698-1313

Angels on Earth
A Guideposts Publication

Angels on Earth publishes true stories about God's messengers at work in today's world. We are interested in stories of heavenly angels and stories involving humans who have played angelic roles in daily life. The best stories are those where the narrator has been positively affected in some distinct way. Look for unusual situations; we have a surplus of stories about illness and car accidents. We are also especially on the lookout for recent stories.

A typical *Angels on Earth* story is a first-person narrative written in dramatic style, with a spiritual point that the reader can "take away" and apply to his or her own life. It may be your own or someone else's story. Observe the following as you write:

1. The emphasis should be on one person, and is usually told from the vantage point of the individual most deeply affected by the angelic experience. But don't try to tell an entire life

story; focus on one specific life event. Bring only as many people as needed to tell the story so the reader's interest stays with the dominant character.

2. Decide what your spiritual point will be. We like to see a positive and specific change in the narrator as a result of the angelic experience. Don't forget: We want our readers to take away a message or insight they can use in their own lives. Everything in the story should be tied in with this specific and inspiring theme.

3. Don't leave unanswered questions. Give all the relevant facts so the reader can clearly understand what took place. Let the reader feel as if he or she were there, seeing the characters, hearing them talk, feeling what they felt. Use dialogue, set scenes, build tension-dramatize the story. Show how the narrator becomes a new, or different, person.

The best rule of all: STUDY THE MAGAZINE!

Payment for full-length stories (1,500 words) usually ranges from $100-$400, and is made when the story is approved and scheduled for publication.

We are always looking for quotes, anecdotes to use as fillers, and material for our short features (50-250 words):

- "Messages": brief, mysterious happenings, or letters describing how a specific *Angels on Earth* article helped you. Payment is usually $25.
- "Earning Their Wings": unusual stories of good deeds worth imitating. Payment is usually $50.
- "Only Human?": short narratives in which the angelic character may or may not have been a human being. The narrator is pleasantly unsure and so is the reader. Payment is usually $100.

Please do not send essays, sermons or fiction. We rarely use poetry and we do not evaluate book-length material. Allow three months for reply. Send submissions to:

Contact Information:
16 East 34th Street
New York, NY 10016
(212) 251-8100

Animals

Overview:

Animals is a full-color, bimonthly magazine written and edited to deliver timely, reliable and provocative coverage of wildlife issues, pet-care topics, and animal-protection concerns. It also publishes natural-history pieces that educate readers about animals' needs and behaviors.

The magazine circulates to a national audience (around 100,000) consisting mostly of direct subscribers, but also of newsstand consumers and some members of the Massachusetts Society for the Prevention of Cruelty to Animals and the American Humane Education Society, its publishers.

What We Publish From Freelance Sources:

About 90 percent of our editorial coverage is from freelance sources.

Feature Stories: Well-researched articles (1,200 to 2,000 words) on national and international wildlife, domestic animals, wildlife/conservation issues, controversies involving animals and/or their use, animal-protection issues, pet health and pet care. Articles must engage readers who are interested in knowing more about a variety of creatures as well as those who consider themselves animal protectionists.

Reviews: Newly released books and videos on animals, animal-related issues, and the environment. These reviews run from 300 to 500 words and are for our Books column.

Profiles: Short pieces on individuals at work to save both domestic and wild animals, to make conditions better for animals, or on others whose interactions with animals makes them of interest to a wide-ranging audience. These reviews run about 800 words and are published in our Profiles column.

What We Pay:

Because payment depends on the length of the article and the amount of research necessary to complete it, payment varies. Our range for features usually starts at $350, plus reasonable and agreed-upon expenses such as telephone and FAX fees. Payment for book reviews start at $75. Payment for profile columns start at $125.

How to Query:

Please query by letter and allow four to six weeks for a response. Query letters should include:

- a pointed summary describing the article's focus, purpose, approximate length, and finish date;
- a list of sources that you plan to contact or have already contacted. When dealing with controversies, sources should be from both sides of the issue;
- writing samples, preferably of comparable pieces;
- information on when and where you may have published, or plan to publish, a similar story, if applicable.

Additional Information: For a sample copy of *Animals* magazine, please send a check in the amount of $3.95, payable to *Animals* magazine, to *Animals*, at the address shown below.

For a copy of *Animals* magazine's photography guidelines, please send a stamped, self-addressed envelope to *Animals*, also at the address shown below.

Thank you for your interest in *Animals* magazine.

Contact Information:

Wildlife/Animal Protection Issues: Joni Praded, Director and Editor
Pets/Issues That Affect Companion Animals: Paula Abend, Managing Editor
350 South Huntington Avenue
Boston, MA 02130
(617) 541-5065 • FAX: (617) 522-4885

Answers
The Magazine for Adult Children of Aging Parents

Editorial Concept

Departments

1. Trends & Talk: (News, Book Reviews)
2. Q&A
3. Readers Tips
4. Letters
5. Product Review
6. Resource Hot Line
7. Marketplace (Classified)

Items for Trends & Talk are always welcome. They should be 50 to 100 words and will be paid for accordingly.

Columns

1. Drug Watch
2. Insurance
3. Legal Affairs
4. Your Emotions
5. Living Arrangements
6. Product Probe
7. Health & Nutrition

Features

1. Columns provide nuts and bolts information about legal affairs, insurance, over medication and more. Features may be written about emotional issues, how-to, or product review oriented subjects.

If you write about a personal experience, it must share solutions that worked for you. For example, what process did you go through in making a specific decision on behalf of your parent, etc.

Features that review products or services that help the caregiver or that help the parent remain independent are encouraged.

Outlines

Outlines must be submitted to ANSWERS before commencement of story writing. Story topics are also welcome.

Technical Presentation

A. Manuscripts

B. Margins should be two inches (left and right)

C. Number all pages and label with author and story title.

D. Columns should be to 800 words.

E. Features can be between 1000 and 1200 words.

F. Use the *Chicago Manual of Style* for style and editing.

G. Stories must be to the point and focused.

H. Only one space after a period. Not two.

I. Please send your story on a floppy diskette (Macintosh is preferable) with hard copy. If you have a modem, we will make arrangements to receive it over the wire.

Deadlines & Payment

A. Articles will be edited and changes may be requested.

B. Deadlines will be assigned when story assignment is made.

C. Columns pay $75 and features pay $100 to $150.

D. Payment is made upon publication.

Resources

Whenever appropriate please include resources at the end of the story that the reader can call and/or write to.

Contact Information:
75 Seabreeze Drive
Richmond, CA 94804
(510) 235-0050 • FAX: (510) 235-0055

Archaeology

ARCHAEOLOGY is the official "public voice" of the Archaeological Institute of America. We reach more than 200,000 nonspecialist readers interested in art, science, history, and culture. Our reports, regional commentaries, and feature-length articles introduce readers to recent developments in archaeology worldwide.

Communicating your scholarly experience to the general public requires deft writing. Please keep the following in mind as you prepare your manuscript:

1. Keep technical terms to a minimum and explain those that you do use.

2. Assume a fairly minimal knowledge of your subject on the reader's part, but don't talk down to them.

3. Be interesting and entertaining, with a strong opening that hooks readers and leads them into your main discussion; avoid the dramatic lead that slips into a site report by page two.

4. Keep in mind that certain articles require a broad historical framework if the reader is to comprehend the importance of the archaeological work.

5. Keep it personal, without being egocentric. Readers are interested in what you do, why you do it, what you have learned, and why they should be interested. They should be led through your material in a way that creates for them the same sense of awe that you have felt about your work.

6. In some form or another, a finished manuscript should contain an EXPOSITION (GUESS WHAT?), DEVELOPMENT (HERE'S WHAT), and a CONCLUSION (SO WHAT?).

7. You should discuss your story idea with an editor before submitting a manuscript. A brief outline, accompanied by samples of available slides or photographs, is helpful.

Other Requirements

- No footnotes
- Separate captions
- Color photographs should be in the form of 35mm original slides or 4" by 5" transparencies. Please supply captions and photo credits.
- Maps can be sketchy, but must show locations accurately. Our art director will make up a final map.
- Permission to reproduce published material must be obtained by the author directly from the publisher.
- Include a brief biographical statement.
- Include a brief, annotated bibliography (up to seven entries). In your bibliography, include remarks on the significance and quality of the references. Categorize and list entries in alphabetical order at the end of your article under the heading "Further Reading." Be sure to include publishers, date, and city of publication as well as title and author.

Examples:

Junius P. Bird, "Treasures from the Land of Gold," Arts in Virginia 24 (1969), pp. 23-33. An uneven but useful review of Peruvian Gold.

Samuel K. Lothrop, *Inca Treasures as Depicted by Spanish Historians* (Los Angeles: University of California Press, 1938). An authoritative, specialized study, 40 years old but still the most complete treatment of breastplates.

- Measurements must be in miles and feet. While archaeologists usually use the metric system, our readers are most comfortable using English measurements.

Contact Information:

Archaeological Features: Peter A. Young, Editor-in-Chief
135 William Street, 8th Floor
New York, NY 10038
(212)732-5154 • FAX: (212) 732-5707
E-mail: ARCHAEOL@SPACELAB.NET

Arizona Business Magazine

Arizona Business Magazine is a full-color, quarterly business publication. We're recognized for our well-balanced articles and high-quality photography. We strive to offer Arizona's business leaders with well-researched, objective articles on the issues facing our state.

Style

Our readers are very busy. To accommodate their schedules we try to make the magazine easy and enjoyable to read. Articles include attractive illustrations or photos with captions that tell a story by themselves. We also use sidebars and bulleted lists to provide quick, encapsulated information.

The articles are written in a powerful, concise and easy-to-read style. The writing style should also be creative and "different," so readers will take the time to read the entire article. This is one reason we use several outside writers each issue-to create a variety our readers will appreciate.

Assignments

Our regular departments are: Health Watch, Environomics, Corporate lifestyle, High Finance, Power of Attorney, Media on Media, High Tech and Newsreel. We also publish several supplements in each issue. These areas are most open to freelance writers. Our cover stories are always staff written.

We have editorial calendars for each department within the magazine. If you're interested in writing one of the stories scheduled, submit an outline at least six months in advance. If you have a suggestion for a new story or topic, please submit a detailed outline of the piece and who you would like to quote. Pre-written articles rarely get published because they generally require revisions to meet our specifications. Your submission will receive more attention if it is brief and direct.

Sources

We generally supply a list of possible sources when we assign the articles. These people and organizations should be contacted first, in addition to any suggestions or contacts the writer may have. If for some reason the people we recommend do not work out, the editorial staff should be notified right away.

Those quoted should be high on the corporate ladder, such as CEO, Executive Vice President, Owner, and so on. If you're not sure, call and ask a member of the editorial staff.

Deadlines

Meeting deadlines are top priority. Although we are quarterly and have a little more flexibility than a monthly magazine, we have a very strict deadline schedule. If problems or delays should arise (and they inevitably do), we ask that the writer keep us up-to-date.

Format

Articles should be submitted in hard copy, as well as on a 3½ inch computer disk. The story should be saved in Microsoft Word or as a DOS text/ASCII file.

The best advice we can give is to read the magazine. Everything you need to know about style and content is there. For a copy of the magazine send a 9"x12" envelope with $1.90 postage to the editorial department.

For more information, speak to someone on the editorial staff, or write to us.

Contact Information:
Jessica McCann, Editor
3111 North Central Avenue, Suite 230
Phoenix, AZ 85012
(602) 277-6045

Arizona Highways

Since 1925 *Arizona Highways* has carried out its mandate: "to promote travel to and through the state of Arizona." A state-owned publication, the magazine has a circulation of more than 425,000, of which 80% is out-of-state, with subscribers in almost every country of the world. Thus, while we are a premier regional photography and travel magazine, we speak to a national and international audience. We expect top-quality writing on subjects of interest to those who visit and love the American Southwest.

SUBJECT MATTER: The main editorial thrust is travel in Arizona. We also buy nature, adventure, history, profiles, quality Indian arts and crafts, humor, lifestyle, nostalgia, and archaeology.

Sections of the magazine for which we purchase copy include:

1. FOCUS ON NATURE - A short feature of 700 words in first or third person dealing with a unique aspect of a single species of wildlife. Preference is for personal experience pieces. Photos are not essential.

2. ALONG THE WAY - A short essay dealing with life in Arizona or a personal experience keyed to Arizona. Length is 800 words. Photos are helpful, but not necessary.

3. PHOTOGRAPH PORTFOLIO - Requires a short introduction of 100 to 200 words to a series of photographs dealing with scenic subjects. Arizona oriented. Contact picture Editor Peter Ensenberger.

4. EVENT OF THE MONTH - A featurette of 600 words dealing with a special event (need not necessarily be an annual event) in one of Arizona's small towns: rodeos, races, regattas, biscuit tossing, etc. Must be a personal experience. Photographs are not necessary. Must include a "When You Go" sidebar. (See #7 below.)

5. BACK-ROAD ADVENTURE - A 1,000 word article dealing with personal back-road trips, preferably off the beaten path and outside major metro areas. Trips should reflect a range of difficulty, from those that can be made in a passenger car to those that require a four-wheel-drive vehicle. One-day trips are preferred but may be two and three days in length. Stories should emphasize traveling to a particularly interesting destination or scenic attraction. A detailed topographical map is required.

6. LEGENDS OF THE LOST - Feature length is 1,200 words. Writer is required to update historical or legendary tales dealing with lost mines or buried treasures, including loot. "Found" lost mines are of particular interest. Requires a source list.

7. HIKE OF THE MONTH - These features are 500 words in length and must be personal experiences on trails anywhere in Arizona. Leave scenery to the photographer. Day hikes preferred. Must include a short sidebar (When You Go) providing necessary information for readers who may want to take the hike: how to get to the trailhead, special clothing, best time of year, a contact telephone number and address for more information, etc.

8. HUMOR - If you've got an amusing story about Arizona, we'd like to buy it to share with our readers. A humorous anecdote about your trip to the state, perhaps. Or a funny incident that happened in the routine of the day. Must have a humorous punch line. We'll pay $75.00 for each piece of humor we publish. We are looking for short stories. No more than 200 words on Arizona topics. Before submitting a query, new writers are asked to review these special sections in back issues, starting with January, 1992, particularly for the style required.

TRAVEL STORIES: We have a style for travel stories that is distinctively *Arizona Highways*. The style starts with outstanding photographs, which not only depict an area but interpret it. So our travel stories need not dwell on descriptions of what can be seen.

Concentrate instead on the experience of being there, whether the destination is a hiking trail, a ghost town, a trout stream, a forest, or an urban area. What thoughts and feelings did the experience evoke? What was happening? What were the mood and comportment of the people? What were the sounds and smells? What was the feel of the area? Did bugs get into the sleeping bag? Were the crows curious about the intruders? Could you see to the bottom of the lake, and if so, what was there? We want to know why you went there, what you experienced, and what impressions you came away with.

The experiences and impressions should be focused in a story with a beginning, middle, and end. We do not want a rambling series of thoughts or vignettes, diary entries, or a travelogue (a piece that begins in the morning, goes hour-by-hour through the day, and ends in the evening). We want a story: one that opens by introducing us to a story line, then develops the tale, and finally concludes. We want an ending, a logical conclusion to the tale we are telling. Just stopping the story won't do.

The story we are telling should be just that: a story, and it should be as interesting and evocative as you can make it. And since it will not be a general guide to an area, we will need a short sidebar containing the service information.

This sidebar, called "When You Go," should explain how to get to the destination, where to stay, restrictions, special requirements, and what to see and do in the area. It also should include places to call for further information.

APPROACH: Our style is informal yet polished, with a readable, literary quality. It should be a story using the techniques of the fiction writer to create a narrative the reader will be unable to put down. We do not want choppy, shallow/Sunday-supplement treatments. First person is okay; present tense, fine. Use strong verbs in the active voice and avoid overuse of the verb "to be" in all its forms.

LENGTH: About 2,000 words or less.

CONTRACT AND PAYMENT: We buy first North American serial rights, and we expect original work. Payment is 35 to 55 cents a word, on acceptance.

SUBMISSIONS: We prefer one-page written queries to unsolicited manuscripts. Telephone queries out of the blue are difficult for everyone. Multiple submissions are not accepted.

Contact Information:

Richard G. Stahl, Managing Editor
2039 West Lewis Avenue
Phoenix, AZ 85009
(602) 258-6641

Army Magazine

Length

- 1,000-2,000 words, which can include one or two separate shorter articles of 250-500 words each.
- The main article must have a two- or three-sentence explanation of why the article is timely, innovative or important as "lessons learned." This is a requirement that helps you more clearly focus the piece and helps us understand what you intended.

Format

- Typewritten and triple-spaced wherever possible. Please send a hard copy and, if possible, a floppy disc of your article and indicate what kind of software you used.
- Original copies only, please.

- Do not submit the same article to any other publication.

Photographs and Other Artwork

- We are interested in photographs or artwork that will enhance your article. We can use black and white or color. Please include caption information with each photograph.

Headlines

- We take your suggestions for headlines seriously. If you think of a good one, suggest it on a separate piece of paper.

Author Biographies

- Biographical information should be submitted with the text of the article. Include as much information as possible, preferably a vita.

Contact Information:
The Editor
Box 1560
Arlington, VA 22210
(703) 841-4300

Army Times

(Please refer to Times News Service.)

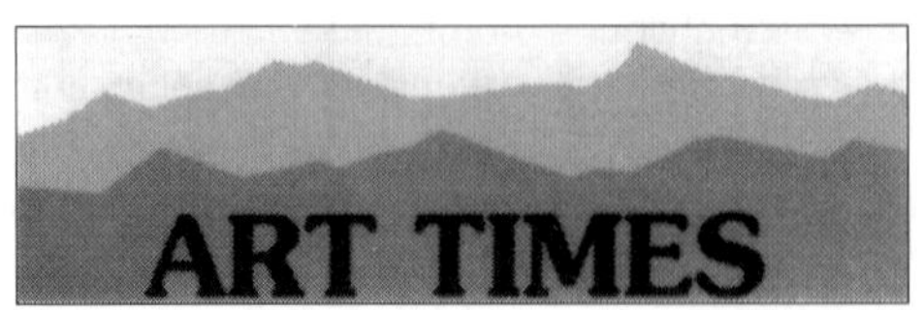

Art Times
A Literary Journal and Resource for All the Arts

Since its establishment in 1984, ART TIMES has been known for its high level of excellence and integrity. In honor of the 10th anniversary of ART TIMES, Governor Mario M. Cuomo of New York issued a special citation recognizing its dedication and commitment to the artistic community of the Hudson Valley. Quoting Governor Cuomo, the citation reads in part: "Born out of love and support of the arts, combined with critical writing skills, Art Times continues to fulfill its goal of establishing a literary arts journal for all the arts and is a valuable resource for both individuals and organizations."

ART TIMES publishes essays about music, dance, theatre, film and the visual arts; reviews major art exhibitions; profiles personalities in the arts; publishes original short fiction and poetry; critiques the work of living artists; and offers brief reviews of new art books and videos. Each issue features an extensive "Cultural Events Calendar" which includes the major museum shows in the Northeast's art centers of New York City, Boston and Washington, DC and an "Opportunities Column" where artists, writers, musicians and actors are alerted to calls for entries. Our popular "speak Out" section offers our readers a forum for airing their personal views on any or all of the arts.

Valued as a reference resource, Art Times has found permanent places in the archives of museums and organizations across the country and has long been made available at cultural reading centers in cities throughout Europe.

Writer's Guidelines (For First Serial Rights)

Fiction: Short stories up to 1500 words. All subjects but no excessive sex, violence or racist themes. Our prime requisite is high literary quality and professional presentation. Pays $25 upon publication, six extra copies of issue in which work appears and one year's complimentary subscription beginning with that issue. WE DO NOT PUBLISH REPRINTS.

Poetry: Up to 20 lines. All topics; all forms. Same requisite high quality as above. Pays in six extra copies of issue in which work appears and one year" complimentary subscription beginning with that issue. WE DO NOT PUBLISH REPRINTS. (We discourage simultaneous submissions of poetry.)

(Note: We are usually on about an 36-month lead.)

Readers of ART TIMES are generally over 40, literate and arts conscious. Our distribution is heaviest in New York State (along the "Hudson River Corridor" from Albany to Manhattan). We are sold by subscription, newsstand; copies may be obtained free at selected art galleries. Subscription copies are mailed across the US and abroad. In addition to short fiction and poetry, feature essays on the arts make up the bulk of our editorial. (Note: Articles and Essays are not solicited.)

Sample copy: $1.75 plus 9x12 Self Addressed Envelope with 3 first-class stamps.

Contact Information:
Fiction: Raymond J. Steiner, Editor
Poetry: Cheryl A. Rice, Poetry Editor
P.O. Box 730
Mt. Marion, NY 12456
Phone/FAX (914) 246-6944

Arthritis Today

Thank you for your interest in writing for *Arthritis Today*. This magazine, which was first published in January, 1987, is a membership benefit of the Arthritis Foundation. It is mailed every two months to about 600,000 people nationwide.

We generally accept six to eight freelance-written articles per issue of *Arthritis Today*. Much of the magazine's content is planned a year in advance, and we often assign these predetermined topics to freelancers. We also welcome query letters and manuscripts on speculation for other topics. If you choose to query, please include one or two writing samples with your letter.

If you need any additional information about *Arthritis Today* or about our criteria for accepting freelance articles, feel free to contact me at this office. We look forward to hearing from you soon.

Editorial Overview

Arthritis Today is written for the almost 40 million Americans who have arthritis and for the millions of others whose lives are touched by an arthritis-related disease. It provides a comprehensive and reliable source of information about arthritis research, care and treatment.

The editorial content of *Arthritis Today* is designed to help the person with arthritis live better today, emphasizing upbeat, informative articles that provide practical advice and inspiration. The magazine also provides hope for the future by describing the latest findings in arthritis research and the most promising new treatments.

Articles in the magazine focus on the physical challenges of arthritis, as well as on the emotional and social issues associated with the disease. Each issue includes at least one profile of a person who is coping with their arthritis in an inspiring way. In addition to being informative, the magazine strives to be entertaining, with articles on lighter topics. A small percentage of the copy in each issue does not relate specifically to life with arthritis, but is of interest to a more general readership. Such general topics would include travel, cooking, entertaining and similar subjects.

We are interested in receiving queries or manuscripts in the following areas:

- General Health/lifestyle issues
- Inspirational articles
- First-person/slice-of-life articles
- Tips/ "How-to" articles
- Research/medical updates

No article or editorial can endorse, or appear to endorse, a specific product. Brand names of products may be mentioned only as references, and should be kept to a minimum.

Of *Arthritis Today*'s 600,000 readers, almost 85% have arthritis or have a loved one with the disease. Our most recent Simmons Custom Readership Study shows that *Arthritis Today*'s primary audience has either osteoarthritis or rheumatoid arthritis and is 55 years old or over, although many articles in the magazine are germane to any age group.

SPECIAL SENSITIVITIES IN WRITING ABOUT ARTHRITIS

The Arthritis Foundation always tries to portray life with arthritis in a positive light and to convey an upbeat, optimistic outlook. Toward that end, we are especially sensitive about the terminology used in our literature. We ask you to respect the following sensitivities in any writing you submit for consideration in *Arthritis Today*.

1. When referring to a person with arthritis, avoid all negative descriptions, such as "sufferer" or "victim." Joints are "arthritic," not people. Use the word "patient" only in the strict sense of a doctor-patient relationship. As a general rule, refer to people with arthritis as just that – "people with arthritis."

2. People are "handicapped" or "disabled" if their arthritis prevents them from doing things other people take for granted, such as driving a car or holding a particular kind of job. Not all people with arthritis are "handicapped," though they may have "pain," "stiffness," "limited mobility" and other problems. People are not "crippled" or "deformed."

3. Avoid portraying people with arthritis who are successful in overcoming their limitations as "superhuman" or "extraordinary."

4. Avoid using emotional adjectives such as "unfortunate," "heartbreaking" and "pitiful" to describe people with arthritis.

5. Emphasize abilities rather than disabilities. For example, say a person "uses" a wheelchair rather than is "confined" to a wheelchair.

6. Never refer to people who do not have arthritis as "normal," "able-bodied" or "whole," thus implying that people who do have arthritis are somehow abnormal.

A Few More Requests:

1. Because the term "arthritis" is used to describe more than 100 different diseases, try to avoid referring to arthritis as a "disease." "Health problem" or "condition" are preferable.

2. Never use the terms "quack" or "quackery." "Unproven" or "untested" remedies are the best alternative descriptions.

3. The current prevalence figures for arthritis are "almost 40 million Americans" or "one in every seven people." Avoid using other prevalence statistics, such as those for individual arthritis-related diseases.

GENERAL WRITER'S GUIDELINES

Length. Articles should be 750 to 3,000 words in length, depending on the topic.

Payment. Payment is made on acceptance, and varies depending on the length of the article, the complexity of the subject, the amount of primary and secondary research needed to write the article, and the writer's particular qualifications with regard to the subject matter. When writing an article on assignment for *Arthritis Today*, please send an invoice for the agreed upon amount with the final manuscript. Please allow two to four weeks after acceptance for processing the check.

Rewrites/Kill fees. If the *Arthritis Today* editorial staff determines that a submitted article is unsuitable for publication, either before or after a rewrite is completed, the author will be paid a kill fee of 25 percent of the original amount plus reimbursement of any agreed upon expenses.

Rights. The Arthritis Foundation will purchase first North American serial rights to each article accepted for *Arthritis Today*, and must be guaranteed exclusive rights for a period of four months following its first publication. We also require unlimited reprint rights in any Arthritis Foundation-affiliated endeavor at no additional cost.

The Arthritis Foundation will buy second rights to an article if the author clearly states where and when the article previously appeared. If the author does not own all subsequent rights to the article, permission to reprint from the previous publication must accompany the manuscript.

Bylines/Author Profile. Bylines will be given for all submitted articles. We include a very brief profile of the author at the end of each article. If you have any special credentials or qualifications that should be included, please provide this information with your manuscript.

Editing/Reviews. All copy is subject to editing—sometimes heavy—by *Arthritis Today* staff. Edited versions will be returned to authors for approval on request only.

Editorial deadlines. The editorial closing date for unassigned articles or queries is four months prior to the date of the issue. Authors will generally be given six to eight weeks for the completion of assigned articles. If an assigned article is not received by the deadline stated in the contract, 10 percent of the payment will be deducted each day it is late unless prior arrangements have been made with the editor.

Verification of information. The author is responsible for ensuring the accuracy of all information in a submitted article. This includes, but is not limited to, the spelling of names; verification of titles, addresses and numbers; accuracy of all medical statements, quotations and other factual information presented. If a source requests approval on an article before it is printed, the author must obtain that approval before the article is submitted. Please supply for our records the address and phone number of any source used in the article, so we can get in touch with them if necessary. If an article should be cut from the original issue for any reason and rescheduled for a later issue, it will be the author's responsibility to provide any necessary updates at the time of ultimate publication at no additional charge.

Acceptance. The *Arthritis Today* editorial staff will review all submitted manuscripts and queries promptly and will respond within four to six weeks in most cases with an indication of interest. We reserve the right to refuse articles without explanation.

Photographs. Most articles in *Arthritis Today* are accompanied by four-color photographs or illustrations. Please feel free to submit any ideas you may have for graphics to accompany your article. If an article focuses on a particular person or references a person extensively, we would appreciate your asking that person if he or she would be willing to be photographed for the article.

Format. Computer printouts are acceptable. We prefer to receive articles on disc whenever possible. We can use 3½-inch discs in WordPerfect 6.0 or 6.1. If you have used a different word processing program, please save the files in ASCII format and indicate the program you have used on the disc. Copy can also be sent to us by e-mail.

Contact Information:
Shelly Morrow, Associate Editor
1330 West Peachtree Street
Atlanta, GA 30309
(404)872-7100 • FAX: (404) 872-0457
E-mail: shorton@arthritis.org.

Astronomy

ASTRONOMY is a monthly popular-level science and hobby magazine with a readership that exceeds 300,000. Our magazine serves both the "armchair" astronomer who wants to keep up on latest discoveries and understand astronomical science, and the amateur astronomer who wants to know what is happening in the sky each month. ASTRONOMY's readers expect a combination of timely observing advice and clear explanations.

ASTRONOMY is not a technical journal. Our readers are college-educated amateurs interested in the natural sciences, with a particular interest in astronomical observing. We strive for a conversational, lively tone. (Some of the techniques we apply are adapted from How to Take the Fog out of Writing, by Robert Gunning and Douglas Mueller.)

1. Use active verbs.
2. Vary sentences in length, but on the average keep them short.
3. If there is a simple way to say something, use it.
4. Write complex ideas in the clearest words you can, but don't limit your vocabulary. Precise words give exact meanings.
5. Use short, concrete words the reader can visualize. Abstract words make writing dull and flabby.
6. Make every word carry weight. Words that don't convey meaning weaken writing.
7. Write to express, not to impress. Avoid showing off a large vocabulary by using needlessly complex terms.
8. Write as you talk. The best written communications have a conversational sound.
9. Build a case starting with what the reader already knows to create a link between your new ideas and older ideas.

ASTRONOMY publishes two types of FEATURE ARTICLES: those on the science of astronomy and those on the activity of amateur astronomy. Feature articles come in a variety of sizes depending on the topic but generally range from 1,000 to 4,000 words.

Science features deepen the reader's understanding of technical concepts, news events, and the human side of astronomy. We use three different approaches:

Descriptive features deal with scientific concepts, explaining them in layman's terms. They focus on a particular type of astronomical object or scientific process (such as galaxy formation or the beginning of the universe). Text length: 3,000 to 4,000 words.

News features focus on an area of research and give the reader an in-depth look at recent events. News features frequently include interviews with scientists. The news topic is fully explained and examined. Text length: 1,000 to 3,000 words.

Human-interest features highlight nontechnical aspects of astronomy (such as personalities and historical events) and multi-disciplinary areas (such as education and archaeoastronomy). Human-interest features appeal to the reader who may not be interested in the science of astronomy. Text length: 2,000 to 3,000 words.

Three types of hobby features present ways for amateur astronomers to get involved in practical aspects of the hobby of astronomy.

Observing features provide information about what the reader can observe in the sky.

Often how-to in approach, these features explain the what, where, and how of observing and are frequently accompanied by sky maps, diagrams, and illustrations. Articles can be aimed at beginning or advanced observers. Text length: 1,500 to 2,500 words.

Technique features give the reader advice on becoming proficient in hobby areas such as observing, photography, and the use of equipment. Length: 1,500 to 2,000 words.

Equipment features focus on astronomical equipment and range from product reviews of new equipment to step-by-step instructions for building equipment. Text length: 1,500 to 2,500 words.

In addition to feature articles, ASTRONOMY runs a variety of DEPARTMENTS each month. Unsolicited manuscripts are accepted for two of these: Viewpoints and Reader Reports. For all other departments, contributions are solicited by our editors; please send a query letter to our editor, Robert Burnham, if you are interested in writing for other departments.

Poetry has been submitted to ASTRONOMY; unfortunately, because of our format we do not accept poetry. Cartoons should be submitted to our art director, Thomas L. Hunt.

Submitting articles to ASTRONOMY can be done in several ways. You may send a query letter an outline or first draft, or a completed manuscript.

Computer diskettes: We have the capability of accessing many word-processing programs, submitted on either 3-½" or 5-¼" diskettes. However, we prefer you send ASCII text file, if not MS Word. Please include a letter-quality manuscript with a diskette.

Typed copy: Use letter-quality printing.

After your submission arrives, we will send you a postcard acknowledging its receipt. Once the article has been received by our editors, it is either accepted for publication (in which case you will receive a contract), returned to you for specified revisions, or rejected. Payment is made upon return of the contract, which outlines the terms of our acceptance. Our editors will consult with you as your manuscript is being edited prior to publication.

Contact Information:
21027 Crossroads Circle
P.O. Box 1612
Waukesha, WI 53187
(414) 796-8776 • FAX: (414) 796-1142

Aviation History

(Please refer to Cowles History Group.)

BackHome

SUGGESTIONS FOR *BACKHOME* CONTRIBUTORS

BackHome is a down-to-earth, how-to magazine whose primary purpose is to help people gain more control over their own lives by doing more for themselves. We are looking for interesting, lively, preferably first-person articles based upon actual experience in the fields of gardening, home construction and repair, workshop projects, cooking, crafts, outdoor recreation, family activities and vacations, livestock, home business, wild-foods foraging, home-based and other education, and community/neighborhood action.

In general, we'll consider any article that will help our readers improve the quality of life—for themselves, their families, their community, and their environment. With few exceptions, we seldom publish essays or basically philosophical contemplations.

We try to answer queries within a reasonable time. You are welcome to send complete articles, but in most cases sending a query in advance gives us a chance to help you develop the slant and focus we want for our readers. It also may save you the trouble of writing an article only to discover that we have a similar one in our files or have assigned the subject to someone else.

We hope to improve our pay scale soon, but at present our standard rate is $25 a printed page, payable upon publication. We pay extra for good clear photographs: color prints, transparencies, or black-and-white. We prefer to buy first North American serial rights, in which case you're free to sell the article after we run it, but because we are at present a quarterly and thus seasonal, we may hold your accepted submission for a considerable time before finding a spot for it. (We sometimes use second-rights material if its previous appearance was not in a major publication.

When submitting an article, please include your full name, address, phone number, and social security number. It is helpful if you can provide your manuscript on computer disk or transmit it by modem, but don't do so unless we request this—just let us know the possibilities. If you haven't seen *BackHome*, we strongly suggest you read at least an issue or two to get a better feel for the magazine before you try to write for us. If you can't find *BackHome* locally, you can order a sample from us for $5.00 or a one-year subscription for $17.97 (four issues).

Thank you very much for your interest in BackHome.

Contact Information:
General: Lorna K. Loveless, Editor
Technical: Richard Freudenberger, Editor
P.O. Box 70
Hendersonville, NC 28793
(704) 696-3838

Back Home In Kentucky

BACK HOME IN KENTUCKY is a beautiful, four-color, statewide publication—the "coffee table magazine of choice" in Kentucky homes. BACK HOME IN KENTUCKY offers a bimonthly glimpse of the state Kentuckians love—whether it's a drive down a country lane or a day spent in one of the state's cosmopolitan cities. Attractive graphics and dynamic editorial content compel readers to pick up the publication, finding a little more of Kentucky each time they browse through it. Kentuckians share a fondness for their history, their scenic beauty, their horse country, the "character" of their people, their wildlife. The magazine addresses these areas of common affection with articles that amuse, educate, and illustrate the benefits of living in the state, connecting the Highlands with the Purchase, the Pennyroyal with the Bluegrass.

GENERAL FEATURES

• Fairs & Festivals – This is an abbreviated listing of events taking place across the state over the two-month period of a particular issue. Color photos and slides are welcomed, as is listing information. No payment is made for information/photos received by this department. Deadline: two months prior to issue date.

• Pursuits – This department features interviews with Kentuckians involved with interesting hobbies and avocations, as well as professional craftsmen and artisans. Past features have included a look at men and women involved in woodworking, quilting, metalworking, basketmaking, photography, and crop dusting. Color photos required. Submissions accepted.

• Cooking – This regular department focuses on interesting dishes for entertaining and family fare, tying each issue's feature to seasonal or other themes. Presently staff written. Anyone interested in working with this department should contact the editor.

• Wildlife/Natural History – These regular departments focus on flora and fauna native to the state of Kentucky as well as other aspects of the Commonwealth's natural history. No submissions being accepted at this time.

• Gardening – This department is presently staff written, focusing on flower and vegetable gardening of interest to readers. Anyone interested in working with this department should contact the editor.

• County Salute – A regular feature, the county salutes generally a county's history, the present picture of the county and its communities, recreational opportunities, etc. We are actively seeking writers for county salutes in a variety of areas. Writers must provide photography to accompany the salute article (may be Chamber or Tourism furnished). Query first.

• Canvas – A special section, this department allows writers to explore their fondness for the Commonwealth, painting a picture of the state they love through personal experiences, events, etc.

HISTORY

• Memories – This department features nostalgic writing submitted by our readers. These pieces, averaging 750 words, should offer the nostalgic flavor of a slower, more friendly time. Must be Kentucky-related. Black-and-white photos may accompany the submission.

• Chronicle – A glimpse at the history of the state, this department explores some aspect of the Commonwealth's past in some depth. Themes have included: Kentucky women, Sports in Kentucky, Kentucky Inventors, Kentucky & World War II, etc. Queries encouraged.

• Profiles – This department captures the personality and characteristics of interesting Kentuckians who are no longer living. We're looking for well-known and lesser-known men and women who have figured in the state's past. Queries and submissions encouraged.

LITERATURE

• Book Nook – This department explores the state's literary scene. Those interested in working with this department should contact the editor.

• Authors – Interviews with or biographical sketches of Kentucky authors provide insight into their writings and explore their connection with the Commonwealth. Submissions accepted.

• Departments for which submissions are most encouraged.

Queries or submissions also being sought for two proposed departments: Kentucky Cooks and Kentucky Gardeners. These would be profiles of interesting Kentuckians in each category.

Writer's Guidelines

BACK HOME IN KENTUCKY is a regional hearth-and-home magazine reflecting a dynamic and contemporary Kentucky, yet one that is rich in history, hospitality, and natural beauty. BACK HOME fosters interest and pride in Kentucky, entertaining and educating the reader. The magazine covers the state's more obvious stories and sparks the interest with the lesser-known. Each issue focuses on one or more themes, which are outlined in the editorial calendar. We emphasize the scenic beauty of the Commonwealth, as well as her wild creatures, natural history, and colorful characters.

We welcome queries and manuscripts on speculation that fall in these general categories: Kentucky history, Kentucky profiles, Kentucky nostalgia, county features, Kentucky crafts and craftspeople, and Kentucky homes. Most articles must be accompanied by attractive, well-focused photographs. Check with the editor to see whether a particular story lends itself to color or black-and-white photographs—generally, all but historical topics require color images. We have regular writers contributing features on wildlife, natural history, and cooking.

County Lines Assignments: The editor assigns all county features for the year far in advance. A writer wishing to write a county feature should contact the editor several months prior to the anticipated publication date.

Special Assignments: There is always room for quality writing on a variety of Kentucky-related topics. Feel free to query the editor about any story ideas you think are feasible.

Payment: Payment for all materials is on publication, unless otherwise negotiated. Payment is for first-time North American rights, unless otherwise negotiated. Writers receive a byline and three copies of the magazine containing their work. Material is placed in the magazine as content merits and space allows. The editor determines the suitability of material for inclusion in BACK HOME and determines in which issue selected material will appear. Payment for articles varies and is negotiable with the editor. Generally, pay ranges from $15-100, depending on department.

Photographs: Photos accompanying articles are paid for as part of the manuscript purchase. Photo essay submissions are welcome. BACK HOME welcomes submissions of color transparencies for cover consideration and color feature photos. We use about 25 photos/issue, less than 10% on assignment. Do not submit any photo without identifying it, and photos will be returned only if a stamped, self-addressed envelope is included with the materials. Payment for these is individually negotiated. Generally, we pay $15/b&w photo, $20/color photo; $50+/cover photo, $15-100/text/photo package. There is no payment for photos submitted for the Fairs & Festivals section, as it is assumed their publication benefits the event.

Deadlines: Because of the nature of the magazine, BACK HOME content is planned several months in advance. If an author wishes his/her work to appear in a particular month, he/she should work closely with the editor. Material should be in the editor's hands no later than ten weeks prior to the month of the issue (that is, we need May/June material by February 15, and so forth).

Don't Forget: ALL SUBMISSIONS SHOULD INCLUDE THE WRITER'S/PHOTOGRAPHER'S PHONE NUMBER for the editor's convenience if questions arise. A word count is required. We accept diskettes of articles in a variety of software—call to see if yours is compatible. Single issue copies available for $3.

Contact Information:
Nanci Gregg, Managing Editor
P.O. Box 681269
Franklin, TN 37068-1629
(615) 794-4338 • FAX: (615) 790-6188

Balloon Life

BALLOON LIFE is dedicated to the sport of hot air ballooning. It is a monthly publication that has news, calendar listing, columns on various aspects of the sport, features, special reports, people profiles and interviews, and coverage of major events and happenings.

GUIDELINES FOR EDITORIAL CONTRIBUTIONS

Articles should be 1,000 to 1,500 words. Shorter articles in the 300 to 500 word range will be considered. Longer articles may be submitted, but are generally reserved for more technical or historical subjects. In addition, the writer may wish to present additional information as a separate item for use as a sidebar to the article.

Types of articles considered for publication:

Balloon events/rallies: May be written from the aspect that the event is about to happen or has just happened. Preview articles should be submitted at least four to five months prior to the actual event. Post-event articles should be submitted as soon as possible after the completion of the event. Types of information to include would be: the event's name, its history, its organizers, participating balloonists, other attractions in the area (famous restaurants, river raft trips, shopping, etc.), value of the event to the community, etc. Short articles (+/-300 words) will be accepted for our Logbook section, which deals with an event that has recently taken place.

Safety seminars: Because this is an educational event, the article should be written as an educational piece that can be used by the readers to further their knowledge. If not being written by the presenter whose information is being used, you must secure his/her permission.

Balloon clubs/organizations: Tell us the history of the organization, what they do, meetings, events, projects, activities, etc. How the club helps to promote the sport of ballooning and handles public relations.

General interest stories: Can be interviews or biographies of people that have made a contribution to the sport of hot air ballooning, or other general interest items.

Crew Quarters: A regular column devoted to some aspect of crewing. May be educational, tell a story of a crew experience, or share some other aspect of the sport. 900 words preferred.

The above contributions should include pictures (color and black & white) with captions (pictures should be able to tell the story), charts, maps, or additional information that would be helpful in conveying the story to the readers.

All material submitted will be on a speculation basis only. The writer will be notified in writing within two-four weeks of receipt of the material whether it is being considered for publication. BALLOON LIFE will only consider articles for publication which have not previously been published. BALLOON LIFE will pay $50 for all, nonexclusive, rights of articles selected for publication, and $20 for short articles (our Logbook section) for balloon events that have recently taken place. Payment schedule for pictures is $15 inside and $50 for the cover.

Freelance pictures that are submitted will be considered for publication, but generally only if they are of an unusual nature or used for the cover photo. Request photo guidelines for more information.

Those individuals who are interested in writing on a specific, technical topic may contact the editor to discuss subject areas, deadlines, and needs of the magazine. For these topics BALLOON LIFE will pay $100-200 for article(s) used on a specific subject, and provide assistance in researching the project.

Contact Information:
Tom Hamilton, Publisher
2145 Dale Avenue
Sacramento, CA 95815-3632
(916) 922-9648

Baltimore Magazine

As a regional magazine serving the Baltimore metropolitan area, we're almost obsessive in our focus on local people, events, trends, and ideas. We sometimes write about state and national issues, but only those of immediate interest to our readers in Baltimore City, Baltimore County, and contiguous jurisdictions.

We need feature stories that are rich with character and drama, or that provide new insight into local events. These stories range from 2,000 to 4,500 words. To propose one, send a query letter and clips.

Unless you've already got a great set of feature clips and a powerful idea, though, the best way to break into Baltimore is through the shorter stories that run before and after the feature well, in departments such as "Sports" and "Body & Soul." These stories range from 1,000 to 1,500 words. To propose one, send a query letter and clips.

Another possible space for writers unknown to us is the essay, which requires a strong personal voice and a risky new take on local life. We're looking for bravery, background research, and, above all, original thought. These essays are 800 words. To submit one, send a cover letter and a completed draft.

We often develop story ideas ourselves and assign them to freelancers. If you'd like to be considered for such assignments, send clips and a letter about your specialties.

Throughout the magazine we need originality, so don't propose anything that you've seen in the *Sun*, the *Baltimore Business Journal*, or other local media, unless you offer a fresh perspective or an unexploited angle. And remember that as a monthly with a copy deadline six weeks ahead of our publication date, we can't do much with breaking news.

You're most likely to impress us with writing that demonstrates how well you handle character, dramatic narrative, and factual analysis. We also admire inspired reporting and a clear, surprising style.

Queries should be no longer than a page. Sorry, we can't return your clips. Send correspondence in care of the appropriate editor, as listed below.

Thanks for your interest.

Contact Information:

Ramsey Flynn, Editor
Fashion, Home, Travel: Lois Perschetz, Executive Editor
Health, Business, Politics: Ken Iglehart, Managing Editor
Essays, Education, Urban Issues: Margaret Guroff, Deputy Editor
Arts, Law, Sports: Jim Duffy, Senior Editor
Short Pieces, Humor: Max Weiss, Staff Writer
16 South Calvert Street
Baltimore, MD 21202
(410) 752-7375 • FAX: (410) 625-0280

Bass West

Our goal is to make BASS WEST the most authoritative reference guide in the West. As western water problems continue to grow and fisheries budgets suffer more cutbacks, bass will become even more important to the western fishing scene. With your expertise, we can make BASS WEST a major resource for bass anglers in the West.

BASS WEST magazine focuses on western techniques for the deep, clear water and tough fishing conditions found in the West. Each issue has three main sections:

• Columns by western bass pros such as Mike Folkestad, Don Iovino, Jay Yelas, and Dub LaShot.

In-depth features of 2,000 to 3,000 words on western techniques, strategies, issues, etc. Additional standard length articles of 750 to 1,800 words about projects, tips and other items of interest to western bass anglers.

• Serious reports on the West's best bass destinations. Up to 4,500 words.

EDITORIAL REQUIREMENTS

- Content geared to both the serious western bass angler and occasional western tournament angler
- The "expert's touch"
- Lots of quotes from other authorities on the subject—guides, manufacturers, biologists
- Specific lures and equipment and identification of manufacturers
- Articles based on current scientific research—western-based biological data
- New facts, not rehashed or outdated opinions

SPECIFICATIONS

- FEATURE ARTICLES: In-depth, hands-on western bass information including seasonal and regional variations—Southwest, Northwest and Intermountain may vary. Educational content is important, as are practical solutions to tough fishing problems. Subjects: techniques, biology, technology, seasonal conditions, etc. Include any slides, photos, charts, maps or illustrations you may have. We also like to clarify subjects with sidebar explanations, illustrations, and charts or graphs.
- STANDARD ARTICLES: Unique projects, tidbits, short technical pieces, innovative projects, etc. If helpful, use quotes from experts. Include slides, diagrams, etc.
- DESTINATION ARTICLES: We want to know the nuts and bolts—why, where, how. Include information on seasonal variations, good detailed maps and interviews with experts—guides, biologists, and major tournament anglers. List lodges, guides, and camping areas with phone numbers.
- PHOTOS AND ILLUSTRATIONS: We prefer slides over prints, but in-focus prints with good contrast are also acceptable. We strongly encourage fishing action shots and photos showing tackle, techniques, rigging, lures, locations (especially western scenic locations) and some big fish photos.
- HUMOR/REAL LIFE ADVENTURES: Creative entertainment.
- PHOTOS: Cover shot must include angler, bass, western scenery, and action in one shot.

RATES

- Feature articles—2,000 to 3,000 words—$200 to $500.
- Standard articles—750 to 1,800 words—$75 to $300.
- Destinations articles—Up to 4,500 words—$200 to $500.
- Humor/real life adventure—750 to 1,000 words—$75 to $250.
- Photos—Inside use: Rate: $25 to $75. Cover shot: angler, bass, scenery, and action. Up to $400.

Contact Information:
350 East Center Street, Suite 201
Provo, UT 84606
(801) 377-7111

Beckett Publications

The Market

Thank you for your interest in Beckett Publications. We publish six monthly magazines: *Beckett Baseball Card Monthly*, *Beckett Basketball Monthly*; *Beckett Football Card Monthly*, *Beckett Future Stars®*, *Beckett Hockey Monthly*, and *Beckett Racing Monthly*. They currently have a combined paid circulation of more than two million. Our readership consists mostly of teenagers and adults. Their common bond is the hobby of collecting sports memorabilia and a love of sports.

Your Opportunity

Most features appearing in our publications are written by freelancers, so we always need good material between 500 and 2,000 words. We purchase First North American Serial Rights. Many accepted articles earn between $150 and $250. We pay upon acceptance, rather than upon publication, after receiving a signed contract from the author. We do not consider simultaneous submissions, and we prefer receiving query letters outlining specific ideas rather than completed manuscripts.

Our Needs

Acceptance of manuscripts is based upon interviews with superstars, excellent writing, solid collecting angles and positive tone. We particularly are on the lookout for articles concerning the hobby itself—autograph collecting, set information, unusual topical subsets, hobby trends and the like. We prefer all hobby stories convey the same message: Collecting should be fun. We have little interest in stories presenting sports cards or memorabilia as investments.

Because of our wide range of readership ranges, articles should not talk down to adults nor bore or confuse our younger readers. Other than that, your best bet for acceptance is to study our magazines. Sample copies are available for $2.95. Our basketball, hockey, Future Stars and racing magazines have fewer stories awaiting publication. Prospective contributors have a better chance of acceptance in those titles. We are, however, always interested in quality baseball and football pieces.

Contact Information:

Baseball, Football, Basketball, Hockey: Mike Payne, Managing Editor
15850 Dallas Parkway
Dallas, TX 75248
(972) 991-6657

Beer, the magazine

Beer, the magazine is an international magazine for beer lovers, aficionados and fanatics. It offers a full-color, tabloid format, as well as articles on:

- Travel
- Adventures in search of the perfect brew
- Columns and departments
- Domestic breweries
- Imports
- Microbreweries
- Brewpubs
- Breweriana
- Homebrewing
- History, lore and legends

Contact Information:

Bill Owen
Beer, the magazine
Box 510
Hayward, CA 94543-0510
(510) 538-9500

Better Homes and Gardens
Meredith Publishing Group

Only about ten percent of our editorial material comes from freelance writers, artists, and photographers; the rest is produced by staff.

We read all freelance articles submitted, but much prefer to see a letter of query than a finished manuscript. The query should be directed to the department where the story line is the strongest. See appropriate editor and department below.

A freelancer's best chance lies in the areas of travel, health, parenting and education. We do not deal with political subjects or with areas not connected with the home, community, and family. We use no poetry, beauty, or fiction. The best way to find out what we do use, and to get some idea of our style, is to study several of our most recent issues.

We buy all rights and pay on acceptance. Rates are based on our estimate of the length, quality, and importance of the published article.

Contact Information:
Building, Remodeling: Joan McCloskey
Food, Nutrition: Nancy Byal
Furnishings, Decorating: Sandy Soria
Garden: Mark Kane
Money Management, Automotive: Lamont Olson, Managing Editor (interim)
Travel: Martha Long
Environment: Steve Cooper
Health/Fitness, Cartoons: Martha Miller
Education, Parenting, BH&G Kids: Barbara Palar
1716 Locust Street
Des Moines, IA 50309-3023
(515) 284-3000

Black Belt Magazine

Please note that we almost never use personality profiles. We prefer style-oriented stories with the person an incidental. We also prefer color prints or negatives with a minimum size of 5" x 7" when possible. Perhaps we'll hear from you in the future.

WRITER'S GUIDELINES

Thank you for your interest in *Black Belt* magazine, the oldest and most widely circulated martial arts publication. The magazine's subjects include training, health and fitness, comparisons of different styles, weapons, historical pieces, fiction, and interviews with prominent martial artists.

Before mailing a completed manuscript to *Black Belt*, it is advisable to send a query letter. Describe your proposed article, including perhaps a sample lead or outline. If the subject is of interest and has not been covered too recently, we may request to see the article on a speculation basis.

Articles must address a specific interest or concern of the serious martial artist. Writing should capture reader interest with a strong lead, then hold it with information that is exact, concrete, and focused around a strong central theme. All quotes and anecdotes should pertain to the central theme.

Black Belt seldom uses first-person accounts. In addition, while many instructors are dedicated and high-ranking, the magazine rarely requests personality profiles. If you do choose to write about an individual, your article should provide that your subject is particularly unique or significant.

All statements and quotes must be accurate and verifiable. Use authoritative sources and cross-check your information. Please define foreign words within the text.

Manuscripts should be from five to ten pages. Payment is generally upon publication, and simultaneous submissions must be identified as such. Depending upon your subject matter, black and white lead and technique photos should be included with the article.

Once again, thank you for your interest in *Black Belt*.

The *Black Belt* staff

Contact Information:
Rainbow Publications
24715 Ave. Rockefeller
P.O. Box 918
Santa Clarita, CA 91380-9018
(805) 257-4066 • FAX: (805) 257-3028

Black Child

(Please refer to Interrace Publications.)

The Bloomsbury Review

The Bloomsbury Review is a magazine about books. *TBR* accepts submissions of book reviews, essays, poetry, interviews, and other articles. Payment is made upon publication. The scale is as follows: book reviews (of 600 or more words) = $10 to $15; poetry = $5 to $10 per poem; essays, features, and interviews = $20 to $30. Submissions of less than 600 words in length are welcome but not paid. Reviewers may also opt for gift subscriptions in lieu of cash.

FORMAT FOR SUBMISSIONS

Our preferred format for submissions is in the form of DOS text stored on a "regular density" – NOT "HIGH DENSITY" – 5-¼" diskette (with one hard copy) formatted in WordPerfect versions 5 or 5.1 or ASCII. We will also accept your review on hard or FAXcd copy.

Please include your name, mailing address, and phone number on page one, and your name only at the top of each following page; allow eight weeks for reply to unsolicited material.

FORMAT FOR BOOK REVIEWS

At the top of the first page, include the following information:

1. Title of book
2. Subtitle (if any)
3. Author/Editor/Translator/Illustrator/Photographer
4. Publisher/price/binding ISBN
   (please include price and ISBN for both cloth and paper editions, when available)
5. The year the book was published

FOR STYLE: Follow *The Chicago Manual of Style*. It is our policy to use nonsexist language. *TBR*'s editors will make minor editorial alterations, if necessary, to conform to the house style. If substantial editing of your review is required, you will be notified and a copy of your edited review can be sent to you for your approval or final changes prior to publication.

LENGTH: Upon assignment of a review or feature, an editor will assign an approximate length (usually from 100 to 1,000 words, as some subjects or books may warrant more or less space).

If you find that a book you have been assigned does not warrant the time and effort it would take to review it, please contact your editor. This does not mean, however, that we will not publish negative criticism provided it is properly substantiated.

QUOTED MATERIAL: It is extremely important to include a photocopy of all materials extracted directly from the text of the book you are reviewing. If you are returning the book to *TBR* you need not include photocopies. Please indicate on your manuscript (in the left margin) the page from which the quote is taken.

REVIEWER INFORMATION: Please include a bio/byline of up to 30 words at the end of each submission.

HEADLINE: Writers are welcome to suggest a headline for their reviews, interviews, or essays, although such will be subject to editorial discretion and space limitations.

TIPS ON WRITING A BOOK REVIEW

As in any good writing, there should be a strong introduction and conclusion, and smooth transitions between paragraphs. The writing should be intelligent without being too pedantic, critical without being condescending, and lively and colorful without being frivolous.

A good book review should tell the reader what the book is about, why the reader may or may not be interested in it, whether or not the author is successful in his/her intent, and whether or not the book should be read.

Never review a book on a subject you are not familiar with. It is not necessary to be an expert on the subject, but a thorough working knowledge of the author or subject matter is imperative.

Be objective. Never review the work of a personal or ideological friend or enemy.

Never review a book you haven't read at least once and understood.

Review the author's ideas, not your own. Do not compete with the subject, react to it.

A review should be more than just a summary of the book's contents. It should be an involved and informed response to both style and theme as well as content.

If you have any questions regarding the writing of a book review or any other feature, please do not hesitate to contact one of our editors. It is our obligation to provide our readers with informative, entertaining statements about books and the ideas presented in them.

The book business is an exciting field, and we welcome your thoughts, comments, and submissions.

Thank you,
The Editors of
The Bloomsbury Review

Contact Information:
1762 Emerson Street
Denver, CO 80218-1012
(303) 863-0406

BlueRidge Country

BLUE RIDGE COUNTRY is a bimonthly, full-color magazine embracing the feel and the spirit of the Blue Ridge region—the traditions and recipes, the outdoor recreation and travel opportunities, the country stores and bed-and-breakfast inns, the things to visit and learn about. In short, it is everything that will allow and encourage the reader to "take a trip home for the weekend" even if he or she has never lived in the region.

Our territory extends from Western Maryland south through Virginia's Shenandoah Valley of Virginia down into northern Georgia and including all territory within about a half day's drive of the parkway. It includes the mountain regions of Virginia, North Carolina, West Virginia, Tennessee, Maryland, Georgia, South Carolina, and Kentucky.

MAIN PIECES (750 - 2,000 WORDS)

PLACES

Everything there is to find out and tell about a great Blue Ridge town, city, or locale. The history, the current economic status, the quaint spots and characters, the best places to eat. A profile so complete our readers can make hard decisions on going to spend a weekend or even moving there.

HISTORY & LEGENDS

From people and events to unexplained occurrences or phenomena, the magazine prints fascinating tales of past and present.

THE BLUE RIDGE PARKWAY AND THE APPALACHIAN TRAIL

There's a wealth of wildlife, beauty, history and future plans involving the parkway and the trail and the areas immediately surrounding each. We bring our readers a new piece of America's favorite scenes highway and favorite footpath in each issue.

GENERAL ARTICLES

Anything that is well-researched, well-written and brings us some of the flavor of the region will get strong consideration. We'll be looking for at-home kinds of things—recipes and craft articles, natural history and wildlife, and especially pieces that embrace the whole of the region. Plus humor, first-person adventure or discovery and the "bests" of the region.

DEPARTMENTS

Very much like the main pieces, but in shorter versions; places to see, things to do, recipes to try, great people doing great things, new books, etc.—anything and everything that contributes to the sense of the place.

RIGHTS

We buy exclusive first North American serial rights until the off-sale date of the issue in which material is published, as well as exclusive rights to the work for promotional and reprint use.

PAY

We pay from $25 (for department shorts) up to about $250 for major pieces. Payment is upon publication. Manuscripts not supplied on disk are paid 20% under the above rates.

Sample copies of the magazine are available. Send $3.00 and a magazine-size SASE.

PHOTOGRAPHY

We use primarily color slides, and pay $25 to $50 for exclusive first North American serial rights until the off-sale date of the issue in which material is published, as well as exclusive rights to the work for promotional and reprint use.

Send queries, ideas, and stories to:

Contact Information:
Kurt Rheinheimer, Editor
P.O. Box 21535
Roanoke, VA 24018
(703) 989-6138

B'nai B'rith International Jewish Monthly

The *B'nai B'rith International Jewish Monthly* explores the social, cultural, historical and political issues that affect the Jewish community in the United States and abroad. The format of the magazine permits the in-depth exploration of subjects accompanied by high quality, four-color photography and other illustration. We try to strike a balance between political, cultural, human interest and service articles in each issue.

We value clear, vibrant, engaging writing which tells a story completely but with a maximum of economy. We discourage generalization, cliché, wordiness and lack of color. Articles should capture the spirit of an idea, person or place, enabling the general reader to appreciate the significance of a story.

We expect writers to work in good faith as journalists: to research thoroughly, to quote accurately, to report objectively and without vested interest, to deliver articles on deadline, and to be open to editorial changes. We are very loyal to writers who meet these standards. We try to include writers in the editorial process as time permits.

We strongly discourage the submission of fiction, political commentary and nostalgia. Query letters should include writer's clips. Articles range from 1,000 to 3,000 words. Submission of commissioned work should be made in hard copy form, accompanied by 5¼" inch or 3½" disks in ASCII or WordPerfect if available. Queries and submissions may also be made by e-mail at the address below.

The *Jewish Monthly* buys first North American serial rights.

A sample copy of the magazine may be obtained by sending $2 to the address below.

Contact Information:
Jeff Rubin, Executive Editor
1640 Rhode Island Avenue, NW
Washington, DC 20036
(202) 857-6646 • FAX: (202) 296-1092
E-mail: jrubin@bnaibrith.org

Body, Mind & Spirit Magazine

Body, Mind & Spirit magazine invites freelance submissions on natural living, health, self-help, spirituality, relationships, prosperity, and metaphysical topics. The material we present is intended to help our readers improve their lives physically, materially, mentally, emotionally, and spiritually. We prefer positive, informative articles that provide insight and practical help for our readers in their daily lives. Please avoid unsupported claims ("the channel told me so") and overly philosophical or abstract instruction.

Since we publish on a bimonthly basis, we need only 8-10 articles every eight weeks to fill the magazine. We receive 60 to 100 queries per issue so most submissions will be declined. That does not mean that your article is not good or that we might not be interested in a similar topic later on.

The best way to see what type of articles we publish is to obtain a copy of the magazine. Sample copies are $3.95 each. Please include a 9"x12" SASE with $1.65 postage affixed.

Queries/Manuscripts

Finished manuscripts are preferred, but queries are acceptable. To query, send a clear, concise outline or description of your idea along with information about the availability of photographs or illustrations (include photocopies if possible). Include up to three sample paragraphs from the beginning of the article. Indicate if you have a resource list to accompany the article (if appropriate) and include a brief biography indicating whether or not you wish to have your address and/or phone number published.

Exclusivity/Copyright

We prefer original unpublished works. Exceptions include book excerpts or adaptations and articles published in small circulation magazines or newsletters.

We buy First North American Rights on original articles.

Rates

We pay 10 cents a word on published words (example: 2500 words = $250).

Payment is made after publication.

Photographs and Illustrations

Photographs and/or illustrations may be submitted with articles. Payment will be included or added to editorial fee. We do accept freelance work; you may send nonreturnable samples for our files.

Contact Information:

Spirituality, Health, Nutrition, Healing: Lisa Colby
P.O. Box 701
Providence, RI 02901
(401) 351-4320 • FAX: (401) 272-5767

Bow & Arrow Hunting

Typically full length articles, as we use them, run six to twelve pages of manuscript. It is not necessary to count the words, as we do not pay by the word.

Manuscripts must be "scanner ready" (typewriter quality print) to be accepted. Dot-matrix printing is unacceptable unless it is NLQ. Gallant Publications will accept 3½-inch floppy disks with hard copy. Query first.

Each typed page should have the author's name and address on an upper corner of the paper. Please include your social security number on the title page. Include your phone number and a suggested time you may be reached, should the need arise.

The likelihood that we will purchase and use a given article is strongly influenced by the quantity and quality of artwork accompanying it. Good black and white or color print photographs of high contrast, together with the necessary information for accurate captions, are essential to us for the magazine.

Submission of color transparencies for possible cover use is encouraged. Transparencies not selected will be returned when accompanied by proper return postage. Payment rates depend upon the content and quality of the individual transparencies.

As to the contents of your manuscript, we recommend that you first review a few copies of BOW & ARROW HUNTING magazine with a view toward absorbing the general writing style employed before submitting a manuscript for consideration.

The primary emphasis must be upon bowhunting. Stories for BOW & ARROW HUNTING should be concerned with various aspects of hunting, including details on archery tackle used. We want our readers to know what was used, when, how and why. The accompanying illustrations should concentrate upon this theme, as well.

Do-it-yourself articles, telling and showing how the reader can make or modify items connected with archery are, always of interest to us. Hunting articles are welcome, both large and small game. We place emphasis on deer hunting for most issues of the magazine. Each story must impart information that will be of interest or benefit to the readers. We tend to put more emphasis upon informing rather than merely entertaining.

We pay upon acceptance and the amount is determined by the length and quality of the manuscript and illustrations as well as, to some extent, the amount of work we have to do to make it suitable for our purposes. If it is weak on artwork and we have to create additional photos, the amount we pay for the story will be correspondingly reduced. As a general guide, payments range from $150 to $300, rarely more than the latter. Expect a reply in sixty to ninety days.

Contact Information:
Roger Combs, Editorial Director
P.O. Box 2429
Capistrano Beach, CA 92624-0429
(714) 493-2101

Bowling Magazine
Official Publication of the American Bowling Congress

TO: WRITERS AND PHOTOGRAPHERS CONTRIBUTING TO "BOWLING MAGAZINE"
FROM: BILL VINT, EDITOR

When making submissions to *Bowling Magazine*, please follow these general guidelines. These general policies will greatly assist us in editing, filing and following up on any matters related to your submission:

MANUSCRIPTS

1. Always leave at least two-inch margins on both sides of your copy.
2. Number each page at the top.
3. On your first page, start typing 3-4 inches from the top of the page. Include the following in order:
   a. HEADLINE: your suggested headline.
   b. SUBHEADLINE: directly below major headline, a very brief subheading related to your story.
   c. BYLINE: By (your credit line, typed in upper\lower case).
   d. Start your copy.
4. On each subsequent page, include a "slug name" in the upper left-hand corner with

page number in upper-right hand corner.

5. At the close of your story, double-double space and then include an "editor's note" explaining who you are. Example: Editor's note—Joe Smith is a sportswriter with the Argon Daily News.

6. Finally, at the bottom of the final page, include your name, mailing address, a telephone number where you normally can be reached during weekday business hours, and your Social Security number.

PHOTOGRAPHS

1. B&W: 5"x7" or 8"x10" photos are acceptable.

2. Color: 35mm or larger transparencies, or 5"x7" or 8"x10" color prints are acceptable (note: for specific assignments, color print negatives may be submitted and we will make prints if detailed caption/photo idents are included with film).

3. QUALITY IS CRITICAL: Bowling Magazine is striving for the highest quality graphics possible, in content as well as in color accuracy and detail.

4. DARE TO BE DIFFERENT: Make certain you first cover the subject matter using traditional journalistic values, but then try something new or different or unique. Our artists are exceptional; we have no fear of trying something different if it works ...

5. PRINTS (color or B&W):

a. Make certain your name is included on the back of every print.

b. Either attach a photo caption to each print, or write a "code" on each print to accompany a corresponding sheet of captions so we can clearly identify photos.

6. COLOR TRANSPARENCIES:

a. Ship all slide/transparencies in plastic sleeves so they are fully protected (in sheet-style holders preferred; please do not ship transparencies in boxes!).

b. Make certain every slide is identified with a code or number. If possible, write your last name (at least) on the slide border in permanent ink.

c. Include a complete caption sheet with slides, corresponding to number, or code on each slide.

7. Include with all photos a separate cover letter including your name, mailing address, a telephone number where you can normally be reached during weekday business hours, and your Social Security Number.

ORIGINAL ARTWORK

Inquire first. We almost never purchase unsolicited, unassigned art work. We do not publish cartoons. Otherwise, follow guidelines under "Photographs" when making submissions.

GENERAL FREELANCE SUBMISSION POLICIES

1. Bowling magazine pays upon acceptance of submissions. You will normally receive payment within 14 days of the acceptance of your materials.

2. Rates paid for written or photographic submissions vary depending upon the nature of the subject, its importance, quality and other factors.

3. All photographs submitted to, and paid for by, *Bowling Magazine* for assigned stories or features become the property of the American Bowling Congress and will not be returned UNLESS specific agreement has been reached regarding the return of unused/unpublished materials.

4. Submission deadlines for assigned stories/photos will be rigidly enforced. Failure to meet deadlines may result in the cancellation of publication of the assigned materials.

5. Bowling magazine retains the full and complete right to edit manuscripts for style, accuracy, length and (if necessary) content and context. We will assume you accept that policy when you submit materials.

Contact Information:
Bill Vint, Editor
5301 South 76th Street
Greendale, WI 53129-0500
(414) 421-6400

Boys' Life

Boys' Life is a general interest, four-color monthly, circulation 1.3 million, published by the Boy Scouts of America since 1911. We buy first-time rights for original, unpublished material.

NONFICTION. Major articles run 500 to 1,500 words; payment is $400 to $1,500. Subject matter is broad. We cover everything from professional sports to American history to how to pack a canoe. A look at the current list of the BSA's more than 100 merit badge pamphlets gives an idea of the wide range of subjects possible. Even better, look at a year's worth of recent issues. We are found in libraries and BSA council offices.

Columns run 300 to 750 words; payment is $150 to $400. Column headings are science, nature, earth, health, sports, space and aviation, cars, computers, entertainment, pets, history, music and others. Each issue uses seven columns, on average. We also have back-of-the-book how-to features that bring $250 to $300.

FICTION. Fiction runs 1,000 to 1,500 words. Payment is $750 and up. All stories feature a boy or boys. We use humor, mystery, science fiction and adventure. We use one short story per issue. Send completed manuscript with cover letter.

Articles for *Boys' Life* must interest and entertain boys ages 8 to 18. Write for a boy you know who is 12. Our readers demand crisp, punchy writing in relatively short, straightforward sentences. The editors demand well-reported articles that demonstrate high standards of journalism. We follow the *New York Times* style of manual and usage.

We receive approximately 50 queries and unsolicited manuscripts per week. Unsolicited nonfiction manuscripts are returned unread.

Please query by mail, not by phone. And thank you for your interest in Boys' Life.

Contact Information:
Nonfiction: J. D. Owen, Managing Editor
Fiction: Shannon Lowry, Associate Editor
1325 West Walnut Hill Lane
P.O. Box 152079
Irving, TX 75015-2079
(972) 580-2366

Boys' Quest

A WORD AT THE OUTSET

Every *Boys' Quest* contributor must remember we publish only six issues a year, which means our editorial needs are extremely limited.

It is obvious that we must reject far more contributions than we accept, no matter how outstanding they may seem, to you or to us.

With that said, we would point out that *Boys' Quest* is a magazine created for boys from 6 to 13 years, with youngsters 8, 9, and 10 the specific target age.

Our point of view is that every young boy deserves the right to be a young boy for a number of years before he becomes a young adult.

As a result, *Boys' Quest* looks for articles, fiction, and poetry that deal with timeless topics such as pets, nature, hobbies, science, games, sports, careers, simple cooking, and anything else likely to interest a young boy.

Writers

We are looking for lively writing, most of it from a young boy's point of view - with the boy or boys directly involved in an activity that is both wholesome and unusual. We need nonfiction with photos and fiction stories - around 500 words, puzzles, poems, crafts, cooking, carpentry projects, jokes and riddles.

Nonfiction pieces that are accompanied by black and white photos are far more likely to be accepted than those that need illustrations.

The ideal length of a *Boys' Quest* piece - nonfiction or fiction - is 500 words.

We will entertain simultaneous submissions so long as that fact is noted on the manuscript. Computer printouts are welcome.

Boys' Quest prefers to receive complete manuscripts with cover letters, although we do not rule out query letters.

We will pay a minimum of 5 cents a word for both fiction and nonfiction, with additional payment given if the piece is accompanied by appropriate photos or art. We will pay a minimum of $10 per poem or puzzle, with variable rates offered for games, crafts, etc.

Boys' Quest buys first American serial rights and pays upon publication. It welcomes the contributions of both published and unpublished writers.

Sample copies are available for $3.00 and a complimentary copy will be sent to each writer who has contributed to a given issue.

Photographers

We use a number of black and white photos inside the magazine, most in support of articles used. Payment will vary, usually $10 per photo used.

Artists

Most art will be by assignment, in support of features used. The magazine is anxious to find artists capable of illustrating stories and features and welcomes copies of sample work, which will remain on file. Our work inside is pen and ink. We pay $35 for a full page and $25 for a partial page.

There's one more thing

Boys' Quest, as a new publication, is aware that its rates of payment are modest at this time. But we pledge to increase those rewards in direct proportion to our success. Meanwhile, we will strive to treat our contributors and their work with respect and fairness. That treatment, incidentally, will include quick decisions on all submissions.

Contact Information:
Manuscripts: Marilyn Edwards, Editor
Manuscripts: Virginia Edwards, Assistant Editor
Illustrations-art: Becky Jackman, Assistant Editor
P.O. Box 227
Bluffton, OH 45817-0227
(419) 358-4610

The Brodingnagian Times

A literary broadsheet published quarterly (June, September, December, March) and a magazine (44 pages) published annually each January.

There are no editorial slants and all submissions are given with equal priority to an editorial committee of five members. We are interested in poetry, primarily free verse of up to 40 lines but all other forms will be considered. We are also looking for short stories as well as other prose (short shorts, autobiography, letters, etc.) and satire. All reviews are done in-house.

Artwork and line drawings are solicited. Previously published and simultaneous submissions are fine if acknowledged. We are an international venue so please, no purposely Irish poems.

Payment is copies if published in the broadsheet and a small honorarium if published in the magazine. Reporting time varies from two weeks to 3 months. Copyright stays with the authors.

Contact Information:
Giovanni Malito, Publisher
96 Albert Road
Cork, Ireland
(21) 311227

Buffalo Spree Magazine

BUFFALO SPREE MAGAZINE is a high-quality, consumer-oriented, quarterly magazine mailed to a literate audience of approximately 21,000 above-average-income residents of metropolitan Buffalo. We publish fiction, nonfiction, and poetry. Except for a few regular features, our editorial is derived solely from unsolicited submissions.

FICTION: We are looking for well-written stories with strong conflicts and well-developed characters. Dramatic and literary as well as light and humorous pieces are welcome. We do not consider pornographic works.

NONFICTION: We are interested in articles of interest to residents of Western New York as well as well as poignant or humorous commentaries and essays.

Ideal length for fiction and nonfiction pieces is 1,000-2,000 words.

Payment is on publication.

We accept but do not encourage simultaneous submissions.

Estimated response time is 1-3 months.

Thank you for your interest. We look forward to receiving your submissions.

Contact Information:
Fiction, Nonfiction: Johanna Van De Mark, Editor
Poetry: Janet Goldenberg, Poetry Editor
P.O. Box 38
4511 Harlem Road
Buffalo, NY 14226
(716) 389-3405

Business Start-Ups

Thanks for your interest in *Business Start-Ups* magazine, the fastest growing small-business magazine in North America.

We've designed these guidelines to help you help us. Read them carefully and design your query to appeal to our ultimate boss—our reader.

FIRST THINGS FIRST

Business Start-Ups pays between $200 and $350 for departments and between $350 and $600 for features. For information about our payment process, see "Acceptance and Payment" below.

THE BSU READER

We're looking for articles that will appeal to two distinct groups: 1) people eager to launch their own companies, and 2) people who run new or very small—but growing—companies.

BSU's 315,000 monthly readers are:

- Fairly young (median age: 41 years old).
- Well-educated (84% attended or graduated college).
- Solidly middle-class (median income about $50K), but with very little capital to invest ($7,700 median).

WHAT THEY WANT

- New Business Ideas. Hence our almost constant theme, "A Million New Businesses You Can Start."
- How-to Articles About Business Start-Up. We're looking for precision: articles that focus on one element of the start-up process—marketing, PR, business plan writing, taxes, financing, selling and the like.
- Homebased Business Tips. Almost three quarters of our readers pick up BSU for our articles on how to run a homebased business. Again, we're looking for precision. The world does not need one more overview on the blessings of working at home.

BSU ARTICLES SHOULD BE:

- *Lessons-oriented.* Get right to the point and tell our readers how to make their businesses operate better.
- *Intelligent.* This means that you should be specific and use real world examples, i.e. entrepreneurs who are successfully using the techniques you are suggesting in your article.
- *Concrete.* Stay away from abstract management theory. Our readers want to know the three things they must do before they hire their first employee, not a rundown on Total Quality Management.
- *Written with self-reliance in mind.* Don't tell our readers to hire someone to write their business plan. Tell them how they can do it themselves.

A good query will convince us that your article is a must-read for *BSU*'s audience. It will show that you have read an issue and know the type of articles we feature and the style in which they are written.

WRITING AND SUBMISSION: A CHECKLIST

- Proofread your article. Check all facts for accuracy before submission. Get full corporate or organization names (and find out if "The" is part of the name). If a name is an acronym, find out what it stands for. Check the exact spelling of the source's name, his or her age, and the month and year the business was started. What does the business do? Where is it based? Ask for financial indicators about the business—where it is now (sales figures!) and where it's going (industry-wide trends).

- Submit your copy on disk or by modem, accompanied by a printed manuscript as well. You may also e-mail your article to us at the address below. Be sure you provide a complete list of all your sources, including their complete addresses and telephone numbers. If you send your story on disk, we need 3-½ or 5-¼ inch disks with the text in ASCII or Microsoft Word format.
- If you wish to modem the article to us, dial (714) 261-9020. Convert your file to ASCII text and send it as a binary file. At the password prompt, type in "Guest." Your filenames must be shorter than eight letters.
- Include your day and evening phone and fax numbers.
- Include a signed writer's contract and an invoice with your name, address, an invoice number (you assign it), the month your article was slated for, the name of the article and the price we agreed upon.
- Include a list of sources (with their addresses and phone numbers) used in the article.
- If you have any questions, please don't hesitate to call us.

ACCEPTANCE AND PAYMENT

BSU pays on acceptance. To eliminate false expectations, here's how the process works:

Your manuscript arrives with an invoice. The story is reviewed, usually within two weeks. If the manuscript requires a rewrite, we'll let you know why. We offer one shot at rewrites; if we're still not satisfied, we'll offer you a 20 percent kill fee.

If we like the manuscript, we'll let you know it's been accepted. We'll ship your invoice to our accounting department and begin the (roughly) 60-day payment process. While we'll work assiduously to move your invoice through the system, there may be delays. We hope this will allow you to calculate your cash flow appropriately.

Contact Information:
P.O. Box 57050
Irvine, CA 92619-7050
(714) 261-2325
E-mail: BSUMag@aol.com

ByLine.

ByLine

A National Magazine Aimed Toward Helping Writers Succeed

About *ByLine*

We believe Erskine Caldwell was right when he said, "Publication of early work is what a writer needs most of all in life." Tenacity is essential to success in writing, but while success as a writer is a great achievement, considerable merit attaches to the effort itself. As in athletics, training is the struggle; victory is merely the affirmation of that struggle. Our message to writers is a simple one: Believe in yourself and keep trying.

Since its founding in 1981, *ByLine* has published the first work of hundreds of fiction writers, poets, and nonfiction writers. We encourage and advise novice writers; we publish the work of beginners and veterans alike. Every month we publish articles on the craft or business of writing, including regular columns on writing poetry, fiction, nonfiction, and children's literature. We also publish short fiction and poetry, and a special feature for student writers.

ByLine sponsors monthly contests with cash prizes, designed to motivate writers by providing deadlines and competition against which to match their skills. In addition, we sponsor the annual *ByLine* Literary Awards as a gesture of appreciation to our subscribers. This contest carries a November first deadline, and a cash prize of $250 in each of two categories, short story and poetry. Unlike the monthly contests, which are open to anyone, the Literary Awards are open to subscribers only. Winners of the *ByLine* Literary Awards are published in the magazine along with brief stories about the authors.

WRITER'S GUIDELINES

Do not submit computer diskettes unless requested.

FICTION—General short fiction, mainstream, literary or genre; 2,000 to 4,000 words. Good writing is the main criterion. Payment is $100 on acceptance. FEATURES—Instructional or motivational articles that could be of genuine help to writers, especially how-to-write or how-to-sell to specific market areas. Length 1,500 to 1,800 words; query or submit full manuscript. We also solicit interviews with editors of freelance-friendly publications for our Inside Information feature. Query with editor's name and sample of his publication; we'll provide specific guidelines. Payment is $50 on acceptance for all features. END PIECE—A strong, thoughtful, first-person essay of 700-750 words, relating to writing. May be humorous, motivational or philosophical. Read several back issues as examples. Payment is $35 on acceptance. DEPARTMENTS—Read the magazine for examples. First Sale carries 300 to 400-word accounts of a writer's first sale. Payment is $20 on acceptance. Writing-related humor of 200-600 words needed for Only When I Laugh. Pays $15 to $25 on acceptance. POETRY—Our poetry also deals with the subject of writing. We lean toward free verse but will accept skillful rhyme if it is not predictable. We get an abundance of short, humorous verse but seek good-quality, serious poetry about the writing experience. Poems about writer's block, "the muse," and inspiration that comes in the middle of the night have been overdone. Payment is $10 for poems of more than five lines, $5 for five lines and under.

We purchase first North American rights only; no reprints. List your full name, address, and telephone in upper left corner of first page of manuscript and an accurate word count (line count for poetry) in upper right corner.

Contact Information:

Fiction, nonfiction: Kathryn Fanning, Managing Editor
Poetry: Betty Shipley, Poetry Editor
P.O. Box 130596
Edmond, OK 73013
(405) 348-5591

C/C++ Users Journal

Types of Stories

C/C++ Users Journal publishes C and C++ related tutorials and stories that take a practical, how-to approach to both theoretical and real-world problems. The typical story runs less than 3,000 words and presents less than 300 lines of code. Stories that cover complex topics may occasionally exceed these limits.

We also print occasional "short subjects." These are very short articles of less than approximately 800 words and 80 lines of code. Examples of short subjects are coding tips, handy utilities, and coding "gotchas" (i.e., mistakes that are very easy to make and very hard to find.)

Book Reviews

When writing a book review give a brief synopsis and answer the following questions :

- Are the topics covered completely? What, if any, are omitted? Are any over- or underemphasized?
- Is the book well organized?
- Is the material accurate?
- Are the examples helpful? Are there enough or too many examples?
- Who is the intended audience? Who should not attempt to read it?
- Is the author's writing style appropriate for the intended audience?
- Is the book easy to read?
- How does this book compare to similar books?

End with a brief overall evaluation, listing the strong and weak points and suggestions for improvement. Keep the length under 1,500 words.

Product Coverage in *CUJ*

C/C++ Users Journal does not print product reviews. Articles that concentrate on evaluation and comparison of products, or make purchasing recommendations are outside the editorial focus of the magazine. Specific products or vendors may be mentioned in articles if they are pertinent to the story. For example, an article may make extensive reference to the Microsoft Foundation Class Library if the author's code uses MFC. *CUJ* also mentions products in User Reports.

A User Report is an article that demonstrates a new use for a product, documents a little-known feature, or presents a work-around for a well-known problem in using the product. In contrast with a product review, the User Report attempts to demonstrate how to use a product, not whether or not to purchase it. Also, the author of a User Report should have extensive experience with the product. This is in contrast to the product reviewer, who typically has time only to gain a general, superficial knowledge of the product h/she is reviewing.

User Reports may also be tutorial in nature. For example, a User Report may educate the reader about special techniques used in embedded systems programming, and use a specific embedded system compiler to illustrate the technique.

If you are considering including specific products in a story, ask yourself these questions as a guide:

- Does the story present factual information about the product (as opposed to personal opinions and judgments)?
- Does the story present useful, "how-to" information?
- Does writing about the product serve an educational purpose?

If you can answer yes to these questions, we may be interested in running your story.

Writing Style

CUJ is not an academic journal. Writing style should be professional of course, but not overly formal. Here are some suggestions:

- Write as if you were talking to a friend who is also a programmer. Assume this programmer is just as talented, intelligent, and knowledgeable about programming as you, but may not know as much in this particular area, or about C and C++ in general.
- Use active voice where possible. Put the actor of the action in the subject position. "getchar takes input from the standard stream." is more forceful and interesting than "Input from the standard stream is obtained by using getchar."
- Feel free to use first or second person. Since you are writing a *CUJ* article for fellow programmers, I and you are acceptable. However, try to avoid the textbook pedantic we. The phrase "Next, we will show you how to allocate memory for... " is better suited to textbooks than to *CUJ*. It is often difficult to describe a program's flow of execution and still avoid passive voice and the pedantic we. Use your best judgment, given these guidelines.
- Don't say the C language. We assume our readers know C is a language.
- Don't try to guess what the reader is thinking. A common problem occurs in weak transitions like "By now you're probably wondering why..."

• Use a subhead to begin a new section instead of composing a weak transition such as "Now that I've explained the factors involved, let's explore implementing them." Instead, just create the subhead Implementation.

• Don't refer to the operating system as DOS. Instead use the full name of your particular operating system (MS-DOS, PC-DOS, AmigaDOS, etc.)

• Explain the "obvious." Don't worry about telling the readers something they already know. Instead, give a full explanation. We know our audience and will edit where appropriate.

• Make the article self-contained. For instance, don't count on readers being familiar with *Knuth Volume 2* or the *IBM Technical Reference*.

Proposing an Article

Before submitting a finished manuscript, consider proposing an article idea. A proposal will help you gauge our interest in a story idea before you invest time producing a polished manuscript.

Each issue of the magazine contains a Call for Papers that describes suggested topics for upcoming issues. The Call for Papers also gives deadlines for proposals. Though we may accept a story on any *C* or *C++* related topic, check the Call For Papers first for our immediate story needs.

A proposal should include a one- to two-paragraph abstract, a one-page outline, and a brief description of the author's background. If possible submit your proposal in electronically readable format, such as on a floppy diskette, or via e-mail.

Submitting a manuscript

Text

Please submit your article via e-mail, or floppy disk. We cannot accept your story unless it is submitted in an electronically readable format.

Disks should be MS-DOS formatted and can be either 3.5-inch or 5.25-inch. All text files must be in RAW ASCII. Do not format text files, except for code listings or fragments. If you use a commercial word processor, use nondocument mode. Make the text flush left and single-spaced. Do not right justify the text. Put a double space between paragraphs.

You may include code fragments in the article text. Since text columns in the magazine are often narrower than columns in code listings, code width in the text is even more restricted. Confine code fragments to 35 characters in width.

Do not put quotes around variable and function names or around keywords. We will print them in special monospace font in the magazine.

You may use sidebars to provide background material on a subject. Sometimes, background information is helpful to a novice, but superfluous to our more advanced readers. A sidebar is an excellent device for letting the reader decide if s/he wants additional information.

Code

Code listings should be submitted in separate files. Width of a listing is restricted by the width of magazine columns. So, keep the width of your code as narrow as possible.

Number each listing at the beginning (i.e., Listing 1, Figure 1, Table 2, etc.). Be sure to refer to your listings at the appropriate places in the article text.

Drawings and diagrams

If your submission includes drawings or diagrams, please submit them in Encapsulated PostScript (.EPS) if possible. If your submission includes bitmaps please submit them in Windows Bitmap (.BMP) format if possible. We can also accept sketches if they are not overly complex. Our artists will use your sketches to produce a drawing in a commercial drawing package.

Biography

Please provide a two- to four-sentence capsule biography to accompany the printed story (include your educational background, areas of expertise, and computer-related interests). Indicate to us whether we may publish your phone number. In any event, please provide us home and work numbers for our records.

Contact Information:
Managing Editor
1601 W. 23rd St., Suite 200
Lawrence, KS 66046
• FAX: (913) 841-2624
E-mail: marc@rdpub.com or mbriand@mfi.com.

The California Highway Patrolman

We are currently in the market for articles on modern or old-time automobiles, boats, bicycles, motorcycles, snowmobiles and other recreational vehicles. We are also looking for stories on transportation and pedestrian safety, travel and recreation in the West particularly California, humor and historical articles on California.

Articles with accompanying photos/illustrations always receive preference.

We are a general-interest publication geared toward the layman - something for the entire family - not a technical journal. Authors should restrict their subject matter to one main theme rather than trying to tackle too many things in one article.

Payment is 2½ cents per word and $5 per photos/illustration. We can use black and white or color prints, line art or transparencies. No negatives please. We pay $20 per original cartoon, which must be CHP-related.

Payment is on publication. We do not pay a kill fee.

We purchase one-time rights. Authors retain all other rights. We have, on occasion, purchased rights to well-written, previously published magazine articles, provided the magazine title and date of publication are furnished. We do not buy fiction, poetry, fillers or reprints from newspapers.

Query or send the complete manuscript, with a cover letter, on speculation. Please do not query by telephone. A sample copy of the magazine will be sent on request provided a 9"xl2" envelope is furnished.

Contact Information:
Carol Perri, Editor
2030 V Street
Sacramento, CA 95818
(916) 452-6751 • FAX: (916) 457-3398

Cape Cod Life

Including Martha's Vineyard & Nantucket

Cape Cod Life, a bimonthly regional-lifestyle magazine, is designed to appeal to year-round residents, seasonal residents, and visitors to this scenic locale.

The editors are looking for articles which capture the unique spirit of Cape Cod, Martha's Vineyard, and Nantucket. The editorial approach is upbeat; articles should inform as well as entertain. Interested writers should read a copy of the magazine prior to sending in story ideas.

Cape Cod Life is published six times a year—February, April, June, August, October, and December. It is 80% freelance written. Each issue has at least four feature articles covering leisure, the arts, history, and a particular theme. The themes are as follows: February/March: Annual Leisure Time Guide; April/May: Lodging; June/July: Dining and Entertainment; August/September: The Arts; October/November: Artisans Report; December/January: Interiors. Other areas of interest include profiles of interesting people and places, legends, the environment, and nautical-related stories.

Editorial

1. *Cape Cod Life* prefers well-conceived query letters with copies of recently published clips. Please include photos to highlight the subject matter, or state availability of such. Photos published in the magazine are usually shot by professional photographers. Seasonal material should be sent six months in advance.
2. Article length varies from 1700 to 3000 words. Manuscripts must show a word count in the upper-right-hand corner. Include name, address, phone, FAX, and social security number on title page. If possible, please query for submission on disk.
3. Payment is based upon 10¢ per word of editorial text used. Payment is made 30 days after publication.
4. Out-of-pocket related expenses, with prior approval only, will be paid to writers working on assignment.
5. A kill fee of 20% will be paid for articles assigned, but not used.

Cape Cod Life buys First North American Serial rights. Contributors receive two sets of tear sheets and a copy of the magazine. Please address correspondence to:

Contact Information:
Laura Reckford, Managing Editor
P.O. Box 1385
Pocasset, MA 02559-1385
(508) 564-4466/(800) 645-4482 • FAX: (508) 564-4470
Web site: www.capecodlife.com

CareerFocus

(Please refer to Communications Publishing Group)

Careers & the disAbled

(Please refer to Equal Opportunity Publications.)

Caribbean Travel and Life

CARIBBEAN TRAVEL AND LIFE is a full-color bimonthly consumer publication devoted exclusively to the unique vacation, travel, recreational, and cultural opportunities offered by the diverse islands of the Caribbean, Bahamas, and Bermuda. It is directed to a sophisticated, upscale audience.

Feature articles should deal with the specific aspects of travel and life in the Caribbean such as travelogues and destination pieces, stories of cultural and historical interest, sports and recreational vacations, special events (festivals, fairs, etc.), special interest stories (historical restoration, flora and fauna, etc.), and personality profiles.

Copy must be lively, entertaining, and stylishly written as well as informative. Articles should be upbeat in tone. We prefer stories that provide an insider's view of the Caribbean with information and expert advice not readily available elsewhere. Avoid guidebook rehashing. We are especially looking for stories with a personal touch or point of view, and lively, colorful anecdotes, as well as strong insight into the people and places being covered. Destination pieces should provide a vivid portrait of a place, synthesized through the writer's own experience there. Detailed consumer information with reviews of upscale hotels, resorts, and restaurants should be provided as a sidebar. Service information should offer a connoisseur's insight and advice.

Each issue contains an in-depth island profile covering the history, culture, geography, and lifestyle of the island. It provides a definitive, insider's view of life on the island.

Feature articles should be 2,000 to 2,500 words and are usually accompanied by a detailed service sidebar. Queries are recommended, though unsolicited manuscripts are welcome. First-time contributors should query the editor with a brief written proposal of their article ideas and must include samples of their published work. Manuscripts should be submitted on a floppy disk if possible, as well as a hard copy.

Payment for first North American rights for feature articles is $550; for shorter articles for department sections, $75 to $200. Payment is made upon publication. Photography is paid separately. A kill fee of 25% of the article rate will be paid in the event that assigned stories are not published.

DEPARTMENT GUIDELINES

POSTCARDS FROM PARADISE: 400 to 600 words

Short essays on great finds in travel, culture, and the good life, such as unique attractions, natural wonders, special galleries, cultural events, travel tips, special travel packages, and other oddities. The section occasionally includes book or film reviews on Caribbean topics related to travel and culture.

DETOURS: 800 to 900 words

A column emphasizing out-of-the-way trips, events, restaurants, and activities that are non-touristy. Usually written in first-person style.

MONEY MATTERS: 800 to 1,000 words plus sidebar

A section on bargain destinations, dollarwise traveling, etc., emphasizing not necessarily the cheapest, but the best value for the money. Past columns have covered how to get the most of your pesos in Cancún, diving deals in the Caymans, comparing all-inclusive resorts.

RESORT SPOTLIGHT: 1,000 to 1,200 words

An in-depth review of one to three resorts focusing on the best or newest accommodations on a particular island. The column should review, evaluate, and describe the resorts, pointing out exceptional strengths and, when necessary, weaknesses.

ISLAND SPICE: 1,000 to 1,200 words

Brief description of the history and origin of a specific cuisine, kind of dish, or ingredient (Creole cooking in Haiti; roti, Trinidad's national dish; multiple uses of breadfruit; Grenada's spicy cuisine) followed by two or three recipes. The column can focus on one outstanding local cook, when appropriate. Also may feature reviews of restaurants on a particular island.

ISLAND BUYS: 1,000 to 1,200 words

A column highlighting shopping on a particular island, with emphasis on handicrafts, duty-free shops, or specialty items unique to the area.

TRADEWINDS: 1,000 to 1,200 words

A column on sailing, boating, and cruising, as well as water sports such as scuba diving, snorkeling, windsurfing, water skiing, and fishing. It should highlight unusual or outstanding offerings and opportunities, new facilities, special events, etc. Focus should not be technical but provide useful information for the layman interested in special sporting and recreational opportunities.

ECOWATCH: 1,000 to 1,200 words

A column highlighting the most worthy conservation efforts taking place in the Caribbean and alerting readers to challenges that need special attention.

JUST BACK: 800 to 900 words

An up-to-the-minute report on all of the tourism news and happenings on one island, such as hotel and restaurant openings, new chefs, new attractions, tourism trends, cultural events, resort expansions, etc.

Payment for departments ranges from $75 to $200.

Contact Information:
Veronica Stoddart, Editor-in-Chief
8403 Colesville Road, Suite 830
Silver Spring, MD 20910
(301) 588-2300 • FAX: (301) 588-2256

Catholic Digest

What kind of material does CATHOLIC DIGEST use?

1. Nonfiction articles: 1,000-3,500 words on almost any topic. Our readers have a wide range of interests—religion, family, science, health, human relationships, nostalgia, good works, and more.
2. We favor the anecdotal approach. Stories submitted must be strongly focused on a definitive topic. This topic is to be illustrated for the reader by way of a well-developed series of true-life, interconnected vignettes.

3. Most articles we use are reprinted—they have appeared in another periodical or newspaper. But we also consider all original submissions.
4 We don't consider fiction, poetry, or simultaneous submissions.
5. Don't query. Send the article itself.
6. Fillers.

A. CATHOLIC DIGEST features six regular fillers each month:

Open Door—Statements of true incidents through which people are brought into the Church. (200-500 words, $50)

People Are Like That—Original accounts of true incidents that illustrate the instinctive goodness of human nature. (200-500 words, $50)

The Perfect Assist—Original accounts of gracious or tactful remarks or actions. (200-500 words, $50)

Hearts Are Trumps—Original accounts of true cases of unseeking kindness. (200-500 words, $50)

Signs of the Times—Amusing or significant signs. Give exact source. ($4)

In Our Parish—Stories of parish life. (50-300 words, $20)

B. CATHOLIC DIGEST also uses other types of fillers: jokes, short anecdotes, quizzes, and informational paragraphs. (1-liners to 500 words, payment by length up to $50)

Address submissions to: Filler Editor

How should I submit articles to CATHOLIC DIGEST?

1. Before you submit a manuscript, study a copy of CATHOLIC DIGEST (available on request) for article tone and style.

2. If you are submitting an article for reprint consideration, send a photocopy of tear sheet, and include the name, address and editor of the original source, the copyright line from the original source, and the date of original publication.

3. If you are submitting an original, send a photocopy or typescript. We try to read handwritten manuscripts, but it's often impossible.

4. Our rates: $100 for reprints, $200-$400 for originals. For reuse in electronic form we pay half of all traceable revenue derived from electronic use to owner/author.

Contact Information:
Filler Editor
or
Articles Editor
P.O. Box 64090
St. Paul, MN 55164-0090

Catholic Near East

Catholic Near East magazine strives to educate its readers about the culture, faith, history, issues and people who form the Eastern Christian churches.

Established in 1974 by Catholic Near East Welfare Association, this bimonthly publication also attempts to inform its readers of the presence and work of the Association and its sister agency, the Pontifical Mission, in those nations that many Eastern Christians call home.

The goal of *Catholic Near East* is to inform, but its contents should not be academic. People, details of contemporary life, history and "local color" should be woven together. Eastern Christians—Catholic and Orthodox—are frequently depicted as relics of the past. Our goal is to portray these communities as living bodies of men, women and children living and coping in a confusing and often troubled world.

Catholic Near East is also a tool of ecumenical and interreligious dialogue. Eastern forms of Christianity, Catholic and Orthodox, should be highlighted. However, the Jewish, Hindu and Muslim communities should not be ignored.

The most successful articles are written by those in the field. Stringers in each PM city and in other CNEWA countries offer the most objective, accurate and sensitive portraits of their subjects. Articles should not exceed 1,500 words. This stipulation allows for the lavish use of color photographs.

Photographers, if they are not writers as well, should work with the respective author (the editor should coordinate these efforts). Photographs must illustrate what is described in the article—people, places, festival, etc. General or thematic illustrations are exceptions.

Submit material on the churches and people of the Middle East, Northeast Africa, India and Eastern Europe to:

Contact Information:
Mr. Michael La Civita, Editor
1011 First Avenue
New York, NY 10022-4195
(212) 826-1480

CATS Magazine

Purpose

CATS Magazine provides our cat-loving audience with timely, practical and well-researched information, delivered in an understandable, enjoyable style. We confront controversial issues and encourage responsible pet ownership through ongoing education. We pay tribute to individuals and organizations that improve the lives of cats and their owners, and we incorporate reader contributions that extol the virtues and pleasures of being friends with our favorite subject —cats.

Readers

We have readers in virtually every age group, but statistically the majority is made up of educated women, ages 35 to 54. Most have owned cats for over 10 years. A large percentage of readers share their homes with non-purebred felines. All have a desire to better their relationship with their furry household companions.

Needs Nonfiction

- Instructional (1,500-2,000 words) - Educate readers on topics of prime interest to all cat lovers. This type of article should include practical advice (e.g. A Feline-Friendly Guide To Holiday Entertaining, December 1995) or answer commonly asked questions on cat-related topics (e.g. Factoring Your Feline's Personality, February 1996). Articles must be well researched and documented. Sidebars that provide relevant information are a plus. Payment varies depending on length, complexity of research involved in writing article, and amount of time *CATS Magazine*'s editors must invest in revising manuscript.
- Human interest (1,500-2,000 words) - Touch the reader's heart; make the reader want to get involved. Features of this type include profiles of outstanding organizations and noteworthy people (e.g. Some Lucky Cats Get Ten Lives, March 1996) or descriptions of unusual cat-related locales (Los Gatos: The California Kitty City, July 1995). Payment ranges from $250 to $500.
- Short Stories (250-1,000 words) - Tell your story so readers can identify with you or

your cat's situation. Focus on a single event as opposed to "Fluffy's Life Story." This section is the best opportunity for new writers, but due to the large volume of manuscripts received, competition is great. Tails & Tales pays $20 to $50.

• Remarkable Cats (1,200 words) - Report a true-life story that is dramatic in nature and describes how a cat overcame insurmountable odds, or performed an amazing feat (e.g. The Greatest Gifts Of All, March 1996). Third person narratives are preferred, but first-person accounts will be considered. Quality color photography must accompany manuscript (6 to 10 different color photos or 35 mm slides). Pays $100 (including photos).

Needs Fiction

• Short Stories (250-1,000 words) - Make the reader believe your story is true. Do not have talking cats, or bring science fiction elements into the story. Stories written from a cat's perspective will not be accepted. Tails & Tales pays $20 to $50.

Poetry

• Express an emotion or evoke an image common to all cat lovers. Avoid breed-specific or long-winded verse. Light, unique or "fun" poetry is used more often than sentimental, memorial pieces. Few Lines 'Bout Felines pays $5 to $30. Do not submit photographs or illustrations with poetry.

Your Submission

Query Letters - Address query letters to the editor. Queries are preferred for feature articles. Do not query for short stories. Phone queries will not be considered.

• Include a brief statement of objectives.
• Define reader interest. (Why would our readers be interested in this idea?)
• List your qualifications.
• Estimate word length and completion date.
• Address completed manuscripts to department (Features, Tails & Tales, Remarkable Cats, etc.).
• Manuscripts are considered for all departments and sections not written by staff members or regular columnists.
• Place name, complete address, telephone number and date in the upper left corner of page 1.
• Specify approximate word count in corner of page 1. Indicate first or second rights. (We rarely buy second rights.) Indicate if manuscript is a simultaneous submission.
• Number each page and include the title and your name on each page.

Computer disk submissions - Address to department and include hard copy of manuscript.

• Microsoft Word, Word Perfect or ASCII files can be submitted on 3½ -inch Macintosh, 3½ -inch DOS or 5¼ -inch DOS floppy disks.
• Label disk with name and complete address.

Photography - Must be pertinent to editorial. 2"x4" transparencies, 35 mm slides or professional quality color prints will be considered. Do not send black-and-white or "instant" photography.

• Label all photographs and slides with your complete name and manuscript title, plus captions, if applicable. Include cat's name, gender, breed (if purebred) and any other pertinent information.

Notes

• Allow at least three months for us to evaluate, respond to, or return your submission. Do not contact us about the status of your submission; we will notify you when we have reached a decision.
• Study our magazine carefully (we suggest 5 to 6 issues), classifying the articles and analyzing them to determine the elements we typically use.

- Seasonal material should reach us 8 to 10 months prior to publication.
- Do not send manuscripts and queries via FAX or e-mail unless specifically asked to do so. Sample issues are available when request is accompanied by a 9" x12" envelope and $3 for shipping and handling.

Policy

- *CATS Magazine* examines all manuscripts on speculation. A positive response to a query does not guarantee purchase.
- By submitting to *CATS Magazine* you grant us the right to edit or abridge your manuscript. You affirm that you are the sole and original author of the article or poem. Payment is offered on publication.
- *CATS Magazine* buys first rights.
- Assigned articles not used for publication receive a 30-percent kill fee.

Contact Information:
Tracey Copeland, Editor
P.O. Box 290037
Port Orange, FL 32129
(904) 788-2770

Celebrate Life
Celebrating and Defending Human Life

This slick, bimonthly magazine, formerly titled ALL About Issues, has been the number-one magazine of the pro-life movement for over a decade. It is distributed worldwide, with circulation over 100,000. *Celebrate Life* is primarily Catholic, but has readers and authors from many Christian denominations. It features a mix of human interest stories, news, devotions and action items on a wide range of pro-life and pro-family issues. The magazine offers writers an international venue for their work.

Celebrate Life is not currently soliciting fiction or poetry.

Celebrate Life purchases one-time rights, and also distributes articles and poems (with the author's copyright notice and a statement that permission must be obtained from the author before reprinting the poem or article) to several electronic bulletin boards.

Multiple submissions and reprints should be identified as such.

Authors should include their name, address and daytime phone number on the first page of the manuscript, along with an approximate word count. The author's name and the manuscript title should also appear on the top of each page of the manuscript.

VOICE

This magazine, launched in 1991, for high school and college students, has been discontinued.

Contact Information:
P.O. Box 1350
Stafford, VA 22555
(703) 659-4171 • FAX: (703) 659-2586

Change
The Magazine of Higher Learning

Should you write for *Change*? Let me encourage the thought by telling you how we operate and what we're looking for.

Scope

Change is an opinion magazine dealing with contemporary issues in higher learning. It is intended to stimulate the thoughts of reflective practitioners in colleges, universities, corporations, government, and elsewhere. Using a magazine style and format, rather than that of an academic journal, *Change* seeks to spotlight trends, provide new insights and ideas, and analyze the implications of educational programs and practices.

The editorial focus of *Change* includes articles and profiles on trend-setting institutions and individuals, innovative teaching methods, economics and finance, administrative practice and governance, public policy, professional development, curriculum, the changing needs of students, educational philosophy, and the social role of higher education.

The editors encourage well-founded discussion of controversial policy issues, whether brief expressions of a controversial point of view—750 to 1,500 words—or more extended articles ranging from 2,500 to 5,000 words long.

Audience

Change, which is published six times a year, is intended for individuals responsible for higher learning in college, university, and other settings, including faculty, administrators, trustees, state and federal officials, students, and corporation, union, and foundation officers.

Manuscripts

What accounts for acceptance or rejection? Few manuscripts fail for general ignorance or poor writing. More typically, they turn up on topics that have been done to death (Bloom and Bennett) or that are too broad (preventing nuclear war) or too narrow (preventing dormitory theft) for our readership. Or they're written in the style of a journal—heavy on jargon and footnotes, light on analysis and point of view.

This last criterion is important. *Change* is a magazine, and the magazine article is a genre unto itself. What characterizes that genre? There's no formula, but a good article compels attention to an important matter. It shows a mind at work, one that reaches judgment and takes a stance. It is necessarily personal: it has a voice that speaks to the reader. It is credible: it knows its subject and the context. And it is concrete: it names people, places, dates, specific statements, and events—these to convey feeling for the subject and for life as it is lived, not as abstracted from an armchair. For models, look to the Atlantic Monthly.

Most writers who submit manuscripts do so with a main feature article in mind, which is fine. But the magazine has a continuing need for shorter pieces—a column (700 words), a profile, even humor. Another department to consider is our front-of-the-book Forum, for which we're after a shorter statement (1,000 to 2,000 words) on a controversial topic, in which you put yourself on the line. We're eager, too, for letters to the editor, to bolster that section of the magazine.

We ask that you adhere to these simple guidelines when preparing your manuscript:

- All manuscripts should be submitted in duplicate. If the article is accepted, at that time we will request a disk of the article in either Microsoft Word 5.0 (or higher) or WordPerfect 5.1.

- Because *Change* is a magazine rather than a journal, footnotes should not be included. References can be worked into the text or given parenthetically when necessary. Lists of "Related Readings" or "Resources" can be provided with the article where appropriate.

• A separate title page should provide short biographical information including the complete address, telephone, and FAX number of the author(s). The first-named author of a multi-authored article will receive the notification of acceptance, rejection, or need for revision.

Review Process

When we receive your manuscript, you will be sent a postcard verifying that your article has entered the review process. All manuscripts will be critically read by a consulting editor and an executive editor, a process that takes from three to four months to complete. (Should the manuscript be held for consideration longer than usual, you will be notified at the end of four months and offered the option of withdrawing the manuscript from consideration.)

If the article is accepted you will be contacted to discuss editing procedures and the production schedule for the issue of the magazine in which your article will appear. Each author receives six complimentary copies of the issue in which the article is included. Authors may also order additional copies or reprints (minimum order of 100). We do not usually pay for unsolicited manuscripts.

Manuscripts should be submitted exclusively to this publication.

Contact Information:
Nanette Wiese, Managing Editor
1319 Eighteenth Street, NW
Washington, DC 20036
(202) 296-6267 • FAX: (202) 296-5149

Charisma & Christian Life
Strang Communications Company

Charisma & Christian Life describes itself as "The magazine about Spirit-led living." Each month more than 600,000 readers turn to the magazine for inspiration, information and instruction.

Meet Our Readers. More than half of our readers are Christians who belong to Pentecostal or independent charismatic churches, and numerous others participate in the charismatic renewal in mainline denominations. Their median age is forty-seven. Seventy-two percent are married, and sixty-six percent have at least some college education. Ninety percent of them have been committed Christians for more than five years, and most are very active in their local church.

Study the Magazine. In order to sell articles to *Charisma & Christian Life*, writers must know the magazine well. A casual examination of a few issues will not be enough. You must study the magazine thoroughly, classifying the articles and analyzing them to discover the elements we typically use. You must catch our vision and get a sense of our readers' interests.

Here's Your Opportunity. Each year freelancers write eighty percent of our articles, but we assign most of these to writers who have established themselves with us. You should avoid sending teaching articles, interviews, issue-oriented pieces or news analyses, as these always originate with the editors. We do not publish sermons, poetry or fiction.

We are, however, looking for well-written articles in the following categories:

• Personality profiles. Our readers want to hear about people who are living the Christian life effectively and with pizzazz. Here we are not looking for complete biographical sketches, but "slices of life" that focus on some noteworthy event or story. Stories should include conflict or challenge, resolution, change and consequences.

• Miracle and healing stories. Our readers are interested in accounts of God's supernatural intervention in ordinary human events. These stories must be thoroughly researched and well told. Healings must be medically documented. Pastor's and other references may be required.

• Trend articles, that discern changes or new direction among Christians or that would be of interest or importance to Christians. Trend pieces must show evidence of exhaustive research. They should be written in a journalistic style and illustrated with anecdotes, facts and quotes from authorities.

• Seasonal articles of all kinds. Our readers enjoy articles that help them celebrate the Christian and secular holidays, including Christmas, Easter and Pentecost, as well as Valentine's Day, Mother's Day, Father's Day, the Fourth of July and Thanksgiving.

• News stories for our People & Events section. We welcome brief (200-700 words) and timely stories about people who have recently done something worthy of note or about events that would be of interest to our readers. Articles must be written in journalistic style and with punch. Facts and quotes must be scrupulously accurate.

With the exception of the short news stories, all articles should be between 1,800 and 2,000 words in length.

Our procedure. *Charisma & Christian Life* accepts query letters as well as completed manuscripts.

The author's name, address, telephone number, and social security number should appear on the top left of the first page on all submissions. An approximate word count should be typed at the upper right of the first page.

Charisma & Christian Life buys all rights. Payment for articles is usually 10 cents to 20 cents per word.

We consider all manuscripts submitted, and we return manuscripts we do not accept with a form letter if the writer has provided a self-addressed envelope with sufficient postage.

We are glad you are thinking about writing for *Charisma & Christian Life*, and look forward to receiving a superb article from you.

Contact Information:
Lee Grady
600 Rinehart Road
Lake Mary, FL 32746
(407) 333-0600

The Chief of Police

(Please refer to Police Times Magazine.)

Child

Child magazine is published 10 times a year, with combined issues in June/July and December/January.

Child provides parents of children from birth to age 12 with the newest thinking, information, and advice they need to raise their families in a constantly changing, time-pressed world.

Freelance writers are invited to submit query letters only, on the following topics:

- children's health,
- parenting and marital relationship issues,
- child behavior and development, and

- personal essays pertaining to family life

Child purchases first-time rights for articles and pays upon acceptance. Fees vary depending on length and positioning of articles.

Writers must include clips of previously published work.

Please allow eight weeks for a reply.

Contact Information:
***Child* Editorial Department**
110 Fifth Avenue
New York, NY 10011
(212) 463-1000

Child Life

(Please refer to Children's Better Health Institute.)

Child of Color

(Please refer to Interrace Publications.)

Children's Better Health Institute

We at the Children's Better Health Institute have a constant need for high-quality stories, articles, and activities with health-related themes. "Health" is a broad topic that includes exercise, nutrition, safety, hygiene, and drug education.

Health information can be presented in a variety of formats: fiction, nonfiction, poems, and puzzles. Fiction stories with a health message need not have health as the primary subject, but they should include it in some way in the course of events. Characters in fiction should adhere to good health practices, unless failure to do so is necessary to a story's plot.

Remember that characters in realistic stories should be up-to-date. Many of our readers have working mothers and/or come from single-parent homes. We need more stories that reflect these changing times but at the same time communicate good, wholesome values.

We are especially interested in material concerning sports and fitness, including profiles of famous amateur and professional athletes; "average" athletes (especially children) who have overcome obstacles to excel in their areas; and new or unusual sports, particularly those in which children can participate.

Nonfiction articles dealing with health subjects should be fresh and creative. Avoid an encyclopedic or "preachy" approach. We try to present our health material in a positive manner, incorporating humor and a light approach wherever possible without minimizing the seriousness of what we are saying.

Word and math puzzles, games, and other activities can also successfully convey health messages if they are enjoyable to young people and are age-appropriate.

We also welcome recipes that children can make on their own with minimal adult supervision. Ingredients should be helpful, so avoid using fats, sugar, salt, chocolate, and red meat. In all material submitted, please avoid references to eating sugary foods, such as candy, cakes, cookies, and soft drinks.

Although our emphasis is on health, we certainly use material with more general themes. We would especially like to see more holiday stories, articles, and activities. Please send seasonal material at least eight months in advance.

Caution: Reading our editorial guidelines is not enough! Careful study of current issues will acquaint writers with each title's "personality," various departments, and regular features, nearly all of which are open to freelancers. Sample copies are $1.25 each (U.S. currency) from the address below.

Turtle Magazine for Preschool Kids (ages 2-5)

Humpty Dumpty's Magazine (ages 4-6)

Turtle and *Humpty Dumpty* use stories and poems, as well as some creative nonfiction. Because these two magazines are designed to be read to children who are not yet reading independently, the editors look for submissions with a good "read-aloud" quality.

Games and crafts should require a minimum of adult guidance. They should also have clear, brief instructions, and use readily available materials. *Turtle* uses simple science experiments; *Humpty Dumpty* features healthful recipes requiring little or no use of kitchen appliances. Nonfiction, which editors always have a need for, must be narrow and specific in focus.

Children's Playmate (ages 6-8)

Jack And Jill (ages 7-10)

Children's Playmate uses easy-to-read fiction for beginning readers, as well as poems, rhyming stories, and nonfiction. *Jack And Jill* is edited for somewhat more accomplished readers; stories and articles are written at about a second- or third-grade reading level.

Both titles are heavy on fiction, using realistic, adventure, mystery, and fantasy. Humorous stories are especially needed. Nonfiction material may deal with sports, science, nature—even historical and biographical articles. Most nonfiction features touch in some way on health and fitness.

Child Life (ages 9-11)

Children's Digest (preteen)

Child Life editors encourage the submission of interesting nonfiction, especially profiles of kids or adults in sports, or active hobbies. Nonfiction articles should be accompanied by professional quality photographs or transparencies; no "snapshots," please. *Child Life* is a good market for offbeat or "slightly wacky" fiction, adventure, or science fiction.

Children's Digest readers want stories that are a little longer and "meatier." Fiction is especially needed: adventure, mystery, science fiction, and humorous stories. Some fiction may have a subtle health message, but this magazine, too, uses factual health features to educate about good health. Games, puzzles, crafts, and hobbies are also welcome, as are nonfiction articles about sports, nature, and the environment.

Manuscript Format

Manuscripts must be typewritten and double- or triple-spaced. The author's name, address, telephone number, date of submission, and the approximate word count of the material should appear on the first page of the manuscript. Title pages are not necessary. Please submit to a special magazine, not just to CBHI.

Please send the entire manuscript. All work is on speculation only; queries are not accepted, nor are stories assigned. The editors cannot criticize, offer suggestions, or enter into correspondence with an author concerning manuscripts that are not accepted, nor can they suggest other markets for material that is not published.

Photos and Illustrations

We do not purchase single photographs. We do purchase short photo features (up to 6 or 8 pictures) or photos that accompany articles and help illustrate editorial material. (please include captions and model releases.) Suggestions for illustrations are not necessary but are permissible. Please do not send drawings or other artwork. We prefer to work with professional illustrators of our own choosing.

Review Time

About three months are required to review manuscripts properly. Please wait three months before sending status inquiries. If a manuscript is returned, it should not be submitted to a different youth publication at this address. Each manuscript is carefully considered for possible use in all magazines, not only the one to which it was originally addressed.

Rates and payment Policies

Turtle and *Humpty Dumpty*, up to 22¢ a word
Fiction/nonfiction—up to 500 words
Children's Playmate, up to 17¢ a word
Fiction/nonfiction—300 to 700 words
Jack And Jill, up to 17¢ a word
Fiction/nonfiction—500 to 800 words
Child Life, minimum 12¢ a word
Fiction/nonfiction—500 to 800 words
Children's Digest, minimum 12¢ a word
Fiction—500 to 1,500 words
Nonfiction—500 to 1,000 words
Poetry—$15.00 minimum
Photos—$15.00 minimum
Puzzles and games—no fixed rates (Send SASE to receive separate guidelines for activities.)

Payment is made upon publication. Each author receives ten complimentary copies of the issue in which his or her material is published.

Rights

We purchase all rights to manuscripts. We buy one-time rights to photos. Simultaneous submissions are discouraged. One-time book rights may be returned when the author has found an interested publisher and can provide us with an approximate date of publication.

Children's Contributions

Except for items that are used in children's columns, the editors do not encourage submissions from children. Even highly talented young people are not usually experienced enough to compete on a professional level with adult authors. There is no payment for children's contributions.

CBHI also publishes *U.S. Kids, A Weekly Reader Magazine*, for readers 5-10. Although unsolicited manuscripts are welcome, editorial content is largely assigned. For more information, send for separate *U. S.Kids* guidelines—free with SASE—at the address below. Sample copies are $2.50 each.

Contact Information:
Editor, (Magazine Name)
100 Waterway Boulevard
Box 567
Indianapolis, IN 46206
(317) 636-8881

Children's Digest

(Please refer to Children's Better Health Institute.)

Children's Playmate

(Please refer to Children's Better Health Institute.)

Chitra Publications

We offer complete directions and diagrams for completing quilt projects, as well as interesting and instructional articles concerning all aspects of quilting. Articles should be informative to quilters, presenting new ideas or techniques. Upon submission of your manuscript, please allow six to eight weeks for a response. Articles are scheduled for publication up to a year in advance. Publication hinges on the quality of photos or the availability of quilts for photography.

SUBMISSIONS

We seek articles with one or two magazine pages of text and quilts that illustrate the content. (Each page of text is approximately 750 words, 6500 characters, or three double-spaced typewritten pages.) Ideas need to be logical, sequential and fully developed. We may ask you to revise or clarify your manuscript to make it publishable.

We prefer original material accompanied by 35mm slides or 2¼" transparencies. Please include detailed photo captions and photo credits. You may send suggestions for a one-line subhead after the title, a pull quote and a cover line of three or four words if you wish, but these are generally written by our editors. Send the names and addresses of your subjects in case we need to contact them for more information.

Please include the following information in the upper right-hand corner of the first page: your name, address, telephone number, Social Security number and the estimated number of words in your article.

Magazines are published six times per year. Specific guidelines for each magazine follow:

Traditional Quiltworks is a pattern magazine offering a variety of instructional features and directions for up to a dozen full-size projects. "What if . . . Design Challenge" is a regular column which encourages quilters to creatively use one pattern in many different ways. "Featured Teacher" is a profile about a quilting teacher accompanied by photos of her/his work. It is followed by "Private Workshop" which contains the teacher's instructions for completing a specific project. We occasionally feature one-page human interest/personality profiles accompanied by quilt slides/photos.

Quilting Today offers feature articles on quilt history, techniques, tools and quilters sharing their knowledge with readers. Articles are accompanied by color slides/photos and sidebars containing helpful tips. The pattern section offers six quilt patterns. Patterns are written according to the established magazine format. Other features include book and product reviews, a calendar of quilt events, a guest editorial and "The Sampler," a news column. Fictional pieces are rarely accepted.

Miniature Quilts offers dozens of patterns for small quilts with block sizes 5" or less. Also included are how-to articles, profile articles about quilters who make small quilts and photo features about noteworthy miniature quilts or exhibits.

EDITING

We reserve the right to edit and/or rewrite for style, clarity, length and adherence to format. When an article is ready for publication, a prepress copy is provided as a courtesy to ensure that all facts are accurate.

PHOTOS

Clear 35mm slides or 2¼" or larger transparencies can be used. Photos should be professional quality. Quilts should be shot straight-on so they do not appear distorted. Include your name and address on all photos. Write "TOP" on all slides. Include the photographer's name for the photo credit if required. Send photos in plastic sleeves or cardboard to protect them.

PAYMENT

Upon preparation of your manuscript for publication, you will be asked to sign a contract stating that your submission is not an infringement on the rights of others. Payment is made approximately six weeks after the on-sale date. Payment varies, depending on the amount of work required to prepare the article and whether or not the article promotes your business. Payment averages $75 per 800 published words, without photos. If your photo is used for a feature article or a pattern quilt, payment is $20. Payment varies for multiple photos. No payment will be made to you for quilts photographed by Chitra Publications. No payment is made for photos shown in the "letters" columns in any of the magazines.

REGULAR COLUMNS

If you would like us to consider your idea for a regular column, please use the following guidelines:

- Submit a description of the proposed feature, indicating its philosophy or goals and indicating why readers would benefit from reading it in sequential issues.
- Submit an autobiography of about 100 words, with an emphasis on quiltmaking, along with a professional-quality photo.
- Submit an outline of one year's columns (six).
- Submit two sample columns, including snapshots of projects or to-scale diagrams, if applicable. Patterns must be written to our format.

Upon acceptance of the feature, we require submission of one year's worth of manuscripts (six) before publication of the first installment. Upon receipt of the installments, we will edit the material and issue a contract. Payment for each installment is made approximately six weeks after the on-sale date. Should we desire the column to continue, a new contract will be issued at the proper time.

Contact Information:
2 Public Avenue
Montrose, PA 18801
(717) 278-1984 • FAX: (717) 278-223

CHRISTIAN HOME & SCHOOL

Christian Home & School

Manuscripts can range from 750 to 2,000 words and should include the author's name and address at the top of the first page. Include a sentence or two about yourself for us to use as a contributor's note; this could include humor.

Christian Home & School has a circulation of 58,000 and is designed for parents in the United States and Canada who send their children to Christian schools and are concerned about the challenges facing Christian families today. These readers expect a mature, biblical perspective in the articles, not just a Bible verse tacked onto the end. Use an informal, easy-to-read style rather than a philosophical, academic tone. Try to incorporate vivid imagery and concrete, practical examples from real life. The style of our articles varies from a reflective or humorous first-person account of a single incident relating to a topic to a more comprehensive, more objective discussion of a topic in general.

Suggested topics are listed below, but don't limit yourself to these ideas. We are interested in articles that deal with timely issues that confront Christian parents—profiles, reviews, or special features (no poetry or short stories, please). In addition to articles about practical concerns of Christian family life, we will consider first-person articles about the challenge of living the Christian life, and historical/biographical profiles of influential Christian individuals. Christian schooling and the relationship of parents and Christian schools are particularly interesting to our readers. Each year we also include seasonal articles dealing with such topics as Christmas, Easter, end of the school year, graduation, summer activities, and vacations.

We pay $75 to $150 upon publication, depending upon the length of the laid-out article, and prefer to buy first rights only.

If you would like a sample copy of our magazine, please send us a 9x12 self-address manila envelope with four first-class stamps affixed. For more information, contact Roger W. Schmurr, senior editor.

***Christian Home & School* Schedule:**

Issue	Author's Deadline
Sept.	June 1
Oct./Nov.	July 1
Dec.	Sept. 1
Jan./Feb.	Oct. 1
Mar./Apr.	Dec. 1
May/June	Feb. 1

Some possible topics for future issues of *Christian Home & School*:

- Teaching your child patience
- What can parents do to foster a good school spirit?
- What educational roles do the home and church play in the life of a Christian school student?
- Enjoyable family vacations—on a budget
- Rewards for good behavior: are they bribes?
- Should I teach my child to be assertive?
- How can the extended family help me in my parenting responsibilities?
- Teenage music: what's hot and why?
- What my parents did right
- How can you open the world to your kids and yet fend off unwelcome influences?
- Sex education at home, church, and school
- Parenting a strong-willed child
- Steering your driven child
- How two-parent families can understand and meet the needs of single-parent families
- Guardian angels: fact or fantasy
- How to teach children to pray
- How do you handle a tattletale?
- What should I teach my adolescent about dating?
- Keeping Christian school students involved in their communities
- Is slowing or speeding up schooling good for the child?
- Co-parenting after divorce
- Resolving sibling rivalry
- How parents can help their children succeed in school

How to avoid nagging
When your daughter says "I don't like the way I look!"
Blending two families after remarriage
Teaching children about money: allowances, spending, saving, giving, family budget, etc.
How Christian schools seek and handle diversity in their student bodies
The role of fantasy and imagination in the development of children
How to talk to your child about bad things: e.g., drugs, AIDS, and violence
Sexual abuse of children: recognizing and dealing with it
Raising secure children: helping children feel spiritually, physically, and emotionally safe
When parents fail: living with the mistakes we've made
The danger of living through your children: parents and their children's achievements
Too much too soon? Pushing early childhood development
Children's friendships: best friends, how friendships change
Kids and work: from household chores to their first paid job
Watching the news: helping children cope with current events
Identifying and handling learning disabilities: attention deficit disorder, etc.
Nurturing creativity in children
Dealing with family crises: death, divorce, serious illness, unemployment
What makes a child popular?
Practical ways to improve the connection between home and school
Learning styles: recognizing and responding to them
Language study at the elementary school level
Cooperative learning
Keeping up with technology: Is it important? Is it worth the cost?
How changing family situations affect schools
Tensions between schools and working parents

Contact Information:
Roger Schmurr, Senior Editor
3350 East Paris Avenue, SE
Grand Rapids, MI 49512
(616) 957-1070 • FAX: (616) 957-5022

Christian Parenting Today

SO YOU WANT TO WRITE FOR *CPT*? That's good news! Even though we assign the bulk of our articles, we're always looking for writers who can provide our readers with helpful information and keep us editors supplied with chocolate. But unfortunately (for you), it will take more than a box of Godiva's finest to get your articles published in our pages. So we need to tell you a few things about *CPT*, our readers, and us ever-picky editors.

WHAT YOU ABSOLUTELY, POSITIVELY NEED TO KNOW

Our goal is to encourage and inform parents of children ages birth to 12 who want to build strong families and raise their children from a positive, authoritative Christian perspective. More specifically, we strive to give parents practical tools in four areas:

1. Encouraging the spiritual and moral growth of their children
2. Guiding the physical, emotional, social and intellectual development of their children
3. Enriching the reader's marriage
4. Strengthening the reader's family relationships.

CPT readers belong to the Buster, Xer, Survivor, call-them-what-you-will generation. Strengthening family bonds, transferring Christian values to their children, and protecting their kids from an unkind world are among their top priorities—a vivid reaction to the difficult latchkey-kid childhoods many of them had. They've had primarily middle-class-American life experiences. Most own their own home (or hope to soon); most have dual incomes, often out of necessity. They are generous, educated pragmatists who take an experiential approach to life. They are "computer babies" who are comfortable with technology and who look at both present and future with attitudes of blunt realism. Their homes are "safe places," retreats from a harsh society where they can look for meaningful tradition. Their Christian churches provide them with friendly communities that give direction on strengthening their faith, families and marriages. Most are married mothers—around 30 years old—who have two young children.

What does such a parent want? Stability. Direction. A strong Christian family. Realistic help raising godly kids. And to do a better job at "family making" than their parents did.

OK, so don't bother sending chocolate. What we editors really crave are writers who demonstrate:

- a desire to assist our readers on both the spiritual and in-the-flesh levels of parenting
- an understanding of our readers and an ability to identify with them on a personal level
- experiential expertise relevant to the topic
- a willingness to work with demanding editors

That's not all. Your manuscript needs to demonstrate a few things too. Please be sure it:

- has a distinctly Christian perspective
- has a strong parenting angle
- applies fresh ideas to familiar issues
- anticipates readers questions
- contains practical, doable, vividly explained suggestions
- doesn't condescend or sermonize
- is authoritative, based on current research from respected and reliable sources
- is brought to life by real people (the voices of everyday parents and kids)
- is personal, speaking to the reader in a one-on-one, chat-over-latte style

If you've read this far, you must really want to write for us. So we willingly offer a few more tips:

- Tell it like it is. *CPT* readers have a "get real" attitude that demands a down-to-earth, pragmatic take on topics. Don't waffle. Don't fabricate sincerity. Don't pretend that the inside of a dirty diaper doesn't smell bad.
- If you've "been there," say so. Transparency is OK. The first-person, used appropriately, is OK. Our readers trust people who have walked in their Doc Martins.
- If appropriate, give your article a developmental spin. Some topics work best when they focus on the needs of certain-age children. We typically work within five developmental brackets: Babies, Toddlers, Preschoolers, Early Elementary Schoolers, and Late Elementary Schoolers.
- Cut out the "four areas" mentioned earlier, highlight them, paste them on neon paper, and tape them to your bathroom mirror next to your Scripture of the day. Ask yourself,

"Does my manuscript specifically address one of these areas?" If the answer is no, chances are ours will be too.

NOW FOR THE TECHNICAL STUFF

We prefer queries, but complete manuscripts are OK. We accept submissions sent via FAX or e-mail; however, we won t respond to them unless we're interested. Please allow eight weeks for us to respond. If we turn out to be no more on time than Alice's rabbit, please drop us a gentle whatintheworldhaveyoudonewithmyarticle! inquiry.

In addition to features, the following departments are open to freelance writers:

YOUR CHILD TODAY (YCT): articles of 300-400 words that address specifics of emotional, physical, social and intellectual development of children in five age brackets: Babies, Toddlers, Preschoolers, Early Elementary and Late Elementary. Send query or manuscript with SASE. Pays $50-75.

TRAIN THEM UP: same as YCT but relegated to spiritual development and values-transfer topics from a Christian perspective.

HEALTHY & SAFE: practical "how-to" articles of 300-400 words that speak to parents' desire to provide their kids with an emotionally and physically safe environment at home and away. Send query or manuscript with SASE. Pays $50-75.

FAMILY ROOM: a back-of-the-book "quit reading and go do something with your kids" activities article of 600-700 words. Should emphasize relationship-building and parent-child interaction. Send manuscript with SASE. Pays $125.

THE LIGHTER SIDE: a humorous look at everyday family life. 600-700 words. Send manuscript with SASE. Pays $125.

THE HOMEFRONT STORE: parent-tested reviews of children's and parenting products. Should demonstrate through practical application how product is relevant to at least one of *CPT*'s four editorial goals. Include price, order info, manufacturer contact. Send slides or artwork if available. Query Colin Miller, associate editor. Phone queries OK. Pays $25-$35.

Submissions to Life In Our House and Parent Exchange are not acknowledged or returned. No SASE required. (No clippings, please.)

LIFE IN OUR HOUSE: an insightful anecdote of 25-100 words about something funny that happened at home. Pays $25.

PARENT EXCHANGE: a tried-and-true parenting idea of 25-100 words. Pays $40.

The technically perfect query includes:

- your name, address, social security number and rights offered (we buy First NAS and Reprint)
- a working title for our reference
- a detailed but tentative outline
- anticipated length

When submitting manuscripts, please:

- include your name, address, social security number and rights offered
- limit your manuscript to 2,500 words (most features published are 1,000 to 2,000 words)
- outline your qualifications for writing the article
- do not send photos, slides or artwork (except to PARENT EXCHANGE or HOMEFRONT STORE)
- do not send fiction, poetry, diatribes, essays, interviews, report cards, or Grandma's treasured nut-bread recipe

And finally:

- We occasionally accept reprints from non-competing magazines. Send a fresh manuscript, a photocopy of the published piece, and the name and date of the publication it appeared in.
- Manuscripts requested via query aren't assignments, but are requested on speculation only.

- Submit seasonal material at least eight months in advance. The earlier the better.
- For a sample copy of our magazine, please send a 9"X12" SASE bearing $3 postage.
- Sorry, we don't have editorial calendars or theme lists available.
- Usually, payment (15 to 25 cents per published word, or a prestated flat rate), is on acceptance of completed manuscript for assigned articles; on publication for unsolicited manuscripts that we have accepted.

"Acceptance" is a loaded word around our offices. It means we've put you through the mill, if necessary, on rewrites and revisions—and we don't apologize for working you hard to meet our readers' needs. Please remember that we love writers, but at the bottom line we love our readers more and will go to (you'll believe) unthinkable lengths to serve them. *CPT*'s best writers are dependable, committed professionals who not only agree with this but join us in commitment to it!

Our Staff: Brad Lewis, Editor • Theresa Fogle, art director • Erin Healy & Collin Miller, associate eds. • Sherry Dixon-Leonard, ed. assistant

Contact Information:
All Except Reviews: Erin Healy, Associate Editor
Product Reviews Only: Colin Miller, Associate Editor
4050 Lee Vance View
Colorado Springs, CO 80918
(719) 531-7776 • FAX: (719) 535-0172
E-mail: CPTmag@aol.com

Christian Single Magazine

Christian Single is a current events magazine that addresses lifestyle issues of single adults from a positive, Christian perspective. The median age of our target audience is 31. We want professionally written articles that are in-depth, well researched with documentation, and thoroughly biblical. Write from a position that touches a felt need. Write to evoke an emotional response. Our intent is to provide practical help, proven answers, and spiritual insight to the spiritual, emotional and physical needs of today's single adult. We address the controversial issues of today by offering Christian solutions to the alternatives of secular society.

Technical Specifications

- Prefer query letter before submission of article.
- We require both hard copy and disk for submission.
- Disk must be 3.5" high-density not double-density.
- Prefer disk on a Macintosh word processing program, but can convert the following from IBM programs:

WordPerfect	Microsoft Word	Wordstar	Professional Write
Leading Edge	PCWrite	Display Write	Office Writer
XyWrite	PFS: First Choice	HP Advance	Write Plus
IBM Writing Ass.	Lotus Manuscript	Wang PC	Volkswriter

- Caution: To protect your disk from erasure, mark on the package, 'DO NOT SCAN."
- Text Specifications: 52 characters per line, 25 lines per page, left-justified.
- Quoted material must be properly documented (publisher, location, date, and page numbers), along with permission verification.
- New International Version is the standard translation used in *Christian Single*.
- *Christian Single* adheres to the *Associated Press, Stylebook and Libel Manual* for writing style.

Departments

Micro-Info: Brief, tips, facts, quotes, humor, etc. related to single lifestyle, household, or work.

Profile: In-depth interviews of well-known single adults who exemplify Christian living.

Single Parenting: Issues or information to help and encourage single parents.

The Body Shop: Health, nutrition, and fitness. Can be single article or collection of brief bits.

Tips for Submissions

1. Please indicate on the manuscript and disk your name, mailing address, social security number, rights being offered (all, first, one-time reprint) and length of article.
2. Length of department articles is 600-1,200 words (except Profile, 1,200-1,800).
3. Length of feature articles is 600-1,800 words.
4. Photographic materials accepted if they relate to article content. Submit captions with photos.
5. Pay is negotiable. Pay is upon acceptance, with three complimentary copies of the issue in which your article appears.
6. Payment and use of photos selected will be determined by the graphic designer.
7. For prose articles, include a thesis statement early in the manuscript.

Contact Information:
Manuscript Submission
127 Ninth Avenue, North
Nashville, TN 37234-0140
(615) 251-5721

Citrus & Vegetable Magazine

Target audience: Commercial citrus and vegetable growers, packers, processors and shippers in Florida.

Articles are aimed at farming practices used by commercial growers in Florida. We are particularly interested in case history type articles where a grower has used a new or unique method and has found it to be especially successful. Our primary mission is to give readers information they can apply to their own operations to make them more efficient and profitable.

We are particularly interested in articles dealing with water management and environmental subjects as they apply to Florida agriculture.

Articles are also sought that relate to the operation of fresh fruit and vegetable packing and processing facilities.

Each issue has a specific focus, i.e. spraying, irrigation, pest control, cold protection etc. An editorial calendar is available.

Articles should usually not exceed 1,600 words. Include the author's name and address at the top of the first page. We prefer articles to be prepared on WordPerfect 5.1 and submitted on 3½" disks with no coding, i.e. bold, italic, etc. Hard copy must accompany disks. When disks are used, copy should be formatted as follows: Set line spacing for 1.5. Set left margin for 1" and right margin for 4.25". Justify right and left. No hyphenation. Indent paragraphs 1 space. Use a hard return only between paragraphs.

Photos: Either color or b/w photos are acceptable. We prefer well composed, high quality color transparencies in 35mm, 2"x2", 6x7cm or 4"x5". Cover photos must be color transparencies and be a vertical format that will bleed off an 8"x10.75" page.

Deadlines: Editorial material must be in our hands not later than the 10th of the month preceding publication.

Payment on acceptance and varies with subject. Author must sign an exclusive rights agreement. QUERY FIRST.

Contact Information:
Gordon Smith, Editor
Scott Emerson, Managing Editor
7402 No. 56th Street, Suite 560
Tampa, FL 33617
(813) 980-6386 • FAX: (813) 980-2871

Classic Toy Trains

Thanks for your interest in writing for CLASSIC TOY TRAINS. We publish articles on all aspects of collecting and operating large scale toy trains: S through G. A look through one or two back issues of CLASSIC TOY TRAINS will give you a pretty good idea of the kinds of material we're interested in.

LETTER OF INQUIRY: Before you submit an article, we recommend that you write to let us know exactly what you have in mind. We can then tell you if your proposed article fits out needs or if we'd like a different approach than what you have in mind. If you have an idea on a subject you haven't seen us cover, write and ask.

The following is a general list of our requirements:

TEXT: Present your subject simply and directly in plain English. Keep it as brief as you can while still covering the subject; the key is to limit your topic to a manageable size. Our payment is based upon the length of the published article, not the length of the submitted article, so there's no advantage to writing long.

It would help us estimate manuscript length if you would set your typewriter or printer margins for 75 characters (e.g., 5 and 80). Type exactly 25 lines per page. Be sure to include a caption for every photo you submit, and number all illustrations and photos in the text with corresponding consecutive figure numbers.

PHOTOGRAPHY: Since two-thirds to one-half of CLASSIC TOY TRAINS editorial space is taken up with photographs, superior photography is critical. We can sometimes improve the text you provide, but we can't do much with weak photos. Part of the attraction of this hobby is the beautiful color of the models, so we prefer color, except in cases where color doesn't enhance your message.

We prefer original 35mm (or larger) color transparencies (slides); we can also use glossy color prints 5"x7" or larger. Most how-to or in-progress modeling or repair photos should be submitted in black-and-white, 5"x7" or larger. Usually it's best to send the negatives along in case we need them; we can return them to you after we use them if you wish. In general, the minimum requirements for submitting publishable photos are that you shoot with a 35mm SLR and put plenty of light on the subject.

We prefer you use one of the following when taking color model photos indoors for publication in CLASSIC TOY TRAINS:

Ektachrome 50 Tungsten, code EPY, made by Kodak

Fujichrome 64 T, code RTP, made by Fuji Photo

Both are "professional" films, which means that the average drugstore film outlet won't have them, but they are available from better camera stores. Both are color-balanced for 3200K tungsten lighting, and both take E-6 processing, which allows quick turnaround from local film labs. Both films are available in 35mm cassettes, 120 (2¼" square) rolls, and larger-format sheet sizes.

Ektachrome EPY has an ISO (formerly ASA) speed rating of 50, while Fujichrome RTP has an ISO rating of 64. Some photographers find that an ISO of 40 is closer to the actual performance of Fujichrome RTP, but if you make adequate bracket exposures you can get good results with a meter setting of either 64 or 40.

For more information on photography, please see PHOTO GUIDELINES (included as part of the COLLECTING TOYS listing in this directory).

DRAWINGS: Clean, neat pencil drawings are fine for how-to illustrations, electrical schematics, and track plans. These will usually be redrawn by our art staff for publication.

PAYMENT: We pay upon acceptance at the rate of $25 per typeset column. Payment for photos is at the same rate based upon the amount of space the photos occupy when published. If the article runs longer than we estimated, we'll make up the difference at the standard rate. We'll return photos and other materials we don't use, but we usually keep everything that's used in the article.

SUBMITTING YOUR MANUSCRIPT: Send everything for one article at one time all in one package, and include a cover letter with your name, address, and phone number where you can be reached during the day. Address your package "To the Editor, CLASSIC TOY TRAINS" and also mark it "MANUSCRIPT ENCLOSED." We'll send you a card acknowledging receipt of the article and try to review it within 60 to 90 days.

Thanks for your interest in CLASSIC TOY TRAINS.

Contact Information:
21027 Crossroads Circle
P.O. Box 1612
Waukesha, WI 53187-1612
(414) 796-8776 • FAX: (414) 796-1142

Cleaning and Maintenance Management

To ensure publication of articles that best suit our readers and advertisers, and to give the best possible presentation of the author's work, we ask authors to carefully review the following:

- Article by author on same topic should not be offered to another magazine in the cleaning/maintenance industry.
- Article must be generic; that is, it must not promote or mention a specific product brand name or company. Generic families or types of products or methods may be discussed, provided they are treated in an evenhanded manner.
- Author and company he/she represents is described in an end-of-article credit that accompanies the author's photo. Please submit author photo with article.
- Recommended feature article length (approximate):

Minimum = 750 words

Maximum = 1,500 words

• Article should be written for facility executives/managers in charge of facility-wide cleaning and building maintenance (contract, in-house or both). It should offer advice on system-wide programs or approaches that reduce costs; improve efficiency; instruct about employee staffing, workloading or training; assist in more professional care of building systems or surfaces; or otherwise upgrade cleaning/maintenance operations. Assume reader is college-educated and needs management-level advice.

• Article text format options:
Typewritten [mailed or FAXed] and/or:
3.5 inch computer disk (IBM-compatible or Macintosh) [mailed]

• We encourage, but do not require, submission of photos (color or b&w), charts, diagrams, "sidebar" or related "breakout" information, etc., that can help illustrate or visually break up the text. Photo prints, slides and transparencies are acceptable.

• Be sure that you and the Editor agree upon an acceptable deadline date and the general topic/approach of the article.

Contact Information:
Anne Dantz, Managing Editor
13 Century Hill Drive
Latham, NY 12110
(518) 783-1281, x3114 • FAX: (518) 783-1386

Club Modèle Magazine

Deadline:
60 days before publication date.
Payment:
Upon publication. $0.05 per word for articles, plus 3 copies of the issue in which article appears. $10 each for each photo or illustration.
Photos:
35 mm color slides or 8" x 1 0" black and white prints preferred. Up to 8" x 10" if used as part of article. All black and white photos must have enough contrast for screening. Captions, subject identifications and model releases required for all photos with identifiable people.
Seasonal Material:
Submit 3 months in advance.
Article Length:
150 to 1,000 words.
Sample Copies:
Copies of each magazine available for $4 each.
Format Accepted:
3-½" high density computer diskettes, PC compatible: txt files, WordPerfect, Word for Windows or PageMaker, e-mail.

Special Conditions:

1. All material subject to editing.
2. All information must be verified and is subject to revision.
3. All articles for which Aquino International pays will be copyrighted by those publications, First North American Serial Rights only, when agreed to in writing by the publisher. Otherwise, all articles will be the exclusive property of Aquino International.
4. Photographers may retain copyrights to their photos. First North American Serial

Rights apply to all photos.

5. Signed model release must accompany any photo submission in which people are identifiable. Articles and/or photos showing models without release forms will be rejected.

6. Captions and identification of subjects required for all photos.

7. Aquino International reserves the right not to publish an article it has purchased and/or to publish it or republish it at a later date.

Tips:

1.) We welcome material for our regular departments as well as for special editorials.

2.) All nonfiction material must be factual and easy to read.

3.) Familiarize yourself with our magazine. Send $4 for a sample copy. It will be sent to you by first class mail.

CLUB MODÈLE is targeted at readers involved in the modeling field. We welcome articles from or about fashion, runway, print, artists or other models, as well as agents, and decision makers in businesses which use models, i.e., magazines, ad agencies, fashion designers, etc. We are also interested in articles on subjects related to the modeling field, such as fitness, health and beauty (vis a vis modeling), business topics, i.e., contracts, royalties, burn out, etc., and general subjects such as information on photo shoots, tips on handling stress and competition, specialty parts modeling, etc. Related photos and model releases must accompany articles.

Kinds of articles for Club Modèle:

Subjects:

1. Modeling agencies, agents, managers, photographers, models (of all types).

2. The business of modeling: fashion, contracts, royalties, licensing.

3. Unusual angle stories, interviews, how-to's, caveats, business opportunities and trends.

4. Travel destinations. Exotic locales around the world. Anecdotes accompanied by off-the-beaten track photos, nontypical tourist spots of interest to photographers.

Readers:

Models, agents, casting directors, ad agency executives, photographers, art directors, fashion designers and executives.

Illustrations & Humor Spot Fillers now welcome. $10.

Contact Information:

Mr. Andres Aquino, Publisher
AQUINO INTERNATIONAL
P.O. Box 15760
Stamford, CT 06901-0760
(203) 967-9952 • FAX: (203) 353-9661
E-mail: aaquinoint@aol.com or aaquino@ix.netcom.com

Coast to Coast

Coast to Coast

As the membership publication for Coast to Coast Resorts, *Coast to Coast* Magazine is mailed to 300,000 readers eight times a year. Coast to Coast Resorts unites nearly 500 private camping and resort clubs across North America. A portion of the magazine is devoted to news about the *Coast to Coast* network: its programs, its products and services, and, of course, its members. The remainder of the magazine focuses on vacation, travel, recreation and good times. It strives to be a fun, unpretentious but well-written publication that offers a balanced mix of articles on things to do, places to visit and ways to ensure a safe and happy trip.

The most important component of stories published in *Coast to Coast* is good writing. While we do seek informative, factual articles, we do not subscribe to the notion that more is necessarily better. Tell a good story—and save the particulars for an accompanying sidebar.

Destination features in *Coast to Coast* should focus on a city or region of North America and should strive to convey the spirit of the place. The most readable place pieces go beyond typical tourist stops to interview locals and synthesize anecdotes and first-person observations in a way that is useful, entertaining, and enlightening. Keep in mind that *Coast to Coast*'s readers already have 500 camping resorts at which to stay, so reporting on accommodations is almost always beside the point.

Activity or recreation features should introduce readers to or rekindle their interest in a sport, a hobby or another diversion. As with the general public, most of our audience can be assumed to possess a basic knowledge of, say, golf or bicycling, but few have experienced rock climbing or skydiving. Nor would they care to, for the most part.

Many of our readers own recreational vehicles, so we generally feature the RV lifestyle in at least one article per issue. This is where lively, concise writing is especially in demand. If the writing is dry, the article will be, at best, unappealing; at worst, deadly. What's essential in these features is that readers identify with the situations they're reading about, that they pick up new information and at the same time are engaged and entertained.

The editors of *Coast to Coast* encourage queries and manuscripts. If you possess the required professional ability and have a lively writing style, please summarize your story idea, supplement it with a few opening paragraphs and forward it to our editorial offices with a selection of your best published clips or other writing samples. The editors are also pleased to review completed manuscripts.

Coast to Coast publishes first North American serial rights; articles must not appear in other publications for 90 days after they are first published in *Coast to Coast*. In accepting an assignment from *Coast to Coast*, writers agree to submit stories on or before the stated deadline and agree to rework the stories, if required, in a timely fashion. Assigned stories should be submitted electronically, either on disk or via modem, with an accompanying hard copy.

Contact Information:

Travel, RVing: Valerie Law, Editor
2575 Vista del Mar Drive
Ventura, CA 93001
(805) 667-4100 • FAX: (805) 667-4217

Collecting Toys

Thanks for your interest in writing for COLLECTING TOYS. As the premier magazine of the toy collecting hobby, we're always looking for superior material. Before you submit an article to us, we recommend you write to let us know exactly what you have in mind. We can then tell you if your proposed article fits our needs or if we'd like a different approach than what you have in mind.

We publish articles on all aspects of toy collecting. Our editorial focus is predominantly on toys from the post-World War II era, but we are interested in material covering all eras of toy production. Again, it's best to contact the editor before you begin. If you have an idea on a subject you haven't seen us cover, write and ask. Here's a general list of our requirements.

TEXT: Present your subject simply and directly in plain English. Keep it as brief as you can while still covering the subject; the key is to limit your topic to a manageable size. Our payment is based upon the length of the published article, not the length of the submitted article, so there's no advantage to writing more material than necessary. It would help us estimate manuscript length if you would set your typewriter or printer margins for 75 characters (e.g., 5 and 80). Type exactly 25 lines per page. Include a caption for every photo you submit, and number all illustrations and photos in the text with corresponding consecutive figure numbers.

PHOTOGRAPHS: Since at least half of COLLECTING TOYS editorial space is photographs, superior photography is critical. We can improve your text, but we can't do much with weak photos. Part of the toy collecting hobby's appeal is the color and look of the toys, so we prefer color, except in cases where color doesn't enhance your message. We prefer original 35mm (or larger) color transparencies (slides). However, we can also use glossy color prints 5x7 or larger.

If you do shoot print film, send the negatives with the prints; if you wish, we can return the negatives after the article has been published.

In general, the minimum requirements for submitting publishable photos are that you shoot with a 35mm SLR and put plenty of light on the subject.

We prefer you use one of the following film types when taking color photos indoors for publication in COLLECTING TOYS:

Fujichrome 64 T, code RTP, made by Fuji Photo

Ektachrome 50 Tungsten, code EPY, made by Kodak

These are "professional" films, which means that they are available from better camera stores. Fujichrome and Ektachrome are color-balanced for 3200K tungsten lighting, and take E6 processing, which allows quick turnaround from local film labs. Both films are available in 35mm cassettes, 120 (2¼" square) rolls, and larger format sheet sizes.

Ektachrome EPY has an ISO rating of 50, while Fujichrome RTP has a rating of 64. Some photographers find that an ISO of 40 is closer to the actual performance of Fujichrome RTP, but if you make adequate bracket exposures you can get good results with a meter setting of either 64 or 40.

PAYMENT: We pay upon acceptance at the rate of $25 per typeset column. Our contract specifies the purchase of all rights to your material; if you prefer to retain rights, payment is reduced. If the article runs longer than estimated, we'll make up the difference at the standard rate.

Send everything for one article at one time and in one package. Include a cover letter with your name, address, and daytime telephone number. Address your package "To the Editor, COLLECTING TOYS" and mark it "MANUSCRIPT ENCLOSED." We'll send you a card acknowledging receipt of the article and will review your material within 60 days.

Photo Guidelines

Attractive photography has made COLLECTING TOYS rise above its competitors. To maintain the quality of photography we publish, we have produced these guidelines to help you take the best possible pictures to contribute to an attractive, creative layout. It is our policy to return only the pictures that are not used in the magazine.

Film

1. We can use glossy color prints, but we PREFER COLOR SLIDES (35mm or larger formats) because they reproduce better than prints. Send duplicates if you want your own complete set.

Background

1. Use a SMOOTH, seamless paper or cloth backdrop.

2. DO NOT use backgrounds that have a texture that will detract from the toy (i.e., carpet).

3. Use a solid, light-colored backdrop, such as tan, light blue, white, or light gray.

4. Use the same color backdrop for all the pictures.

5. Be sure the backdrop is big enough to fill the frame of the picture so you don't see the edge or the area beyond the backdrop when looking through the camera.

Technical info

1. Avoid shadows. For best results, place lights slightly above the subject.

2. Get the entire object in focus. If you have a point-and-shoot camera, read the manual to see how close you can get to an object and have it remain in focus. Experiment and take a number of pictures at varying distances and exposure lengths.

3. If you have a more advanced camera, use a 55mm close-up lens. It will produce the best results. To get the entire toy in focus, use the smallest F-stop possible (i.e., F-32 or smaller).

4. Use a tripod and cable release, if possible.

Viewpoint

1. At least one picture of each toy should be taken straight on from the front. To do this, place the camera at the level of the toy or just slightly above it.

2. Shoot toys from a variety of angles.

3. If the toy has a "nose" (like a car, boat, or action figure), also take angle shots, one with the toy angled left and one with it angled right.

Frame

1. Get close to the toy, but be sure the ENTIRE toy is inside the frame of the picture and not touching the edge of the picture. For example, if a toy has a tail or antenna, be sure it is also well within the frame.

2. When taking pictures of flat things (like posters, instruction sheets, or illustrations) photograph them straight on (from above, looking down at them).

3. Group shots are fine if they aren't cluttered and every item is completely in the frame.

4. If you take a group shot, also take individual pictures of each item in the group shot. (Exceptions to this apply to toys like playsets. We don't need individual shots of playset figures unless they are rare or unusual.)

Thanks for your interest in contributing to COLLECTING TOYS.

Contact Information:
Editor
21027 Crossroads Circle
P.O. Box 1612
Waukesha, WI 53187-1612
(414) 796-8776 • FAX: (414) 796-1383

College Preview

(Please refer to Communications Publishing Group.)

Colonial Homes

Colonial Homes

Thank you for your interest in writing for *Colonial Homes*. To better understand what we expect from our freelancers, the following paragraphs provide information on our readers and what is published in the magazine. No guidelines sheet is a substitute for reading back issues, which will help writers to learn the scope and style of the articles we publish.

Our readers generally are married, college-educated, employed men and women who have a passion for history and design. The magazine offers readers a celebration of America's spirit with articles featuring antiques, art, architecture, historic homes, interior design, travel, and profiles of historical figures.

We look for articles on topics that have not been covered in our magazine—or other publications—for a substantial period of time. Our use of freelance writers is minimal, so a well-researched history and a new or unusual angle to a story are imperative. Most of our articles are produced by assignment only, so we accept no unsolicited manuscripts. Instead, we request that you query us with an idea. Your query should include:

1.) Your resume

2.) A variety of your published works/clips

3.) A one-page summary of the topic and proposed scope of the article

4.) At least one of the following—Copies of photographs or illustrations that might accompany the article; a list of proposed photographs; a list of potential suppliers of artwork to accompany the article

Queries should be mailed, FAXed, or e-mailed. No telephone calls!

Please keep in mind that we want a colorful, informative approach, with quotes from noted authorities on a subject. Our readers already know quite a bit about all that is Colonial, so use adjectives that describe an item in detail, such as "Chippendale" or "Georgian," not "nice" or "old."

Use the following checklist as a guide to creating a query and, if assigned, an article for *Colonial Homes*.

1. Study several issues of the magazine to familiarize yourself with our tone, style, and content.

2. Most articles run from 400 to 1,000 words long (depending on pages allotted), so plan the scope of your article to fit.

3. Generally, we use commissioned photographers to photograph a site or topic BEFORE a writer is assigned to a story. Therefore, we must be certain that appropriate photography can be secured before committing to a story. Along these lines, writers should provide a list of sites or examples that can be photographed to support your story.

4. All materials should be labeled with your name, address, and phone number.

5. *Colonial Homes* does not publish fiction, so please no queries in this area.

6. As a guide for spelling and style questions or concerns, writers can refer to *Webster's Ninth New Collegiate Dictionary* and the *Chicago Manual of Style*.

7. We regret that materials sent to us will not be returned.

8. Please send any background materials (for example, old newspaper clippings, information sheets, copies of relevant pages in publications covering your topic, etc.) along with your query.

9. Allow plenty of time for your query to be addressed; Articles should be queried a minimum of six to nine months before publication.

10. It is important not to take what a homeowner (or any other contact) says as a fact. Make sure that what you are given about style or history is correct by confirming it with another source or (if appropriate) asking them for their source of the information.

We look forward to hearing from you.

Sincerely,

Contact Information:
Audra Shanley, Chief Copy Editor
1790 Broadway, 14th Floor
New York, NY 10019
(212) 830-2900 • FAX: (212) 586-3455
E-mail: ashanley@hearst.com

Colorado Business Magazine

Dear Freelancer:

It's time to distribute our editorial calendar, along with some basic writer's guidelines.

This should make both of our jobs easier. It will strengthen your marketing efforts since you'll have a better idea of our needs, and we'll be spared unnecessary inquiries. [AUTHOR'S NOTE: *Colorado Business* hires freelance writers from Colorado only.]

We're always open to calls – and then query letters – that reflect well-planned story ideas. Our editorial content is not restricted to the editorial calendar, but be aware it will fill a high percentage of our news hole. Besides articles, you can pitch ideas for our departments: Turning point is about an individual who has made, or is making changes, in his/her life and business. On Target is an advice column for business owners and entrepreneurs. Both are about 1,000 words.

We assume you are steady readers of the magazine. That's by far the best way to understand the stories we seek.

Our readership is a high-end audience, with average salaries of $142,000. Many are CEOs, business owners, or highly placed executives or managers. Our readership is 75 percent male, but our female readership includes many very successful women business owners and operators.

They seek information on any business development that's new, interesting and useful to their business life or personal life. They want to read about trends, and interesting individuals and businesses. They're especially hungry for information on finance, health care and small business, and we're going to meet that need with a new quarterly focus.

Most of you are accustomed to an 1,800-word limit on our features. Frequently, we will ask for 1,500 words instead, especially during the thin months.

We plan the magazine four months in advance. Stories are due two months in advance, i.e., Sept. 1 for the November issue. Stories should be submitted on a 3½-inch disk, PC format (Microsoft Word is our preference). We can, however, convert Mac disks into our format, so don't buy a whole new computer just to suit us.

Your submission should include the disk, a hard copy of the story, your invoice (including a social security number), phone numbers of people quoted, a photo suggestion list if the spirit moves you, and separate backing for statistics. We fact-check, so be prepared to be questioned.

We have sped up the payment process. Instead of paying on publication, we're now paying on acceptance, which we define as the day the magazine goes to the printer – that signals our final acceptance of the story. We pay, on average, 22 cents per word.

In addition, we will add $25 to payments to cover anticipated revenue from electronic pickups. We get paid an average of $2 to $3 royalties when a story is picked up and split the revenue 50-50 with you. So we're assuming a story will be downloaded 20 times—a high estimate—in paying the extra $25. Only one of the electronic services provides a story-by-story printout of what's picked up, so we're doing this as fairly as we know how.

If the electronics services move to a clearer accounting practice, we'll change our method of payment to keep it fair for all concerned.

If you are also a public relations consultant, please don't try to write about your clients for *Colorado Business*. You can pitch them to us like any other PR person, but you can't write about them for us.

The 1996 editorial calendar included:

JANUARY: 1996 economic forecast (assigned); aviation; quarterly financial focus.

FEBRUARY: Best of *Colorado Business* (assigned); environmental business; quarterly health care focus; *Colorado Business* Reference Guide (we handle that one).

MARCH: Annual Arts Awards (we handle); computing; franchising; quarterly small business focus.

APRIL: Golf; business on-line; quarterly financial focus.

MAY: Hotels – meeting and convention planner; top 100 women-owned companies (we handle); quarterly health care focus.

JUNE: Top 250 public companies (we handle); real estate – corporate relocation; quarterly small business focus.

JULY: Economic development; top 100 minority-owned businesses (we handle); quarterly financial focus.

AUGUST: Company of the Year winners (we handle); architecture, engineering and construction (that's one story); quarterly health care focus.

SEPTEMBER: Top 250 private companies (we handle); computers; quarterly small business focus.

OCTOBER: Banking; telecommunications and cable; quarterly financial focus.

NOVEMBER: Taxes and finance; employee benefits, quarterly health care focus.

DECEMBER: Education; information highway; quarterly small business focus.

Please feel free to call me at ext. 223, with questions, comments, ruminations, etc.

Contact Information:

Bruce Goldberg, Managing Editor
7009 So. Potomac Street
Englewood, CO 80014
(303) 397-7600 • FAX: (303) 397-7619

THE COMICS JOURNAL

The Comics Journal
The Magazine of Comics News & Criticism

For more than 15 years, *The Comics Journal* has provided a lively, intelligent and challenging look at the art form of comics. It has always been our belief that comics have the potential for artistic depth and greatness—that they're not merely a commodity but rather a vital, relevant medium of expression. To this end, *The Comics Journal* has subjected comics to the same critical treatment as fiction, film, and fine art. Our readership primarily consists of intelligent readers who share the magazine's desire to improve both the art form of comics and its critical consideration.

Therefore, *The Comics Journal* is interested in supporting and spotlighting the more intelligent, mature, and experimental form of comics art. We are simply not the place to publish articles about Spider-Man or Teenage Mutant Ninja Turtles.

REVIEWS

We enthusiastically welcome intelligent, analytical and entertaining reviews of current comic books, comic strips, anthologies, reprint collections, comics-related books, films and videos, and comics-related art exhibits. We have no real interest in plot synopses or simple "book reviews." *The Comics Journal* strives for criticism which addresses the themes, techniques, and artistic intent of comics, with equal attention given to both the visual and narrative elements of each work. The reviewer must be articulate, insightful, and lucid, with enough solid knowledge of the comics art form to present opinions with conviction and reliability. We are not looking for rambling, self-obsessed, "new journalism" style reviews. We are interested in substantive, intelligent, and far-reaching critical pieces ranging in length from 1,000 to 3,000 words.

FEATURES

We are seeking feature articles on a broad range of comics-related subject matter including overviews of comics trends, developments of genres, exposes, profiles of creators, essays, and illuminations of lesser-known aspects of the medium. We publish features on current mainstream comics only if they offer an exceptionally novel or interesting slant.

Recent examples of feature articles in *The Comics Journal* include Samuel Joyner's discussion of his long career (#150), an expose of the hidden sexual symbolism in Al Capp's L'il Abner (#147), an examination of religious comics produced by Jack T. Chick (#145), and an examination of censorship in Mexican comics (#157).

Features may range in length from 2,000 to 5,000 words.

COLUMNS

The Comics Journal is always seeking essays for its "Opening Shots" column which features guest editorials by freelance writers or industry insiders. These pieces generally examine everything from controversial issues within the comics industry to reevaluations of accepted practices in comics. Additionally, the column will occasionally take issue with views expressed in previous articles published in *The Comics Journal*. "Opening Shots" columns range in length from 1,000 to 1,500 words.

We are also interested in featuring continuing columns of comment and criticism from informed writers. Among our current columns are "Funnybook Roulette," R. Fiore's irreverent look at the comics scene; "Reruns and Revivals," a critical analysis of important works in comics history by R.C. Harvey; and "Minimalism," an examination of the mini-comics genre by Robert Boyd.

DOMESTIC NEWS

Because *The Comics Journal* is a monthly magazine and therefore experiences an extended lead time, we compensate for a lack of timeliness in our news section by concentrating on depth and breadth of coverage. We pursue detailed investigative reports on major events in creator/company relations, publishing, marketing, syndication, distribution and retailing. We don't cover "events" within comic books series (developments in storylines, new characters, etc.) unless such events create an impact on the society at large. The watchwords in our news stories are independence (from any publisher), accuracy (an obvious must), and fairness (allowing the truth to surface by providing a full view of the facts and issues, not from partisan advocacy more appropriately suited to editorials or essays). We neither curry favor with nor step lightly around the major comics publishers. We believe that a rigorous standard of fairness justifies tough reporting. As a result, we request reporters who are aggressive, persistent, analytic, and reactive. Journalism experience is preferred; please query first. News stories range in length from 500 to 2,000 words, depending on importance and complexity.

INTERNATIONAL SECTION

The Comics Journal reports on comics from around the world, necessarily with the help of international correspondents. The international news section features short spotlights on con-lies trends, creators, and companies as well as breaking news from the world arena. Additionally, we seek feature articles and reviews which follow the previously staled guidelines.

PHOTOGRAPHERS

The Comics Journal is in need of photographers. While we've consistently expanded our photo library and continue to do so, we often miss photo opportunities at many newsworthy events such as conventions, speeches, and exhibits. Please do not send unsolicited photographs; query first. We are especially interested in finding reliable regular photographers to cover specific beats.

We buy prints (you keep the negatives at the rate of $15 per photo with rights to publish at any time, and $10 for each subsequent use of the photo).

INTERVIEWS

Each issue's center piece is an extensive, in-depth interview with a major figure from the comic book, comic strip, or animation fields. We also feature shorter interviews with up-and-coming creators. We prefer that the interviews be transcribed before submission, but we do make occasional exceptions. Interviews generally fall between the two to four hour range. After the process of editing by both our staff and the interview subject, this length generally translates to approximately 30 pages for a major figure, and somewhat less for a secondary interview. For shorter interviews, one to one and a half hours is an advisable length.

We are especially interested in interviews with major political cartoonists and significant comic strip and panel cartoonists. We are also open to short interviews with newer creators who may not yet be accomplished enough to merit a major interview, but whose work is worthy of a short discussion.

Prospective interviewers should be well-versed in their subjects work before conducting the discussion. Please query first before submission.

GENERAL INFORMATION

Payment for articles, essays, and columns is two cents per word, plus reimbursement for any documented expenses. Writers are paid upon publication. Payment for interviews varies and is negotiable. Replies to submissions and queries are generally received within two months. Feel free to contact us with story or interview ideas, but to avoid duplication of articles, it's best to check first before submitting final manuscripts.

We prefer that manuscripts be submitted on a Macintosh floppy disk, as Microsoft Word documents or MacWrite documents, together with a printout. We can read the IBM WordPerfect format as well, but disks must be the hard-shelled 3½-inch variety. Include your name, address, telephone number and social security number in the upper left corner or the first page of your submission, and your name, article title or subject, and page number across the top of each subsequent page. Additionally, include photocopies of any artwork relevant to your article and, in the case of reviews, you must include the name and address of the publisher of the particular work which you are reviewing. We also require that you submit a three to four sentence statement summarizing your professional background for use in our Contributors' Notes section.

Contact Information:
Tom Spurgeon, Managing Editor
7563 Lake City Way NE
Seattle, WA 98115
(206) 524-1967 • FAX: (206) 524-2104

Commonweal

COMMONWEAL is a biweekly journal of opinion edited by Catholic lay people. Founded in 1924, the magazine welcomes original manuscripts dealing with topical issues of the day on public affairs, religion, literature, and the arts. We look for articles that are timely, accurate, and well-written. Articles fall into three categories:

1. "Upfronts," running between 750-1,000 words, are brief, "newsy" reportorials, giving facts, information, and some interpretation behind the "headlines of the day."

2. Longer articles, running between 2,000-3,000 words, are more reflective and detailed, bringing new information or a different point of view to a subject, raising questions, and/or proposing solutions to the dilemmas facing the world, nation, church, or individual.

3. "Last Word" column, a 750-word reflection, usually of a personal nature, on some aspect of the human condition: spiritual, individual, political, or social.

Please send a query with outline and resume. We do not consider simultaneous submissions.

Articles should be written for a general but well-educated audience. While religious articles are always topical, we are less interested in devotional and churchy pieces than in articles which examine the links between "worldly" concerns and religious beliefs.

Notes and footnotes are discouraged. Please allow 3-4 weeks for an editorial decision.

Those with MS-DOS or Macintosh systems are encouraged to send the article on a diskette, along with hard copy. The diskette will be returned. Payment for articles is generally made on publication.

Poetry: We publish about thirty high quality poems a year.

Contact Information:
Patrick Jordan, Managing Editor
15 Dutch Street
New York, NY 10038
(212) 732-0800

Communications Publishing Group, Inc. (CPG)

Communications Publishing Group provides publications designed to inform and motivate minority youth and young adults (16-49) on higher education, career preparation and challenging opportunities. All publications are nationally distributed by subscriptions, direct and bulk mail.

Publications and Audiences

CAREER FOCUS . . . "The Briefcase Mentor" designed for today's rising Black and Hispanic professionals provides information on job search techniques, career development and skills for advancement. By profiling successful Black and Hispanic professionals in different fields, CAREERFOCUS provides insider secrets about career prospects for these recent graduates and aspiring executives. This unique magazine highlights corporate promotions, outstanding achievement, and career success. Published bimonthly.

COLLEGE PREVIEW . . . A resource guide for Black and Hispanic junior and senior high school students, this magazine offers helpful tips and advice on college preparation, financial aid, admissions and career planning. Published four times a year in January/February, March/April, September/October, and November/December.

DIRECTAIM . . . For the Black and Hispanic college students at traditional, nontraditional, vocational and technical institutions. This magazine informs students about college survival skills and planning for a future in the professional world. Published four times a year in January/February, March/April, September/October, and November/December.

FIRST OPPORTUNITY . . . Designed for Black and Hispanic high schoolers, this magazine prepares students for higher education and careers in vocational, technical, math and science fields. Published four times a year in January/February, March/April, September/October, and November/December.

VISIONS . . . A resource guide for Native-American high school and college students offering helpful tips and advice on college preparation, financial aid, admissions and career planning. Published semiannually in March and September

FOCUS/Kansas City . . . Published for the regional Kansas City area minority business and professional minded. Focuses on entrepreneurship, professional development, personal growth, and life management skills.

Editorial Topics

Profiles of outstanding, successful students, business people or corporate professionals who serve as positive role models to our audiences. Persons profiled must be Black, Hispanic, Asian American or Native American, preferably ages 16-35. Color photographs or slides must accompany manuscript.

For college graduates and rising professionals: hot career prospects, resume writing tips, interviewing techniques, office politics, managerial styles, career advancement, higher education, entrepreneurship and resource lists.

For high school juniors, seniors and college students: college preparation and selection, financial aid information, money management, study methods, campus living, extracurricular activities, higher education, hot career prospects.

For all audiences: news items from college campuses, current events, fads and trends, politics, fashion, sports, technology, entertainment, multi-cultural information, and minority business development.

Style and Tone

Articles should be informative and motivating, yet entertaining and easy-to-read. Format should take a who, what, where, when, and why approach to achieving goals. Providing tips or a checklist as a sidebar is acceptable. For example, "10 Tips on Money Management" could follow an article on "Financial Planning in the 90s."

Second or third person preferred in features and short stories; first person accepted in an essay of widespread interest.

Taboos

Assuming readers are totally unsophisticated; overly ponderous or "cute" writing styles;

preaching; or casual mention of drug and alcohol abuse or sex. However, drug, drinking or sex may be treated responsibly in a short story or feature.

Article Length

Features: 1,000 to 2,000 words.

Profiles: 500 to 800 words. Subjects must be Black, Hispanic, Asian-American, or Native-American and a suitable role model for youth. Must include color photos, slides or B&W glossies. Snapshots are unacceptable.

News Briefs: 100 to 500 words. Timely information that will be of widespread interest.

Fillers: 25 to 100 words. Tasteful quotes, cartoons, poems and jokes relevant to college or professional life.

Announcements: 25 to 200 words for promotions or other noteworthy achievement.

Professionals & Students on the Rise: 100 to 500 words.

Manuscripts

All first-time writers with CPG must submit full-length manuscripts, resume and other published work in order to be considered by CPG editors. Manuscripts will not be returned unless specifically requested. Address to a particular magazine and direct to the attention of the editor.

Submissions

Submitting manuscript along with disk (PC—WordPerfect or ASCII file or Word/Mac) will enhance your acceptability. CPG pays additional for disk. All manuscripts must include the following on first page: name, address, telephone number, social security number, word count, and title. Number and staple pages together.

Queries

Queries are reserved for writers who have had at least two articles published by CPG. Queries should detail the topic, how the writer plans to approach it, and how it will benefit our readership. Telephone calls are not accepted for queries.

Hold Status

After reviewing a submitted manuscript, CPG may decide to hold it for further consideration for an upcoming issue. A manuscript may be held up to six months as some articles are timeless and appropriate for any CPG publications. Notice of this hold status will be mailed to you. However, hold status does not constitute an acceptance. If these conditions are unacceptable or if the manuscript has been accepted by another publication, please notify our editorial staff immediately.

Acceptance

All articles are reviewed by our editorial staff who make recommendations for publications. As all CPG publications are published as a series of editions, all accepted articles can be utilized in one or more editions in the same series. For example, any articles on college preparation may appear in the spring editions of *College Preview*, *First Opportunity* and/or *Visions*. It will not appear in the fall editions. Therefore, CPG purchases one-time rights for use in our series of magazines.

Bylines and brief biographies of author are given generously at the discretion of the editor.

CPG reserves the right to edit all editorial for clarity and length.

Please allow eight to twelve weeks for a follow-up on queries and manuscripts. Acceptance is upon publication.

Payment

Notification of acceptance will be mailed along with payment. Pay rate is 10 cents per word, not to exceed $400.00 for a full-length feature. Pay rate is $10-$25 each for accepted poems, puzzles, jokes, cartoons; $25.00 each for color photos/slides; $20.00 each for B&W photos. CPG does not pay for photos supplied by public relations agencies or other entity seeking public service promotion.

$10 for each disk. If multiple submission, place all articles on one disk.

Art Submission

Art or suggestions for art to accompany a submitted manuscript are encouraged, but not mandatory. However, manuscripts submitted with color photos and/or illustrations have a greater chance of acceptance.

B&W Photos: Glossies, 5"x7" or 8"x10"; transparencies, no snapshots.

Color Photos: Transparencies preferred, glossies accepted; no instant photos.

Contact Information:
Cheri LeBlond, Assistant Editor
250 Mark Twain Tower
106 West 11th Street
Kansas City, MO 64105-1806
(816) 221-4404

THE COMPUTER JOURNAL

The Computer Journal

THE COMPUTER JOURNAL (TCJ) focuses on current issues in business, technology and computers, and offers a view of how computing technology and trends impact business. Because we are targeting a business audience, we cut through the computer-industry jargon and present topics for the nontechnical business person.

TCJ is a national monthly (12 pages, tabloid) customized for individual computer dealers in various regions and distributed free to their clients and prospects. The same editorial appears in each version. Total circulation is approximately 30,000.

- Use the following guidelines for gauging the length of articles:
  - Short Pieces (i.e., "Business of Computers" department): <100 words
  - News Items: 100 - 500 words
  - Departments: 250 - 750 words
  - Features: 750 - 1,250 words
- Articles should be slanted toward the business computer user (not "techie" types or MIS managers), and should explore computing trends that impact business, new technologies, basic computing concepts, ways to improve productivity, etc. While the range of possible topics is wide, a business-orientation is essential.
- Our readers want in-depth information that's clear, concise and easy to read. Generally, features longer than 1,250 words are not accepted, although multipart (serial) features may be considered.
- Articles should not be too product-specific. Examples of products related to the subject may be mentioned, preferably in a sidebar (each manufacturer's name, city and phone number should be included). Product reviews and product comparisons are not accepted.
- All jargon words should be defined. If the article contains only a few jargon words, they may be defined parenthetically within the text. For longer articles on more complex topics, terms may be defined in a sidebar. Highly technical material is not accepted.

Publication Rights and Payment

• Queries are preferred. Adventure Publishing pays 5¢-10¢ per word, upon acceptance, for assignments resulting from queries, and 3¢-5¢ per word upon publication, for unsolicited manuscripts.

• Adventure Publishing retains first North American serial rights. Because the same editorial appears in each customized version of *TCJ*, publication of an article in a given "issue" means that the article will appear in each version produced for that monthly issue. (The number of versions and total circulation varies.)

• Writer should submit an invoice to Adventure Publishing upon acknowledgment of acceptance of final manuscript (or upon acknowledgment of publication, for unsolicited manuscripts). Invoice should detail the total number of words in the manuscript and the contracted rate per word. The writer's Federal Tax ID or social security number must be included. Payment will follow within two to four weeks of receipt of invoice.

• Adventure Publishing will provide the writer with copies of each publication in which her article appears.

Press Releases

Companies are encouraged to send press releases to *The Computer Journal*. Use the above editorial guidelines as a reference. The information must have a business slant in order to be considered. Highly technical material is not appropriate. We will try to send tear sheets when press releases are used.

Contact Information:
Cheryl Cooper, Editor-in-Chief
P.O. Box 700686
Tulsa, OK 74170
(800) 726-7667 • FAX: (918) 621-2134

The Construction Specifier

The Construction Specifier is a monthly magazine for construction professionals who deal with commercial, institutional, industrial, and renovation building projects. Our readers include architects, engineers, specifiers, contractors, and product manufacturers.

Writers may request a complimentary sample issue and thereafter submit a query letter outlining the scope of the intended article. Once accepted, an article may be held for several months before being published. Articles that have time-oriented significance should be flagged as such.

The editors must receive articles no later than ten weeks before a scheduled issue date. The editors will make every effort to review articles and inform writers of their decision regarding publication within six weeks.

Manuscript Preparation

Submissions should be:

• typed, with 1-inch margins

• submitted on diskette—3½-inch, if possible (we prefer WordPerfect submissions, though we can accept ASCII and most popular word processing programs)

• accompanied by a two- to three-sentence autobiographical sketch

• supplemented with photos, diagrams, charts, etc. (all measurements in manuscripts, tables, and charts should be in both metric and inch/pound units)

• referenced with footnotes and bibliography when necessary—consult the *Chicago*

Manual of Style

Features average 2,500 words; columns and departments average 750 to 1,500 words. All manuscripts are subject to editing as a condition of publication. Submission of an article or column implies permission to publish insofar as copyright is concerned, but the editors require authors to return a signed copyright permission form (provided by the magazine) within five days of notification that the manuscript has been accepted for publication.

Artwork and Captions

We strongly encourage authors to submit photographs and illustrations (line drawings, graphs, charts, and tables) to reinforce the content of their articles. Captions should be typed on individual pieces of paper and attached to the appropriate photographs or illustrations. The source of each photo or drawing should also be noted. If a person in a photo is identifiable, a signed model release form must be provided. A letter of permission must accompany all illustrative material copyrighted elsewhere.

Slides, transparencies, and black-and-white or color prints are welcome. Digitized high-resolution (no less than 300 dpi) black-and-white scans in Adobe Photoshop are also accepted. Drawings may be submitted in .tif or .eps format. Embedded graphics are not acceptable.

When preparing tables and charts, place them on separate pages, labeled with reference to the text ("Table 1," "Table 2," etc.). If a table requires more than one page, repeat all headings and subheadings. Each table and chart should have a caption.

No material is returned to the author unless arrangements have been made in advance.

Rights and Obligations

Authors are responsible for all original statements made in their work. Manuscripts are submitted with the understanding that they are not under consideration elsewhere. If your manuscript is being considered by another publisher, we need prompt notification to avoid embarrassment and possible copyright infringement.

Accepted manuscripts become the property of The Construction Specifications Institute. We require one-time world serial rights. The magazine is copyrighted as a collection and retains all rights to editorial changes, design, and artwork used in an article.

Payment for articles, if authorized, is made upon publication.

Contact Information:
News, Exteriors, Specifications, Renovations, Infrastructure:
Anne Scott, Senior Editor
Info Tech: Diane Mossholder, Production Editor
Products, Engineering, Failures, Interiors:
Dianne Baldwin, Assistant Editor
Letters, Law, Opinion: Jack Reeder, Editor & Publisher
601 Madison Street
Alexandria, VA 22314
(703) 706-4790 • FAX: (703) 684-0465

Cook's Illustrated

COOK'S ILLUSTRATED is a magazine about the techniques of home cooking. Because all our income comes from subscribers we are uniquely free and obligated in all our stories to provide useful, accurate, and thoroughly tested master recipes for home kitchens.

Our readers look to every issue for practical, everyday dinners and family-occasion specialties. Our most successful stories sift through the food fads and the "culinary literature" to get at the basics. We use the phrase "weeknight suppers" to remind us to keep our recipes to reasonable preparation times. Our competition is not the gourmet-cooking magazines but the canned and frozen entrees on the supermarket shelves.

A story for us should contain something new. Or it may clear away decades of received wisdom to find that a standard technique is the best, easiest method after all. It should empower the reader with a method or master recipe that gives a superior result more quickly, or more easily, or with more readily available foodstuffs.

Although we may have headlines like "The Best Cupcake" or "Frittatas Made Easy," or "Our Favorite Lobster," what we really need are cupcakes beyond the best published recipes, and frittatas made more easily than ever before yet as good as the best made the old-fashioned way, or a rigorous demystification of lobster lore.

Story concepts should be narrowly focused, so the author can test and explain them in depth—how it really works, not how we have been told it works. Most stories and all proposals should begin by defining the goal, setting a standard. Pay attention to texture (or appearance) and flavor.

Most stories and all proposals should then set out a series of experiments, leading to a master recipe. Along the way, the writer may consult experts from scientists to street vendors, testing their advice. Humor and color arise from kitchen failures, so one must be open to all possibilities.

Hints accumulate until the goal is reached with a master recipe, and variations. Scientific explanations and unusual tips and findings make good sidebar material. But culture, history, or travel-related information are important only insofar as they might guide the search or set the standards.

Our readers are home cooks who prefer to cook from scratch with fine ingredients and effective equipment. But they are not necessarily wealthy sensation-seekers or "early adopters." If your story requires mail order ingredients or single-purpose equipment, you must make a powerful case that the results fill a need that cannot be satisfied from the supermarket and typical kitchen tools.

A story about the food of Uruguay, then, would not interest us, even though Uruguay might have some unknown herb with which you can make a great dish. But if there is a style of one-pot stewing that is particular to Uruguay and can be applied here, we'll jump at it.

What about healthfulness? Like everyone else, we are certainly concerned with it. However, we are not interested in perverting great recipes by, say, removing the fat.

Lastly, but always, the name of the magazine is COOK'S ILLUSTRATED, so writers should think about visual possibilities, especially including steps of preparation.

Now, process: Begin with a query. We may then request a 2-3 page proposal. This is a headline and a sub-headline, and an outline of questions and tests you intend to pursue. It is not uncommon to lay out 15-30 kitchen experiments. If your proposal is accepted, we will negotiate an assignment and send you a contract.

We should warn you that writing for COOK'S ILLUSTRATED is not necessarily fun or easy. When you think you are done with the piece, it is almost certain that we will find several more issues to raise. We say this not to discourage you but to remind you that coming up with the "best" way to do anything is a long, ongoing process that requires a great deal of trial and error.

We look forward to seeing any article proposals that you feel meet these general guidelines.

Contact Information:
Elizabeth Cameron, Editorial Assistant
17 Station Street
P.O. Box 569
Brookline Village, MA 02147
(617) 232-1000 • FAX: (617) 232-1572

Cornerstone

We appreciate your interest and hope you will find these guidelines useful.

Articles

The kind of article we are looking for is the well-documented piece dealing with contemporary issues. This kind of writing takes time to prepare, i.e., research, interviews. We use 2-3 unsolicited manuscripts per year with up to 4,000 words maximum and pay 8-10 cents per word.

Opinion Pieces/Reviews/Cartoons

We welcome various opinion pieces, personal testimonies, cartoons and reviews that reflect a Christian world point of view. These items should be between 500 and 1000 words, and, again, we pay 8-10 cents per word. We also publish book and music reviews. These should feature a recent publication or artist focusing on the work and/or the artist's world view and value system.

Fiction

We are looking for high quality fiction with skillful characterization, plot development, and imaginative symbolism. We welcome material which touches on current social and theological issues. We are open to all types of fiction from the traditional to experimental pieces. Manuscripts should be from 250 to 4,000 words, though this can be negotiated. We, again, pay after publication 8-10 cents per word.

Poetry

We accept avant-garde, free verse, haiku, light verse—though we have no room for epic poetry. We usually print 5-6 poems per issue at $10.00 per 1-15 line poem, $25.00 per 16+ line poem. We are looking for good use of imagery, words that elicit a sensory response in the reader, a poem that has memorable quality.

Response Policy

Due to the volume of material we receive, we cannot return your work. We will contact you only if we accept your manuscript for publication, so please do not send a SASE. Our response time is two to three months.

Mark your envelope "Attn: Misty Files, Submissions Editor" or for poetry, "Attn: Tammy Boyd, Poetry Editor." (You are also welcome to FAX your submission.) Because Cornerstone publishes only four issues a year, it often takes some time before we are able to use manuscripts, but rest assured, all material sent to Cornerstone is read and considered.

We look forward to hearing from you soon.

Contact Information:
Fiction/Nonfiction: Misty Files, Submissions Editor
Poetry: Tammy Boyd, Poetry Editor
939 West Wilson Avenue
Chicago, IL 60640
(312) 561-2450 • FAX: (312) 989-2076

Country America Magazine

CIRCULATION: 900,000

PUBL. SCHEDULE: 10 times annually

EDITORIAL PHILOSOPHY:

Country America celebrates and serves the country way of life including country music.

***COUNTRY AMERICA* READERS:**

Mainstream America whose values include freedom, honesty, patriotism, individuality and loyalty. They are people who consider themselves down-to-earth, straightforward, neighborly, hard-working and honorable.

What makes a good *Country America* article? The ideal *Country America* article will be tightly written with potential for several color photographs. Think visually. The magazine serves the needs and interests of people who live in the country or identify with traditional country values and lifestyles found throughout the nation. *Country America* provides feature stories on country music and country entertainers, travel, cooking, recreation, outdoors, crafts, homes, traditions and people.

WRITING SUGGESTIONS:

1) Remember to keep a national audience in mind. Don't narrow the articles so much that they only interest a small segment of our audience. Country is not only a location but a state of mind.

2) Use many examples.

3) Use multiple sources. A good story will contain diversified and unique quotes. Differing perspectives lend credibility and balance to stories.

4) Write in a conversational, easygoing manner to make for enjoyable reading. Many of our readers are do-it-yourselfers; "how-to" sidebars are desirable.

5) Make it easy for the readers to take action by providing addresses and phone numbers telling them where to get more information.

FACT CHECKING:

All articles must be checked back and cleared with the sources before submission to *Country America* to ensure the accuracy of information. It is also highly recommended that the reputations of sources be checked in the community.

RIGHTS:

Articles written for *Country America* are lifetime – we buy all rights. We very rarely reprint an article.

QUERIES:

It is strongly recommended that freelance writers first query *Country America* with their story ideas before writing. Keep in mind that an original article is more valuable than one assigned by the editorial department. The respective editors are:

- BILL EFTINK: general inquiries.
- ROBBIE PETERSON: country people, country lifestyle, almanac, travel, comedy.
- NEIL POND: country entertainment, entertainer's lifestyles and events.
- DICK SOWIENSKI: general interest, personalities, country essays, travel.
- DIANE YANNEY: foods, recipes, country crafts.
- BOB EHLERT: heritage and traditions, country places, country people.

SAMPLE COPIES: For a sample copy, send $4.95 to *Country America*, 1716 Locust Street, #439, Des Moines, Iowa 50309-3023.

PAYMENT/TERMS: *Country America* pays between $.35 and $1 per word and buys lifetime rights on acceptance within three weeks. All freelance contributors must sign a standard freelance contract form and provide Social Security number or tax ID number before payment can be made.

PHOTOS: Color transparencies are required. Rates start at $75 for color photos and

$50 for black and white. Photographers are required to obtain signed photo releases of all subjects before payment can be authorized.

Contact Information:
Bill Eftink, Managing Editor
1716 Locust Street
Des Moines, IA 50309
(515) 284-3787

Country Connections
Seeking The Good Life-For The Common Good

We encourage submissions of articles, column ideas, essays poems, short stories, book reviews, and drawings. Word count for articles generally does not exceed 2,500. Please query us before submitting a feature, article, book review or new column. All other material may be submitted directly for consideration.

Because of the unique nature of our publication, it is important that contributors read the magazine and become familiar with our direction. (Sample copies are available for $4.00. Subscriptions are $22 per year.) We look for a strong, personal point of view, original thinking, and focused, accomplished execution. Humor is also appreciated.

All non-art submissions should include a word count, and the writer's name, address, and telephone number on the first page. We have listed below in order of preference the methods for submission of written material:

1. Attach Microsoft Word for Mac file and send to our e-mail address.
2. Include submission as part of message to our e-mail address. (We will respond via e-mail for 1 and 2.)
3. Typed or printed copy.

Graphics should be submitted in black ink on white paper for best reproduction. All originals will be returned upon request and with SASE.

BOOK REVIEWS FOR COUNTRY CONNECTIONS

A BIBLE

In book reviews for COUNTRY CONNECTIONS we look for subject and tone very different from the standard reviews published in *The New York Review of Books* or *The New York Times Book Review*, for example.

First, we want to publish reviews of books—primarily nonfiction—that the reviewers and publishers of COUNTRY CONNECTIONS want to recommend to the readership. While there are probably areas in any book that have problems, we are not interested in a "why this book is stupid and doesn't work" piece. If after reading, the book doesn't appear worthwhile to the reviewer, or fails to generate a passion for writing about it, let the publishers know as soon as possible. Life is too short, and there are plenty of other books. We want the enthusiasm to show.

Second, we consistently try to match a reviewer's interests with a book's subject. Not only do we want a lively and interesting piece, but our review should actually be a kind of personal essay with the book as the jumping off point. The book's premise should be filtered through the reviewer's experience, expertise, and strong personal point of view. Not only what the book is saying is to be discussed, but why it is has meaning to the reviewer and why it should be of interest to the *CC* readership. We are looking for writing with a personal edge that is honest, compelling, clear and original. A journalistic or academic style is not what we're after.

Third, reviews should be informed by cultural, political, or social commentary. The book's context in this broader view of issues is important to describe. How does it connect with the topics explored regularly in the magazine?

Finally, reviews should generally run around 800 words, or 1,600 words for a double (two book) review. An excerpt from the book of approximately 200 words should be selected and submitted by the reviewer along with the review. A title for the review should be suggested.

Contact Information:
P.O. Box 6748
Pine Mountain, CA 93222-6748
(805) 242-1047 • FAX: (805) 242-5704
E-mail: countryink@igc.apc.org

Cowles History Group

Cowles History Group, a Division of Cowles Magazines, Inc., in Leesburg, Va., publishes six full-color historical magazines: *America's Civil War*, *Aviation History*, *Military History*, *Vietnam*, *Wild West*, and *World War II*. Prospective contributors should be familiar with the individual magazines before querying. *America's Civil War*, *World War II*, and *Vietnam* cover strategy, tactics, personalities, arms and equipment for the appropriate period. *Military History* deals with war throughout human history. *Aviation History* covers military and civilian aviation from man's first attempts at flight to the present. *Wild West* covers the American frontier, from earliest times through its westward expansion.

Historical accuracy is imperative. We do not use fiction or poetry.

STYLE: The two paramount considerations in all Cowles History Group publications are: absolute accuracy and highly readable style. Give proper attribution in the manuscript when using other author's work and cite your major sources for our review. We like to see action and quotes where possible to heighten reader interest.

QUERY: Submit a short, self-explanatory query summarizing the story and its highlights. Also state your sources and expertise. Cite any color and black-and-white illustrations and primary sources of illustrations (museums, historical societies, private collections, etc.) you can provide. Photocopies of suggested illustrations are extremely helpful. Illustration ideas are an absolute must. The likelihood that articles can be effectively illustrated often determines the ultimate fate of manuscripts. Many otherwise excellent articles have been rejected due to a lack of suitable art.

FORMAT: We strongly urge authors to submit with manuscripts computer disks that are IBM or Macintosh compatible. Name, address, telephone number and Social Security number should be on the first page. Indicate sources and suggested further reading at the end of your manuscript. Include a 1-2 paragraph biography of yourself. All submissions are on speculation.

LENGTH: Feature articles should be 3,500-4,000 words in length, with a 500-word sidebar. Departments should be 2,000 words. Cowles History Group retains the right to edit, condense or rewrite for style.

PAYMENT: Payment, which is made on publication, varies by magazine and ranges from $200 for *World War II* features to $400 for *Military History* features and $100 to $200 for departments. We also use book reviews, payable at a per-published-word rate. Cowles History Group buys exclusive worldwide publication rights, and the right to reprint the article in all languages, in hard copy or through electronic means.

REPORTING TIME: Please allow six months' response time for queries and manuscripts. If you want immediate verification that a submission has been received and is being considered, please enclose a stamped, self-addressed postcard containing the title of your submission.

WE DO NOT PUBLISH REPRINTS.

COWLES HISTORY GROUP EDITORIAL PHILOSOPHY

Cowles History Group is committed to creating accurate, entertaining, and informative magazines, books, and products. It is our responsibility to ensure the loyalty and confidence of our customers by maintaining the highest editorial standards. To this end, our editorial content is never used as a sounding board for political partisanship, religious points of view, or social agendas. Our mission is to present an undistorted view of history and to encourage understanding and appreciation for the events, personalities, and artifacts of the past.

THE READER IS NUMBER 1

Just as writer's guidelines provide the mechanical requirements for submission of a manuscript, the following tips are intended to provide more subjective guidance for the preparation of copy that is editorially "clean" and enjoyable to read.

- Please give the reader a little excitement, some sense of being there, with lively—but always factual—anecdotes. Lead with one of these, if possible, to foster the reader's interest in seeing more of your story and to let him or her know that here is an article that is going to be worth reading.
- Know what the reader expects from the publication in terms of subject matter and style of writing. Be very careful to keep technical terminology in the proper context.
- Start most paragraphs with a simple, active sentence—so many begin with As, When, Because, After, or other passive openers. Active writing keeps readers' eyes open. Our aim is to bring life to history, not to use it as a bedtime soporific. The same goes for ". . .ing" verbs; use them sparingly, as you do with sleeping pills, to which their effects are related.
- Keep your facts straight.
- Provide each paragraph with more than one sentence, except to make an occasional emphatic point. Break a paragraph before it runs on and takes up half a page.
- Keep your facts straight.
- Keep to your story, and tell one story at a time. If there is a related aside, put it into a sidebar rather than break the flow of the main story.
- Maintain a smooth flow of information. It's fine to begin with an attention-getting action lead and a flashback, but from then on proceed straight through the story rather than jump around chronologically. If you make it difficult for the reader to follow your story, he will desert you; if you do that to the editor, he will protect his readers from a similar experience.
- Watch your spelling and grammar. You may be an expert in your subject, but your credibility can be shattered by sloppy copy.
- When you—either in exhaustion or exultation—finish the last keystroke, never, never rush the manuscript into the mail in an I'm-so-glad-to-be-finished dismissal. Put the manuscript aside and out of your mind at least overnight; then get back to it in a day or two and play editor. Go through the entire manuscript slowly, thoroughly and critically and correct all spelling errors. Question the spelling of every name—person, thing, company—all of them. Read it through as if you were the reader who has never seen it before and does not know what you are trying to get across. Does it flow smoothly? Does it say what you want it to say? Does it proceed logically through a basic beginning, middle, and end? Is it simple and clear rather than flowery and hobbled by descriptive adjectives? Are your facts straight?
- What you are doing here is just what the editor will do when he receives your material. His job is to select quality material that will hold the interest of his readers. If your submission is unprofessional, it may be returned unread with a standard rejection letter. A profes-

sional presentation of a well-written and researched manuscript has a better chance of being reviewed and seriously considered. From then on, the appropriateness of the subject, the writing and the facts will influence whether the editor believes your manuscript will please the reader—and will determine its acceptance.

- Keep your facts straight.

Contact Information:
Editor, (Magazine)
741 Miller Drive SE, Suite D-2
Leesburg, VA 22075
(703) 771-9400

Crochet World
Designer Guidelines for Crochet Patterns

I am pleased to review and consider crochet designs for publication in *Crochet World* and *Crochet World Special Issues*, which are published by House of White Birches, publishers of 20 internationally distributed magazines. The company also produces newsstand special issues and pattern sets relating to many crafts, including crochet.

Other crochet publications published by House of White Birches, which I do not edit, are *Crochet Digest* (contact: Laura Scott, House of White Birches, 306 East Parr Road, Berne, IN 46711) and *Old-Time Crochet* (contact: Anne Morgan Jefferson, 4 Oak Drive, P.O. Box 158, Hampton Falls, NH 03844).

- *Crochet World* is a bimonthly publication which features a wide variety of crochet designs geared for the beginner to the intermediate crocheter with very few advanced designs offered. Designs include afghans, toys, clothing, household items, baby items, gift and bazaar items, and more.
- *Crochet World Special Issues* is published quarterly, and in addition to the above items, it specializes in featuring the different seasons and holidays for each quarter, with lots of attention to quick and easy design.

WHAT I WANT

Only original, never-before-published crochet designs for which we can buy all rights.

SUBMISSION GUIDELINES

Preparation: Typewritten or printed via a computer. Or, you can submit a 3½ -inch floppy disk provided you use the WriteNow 4.0 or Microsoft Word 4.0 program. Include your name, address (including a UPS street address), telephone number and social security number on the top of the first page and your name and address on the top of additional pages. Leave 3 inches at the top of the first page and 1 inch at the top of all additional pages. Number each page. Indent paragraphs five spaces.

Introduction: Describe your design. List its specific qualities, why you decided to create it and how the reader can best use it—for personal use, home decor, gift giving or bazaar selling.

Directions: Indicate the skill level needed for a crocheter to make your design—easy, intermediate or advanced.

Size: When designing clothing, such as a sweater, please offer a size range (such as S,M,L), not just one size. Clothing submissions offering just one size will be returned.

What is the finished size of your model design? We need to know this in order to line up the correct size model.

Materials: List all supplies and materials necessary to complete your design. List the hook size(s), amount, size, color, etc., needed. Use readily available yarns and threads and list the company name you choose and the color numbers. Make sure that your design uses current materials that will still be part of a company's line when the article is published, not discontinued yarns and thread.

Gauge: A stitch gauge is mandatory. (Example: With crochet hook size F, 4 sc = 1 inch; 5 sc rows = 1 inch.)

Instructions: Please familiarize yourself with our format of direction writing and use the standard crochet abbreviations as indicated in the "Stitch Guide" which appears in each issue.

Diagrams: Provide diagrams only when absolutely necessary to make the instructions clear. They should be done on white paper in black ink, separate from the typewritten copy. Label accurately as Diagram A or Diagram B, making sure the labels correspond to your instructions. Add easily understood cutlines, such as "fold Line" or "cut here."

Graphs: Use a two-square border of graph paper around the design. Please be legible! We prefer symbols to colored squares. Make sure you keep a copy for your files.

Photography: House of White Birches will be responsible for all photography.

GENERAL INFORMATION

Multiple Submissions: We DO NOT accept patterns you are submitting to other publications at the same time.

Electronic Submissions: Must be on 3½-inch diskette using WriteNow version 4.0 or Microsoft Word 4.0 for Macintosh. Actual item must accompany the diskette.

Send Item: Instructions should accompany the actual crocheted item itself. Be sure your sample is of top quality workmanship. In the case of heavy, bulky items such as afghans, you may send a good, clear photocopy as a query. If accepted, you will have to send the actual item.

Shipping: Send UPS or first class mail. Include return postage.

Labeling: Make sure each item is tagged with a stringed tag that includes your name and address on one side of the tag, name of design on the other. In the event of multiple pieces, make sure each piece is tagged with above information.

Proofread: Proofread your pattern several times to eliminate possible errors. Suggestion: Have a crocheting friend read over your pattern to help spot errors or hard-to-follow sections.

Keep in Mind: Each set of instructions must stand alone. When writing instructions, you must assume that this is the first project of its kind the reader has ever done.

Copies: Be sure to keep a copy of the pattern for your file!

Payment: We pay competitive rates for original, top quality designs.

Contact Information:
Susan Hankins, Editor
6 Pearl Street
P.O. Box 776
Henniker, NH 03242-0776
(603) 428-7289

Crone Chronicles
A Journal of Conscious Aging

Crone Chronicles is a quarterly magazine by and for women who wish to move through the aging process in a conscious manner. "Crone" is identified as the third aspect of the ancient Triple Goddess: Maiden/Mother/Crone. Crone symbolizes the wisdom present in a woman of any age, but which usually becomes stronger as she grows older.

The patriarchal culture's valuation of the female is based on the youthful beauty of her bodily appearance, her "image." By this measure, the older a woman becomes, the less she is valued. Rather than accepting our culture's devaluation of women as they age, *Crone Chronicles* was founded to transform our way of understanding the aging process altogether.

To understand the Crone stage of life consciously is to look beyond appearances to reality, the reality of a long full life, through which much learning has been gleaned. To evaluate the Crone stage of life consciously is to see this phase as the crowning glory, the time when a woman enters into her full maturity, inside and out. By this new (and very ancient) measure, the Crone is the most revered stage of life, rather than the least; she is the most honored, not the most ignored. Distilling wisdom from her experience, her words, attitudes and actions can now serve as examples to others.

Our readers are women (and a few men!) from their early 30's to 100, the majority of them from 40 to 80. Some come from New Age backgrounds, others are much more traditional. What we all have in common is a commitment to conscious aging, which includes transforming the derogatory meaning of the word "Crone." If you feel this kind of commitment yourself, then we welcome your contributions to the *Crone Chronicles*. Most of each issue is created from readers' contributions, so your willingness to share is vital to this journal!

Crone Chronicles is geared mainly towards women. However, we do not wish to limit our readers to women, nor to assume that men are excluded from the wisdom of Crone. Indeed, on an archetypal level, we assume that as each woman includes male and female elders within her, so does each man. With that understanding, both men and women are welcome to submit to this journal for possible publication.

The following guidelines may help you gear your submission to the context of *Crone Chronicles*.

Subject Matter

All submissions—whether written or artistic—should focus in some way on issues relating to the aging process itself or to perceptions of any subject which are altered or filtered through the process of "growing older." What we are looking for is the expression of "one's own unique Crone point of view." In other words, we wish to publish the wisdom you have gained from your experience, and strongly prefer submissions which are either written entirely from a personal point of view, or at least include personal experience as an example of what is being talked about. Thus, most of what we publish is nonfiction. Fiction and myth will be considered, but only as they are particularly relevant to Crone.

Please realize that your contributions to the *Crone Chronicles* need not be limited to the theme of any issue. Though one section of each issue is theme-based, there is room for other contributions as well. Seasonal topics and articles on any aspect of the emergence of Crone in any form are always welcome.

Written Submissions

All written submissions should be the original work of the author. We prefer double-spaced manuscripts but will also accept neatly handwritten pieces. We are also able to accept computer disks. If you work on a computer, please send both the disk and a written copy of the manuscript. We are Macintosh-based and will accept 3.5 inch disks with text in either Text or Microsoft Word 4 formats. We can also read 3.5 inch IBM-compatible disks in ASCII (.txt) format.

We publish articles ranging from 100 to 6000 words; please keep in mind that very long manuscripts are less likely to be published, due to space limits. Please include the author's name, address and phone number on each page. Please be clear about the name under which you wish us to publish your material if we decide to use it.

We do edit for clarity, grammar, and sometimes for length at the last minute before publication. Any other significant editing will be done in conjunction with the writer, or with the writer's permission. If you do not want your article edited in any way, please write "Do not edit" on the manuscript clearly and in large letters. We will respect your wishes; however you should be aware that manuscripts so marked are far less likely to see publication in our pages.

Writers: here is your chance to tell your stories! Personal essays, reviews, journal entries, dreams, jokes, cartoons, asides—all are welcome. *Crone Chronicles* is here to help document and report on the Crone archetype as she resurrects Herself within the ashes of the patriarchal culture.

If you have something to say, and would rather talk about it than write it down, you are welcome to send us a tape for us to transcribe. If you know any older women who can serve as models for the rest of us, we will also transcribe your interviews of these tapes. Besides the magazine, we are also collecting interviews of interesting crone women for possible inclusion in a book.

We receive lots of poetry, all of which goes in a file for possible use in some future issue.

Graphic Art

All graphic art submissions should be the original work of the artist. Clear, black and white drawings are best, but penciled or colored works are sometimes acceptable. Please be aware that all artwork will be reproduced in black and white only except for pieces used on the outside cover. Our covers are usually commissioned works, but feel free to submit colored photocopies or slides of your color work for possible use on the cover. Please send us clean copies of your artwork only—we cannot be responsible for original artwork.

We are always looking for new artists. If you have a portfolio of your work, feel free to send it; when doing so, please let us know if any of the pieces have been previously published or are not available for publication. We keep files of artwork, by artist, and when an issue is in production we find the pieces of artwork on file that fit each article, and then inform the artist that we will be publishing that piece of work. This means that artwork is on file for months, even years—and may, sooner or later, still be published. Please let us know if this does not work for you, and we will make other arrangements.

Photography

All photographic submissions should be the original work of the author. If persons other than the photographer are shown, a signed release form said person(s) must be included in order for us to publish the photo. Please send standard prints. We cannot publish from negatives or slides. Photographs may be in black and white or color—but please be aware that all photographs will be reproduced in black and white only, unless the photo is selected for the cover. We are especially interested in photos of old women whose beauty of character shows in their faces and bodies; also in subject matter which reminds us in some way of Crone. (For example, old trees, plants in their winter appearance, crossroads, gateways, etc.)

Special Note to Artists and Photographers

Crone Chronicles is one arm of the Crone Corporation. The other arm is Crone Art (formerly known as Crone Creations) which is seeking images of Crone for a full line of Crone greeting cards. Images can be either in color or black and white. Color is preferred. Contact Claudia Kimball, Box 2344, Vashon Island, WA 98070.

General Information

If we are interested in using your material in some future issue, you will be notified. Otherwise, you will not be notified unless you have sent us an SASE for that purpose. Please realize that we cannot guarantee publication of anything, and that even when we have decided to use your piece, it may or may not get into any particular issue, as there are sometimes enormous changes at the last minute. Remember also that poetry, artwork, and photos are filed sometimes for years, before being used. If you do not wish us to keep your artwork on file, please let us know and we can make other arrangements.

We prefer material which has not been previously seen or published—please inform us of multiple submissions or previous publication.

Crone Chronicles is published quarterly. All material should be sent to the attention of the Editor. Upcoming issue themes and deadlines at the end of this letter.

Compensation and Rights

At this time, *Crone Chronicles* is unable to offer cash compensation for unsolicited artwork, photography, or written work. Given our growing circulation, we assume this will change in the future. At this point, funds left over from printing, postage, rent, utilities and supplies all go into marketing efforts to support increased circulation, as well as beginning to pay staff salaries.

If your material is accepted, you will receive a free copy of the issue in which your work appears; if you are a subscriber this will be in addition to the copy you receive as part of your subscription.

Copyright for all work reverts to authors and artists upon publication. However, we may also wish to reprint it in future *Crone Chronicles* collections. Please let us know if this is not possible.

If there are any questions which these guidelines do not cover, please feel free to call or write for more information, or simply to try out your ideas on us! Please leave a message if we are not here to receive your call.

Thanks for your interest in *Crone Chronicles*. I look forward to hearing from you soon.

Blessings,
Ann Kreilkamp

Contact Information:
Ann Kreilkamp
P.O. Box 81
Kelly, WY 83011
(307) 733-5409

Cruise Travel

The Worldwide Cruise Vacation Magazine

WHO READS *Cruise Travel*? Readers are primarily in the 40-to 60-year-old age bracket, have already taken one cruise and thoroughly enjoyed it. It should be emphasized, however, that continuous letters to the magazine also indicate a steady and growing interest in areas of family cruising, cruising for singles and cruising as a means to meet those of the opposite sex—all indicating a younger (20- to 40-year-old) audience. Overall, readers tend to display an avid, sometimes fanatical, interest in shipboard vacations and direct specific inquiries about officers, crew, special themes, etc. even in regards to a ship's former name(s) and historical background. In short, our readers are sophisticated and knowledgeable travelers not easily put off with "fluff."

The Format: Over a period of years, we have developed and refined an article and departmental content that, at present, satisfies this audience.

Each issue contains these features:

- Ship of the Month
- Port of the Month
- Cruise of the Month

Each issue may contain, in addition:

- Updated seasonal Cruise Calendar
- Interviews at Sea (Captain, Purser, Cruise Director, etc.)
- Cruise Roundups
- Cruise Guides
- Cruise Company Profiles
- If You Only Have a Day In ....

These format features are reviewed on the following basis:

A total, in-depth review of a popular and prominent major line. All aspects of the ship's "personality" should be covered, such as physical size, spaciousness, decor, etc., with special attention to public room areas. It is important to portray one's feeling aboard. Each ship is uniquely different and conveys this feeling or atmosphere. These differences could range from gaudy and loud to laid-back and refined, from intimate and subdued to wide-open and bright. Most ships will contain a cross-section mix of varied atmospheres reflected in public lounge/bar/disco areas, but overall will usually fall into a definable category. The good writer will capture this identifiable feeling in their first-person review. A "facts & features" sidebar must be included. Also send all photos, brochures, PR material, etc. (1,500-2,000 words)

Port of the Month: Choice is made on a mass appeal basis. For example: St. Thomas not Capetown, South Africa; Aruba not Honolulu. The key here is cruise lines (ships) serving the area. Generally, areas in order of importance would be the Caribbean, Yucatan-Mexico, Mediterranean. Of course, there are those ports that, although lacking in heavy cruise visits due to cost, time, etc. are nevertheless still to be considered because of universal appeal and awareness. These might include Hong Kong, Cartegena, etc. Note: New writers to *Cruise Travel* would do better to avoid this category, aiming instead for a "general" port article or "Cruise of the Month." The "Port" feature is usually assigned to writers well established with us through prior articles. Port aspects would include: a "fast facts" sidebar, history (brief unless interesting), sights, shopping (in article or as a "beefed up" sidebar). Emphasize shore excursions, side tours, things done within time of ship visit. (1,200-2,000 words)

Cruise of the Month: An area/itinerary coverage including ports-of-call, available "best buys" shopping, brief history, side tours and excursions, etc. Main function of this feature is to familiarize readers with lesser known, less popular ports in a popular area. Examples: Alaska's Inside Passage, Indonesia, China, North Africa, Panama Canal Transit, etc. Point of view would be from a specific line's ship, with background or sidebar about other major lines to the area. The benefits of a cruise vacation are made clear as readers are exposed to these multi-port itineraries. This category could also include major inland waterways like the Rhine, Danube, Mississippi, etc. Also be aware of possible stopover/stayover pre- and post-cruise options (at article's close or as sidebars). Examples: stopover in Orlando's Disney World or two- to three-day package stay in New Orleans, etc. (1,200-2,000 words)

The Exotic and Remote: A chance to cover the unique. Well received first-person adventure pieces from past issues have been: a side tour to the Lost City of Petra, Lindblad's North Cape, the Orinoco River, etc. Anywhere in the world is available to the creative writer so long as a cruise is somehow connected. Side tours offer excellent subject possibilities (Africa's Wild Game Preserves, Mayan Ruins, River Rafting, etc.). Obviously, good color photos with detailed captions are essential. Piece must include sidebar material about ships, airlines, hotels, general conditions pertinent to the area. Note: Preferred article (more of a story) would capture the romance and intrigue of the destination, since many readers express interest in these pieces even though they have never thought of taking a cruise—a form of armchair escape to the unusual. (800-2000 words)

General Ship or Cruise Features; This type of piece will usually revolve around a definite theme. Examples: The Short Cruise Introduction to the Good Life, Selecting a Stateroom, Choosing a Ship, Big vs. Small, Single Cruises, Honeymoon Cruises, Party Ships, Cruising With Kids, etc. Note: *Cruise Travel* readers are sophisticated and knowledgeable. These "general" information articles, although covering basics, should be "meat" not "fluff." A very basic or sketchy submission will be rejected. Always consider sidebars, charts, listings, maps, etc. (800-1,500 words)

Other Features: Cruise Line Profiles should cover the history of the line; describe the ships and itineraries, the company's current and future plans, etc.- and should include quotes from the line's officers as well as shipboard personnel; each line is unique and the profile should tell readers why. If You Only Have A Day In ... Will detail exactly what a passenger can do in a particular port within a certain amount of time-, focus can range from pursuing a single purpose to a "do it all" whirlwind; must be very specific and detailed. We will also consider subjects pertaining to travel in general. Examples include: Palm Trees of the World, Island Flowers (or Birds, Jewelry, Crafts, etc.). Others would include: Products—such as luggage, photography, wines; items of port shopping interest—jewelry, collectibles, art, etc. (500-1,500 words)

Sample Copy: $3.50 with self-addressed, stamped (6 oz., first class) 9 x 12 envelope.

Editors' Hints:

New writers can "break the ice" more easily by jotting down and mailing in a list of four to six article ideas they feel comfortable in developing. Include SASE, home and work telephone numbers for possible contact discussion, and social security number. Related tearsheets of published pieces are very helpful and, in many cases, lead to immediate reprint purchase. Whenever possible, include any brochures, PR material, photos etc. that relate to your stories.

Writers must be aware that issue material is developed six to eight months in advance. For example, your Alaska article, if submitted in spring would not run possibly until fall, thus schedule/itinerary information should pertain to the following year.

Features accompanied by good, well-captioned slides (color slides preferred to color prints) receive prime consideration as we are sometimes unable to generate our own pictures on "exotic" locales.

Clean photocopied submissions are fine. Copy need not be "letter perfect," i.e. minor, handwritten corrections are okay if they're neat and legible. Clearly title and number each page. Writers are encouraged to submit suggested headlines, subheads, grabbers, etc. It should go without saying that manuscripts must be grammatically correct. We use the *Associated Press Stylebook* and *Webster's New World Dictionary* as references.

Writers should aim for an active, breezy, light, conversational, even "folksy" style; avoid passive voice and pedantic or "stuffy" phrasing. Be informative and descriptive; avoid effusive but empty adjectives (elegant, luxurious, marvelous) unless backed up with descriptive fact (not just—"the elegant hardwood furniture in the main dining room" but rather "the elegant, French Provincial style, dark cherrywood furniture"). You can best capture the flavor of *Cruise Travel* by studying current issues.

I cannot stress enough the fact that high-quality photographs not only greatly enhance the article of which they are a part, but also serve to increase the chances that the submission package of which they are a part will be received more favorably than would be the case without such photos. We are always in need of quality photographs.

Payment: Upon acceptance.

Contact Information:
Charles Doherty, Managing Editor
WORLD PUBLISHING
990 Grove Street
Evanston, Illinois 60201
(708) 491-6440

Database Magazine

DATABASE is edited and written for the "information professional"—librarians or subject specialists who routinely use online services. Our articles are directed to the "hands on" searcher and to managers of information facilities. DATABASE stresses practical, how-to advice on the effective, efficient use of online databases. Both emphasize innovative tips and techniques and new technologies and products.

DATABASE covers the entire range of online topics including online industry trends, new technologies, the Internet and practical online searching tips and techniques for online searchers. It seeks a balanced mix of industry and technology coverage with practical, how-to articles, and articles on online management topics. It covers online systems, enhancements to the systems, and microcomputer hardware and software as they are used for online searching and management of online search services.

EDITORIAL PRACTICES

- We assume you are using a word processor; please also use a spelling checker.
- Write in simple, straightforward English
- Begin the article with a paragraph or two to attract the reader's interest. Boring, background introductions are not appropriate.
- Write tersely in "Reader's Digest" style, not in wordy, academic prose.
- Short, pithy, fact-filled articles are much better than long, wordy pieces.
- Stress "dos and don'ts" and "tips and techniques" that can be applied to readers' situations.
- Use examples to enhance the text; gather comments from colleagues or patrons when appropriate and include them.
- Provide photos whenever possible, also diagrams and graphs.
- Use subheads frequently to break up text (make them descriptive—not just a single word).
- Do not capitalize database names unless the producer does; if necessary check with the producers about preferred style and exact wording for names.
- Keep cited references to a minimum, and follow our preferred style.
- Identify references in the text [e.g., "Sally Smith, writing in the Nov. 1996 DATABASE, noted that..." then add a [1], [2], etc. for the full reference (Note: Use square brackets.)
- We stress original work (as opposed to a synthesis or overview based on previously published work).
- The byline should include the author's full name, title, and affiliation.
- The article should conclude with "Communications to the author should be ad-

dressed to...Name, Title, Affiliation, Mailing Address, Phone, and Electronic Mail Addresses" - (a photo and biographical sketch are optional). Type your phone number as 888/888-1234 using slash instead of parens.

- Keep printouts to a minimum and annotate the major points in printouts
- Some preferred terms are as follows: online, microcomputer, database, offline , World-Wide Web, printout, update, logoff, logon, FTP, disk, e-mail, hardcopy, host, archie, end-user, CD-ROM, MS-DOS, PC-DOS, multimedia, user-friendly, in-house, U.S., menu-driven , free text, MB (4MB), KB (24KB). Also use databank or online service ("vendor" is not acceptable).

MECHANICAL REQUIREMENTS

- All parts of an article must be submitted in electronic format, either on disk or via e-mail. This includes sidebars, biographical material, tables, charts, printouts, etc. Exceptions may be made for laser-printed illustrations after consultation with the editor.
- Two hardcopies must be submitted, in addition to a copy on disk in one of the major IBM or Macintosh word processing formats, or in ASCII. If you chose to e-mail your manuscript, send two hardcopies in the U.S. mail at the same time.
- Length should be from 12K to 30K characters, according to your discussions with the editor. Check the file length on disk, but disregard padded character counts for word processor formatting.
- Use as little formatting as possible in the manuscript since often it must be removed and revised to suit our style.
- Use carriage returns only at end of paragraphs, not after every line.
- Do not indent at beginning of paragraphs, instead use a double linefeed between paragraphs.
- The manuscript galley will be sent to the author for proofing if time allows. (Revisions or rewriting after the manuscript is edited are strongly discouraged and will be permitted only at the discretion of the production staff, and in consultation with the editor. Only necessary corrections should be made at the galley stage.)

CHARTS, GRAPHS, PRINTOUTS, ILLUSTRATIONS

- Submit graphs, charts, and other illustrations on disk if possible or in laser-printed format. Discuss acceptable graphic file formats with the editor.
- Charts and tables should have tabs, not spaces delineating the columns. Set the appropriate tabs on your word processor, using one tab per column. Do not use the Table feature in your word processor unless the editor gives approval.
- Keep the length of printouts to a minimum, using vertical ellipses where possible to eliminate repetitious parts. Printouts should be annotated.
- If you include search printouts or search examples, format them as separate figures. Search printouts cannot usually fit in our three-column text format, and must be handled separately.
- Each printout and figure must be numbered (i.e., FIGURE 1), and must have a descriptive title, and a line or two of explanation since it is possible it will appear elsewhere than near the part of the article where it is mentioned.
- Submit good copies of original printouts and search statements for proofreading of spacing, etc.
- Screen dumps must be laser-printed/camera-ready copy.
- Good photographs or other illustrations are welcome and encouraged. Discuss formats with the editor.

CITATION FORMAT

- Journal citations: Refer to a "Journal Watch" column in the magazine for the correct style. Cite the volume, the number, and the complete date of the journal article. All three elements are essential. (Example: Walker, Dana "Using Online Services." DATABASE 14, No. 3 (June 1996): pp. 104-106.)

• Book citations: Example— Glossbrenner, Alfred, and Anis, Nick. Glossbrenner's Complete Hard Disk Handbook. Berkeley, CA: Dvorak Osborne/McGraw-Hill, 1990. 814 pp.

DEADLINES

Manuscript deadlines are set by the editors of the magazines, and are staggered according to their publication schedules and work flow. Missing the scheduled deadline for your article may jeopardize publication of your article since timeliness is often of critical importance. Lead time for actual production is about three or four months due to the rigorous editing, proofing, and production efforts expended on each manuscript. If a manuscript needs fact checking or review by outside experts, editorial board members, database producers, or online services, additional time is required to complete the editorial process.

PAYMENT AND COPYRIGHT

Payment for a manuscript varies according to the article's complexity and original research. All authors are paid except those employed by online suppliers (and consultants to suppliers) who are writing about their employers' products and services. In some cases authors reviewing software that we supply may keep it as their payment. Payment is made upon publication; a check, tear sheets, and a complimentary copy of the issue are sent to the author on publication.

Authors will be asked to sign a publication agreement prior to the editing process. Copyright of DATABASE magazine as entities resides with Online, Inc.

If you'd like to write for DATABASE, please contact me to discuss an idea. I'd also be happy to review an outline or draft proposal. Send manuscripts intended for DATABASE to:

Contact Information:
Paula Hane, Editor
5917 Royal Palm Drive
Plano, TX 75093
(214) 403-0604
E-mail: phane@well.com

Decorative Artist's Workbook

Decorative Artist's Workbook (DAW) is a bimonthly publication for decorative painters of all skill levels. The magazine covers a wide range of tole and decorative painting subjects, including early American/Pennsylvania-Dutch stroke work, Rosemaling, bronzing techniques and faux finishing methods, just to name a few. In addition, articles on stenciling, theorem painting and the historical background of a painting genre are also covered. Paintings are done on such surfaces as tin, wood, canvas, fabric and glass. Whatever the medium or surface, we're seeking the new, the unique and the traditional presented in a fresh way.

FEATURES

Our most consistent need is for instructional articles. We use between six and 10 features per issue, and all features (except for those with a strictly historical emphasis) should emphasize the how-to: how the artist works and solves problems to complete a project or master a technique. These features range from 1,200 to 2,500 words in length, but we certainly welcome short features on quick projects that can be explained in one or two pages.

Historical articles can be either a history of an art form (such as stenciling or Bauernmalerei), or a history combined with technique. This type of article is used most often, and explains how a technique originated (its purpose, materials used, etc.), and how it can be completed today.

Pay for all features ranges from $125 to $250, and is, of course, dependent upon the quality of the artwork (if used), the writing, length of the article and the total package submitted by the writer.

COLUMNS

Opportunities with DAW lie basically with feature articles and with "The Artist of the Issue" (a column profiling an up-and-coming painter). Most of the other columns are written by our contributing editors and editorial board members. We will, however, accept queries for "By Design," and two of our newest columns—"Home Painting" and "Creative Painting." Submissions for columns should follow the same format as for features.

"The Artist of the Issue" runs about 500 words. Pay for the column averages $85 and depends on the quality and length of the work. Other columns pay more depending on their length and content.

Our "Ask the Masters" column features advice and answers to all of your painting questions from some of the country's top decorative artists. To participate, simply send your questions to "Ask the Masters," Decorative Artist's Workbook (See address below.)

QUERIES

Please query in advance rather than send unsolicited manuscripts and artwork. Although you're welcome to submit several ideas at once, we ask that you present each query on a separate sheet of paper. Your query should include:

- A color photo or slide of the project.
- A list of all materials (you should only use products easily available).
- A brief outline of the proposed article.
- A brief summary of the techniques used to complete the project and the photos/step-by-step worksheets you'll supply to illustrate the project.
- A short biographical sketch. Include your painting accomplishments, address and a daytime phone number.

Once your article query has been given the go-ahead, here's what you'll next need to send:

MANUSCRIPT SUBMISSION

Place your full name, address and phone number on the first page. Your manuscript should include the following:

1. Title
2. Introduction: Describe an important point about your project or subject. What made you develop the idea or design for it? You might note an unusual technique, surface or media, how it can be used or why it's one of your favorites.
3. Preparation: Explain any necessary pre-painting steps such as sanding, sealing, etc.
4. Painting Instructions: Go step-by-step through the painting process, explaining each point clearly and concisely, as if a beginning painter were looking over your shoulder. Make sure you include every detail and write in a conversational style. Spell out the full names of paint colors and please don't shorten terms (e.g. P.G. for Paynes gray).
5. Finishing: Give complete instructions on how to finish the painted project (varnishing, sanding, heat setting, etc.).
6. Closing: Close your article with a brief statement to tie everything together.
7. Materials: Please provide a list of the following:

- Palette: paint brand name, media and colors (be sure that these are spelled correctly).
- Brushes: brand name, type and size.

Surface: size (if applicable), supplier's name, address, phone number and the price of the surface (note shipping charges).

• Miscellaneous: note every other item used, from pencils to glue and sprays. Please list brand names as they appear on their packaging.

8. "About the Artist": This sidebar runs with every feature. Just tell us about yourself and include the following information:

- How long have you been painting and how did you get "hooked?"
- Have you won any awards?
- Have you published any painting books or pattern packets?
- If you teach, give the what, when and how.
- Any anecdotes about painting and your family.
- Your philosophy regarding decorative art.
- Your advice for beginners.
- A photo of yourself.

SUBMIT WITH MANUSCRIPT

- Visual aids are an important part of instruction and are essential for project articles, so remember to submit well-photographed illustrations (clearly labeled color slides or transparencies are preferred) or step-by-step painted examples of key painting steps. Instead of writing instructions directly on art/illustrations, place any copy describing the process or technique shown on a tracing paper overlay. This information will be compiled as captions. Worksheets should be painted on canvass, canvasette or oak tag paper, and should be neat and easy to see. Keep plenty of blank space around each step. Be aware that we often have to cut out illustrations for art purposes.
- If a certain technique is important in the painting of your project, make a suggestion for a special "sidebar" showing that technique. (Sidebars, such as the "Materials" and "About the Artist" sections of DAW usually appear near the main text and serve as important sources of additional information.)
- A "drawn-to-scale" ink drawing of the pattern (neatly drawn with a technical pen) for inclusion in the Special Design Insert section of the magazine.
- The completed project, ready to be photographed. (If the project is on canvas or watercolor paper, please frame it.)

All artwork, photos and drawings will be returned.

ORIGINALITY AND RIGHTS

All material submitted must be original and unpublished. DAW purchases First North American Serial Rights for one-time use in the magazine, and all rights for the use of the article (both text and illustration/art) in any F&W promotional material/product or reprint.

You always retain the copyright of your work, and are free to use it in any way you wish after it appears in the magazine. We ask, however, that you not publish this material for at least six months from the time it appears in our publication.

Contact Information:
Sandra Carpenter, Editor
1507 Dana Avenue
Cincinnati, OH 45207
(513) 531-2690

Destination:
Vietnam

Destination: Vietnam

Destination: Vietnam is a bimonthly, 56 page full color magazine for American travelers headed for Vietnam. We began publication with the September/October 1994 issue. Our mission is to show the best of the country and provide our readers with information so that they can intelligently plan their trips to Vietnam. For the first time traveler, we want to showcase Vietnam through its extraordinarily scenic countryside, its rich culture and art, and its very friendly people. We also provide the basic facts on how to plan a trip and on getting there. For those who have already been there, we include topics which will lure them back again.

Our readers

The *Destination: Vietnam* readership in the United States consists of two primary groups: individual travelers with a strong interest in Vietnam; and travel professionals who are involved in the Vietnam travel market. In Vietnam, *Destination: Vietnam* is imported and distributed by Xunhasaba, and is available at newsstands and hotel gift shops in Hanoi and Ho Chi Minh City.

The press run as of January 1995 has been 25,000 copies per issue. Distribution is by mail to individual and travel business subscribers. *Destination: Vietnam* is also available to members of various organizations such as the Vietnam Business Association of Hong Kong, the California-Southeast Asia Business Council, the San Francisco World Trade Center, Pacific Rim Expatriates, and the International Trade Association. *Destination: Vietnam* is often distributed at Vietnam trade shows and seminars both in the United States and in Vietnam.

Our writers and photographers

Our writers and photographers are all Americans who are well traveled. As the list of our current contributors shows, they come from a broad range of professions and traveled to Vietnam either in the course of business or out of strong personal interest. Most of them are amateur writers and photographers and were moved to contribute articles and pictures to *Destination: Vietnam* by the country's beauty and the friendliness of its people. Several of our regular writers have studied Vietnamese culture and art in depth. Some of our current contributors are recognized experts on Vietnam in their respective fields.

What makes up each issue of *Destination: Vietnam*

Each issue of *Destination: Vietnam* has a general theme, such as Tet and festivals for the "New Year" issue, or Mekong and Cruising for the "water" issue. Every issue has three feature articles, with five to ten departments.

Features are made up of articles of between 2,000 and 3,000 words, illustrated with pictures, or photo essays of 10 to 15 pictures accompanied by a short introduction and long photo captions. Features range from 5 to 15 pages long. Features highlight first-hand personal accounts of travel in Vietnam.

The current line up of departments include: Arts, Book/Video/Film reviews, Cuisine, Culture, Directories, Happenings, Maps, Nice Finds, Postcards, Side Trips, Touring, and Travel Tips. Departments are one to three pages, up to 1,000 words, and are chosen to complement and balance the features and the general theme of each issue.

What we look for

We want to promote Vietnam in a positive light because we believe it is a fantastic travel destination. We look for personal accounts of American travelers in Vietnam or destinations on the way to and from Vietnam.

These stories should be relatively current (within the last two years). Our readers would like to know a little about you, the writer, why you happen to be in Vietnam, where and how you traveled, the people you met, and what you enjoyed, and your feelings about your visit. The topics you cover could be anything you have an expertise or interest in.

In the Arts department, we have written about an old embroidery shop in Hanoi, and about the history of woodblocks. Both traditional or contemporary art would be of interest.

We have reviewed books such as *A Passage to Vietnam* and *Seeing Vietnam*; and have written about early traveler's tales, a look at travel in Vietnam in older books. We are always looking for new publications (books, newsletters, CD, video, software, movies) to review.

The Cuisine department has presented popular Vietnamese recipes as well as reviewed various cuisines such as pizza in Hanoi.

Our culture experts deal in subjects such as the Temple of Literature, the history and meaning of prayer flags, and the long lost musical art form of Ca Tru.

A new department, Happenings, debuts with an article on the recent Hanoi marathon. If you just came back from a cycling trip in Vietnam, or a surfing competition, we would love to hear from you.

In Nice Finds, we describe places where a seasoned traveler might hang out: Cafe 252 in Hanoi, the famous Rex roof top restaurant, Le P'tit Bistrot in Ho Chi Minh City or the Q-bar.

Side Trips gives accounts of places one might visit either on the way to Vietnam or on the way home, such as Vientiane, Myanmar, or riding the Eastern & Oriental Express from Singapore to Thailand.

Touring takes the reader golfing or cycling around Vietnam. Good topics would be: road trips, scuba diving or sailing the coast of Vietnam.

What to send us

If you think you have something we can use, do not hesitate to call to discuss your idea or to send it in.

Please include photographs (with captions), illustrations, charts or maps that can be used with your article, together with a photo and a bio of yourself (for the contributors page). We can take photos in prints (black & white or color), negatives or slides. Slides are preferred.

Ideally, your article and bio should be in a IBM/PC disk (3.5"), in ASCII, WordPerfect or Word format. No special formatting such as boldface, underline, italics, headers, footers, page numbering, columns, paragraph titles, etc. are needed. If you use Vietnamese words, please make sure you have the correct spelling, or note otherwise. Please also include a hard copy of the article with the disk.

We will acknowledge receipt as soon as we receive it. It takes us several weeks to review an article, and three months to publish one.

Writers Pay Rate

Pay rate is 10 cents per word, based on final edited length, upon publication. Length for Department articles is between 400 to 600 words. Features should be between 2,000 and 3,000 words.

There is no pay for photos but if you have some good ones that can be used with the article, it may enhance the chance of acceptance of the article.

Contact Information:
Global Directions, Inc.
116 Maiden Lane, Second Floor
San Francisco, CA 94108
(415) 333-3800

Dialogue Magazine

Blindskills, Inc. welcomes the submission of freelance material from visually impaired authors for possible publication. The best way to get an idea of the kind of material we publish is to purchase a sample copy and review it.

Current Needs: Interviews of interest or assistance to newly blind and other visually impaired persons, examples of career and leisure experiences, fiction, humor, and poetry.

Material that is religious, controversial, political, or contains explicit sex, is not acceptable.

Payments: Since DIALOGUE is entirely dependent upon public contributions for its support, payment is necessarily low. We think we offer an unusual opportunity for beginning writers. We send an explanatory letter along with each returned manuscript. A copy of the large-print edition of the magazine will be sent to each article contributor. Payments for fiction or nonfiction articles will be made at the rate of $15 to $50. Payment for poetry will be $10 to $15. All payments for articles used in a given issue will be made after all formats of DIALOGUE have been shipped.

Rules:

1. No simultaneous submissions to other publications are allowed while being considered by DIALOGUE.

2. We reserve the right to do minor editing.

3. Manuscripts must be the original work of the writer, and, in most cases, must not have been previously published. If material has been previously published, state where and when.

Rights: We buy all rights with a generous reprint policy.

Deadlines: For publication in the Spring issue, material must be received by January 1; for the Summer issue - April 1; for the Fall issue - July 1; and for the Winter issue - October 1.

SPECIFIC GUIDELINES:

Nonfiction: Though the freelance portion of any issue is generally representative of the kind of material we are buying, freelance pieces on subjects now being staff-written are always welcome. Currently, we are especially interested in first-person accounts of travel experience, articles about participation in sports, information on new products useful to the blind, features on homemaking, and descriptions of feelings and methods experienced by those losing vision or recently blind.

Fiction: Fiction pieces that promote the purposes of DIALOGUE will be printed. We are interested in well-written stories of many types: mystery, suspense, humor, adventure, romance, fantasy, science fiction, and mainstream. We prefer contemporary problem stories in which the protagonist solves his or her own problem. We are looking for strongly-plotted stories with definite beginnings, climaxes and endings. Characters may be blind, sighted, or visually in-between. Because we want to encourage any writer who shows promise, we may return a story for revision when necessary. Fiction pieces should not exceed 1800 words.

Poetry: We are eager to find new poets. Our readers enjoy traditional forms of poetry such as blank verse and free verse. Submit one poem, complete with title, date, and name and address of author to a page. Poems should not exceed twenty (20) lines in length. Poems may mention a supreme being, but will not be accepted if their theme or nature is religious. Submit no more than five poems at a time.

Recorded Interviews: Taped interviews should be recorded on a cassette recorder of very good quality at 1-7/8 IPS. The interview should be professionally conducted and should not be over twenty (20) minutes in length unless the subject or the guest has outstanding significance. The taping session should be preceded by careful research, and at least some of the questions should be prepared in advance. Where possible, submit the original tape. Tapes which are not accepted will be returned as promptly as possible. Each tape interview submitted will be evaluated on the basis of timeliness, content, and technical quality.

Short Items/Fillers: Specify what department the item is for— "ABAPITA," "Connie's Kitchen," "Classified," "Resources, New and In Review," "Department K-9," etc.

Manuscripts: Material should be submitted on a low-density IBM compatible disk in WordPerfect format. Include a hard-copy. If you do not have a computer, material may also be submitted in typed, brailled, or recorded form.

On the first page of your submission be sure to type your name, complete address, and date of submission in the top left-hand corner. Type the title of the article below these identifying data, preferably in the center of the page. On all subsequent pages, be sure to include your name and the title of your submission in the top left corner and the page number in the top right corner. Edit material on tape as carefully as you would a typed manuscript, making certain that each word is exactly as you intend it to appear in print. Spell any unusual words and proper nouns whose spelling is unclear or variable.

Length: Due to space limitations necessitated by quarterly publication, shorter lengths are preferred both for fiction and nonfiction. Stories and articles of more than 1,800 words are rarely used. We do occasionally run long nonfiction articles if the importance of the topic or nature of the material warrants it. In these cases we divide articles into two or three parts and carry them over from issue to issue.

Time Needed For Reply: At least one month.

Where To Send Freelance Material:

Contact Information:
Carol M. McCarl, President
Blindskills, Inc.
P.O. 5181
Salem, OR 97304-0181
(800) 860-4224 • FAX: (503) 581-0178
E-mail: blindskl@teleport.com

Direct Aim

(Please refer to Communications Publishing Group.)

Discipleship Journal
A Ministry of the Navigators

OUR PURPOSE

Discipleship Journal strives

- to help believers develop a deeper relationship with Jesus Christ, and
- to provide practical help in understanding the Scriptures and applying them to daily life and ministry.

CONTENT

Most of the articles we publish fall into one of three categories:

- Teaching on a Scripture passage, such as a study of an Old Testament character or a short section of an epistle, explaining the meaning and showing how to apply it to daily life

- Teaching on a topic, such as what Scripture says about forgiveness or materialism
- How-to, such as tips on deepening your devotional life or witnessing in the workplace

We do not publish testimonies, devotionals, purely theological material, book reviews, news articles, or articles about Christian organizations. We occasionally use profiles of lay people who exemplify a quality treated in a theme section.

TOPICS

About half of each issue is devoted to a theme section, which explores in-depth a subject such as time pressures, evangelism, or leadership. Send a self-addressed, stamped envelope (SASE) to request a theme list. Theme articles require a query at least three months before the issue deadline.

We encourage first-time writers to write non-theme articles, which can touch on any aspect of living as a disciple of Christ. Recent issues have dealt with subjects such as rekindling passion for God, judging others, stages of development in personal discipling, overcoming bitterness, and Jesus' principles for small group leadership.

We'd like to see more articles that (1) encourage involvement in world missions, (2) help readers in personal evangelism, follow-up, and Christian leadership, or (3) show how to develop a real relationship with Jesus.

OUR READERS

Be sure to consider our audience as you choose a topic and approach:

- Slightly more than half are women.
- About half lead a small group Bible study.
- Median age is 42.
- More than half meet individually with younger Christians to help them grow.
- Most are professionals with at least some college education.
- Many consider busyness the greatest obstacle to their spiritual growth.
- Nearly all have regular personal devotions.

TIPS FOR SUCCESSFUL ARTICLES

- Derive your main principles from a thorough study of Scripture. You will probably want to include some personal experience and quotes from others, but these should not form the basis for your article. You need not always quote a verse or reference, but you should be able to support your assertions from the Bible.
- Illustrate each principle. Use analogies, examples, and illustrations to help the reader gain understanding.
- Show how to put each principle into practice. Show the reader what applying this principle would "look like" in everyday life.
- Be vulnerable. Show the reader that you have wrestled with the subject matter in your own life. Write from the perspective of a fellow pilgrim, not someone who has "arrived."

HOW TO SUBMIT AN ARTICLE

Due to an increasing volume of submissions, we can no longer accept unsolicited manuscripts. Please send a query letter first. Phone queries are discouraged.

Queries. Please include (1) the working title, (2) a clear statement of purpose, (3) a tentative outline, (4) some indication of the style and approach you plan to use, (5) the prospective length, (6) a short description of your qualifications to write the article. If possible, include a few samples of your published work.

Manuscripts. (Submit a manuscript only after receiving a positive response to a query.) Dot matrix submissions are acceptable. On the first page, in the upper left-hand corner, type your name, address, phone number, and social security number. At top right, indicate an approximate word count and rights offered (first or reprint). We prefer Bible quotes from the

New International Version.

Length should be from 500 to 3,000 words; most articles are between 1,500 and 2,500 words. Response time is usually within four weeks. Feel free to drop us a note if you haven't heard from us after two months. Payment of 20 cents per word for first rights or 5 cents per word for reprints is made on acceptance. Reprints from non-competing publications are acceptable; be sure to indicate the publication in which the article originally appeared and the date of publication. Simultaneous submissions are discouraged.

• Before you submit an article, be sure to study several recent issues of *Discipleship Journal*. Look at the types of articles we publish, common writing styles, and the way our writers approach their topics. To obtain a sample copy, send a self-addressed 9"x12" envelope with $2.24 in postage to Diane Sevcik at the address below. If you have other questions, write to editors Susan Maycinik or Jonathan Graf at the same address, or call us at the number shown below.

Contact Information:
Jon Graf, Managing Editor
P.O. Box 35004
Colorado Springs, CO 80935
(719) 531-3529 • FAX (719) 598-7128

E
The Environmental Magazine

1. We strongly prefer a written query to a phone call. It is advisable first to review copies of *E* to judge which section your idea might be appropriate for. Write to us about your idea, its approximate length, and whether or not you would require payment. Then we'll let you know if we think there's a fit for it. We also need to see writing samples so we can determine whether or not your style is appropriate for *E*.

2. Payment (if required) is negotiable depending on the section of the magazine the article will be used in and upon the amount of work the writer must undertake to complete the assignment. We pay upon publication, unless other arrangements are made in advance.

3. Articles should be submitted with an approximate word count indicated on the printout; FAX transmissions are acceptable. We also request that the article be sent on an IBM-compatible disk.

4. Articles for *E* should be written in a journalistic style so as to be easily understood by those not immersed in the environmental movement. Unfamiliar terms, scientific language, and jargon should be avoided or explained for the benefit of the lay reader. Although *E* is an "advocacy" magazine, we are not interested in strident, opinionated writing. We want a balanced tone that will not alienate the casual reader; E's mission is to broaden the base of the environmental movement, not to preach to the converted.

5. We are interested in articles dealing with environmental issues, currents of environmental thoughts and action, and the dynamics of the movement (see "Section Guidelines" below). We are also interested in articles that explore the connections between environmental and other social change/humanitarian issues. We rarely publish poetry, fiction, or nature writing. We like articles which give readers ways to become involved (i.e. places to write letters of support or protest, contact names and addresses, resources to tap).

6. If photos and/or artwork are available, please indicate so in your query. PLEASE DO NOT SEND ANY ART MATERIALS UNLESS THEY ARE REQUESTED. Also, please include a few sentences about who you are for the brief "author bio" we include at the end of

most articles.

7. We reserve the right to edit for brevity, clarity, and tone. We prefer gender-neutral phrasing—i.e. "humankind" instead of "mankind."

Section Guidelines

E Magazine seeks submissions for the following sections, with word lengths as indicated. Please examine back issues of *E* to get an idea of the style, tone and content of the articles we publish.

Features: In-depth articles on key national environmental issues; often broadly themed (i.e. population, transportation, energy). 2,400 to 4,000 words.

Conversations: Question-and-answer interviews with environmental "movers and shakers." 2,000 words.

Currents: Medium-length news stories, 1,000 words.

In Brief: Shorter news items with a what to do/who to write emphasis. Upcoming events and concerts are listed here, too. 200 to 400 words.

Green Business: Explores the relationship between the environment and business. 800 words.

Eco-Travel: A new section about the fast-growing vacation option of eco-tourism. 800 words.

Consumer News: Examines consumer products and services, including what industries are doing in response to growing environmental concerns (i.e. recycled paper, natural cosmetics, energy-efficient appliances, etc.). 1,400 words.

Eco-Home: A new section goes inside the green home. 800 words.

Health: Explores environmental aspects of personal health. 1,000 to 1,200 words.

New Products/Reviews: Quick mentions of new products and publications. 100 words.

Contact Information:
Doug Moss, Publisher
Jim Motavalli, Managing Editor
28 Knight Street
Norwalk, CT 06851
(203) 854-5559 • FAX (203) 866-0602

Early American Homes

Early American Homes is a bimonthly magazine about the details of the American domestic past. Our time period ranges from the Pilgrim Century to 1850 and extends later if the subject warrants it.

Our readers are interested in material and social history. They value what this information adds to their own lives and surroundings. They want to know more, in-depth, about the history inherent in objects—houses, gardens, textiles, painted decoration, furniture, pottery, food—indeed every element that was commonplace to early America. They like to see, and read about, the details.

This magazine is about reproductions as well as antiques. Fine craftsmanship—the work of someone who lived and worked at a certain time in a particular place—is integral to the value of objects past and present. We feature new houses, textiles, furniture, ceramics and other decorative objects and techniques made with attention to their historic precedents. Projects our readers can try themselves are also appealing, provided they, too, have an early American background.

We're receptive to articles that explore travel to historic places, discuss preservation issues, the antiques and reproductions market, journals, diaries, and inventories. We are always interested in articles that examine the human dimensions of American history; in the regular department called Early American Life we explore what went on day to day in a particular place in a certain period. Academic writing and images of past grandeur do not appeal.

Photographs accompanying article queries are helpful to us; their quality need not be professional, just informational. We do return them. We pay for articles on acceptance and buy first-time North American rights.

Contact Information:
Mimi Handler, Editor
P.O. Box 8200
Harrisburg, PA 17105-8200
(717) 657-9555 • FAX: (717) 540-6706

Electronic Servicing & Technology

These writers' guidelines describe the kinds of articles published in *Electronic Servicing & Technology*, give some idea of the recommended length, and suggest a format for manuscripts.

Also included is a list of possible article subjects as well as a list of vocabulary words that we would like to define in depth in the magazine. These are meant as idea starters, and are not intended to exclude from consideration subjects that are not on the lists.

Also included are specific guidelines for preparing materials for publication in the SYMCURE and Troubleshooting Tips departments.

Here is a list of the contents of these guidelines:

- Writers' Guidelines
- Symcure Guidelines
- Troubleshooting Tip Guidelines
- Article Ideas
- Vocabulary
- Computer Considerations

General Information

Electronic Servicing & Technology is written primarily for servicing technicians who sell, install and service home electronics equipment.

Articles should be technical in nature and be about an electronics or electronics-related subject. Articles published in *ES&T* ordinarily fall into the following general categories:

- Specific servicing procedures for specific electronic products.
- General troubleshooting/servicing procedures.
- Theory/operation of specific items of test equipment.
- Reports of new electronics technology of interest to electronic servicing technicians.
- Tutorial articles on electronics theory.
- Symptom/cure type brief articles.
- Troubleshooting tips.

ES&T article coverage is not limited to these subject areas, however, and we welcome inquiries from prospective authors.

We use drawings, schematics, and photos, both B&W and color. For color photos, we prefer transparencies, although we can work from prints. We have access to artists who can create finished art, so don't be hesitant to include rough hand drawings. We can put them in final form.

We especially welcome articles that are on computer disk. We use IBM format, and can accept either 3-½ or 5-¼ inch disks. Preferred format is ASCII, but we can usually accept output from any word processor. Please be sure to include information that tells us what word processor you used to create the document.

Article length for a feature article should ordinarily be between three and fifteen typewritten pages. That's just a rough guide, though, not a hard and fast rule. Articles should be as long as they have to be to cover the subject thoroughly. Other manuscripts like Symcure, Troubleshooting Tips and others may be very brief.

It might be to the writer's advantage to submit a query beforehand, outlining a proposed article. That would allow the editors to comment specifically on whether an article is appropriate and/or needed, as well as to suggest to the writer information that should be included.

In any case, do not hesitate to write or call the editors to request comments and guidance on writing for *ES&T*.

Manuscript Preparation

There really are few stringent requirements for preparation of manuscripts for *ES&T*, but here are a few suggestions for writers who submit manuscripts on computer disc, that will make it easier for the editors.

1. If you feel that a term, or some kind of description requires emphasis, make a note of it on the manuscript, with your suggestion of the type of emphasis: italic, boldface, etc. Please don't include such things as underline or all caps, because we don't do that kind of emphasis in the magazine. And don't include that kind of emphasis in your document if you're submitting it on disc, because we would have to eliminate those imbedded commands and change to our typesetting codes for that emphasis.

2. Don't leave large open spaces in the text to show where figures go. Simply refer to the art in the text, for example "see Figure I." The art department will try to put the art in the right place.

3. Don't put the caption at the point in the article text where the art goes. At the end of the article type in the word Captions, leave a couple of line spaces, and type in the captions, like this:

Figure 1. Connect the probe of the oscilloscope to.........

4. If you're submitting hand drawn art to be prepared in final form by the *ES&T* artist, it would be very helpful to the editors if you could type the callouts for all of the art on a separate sheet of paper, as well as writing them in on the hand drawn diagram in all capitals. This has to be done by someone before the callouts can be sent to the typesetter.

Symcure

The term Symcure is a contraction of the two words: Symptom/cure. Problems that are published in *ES&T* in the Symcure department are those that have occurred more than once.

This is the kind of problem that you can solve without even a second thought because you've already seen so many of that particular brand and model of set with those symptoms and in almost every case it was the same component that had failed, or the same solder joint that had opened.

Because of the manner in which we publish Symcure, submissions, if they are to be considered, must follow these rules:

1. Each submission must consist of seven individual symptom/cure units on a single brand and model of television set. Seven are requested so we may choose the most appropriate for publication.

2. We must have the following information about the set:

• Manufacturer's name

• Model and chassis number or ID

• Sams Photofact number if you know it

• A rough sketch of the schematic where the fault was found. Each sketch should contain a major component such as a transformer, a tube, a transistor or an IC to provide a landmark for the *ES&T* staff.

3. Because the very nature of Symcure is based on schematics, if for any reason there is no Sams Photofact on the unit, we cannot accept the submission.

Article Ideas

This is a list of ideas for articles for *Electronic Servicing & Technology* that readers have suggested, and that the editorial staff has added to. It is not meant to limit articles in *Electronic Servicing & Technology* to these subjects, merely to serve as a list of possible articles and idea starters.

• One type of article that many readers have requested is the article, or more usually a series of articles, that examines a relatively new model of TV set from end to end, describing all of the circuitry, and especially dwelling on any new type of circuitry.

• Other article subjects:

TELEVISION

Troubleshooting HV and LV circuits and how they work; Understanding and servicing TV shutdown circuits;

Understanding TV startup circuits; Understanding TV voltage regulator circuits; Troubleshooting horizontal circuits; Troubleshooting vertical circuits; Troubleshooting TV power supply Circuits; Specific troubleshooting procedures for specific brands and models of TV; Dealing with newer more exotic TV

Understanding the NTSC waveform; Servicing projection TV; Multichannel TV sound; The new multistandard TVs; Identifying sources of TV interference and correcting problems; TV tuner repair

Troubleshooting older TVs

Here's an idea I've toyed with from time to time: Would it be possible to start with a bare bones TV receiver and add colored overlays showing how TV has evolved from its inception to today?

VCRs AND CAMCORDERS

Servicing VCRs; Understanding and servicing VCR control systems; Servicing video cameras/camcorders

What is "HQ" circuitry in VCRs

POWER CONDITIONING

OFFICE EQUIPMENT

Servicing Cellular telephones; Preventive maintenance for printers; Understanding electronic tuners and tuning

PERSONAL COMPUTERS

IBM PC computer servicing; The personal computer as a servicing tool; Personal computer servicing: general and product specific

MOTORS

DC motor control

SATELLITE TV

Servicing TVRO: downconverters, LNAs, actuators

TWO WAY AND CB RADIO

Servicing two-way radio; Servicing CB radio

AUDIO

Servicing audio equipment; Servicing compact disc players

CIRCUITS, GENERAL

Understanding new circuitry: SAW fibers, phase-lock loops, comb fibers; Detailed descriptions of how circuits work; Do it yourself circuit construction

TROUBLESHOOTING

Using a spectrum analyzer in troubleshooting; Suggested general troubleshooting techniques/tips/hints; A step-by-step approach to troubleshooting: using the senses, what's the next step, etc.; Signal injection/signal tracing; Component testing: resistors, capacitors, inductors, diodes, transistors, ICs; Troubleshooting using an oscilloscope

FUNDAMENTALS

Fundamentals of electronics; Fundamentals of electronic servicing

TEST EQUIPMENT

Test equipment use and operation; Inexpensive test equipment/accessories; Testing methodology; Servicing, repair and calibration of test equipment; Equipping a test bench

SOLDERING/DESOLDERING

New methods of soldering/desoldering for new soldering technology

COMPONENTS

Suggestions on finding/tailoring general replacements when exact replacements are no longer offered by manufacturer; Sources of replacement parts

COMPUTERS AND DIGITAL CIRCUITS

Troubleshooting/repairing digital circuits; Understanding digital circuit design and operation; Test equipment for personal computers; Understanding digital circuit test equipment; Troubleshooting logic circuits with logic probes, pursers, etc.

ANTENNAS

Diagnosing antenna problems; dB calculations for MATV

MISCELLANEOUS

Servicing consumer electronic instruments: keyboards, organs, etc.; Servicing microwave ovens; Lightning and surge protection; Electronics in home appliances: what they are, how to fix; Servicing mechanical components; Understanding wire and cable

Contact Information:
Conrad Persson, Editor
P.O. Box 12487
Overland Park, KS 66282-2487
(913) 492-4857

Endless Vacation

Endless Vacation **is . . .**

Endless Vacation is a magazine for vacation travelers. It is not for business travelers or armchair travelers. *Endless Vacation* shows readers where to go and what to do on vacation, and perhaps most important, why. *Endless Vacation* also addresses the issues of timeshare ownership and timeshare exchange and offers travel information geared to increasing the enjoyment of our readers, who own a timeshare condominium.

Freelance writers contribute three to five features of 1,200 to 2,200 words in each issue. In addition, there are several departments of 800 to 1,000 words each.

Our features focus primarily on domestic vacation travel, with some mainstream international vacation articles. Features should cover new and interesting vacation options, and should have a solid angle. Topics range from Colorado resorts in the fall to Civil War steamboating. Although limited, the international features cover easily accessed areas of Europe, South America, Africa, and the Pacific. We are not looking for Nepalese mountain treks or hiking the wilds of Vietnam—however, the romantic towns of Bavaria or shopping in

Singapore might turn our heads.

Department topics for which *Endless Vacation* accepts some freelance contributions include weekend travel destinations, health and safety on the road, short travel service and news-oriented pieces, and hot news tips and trends in travel.

Before You Write Your Manuscript or Query

1. The editors strongly suggest that you read the magazine thoroughly to get an understanding of our style and approach. Reading the magazine may also prevent you from querying us on a topic that has recently been covered.

2. Because our readers are doers, not dreamers, your article should cover destinations they can visit and activities in which they can participate.

3. Features should have a narrow focus but not be so limited as to have a parochial appeal. An article on the renaissance of a city is good; an article on a common event or festival in a city usually is not.

4. Articles should provide a fast read, packed with anecdotes, examples, and mini-stories. We are not looking for guidebook material, but finely-written, well-constructed travel stories. Personal observations and experiences, interviews with other vacationers or local guides, and solid facts are articles we look for. Many, many publications are competing for our readers' time. Brevity, clarity, and conciseness should be hallmarks of your article.

5. Audience (based on 1994 demographic study by MRI)

- Sex: 42 percent male; 58 percent female
- Median Age: 42.3
- College graduates: 32 percent
- Married: 65 percent
- Income: $57,000 median
- In addition, other research shows that 99 percent own a timeshare condominium and rank their most important activities while on vacation (in descending order) as: leisure time, visiting local tourist attractions, dining, shopping, swimming, sports activities, cultural activities, and entertaining.

For more information, *Endless Vacation*'s media kit, which includes a copy of the magazine and an 18-page demographic profile of readers, is available for $10. Single copies of the magazine are $5 each, and subscriptions are available to freelance writers for $33.50 (standard subscription rate is $67). Please mail requests to the attention of Joyce Moore.

How to Submit Manuscripts and Queries

Our editorial calendar is booked many months in advance, and currently we have extremely limited space for freelance submissions. We will review manuscripts on speculation, and for a writer who is unfamiliar to us, this may be the best entrée to our publication. The lead is crucial. If the first sentence does not catch our attention, we may never get to the second one.

If you are interested in submitting a query for a specific issue, please submit your query as early as possible. A year in advance is suggested.

Query letters should include three to four concise paragraphs indicating the focus and tone of the proposed article. Please include samples of your travel writing so that we may give your query full consideration. We generally respond to queries by letter in 30 days.

Please do not telephone us with your query. It is necessary for us to have queries in written form.

Photography

Photographers should submit a stock list and printed samples to the photo editor. (We cannot guarantee the return of unsolicited slides and transparencies.) The photo editor will contact you if your portfolio matches our needs.

If you are asked to submit materials, please make sure that your name and some form of ID number are on each 35mm slide and color transparency. Photos must be identified on the slide mount or with a caption sheet.

Payment for photos generally ranges between $100 and $500 per photo used, depending on size. Cover photos earn more.

Model releases are required.

If a writer submits slides with a story, they will be considered by the photo editor, and if selected, payment will be negotiated separately from the article. We do not, however, encourage writers to submit photos.

Manuscript Payment

Payment is negotiated upon assignment and tendered upon acceptance. The following ranges will give you an idea of our rates:

- Feature articles (including sidebars): $500 to $1,000
- Departments: $300 to $800
- News Briefs: $75 to $100

Expenses are not guaranteed and are negotiated individually.

If you are assigned an article, you will be sent a contract with a brief description of the topic, terms, and payment. Sign the contract and return it immediately. We cannot send payment without a signed contract on file.

Assigned deadlines are absolute. Failure to meet them may result in the cancellation of the assignment.

Contact Information:
Manuscripts or Queries: Elizabeth LaPlante, Senior Editor
Photographic Inquiries: Tom Heine, Photo Editor
P.O. Box 80260
Indianapolis, IN 46280-0260
(317) 871-9504

Entrepreneur Magazine
The Small Business Authority

Focus

Entrepreneur readers already run their own businesses and are seeking innovative methods and strategies to improve their business operations. They're also interested in new business ideas and strategies.

Types of Articles

- Profiles of entrepreneurs with unique businesses and stories to tell.
- Articles offering how-to advice for running a business or explaining how a current business issue, such as the health insurance crisis, affects the operation/management of a business.
- Psychological topics such as coping with stress or how personality affects management style.
- Industry round-ups covering the state of a particular industry and the future trend of that industry.
- Columns are not open to freelancers.

Where to start

- You must read the magazine before attempting to query an article.

- Submit queries only. Full-length manuscripts are discouraged.
- Queries should describe the topic clearly and concisely.
- Allow a minimum of 6-8 weeks for a response. No phone calls please.
- Entrepreneur Group buys first worldwide rights and pays upon acceptance.

Contact Information:
Rieva Lesonsky, Editor-in-Chief
P.O. Box 57050
Irvine, CA 92619-7050
(714) 261-2325

Equal Opportunity

(Please refer to Equal Opportunity Publications.)

Equal Opportunity Publications

Thank you for your interest in writing for our career-guidance magazines, which provide college-level and professional women, minorities, and people with disabilities with information on how to find employment and develop their career potential.

CAREERS & the disABLED: Published four times a year with Fall, Winter, Expo, and Spring editions. It is devoted to promoting the personal and professional growth of individuals with disabilities.

EQUAL OPPORTUNITY: Published three times a year with Fall, Winter, and Spring editions. It is dedicated to advancing the professional interests of blacks, Hispanics, Asian Americans, and Native Americans.

MINORITY ENGINEER: Published three times a year with Fall, Winter, and Spring editions. It is focused on advancing the careers of minority engineering students and professional engineers.

WOMAN ENGINEER: Published three times a year with Fall, Winter, and Spring editions. It is aimed at advancing the careers of women engineering students and professional engineers.

WD—Workforce Diversity: Published quarterly with Fall, Winter, Spring, and Summer editions. It addresses professional women, minorities, and people with disabilities about how they can succeed as part of a diversified workforce.

Articles sought for recruitment magazines: Career-guidance articles on job hunting; overview articles of particular career disciplines such as health care, nursing, engineering, sales, government, accounting, banking, communications, and insurance; role-model profiles of professional women, minorities, and people with disabilities working in the field; and mini profiles of women, people with disabilities, and minorities for the "People On The Move" section.

Rights: First North American serial rights are owned by Equal Opportunity Publications, Inc. Previously published articles to which you have retained reprint rights are also acceptable if they have not appeared in a competitive publication.

Photographs and artwork needed: We need photographs of professional women, minorities, and people with disabilities at work to be used on the covers of the magazine. Please submit vertical 35mm slides or transparencies. In addition, we need photographs and cartoons for the interior of the magazines.

Rates: The rate for articles is ten cents per word paid within six weeks after publication. The rate for each photograph used is $15. The rate for cartoons is $25. All manuscripts and photographs are submitted on speculation.

Queries: We prefer to receive an article proposal and/or outline rather than a completed manuscript, except for humor and filler pieces. After reviewing your idea, we will let you know as soon as possible if it meets our editorial needs. Once you receive our go-ahead, follow the procedure for submitting manuscripts.

Manuscripts: Since all of our magazines are produced electronically, manuscripts should be submitted on a 3½" floppy disk, either in a Macintosh program or saved in ASCII on a PC. (5¼" floppy disks are unacceptable.) In addition, we request that you send a printed version of your manuscript that includes your telephone and social security numbers. In the event that you cannot meet these requirements, you can submit a typed manuscript (no dot matrix submissions).

Contact Information:

Forward your query to the following editors:
WOMAN ENGINEER: Anne Kelly, (516) 421-9478
WD—Workforce Diversity: Eileen Nester, (516) 421-9467
CAREERS & the disABLED, EQUAL OPPORTUNITY, MINORITY ENGINEER:
James Schneider, (516) 421-9469
1160 East Jericho Turnpike
Suite 200
Huntington, NY 11743
(516) 421-9421

Essence

Thank you for your interest in writing for ESSENCE Magazine. ESSENCE publishes provocative feature-length articles for African-American women, on subjects that are important to our personal development and empowerment. We are interested in well-written self-help articles as well as celebrity profiles and essays on personal, political and social issues. We are looking for how-to articles on careers, money, health and fitness, electronics, computers and cars. We also run freelance-written short gazette items on health, work, money, parenting, computers, people in the arts and community activists. Word length is given upon assignment.

Please send a query letter rather than submitting a completed manuscript. If we have recently done a story on your topic, if we would like you to approach the topic from another angle, or if we cannot use your story idea, a query letter will save you the time and effort of preparing a manuscript. The only exceptions are for Interiors, Windows, Brothers and Back Talk columns; essays submitted for these pages should run no longer than 1,000 words and should be clearly addressed to the editor of the column.

Be sure to include in your query your name, address and daytime phone number. Give us a clear and concise outline of your story; one page is sufficient. It will help if you include a brief bio that describes your writing experience. Clippings are welcome.

If you wish to submit more than one idea to us, write a separate query for each topic and send each one to the appropriate editor. Check our masthead in the current issue to learn which areas each editor covers.

If we feel your subject will be of interest to our readers and you are a writer new to ESSENCE, you will be asked to submit the completed manuscript on speculation. Manuscripts are then read and a decision is made by our editors. Payment for articles is made upon acceptance for publication. Please allow six weeks for review.

We look forward to hearing from you.

Contact Information:
THE EDITORS
1500 Broadway
New York, NY 10036
(212) 642-0600 • FAX: (212) 921-5173

Executive Female

Executive Female is the award-winning bimonthly publication of the national Association for Female Executives (NAFE), the largest businesswomen's organization in the country. The readers of *Executive Female* are members of NAFE. They are well educated (with at least a four-year college degree), sophisticated professionals, managers or entrepreneurs. They have a median age of 38 and personal incomes of more than $42,000 a year.

Executive Female's mission is to provide the already accomplished businesswoman with sophisticated and informative articles on management, career strategies, entrepreneurship, business trends and personal finance that will help her become a more expert and confident manager—of other people, of her own business, of her career. It speaks to the readers as an equal, with the voice of a trusted and savvy colleague—smart, informed, eager to share strategies and stories, to pass on useful information.

Feature articles in the magazine cover issues that are relevant to managerial and entrepreneurial women—for instance, the latest managerial practice or career strategy, an innovative remedy for the salary gap between men and women or the saga of how someone started a business. *Executive Female*'s readers are very success-oriented: They know women still face a tough time in the workplace but they are focused on solutions. Every article must therefore provide in-depth information the reader can put to use to make her job and/or life better.

Stories may be told through the example of a particular woman manager or entrepreneur or they may be built around a particular company or industry. Quotes from real-life women managers and experts are important ingredients of every article. Actual examples, rather than hypothetical "cases," are necessary. Profiles always include interviews not just with the profile subject but with those who have worked with her, as well as industry experts. Pertinent statistics about the size of her industry, her salary, the budget she commands and annual profits should be included. Any company profile must include as many financials as possible. Feature ideas should be sent to Carol Wheeler, Features Editor, or Patti Watts, Executive Editor.

The magazine also has the following departments in each issue:

Your Business: Starting It, Growing It—An 8-page entrepreneurial section covering small-business management strategies, franchise opportunities and financing methods. Address queries to Laurel Touby, Small Business Editor.

Managing Smart—Addresses the reader in her role as manager of other people and head of a department or division. Send queries to Patti Watts, Executive Editor.

Your Money—How to manage and invest money. Mutual funds, insurance, financial planning, tax planning, stocks and bonds, real estate and more. Send ideas to Patti Watts, executive editor.

Latest Technology & Equipment—Information on how to use technology to solve various business problems; software to make your business run smoothly; equipment that can improve productivity and performance; and advice on how to navigate in cyberspace. Send queries to Carol Wheeler, Features Editor.

The Working Life—Focuses on creating a more balanced life, including self-management of a woman's on-the-job performance, career and personal time. Send queries to Dorian Burden, Managing Editor.

Writers who wish to contribute to *Executive Female* should read the magazine to get an overall sense of its focus before submitting queries. (Sample copies are available for $2.50 each, and can be obtained by sending a check to the address below.) Send queries rather than completed articles, including published clips and a detailed outline of the piece you propose, including who you plan to interview and why your idea is a timely topic to cover. Replies will be sent out within six weeks.

The national Association for Female Executives is in the process of constructing a Web site, Women@Work. The best way to get an idea of what we'd use is to take a look at the site (address below). Queries for online material, separate from the magazine, should be directed to Heather Ekey, Web Site Associate, at the Web address.

Contact Information:

Career, Personal Time: Dorian Burden, Managing Editor
Technology, Software, Cyberspace: Carol Wheeler, Features Editor
Management, Money: Patti Watts, Executive Editor
Entrepreneurs, Franchises: Laurel Touby, Small Business Editor
30 Irving Place, 5th Floor
New York, NY 10003
(212) 477-2200 • FAX: (212) 477-8215
E-mail: http://www.nafe.com

Family Circle

Dear Reader:

Writers are sometimes surprised to find out that most of the articles FAMILY CIRCLE publishes are written by freelance writers. We are always looking for new contributors.

If you want to submit an article proposal to FAMILY CIRCLE, please pay careful attention to the following points:

1. Take a close look at FAMILY CIRCLE for some knowledge of format and an understanding of subjects we have tackled in the past, remembering that we are a general interest women's magazine which focuses on the family. We are looking for family-oriented stories with strong plot lines and characters with whom an audience composed primarily of women would identify. We are especially interested in women who make a difference in their community, news and information on health, childcare, relationships, finances and other matters of concern to today's family, and dramatic personal experiences.

2. Submit a detailed outline first, and include a brief cover letter describing your publishing history with two representative clips. Remember to consider our lead time (usually three months) when proposing articles; for example, we finish our back-to-school issue in June and our Christmas issue in September.

3. Maximum length for articles is 2,500 words.

4. Though we try to review queries quickly, please be patient. We receive thousands of proposals per year and we consider them all very carefully before making decisions.

Again, thank you for your interest.

Sincerely,

THE EDITORS

Query individual category editors listed on masthead.

Contact Information:
110 Fifth Avenue
New York, NY 10011
(212) 463-1000

The Family Digest

Thank you for your interest in our bimonthly publication. This writer's guideline is yours to keep in your writer's portfolio. It outlines our editorial needs and requirements for this parish-oriented publication.

Types of articles we're looking for:

The *Family Digest* is dedicated to the joy and fulfillment of Catholic family life. The *Family Digest* is looking for articles of interest to the Catholic family, particularly in its relationship to the Catholic parish. We are especially looking for upbeat articles which affirm the simple ways in which the Catholic faith is expressed in daily life.

Article topics include:

- Family life
- Parish life
- Spiritual life
- Church traditions
- Seasonal
- Prayer
- Inspiration
- How-to

Word length and seasonal articles:

Writers are encouraged to submit articles between 700 and 1,200 words in length. The *Family Digest* prefers to purchase and publish previously unpublished articles, but will consider previously published pieces. Please include the publication history with your article submission. Articles on seasonal or holiday themes should be submitted seven months prior to date of issue. The *Family Digest* does NOT publish poetry or fiction.

Rates of payment:

- Articles: 5 cents per word
- Cartoons: $20.00
- Humorous anecdotes: $10.00 for exclusive, unusual stories drawn from personal experiences (25 to 125 words)

The *Family Digest* pays for accepted articles, cartoons and anecdotes within one month of acceptance.

Response time:

Writers can expect to hear back on submitted articles within four to eight weeks. Due to the sheer volume of manuscripts received, personalized replies are not possible.

Reading the articles published in The *Family Digest* will give you the best sense of the types of articles The *Family Digest* accepts. Best wishes in your writing efforts!

Contact Information:
Corine B. Erlandson, Editor
P.O. Box 40137
Fort Wayne, IN 46804

FamilyFun

Thank you for inquiring about freelance opportunities at *FamilyFun*. We are a magazine for parents of children ages three to twelve and we cover all the great things families can do together: travel, educational projects, holiday celebrations, crafts projects, and more. Our goal is to provide our readers with all of the practical information they need to carry out our ideas with their own resources such as related books and contact phone numbers. We deem an idea a good one when it is fun for the whole family, it is inexpensive, and it is not time-consuming for a parent to plan. FamilyFun's style is upbeat and straightforward. Ours is not a child-rearing magazine—we do not give out advice about health, discipline, or other concerns in child development—so we do not consider queries on those topics or quote psychologists or other experts.

We rely primarily on our staff members and regular contributors for features and feature ideas, but we welcome freelance queries for a number of sections in the magazine. With each query or manuscript you send, please include a short cover letter and two or three relevant clips for our review. We generally take four to eight weeks to respond and regret that we cannot, under any circumstances, consider queries over the telephone.

FAMILY ALMANAC is scheduled and assigned several months before the issue date. This section is meant to provide readers with simple, practical ideas and projects (outings, craft projects, games, nature activities, learning activities, and cooking with children). FAMILY ALMANAC also provides the resources—activities, phone numbers, books—to carry out those ideas. FAMILY ALMANAC is direct and cheerful in tone and is never written in the first person. We read freelance manuscripts and queries for FAMILY ALMANAC, and payment is $150, on acceptance, for approximately 300 words.

FAMILY TRAVELER consists of very brief, newsy items about family travel—what's new, what's great, and especially, what's a good deal. This section is informative and to the point in tone and covers very specific topics (e.g. a new program at one hotel, rather than a round-up of hotels around the country). We cover resort news, festivals, museum exhibits, outdoor outfitters, specialized travel agencies, educational trips and programs, etc. Because we are budget conscious, we rarely cover international travel or expensive American resorts or programs. We read freelance manuscripts for FAMILY TRAVELER and pay $75 for 100 to 150 word pieces.

READ ALOUD STORY is for children ages two to six. We will read complete manuscripts only, of approximately 500 to 750 words, and are happy to consider reprinting previously published stories. Topics we choose often touch on, with humor or sentiment, the positive aspects of family life. Payment is $500 on acceptance. Please do not send original art.

We rotate three front-of-the-book, first person columns in *FamilyFun*. We are happy to consider not only queries but also completed manuscripts.

FAMILY TIES is a humorous or inspirational first-person column that looks at the writer's life with his or her own children. Topics here range widely. In the past, for example, one writer covered the development of folklore in his own family; yet another wrote about passing his love of baseball on to his son or daughter; another explained her family's tradition of taking off on spontaneous weekend jaunts. This column runs 1,500 words and pays $1,000 and up.

NATURE & KIDS, also a humorous or inspirational first person column, is a new section that will look at the writer's experience of sharing nature experiences with his or her own children. Possible topics might be learning to birdwatch with kids, the first family campout, or a family tradition of tidepooling. This column will run 1,500 words and will pay $1,000 and up.

MY GREAT IDEA, our third column, explains fun and inventive ideas that have worked for a writer's own family. Two examples from previous issues are a game that gets children engrossed in museum-going and a chain letter that brings an extended family together. The simpler and more clever the idea, the better. The column length is 800 words, and pays $500 to $750 on acceptance. We would consider any ideas for this column in query, letter, or manuscript form. In addition to the column, we publish the best letters from writers and readers at the end of the column. MY GREAT IDEA LETTERS run 100 to 150 words, and will pay $25 upon publication.

We will announce in the magazine any invitations for photographic submissions. Do not send any slides or photographs that you wish to have returned!

If you would like to receive a SAMPLE COPY or order a SUBSCRIPTION to *FamilyFun*, please call 1-800-289-4849 or write to:

FAMILY FUN
P.O. Box 10161
Des Moines, IA 50340-0161

The cost per sample copy is $3; a year's subscription is $14.95.

Thank you for your interest in *FamilyFun*.

Contact Information:

FAMILY ALMANAC: Cindy Littlefield, Assistant Editor
FAMILY TRAVELER: Rani Arbo, Associate Editor
READ ALOUD STORY: Deanna Cook, Senior Editor
FAMILY TIES: Clare Ellis, Editor
NATURE & KIDS: Lisa Stiepock, Senior Editor
MY GREAT IDEA: Rani Arbo, Associate Editor
Photography: Dave Kendrick, Art Director
244 Main Street
Northampton, MA 01060
(413) 585-0444

Family Life

A Publication of Hachette Filipacchi Magazines

Thank you for your request for *Family Life* guidelines.

Our readers are parents of children ages 3-12 who are interested in raising their kids in the most educational, innovative environment available today. Most are college educated and work hard at a full-time job. We want fresh articles dealing with the day-to-day issues that these families face, with personal insight and professional opinion on how to handle them.

Our "Family Matters" section in the front of the book consists of newsy shorts on noteworthy individuals, new educational programs, cool travel destinations and the latest on health issues; pieces run from 150-250 words.

Individual columns run from 1,000-1,500 words, and are divided accordingly: "Why We Live Here" highlights particular communities that lend themselves favorably to family life. "First Thoughts" is our first-person essay about life with children. "A Child's Eye" discusses the personal issues children face while growing up; "Family Affairs" deals with those issues which crop up in a couple's relationship as parents. "School Smart" discusses today's educational issues. "Family Strategist" deals with family financing. "What-to-Do" highlights interesting activities for the kids. "House Calls" is our health column and "Chip Chat" addresses the latest in family computing.

Features run from 2,000-3,500 words. We prefer a written proposal of your idea, accompanied with several previously published clips.

The Children's Hour reviews books, videos, TV, movies, music, software and other entertainment for children or parents. Please send information or review items to the attention of The Children's Hour editor.

We appreciate your interest in *Family Life*.

Contact Information:
Peter Herbst, Editor-in-Chief
1633 Broadway
New York, NY 10019
(212) 767-4918 • FAX: (212) 489-4561

Fast and Healthy Magazine

Fast and Healthy Magazine is a family-oriented food magazine with healthful recipes for active people. Its emphasis is on Monday through Friday cooking. All recipes can be prepared in about 30 minutes or less and meet the U.S. Dietary Guidelines for healthful eating. *Fast and Healthy Magazine*'s editorial reinforces the health and convenience aspects of the recipes.

If you are interested in proposing an article for *Fast and Healthy*, please consider the following:

• CONTENT - *Fast and Healthy* is a mainstream magazine about everyday healthful cooking; it is not a diet magazine or a gourmet cooking magazine. The majority of *Fast and Healthy*'s features and departments are comprised of recipes with supporting editorial. The editorial is consumer-oriented with news and tips about quick and healthy cooking. We occasionally include non-recipe articles that also focus on quick meat preparation and healthy cooking and lifestyles. Article length can range from 200 to 1,500 words, but most often the editorial is short and is divided into smaller blocks of information, with frequent use of sidebars and charts.

• STYLE - Our editorial voice is upbeat, friendly, straightforward and consumer-oriented.

• STORY IDEAS - While feature ideas are generated by the editors, we are open to proposals from experienced writers or writer/recipe developers. Please do not send completed manuscripts. Instead, present your idea in a concise paragraph or two and accompany it with a resume and representative clips. If you are experienced in recipe development and are proposing recipe ideas, please keep in mind that recipes must meet our nutrition and time criteria to be accepted. (Detailed information is provided to those given an assignment.)

• RIGHTS/PAYMENT - We buy all rights to editorial material and recipes. We pay upon acceptance. Rates vary depending on length and difficulty of the assignment. A kill fee of 20% is offered.

• SAMPLE COPIES - A sample copy is available for $3 from the address below. (Fast and Healthy Magazine also is available on newsstands.)

Thank you for your interest in *Fast and Healthy Magazine*.

Contact Information:
Queries: Betsy Wray, Editor
200 S. 6th St., M.S. 28M7
Minneapolis, MN 55402
(612) 330-4475 • FAX: (612) 330-4875

Fate Magazine
True Reports of the Strange and Unknown

Thank you for your interest in writing for FATE. We are always interested in new writers and hope that you will be one to help us share factual information that takes our readers beyond superficiality to a serious but popular presentation of the most important and amazing subjects ever presented to the public.

We've prepared these guidelines to address what we are looking for and how manuscripts should be prepared. Submit your article along with the information we request at the end of the guidelines. If you have a book to submit, please write to Llewellyn Worldwide at the address below and ask for "Book Submission Guidelines."

FORMAT

1.) We encourage submissions on Macintosh- or IBM-compatible disks. Label disks with your name, title of the article, the word processor program used, version, etc. (or ASCII, and whether IBM compatible or Macintosh). Include a printed copy.

2.) Whether you use a typewriter, word processor, or computer, output should be letter quality (laser, high-quality inkjet, or very high quality dot matrix). Use a standard typeface.

3.) Place identification at the top of each sheet to prevent mix-ups. Include your last name, the article's title, and consecutive page numbers.

4.) Include a cover sheet with your name and address.

5.) If return postage is not included and your submission is not accepted, you will receive notification but your article will be discarded.

6.) We want FATE to be as visual as possible. Articles with accompanying photographs and illustrations are more likely to be accepted and published faster.

A.) They must be legally reproducible. If you are taking illustrations, photos, or text from other published sources, they may fall under copyright law. You are responsible for obtaining permissions for use from either the publisher or copyright holder before the manuscript is accepted for publication. We cannot assume they are in the public domain unless you tell us so and give the source and year of publication.

B.) We prefer good quality black & white photos. In FATE's present format, black and white photos reproduce best and will most strongly complement your article. If you have good color photos available as well, please note that with your submission and we will request them if needed.

C.) Put your name, the story title, and captions on the back of photos and illustrations.

D.) Photos and illustrations that are used will be paid for after publication, at a rate of $10.00 per photo or illustrations. We may or may not use the photos. (See sections 15 and 18, below.)

7.) The preferred length of feature articles is 1,500 to 3,000 words.

A.) "Brief" articles are from 500 to 1,000 words.

C.) "Fillers" are less than 500 words and are used at the end of articles and other places in the magazine where a "tidbit" is needed to fill the page. Very short ones, of 150 words or less, are particularly needed at this time.

STYLE

8.) Articles should be lively, personal, experiential, and informative. They should play up the wonder of the subject matter and/or develop practical benefits, show "how-to," and so on.

9.) FATE is nonfiction. Consequently, articles should be documented in the following ways:

A.) Personal experience articles should include full details of names, dates, times, and places. Although some of this material may be withheld from publication if you specifically request it, we must have it all correctly documented for our files.

B.) You may be asked to provide contact information for all participants if you have not included it in the article. You may be asked for a sworn and notarized statement from yourself and other participants/witnesses verifying facts described. You will be reimbursed for this cost after publication.

C.) Sources for quotes must be footnoted or be given in the body of the article (although we may choose not to use this information in the published article).

D.) When appropriate, include a bibliography. It should include author, title, publisher, place, and date of publication. If sources are other than published works (i.e. personal research or interviews), this too should be detailed.

10.) Although FATE publishes relatively brief articles, we are looking for depth of content. We do not want "round-ups" that merely list a variety of sightings or events. Rather, focus on one event, time period, and so on, in detail.

11.) Topics and Content:

- Psychic phenomena: reports, investigations, experiments, theory.
- Recent UFO information: activity, investigations, disclosures.
- Recent Fortean phenomena: strange creatures, mysterious events, unexplained coincidences, etc.
- Ghosts, poltergeists, mediumship, survival after death.
- Alternate forms of spirituality.
- Alternative healing systems, including acupuncture, herbalism, suggestion, etc.
- How-to articles on healing, divination, mediumship, dowsing, ghost hunting, spiritual growth, etc.
- Practical applications of astrology, dream analysis, graphology, visualization, etc.
- Modem archaeology as well as myths, folklore, etc. Write the article in a lively, descriptive style rather than a dry, academic manner.
- New scientific breakthroughs, including "free energy," Tesla, lost continents, new discoveries about matter, energy, ancient religions and cultures, ley lines, mind machines, etc.

Consider this a partial list. We are open to receiving any well-written, well-documented article.

12.) Articles for the "True Mystic Experiences" and "My Proof of Survival" departments should be 500 words or fewer and include a photo of the author*. These are either personal mystic or psychic experiences or evidence of survival after death. All the details described must be true. You will be required to send a notarized affidavit attesting to their authenticity and that you personally experienced it as described. Current payment for these articles is $25.00 including the use of the photograph, which will be returned to you (see also sections 15 and 18, below). FATE will reimburse you for notarization costs after publication.

*Remember that your photo is likely to be published in this international publication. Black/white reproduces best; if color is all you have, make sure the picture has good contrast and detail. A plain background is best; make sure your face shows and is not shadowed by hats, trees, etc. A picture of you alone is best, unless the other person/s in the photo are also part of your story. If that's the case, be sure to clearly identify each individual in the photo.

PAYMENT

13.) FATE purchases the right to assign copyright and all rights, literary and otherwise, to all articles and photos we accept. (See also section 18, below.) (If you have questions on this, please write and let us know your specific questions and a detailed reply will be provided.)

14.) The standard rate of payment is $0.10 per word in U.S. currency, payable after publication. FATE does not pay kill fees if an article is not used, except in cases of contracted, assigned articles where an arrangement has been specified in writing in advance.

15.) We will send you three copies of the issue in which your article appears, with an offer for more copies at a discounted rate.

16.) FATE will retain all rights to the articles, illustrations, and photographs that we publish. This entitles FATE to use the article again, in print or in any other media, including but not limited to radio, film, and electronic media. It also entities FATE to sell the article.

We like to see our writers published! If you are having a book published that includes material from an article you have published in FATE, written authorization for you to use the article will be given at no charge as long as FATE is credited as the original source (month and year of issue).

17.) Original manuscripts, photographs, illustrations, documentation, etc., that are published will remain the property of FATE.

18.) Complete the attached Author Biographical Information and include it with your submission.

FATE looks for new writers and encourages them. We hope that your inquiry is the beginning of a long and mutually beneficial relationship.

AUTHOR INFORMATION

Please type or print all information clearly.

Note: If article is co-written by two or more authors, include information for all authors.

1.) Writer's legal name as used in contracts

2.) Writer's legal address as used in contracts

3.) Writer's preferred mailing address if different from above

4.) Writer's social security number, or similar number for tax reporting purposes if resident of nation other than the U.S. (Note: although we do not deduct taxes from payments, we may have to report them according to IRS rules) (If more than one author, please indicate how payment is to be made-i.e., to which author. Be sure his/her social security number is listed.)

5.) Phone numbers where writer may be reached day, evening, FAX, and e-mail

6.) Current legal citizenship

7.) Birthplace; date of birth

8.) Writer's name as it should appear on the article: preferred style, pen name, etc., if different from legal name

9.) Writer's current occupation

10.) College degrees, honors, etc., if any

11.) Recent books or articles by writer, if any, that have been published and who published them

12.) Field(s) in which you are an expert and why you are an expert in that/ those fields

Contact Information:
M.T. O'Neill, Editor-in-Chief
P.O. Box 64383
St. Paul, MN 55164-0383
(612) 291-1970

Fiction Writer's Guideline
the Newsletter of Fiction Writer's Connection (FWC)

FWC is a membership organization providing practical assistance and information to writers pursuing the craft of fiction. Among the benefits to members is a monthly newsletter, *Fiction Writer's Guideline*.

TOPICS: How-to Articles on the craft of writing fiction and practical tips and advice on getting published. Success stories; Interviews with Authors, Agents, and Editors (See below for required and suggested questions).

RATES: *Fiction Writer's Guideline* is a fledgling publication. As circulation increases, so will writers' fees. Fees currently range from $1 to $25, depending upon length and subject matter. Payment is within two weeks after publication.

RIGHTS: One-time rights or reprint rights.

WORD COUNT: From 250 to 1000 words.

MANUSCRIPT SUBMISSION: All articles will be considered "on spec." Please submit complete manuscript. All manuscripts must have the exact word count typed in the upper right hand corner of the first page. Be sure to include your name, address, and telephone number.

AUTHOR INTERVIEWS: You are free to choose the authors you interview. The only requirements are that he or she is an author of fiction and has been at least moderately successful. Ask each author how he or she became interested in writing as a profession and detail how he or she got started. How did they get heir first book published—did they go through an agent—or submit to editors themselves? How many places did they submit their manuscript to until it was accepted—any interesting anecdotes/feedback/comments in the process? How were they notified of their first sale—phone/mail etc.? How much did they get paid—advance/royalty % for their first sale? For the latest sale? Advice to aspiring writers? Next project in the works?

AGENT INTERVIEWS: Agents interviewed must handle fiction, be open to new writers, have room to add new clients to their list, and must not charge a reading fee. The following information must be obtained during your interview: genres they are most interested in; how they prefer to be approached, i.e. telephone, query; what they want to see, i.e. synopses, the first 3 chapters/50 pages, etc.; response time; recent sales (if available); commission charged; any photocopying/ FAX fees, etc.; advice to FWC members.

EDITOR INTERVIEWS: Editors interviewed must handle fiction and be willing to accept unagented submissions. The following information must be obtained during your interview: genres they are interested in; how they want to be approached initially, response time, submission do's and don'ts, advances, royalties, advice, etc.

Contact Information:
Ms. Blythe Camenson, Editor
P.O. Box 4065
Deerfield Beach, FL 33442
(954) 426-4705

Field & Stream

FIELD & STREAM is a tightly focused magazine. All material is related to hunting and fishing, with the articles ranging from the basic how-it's-done pieces to finely written features with a philosophical edge. While we are always on the lookout for good technique articles, freelancers may find a better market in specific categories such as humor, mood or nostalgia (see "Guest Shot," in particular), Field Guides (hunting or fishing related natural history), Sportsman's Projects (related to hunting, fishing, camping, boating, bowhunting), and personal essays suitable for the "Finally . . ." department on the last page of the magazine. Another possible market is the F&S Jr. Section, which runs short "features" designed for young sportsmen (9-12), including how-to, natural history, outdoor lore, fishing and hunting tips, projects, and puzzles and games related to hunting and fishing activities. We also buy a variety of short features and tips for the "By The Way" pages and the Regional Sections (see separate guidelines below).

Writers are encouraged to submit queries on article ideas. These should be no more than a page, and should include a summary of the idea, including the angle you will hang the story on, and a sense of what makes this piece different from all others on a same or similar subject. Pieces that depend on writing style, such as humor, mood and nostalgia, or essays often can't be queried and may be submitted in manuscript form. The same is true of short tips. All submissions to FIELD & STREAM are on an on-spec basis.

Before submitting anything, however, we encourage you to study, not simply read, the magazine. Many pieces with good potential are rejected because they do not fit the tone or style of the magazine, or fail to [be] specific [about how the] subject of the article [fits in] with the overall subject matter of FIELD & STREAM.

Feature articles generally run from 1,500 to 2,000 words, and short features run from 750 to 1,000 words. Payment depends on the experience of the author and the quality of the work, and ranges from $800 on up for features and $450 for other short articles. Pay for fillers and F&S Jr. Varies. Payment is on acceptance.

Above all, study the magazine before submitting anything.

REGIONAL EDITIONS

FIELD & STREAM includes a regional section in each issue. It carries editorial geared to the fishing and hunting scene in that particular region of the country. Regional features are between 100 and 750 words apiece. In addition to where-to and how-to articles, the section includes state- or region-specific conservation articles, personality/profiles, and hunting-and-fishing politics.

Contributors should limit where-to articles to one or a few bodies of water, WMAs, national forests, river stretches, or species. For example, an article, "Record Public-Land Bucks of the South," in which the writer presents three WMAs consistent Boone and Crockett-quality public areas for hunting whitetails has a better chance of being accepted than an article with listings for the whole Southern region.

Pay rates for regional feature begin at $100 for up to 100 words, and climbs to $500 (occasionally more) for pieces of 500 or more words.

Assignments are made five to six months in advance of publication. For where-to and how-to material, time your query/submission to fit what you believe to be the best month/season for a particular activity. Mistimed queries will be returned with a note asking the contributor to resubmit at the appropriate time. Nonseasonal queries, such as profiles, should arrive in Houston on or before the first of each month.

Queries should tell the best timing for the idea and why it deserves mention at all. Specify locations, access, and species as appropriate. Also mention the availability of maps, photos, charts or other illustration ideas that would suitably accompany your article. Furthermore, also state your ability to submit computer-ready copy. We accept hardcopy manuscripts, but prefer electronic copy delivered on disk or sent by modem.

There are four regional sections. EAST: CT, DE, ME, MD, MA, NH, NJ, NY, PA, RI, WV, VT, New Brunswick, Quebec, Maritime Provinces. MIDWEST: IL, IN, IA, KS, MI, MN, MO, NB, ND, OH, OK, SD, WI, Manitoba, Ontario, Saskatchewan, Northwest Terr. SOUTH: AL, AR, FL, GA, KY, LA, MS, NC, SC, TN, TX (eastern), VA. WEST: AK, AZ, CA, CO, HI, ID, MT, NV, NM, OR, TX (western), UT, WA, WY, Alberta, British Columbia.

NATIONAL/REGIONAL PAGES

In addition, FIELD & STREAM devotes three pages to short articles of national interest that will run in all regional sections. Examples of articles included in this section are How-It's-Done and Do-It-Yourself projects, short Myths and Misconceptions and Field Guides, occasional new product reviews, natural history items, personality profiles, special events, and conservation issues that, while regional in nature, involve a principle or problem which makes them of national interest.

Article length is from 100 to 500 words, depending on the strength of the idea. We are looking for efficient, to-the-point writing. Payment for articles will be based on the rate of roughly $1 per word.

We also run very short (up to 100 words) tips and How-It's-Dones. Examples include Tap's Tips-like material in a slightly expanded form, items of natural history lore or other interesting facts that pertain to hunting and fishing, and simple Do-It-Yourself projects. Payments for such submissions will be $75.

Scrap art and photos are welcome with all submissions.

We urge writers to first send queries of a maximum length of two paragraphs. Should we accept your idea, we will specify the word count and base your payment on our specification. If you believe that the requested length is unreasonable, please let us know before you submit the piece so that we can reach a satisfactory agreement.

Contact Information:
The Editor
Two Park Avenue
New York, NY 10016-5695
(212) 779-6000
Regional Editions: T. Woodard
FIELD & STREAM — Houston
14311 Wickersham Ln.
Houston, TX 77077-5227
National Pages: Cathy Meyers
FIELD & STREAM
2 Park Avenue
New York, NY 10016

Film Comment

Dear Writer:

Thank you for your inquiry. We have no writer's guidelines, but maybe the following remarks will serve.

We make no formal demands regarding the state of manuscripts; if we can read it without eyestrain and without getting our hands dirty, we are content. It is not necessary to send articles on disk, though if anyone cared to, we speak Word Perfect 5.1 and Microsoft

Word 6.0 (which can convert a lot of formats). Files can be attached to e-mail sent to our e-mail address below.

As a glance at any issue will discover, we print a wide range of articles, on films new and old, foreign and domestic; on directors, performers, writers, cinematographers; on studios, national cinemas, genres; opinion pieces, history pieces. We are more or less impervious to "hooks," don't worry a whole lot about "who's hot and who's not" or tying in with next fall's surefire big hit (we think people should write about films they've seen, not films that haven't even been finished). We appreciate good writing (writing, not journalism) on subjects in which the writer has some personal investment and about which he or she has something noteworthy to say.

We read and consider anything sent to us; few issues have lacked for a piece, or pieces, that just "came in over the transom" and seemed worthwhile—occasionally terrific—and found a home in our pages. We almost never commission pieces from writers with whom we have not established a relationship (can't afford to), so the query process is somewhat limited in utility. We can save the writer and ourselves some bother by saying "That doesn't sound like something we'd be interested in" or "That sounds like something we'd be interested in—in fact, we already have two articles about it in the forthcoming issue." We may say, "We're interested and we think you ought to play up this aspect and play down that one—but you'll still be writing on spec."

I hope this is at least approximately what you wanted. Best of luck.

Yours truly,

Richard T. Jameson, Editor

Contact Information:
70 Lincoln Center Plaza
New York, NY 10023
(212) 875-5615
E-mail: RTJ FC@aol.com or RTJ_FC@msn.com

Fire Chief

FIRE CHIEF is the management magazine of the fire service, so our readers are predominantly chief officers, especially chiefs of department. We're potentially interested in any article that can help fire chiefs and fire officers do their jobs better, whether that's as incident commanders, financial managers, supervisors, leaders, trainers, planners, or ambassadors to municipal officials or the public.

Our authors are usually fire chiefs, although our contributors over the last several years have included other fire officers, firefighters, civilians and academics.

Article ideas

Unless you're quite sure your article will work for us, it's a good idea to query us first. Even if we like your idea, we can often fine-tune it before you actually write the article, saving both you and ourselves some work in the long run. Your best way to estimate what we're likely to publish is to review some back issues.

The most common reason we reject a manuscript or ask the author to rewrite it is a lack of focus. Writers often tackle too large a topic, with the result that the article winds up too shallow and basic. Narrower and deeper is usually the way to go. Remember that many of our readers are highly experienced officers, often with college degrees and/or training at the National Fire Academy.

Someone recently asked why, since we're the fire service's management magazine, we don't publish more articles on management theory. The answer is that we don't get many management-related articles. It's easy to string together some quotes from books by people like Peter Drucker or Stephen Covey (or from "Reinventing Government") along with some general observations about how they relate to the fire service, but our readers won't get much from the resulting article.

On the other hand, if your department has made some changes in its structure, budget, mission or organizational culture (or really did reinvent itself in a serious way), an account of that process, including the mistakes made and lessons learned, could be a winner. Similarly, if you've observed certain things that fire departments typically could do a lot better and you think you have the solution, let us know.

One possible source for article ideas is to ask yourself what your department is really good at. What does your department have a solid reputation for? What does your department do that other departments don't, but possibly should?

One caution in regards to that last point. Often, someone will call or write us to propose an article about a new program his or her department has just put into operation. In such cases, we almost always ask the prospective author to contact us again in six months or so. Napoleon once said that no battle plan survives the first contact with the enemy intact, and similarly, new fire department programs almost invariably go through a phase of fine-tuning once they're up and running. Once you've made those mid-course corrections, you'll be in much better shape to tell our readers how to carry off a similar program.

Another suggestion for article ideas is any courses you might have taught, or any presentations you might have given at a fire service (or similar) conference.

We do not publish fiction, poetry or historical articles.

We also aren't interested in straightforward accounts of fires or other incidents, unless there is a specific lesson to be drawn from a particular incident, especially a lesson that's applicable to a large number of departments. If you want to write an article like this for us, be prepared to discuss what went wrong and how it will be handled differently next time.

Feature articles

For features, length is highly flexible. We've run features shorter than 1,000 words and longer than 10,000, though most fall between 2,000 and 3,000 words.

Some of the pieces we have published started out as Executive Fire Officer papers, master's degree theses or similar academic writing. While the content in these is often good, they usually need extensive rewriting to change the academic tone to one that's more appropriate to a magazine article. Normally we ask the author to take the first shot at this. Also, in anything adapted from academic writing, we ask our authors to keep footnotes to a minimum or avoid them entirely. When they are needed, we reformat them as endnotes.

One of the most common problems with academic papers is a lack of specific examples to illustrate the theoretical points. One way to organize a feature article is by roughly alternating "important, interesting, important, interesting," which can also be thought of as "theory, example, theory, practice." All theory makes for a dull, arid article, while all examples can come off as a disjointed series of war stories. Combine them intelligently for the best results.

Columns

Most of our regular columns are written by standing columnists, although three, "Training Perspectives," "EMS Viewpoints" and "Sound Off" are open to outside writers. Typical length is 1,200 to 1,800 words.

If you have a proposal for a training column, contact the editor or Gary Wilson (University of Kansas Fire Service Training, 913-864-4467, gwilson@falcon.cc.ukans.edu).

If you're interested in writing an EMS column, contact the editor or Kevin Brame (Orange County (Calif.) Fire Department, 909-371-3335).

In our guest editorial, "Sound Off," which runs on an occasional basis, a point of view is important, but we also look for columns that go beyond merely opinion and constructively address some issue in the fire service.

Editing

Your article will be edited by one of our staff editors, who will contact you about any areas that need to be clarified or expanded. If your article is typical, you'll probably notice that after editing it's shorter than it was, yet still contains 90% to 100% of the original information.

Time permitting, when an article has gone through heavy editing, or the author has requested it, we will FAX a copy of the completed edit (but before final proofreading) to the author. It will be the author's responsibility to get back to us promptly with any final changes or questions.

Artwork

Authors are normally responsible for supplying any art to illustrate their articles, especially photos.

Charts and graphs will be redrawn by our art director or staff artist, and tables will be typeset by someone on our editorial staff.

If there are no photos to go with an article, we will sometimes arrange to have a staff or freelance artist do an illustration in black-and-white or color to go with the article. We encourage authors to work with us in developing ideas for this kind of artwork, but we reserve the final decision as to the form and appropriateness of editorial illustrations.

Copyrights

When your article has been accepted for publication, you'll receive a copyright release form, which you should sign and return to us promptly.

If you have any questions about the form, or if its specific wording might cause any problems, please call us. Although the specific terms of copyright release can sometimes be altered, we must have a signed copyright release on file before we can print your article.

One problem prospective authors should be aware of, but often aren't, is when they send the same article or query to more than one publication at a time. In the magazine business, this is called simultaneous submission, and it's a real no-no. The best approach is to decide which publication is the one you most want to submit your article to, and stick with them until they decide whether to publish it.

Scheduling

If you haven't heard from us within 60 days of sending your query or manuscript, please call, FAX, or e-mail us to follow up. We have a small staff, and we sometimes fall behind in reviewing queries and articles.

Articles are sometimes accepted with our intent to publish them in a specific issue or with one or more articles as part of a specific editorial package. In other cases, an article on an "evergreen" topic will be accepted with our intent to use it in the next suitable issue. (In case planned articles fall through at the last minute, we try to always have several edited articles in reserve, ready to go.)

In either case, circumstances beyond our control can delay an article's publication, sometimes for several months. Combined with deadline pressures, this can lead to the "Hurry up and wait" situation familiar to military veterans, but we ask authors to please understand. An author whose article has been accepted for publication is always welcome to call us and ask for the current schedule on his or her article.

Submissions

We prefer article submissions on a 3.5-inch diskette with a hard copy, but can make other arrangements. Queries and article submissions can also be e-mailed.

Contact Information:
Scott Baltic, Editor
35 East Wacker Drive, Suite #700
Chicago, IL 60601
(312) 726-7277
E-mail: firechfmag@connectinc.com
© Fire Chief Magazine

First Opportunity

(Please refer to Communications Publishing Group.)

First Things
A Monthly Journal of Religion and Public Life

FIRST THINGS does not accept unsolicited manuscripts. Guidelines are as follows:

Opinions:	800-1,500 words.	Honorarium of $125.
Articles:	4,000-6,000 words.	Honorarium of $450.
Book Reviews:	800-1,500 words.	Honorarium of $125.
Review Essays:	4,000-6,000 words.	Honorarium of $450.

Contact Information:
James Nuechterlein, Editor
156 Fifth Avenue, Suite 400
New York, NY 10010
(212) 627-1985 (or -2288)

Fly Fisherman
A Publication of Cowles Magazines

Fly Fisherman is the nation's first and largest consumer magazine devoted solely to the sport of fly fishing. Most other national outdoor magazines give coverage to hunting, camping, boating and other sports or, in the case of general fishing publications, give coverage to other types of fishing in addition to fly fishing.

We don't assume that all of our readers are expert fly fishermen, nor do we assume that they are all novices. We select material for publication that, overall, provides stimulation to the accomplished, instruction to the beginner, and even an invitation to non-fly fishermen. Similarly, we provide geographic coverage that meets our responsibility as an international publication.

Almost all of our contributors are avid readers of the magazine, and their submissions reflect a familiarity with the style and content of material used in the magazine. Potential contributors should. likewise familiarize themselves with the kind of material *Fly Fisherman* uses by looking over recent issues.

Eighty percent of *Fly Fisherman*'s readers are college educated, and nine out of ten of them are male. However, the magazine is regularly read by other members of the household—including non-fly fishermen. Our readers fish for almost any species of fish that will take a fly in fresh or salt water.

Editorial Format

The general types of articles that we normally publish include:

1. Main features of 2,000-3,000 words, illustrated with black-and-white prints or color transparencies or both. These articles embrace a wide variety of subjects, including major destinations—where to fish; instruction about fishing techniques, and how to tie flies. Fiction, humor and personality profiles are used infrequently and represent a very small portion of the articles we purchase each year.

2. Short features of about 750-1,500 words, usually illustrated in black-and-white or color. These articles highlight a specific aspect of the sport; most are short destination or how-to-do-it stories. The short feature is an important component of our magazine. It allows us to present a wide variety of information and topics to our readers.

3. Technical feature articles of about 2,000 words, illustrated in black-and-white or color, deal with subjects that lend themselves to presentation in the "Fly Tier's Bench" or "Tips From The Experts" departments. Sometimes these are used in the main feature section of the magazine. The text usually includes step-by-step instructions (such as fly-tying instructions), and if such instructions are included, appropriate photos, illustrations, or diagrams should accompany the text.

4. Mini-articles of 100-800 words concentrate on a very specific experience or aspect of the sport. These stories are illustrated in black-and-white (if they are illustrated at all) and may deal with a range of topics similar to those mentioned under short feature articles; but the mini-article is much more crisp and to the point in its presentation of information.

All submissions to *Fly Fisherman* containing factual information must be thoroughly and carefully documented. Double-check stream or lake locations and names (especially spelling); if you're unsure of any factual detail and can't document it, leave it out. When referring to insects or fish by their Latin names, consult a standard college text for correct spelling and nomenclature.

Photographs and Artwork

We can't overemphasize the importance of quality illustrations to accompany submissions. Color photographs should be in the form of 35mm slides or 2 ¼" x 2 ¼" transparencies, as color prints do not reproduce satisfactorily. The preferred format for black-and-white photographs is 8" x 10" glossy prints. Articles are best accompanied by both black-and-white and color, giving us the option of using one or the other or both to illustrate your work.

If you don't have photos, send the article anyway—we may have the appropriate illustrations on file. However, good photos often sell an article that is less than the ultimate coverage of a topic.

Quality color or black-and-white art is always welcome. Often we request permission to keep a selection of such submissions on file here so that we can draw from them to illustrate appropriate stories.

All photographic submissions should be accompanied by a caption sheet. Such sheets should identify each slide (or black-and-white print) and include an appropriate credit line and the names of the water, fish species, insect species, etc., that are pictured. A credit line and general location information should be written on the border of each slide or on the back of each black-and-white print.

If we request permission to hold your photos on file here, payment is not made until publication. Naturally, if you request any or all submissions on file to be returned, we will do so promptly. If you wish to submit color photographs for consideration as covers, they must be of exceptional quality and must be appropriate for vertical format.

Maps and diagrams should be submitted with articles when called for by the text. When submitting fly-tying articles, drawings or black-and-white prints showing tying steps should be included when appropriate.

Submissions of cartoons are welcome.

Preparation of Material and Submission Procedures

We do not accept photocopies of original manuscripts. Computer printouts are acceptable. We also accept manuscripts on computer disk. Manuscripts on 5¼" or 3½" disks in WordPerfect, WordStar, MultiMate and Display Write can be accepted directly. Other files on disk must be in the ASCII or Text format. The name, address and phone number of the author should be on the first page of the manuscript. The name of the story, the name of the author and the page number should be on each ensuing page of the manuscript. The author's name and credit line (if different) should be on each piece of photographic material or artwork submitted, and care should be taken to package all material properly before mailing.

We strongly recommend that you query us in advance on a specific article or article idea. A query allows us to suggest a slant on the article, or at least to inform you in advance of our interest in your proposed story idea.

Reporting on the status of submissions adheres to the following schedule. Upon receipt of a submission we'll send an acknowledgment—within six to eight weeks after receipt, material will either be returned, purchased or we'll ask for permission to retain it pending further consideration. Article queries will be answered within four weeks, and queries concerning the status of submissions (after our reply deadline of six to eight weeks) will be answered immediately.

Payment

Payment is made within 30 days of publication or acceptance of material. *Fly Fisherman* buys First Time North American Rights. *Fly Fisherman* does not accept simultaneous submissions or previously published material. Shortly after publication, all photos, illustrations, diagrams, maps, etc. will be returned. Original manuscripts will be kept here on file. (Writers who regularly make submissions to any publication should familiarize themselves with the current copyright laws.)

Fees to contributors vary according to the manuscript's professional level, frequency of accepted contributions, and length of article. The same applies to photographs and artwork. Fees range from $300 to $500 for main features, from $100 to $250 for short features, from $200 to $300 for technical features and from $50 to $100 for mini-articles.

Fees are paid for complete packages, which include manuscript, artwork, and photographs. Payment for photographs and artwork purchased without manuscripts is determined by the size and use inside the magazine and ranges from $35 to $200. We pay $500 for a photograph used on the cover of the magazine.

Publication Schedule

Fly Fisherman magazine is published six times per year. The editor usually purchases manuscripts one year in advance.

Months of Issue

- February
- March
- May
- July
- September
- December

Please advise us of any change in your address or telephone number so that we may keep our files up-to-date and ensure that your submissions are returned safely. Include both home and office phone numbers as well as any seasonal addresses.

Style Guide for Potential Contributors

1. Indent the first line of each paragraph.
2. Show the end of a story by writing End, The End, 30, #, or similar mark.
3. Use standard scientific nomenclature when referring to insects: Consult standard references, such as "Mayflies of North and Central America," Edmunds et al, for correct spellings.
4. The common names of insects are lower case, the proper names of fly patterns are capitalized: The black gnats were a nuisance that night, but I caught four trout on a Black Gnat dry fly.
5. The common names of fish are lower case unless the name includes a proper noun: I like to fish for coho salmon, Chinook salmon, Atlantic salmon and brown trout.
6. Some preferred spellings: caddisfly, drys (dry flies), fish-for-fun, fly-fishing, fly-fishing-only, fly rod, flyrodder, fly tier, fly-tying, Matuka, marabou, mayfly, mylar, no-kill, Opening Day, snowmelt, snowpack, stonefly, whip-finish.

An excellent, concise and handy guide to style is The *Elements of Style* by William Strunk, Jr. and E.B. White (2nd ed., Macmillan Publishing Co., New York, 1972, $1.95) and we recommend it highly.

All editorial submissions and correspondence should be addressed to:

Contact Information:
The Editor
Box 8200
Harrisburg, PA 17105-8200
or
6405 Flank Drive
Harrisburg, PA 17112

Focus/Kansas City

(Please refer to Communications Publishing Group.)

Games

GAMES is a bimonthly magazine of verbal and visual puzzles, quizzes, game reviews, contests, and feature and short articles. Our readers tend to be adults (average age 42), although the age range is very wide; and both sexes are represented about equally. What all our readers share is the joy of exercising their minds in new and playful ways.

Our feature articles can cover almost any subject, from game- or puzzle-related events or people, to wordplay, humor, mystery, and human ingenuity in all its guises. For example, recent features have included Internet scavenger hunts, who really wrote the Shakespeare plays, walk-through mazes, crosswords by computer, America's funhouses, deciphering ancient languages, a profile of chess champ Judit Polgar, and April Foolery in various publications.

We prefer queries for feature articles, but will consider completed typewritten manuscripts of 2,000 to 2,500 words. Avoid dry, historical coverage—a light, humorous, informative tone is best. Accompanying photographs are welcome but not required—we can do photo research or assign illustrations, as needed. Payment for accepted manuscripts ranges from $1,500 to $2,000 for all rights to the work. The fee is based on the subject, story length, and difficulty of the assignment. We run one feature article per issue.

Our "Gamebits" page offers three short articles per issue. Pieces range from 200 to 350 words. Payment ranges from $150 to $250. Queries are preferred, as are stories accompanied by eye-catching visuals. Topics include game- or puzzle-related trends, news, and events; playful people with creative occupations; and other ingenuities. Recent Gamebits have covered puzzle consultants for movies, man-versus-machine checkers matches, designers of Lego displays, crossword puzzle cravats, the World Scrabble Championship, the phenomenon of Magic: The Gathering, scientific research through videogames, and a traveling exhibition of quilts based on a deck of playing cards.

Puzzles, tests, quizzes, and other "doable" features may be of any length from 1/12 of a page to a two-page spread. We look for fresh, lively ideas, carefully worked out for solvability and unique solutions. Visual appeal, a sense of humor, and the incorporation of pictures/objects from popular culture and everyday life are big pluses. Novelty is essential. For visual puzzles, submit rough drawings or written descriptions of photos/pictures-we can assign finished art or photography, as needed. Payment varies.

GAMES also accepts contributions of original two-player games, pop-out puzzles, contests, and fake ads. Please check the magazine for style. Game reviews are done on assignment only. Prospective reviewers may contact the Games & Books editor.

Please allow six to eight weeks for a response.

Thank you for your interest in GAMES. We look forward to your imaginative proposals.

Sincerely,

The Editors

Contact Information:
19 West 21st Street
New York, NY 10010
(212) 727-7100 • FAX: (212) 727-7661

GEICO Direct

GEICO Direct magazine is published twice a year by K.L. Publications, Inc. for Government Employees Insurance Company and distributed to federal and military employees, as well as general policyholders, throughout the country.

The magazine's editorial focus is on lifestyles, financial, recreational, automotive and travel subjects of interest to GEICO policyholders. In most cases, the articles are geared to automotive information and safety with respect to travel and home.

We prefer to receive queries rather than finished manuscripts or phone calls.

Story Length: 1,000 to 1,800 words for features
650 to 1,000 words for departments

Style: Writing should be tight, reportorial and colorful, but don't sacrifice accuracy for adjectives.

Taboos: No poetry or fiction or cartoons. No satire or humor.

Photography: Buy mostly color, but some black and white. Black and white glossies and 35mm (or larger) color transparencies. No color prints. Also use illustrations.

Manuscript Rates: $350 to $500 for feature articles, depending on length, quality of writing and research required. $275 to $375 for departments. All but speculative articles are assigned with contract.

Rights: K.L. Publications buys First Serial Rights. We are not a market for reprints.

Sample Copy: To receive a sample copy of GEICO Direct, send a 9x12 self-addressed, stamped envelope (4 stamps) with your request.

Contact Information:
Bernadette Baczynski, Editor
2001 Killebrew Drive, Suite 105
Bloomington, MN 55425
(612) 854-0155 • FAX: (612) 854-9440

German Life

German Life is a bimonthly, written for all interested in the diversity of German culture, past and present, and in the various ways that the United States has been shaped by its German element. The magazine is dedicated to solid reporting on cultural, historical, social, and political events.

Writers / Reporters

Starting Out—To suggest a story send us a query letter with backup clips. Refrain from sending us a lengthy, wordy proposal. Three or four concise paragraphs should be enough to pitch your idea. Keep in mind that we receive numerous solicited and unsolicited manuscripts. The more directly and quickly your proposal stands out, the better your chances to be recognized.

Timing is Everything—Each issue of *German Life* is bound by our editorial calendar and seasonal events. For example, a summer travel piece would likely find its way into the April/May issue, which typically covers topics for summer but also fall travelers; our October/November issue is dedicated to Oktoberfest. Depending on your interests, plan accordingly! Given scheduling restraints, we prefer that you submit your work several months prior to the appropriate issue.

Manuscript Mechanics—Your manuscripts should not exceed 2,000 words. Longer pieces will be considered solely at the editor's discretion. Manuscripts considered too lengthy will be immediately returned for revision. Smaller tidbits fit for a sidebar or one of the magazine's anecdotal departments should range between 300-800 words. Book reviews average 250-350 words.

Due Credit and Accuracy—Please ensure that we are the sole recipients of your manuscript. If the piece is being considered by other publishers or has already been published, we will return it to you. Moreover, please guarantee your work's originality. Give proper credit for any other author's ideas you may use. If your article only recounts firsthand experiences, references are seldom necessary. In all other cases, cite the direct source on a separate sheet of paper, following the *Chicago Manual of Style*. Check the accuracy of your items carefully!

Submission—On the title page, include each author's name, current position, mailing address, daytime telephone, and FAX number.

Please submit manuscript BOTH on disk and as hard copy. We accept IBM-compatible 3.5 inch or 5.25 inch high density disks. Submit the original(s) (including photos, slides, and/or illustrations) to the address below.

Photographers / illustrators

Starting Out—With or without manuscript, feel free to submit photographs, transparencies, or illustrations that are in accordance with the magazine's direction and style. We look for pictures that capture and/or detail the diversity of German(-American) life and culture, including images of everyday life, landscapes, people, architecture, art, festivals, and so on.

Timing is Everything—Please read carefully the notes on timing in the Writer's section of these guidelines.

Photo/Illustration Mechanics—Photos should be black-and-white or color glossy prints, 5"x7" or larger, with excellent focus, fine grain, and clear contrasts. Tape an identifying label to the back of each photo. Do not write on back of photos—ink stamp or paper clip labels to them.

Transparencies are the most frequently purchased photographic material without manuscripts. 35mm slides are acceptable. (For best reproduction on press, slides should be perfectly exposed or slightly underexposed.) Identify slides by writing your name, the location, and the subject on the margins.

For illustrations, any medium is acceptable. With four-color art, please send 35mm transparencies. Computer illustrators may send four-color laser printouts of their work (e.g., maps, charts, and graphs) for consideration. In the case of black-and-white art, we prefer to first see photocopies. However, unless you are (have) a professional artist (available), submit only rough sketches for figures and diagrams. Type captions on separate sheet of paper, along with any credit lines.

Due credit—Please note that any photograph or illustration with an article must be credited and a photograph release form must be included. A release must also be signed by the person or party responsible for object(s) not open to public photography (e.g., special museum items). In addition, to avoid legal complications and embarrassing situations, please alert us to any purchase of your work by other publications.

Submission—Include with each submission all relevant contact information, such as the artist's name, current position, mailing address, daytime telephone, and FAX number if available.

For each photograph, submit on separate piece of paper a description and photo credit. Please do not submit more than 25 glossies at a time. The same goes for transparencies. On separate sheet of paper, include a description and photo credit for each. Place slides in individual plastic protectors and in a plastic slide sleeve fit for 20 slides. Limit your submission to 80 slides or four slide sheets at a time. Send all submissions to the address below.

With your permission, we will keep visual materials of appropriate quality and interest for our files. Photographs, slides, illustrations, and sketches are returned only upon request.

The Editorial Process

Acknowledgment—Expect acknowledgment of your submission within one to two weeks from the date of receipt. The editorial staff considers all manuscripts, solicited and unsolicited, without obligation for publication. Within four to six weeks of acknowledgment, the Editor will notify you of the decision on your submission—revision request, acceptance, or rejection. Manuscripts requiring revision are either returned in original form or first edited and then sent to the author for approval.

Acceptance—If your submission is accepted, you will receive notice within one week of our decision. *German Life* purchases over 60 manuscripts annually. Most manuscripts are published from three months to one year after acceptance. Publication of photographs/illustrations depends on need and topic.

Please be advised that all manuscripts at the acceptance stage, including solicited works, are considered on speculation. You will be duly alerted when your accepted manuscript/ photo/ illustration has been scheduled into an upcoming issue.

Payment ranges from $300 to $500 for feature articles, to $80 for short pieces and fillers. In exchange for remuneration, *German Life* retains first English/German language serial rights.

Final Status—All manuscripts are edited for style, consistency, and clarity. The editorial staff will send you a copy of the edited manuscript for approval shortly before publication. The final title of the published article, subheads, captions, photographs and illustrations, and other elements that attract attention to an article or contribute to the tone and appearance of the magazine are the Editor's prerogative.

The Publisher reserves the right to change these policies at any time.

Contact Information:
Heidi L. Whitesell, Editor
1 Corporate Drive
Grantsville, MD 21536
(310) 895-3859

GiRLFRIENDS

Girlfriends Magazine

Girlfriends Magazine is America's fastest-growing lesbian magazine. Our mission is to provide its readers with intelligent, entertaining, and visually pleasing coverage of culture, politics, and sexuality—all from an informed and critical lesbian perspective.

The sections for which we encourage freelance submissions are:

Parenting: 600 words from a first-person perspective. Anecdotal, controversial, and challenging pieces encouraged. Tell us what is different about your parenting experiences, your children, or your family structure. Give us examples. Must include two or more photos of you and your child(ren)/family.

Travel: 800 words in main text; 180 word sidebar on "best of" the profiled area. You must tell us something unique about the area; tell us something no one else could tell us.

Fiction: 1,300 words maximum. All styles considered.

Humor: 800 words; must have some relevance to lesbian readers.

Sports: 800 words; action-oriented profile of a particular athlete, team or group involved in a sport that has some interest among lesbians. Tell us what is unique about this particular athlete.

Spirituality: 600 words; profile-oriented piece on a religious leader or activist that has some relevance to lesbians. Profiles of unusual or under-represented religions also encouraged if they have some particular meaning for lesbians.

Health: 600 words; essay or how-to article on socio-political health issue (is Prozac good?) or on a particular ailment that affects lesbian women (breast cancer, yeast infections).

Authors are encouraged to query the editorial staff via letter or e-mail before they submit unsolicited material. Please make sure you study the magazine's style and previous articles before you send us unsolicited work. (Note: some book, video, movie, music & multimedia reviews may also be written on assignment; query with clips of work.)

Fees: *Girlfriends Magazine* pays ten cents per word for all written contributions.

Please keep in mind that we use *Chicago Style Manual* in considering the editorial clarity of our contributions. It is strongly encouraged that you read an issue of the magazine before you send material in for consideration.

For editorial submissions, we would like copy to arrive on floppy disc, formatted in Microsoft Word for the Macintosh. Traditional and express mail are acceptable. If you have access to a FAX or electronic mail, contact us via those means. Please allow six to eight weeks for a response.

Contact Information:
Diane Anderson, Managing Editor
3415 Cesar Chavez Street, Suite 101
San Francisco, CA 94110
(415) 648-9464 • FAX: (415) 648-4705
E-mail: staff@gfriends.com or http://www.gfriends.com

Glimmer Train Stories

REGULAR SUBMISSION GUIDELINES

- 1,200 - 7,500 word limit.
- Our issues have no themes.
- Please, no heavy dialect, story fragments, poetry, children's stories, or nonfiction.
- We tend to choose stories for their ability to move us emotionally and for their absolute clarity in storytelling.
- Simultaneous submissions are okay.
- Send your stories during the months of January, April, July, and October.
- We pay $500 for first publication and nonexclusive anthology rights. Payment is made upon acceptance.
- Please include a single stamped envelope if you would prefer we send a response only.
- Single issues available for $9 in most bookshops or directly from us payable by check.

GLIMMER TRAIN SHORT-STORY AWARD FOR NEW WRITERS

- See first six regular submission guidelines.
- Held twice yearly and open to any writer whose fiction hasn't appeared in a nationally distributed publication with a circulation over 5,000.
- $11 reading fee (covers up to two stories sent together in the same envelope). Please be sure address on your check is correct.
- Entries must be postmarked during the months of February/March or August/September.
- First page of story to include your name, address, phone.
- Please staple (rather than paper clip) your story's pages together.
- Please write "Short-Story Award for New Writers" on the outside of your envelope.
- Winner receives $1,200 and publication in *Glimmer Train Stories*.
- First/second runners-up receive $500/$300, respectively, and honorable mention.
- Winners telephoned by July 1 (for Feb./March entries) and Jan. 1 (for Aug./Sept. entries).
- Please do not send a SASE, as materials will not be returned.
- We cannot acknowledge receipt or provide status of any particular manuscript.
- All entrants receive a copy of the issue in which winning entry is published and runners-up announced. (Please advise us of address changes.)

Contact Information:
710 SW Madison, Suite 504
Portland, OR 97205
(503) 221-0836 • FAX: (503) 221-0837

Gnosis

A Journal of the Western Inner Traditions

GNOSIS welcomes the submission of material dealing with all aspects of the esoteric and mystical traditions of the West. In order to make our efforts compatible, please keep the following guidelines in mind.

- We prefer that manuscripts be typewritten (or computer-printed), with your name, address, and phone number in the upper right-hand comer of the first page. If you write on an Apple Macintosh, it would be helpful if you could send a disk containing your article, in the event we accept it, so that we don't have to retype it. (If you use an IBM-compatible computer, we request articles in ASCII or MS Word format on a three-and-a-half-inch disk.)
- It is OK to send us a photocopy or printout of your manuscript; be sure to indicate if it has also been submitted elsewhere. We do not return manuscripts that have been submitted without a return envelope and postage. We prefer that submissions not be made simultaneously to several publications at once.
- We try to respond promptly to all submissions. At most we try to take no more than two months to respond. Please be patient and allow up to ten weeks before expecting to hear from us. Our response to submissions may be delayed during production—the five weeks before each issue's publication.
- Though we work to maintain a high level of scholarship, GNOSIS isn't an academic journal per se. Our goal is to bring the discussion of the esoteric and mystical traditions to an interested general public. Accordingly, you are encouraged to write in an accessible, informal manner, as if you are talking to an intelligent, interested friend. Displays of enthusiasm, emotion, or subjective opinion are not taboo, though you should keep in mind that GNOSIS is more interested in exploring points of agreement or clarifying differences between traditions and paths than in sponsoring wrestling matches. Since space is always at a premium, we prefer writing that is concise, to the point, and engaging. It is very helpful if you familiarize yourself with the kind and style of material that we publish before submitting your own.

We are looking for the following kinds of material:

- first and foremost, articles that fit within the themes of upcoming issues
- articles on esoteric traditions and practices, past and present (up to 5,000 words)
- news items relating to current events in esoteric spirituality (up to 1,000 words)
- book reviews of new spiritual and occult books rarely reviewed elsewhere (up to 1,000 words)
- interviews with spiritual teachers, authors, and scholars (varying lengths)
- letters to the editor (up to 250 words). We do not pay for letters.

All lengths indicated are approximate.

- If you have a topic you would like to pursue, we encourage you to send us a short query letter before you begin writing. If possible, include a clipping or photocopy of writing you've done, if you think we may not be already familiar with your style. All published contributors receive contributors' copies, and a complimentary four-issue subscription. In addition, we are presently paying $100-250 per article, depending on length, editing requirements, and other considerations. Book reviews receive $50 per book. Please note: we cannot pay "kill fees." All submissions are "on spec." Payment is upon publication.
- We reserve the right to copy-edit material for style, grammar, and conciseness. If major rewriting or editing are called for, we will try to contact the author before publishing. We generally try to avoid cuteness, recycling of material available elsewhere, or story ideas more appropriate to other focused publications such as Yoga Journal or Shaman's Drum. Please see below for additional style tips.

• GNOSIS buys first-use rights and nonexclusive reprint rights. Contributors reserve other rights. We reserve the right to post selected articles and reviews on-line through the GNOSIS conference on The WELL (Whole Earth 'Lectronic Link), our gopher site on the Well and on the World Wide Web. Our contributors retain their own copyrights.

Sample copies of GNOSIS are available for $7 (plus $2 postage) from the address below. Subscriptions are $20 per year in the U.S., $25 per year for foreign readers. GNOSIS is published quarterly.

GNOSIS WRITER'S STYLE SHEET

GNOSIS style generally follows *A Manual of Style* by the University of Chicago Press; ideally you should familiarize yourself with that. If you haven't, just make sure to be as meticulous as possible in following generally accepted rules of spelling and punctuation.

It isn't necessary in all cases to provide references for your sources, since GNOSIS is not an academic journal as such. But if you do want to quote or cite printed sources, it's best to use footnotes so as to provide the most information and authentication for our readers.

Follow the examples below for footnotes:

1. Steven Foster and Meredith Little, *Book of the Vision Quest* (Spokane, Wash.: Bear Tribe Publishing, 1980), p. 35.

8. Colin Wilson, "The Laurel and Hardy Theory of Consciousness," in *The Essential Colin Wilson* (Berkeley, Calif.: Celestial Arts, 1986), pp. 168-179.

Footnotes should run at the end of the story. It's extremely important that you include all the elements of a footnote and that you document them correctly; it's very hard for us to do this, as we usually don't have the books you're quoting from. Please note that we include the name of the publisher as well as their city and state in footnotes. This may be more information than you are used to providing, but we request it in order to assist our readers in their researches.

We will also make every effort to check spellings of proper names, but in many cases, especially with more esoteric or little-known names, it may be difficult or time-consuming to do this. Please make sure that all proper names are spelled correctly (and their identity noted, if necessary).

In keeping with the best editorial practice, we won't change spelling or punctuation on material you're quoting directly from other sources. It's thus extremely important that you check this, since you have the material in front of you and we don't.

In addition, it'd be helpful if you could include a one sentence author blurb at the end of your piece that identifies who you are. In sending in article queries, you may also want to describe why you're qualified to write on the subject if you think we may not be familiar with you.

GNOSIS is a small magazine, and we don't have the resources to hire fact-checkers to go over your material. On the other hand, we are committed to publishing as accurate and factual a magazine as we can. That puts a lot of responsibility on you to make sure all facts are correct and double-checked. By being as careful as you can with this, you can help assure your credibility and ours.

For book reviews, follow the style below for access info at the beginning of a review:

Adam, Eve, and the Serpent by Elaine Pagels. Random House, 201 E. 50th St., New York, NY 10022, 1988; 189 pp., $17.95.

It's very important that you include the publisher's address with your review. Many of the books we review aren't easily found in bookstores, and interested readers may need to contact the publisher directly in order to obtain a copy. We also ask you to return the book with your review so that we can take a picture of it to run with the review; the book will be returned to you along with your contributor's copies after the issue is published. In some cases we may have an office copy of the review book in hand, so it is best to check with us on this first.

For best luck in writing reviews, as with articles, please query us first to find out whether we want a certain book reviewed or not.

We appreciate your interest and look forward to hearing from you. You can address your queries and submissions to:

Contact Information:
Richard Smoley, Editor
P.O. Box 14217
San Francisco, CA 94114
(415) 974-0600 • FAX: (415) 974-0366
E-mail: smoley@well.com.

Gold and Treasure Hunter Magazine

Writers' & Photographers' Guidelines

Written Material:

The editorial staff of *Gold & Treasure Hunter* is looking for how-to articles on gold mining and treasure hunting, fiction and nonfiction stories about mining and treasure hunting experiences, or about experiences in the great outdoors. Fiction material must be labeled as such. We also publish interesting profiles about people within our industry. Since we are a membership organization dedicated to preserving our rights to mine gold and recover treasure, we are also interested in articles concerning our legal rights, politics and issues. We publish some historical articles and routinely review products on new equipment within the industry.

Important: We do not print stories or articles which are primarily oriented toward the promotion of a product or service. However, we do not object to the author mentioning the type of equipment used during a gold find or treasure discovery or who to contact for more information about locations to visit or other services written about in an article.

Preferred Material:

Our general readership is comprised mostly of individuals who are actively involved in gold mining or treasure hunting, or people who are interested in reading about others who are active and successful in the field. True stories of actual discoveries, along with good color photos—particularly of gold—are preferred. Also, valuable how-to information on new and workable field techniques, preferably accompanied by supporting illustrations and/or photos.

Rate of Pay:

We purchase your material for three cents per published word, $10 for each black and white photo used, $10 to $25 for each illustration/cartoon used, $25 for each color photo used, and $50 for the main cover photo if used alone or as a full bleed. Payment is made upon publication, along with a copy of the magazine. Please include your social security number along with your submission if you wish to receive payment.

Internet Publishing and Rates:

We reserve the right to republish any of our previously-published and paid for material inside our Internet publication, *Wonderful World of Gold and Treasure Hunting*. Any material which we publish on the Internet that has not yet been printed in our magazine will be paid at the rate of $.02 per word and $10 per photo used, with the balance of magazine rates to be paid if and when the same material, or a portion of it, is published in the printed magazine.

Photographs:

Since our magazine is very much a graphically oriented publication, good quality photographs are vitally important. Probably more manuscripts are rejected for poor illustrations or poor quality photography than for any other reason. All photos should be sharp with good composition and include captions. Please do not write or mark on front or back of photos! We prefer good quality prints rather than negatives—although we can work with the negative if you are sending us a print that is damaged or poorly developed. We also work with 35mm color slides.

General Copy Requirements and Length:

IBM compatibles 5¼" or 3½" disks along with computer printout are also acceptable. We also work with Macintosh formatted 3½" disks. All disks will be returned once we are finished with them. Copy should be as sharp and clear as possible in order that our scanning equipment will be able to read it with minimum error. Please send original printed matter. Manuscripts can be up to 2,000 words in length, but 1,500 words or less is ideal (include number of words on manuscript). Do not submit previously published material or material which has subsequently been submitted to any other publication. All manuscripts should be sent to the address below.

Acceptance:

Manuscripts submitted are considered "accepted" when published. All editorial material being held for future issues is subject to change or rejection right up until the time of printing. All material is subject to light editing according to the needs of our publication. It is understood that any material submitted is original, free and clear of all copyrights, and does not infringe upon previously published works. All material must be submitted with the agreement that upon publication, either in our printed magazine or our Internet publication, we are buying all rights to the material and photos published, without exception. The author, in submitting material, acknowledges this agreement.

Contact Information:

Marcie Stumpf, Managing Editor
P.O. Box 47
Happy Camp, CA 96039
(916) 493-2062, -2029 • FAX: (916) 493-2095

Good Housekeeping

Good Housekeeping addresses 24 million married women, most of whom have children (anywhere from newborn to college age) and who work outside the home.

Areas of interest covered include consumer issues, human interest, social issues, health, nutrition, relationships, psychology and work/career.

Several sections are especially well suited to freelancers: Better Way, which is comprised of 300 to 500 word how-to pieces; Profiles, 400 to 600 word features on people involved in inspiring, heroic or fascinating pursuits; and "My Problem and How I Solved It," a first person or as-told-to format, in which a woman (using her real name) relays how she overcame an especially difficult impasse in her life.

It's best to familiarize yourself with the tone and content of *Good Housekeeping* before you query us. The most successful queries or manuscripts are those that are timely, appropriately researched, engagingly written, freshly angled, and tailored to *Good Housekeeping* readers in particular.

Manuscripts and queries submitted on speculation should, when possible, have clips of previously published articles attached. Please allow 2 to 3 months for a response due to the large volume of unsolicited queries we get.

Contact Information:
Diane Salvatore, Deputy Editor
Profiles Section: Evelyn Renold, Articles Editor
Better Ways Section: Lisa Benenson, Better Ways Editor
959 Eighth Avenue
New York, NY 10019
(212) 649-2200 • FAX: (212) 265-3307

Good Times

The Lifestyle Magazine For Mature Pennsylvanians

Good Times, the lifestyle magazine for mature Pennsylvanians which is published 10 times a year, provides general interest information to people who have retired or are contemplating retirement. Articles focus on legal and financial rights, health and medical issues and news, lifestyle and relationships, cuisine, travel, fashion, celebrities, hobbies and leisure activities, gardening and more.

Writing for *Good Times*

There are five steps to writing for *Good Times*:

1. Submit a query letter, together with your resume and a few writing samples.
2. If we are interested in your article, we will discuss it with you.
3. Or, we may ask you to write an article on another topic that suits your experience as well as our audience.
4. When we agree on topic, article length and compensation, we will send you a letter, setting forth the terms, for you to sign and return.
5. Submit your article by the predetermined date, and send us an invoice, including your Social Security number, for your payment.

Topic Selection

Your article should focus on topics of interest to retired persons and persons planning retirement. Your article should address concerns of the readership and offer practical advice, recommendations and solutions to the readers. As appropriate, your article should offer readers sources for additional information.

Writing Style

Your writing should be clear and concise, using terms that are easily understood by the reader. Spell out acronyms and abbreviations on first reference. After you have completed your article, review it for places where you can eliminate wordiness.

Graphics

Diagrams, tables and photographs can add impact to your article. Reference all graphics in the text, indicate the source if appropriate, and include a caption. We can also accept sketches if they are complete and accurate. Our design and production department will convert your sketches into color graphics. We can accept photographs as transparencies, slides or prints, in that order of preference. We prefer four-color photographs to black-and-white, and we cannot accept negatives.

Submitting Your Article

Submit your article as a standard word processing document on a Mac or IBM 3½-inch floppy disk. When formatting disks on a DOS computer, always format standard double-sided disks in the 720K format; always format high-density disks in the 1440K format.

Contact Information:
Centre Square East, 12th Floor
1500 Market street
Philadelphia, PA 19102
(215) 246-3433 • FAX: (215) 665-5723

Graduating Engineer

GRADUATING ENGINEER magazine is a career publication for junior and senior engineering undergraduate students and those attending graduate schools. The magazine is sent to the deans and professors of engineering at every accredited engineering school in the United States. The deans and professors distribute the magazine, which is sent free of charge to their colleges and universities.

Queries

Please send a list of topics you are experienced writing about as well as recent clips.

We prefer written queries from authors. The query should consist of a tentative title and a brief description—two or three short paragraphs—outlining the article.

Unsolicited Manuscripts

Occasionally we publish unsolicited original manuscripts or features which have been previously published and to which you own the rights. Fee: $200.

Assigned Features

Assigned full-length features normally contain 2,000 or more words. Where feasible, submit a typed manuscript plus a floppy disk (Macintosh compatible 3½" disk is preferred with copy in MS. Word, MacWrite, WordPerfect or text file). Fee: $400 to $600 depending on the author and article.

Editorial Calendar

GRADUATING ENGINEER is published eight times a year with the following schedule of editorial focus:

September: general career topics for engineers getting ready to enter the workplace
October: African-American, Hispanic, American Indian engineering career issues
November: advanced education topics
December: career topics for engineers/scientists with disabilities
January: advanced technology
February: women engineer career topics
March: engineering careers in government
April: African-American, Hispanic and American Indian career issues

Feature Topics

CAREERS. Articles addressed to the particular career needs of entry-level engineers leaving the college environment and moving into professional life. The features cover both short-term topics such as how to get the best job and interviewing tips to long-term career planning.

ON-THE-JOB. Articles about career issues for engineers entering their first few years of a job. Topic areas cover dealing wit co-workers to business etiquette.

AFRICAN-AMERICAN, HISPANIC, NATIVE AMERICAN ENGINEERS. Articles on career topics pertinent to African-American, Hispanic and Native American entry-level engineers or articles about successful minority engineers already on the job who can provide career advice or be role models. We are also particularly interested in African-American, Hispanic and American Indian writers who can address these career subjects.

WOMEN ENGINEERS. Articles about the specific career needs of women entry-level engineers. Interviews or articles about successful women engineers.

ENGINEERS AND SCIENTISTS WITH DISABILITIES. Articles for the person with a disability who is either a working engineer, scientist or mathematician or is about to graduate in any of the above disciplines. Career topics range from on-the-job needs to interviews as well as articles about specific job situations and career preparation for people with disabilities.

HIGH-TECH TOPICS. Articles about "cutting edge" engineering topics or unusual projects or engineers with interesting jobs. Features also discuss technology's impact on careers, the workplace, the environment and the role engineers play in creating, implementing and managing it.

PERSONAL DEVELOPMENT. Articles which discuss the personal development needs of the college senior engineer such as the importance of self-esteem to communications skills to fitting into corporate life.

LIFE-STYLE. Articles about living arrangements and finances to topics about moving from college student to young professional.

MANAGEMENT. Articles that deal with management in the business world such as the decision to go into management to how to know if you're management material.

ON CAMPUS. Articles about campus life from talking to students and deans at specific schools to topics covering a student's last two years at college.

Contact Information:
Charlotte Thomas, Editor-in-Chief
Peterson's Magazine Group
202 Carnegie Center
Princeton, NJ 08543
(719) 573-4105

GreenPrints
"The Weeder's Digest"

Thanks for your interest! GREENPRINTS lives because people like you care about gardening—and about sharing with other gardeners. Without your contributions, the magazine simply would not exist. Still, it almost feels like a contradiction in terms to offer Writer's Guidelines for GREENPRINTS (after all, what we want is special, exciting, provocative, sparkling, unordinary writing—and how do you prescribe that?). But people do ask, so I better be a good fellow and come up with something! To wit:

1. We want the best, personal (key word, that) garden writing we can find. Expressive, thoughtful, humorous, angry, contrite, flippant, searching, witty, observant, sad, inviting—whatever! We focus on the human, not the how-to side of gardening. On the people as well as the plants. After all, gardening is a relationship, not a recipe. GREENPRINTS explores that relationship, not by instructing, preaching, or lecturing about it. Instead, we celebrate it . . . by

sharing the stories and experiences we all have trying (and sometimes failing) to get along with plants.

I can put what we want in one word: Storytelling. Or maybe storyshowing. The most common shortcoming I see is people who forget the old high school English-class dictum: Show, don't tell. Take us through the experiences with trenchant details and descriptions. Don't tell us how profound or funny or beautiful it was: make us experience the feeling.

2. We're not opposed to essays, but the good ones a) evolve directly from personal experience and b) offer new insights or at least new ways of expressing old insights. We're not opposed to fiction, either, but don't you agree that it should offer something special that the nonfiction stories we get wouldn't? (i.e., don't just imitate realty).

3. One thing for sure, we don't want sappy, gooey writing. Tender, moving, poignant is wonderful. But syrupy is the biggest trap GREENPRINTS has to avoid. (Trap #2: preachy. We can all read lectures and sermons plenty of other places, n'est-ce pas?)

4. Length? I don't know. Since we're digest-sized, most of our pieces have been no more than 2,000 words. But write what you have to. If it's good, we'll work out length problems.

5. Payment? Did you have to ask? We pay miserably; top payment right now is $100 and we often pay less. (No payment for "Cuttings," for instance.) I apologize. You deserve more. When GREENPRINTS starts making money, I intend to share it. Right now, I'm working for free and hanging in there until this different little gardening gem takes off. We pay on acceptance; buy First North American Serial Rights (unless you've already published it somewhere else first; we're happy to reprint pieces—long as they're good!). SASE? Oh, yes please.

6. Poetry: Well, we run about 1 poem per issue. That's 4 per year (in contrast to 50 or more prose pieces), so let's admit there's not much chance I can accept your poem. The ones I do take tend to be a) not too hard to follow, b) not too saccharine, but most of all, c) clever. Innovative. Offering well-expressed, detail-dressed new twists or outlooks on this magazine's very old topic. Pay: $10.

7. One last thing: Are you a subscriber? If not, would you please consider becoming one ($17.97 a yr.)? Not only does it get you a wonderful little magazine and the best possible feel for the type of writing we run, it also helps us survive so we can run your writing!

Thanks again. Best to you with prose and plants—and the rest of life, too.

P.S. Oh, one more thing: Often I can't find time to read submissions until after an issue deadline: Nov., Feb., May, & Aug. Sorry.

Contact Information:
Pat Stone, Editor
P.O. Box 1355
Fairview, NC 28730
(704) 628-1902

Grit
American Life & Traditions

GRIT is the country's leading publication for people living in small towns, rural areas, major cities, and outlying suburbs who share a common interest in preserving the best of American life and traditions.

Building on more than 100 years of publishing history, GRIT is edited expressly for Americans who want a publication that accentuates a positive outlook and that provides guidance in ways to improve the quality of life.

Each issue of GRIT focuses on the values, lifestyles, traditions, and social issues important to those concerned about themselves, their families, and their communities. Articles provide readers with an informative yet entertaining look at life in America—past and present. Every issue also provides readers with an opportunity to share their ideas with one another through various departments.

Most important, GRIT accentuates the qualities of courage, dedication, and determination to make a difference. These are the qualities of GRIT . . . and the hallmark of GRIT.

GRIT accepts reader contributions and freelance material appropriate for the publication. If you are a freelance writer and/or photographer, we encourage you to become familiar with recent issues. Copies may be obtained through subscription or by requesting a sample copy directly from GRIT at the address below. (Please include $4 for postage and handling plus a self-addressed 9x12 inch envelope.

FEATURE ARTICLES

GRIT publishes feature-length articles (1,200-2,000 words) about topics relevant to today's families, such as:

- American values and the quality of life
- Outstanding people and interesting places
- Parenting and grandparenting in the '90s
- Family-oriented, books, television, and movies
- Working at home or starting your own business
- Family lifestyles and home improvements
- Community involvement or service
- Holiday and vacation planning and sites
- Americana and nostalgia
- Collectibles and antiques

In addition, GRIT publishes features about American history, traditions, and culture—particularly those articles accenting positive aspects of our past.

SHORT STORY, ESSAY, POETRY AND LOOKING BACK

GRIT regularly publishes short fiction of about 2,000 words, as well as poetry of no more than 16 lines. Occasionally, GRIT publishes fiction of about 500 to 1,200 words. Short stories and poetry should emphasize the positive aspects of American life.

Essay stories are 800- to 1,200-word first-person accounts about a particular event, situation, or feeling.

Looking Back features personal reflections of America's past. Submissions (50-250 words) should include a sharp, clear black-and-white photo of good quality.

GRIT also publishes Talelites: short, humorous anecdotes.

Be sure to address the envelope Looking Back, Attn: Fiction Dept., or Attn: Poetry Dept. as appropriate. Do not send fiction, Essay, or Looking Back queries.

GRIT DEPARTMENTS

Each issue of GRIT offers a variety of departments, each approximately 800-1,000 words in length. These include the following:

- Today's Family - various aspects of families, parenting, grandparenting, and children's issues.
- Book Reviews - reviews of recent and classic books.
- Media and Movies - a look at newspapers and magazines, radio and television programs, and movies - both current and vintage.
- Profile - character profiles of individuals who demonstrate grit: strength of character, self-reliance, dedication, courage; or of individuals who are involved in unusual activities that reflect an aspect of American life and culture.
- Home Life - home lifestyle articles, including decorating, remodeling, gardening, and entertaining.

ODD, STRANGE & CURIOUS AND PANORAMA

GRIT features two special sections filled with 100- to 300-word articles plus color photos. Please send complete manuscripts and an assortment of color slides or prints for these departments. Occasionally, black-and-white photos may be accepted as well. With manuscripts, include complete addresses and phone numbers of the subjects.

• Odd, Strange & Curious - A funny and nostalgic glimpse into odd, strange, and curious people, places, and things.

• Panorama - A colorful look at out-of-the-way museums, travel spots, landmarks, and other unique places off the beaten path of America's landscape.

Be sure to address the envelope Odd, Strange & Curious or Panorama as appropriate. Do not send Odd, Strange & Curious or Panorama queries.

ASSIGNMENTS, SUBMISSIONS, PHOTOS, AND PAYMENT

GRIT makes assignments to proven freelancers but welcomes unsolicited submissions from published writers. Please query, including a personal resumé and samples of your published work. Suggested article topics should include approach and theme.

Please let us know if you are a professional photographer or work with one and what art is available for each story. GRIT uses professional-quality color transparencies and good black-and-white glossy photographs. Please do not submit snapshots, Polaroids, or any photograph that is not up to professional standards. Attach your name, address, telephone number, and caption information to each photograph submitted.

GRIT pays by the word unless other arrangements are made. The rate for unsolicited manuscripts is not as high as for assigned articles. For articles published from assigned queries, the rate is 22 cents per published word. Slightly higher rates are paid to GRIT correspondents, those who write for us on a regular basis. Rate for fiction and essay pieces is 15 cents per published word.

Articles are occasionally accepted for reprint rights if first publication was strictly local or regional. Second rights pay at the rate of 15 cents per word. Payments are made upon publication of materials.

Submissions often are evaluated within 60 days of receipt; seasonal and topical materials may be held longer. Please allow 90 days for fiction and essay evaluations.

GRIT assumes no responsibility for any material that is lost or damaged.

TIPS FOR NONFICTION WRITERS

• Articles should be informational, educational, inspirational, entertaining, and/or instructional. Articles that focus on community spirit, American heritage, family life, and individual commitment are of particular interest.

• Articles should help readers make wise decisions and solve personal problems. Articles may also help readers understand complicated issues and discover positive ways to approach a problem. Articles should emphasize the best of American values and traditions.

• Professional quality photographs increase acceptability of and payment for articles. Please provide photo releases. Color slides or black-and-white prints are preferred.

• With your article, include your daytime telephone number and information regarding the best time to reach you.

• Please attach the names and telephone numbers of all sources for fact-checking purposes. Identify sources fully, including credentials, titles, or reasons sources are qualified to comment on this subject. Also, provide full references for any publications used as sources.

• Most articles should have at least three sources. Sources should give a complete picture to readers.

• Third-person accounts are preferred. First-person stories are generally not appropriate, except in the case of Looking Back and Essay.

• Information in sidebar or graphic form is appropriate for many stories: lists of tips, resources, or questions to help readers understand the topic. For example, five ways to . . .

Submitting freelance materials to GRIT

- Include your full name, address, and telephone and social security numbers on each page, and a paragraph-long personal bio.
- We prefer material submitted on a 3.5 inch Macintosh disk with a hard copy, but this is not required. Please include your name and submission title on each page.
- Material should be mailed to the address below. If appropriate, direct materials to Fiction, Poetry, Looking Back, or to the appropriate department.

Contact Information:
Anything not listed below: Michael Scheibach, Editor-in-Chief
Health, Travel: Prisella J. Adams, Assistant Editor
Family, Fiction, Poetry: Donna Driscoll, Assistant Editor
Gardening: Janis Keen, Assistant Editor
1503 S.W. 42nd Street
Topeka, KS 66609-1265
(913) 274-4300 or (800) 678-5779

The Growing Edge

Dear Contributor,

Thank you for your interest in The Growing EDGE magazine.

The Growing EDGE offers the latest in high-tech indoor and outdoor gardening for professional commercial growers and serious amateurs. Thus, some previous experience, special knowledge, or at least very careful research is necessary for most successful articles.

Our goal is to build a permanent list of experts and general interest writers to help us make the magazine what it can and should be. We look forward to growing with you.

General Information

- Manuscript format: Dot matrix is OK. Manuscript on disk is preferred (include hard copy).
- Software: We can transfer from most Macintosh, IBM & IBM-compatible word processing programs.
- Frequency/Content: Published quarterly, 80-88 pages, approximately 80% freelance written.
- Buys First World Serial rights, First Anthology rights and Electronic rights.

Editorial Copy Guideline

- Articles should be directly related to high-tech cultivation indoors or out. We are looking for new and interesting developments in organics, hydroponics, greenhouse/grow room operation, high intensity lighting, organic and chemical fertilizers, new or unusual plant varieties and similar "growing edge" developments in commercial and personal gardening. Other stories may be considered. Advance consultation with the editor is encouraged, although we do accept unsolicited material on speculation.
- Address queries to the editor. New contributors should include a writing sample.
- Bylines are given, except where extensive rewriting or short length make them inappropriate. Please specify desired byline in your MS. Include a 1-2 sentence "author bio;" for example, "George Smith is a freelance writer and hobby gardener living in Macon, Georgia."

• Payment for articles is 10¢ per published word, paid on publication.

Photo Guidelines

• Photos should be related in some way to the general subject areas listed above.

• Black & white prints and negatives, or clear color slides are preferred. Number each photo. Undeveloped rolls should be clearly marked to indicate film type and speed.

• When possible include a complete description (plant variety, age, system/product used, etc.) for each photo on a separate sheet, with captions for each.

• Photos may be credited. Submit credits on a separate sheet.

• Photo Tips:

• Check focus and depth of field carefully, especially in close-ups.

• When shooting B&W, a green filter helps bring out highlights and detail in foliage.

• Photographing under artificial lighting can be difficult with automatic cameras. When possible use "manual" control and bracket exposures under and over the meter's setting.

• Payment is $25–50 per published photo, $175 for cover photos. Payment is on publication. Payment for assignment photography is negotiated on a case-by-case basis.

Cartoons, Diagrams and Other Graphics

• We do not solicit original cartoons.

• Diagrams and other graphics used to illustrate your text should be submitted after consultation with the editor. In most cases, finished drawings can be produced in-house from rough sketches.

• Payment for original line art and any other illustration will also be negotiated on a case-by-case basis.

Contact Information:
Trisha Coene, Editor
P.O. Box 1027
Corvallis, OR 97339
(541) 757-0176

Gryphon Publications

Dear Contributor,

Thank you for letting me get a chance to see your work. Until now I've usually commented on each and every manuscript sent to me, anything from a few encouraging words to a one page letter. I know how important it is to get feedback on your work. However, lately, the volume of manuscripts has reached critical mass, and it has become impossible to comment on an individual manuscript any longer. I hope this short letter will help you get a better understanding of what my needs are for various Gryphon Publications.

Please read carefully before sending anything.

HARDBOILED: I'm looking for very hard, cutting-edge crime fiction, usually under 3,000 words (longer would have to be extraordinary) and with impact. The kind of story that stays with a reader, that might just change that reader. The competition is rough, you're up against some of the best of the Pros, so only send me your best, but there is always room for newcomers. Each issue of HARDBOILED is 100+ pages, typeset, with color covers, and has many stories by unknown and first-time writers. Your work is what's important, not your name. Payment is in two free copies of the issue you appear in and a nominal cash payment by contract upon publication.

Sample copies and all back issues are $7 each; subscriptions 6 quarterly issues @ $35 by third class; outside USA $8 each and 6/$42 surface mail.

PAPERBACK PARADE: needs all types of nonfiction, articles, essays, book lists, interviews, etc. about collectible paperbacks, authors, artists, publishers, etc. This is a magazine for book lovers, published since 1986, with 42 issues so far, 100+ pages, typeset, with color covers! A great place to showcase work, but only the best and most detailed bibliographical material are needed. Query first.

Sample copies and back issues $7 each, subscriptions: 6 bimonthly issues $35 third class; outside USA, $8 each, 6/$42 surface mail.

OTHER WORLDS is an annual paperback magazine, perfect-bound, 100+ pages. I'm looking for short, hard SF shockers, stories with impact, usually under 3,000 words. Science Fiction or Science Fiction Fantasy, also some SF horror. No outright fantasy, horror or supernatural at all. Payment in one free copy of the issue you appear in.

Sample copies of #1-4 @ $4 each; #5 and #6 are 100pp perfect-bound paperback issues @ $9.95.

GRYPHON DOUBLES showcase two longer works, back-to-back like the old Ace Doubles. A cover for each story. I need only extraordinary longer works. Only quality material. All types of work here, 10,000 to about 20,000 words. DO NOT SEND MS. Send only a one-page letter about the work.

Samples of Doubles are $9.95 each, subscriptions: 5 issues as they appear for $45.

GRYPHON BOOKS: I also publish, from time to time, hardcover and paperback (trade size) books on certain special subjects. DO NOT SEND MS. Send only a one-page letter about the book.

The best way to break into writing for a publisher is to be familiar with that publisher's product. I suggest you try a recent copy of HARDBOILED or PAPERBACK PARADE, or try a GRYPHON DOUBLE. See what they're about. The stories in HARDBOILED are all interesting and may open your eyes to a new and better way to say what you want to say in your own work. The articles in PAPERBACK PARADE will give you an added perspective too few writers wanting to break into the field have today. To their disadvantage. Some of the best work being done today is appearing in these publications, it's just plain good writing, good reading, and fun stuff.

Contact Information:
Gary Lovisi, Owner and Editor
P.O. Box 209
Brooklyn, NY 11228-0209

The Guide

CURRENTLY NOT BUYING FICTION

The Guide is published monthly with a press run of over 30,000. We are distributed throughout the United States, Canada, and selected cities in Europe. Contents include politics, travel, humor, and sex.

We pay based on length and intended use in the magazine. Column length pieces (~1,000 words) pay $50-100; secondary features (~1,000-3,000 words), $100; and cover-story length pieces (~3,000-5,000 words), $200.

Article ideas are welcome. They should be accompanied by a writing sample or clips of previously published work. Unsolicited submissions and phone inquiries are also welcome. Response time for manuscripts is 2-6 weeks.

Payment is upon acceptance of the final manuscript.

Dot matrix printouts are acceptable. We publish on the Macintosh. Accepted articles submitted on disk (any format) or via e-mail are greatly appreciated.

If you have any further questions, please feel free to call or write.

Contact Information:
Frank Well, Editor
P.O. Box 990593
Boston, MA 02199
(617) 266-8557

Guideposts

Guideposts® magazine, A Practical Guide to Successful Living®, is a monthly inspirational, interfaith, nonprofit publication written by people from all walks of life. Its articles present tested methods for developing courage, strength and positive attitudes through faith in God. Our writers express viewpoints from a variety of Protestant, Catholic and Jewish faith experiences.

A typical *Guideposts* story is a first-person narrative written in simple, dramatic, anecdotal style with a spiritual point that the reader can "take away" and apply to his or her own life. The story may be the writer's own or one written in the first person for someone else. Even our short features, such as "His Mysterious Ways," "What Prayer Can Do," "Angels Among Us" and "The Divine Touch" use this format. Writing a short feature is often the easiest way of making a sale to Guideposts.

Please observe the following in writing your Guideposts story:

- Don't try to tell an entire life story in a few pages. Focus on one specific happening in a person's life. The emphasis should be on one individual. Bring in as few people as possible so that the reader's interest stays with the dominant character.
- Decide what your spiritual point, or "takeaway," will be. Everything in the story should be tied in with this specific theme.
- Don't leave unanswered questions. Give enough facts so that the reader will know what happened. Use description and dialogue to let the reader feel as if he were there, seeing the characters, hearing them talk, Dramatize the situation, conflicts and struggle, and then tell how the person was changed for the better or the problem was solved.
- Most important: Study the magazine.

Payments:

- Full-length manuscripts (750-1,500 words): $250-$500, occasionally higher.
- Shorter manuscripts (250-750 words): $100-$250.
- Short features and fillers (under 250 words): $25-$100. These include "What Prayer Can Do" and heavenly encounters such as "His Mysterious Ways," "Angels Among Us" and "The Divine Touch."

We do not use fiction, essays or sermons, and we rarely present stories about deceased or professional religious people. We do not evaluate book-length material.

We receive thousands of unsolicited manuscripts each month, so allow two months for a reply.

Contact Information:
16 East 34th Street
New York, NY 10016
(212) 251-8100 • FAX: (212) 684-0679

Guitar Player

Our goal is to enable readers to become better guitarists, more successful musicians and more informed equipment buyers. If you write for us, this is your goal too.

The essential question: What can the reader take away from a story to become a better player? This can include insights into an artist's technique, equipment use and recording tricks, and general information like creative philosophy, career tips and influences. The article must be detailed and accurate.

Guitar Player is about music, not pop culture. Merely recounting a player's or band's background or latest CD is inadequate. Artist interviews should include comprehensive information about technique and equipment, including model names and numbers for all gear mentioned. Readers should learn how the artist uses the gear, not just what's used. For longer features, musical examples—scales, modes, chord diagrams, whole pieces—should be included when possible.

We address a variety of topics on guitarists and instruments. In addition to interviews with guitarists in all styles, we run historical and analytical pieces, how-to articles about musical technique and equipment, and profiles of instrument makers, composers, and teachers important to guitarists. A story must appeal to dedicated musicians, but that's no excuse for dry writing. A colorfully written story is preferable to a dull one—if it meets all other requirements.

Verify the spelling of all names and other proper nouns. Include correct titles and labels of record albums mentioned, and provide the address of lesser-known independent labels. Style: album title in italic, song title in quotation marks, record label in brackets—"Beck's Bolero" from Truth [Epic].

Do not submit a story if any part has been previously published or if any part has been submitted to any other publisher.

Send us the address and phone number of the person interviewed so we can follow up if necessary and send tearsheets. Let us know if you have leads for photos.

Payment is generally $250 for Intros, $350 for Profiles, and $450 and up for Features. GP buys first-time and reprint rights. Payment is on acceptance. We can provide freelancers copies of issues in which their features appear.

Article categories and approximate lengths:

- Intro, 1,600-2,000 characters (250-300 words).
- Profile, 3,500-6,000 characters (550-1,000 words).
- Feature, 7,000 characters (1,100 words) and up.
- Lesson, usually 20-40 measures of examples with explanatory text.

The preferred form of submission is Microsoft Word for Macintosh, though we can translate PC files and other text programs. Files may be modemed, e-mailed or mailed on disc along with a hard-copy version. Printed manuscripts can be FAXed. Submissions should be accompanied by an invoice that includes your social security number.

Article ideas should first be submitted in writing. DO NOT contact artists in GP's behalf before a story has been assigned. Submissions will be responded to as soon as possible.

Contact Information:
Miller Freeman, Inc.
411 Borel Avenue, Suite 100
San Mateo, CA 94402
(415) 655-4134 • FAX: (415) 358-9216

Guns Magazine

GUNS magazine is primarily freelance written, but most of our material comes from a core of regular contributors. It is quite common for us to be sufficiently stocked with articles for GUNS six to twelve issues in advance. If you have professional writing skills, a thorough knowledge of your subject and, most importantly, something significant to say to the knowledgeable gun enthusiasts who read our magazine, then we would be interested in hearing from you.

Please start with a query letter that includes a brief outline of your idea or a short menu of topics. Unsolicited manuscripts are given low priority.

Remember that we are a "gun magazine" first and foremost. Most of our articles focus on the firearms themselves: test reports, firearm design, shooting technique, ammunition performance and essays on guns for specific purposes. We are not a hunting magazine. Our occasional hunting articles center on guns for various types of hunting but not on hunting techniques, tracking or calling games, dressing your deer, etc.

If we agree to look at your manuscript and consider it for publication your chances of getting it accepted will be significantly increased if you provide sharply focused, well-lighted photographs accompanied by detailed captions. When we agree to take a look at your article, we will let you know if we want color slides, black & white photos or both. I cannot stress too strongly how important photo quality is to us. If you haven't already familiarized yourself with our photo standards, please study some recent issues.

We edit on Macintosh computers and prefer to get our submissions on disk (double-sided 3½" or 5¼", not high density) along with a hard copy. Our first choice is Microsoft Word 5.0, but we can convert WordPerfect and most ASCII programs. If you don't have a computer, send your article typed.

We pay on publication and usually buy all North American rights to the manuscript and photos. Our rates range from $250 for a 1,000-word piece with one or two b&w photos to $600 or more for a 3,500-word article with a six- or eight-page color layout.

Some other tips: most GUNS readers are quite knowledgeable about firearms and are more interested in advanced topics than the fundamentals. Don't talk down to them. Keep your article brief and to the point; 2,000-3,000 words is usually sufficient. Be very sure of your facts and numbers, especially regarding technical and reloading data.

Thanks for your interest. And good luck!

Contact Information:

All Firearms, Ammo: Scott Farrell, Editor
591 Camino de la Reina, Suite 200
San Diego, CA 92109
(619) 297-5352

Handcraft Illustrated

About Our Readers

Our audience is primarily made up of college-educated women in their late 30s or older. They read *Handcraft Illustrated* for ideas on how to personalize their home with relatively quick, hands-on projects. As they complete each project, they're also learning basic handcraft skills. When writing your article, you should assume that the reader has no previous experience with the project or technique at hand, nor a great deal of time to complete the process. Any terms, tools, or processes specific to your area of expertise should be defined and explained.

Basic Requirements

1. Manuscripts should be submitted on disk. We prefer files stored as Microsoft Word documents in Macintosh format, but we also accept PC (DOS or Windows) disks with files saved in ASCII (.txt) format. If you have questions, phone Barbara Bourassa. When sending articles on disk, be sure to include a printed copy of the piece.

If you do not have access to a personal computer, we will accept articles that have been typed. We do not accept handwritten articles.

If sending sketches or diagrams, please make them as clear as possible, mark important references and include all captions.

2. All articles should be accompanied by the following items, unless otherwise noted in the assignment process:

a.) A photograph of the project, or the project itself.

b.) A complete list of materials. Every tool, supply, or material used in the project should be listed in the order in which it will be needed. Give as much detail as possible when listing the materials—i.e., 1 quart latex paint, 1 ½ yard fabric of choice, etc.

c.) Step-by-step instructions. The instructions should be written strictly in order, and should take the reader through the entire project, from laying down newspaper to protect the work surface, for instance, to tying the finishing bow.

d.) Mail-order sources. Every article should be accompanied by a list of mail-order sources for each tool, supply, or material used in the project.

Payment

We pay authors 60 days from final acceptance of an article or receipt of invoice, whichever comes later.

Sending Your Manuscript

All completed articles, projects, photographs, and diagrams should be sent to the attention of Barbara Bourassa at the address shown below.

A Few Simple Suggestions

1. Your writing should be personal, but remember to keep the focus on the project, not on yourself. Be friendly to the readers and try to make them feel at ease. They should feel like this project is something they can do. Otherwise what's the point in you writing about it?

2. Write in a way that comes naturally. Write as you would speak, in common, everyday language. Don't try to adopt a "literary" style. Don't use a long word where a short one will do. Keep your sentences simple and clear.

3. Define every term the reader might be unfamiliar with. If you define the term the first time you use it, that will give the reader a sense of confidence, not only in his or her ability to do the project, but also a sense of confidence that you know what you're doing.

4. Do everything in order. Many readers won't read all the way through the instructions before they start, so be sure that every material and every instruction is given in exactly the order needed.

5. Be careful with prepositions and words like "top" and "bottom." They are the words most likely to be misinterpreted. UP means away from the pull of gravity; the TOP is the surface facing UP. If the project involves, for instance, a piece of paper which has been laid out on the table, do not refer to the top of the paper unless you mean the surface of the paper facing away from the table. If you mean the end of the paper away from you (or the reader), say so.

6. Be consistent. If you call a spade a spade in the first part of the article, don't start calling it a shovel in the latter part. Pick words that mean what you want them to mean, then define them (if necessary), and stick with them. You'll be doing your readers a service.

7. When you have written your article, reread it trying to put yourself in the position of an inexperienced reader. See if there's a way to misinterpret anything you've written. If there is, correct it. The true measure of your own expertise is in how well the reader can complete the project using your instructions.

Contact Information:
Barbara Bourassa, Executive Editor
17 Station Street
P.O. Box 509
Brookline Village, MA 02147
(617) 232-1000 • FAX: (617) 232-1572

The Healing Woman
The monthly newsletter for women survivors of childhood sexual abuse

Contributors' Guidelines for Writers and Healing professionals

Important Note

In order to write for THE HEALING WOMAN, you must be either:

- A survivor of childhood sexual abuse
- A family member or close friend of a survivor
- A professional who works with survivors to help them heal

Topics for Articles

THE HEALING WOMAN is looking for stories that provide information, self-help, and support for women recovering from the trauma of childhood sexual abuse. We want articles that validate our readers' experience, offer suggestions and tools to help them work through their issues, and remind them they are not alone on their difficult journey.

Articles should be more storytelling than lecture. In other words, articles should include your own—or your clients'—first-person experiences in struggling and coping with the issues you are writing about. Specific examples should be used to illustrate your points, and the more the better. This is extremely important to us.

The focus of THE HEALING WOMAN is on healing, not on suffering. Our tone is positive and encouraging but we do not minimize or deny the horror and the pain our readers suffer.

THE HEALING WOMAN publishes feature articles, book reviews, and interviews. Interviews may be with women who have completed their recovery from childhood sexual abuse or with professionals whose work with survivors has either had a major impact or is unusually interesting.

(We also publish poetry and first-person stories by survivors in our "Survivors Speak Out" section. Payment for this section is in copies. See Contributors' Guidelines for Readers Who Want to Share Their Stories and Poetry, below.)

We strongly recommend you read an issue of THE HEALING WOMAN before querying or submitting a story. To get a sample issue, send us a check for $3.

How to Query

If you have an idea for an article, a book review, or an interview, please send us a query letter before you start writing. Be sure to state your qualifications (whether you are a survivor, a family member or friend, or a professional), as well your professional and/or writing credentials. We are willing to work with unpublished writers.

Responses to queries usually take about four weeks.

Length of Articles

Feature articles and interviews run 1,000 to 1,500 words. Book reviews run 400 to 700 words, depending on the book. Please do not exceed these limits without consulting the editor!

How to Submit An Article

All articles, unless we have agreed otherwise, are done "on spec," which means that we will not make a decision about accepting your work until we have seen the completed piece. We will try reply to your submission within a month, but sometimes its takes longer. Please be patient.

Be sure to put your name on each page of your manuscript. Indicate the approximate word count on the first page. If you use a computer, you can make yourself very popular with our editors by sending us your story both in hard copy and on floppy disk (either 3.5" or 5.25" IBM or Macintosh) as unformatted ASCII text.

If we choose to publish your article, we will keep your original manuscript for our files. Even if you don't want your manuscript returned, please include a self-addressed, stamped envelope for our response to your submission. All floppy disks will be returned at our expense.

Editing

We will edit for length and clarity. If in the process of editing we make substantial changes to your article, we'll check with you before publishing.

Copyright

As the author of your article, you hold the copyright to it, even though you give us permission to publish it. Your permission gives us first North American serial rights; it also allows us the option of reprinting your work one time only in hard copy and/or electronic form.

Privacy Issues and Legal Requirements

For each article or piece of writing you submit, you need to complete a 'Permission to Publish' form (available for a SASE). This form asks for some personal information (name and address), which we will keep confidential. It also asks you to certify that your piece is original, truthful, and so on. This is for your legal protection and ours.

Payment

We buy first North American serial rights; we also retain the option of reprinting your work one time only in hard copy and/or electronic form. We pay $25-50 for feature articles and interviews, $25 for book reviews (and you can keep the book). Payment is upon acceptance. When we publish your article, we will send you three copies of the issue in which it appears.

A healing professional (therapist, body worker, etc.) may choose to have payment in the form of an extended byline of 3-5 sentences, which describes the services she or he offers, the location of her or his office, and phone number. This extended byline should be factual ("so-and-so facilitates a weekly therapy group for women incest survivors") rather than promotional ("so-and-so facilitates an excellent therapy group . . .").

Contributors Guidelines for Readers Who Want to Share Their Stories and Poetry

THE HEALING WOMAN encourages its readers to write about their problems and their successes in recovering from childhood sexual abuse. In telling your story, you may need to talk about the abuse and the pain you suffered, but the focus should be on the healing that you are doing. We want to hear about the ways in which you are coping with and recovering from your own traumatic past.

Remember that your writing style isn't as important as your thoughtfulness and sincerity.

Survivors Speak Out

Readers share their stories and poetry in a section called "Survivors Speak Out." Some readers write about their pain and their determination to heal; some share how they are recovering their inner child; others write about the things they have used to heal themselves.

Because THE HEALING WOMAN is a community of survivors and pro-survivors, and because the "Survivors Speak Out" column is a forum for this community, only those "Survivors Speak Out" submissions that come from members of our community will be considered for publication. In other words, you must be a subscriber (member of THE HEALING WOMAN community) in order to have your work considered for publication in "Survivors Speak Out."

If you are considering submitting your writing, the best advice we can give you is to read several issues of THE HEALING WOMAN, focusing on "Survivors Speak Out."

The Nuts and Bolts of Sending Us Your Writing

How to Submit Your Writing

Your submission for "Survivors Speak Out" should run about one or two pages long (200-400 words). (If your submission is poetry, you may submit a maximum of five poems; the maximum length for poems we accept is 40 lines.) If you don't type, please print clearly. Be sure to put your name on each page.

Because of space limitations, we need to be strict about story length. As a result, we cannot consider work that exceeds the word and line-length limits noted above.

You can expect a reply from us in about 8 weeks. Please understand that we receive many submissions and it takes a while for us to read through them and respond.

If you can, PLEASE use a computer and send us your story on paper and on floppy disk (either 3.5" or 5.25" IBM or Macintosh) as text only, DOS text, ASCII text or unformatted text. (These all mean the same thing.) Please put your name on your disk (We will return it!)

Editing

We will edit your story for grammar, spelling, and clarity. Because of space limitations, we may also need to shorten it. If in the process of editing we make substantial changes, well check with you before publishing. Except for obvious errors, we do not edit poetry.

Copyright

As the author of your story or poem, you hold the copyright to it, even though you give us permission to publish it. Your permission gives us first North American serial rights. This means that THE HEALING WOMAN gets to publish your work for the first time in any North American periodical. Your signature on the "Permission to Publish" form also allows us the option of reprinting your work one time only in hard copy and/or electronic form.

Privacy Issues and Legal Requirements

For each article or piece of writing you submit, you need to complete a 'Permission to Publish' form (available for a SASE). This form asks for some personal information (name and address), which we will keep confidential. It also asks you to certify that your piece is original, truthful, and so on. This is for your legal protection and ours.

Payment

When we publish your story in "Survivors Speak Out," we will send you three extra copies of that issue.

P.S. Once you have contributed to 'Survivors Speak Out,' you may wish to write a more formal article for THE HEALING WOMAN, such as a book review or a self-help article on an issue you are working on in your own recovery. If so, please review the Contributors' Guidelines for Writers and Healing Professionals, above.

Contact Information:
Brenda Anderson, Editor
P.O. Box 3038
Moss Beach, CA 94038
(415) 728-0339 • FAX: (415) 728-1324

HealthQuest
The Publication of Black Wellness

WHO

HealthQuest is looking for writers who have a strong interest in the well-being of black people. Experienced writers are preferred, but we have a history of working with new writers whose work exhibits style, skill and promise.

So that we can get a sense of what your writing is like, and how your mind works, send us samples of your nonfiction writing along with a query letter that outlines your story idea(s).

WHAT

In each issue, our Focus Section comprises several stories and sidebars related to a single health issue. Features and departments cover fitness, nutrition, image, travel, spirituality, disease and other issues that affect black health. (See Editorial Sections attached.)

If you have an idea that fits our editorial goals, sent us a query letter. We prefer a query to articles that are sent "on spec," but we will review and consider unpublished manuscripts. We can't promise to return your unsolicited manuscript, but you can be sure that we won't print your story without contacting you first. If you haven't heard from us about the status of your story, contact the Managing Editor.

WHEN

We plan Focus Sections at least one year in advance of publication and other features and departments as much as six to eight months out. If you're assigned a story, your deadline will be approximately 3 months before the magazine hits the newsstand. Keep this schedule in mind if you are querying us about a story that has a seasonal slant.

Writers are paid in full within 30 days after publication. If, for any reason, we aren't able to run a story we've assigned, we'll either pay you a kill fee as agreed upon in the contract, or we'll arrange to hold the story to run in a future issue.

WHY

When you write for *HealthQuest*, you'll be associated with a top-quality publication. We are the only nationally-distributed, black-owned magazine that covers African-American health issue—and our concern for black health shows in the depth and quality of the articles we publish. Writing for us puts you in league with Dr. Joycelyn Elders, Iyanla Vanzant, Pearl Cleage and others who have written for us. Good writers make for a good publication—so we value strong skills and we pay competitively.

HOW

We emphasize strong reporting and creative writing. Our writers take a conversational, reader-friendly tone without being too colloquial. We encourage writers to be as creative as possible—taking into consideration the nature of the story. Don't feel repressed; your writing should be interested and interesting. Dig-in reporting covers all sides of an issue—often health issues aren't black and white, but all shades of brown. And we take a holistic approach to the way we look at specific treatments and health in general—emphasizing the importance of physical, mental, emotional, spiritual and social wellness.

WHERE

If you want to get to know *HealthQuest* a little better, you can find us at fine bookstores and newsstands nationwide. When you're ready, send samples and queries to:

Contact Information:
Tamara Jeffries, Managing Editor
200 Highpoint Drive, Suite #215
Chalfont, PA 18914
(215) 822-7935

Heartland Boating

Readership description: *Heartland Boating* magazine is devoted to both power and sail boating throughout middle America. Primary geographic readership areas include Tennessee, Kentucky, Alabama, Mississippi, Illinois, Missouri, Georgia, Arkansas, Indiana, Iowa, Ohio, Louisiana, Michigan, Wisconsin, Pennsylvania, Kansas, Minnesota, Nebraska, Florida, South Carolina and North Carolina.

Publication description: *Heartland Boating* is the official magazine for the boater who isn't going around the world. The content is both informative and humorous—describing boating life as the heartland boater knows it. We aren't pretentious. But, we are boating and enjoying the outdoor, water oriented way of life. The content reflects the challenge, joy and excitement of our way of life afloat.

Freelance submissions: *Heartland Boating* welcomes submissions of photographic, art and written material for possible publication. Our focus is on the freshwater inland rivers and lakes of the Heartland. . . primarily the waters of the Tennessee, Cumberland, Ohio and Mississippi rivers, the Tennessee-Tombigbee Waterway and the lakes among these rivers. The magazine caters to all kinds of boating: sail, houseboats, cruisers, runabouts, pontoons, etc.

No Great Lakes or salt water material will be considered unless it applies in some way to our area. Example: "What the fresh water boater should know about salt water cruising."

Writers not familiar with *Heartland Boating*'s style should write for a sample issue. Enclose $5.

We are looking for material with fresh "snap." Don't be afraid to let your personality show. Please be Correct, Concise, Clear and Colorful.

Regular features open to freelance writers:

(1) Marina Profile: A regular feature highlighting a marina in the area already described. Writers should provide comprehensive information about marina facilities, restaurants, services, things to do, etc. . . . the kind of information traveling boaters want to know about marinas they might visit. Articles should be accompanied with a good selection of sharply focused color and b/w photos. 1,000-1,200 words.

(2) Near the Water: A regular department featuring shore based, close-to-the-water places of interest to boaters. Places that are near, but not necessarily on the water. (Guard against a "touristy tone.") Articles should be accompanied with a good selection of sharply focused color and b/w photos. 1,000-1,500 words.

(3) Books Aboard: Reviews on nautical books. Book reviews don't have to be dry and boring. Prove it. 600-800 words.

(4) Maintenance/Nuts and bolts (boats) articles: Technical articles on boat maintenance/repair. Supply charts/graphics. 500-1,000 words.

(5) Environment/Ecology: An aid to education of boaters on how to do our part in keeping our waters clean for boating and swimming. (Tear-out sheet that might be posted on a marina bulletin board.) 600-800 words.

(6) Electronics: Technical articles. 300-1,000 words with art if possible.

(7) Miscellaneous: Anything not already mentioned which would be of interest to boating enthusiasts. Query first.

Manuscript specifications: We prefer that prospective contributors query an idea first rather than submit an unsolicited manuscript.

Manuscripts must be typed (dot matrix OK but not preferred). Please indicate the approximate number of words and mark all sheets with the page number, feature title and author's name. Those using Macintosh personal computers are asked to submit a Macintosh computer disk (MacWrite or Word OK or indicate what application you used) along with the hard copy. For IBM DOS—save as text file.

Freelance photographers: *Heartland Boating* buys a limited number of photographs each issue. Freelance photographers query first with sample of your work.

Black and white photos: 8x10 glossy prints preferred. High quality with moderate contrast and sharp focus. Contact sheets can be submitted for consideration.

Color: Good quality transparencies are acceptable for editorial use. Color prints are preferred if submitted with negatives. Consideration will be given to 35mm for possible use as covers, but large format transparencies are preferred. Photo essays are very occasionally awarded to an artistically outstanding series centered on a single facet of boating in our editorial area.

Freelance Illustration: *Heartland Boating* has few requirements for illustration and works with illustrators on an assignment basis only. Professional illustrators interested in being considered for the magazine should have a well developed style, strong in line art and be familiar with the contents of the magazine. Nonreturnable standard file sized samples of work should be accompanied with a brochure or resume which can also be kept on file.

Freelance Cartoons: *Heartland Boating* occasionally uses freestanding single panel or gag cartoons. Submissions should be prepared in black line art on 8½" x 11" paper. Remember, send only material slanted for this specialty audience.

General: *Heartland Boating* pays for all contributions on publication.

We are specifically looking for a core of freelancers who are also boating in the inland waters of middle America.

Contact Information:

Editorial, Photographic Material: Molly Lightfoot Blom, Editor
P.O. Box 1067
Martin, TN 38237-1067
(901) 587-6791 • FAX: (901) 587-6893
Illustrations, Cartoons: John R. Cassady, Art Editor
P.O. Box 340568
Tampa, FL 33694-0568

Heartland USA

HEARTLAND USA is a general-interest, bimonthly magazine with a circulation of over 750,000 and a readership exceeding 2 million. Targeted primarily at blue collar working people, the publication regularly includes short, easy-to-read articles on spectator sports (motorsports, football, basketball and baseball), hunting, fishing, how-to, travel, music (both C&W and soft rock), gardening, wildlife, the environment, as well as stories about everyday American heroes and towns—with emphasis on the upbeat, touching, or humorous.

Articles focus on interesting aspects of life in these United States. Clean and simple design elements, compelling photographs, and entertaining cartoons characterize each issue.

Please keep in mind that our average reader is a working person with a high school education. We have consciously chosen not to "write down" to our readers, but rather to pursue an editorial style that reflects a relaxed, jocular, "Main Street" familiarity. The liberal use of anecdote or interesting quotations—anything to breathe some life into a piece—is looked upon favorably.

The target length for feature articles is 1,200 words, with payment varying from $250 to $950. Feature-length pieces must lend themselves to strong photographic support.

Department-length articles (generally 550 - 1,200 words) pay from $140 to $950.

We pay on acceptance (20% kill fee), purchase the first or second North American serial rights and copyright our publication. Dot-matrix computer printouts (if legible) are acceptable, as well as electronic submissions via Microsoft Word, WordPerfect, or MS-DOS ASCII only. Simultaneous, photocopied, and reprinted submissions are okay. Please query with clips of published work and include your social security number with the manuscript or cover letter. Response to your query or submission will be within 4-6 weeks. Sample copy, $3.

Contact Information:
Brad Pearson, Editor
1 Sound Shore Drive
Greenwich, CT 06830
(203) 622-3456 • FAX: (203) 863-5393

Hemispheres
The World Brought to You by United Airlines

HEMISPHERES, the award-winning inflight magazine of United Airlines, is published by Pace Communications, Inc., for the approximately 72 million passengers who fly United each year. The magazine's 500,000 monthly copies reach 1.9 million readers. Articles for the magazine are written primarily by freelance writers. In October 1992, HEMISPHERES supplanted the previous magazine, VISàVIS. Virtually nothing about the two magazines is the same.

HEMISPHERES is edited for an active and global mix of business and leisure travelers. United's international route system means that the magazine is being read around the world. Thus HEMISPHERES is in the unusual position of being able to accurately describe itself as a truly international magazine. We seriously pursue the goal of meshing that circulation with an emerging concept of a "global magazine." We want HEMISPHERES to be much more than an American magazine read around the world. We try to achieve that with everything from a policy avoiding use of words like "foreign," to specifically choosing writers and perspectives that impart a sense of cultural political, business, and cultural "worldwideness." We eschew "general travel," in style and substance, leaning instead toward "insider" articles written by residents or writers with expert credentials.

Reader service is paramount, so articles must provide solid, practical, and well-researched information for travelers. Good-natured humor and sophistication infuse a mix of travel, business, family, and leisure subjects.

What We're Looking For

We look for intelligently written, lively, and entertaining articles with a global perspective.

HEMISPHERES is a heavily departmentalized magazine with a preferred format for most departments and some features. Queries that capture the concept of those categories often win assignments. Please study sample copies, which are available for $5 each from Ellen Kerr at our address.

Because of HEMISPHERES' global circulation and service orientation, we place a premium on documentation and accuracy. Background information is always required for fact checking. With your article, we must receive copies of brochures, business cards, menus, and other printed material to verify basic information about the people and places that appear in print. We need the phone and FAX numbers of everyone you quote and photocopies of pages from books or other resources from which quotes are taken. Where appropriate, prices should be listed in foreign currencies and U.S. dollar equivalents. The magazine's international coverage and the difficulty of telephone checking makes such documentation necessary.

In general, articles include phone numbers, addresses, and a map (the Three Days article, Roving Gourmet and Savvy Shopper departments require street maps, the first two marked with the locations of featured locations). Specific requirements vary by department, but a Details, Details, Details section usually follows the piece. Assigned writers will be expected to provide copy that conforms to that format and punctuation. Writers should add a bio blurb, (hopefully witty, provocative and creative), to the end of their articles.

All queries should be brief and concisely written. First-time writers should supply a few of their most impressive and representative current clips. We try to report on queries within eight weeks.

After a telephone discussion with the author, assignments are finalized with a contract and/or an assignment letter. Most deadlines are one month after the assignment. We rarely send writers on assignment, but will pay telephone and certain other agreed-upon expenses.

We must receive assigned articles on a 3½ - or 5¼-inch computer disk along with a hard copy. We ask writers to file stories in Microsoft Word or ASCII, but we can convert other programs. We are also able to receive stories by modem. Editors will provide details.

Payment for articles varies (by length, location in the magazine, and other factors) and is negotiated with the writer. Due to our world-wide circulation, we buy First Global Serial Rights for most articles, exclusive rights for "3 Perfect Days In . . ." "Roving Gourmet" and "On Location" articles, and pay upon acceptance.

First-time writers may be asked to provide a proposed story on speculation. After a requested rewrite, we pay a kill fee of 20% for an unacceptable article. Please furnish articles at the assigned length.

The Magazine

HEMISPHERES usually provides four major features and a variety of department stories that are written by freelancers.

MAIN WELL

A 1,500-2,000 word feature called "Three Perfect Days in . . . " anchors the main well. This highly reader-service-oriented article provides a romantic, day-by-day itinerary for a sybaritic, insider's tour of a world-class destination city. The writer should be a resident or live close to the featured city.

Freelancers write three or four other 1,200-1,500-word features that sometimes include fiction. These articles span travel and other categories, among them action/adventure experiences, exotic destinations, family travel, articles on nature/environmental topics and trips, and pieces that focus on the discovery of human cultural diversity. We also want to publish stories that feature trips by rail, cruise ship, and unique modes of travel.

DEPARTMENT pieces range from 800 to 1,400 words.

Making a Difference is a front-of-the-book Q&A format interview with world leaders, movers, and shakers. A 500-600 word introduction anchors the interview. We want to profile an international mix of men and women representing a variety of topics or issues, but all must truly be making a difference. No puffy celebrity profiles.

On Location is a snappy selection of one sentence, "25 Fun Facts" that are obscure or intriguing facts or travel-service-oriented items that the reader never knew about a city, state, country, or destination. These should be separate items, not running together by subject or relying on the one before for meaning.

Executive Secrets lets us in on the things that top executives know. Topics have included how to use an interpreter, strategies for those breaking into business behind the former Iron Curtain, active listening, morale building, volunteering time when busy.

In Case Study, we learn how companies or organizations have found their niche, beat the competition, achieved a remarkable marketing objective, or rebounded from the brink of bankruptcy. No lionizations of CEOs that become profile pieces. After profiling the company's success, the writer could almost bullet prominent strategies the firm has followed and it would be a winner. Strategies should be the emphasis. We want international candidates.

Weekend Breakaway takes us just outside a major city for a physically active, action-packed weekend. This isn't a sedentary "getaway" at a "property." We've covered sea kayaking from Miami, mountain biking from Albuquerque, hiking from Melbourne, windsurfing from Honolulu.

Roving Gourmet is an insider's guide to interesting eating in a major city, resort area, or region. The slant can be anything from ethnic to expensive, best to biggest, or anything else the author can support. The writer should be a resident. We've done Chicago ethnic eateries, Miami's new cuisine, Seattle seafood, Denver frontier dining, Tokyo's Japanese eateries, dining well at Disney World, a "hot spot" neighborhood in Philadelphia, New York's jazz dinners and brunches. Usually four featured eateries span a spectrum from "a hole in the wall," to "expense account lunch," and on to "Big Deal Dining."

Collecting will alternate between a photo with a lengthy caption and an occasional 800-word story. The focus will be on collections and collecting, of all kinds.

Eye on Sports will be a literally global look at anything of interest in the world of sports. Topics have included arcane football teams, global hockey contests, athlete comebacks, the game that changed the Super Bowl, the World Cup of soccer, the emerging seniors tennis tour.

Vintage Traveler appeals to the traveler who wasn't born yesterday. This is for mature, experienced travelers who perhaps are interested in, or can afford, more gracious, luxurious, or enlightening options that the rest of us.

Savvy Shopper steps beyond all those stories that just mention the "great shopping" at a particular destination. This piece will give us an insider's shop-by-shop, gallery-by-gallery tour of the best places in the world to shop for everything from expensive rarities to bargains. Residents preferred. We've done China's Silk Road, New York, Florence, London, the international appeal of outlet malls.

Science and Technology alternates with Computers. Neither is just another column on audio components or software. They are substantive, insightful stories. Articles will explore everything from how a medical breakthrough happened to emerging technology and its impact on the future. This could have a travel slant, but doesn't need one. Past topics have included ergonomics, virtual reality, smart cars, digital compression, computer-designed drugs.

Aviation Journal is an opportunity to enthrall all of those fliers who are fascinated with aviation. Topics will range widely. Stories have covered the history of the classic DC-3, the next generation of airliners, airport identifiers (LAX, etc.), computer flight simulators, airport traffic lights.

Of Grape And Grain explores the world of wine and other spirits with an emphasis on education, not one-upmanship. We'll take a travel approach with tours of viticultural areas (please no overexposed candidates), wine festivals, etc. Topics have included wine art labels, Beaujolais Nouveau, cognac's rituals, Virginia wine country, the boom in micro-brewed beer, and wine snobs.

Show Business looks insightfully at the world of films, music and entertainment. We've explored the growing family appeal of Las Vegas, the internationalization of music marketing and the Academy Awards, and Chicago's Blues Clubs.

Musings features humor, or just curious "musings." Articles have highlighted the tradition of April Fool pranks in Britain, and explored the lessons learned by that official nobody, the father of the groom.

Among other amusements at the back of the book is a Quick Quiz. This might tell well-traveled readers how much they know about geography or whether they'd do well on the Law School Aptitude Test. We'd be interested in any existing tests or ones devised by writers that might amuse and educate.

We also run reader-service Travel News items as space permits. These widely ranging tips should be brief, practical, invaluable, and trend oriented.

Photography

HEMISPHERES works solely with professional photographers and photo stock houses. We discourage writers from sending their own photos or stock lists. Please do not send unsolicited selections of photography. Only assigned writers who are also published photographers should submit color transparencies with their articles.

Contact Information:
Queries: Kate Greer, Editor-in-Chief
Travel News: Lisa Fann, Associate Editor
Pace Communications, Inc.
1301 Carolina Street
Greensboro, NC 27401
(910) 378-6065 • FAX: (910) 275-2864

Highlights for Children

We appreciate your interest in *Highlights for Children*. *Highlights* is published monthly for children 2 to 12. Circulation is nearly 3 million.

Please note:

- We do not pay persons under age 15 for contributions.
- We buy all rights, including copyright, and do not consider material previously published.
- We prefer to see a manuscript rather than a query.
- All material is paid for on acceptance.
- We accept material year round, including seasonal material.

FICTION should have an engaging plot, strong characterization, and lively language. Stories for younger readers (ages 3-7) should be 400 words or less. Stories for older readers (8-12) should be 900 words or less and be appealing to younger readers if read aloud.

- We prefer stories that teach by positive example, rather than by preaching.
- Suggestions of crime and violence are taboo.
- Frequent needs include humor, mystery, sports, and adventure stories; retellings of traditional tales; stories in urban settings; and stories that feature world cultures.
- We seldom buy rhyming stories.

Payment: $100 and up.

REBUS STORIES are a monthly feature for beginning readers, featuring a variety of familiar words that can easily be shown as pictures. Rebuses should be 125 words or less.

Payment: $75 and up.

NONFICTION includes biography, autobiography, and various approaches to the arts, science, history, sports, and world cultures. All articles should be 800 words or less.

- Focused articles are more successful than broad factual surveys.
- We prefer research based on consultation with experts or firsthand experience.
- Writers with an extensive background in a particular field are encouraged to share their experiences and personal research.
- Articles about cultural traditions and ways of life should reflect a deep understanding of the subject.
- Biographies of individuals who have made significant artistic, scientific, or humanitarian contributions are strengthened by the inclusion of formative childhood experiences. We prefer biographies that are rich in anecdotes and place the subject in a historical and cultural context.
- Nonfiction articles geared to our young readers (ages 3-7) are especially welcome. These should not exceed 400 words.
- References or sources of information must be included with submissions.
- Color 35mm slides, photos, or art reference materials are helpful and sometimes crucial in evaluating submissions.

Payment: $100 and up.

CRAFTS should appeal to a wide age range, with clear, numbered directions, typically not more than five steps.

- A well-made sample should be submitted with each craft idea.
- Projects must require only common household items or inexpensive, easy-to-obtain materials.
- Projects should result in attractive, useful gift items, decorations, toys, and games.
- Crafts that celebrate holidays or religious traditions are welcome. Crafts from world cultures are a current need.

Payment: $25 and up.

FINGER PLAYS/ACTION RHYMES should have plenty of action and minimal text. They must be easy for very young children to act out, step-by-step, with hands, fingers, and body movements.

Payment: $25 and up.

PARTY PLANS should give clever, original party ideas organized around a single theme, clearly described in 300 to 700 words. Plans should include invitations, favors, decorations, refreshments, and a mix of quiet and active games. Materials used should be inexpensive. Include drawings or samples of items.

Payment: $50 and up.

VERSE is purchased sparingly. It is rarely longer than 16 lines and should be meaningful for young readers.

Payment: $25 and up.

Contact Information:
Beth Troop, Manuscript Coordinator
803 Church Street
Honesdale, PA 18431
(717) 253-1080

Highways
The Official Publication of the Good Sam Club

Thank you for your interest in *Highways*, the official publication of the Good Sam Club. *Highways* is published 11 times a year by TL Enterprises Inc. and is a sister publication of *Trailer Life* and *MotorHome*.

Highways is a specialty magazine for RV enthusiasts and has a circulation of more than 900,000. We suggest that potential writers study recent issues before sending us queries or manuscripts. All manuscripts must be submitted on a 3.5 inch diskette (most word processing programs are acceptable) and in printed form. Photocopy submissions are OK. Please allow eight weeks for replies on unsolicited submissions.

Payment is on acceptance for publication. However, we reserve the right to hold sidebars and other related material until the feature layout is designed. Sidebar fees are negotiated by the editorial staff on an individual basis. *Highways* buys first North American serial rights and electronic rights. The editors reserve the right to edit and even rewrite any article in order to make it suit the theme or space limitations of a specific issue. Major alterations will be discussed with the author when possible.

TRAVEL FEATURES:

The easiest way to sell your work to *Highways* is to write an interesting and tightly focused RV travel story. Please do not send us 500-word descriptions of cross-country RV trips. We need features that evoke the sights, sounds, smells and even tastes of specific travel destinations. Consequently, we'd much rather have a tight 2,000 words on traveling to Anchorage in the spring than on all of Alaska. The maximum length for travel features, unless cleared by the editorial staff, is 2,500 words. We accept queries, not manuscripts, via CompuServe. Our address on the RV Forum is 73324,2656.

Highways' special interest and travel feature stories are usually in color, while technical and humor stories are usually in black and white. All stories (excluding humor) should be accompanied by a comprehensive selection of clear, color transparencies with captions. When possible, the transparencies should feature RVs against a scenic backdrop. Think cover shot (vertical) when taking these photos and remember lighting is crucial to the overall effect. Focus your photography on scenic or panoramic views for the opening layout and points of interest, local color and activity shots for the carryover pages. Fees for full-length travel features with photos start at $300. Higher fees are negotiable. Short travel features start at $100 and max out at $250.

MAINTENANCE AND TECHNICAL:

Highways publishes several types of technical stories.

• Maintenance: RV maintenance stories should be 1,800 to 2,500 words long and written so that they are of interest to both the novice and the veteran RVer. Color transparencies showing the maintenance procedure are essential.

• How-to: These features for handy RVers should be 1,500 to 2,500 words and include step-by-step instructions, diagrams and slides.

• RV Safety: An example of this type of a story includes a look at extension-cord use by RVers. Stories should be 1,000 to 2,000 words and be accompanied by a selection of slides.

• RV Accessory Overviews: If you know a lot about RV air conditioners, tires, batteries, and/or generators, you may be able to create this kind of feature. However, it is guaranteed to be a tough sale. Overview features tend to be lengthy (1,500 to 2,500 words) and should be as comprehensive as possible. An example of this is the holding tanks story in our January 1995 issue. Before writing a technical story of this type, it is best to send a query letter to the editor. Be sure to include clips of similar published features.

• Product Evaluations: All product evaluations are assigned by the editorial staff. If you are interested in writing such a story, query the editor and include published clips of similar work. Product evaluations must be fair and unbiased. Queries by any representative of the product's manufacturer or distributor will be rejected and all product claims must be independently substantiated. No writer is to contact a manufacturer or distributor as a representative of *Highways* without explicit permission of the editorial staff.

If you are assigned a story by the editorial staff, please keep in mind that you now represent *Highways*. Be conscious that if you receive information or materials about the subject/area you are covering, you must still write an ethical, objective story.

VEHICLE TESTS:

Highways does not publish full-length vehicle tests. Capsule vehicle tests and previews are staff written.

All technical copy is reviewed by the technical editor of *Highways* for accuracy. Payment for technical stories ranges from $250 to $600, depending on complexity of the story and quality of the manuscript.

SPECIAL INTEREST:

Highways' editorial focus can be expanded to include hobbies, crafts and other recreational activities that are popular among RVers. Recent stories have covered vintage vehicles, the Iditarod Trail Sled Dog Race, computers and other hobbies. Special interest features should be 1,200 to 2,500 words and pay $250 to $450.

RV HUMOR:

In each issue of *Highways*, we try to include a humorous vignette on some aspect of the RV lifestyle. Humor stories should be directly related to the RV experience. Maximum length for humor stories is 1,500 words; minimum, 800 words. Do not send photographs. All humor stories are illustrated by line drawings. Fees start at $150. Higher fees are negotiable.

COLUMNS:

All *Highways* columns are assigned. If you have a column idea and wish to discuss it with us, write us several sample columns and we will consider them. Columns are a tough sale and we do not foresee a need to add any new columns to *Highways* in the near future.

HUMAN INTEREST:

Highways generally does not publish personality features.

POETRY AND FICTION:

Highways does not publish poetry or fiction.

PHOTO REQUIREMENTS:

Travel features should be accompanied by a minimum of 15 color transparencies, all originals. All transparencies should be numbered with an accompanying caption sheet identifying each subject. Photos and slides supplied by someone other than the manuscript author should be clearly identified for photo credit. All photos and slides will be returned after publication when possible. Please include a self-addressed, stamped envelope for this purpose.

Contact Information:
Ronald H. Epstein, Editor
P.O. Box 8545
Ventura, CA 93002
(805) 667-4100 • FAX: (805) 667-4454

The Home Shop Machinist
A Bimonthly Magazine Dedicated to Precision Metalworking

The *Home Shop Machinist* is a magazine with very specific content. Our audience is the hobbyist who works primarily with metal, though other materials enter in from time to time, such as plastics, glass or ceramics. Subject matter in the magazine is virtually all directed toward "how to." Our aim is not to feature people, but projects, hints, tips and guidance that will improve skills, enhance the shop machines or environment, or provide a challenge.

We like articles about jigs and/or fixtures of original design (yours) that is of a general enough nature that others may find some application to their own situation now or later. We also like practical (and safe) shortcuts and money-saving ideas. For example, we have done features on designs for milling attachments for your lathe, or milling on your drill press, or fabricating your own boring head, fly cutter, lathe carriage stop, etc. We publish articles on foundry work frequently. There is growing interest in the subject. Computers with shop applications have become more popular, too. We (and the readers) also like to have at least one "hobby" project running all the time. Examples of past articles include a firing model Civil War cannon, a small horizontal steam engine, a Stirling cycle engine, a model airplane engine, a hit-and-miss engine, rifle action, and more. Just about anything that can be machined, cast, or welded out of metal will be considered for publication.

I must discourage you from writing historical articles, even though we have published one on a couple of occasions. The same goes for people features. Fiction, poetry, and the like are not considered.

COPY: While we don't mind a little more "friendly" style of writing—this being a hobby magazine—it is essential that you organize your article so descriptions of your subject are logically sequential, and written in a technical style as much as possible. Be concerned about the way you use familiar or idiomatic expressions or abbreviations that are not universally used and accepted. (Owning a Machinery's Handbook may be the best investment you ever made as an author or as a machinist. It's our favorite reference.) Your information must be thorough. Our readership ranges from novice to skilled machinist and engineer. A bill of materials is essential if your article describes the construction of some item. You may want to mention your favorite source for those materials, too, along with an approximate cost.

Your articles are most likely to be accepted by us if they are typed and double-spaced. If you don't have a typewriter, don't worry; we can work from neatly done handwriting, too. We have PC and Macintosh computers in our office, so a disc (either size) is welcome, but must be accompanied by hard copy. DO NOT SEND A PHOTOCOPY OF YOUR ARTICLE. We have a type scanner that will put your article on computer. It does not read photocopies very well, so send us the original and keep the photocopy. Hand written text is discouraged and may be rejected.

PHOTOGRAPHS: Your photos can make or break your article. We strongly prefer black and white glossy prints. We can, however, work with color prints that have average contrast and a clear image. Make certain your depth of field (focus) is great enough to have your entire subject clearly detailed. Color slides are not welcome. We only return photos at your request.

Your work may be republished in book form later, so we keep photos here.

AVOID WRITING ON THE BACK OR FRONT OF PRINTS WITH INK. Number your photos with a crayon. Ink transfers onto the emulsion of the photo beneath it when stacked. The photo is then ruined for our purposes. If you need captions for your photos, type them on a separate sheet of paper, along with photo credits, or attach the typed caption to each photo with clear tape. Be sure the photographer is identified so we can recognize him/her in the article. The size of the photo is unimportant so long as the image is clear. Polaroids or other instant prints are not recommended. When you are shooting, be aware of flash glare off of shiny surfaces. It's better to bounce your flash or use a diffused light source.

DRAWINGS: We are extremely picky about drawings! Most authors will simply send us sketches or blueprints of their working drawings, and we then have our draftsman redraw them to our size and line weight specs. Most important is that you DOUBLE-CHECK FOR ERRORS, whether they be in dimensioning or important omissions of lines. We hate writing errata! Make your drawings as clear and detailed as you possibly can. Drawing all necessary side, top and bottom views is much preferred to dimensioning hidden (invisible) lines. Even it we want to use your article, we may have to send the drawings back to you for more work before proceeding with publication. A construction article without drawings is virtually useless, so I would encourage you to include them.

We pay nearly double our per-page rate for finished, inked (or CAD) drawings we can use without having to pay a draftsman to redraw. You are welcome to try it, but don't be disappointed if we decide to have them redone after all your work. Take a careful look at the style of drawings already published in *The Home Shop Machinist*. Let them be a guide for you. Unless you can do your lettering with a Leroy template (or a sans serif font in CAD), just use a light blue pencil for dimensions and callouts. We will have them set in type here. You might consider attaching a transparent tissue overlay, and indicate the callouts there rather than writing on your original. If you're doing them on computer, we use Helvetica or Arial as our type fonts. The drawings you see on our pages have been reduced to half their original size. Whatever you draw would also be reduced 50%, so you need to scale your drawing so it fits on a page comfortably. Basically, we stick to the ANSI drafting standards as a guide. You can get a set of those standards by writing to the American Society of Mechanical Engineers (ASME), United Engineering Center, 345 E. 47th St., New York, NY 10017.

ORGANIZING YOUR ARTICLE: When you're putting your article together, keep your drawing and photo numbering system simple. Just begin with No. 1 and follow consecutively, whether it is a photo, a figure, or a table. Figures refer to drawings, charts, or other visuals that are not photos.

Regarding titles, you are welcome to suggest a title for your article, but we reserve the right to change and use our own instead.

Regarding copyright, *The Home Shop Machinist* buys First North American Serial Rights. That means we have one-time use of the article. You retain copyright. Your article may be one we choose to reprint in one of our Projects books, but we will seek your permission before doing so. Payment for the reprint comes in the form of a complimentary copy of the book only.

We do not accept simultaneous submissions. I cannot recommend you ever do that with any magazine. Some very embarrassing situations have come up in the past for authors who did so.

We pay upon publication for all articles used. Please be aware that it may take many months—even up to two or three years—for your work to be published. There is a substantial backlog of articles awaiting publication.

Your article may be chosen to be published in *Projects in Metal* rather than *The Home Shop Machinist*. If it is accepted, it's automatically eligible to be printed in either one. It would not be used in both, however.

We appreciate the fact that you are interested in sharing your knowledge and expertise with our readers (your fellow machinists). I am available by phone or mail to assist you as you get underway. Thank you for your interest.

AUTHOR'S PAY

Minimum per full published page $40.00
Published photos with feature articles (each) $ 9.00
Cover photo* $40.00
Published pages with finished drawings** $70.00
(not requiring redrawing by our draftsman)
Short columns or articles less than full page $30.00
Filler items (less than half page) $15.00
Book reviews (We do not accept unsolicited reviews.) $30.00
Items submitted to "Chips & Sparks" are considered gratis.

**The Home Shop Machinist* rarely accepts cover photo submissions that are unaccompanied by feature articles material.

**This is not necessarily to say that a tiny square drawing appearing on a page (for example) justifies $70 rather than $40. The editor has the final judgment on what constitutes a $70 page.

Payment is made upon publication of the article. Pay rates are subject to change without notice.

Contact Information:
Joe Rice, Editor
P.O. Box 1810
Traverse City, MI 49685
(616) 946-3712

Home Times
Family Newspaper

Home Times is a monthly tabloid newspaper, distributed locally and nationally by U.S. Mail to paid subscribers and requestors, covering world & national news & views, home & family, arts & entertainment, and religion, all with a Biblical worldview. It is pro-Christian and pro-Jewish —but not religious.

We are a NEWSpaper, so content is generally keyed to current events and hot issues of the day. It is aimed squarely at the general public and written for them, though it receives most of its support from Christian readers. The news articles are often what we call "virtual exclusives," stories unpublished or under-published in the regular news media, often reporting on trends months, even years before they find their way into the regular press. Features on family, education, parenting, entertainment (movies, books, TV, videos) are practical, not preachy, related to issues and pro-values.

Home Times is non-denominational and non-doctrinal, free of religious clichés or churchy or preachy perspectives. It tries not to moralize but to just be practical and Biblical in perspective. Our goal is to publish godly viewpoints in the marketplace, and to counteract the culturally elite of media and politics who reject Judao-Christian values, traditional American values, true history, and faith in God.

Home Times is different from all other "Christian" publications – we strongly suggest you read these guidelines AND sample issues. Once you understand our slant, and if this is your kind of writing, you'll enjoy writing for *Home Times*! We make it easy for you to "test ride" *Home Times*: send $3 (no SASE required) and we'll mail you the upcoming three issues;

ask for Writer's Trial. Or as a prospective *HT* writer subscribe at $9 (regularly $12) for 12 issues.

We encourage new writers at *Home Times*. We do not pay much—but it is a great opportunity for writers, especially new writers, to hone their skills. The editor has even written a 12 chapter report for new writers entitled "100 reasons why I reject your mss" —which is an effective training course for freelancers written in a lighthearted vein.

General Requirements: We want complete manuscripts – no queries please. Photos and illustrations may enhance a story if appropriate. No slides, negatives, or computer disks, please. Pay is upon publication and ranges from $0 to $25 ($0 to $10 for reprints – which are accepted). Photos if used are paid at $5 each. Seasonal materials: 4-6 weeks in advance. LENGTH: as brief as possible, 500-800 words. Major stories up to 1,000 words are accepted but not as readily. We reserve the right to shorten your story and edit it somewhat to fit our slant and style. REPLIES: we're understaffed and overworked so sometimes we get back to you in a few days, sometimes in a month. Holler if you don't hear in 6-8 weeks.

Special Opportunities: We want personal features in these categories: Miracles! and Human Heroes, true-to-life stories 500-800 words with photo(s), generally about ordinary people who do extraordinary things, or about the goodness of God in our lives; Light One Candle: little people who do something to change our world for the better. Also: Sports Essays, brief (300-750w), on the values or issues side of sports. These pay the usual rate.

Local Opportunities: Local People Stories, local events; local calendar, local issues and news events of importance to the family; usually with a slant that is of interest to families everywhere. These kind of stories are often assigned, or suggested to the editor by phone if you are local and have been accepted on assignment status; they are not available if you are not local (southeast Florida). Quite frankly, we need some volunteers in this area, too.

Some Non-Cash Opportunities: We generally pay for the following with a six-issue subscription: (1) Our Interactive Columnist Tina Krause is open to your responses – see her column. (2) We want briefs of all sorts, anecdotes in various categories such as: Family Life (funny stories from parents and kids), Tales Out Of School (funny incidents from teachers & students, all grades through college), In The Pew (funny things that happened in church or synagogue), First Grade Jokes (clean, corny kid stuff), America! (funny stories about Americans), and Good News Only sharing faith in God and Jesus Christ; ALSO: (3) Great Shots! (photos of babies, kids, family, pets, action, news events that are cute, funny or unusual); and (4) Letters to the Editor (to 200 words) and (5) Op-Eds (to 400 words).

Some Do's & Don'ts:

- Don't preach. No devotionals.
- We do accept poetry (traditional or light verse to 16 lines) and short fiction (up to 800 words) but it's best to read "HT" samples to see what we like.
- The Religion section is more spiritual and wants articles on prayer, unity, revival and harvest.
- We run Special Emphases but they are usually tied into current events and rarely planned ahead.
- Internships/Volunteers: We are interested in talking to students interested in a career in our kind of journalism, for summer or school-year internships. We also have a small corps of volunteers who help with writing, layout, distribution, phone work, etc. "HT" is more than a business – it is a ministry to our nation, seeking to restore our godly roots – please call if interested!

Contact Information:

Dennis Lombard, Editor & Publisher
P.O. Box 16096
West Palm Beach, FL 33416
(561) 439-3509

Hopscotch For Girls

A WORD AT THE OUTSET

Every HOPSCOTCH contributor must remember we publish only six issues a year, which means our editorial needs are extremely limited. An annual total, for instance, will include some 30 to 36 nonfiction pieces, 9 or 10 short stories, 18 or so poems, six cover photos, and a smattering of puzzles, crafts, and the like.

It is obvious that we must reject far more contributions than we accept, no matter how outstanding they may seem. To you or to us.

With that said, we would point out that HOPSCOTCH is a magazine created for girls from 6 to 12 years, with youngsters 8, 9, and 10 the specific target.

Our point of view is that every young girl deserves the right to be a young girl for a number of years before she becomes an adult.

As a result, HOPSCOTCH looks for articles, fiction, and poetry that deal with timeless topics such as pets, nature, hobbies, science, games, sports, careers, simple cooking, and anything else likely to interest a young girl. But we leave dating, romance, human sexuality, cosmetics, fashion, and the like to other publications.

Writers

We are looking for lively writing, most of it from a young girl's point of view – with the girl or girls directly involved in an activity that is both wholesome and unusual. Examples have included girls in a sheep to shawl contest, girls raising puppies that are destined to guide the blind, and girls who take summer ballet lessons from members of the new York City Ballet.

While on the subject of nonfiction –remembering that we use it 3 to 1 over fiction – those pieces that are accompanied by black and white photos are far more likely to be accepted than those that need illustrations.

The ideal length of a HOPSCOTCH nonfiction piece is 500 words or less, although we are not about to turn down a truly exceptional piece if it is slightly longer than the ideal. We prefer fiction to not run over 1,000 words.

We will entertain simultaneous submissions so long as that fact is noted on the manuscript. Computer printouts are welcome.

HOPSCOTCH prefers to receive complete manuscripts with cover letters, although we do not rule out query letters. We do not answer submissions by FAX.

We will pay a minimum of 5 cents a word for both fiction and nonfiction, with additional payment given if the piece is accompanied by appropriate photos or art. We will pay a minimum of $10 per poem or puzzle, with variable rates offered for games, crafts, cartoons, and the like.

HOPSCOTCH buys first American serial rights and pays on acceptance. It welcomes the contributions of both published and unpublished writers.

Sample copies are available for $3.00 and a complimentary copy will be sent each writer who has contributed to a given issue.

Photographers

We use a number of black and white photos inside the magazine, most in support of articles used. Payment is $10 per photo and $5 for color slides.

Artists

Most art will be by assignment, in support of features used. The magazine is anxious to find artists capable of illustrating stories and features and welcomes copies of sample work, which will remain on file. Payment is $25 for partial illustrations and $35 for full page illustrations.

Incidentally

Although we are working far into the future, we occasionally have room for one or two pages.

One More Thing

We are in need of cute recipes, well written and illustrated crafts, and riddles and jokes.

Contact Information:
Manuscripts: Marilyn Edwards, Editor
Manuscripts: Virginia Edwards, Assistant Editor
Art & Illustrations: Becky Jackman, Assistant editor
P.O. Box 164
Bluffton, OH 45817
(419) 358-4610

Horticulture
The Magazine of American Gardening

Published: 10 times per year
Circulation: 320,000
Query response time: 8 to 10 weeks
Number of articles purchased: About 15 a year from the approximately 900 unsolicited queries and manuscripts received.
Rights purchased: One-time, first North American serial
Expenses: Reasonable expenses paid if previously arranged with editor
Kill fee: Depends on final fee

Rates:	Type of Article	Word Length	Payment
	Features	1,500-3,500	$600-$1,000
	Departments	1,000-1,500	$50-$600

The Magazine

Horticulture, the country's oldest gardening magazine, is designed for active amateur gardeners. Our goal is to offer a blend of text, photographs, and illustrations that will both instruct and inspire readers. While we place great emphasis on the style of our contributor's work, we believe that every article must offer ideas and illustrate principles that our readers might apply to their own gardens. No matter what the subject, we want our readers to become better, more creative gardeners.

We prefer that our writers, like our readers, have an interest in and some experience with gardening. We look for and encourage personal experience, anecdote, and opinion. At the same time, a thorough article should to some degree place its subject in the broader context of horticulture.

Query Letters

One page is preferred. Tell us why you think your idea belongs in *Horticulture* and give us the general outline of your piece. Please let us know your personal involvement with the subject. If the article will require research or reporting, give us a brief description of the work you'll need to do.

We appreciate receiving any other background material (photos, newspaper clippings, brochures) you have that will help us assess the appropriateness of your idea. We would also like to see a sample of your writing.

Queries with a seasonal angle should be submitted at least 10 months in advance of the proposed publication date.

Manuscript Submissions

We prefer that a query precede any manuscript. Manuscripts should be accompanied whenever possible by a computer disk. Include your name at the top of each page.

Thank you for your interest in *Horticulture*.

Contact Information:
Thomas Fischer, Executive Editor
98 North Washington Street
Boston, MA 02114
(617) 742-5600 • FAX: (617) 367-6364

The Human Quest

A bimonthly, independent journal of religious humanism, under the sponsorship of The Churchman Associates, Inc. It is edited in the conviction that religious journalism must provide a platform for the free exchange of ideas and opinions; that religion is consonant with the most advanced revelations in every department of knowledge; that we are a fraternal world community; and that the moral and spiritual evolution of man is only at the beginning.

Contact Information:
Edna Ruth Johnson, Editor
1074 23rd Avenue N.
St. Petersburg, FL 33704-3228
(813) 894-0097

Humpty Dumpty

(Please refer to Children's Better Health Institute.)

The Iconoclast

Mission: To serve readers stranded between the low intellectual level of commercial publishing and the arcana printed by the universities. To have a sense of humor. Not to have an agenda, save for the exploration of thought and emotion in the hope of reflection, leading to wisdom, personal accountability, and sheer delight.

Appearance: 28-32 8½" x 5½" white pages double-stapled, professionally photocopied.

Needs: Poetry and prose from writers more interested in the sharing and transmission of ideas, imaginings, and experiences than in career advancement or self-recognition. Impress us with clarity and sincerity of thought, not lists of credits.

PROSE: To 2,500 words. Subject matter and style completely open within the dictates of public taste—ask yourself: Would I read this aloud to my parents or teenage children?

No zealotry, militancy, cruelty, or intolerance—unless in the service of fiction—and then there'd better be a positive revelation. Needless profanity is annoying.

We like work to have a point (or more). We don't care for the 'slice of life' type of story, which reminds us of virtual reality, which, aside from technical applications, is a poor substitute for the original. Entertainment (as in humor, lovable characters, and unusual vertuosities) can, when well done, be a point in itself. Sensationalism or the gross cannot.

Please don't send preliminary drafts. Or work which leaves the writer indifferent.

One submission a month is quite adequate. Simultaneous/reprint submissions are OK. But be honest. We don't want to publish anything within at least a year of anyone else. Only one time publication rights are desired at present. Reports: 1 day to 1 month. OTHER INDICATIONS OF PROFESSIONALISM AND SOCIAL GRACEFULNESS ARE APPRECIATED.

POETRY: To 2 pages. Everything above applies. Try for originality; if not in thought, then expression. No greeting card verse or noble religious sentiments. Look for the unusual in the usual, parallels in opposites, the capturing of what is unique or often unnoticed in an ordinary, or extraordinary moment. What makes us human—and the resultant glories and agonies.

ART: Drawing is a lost craft among the populace. Maybe people just don't have the time or patience for sketching as a self-entertainment or communication skill. As a result, we're always starved for decent line art: simple black and white drawings to use as features, illustrations, cartoons, or fillers.

Payment: Generally—PROSE, 2 copies. ART and POETRY, 1 copy. 40% discount for additional copies. Monetary payment will begin six months after we've gone into the black.

Reality Check: People who buy, read, and subscribe to the ICONOCLAST keep it alive and available to those who seek publishing. This is not a government program, but an abstract community of folks interested in a freewheeling approach to life. No interest, no zine. If the ICONOCLAST is good enough to send your work to, is it good enough to buy?

Single copy:	$1.75
Subscription:	$12 for 8 issues (1 year)
	$23 for 16 issues (2 years)

Contact Information:
1675 Amazon Road
Mohegan Lake, NY 10547

ID Systems
The Magazine of Automated Data Collection

Thank you for your interest in writing for ID Systems magazine. ID Systems readers are buyers, specifiers, and users of automated data collection products. Our editorial mission is to provide them with authoritative and accurate information on that technology. Coverage includes bar code, magnetic stripe, OCR/OMR, radio frequency data communications (RF/DC), radio frequency identification (RF/ID), smart cards, touchscreen, and voice.

Feel free to contact Joseph Fatton, editor-in-chief, with your article ideas or for further assistance. Please submit your application/case history ideas on our ID Systems "Article Proposal" forms.

Following is a description of the areas in which ID Systems welcomes submissions:

APPLICATION FEATURES/CASE HISTORIES (approximately 1,500 words) profile automated data collection systems in use, and detail their benefits. Please include resources—listing name, address, and phone number of hardware and software vendors, as well as the systems integrator or VAR if appropriate.

TUTORIALS (1,500 to 2,000 words) address the educational needs of both novice and veteran end users by presenting overviews on current and emerging technologies. If possible, a roundup of available products, along with manufacturers' names and addresses, should be included.

READERS' SUCCESS STORIES (1,500 to 2,000 words) present first-person accounts by end users on installing automated data collection systems in their companies. (Please include photo of author.)

OPINION PIECES (500 to 700 words) offer issue-oriented viewpoints on technologies, industry trends, and events that are shaping the automated data collection marketplace. (Please include photo of author.)

Writer's Guidelines

Here are some style notes to help you write your article once your idea has been accepted:

- For application features and case histories, include the following:—Briefly describe company implementing the system, including annual sales or size.
- What problem was solved?
- Get details on how the technology was chosen, what its advantages are, and what technology or manual system it replaced.
- What system was selected (include details on computer system, printers, etc.) and why? Include the manufacturer, name, address, and phone number for all equipment used.
- What bar code symbologies and scanners are used?—To what computer is the system interfaced?
- How was the system set up, designed, and installed? Were there problems encountered during installation? How were they solved?
- What, if any, national or international bar code labeling or EDI standards apply?

• Has the system achieved payback? Anticipated payback? What were the gains in accuracy and productivity?

• What would the company do differently?

• Focus on the application, not the company.

• Look for attention-getting lead paragraphs and quotations from your information source.

• Obtain photos of the system in use—black and white or color prints or transparencies.

Important: Names, addresses, and phone numbers of everyone quoted in the article or contacted for the article should accompany your manuscript.

Additional Instructions:

1. Articles should be submitted on 3.5-inch disks (Mac format preferred), with data stored in straight ASCII or Microsoft Word, accompanied by printed manuscripts.
2. Color photos or transparencies (2¼ -inch format minimum) related to feature articles may be submitted as possible cover candidates, but consult with the editor first. Submissions should be professionally generated. Format should be 2¼ -inch or 4- by 5-inch transparencies. Photo submission does not guarantee acceptance.
3. Figures accompanying articles must be camera ready.
4. Submit a short bio of author.
5. Acceptance of article does not guarantee publication.
6. Helmers Publishing, Inc., requires transferal of all rights to accepted material.

Contact Information:
Joseph Fatton, Editor
174 Concord Street
Peterborough, NH 03458
(603) 924-9631 • FAX: (603) 924-7408

Illyria
The Albanian-American Newspaper

Illyria, the leading Albanian-American newspaper in the world, published every Wednesday and Saturday in both English and Albanian, seeks articles on almost any subject providing they have an "Albanian angle."

Articles are considered on current events, history, arts, science, sports, personalities, travel, etc. Please query first to discuss terms, length, payment, etc.

We also seek relevant photos.

Writers can query us at the Internet address below.

Contact Information:
Joseph Finora, Managing Director
2321 Hughes Avenue
Bronx, NY 10458
(718) 220-2000 • FAX: (718) 220-9618
E-mail: 73160.3256@compuserve.com

In Touch

GENERAL INFO

Emphasis is on the lighthearted, romantic, erotic, provocative and entertaining. No limits on sexual content or explicitness in fiction, although safer sex must be depicted. Please refrain from submitting stories involving fantastical characters (i.e. vampires, ghosts, Tarzan).

ALL INDIVIDUALS MUST BE 18 YEARS OF AGE OR OLDER WHETHER THEY ARE MODELS OR CHARACTERS IN FICTION. ALL SUBMISSIONS ARE SUBJECT TO EDITING.

Sample issue is $5.95/postage paid.

EROTIC FICTION ARTICLES

3,000 to 3,500 words
fiction or nonfiction
may be submitted on Mac computer disk or via modem (please call for details)
Fee Paid: $75

FEATURE ARTICLES

2,500 to 3,500 words
MUST BE PRE-APPROVED BY EDITOR
Fee Paid: $100

SHORT ARTICLES & CARTOONS

Under 2,500 words, size variable, short items, etc.
Fee Paid: $25 - $50

NON-MODEL PHOTOGRAPHY

Color or B&W prints acceptable
Slides or transparencies preferred
No Polaroid or Instamatic, please.
Fee Paid: $25 - $35 per shot

Submissions for Touch & Go are not compensated, unless prior arrangements are made

MODEL PHOTOGRAPHY

Call or write for Photographer Guidelines

Fees listed are for one-time usage, first North American rights, paid upon acceptance (photographs/illustrations) or publication (stories/articles/cartoons).

Thank you.

Contact Information:
Alan Mills, Editor
13122 Saticoy Street
North Hollywood, CA 91605
(800) 637-0101

Interrace Publications

INTERRACE (founded November 1989; circ. 25,000; bimonthly) focuses on issues concerning interracial, intercultural, interethnic couples—married or dating—families, and multiethnic people.

CHILD OF COLORS

(founded January 1996; circ. 5,000; quarterly) is a parenting/child care magazine for parents of children of all colors, cultures and ethnicities. Formerly *Biracial Child.*

BLACK CHILD

(founded September 1995; circ. 50,000; bimonthly) is a parenting/child care magazine for parents of African-descent children.

I. WRITERS

For INTERRACE, submissions . . .

1.) . . .must have an interracial, intercultural or interethnic theme.

2.) . . .can be nonfiction, news event, commentary, success story, research/study, personal account, exposé, historical, entertainment, music, art, literature, love interest, friendship, race relations, interview, fiction, short story, poetry.

3.) . . .are not limited to black/white issues. Interaction between blacks, whites, Asians, Latinos, Native Americans, etc. is also desired.

4.) . . .should be original. Previously published work acceptable.

LENGTH: Articles: 800-plus words; Fillers accepted.

PAY RATE: Subscriber-supported; advertisement-free; no payment; national exposure; can supply up to 5 complimentary copies and/or free one-year subscription upon request.

For CHILD OF COLORS, submissions . . .

1.) . . .must have a parenting or child care theme.

2.) . . . can be nonfiction, news event, commentary, success story, research/study, personal account, exposé, historical, multimedia reviews, race relations, interview, fiction, short story, poetry.

3.) . . . are not limited to black parenting issues. Parenting issues affecting whites, Asians, Latinos, Native Americans, multiethnic children, etc. is also desired.

4.) . . . should be original. Previously published work acceptable.

LENGTH: Articles—800-plus words; Fillers accepted.

PAY RATE: New magazine; no payment at this time; national exposure; can supply up to 5 complimentary copies and/or free one-year subscription upon request.

For BLACK CHILD, submissions . . .

1.) . . . must have a parenting or child care theme.

2.) . . . can be nonfiction, news event, commentary, success story, research/study, personal account, exposé, black history, multimedia reviews, race relations, interview.

3.) . . . are not limited to black parenting issues.

4.) . . . should be original. Previously published work acceptable.

LENGTH: Articles—800-plus words; Fillers accepted.

PAY RATE: $35- $50 for articles featured on the cover only; national exposure; can supply up to 5 complimentary copies and/or free one-year subscription upon request.

Please Note:

1.) Our staff is limited to two people, so please be patient and allow 4-16 weeks for review.

2.) Sample copies are $2 each.

3.) Include name, address, and phone number on submitted material.

4.) No vulgar or sexually explicit material considered for publication.

Contact Information:
Candy Mills, Editor
P.O. Box 12048
Atlanta, GA 30355
(404) 364-9690 • FAX: (404) 364-9965

Jack And Jill

(Please refer to Children's Better Health Institute.)

Jewish Currents
A Progressive Monthly

JEWISH CURRENTS prints articles, reviews, fiction and poetry pertaining to Jewish subjects or presenting a Jewish point of view on an issue of interest. Pieces submitted should be ideally 3-4 magazine pages in length but in any case should not exceed 5 such pages. (A magazine page contains, very approximately, 600-700 words.) Submissions must be accompanied by a brief biographical note including the author's publishing history.

Because of our very large backlog of fiction and poetry already accepted and awaiting publication, contributors in these categories are warned that it is virtually impossible for us to consider any new acceptances in these areas at this time.

Finally, JEWISH CURRENTS is unable to pay its contributors beyond a year's free subscription plus six copies of the issue in which they appear.

Contact Information:
Morris V. Schappes, Editor
22 East 17th Street, #601
New York, NY 10003
(212) 924-5740

Journal of Christian Nursing

Journal of Christian Nursing is a practical quarterly journal for nurses who care about the spiritual needs of patients and want to meet ethical dilemmas in nursing in a consistently biblical way.

All articles must have a strong faith component and be directed to Christian nurses.

Contact Information:
Melodee Yohe, Managing Editor
P.O. Box 1650
Downers Grove, IL 60515
(708) 887-2500

The Kenyon Review

The Kenyon Review

The Kenyon Review, an international journal of literature, culture, and the arts, is published triquarterly at Kenyon College, Gambier, OH 43022.

It seeks to publish the best new writing of established and emerging writers with a diversity of background, perspective, genre and style.

SUBMISSIONS: Only material offered for first publication is considered. Simultaneous submissions are not accepted. We consider short fiction and essays (up to 7,500 words), poetry (up to 10 pages), plays (up to 35 pages), excerpts (up to 35 pages) from larger works and translations of poetry and short prose. The original-language work must accompany the translation and the translator is responsible for author permission. We do not consider unsolicited reviews or interviews. Unsolicited manuscripts are read September through April. Review of submissions takes up to four months. We generally follow the *Chicago Manual of Style* and *Webster's Ninth New Collegiate Dictionary*. Authors planning to use end notes and/or citations may send a stamped, self-addressed envelope for our citation style guide. Send submissions to Submissions Editor at the address below.

PAYMENTS: (Per Printed Page)

Prose	$10
Poetry	$15
Minimum per poem	$15
Book Reviews	$10
Drama	$10
Translations	$10 to translator & $5 to author

Payment, plus two copies of the issue in which the material appears, will be mailed upon publication. Additional copies of the issue are available to authors at $5.00 each.

Contact Information:
Submissions Editor
Kenyon College
Gambier, OH 43022
(614) 427-5208

Kinesis
The Literary Magazine for the Rest of Us

kinesis *suff.* 1. Motion.

There's quite a relaxed atmosphere here at our editorial offices. One of our editors is cranking away at his computer every morning by 7:30am, another doesn't even show up until noon. There's usually a dog asleep under a desk somewhere. We like to listen to music while we work, and we put away endless pots of coffee. We don't have too many rules, but we have a philosophy — If it moves, print it! We don't have any "types" of writing that we will or won't print. We judge everything on whether it moves. It has to move!

What does that mean? It means we don't like inquiries. We'd rather see the piece. Inquiries don't convey movement. Only the actual words you've chosen can do that. It means you shouldn't be afraid to send us anything. Whether fiction, poetry, essays, book or movie reviews, illustrations or photography, we judge it all by the same criteria: Movement! Remember, the words you use, how you use them, is infinitely more important than what your piece is about. Please do include a cover letter with your submission. We like to know a little about you, it makes our day more interesting.

We realize this isn't all that helpful. You wanted guidelines and we're giving you philosophy and mumbo jumbo. What might be helpful is reading the magazine. That's the best way to learn what we're all about. Subscriptions are $20 for one year—12 monthly issues. Sample copies are available for $4.

We generally print 3-4 short stories, 6-10 poems, 2-3 essays and 2-3 book reviews each issue. In addition we have four columnists who write for us each month. We respond to submissions within 6 weeks, usually a lot sooner. Don't worry about length. If it moves, we'll make room.

We have a readership of more than 7,000 and we're distributed by subscription and sold in bookstores, art galleries and coffee houses. We're in stores large and small, including urban centers like Seattle, Portland, San Francisco and Manhattan; places like Spokane, Missoula, Sausalito and New Hope, and in many university bookstores, ranging from the University of Washington to Rutgers.

Payment — One year's subscription and 5 copies.

We hope to hear from you soon!

Contact Information:
Leif Peterson, Editor
P.O. Box 4007
Whitefish, MT 59937
(406) 756-1193

Kiwanis
A Magazine for Community Leaders

KIWANIS magazine is a monthly publication, except for combined June/July and November/December issues. It is distributed to the 275,000-plus members of Kiwanis clubs in North America, as well as to clubs in more than seventy overseas nations. Though KIWANIS is the official magazine of Kiwanis International and is responsible for reporting organizational news, each issue also includes five or more feature articles geared to other interests of Kiwanians and their families and friends.

Kiwanis club members are business and professional persons who are actively involved in community service.

Freelance written materials submitted to KIWANIS may deal with almost any topic of interest to an intelligent readership. Editorial need primarily is for articles on current business, international, social, humanitarian, self-improvement, and community-related topics. Other subjects of continuing appeal include health and fitness, family relations, young children's needs, sports, recreation, consumer trends, education, and transportation.

The magazine has a special need for articles on business and professional topics that will directly assist readers in their own businesses and careers.

Some of KIWANIS magazine's recent titles have included: "Operation Zero-Defect

Marketing," "Shots for Tots," "The Downsizing Myth," "Withstanding the Coastal Crunch," "One's Quest for Self-Renewal," "Farming Fields of Dreams," "Preventing Lead's Poisonous Legacy," and "Organ Donations: A Thin Harvest."

DEMOGRAPHICS

To help you identify the audience to which you are writing, here are some statistics on KIWANIS magazine readers:

- Median age—56
- Graduated high school—98%
- Attended/graduated college—87%
- Post-graduate degree—29%
- Median household income—$57,100
- Married—90%
- Manager—61%
- Professional—29%
- Owner/Partner—15%
- Own a home—88%
- Market value of home—$142,000
- Median size of company/business—26 employees

Articles published in KIWANIS magazine are of two general types: serious and light nonfiction. (No fiction, poetry, filler items, jokes, opinions, or first-person accounts are used.) Manuscripts should be between 2,000 and 3,000 words in length (eight to twelve pages, typed double-spaced). Payment is on acceptance, ranging from $400 to $1,000 depending on current editorial need, depth of treatment, appeal to the magazine's readership, and other factors. Queries are preferred to manuscript submissions.

Proposed articles are tested against two major criteria: (1) be about an overall subject rather than an individual person, place, event, or organization, and (2) have applicability in the lives and concerns of KIWANIS magazine's readership.

In addition, an article, when feasible, should be international in scope, providing information from various world regions. Writers should be aware that KIWANIS magazine is not an exclusively US magazine; it has readers in Canada, Europe, Central and South America, Australia, Africa, and Asia as well. Terms such as "our nation" and "our president" must be avoided. Articles on global topics, particularly if they have a strong bearing on current US developments, could be ideally suited for KIWANIS magazine.

In all manuscripts, a writer's treatment of a subject must be objective and in depth, and each major point should be substantiated by illustrated examples and quotes from persons involved in the subject or qualified to speak on it. The question "why?" should be as important as "what?" and perceptive analysis and balanced treatment are valued highly. Serious articles should not contain intrusions of the writer's views. Writing style should not be pedantic but rather smooth, personable, and to the point, with anecdotes, descriptions, and human detail where appropriate.

Treatment of light subjects must be as authoritative as serious topics, but humorous examples and comparisons and a lighter writing style are valued where needed.

An article's lead must be strong, drawing the reader's attention and setting the tone of the piece. It should be followed by a clear statement of the article's central thesis: Readers quickly should know what they are going to read about and why.

Manuscripts also should contain pertinent background and historic information, as well as a balanced presentation of issues. Firsthand interviews as well as research of published sources are essential. All information should be the most current available on the subject. And the article's conclusion should summarize the consequences of what has been said.

Photos are not essential, but they are desirable when they are high quality and add substantially to the impact of the text. Black-and-white photos should be 8-by-10 inch glossy prints; color transparencies and color slides also are used. All photos should be captioned and are purchased as part of the manuscript package.

Writers are encouraged to study a recent issue of KIWANIS magazine for a better understanding of the writing styles and story subjects used in this publication. To receive a sample copy, send a self-addressed, stamped (five first-class stamps) large envelope to the address listed below.

Your interest in KIWANIS magazine as a market for your work is appreciated.

Contact Information:
Chuck Jonak, Managing Editor
3636 Woodview Trace
Indianapolis, IN 46268
(317) 875-8755

L.A. Parent Magazine

Thank you for your interest in our parenting publications. For a sample copy, send $2 to *L.A. Parent* magazine at the address below.

L.A. Parent, *Parenting* (Orange County) and *San Diego Parent* are city magazines with a strong service-to-parent slant.

Always query first, to save your time and the editor's. Phone calls are difficult due to an editor's tight production schedule. A letter allows more time for valid decision-making.

Include one or two clips of previously published work. An unpublished manuscript will be considered but may take longer for evaluation. Even though your query may be rejected, you may be matched up with future assignments.

Recent titles published include: Is My Kid a Klutz? The Too Precious Child, The Public School Crisis, Bed and Breakfasts that Welcome Children, Nurturing a Creative Youngster, Evaluating Test Scores and Weird Places to Take Your Kids. The Woman's Pages section focuses on issues affecting women from home to the workplace. Family Health is a quarterly section devoted to children's and parents' well-being.

When dealing with generic parenting articles we often quote regional and national sources. Balanced reporting is a must. Local writers should quote San Diego and Orange County sources when appropriate.

Payment

Unless otherwise indicated, we pay 20 cents a word (see below for special circumstances). We will cover some expenses (phone calls, mileage at 25 cents per mile in excess of 20 miles, etc.), but these must be pre-approved by your assigning editor. Unless otherwise indicated, when we make an assignment it is with the understanding that it is for first-time use in all our editions (currently, *L.A. Parent*, *Parenting* and *San Diego Parent* magazines).

Feature Articles

The average length for a feature article is 1,100 words. We pay $300 for these stories. We reserve the right to assign a sidebar if, upon reading your manuscript, the editor decides the story would be incomplete without one. This is considered part of your assignment and is included in the flat $300 rate.

Flash Facts

From childcare advice on the Internet to the Daddy Saddle, Flash Facts covers what's new on the world of parenting. Writers should aim for a tight and breezy style.

- We pay $25 for straightforward product reviews; average length is 100 to 150 words.
- For more involved assignments (those that require field work or interviews), our rate is $50. Word count is between 150 and 300 words.
- Occasionally, we run lengthier articles (up to 500 words) on topics requiring more extensive research (Aromatherapy for Kids, Parents on the Net). For those assignments we pay our standard rate of 20 cents per word.

Entertainment Pages

This column includes movie, video, audio, theater and multimedia reviews. We generally do not cover mileage and parking expenses for these assignments.

Parenting People

These 200 to 500 word interviews profile individuals with something significant to say about the challenges of parenting. Typical candidates are experts and celebrities with a provocative and/or novel viewpoint. Bear in mind that we generally like to set up a photo session with the person you're interviewing (this can be tricky if that individual is a Big Star or resides in Tahiti). We pay $50 ($60 if you come up with the idea.)

Other Columns

Freelance writers are rarely used for Kids Cuisine, HealthNotes, etc. When we do assign out a story, we pay our standard rates.

Artwork/Photographic

We generally pay $50 plus processing expenses (not to exceed $12) for black and white photos. For inside color, our standard rate is $75. The cover is $300, expenses included. Stock photos used on the cover are paid at $150. Four-color fashion spreads are reimbursed at the rate of $350, expenses included.

Artwork/Illustration

For spot art we pay $50, $75 for more detailed line art.

Is the Check in the Mail?

You will generally receive payment 30 days after acceptance of the manuscript or artwork. We require that you submit an invoice stating your name, address, phone number, social security number and assignment to process your request. Failure to do so may delay payment.

Contact Information:
443 East Irving Drive
Burbank, CA 91504
(818) 846-0400

La Revista Aquino

Deadline:

60 days before publication date.

Payment.,

Upon publication. $0.05 per word for articles, plus 3 copies of the issue in which article appears. $10 each for each photo or illustration.

Photos

35mm color slides or 8" x 10" black and white prints preferred. Up to 8" x 10" if used as part of article. All black and white photos must have enough contrast for screening. Captions, subject identifications and model releases required for all photos with identifiable people.

Seasonal Material:

Submit 3 months in advance.

Article Length:

150 to 1,000 words.

Sample Copies:

Copies of each magazine available for $4 each.

Format Accepted.

3½" high density computer diskettes, PC compatible: txt files, WordPerfect, Word for Windows or PageMaker, e-mail.

Special Conditions:

1. All material subject to editing.
2. All information must be verified and is subject to revision.
3. All articles for which Aquino International pays will be copyrighted by those publications, First North American Serial Rights only, when agreed to in writing by the publisher. Otherwise, all articles will be the exclusive property of Aquino International.
4. Photographers may retain copyrights to their photos. First North American Serial Rights apply to all photos.
5. Signed model release must accompany any photo submission in which people are identifiable. Articles and/or photos showing models without release forms will be rejected.
6. Captions and identification of subjects required for all photos.
1. Aquino International reserves the right not to publish an article it has purchased and/or to publish it or republish it at a later date.

Tips:

1) We welcome material for our regular departments as well as for special editorials.
2) All nonfiction material must be factual and easy to read.
3) Familiarize yourself with our magazine. Send $4 for a sample copy. It will be sent to you by first class mail.

LA REVISTA Aquino focuses on Hispanic people involved in

1. Art
2. Fashion
3. Lifestyle
4. Entertainment
5. Travel destinations: exotic locales around the world. Anecdotes accompanied by off-the-beaten track photos, nontypical tourist spots.

Readers: Hispanic business owners, young professionals, bilingual people.

Illustrations and humor spot fillers now welcome. $10.

Contact Information:

Mr. Andres Aquino, Publisher
AQUINO INTERNATIONAL
P.O. Box 15760
Stamford, CT 06901-0760
(203) 967-9952 • FAX: (203) 353-9661
E-mail: aaquinoint@aol.com or aaquino@ix.netcom.com

Lakeland Boating

READERSHIP

Lakeland Boating is devoted to boating throughout the Great Lakes and the area that encompasses them. Principal areas of readership include Illinois, Indiana, Michigan, Minnesota, New York, Ohio, Pennsylvania, Wisconsin, surrounding Midwest and Mid-South states, and the southern parts of Ontario and Quebec provinces of Canada. *LB* publishes cruising features, boating-related technical articles, boat tests, historical pieces, personality profiles, photo essays, and other boating- and Great Lakes-related information of interest to readers in these areas.

Nearly 80 percent of *LB* readers own a powerboat of some type, the majority of which are 19 feet or greater in length; 20 percent of *LB* readers own a sailboat. Because of this ratio, *LB* orients most of its editorial features toward powerboating.

SUBMISSIONS

We prefer that contributors query an idea first rather than submit unsolicited manuscripts. Payment for articles varies according to length, generally within a range of $50 to $500.

Prospective contributors are asked to submit a query that outlines the nature of the proposed manuscript and explains why it would be of interest to *LB* readers. Please include at least two sample clips of previously published writings and any other personal and professional information that might be useful to the editor.

We prefer to work with freelance writers who are skilled photographers and are able to submit photography that will complement their manuscripts.

Regular features that are open to freelancer contributions include:

• CRUISING

LB publishes at least one cruising feature per month dealing with Great Lakes area ports, lakes, rivers, and other waterways.

"Port O' Call" articles, which are generally 2,000 to 2,500 words in length, should 1.) contain a good description of the port and its location, facilities, and particular attributes; 2.) provide a balanced, in-depth report on the surrounding area; and 3) describe what makes it a great place for a major cruising trip: location, scenic appeal, interesting history, things to do, restaurants, and so on. Include information on any other nearby places worth visiting.

"Weekender" articles (1,200 to 1,500 words) feature smaller lakes, rivers, and other waterways. They should 1) provide comprehensive information for all boaters, especially trailer boaters, about the area and how it's best reached by land; and 2) contain good information on launching ramps, docks, and other facilities in the area.

• GREAT LAKES HISTORICAL SUBJECTS

LB occasionally publishes articles dealing with marine and boating history in the Great Lakes region, including such subjects a s shipping, exploring, treasure hunting, shipwrecks, settlements, naval battles, and the like.

• THE ENVIRONMENT

Features about the physical character of the Great Lakes and the surrounding landscape are of interest to our readers, particularly the shorelines, water levels, pollution, marine wildlife, and so on.

• "BOSUN'S LOCKER"

Every month *LB* publishes this instructive, technically oriented section composed of brief tips and vignettes on boat and engine maintenance, trailering, safety, gear, weather, navigation, seamanship, marine electronics, and other practical subjects.

- **ANTIQUE AND CLASSIC BOATS**

Noteworthy antique boats and their owners; antique and classic boating events; and companies involved with antique boats are the subject of brief, photo-oriented pieces.

- **PROFILES**

LB publishes at least one brief article (approximately 800 words) each month on noteworthy individuals involved in boating and boating-related activity in the Great Lakes area. One photograph accompanies each profile.

MANUSCRIPTS

Macintosh users may provide text in WordPerfect, Microsoft Word, MacWrite, or Quark Xpress. MS-DOS users are asked to convert the text to ASCII format, or there may be difficulty in capturing all of the material. All page format (hard returns, justification, etc.) and printing commands must be removed. Writers who do not use personal computers should submit hard copy on medium-stock paper (no photocopies). *LB* will also accept manuscripts via telephone modem. Contact our office for procedures.

PHOTOGRAPHY

Photos of individuals must be accompanied by signed releases for use in the magazine. For production purposes, we greatly prefer receiving 35mm slides to color prints. Negatives are unacceptable. Please label slides with the photographer's name. Photos must be clear and well focused.

PAYMENT

LB pays for most contributions upon acceptance. Material scheduled to appear in a specific issue must be submitted at least eight weeks prior to issue date.

Contact Information:
Randall Hess, Editor
1560 Sherman Avenue, Suite 1220
Evanston, IL 60201
(708) 869-5400 • FAX: (708) 869-5989

The Lawyer's PC

Acceptance of an article for publication in *The Lawyer's PC* or *The Perfect Lawyer* is conditioned on the following terms:

The author would retain the copyright. The newsletter would have a.) the right of first publication of the article, b.) subsequent, multiple reprint rights, including electronic media, and c.) the rights to grant access to the article, its title and other bibliographic citation material stored electronically in public databases, and to furnish printed copies thereof requested through such public databases. If the author subsequently grants reprint rights to another publication, we request but do not require that the subsequent publication include credit for the newsletter as original publisher.

We presume the article is being submitted for exclusive consideration. We will not consider articles which are submitted simultaneously to other publications.

We reserve the right to change the title of any article accepted, and to edit the text of the article.

By submitting the article, the author warrants and represents that a) the author has included no material in the article in violation of any rights of any person or entity, and b) the author has disclosed all relationships of the author to any person or entity producing or marketing any product or providing any service referred to in the article.

We pay for accepted articles at the rate of approximately $30-50 per published newsletter page, at the end of the month of publication.

Contact Information:
Dan Harmon, Managing Editor
P.O. Box 1108
Lexington, SC 29071
(803) 359-9941

Learning®
Successful Teaching Today

Interested in writing for *Learning*? We're interested in you! Here's how to prepare and submit an article.

Learning articles must be written for teachers of grades K-8. Our articles generally fall into these three categories:

- How-to articles present techniques or materials that have proven effective in the classroom and that readers can use in their classrooms. These ideas must be innovative and fresh, not tried and true.
- Why-to articles analyze and evaluate educational issues, theories, philosophies, and trends in a way that provides readers with new insight and understanding.
- Personal experience articles tell either how you coped with a difficult person (student, parent, colleague, administrator) or how you overcame a situation that hampered your effectiveness as a teacher (curriculum constraints, unrealistic guidelines, difficult surroundings, and so forth).

To get a sense of *Learning*'s style, read recent issues, especially the articles similar to the kind you want to do. Please keep these tips in mind:

- Avoid jargon—use clear, simple language.
- Make your point with specific information, not generalities.
- Talk directly to the reader—keep the tone as conversational as possible.
- Please note that we do not publish worksheets, poetry, or student work.

Learning articles typically run from 500 to 2,000 words.

Send your manuscripts to the address below. Because of the high volume of manuscripts we receive, decisions normally take up to nine months. If photos are available, please indicate this in writing instead of sending them with the manuscript.

We pay between $10 and $300 for articles, depending on their length and quality. Payment is made on acceptance, and gives us the exclusive right to publish your manuscript. Articles will be edited to fit *Learning*'s voice and style. In most cases, we'll be in touch with you prior to publication of your article. Once the article is published, we'll send you a copy of your work.

Contact Information:
Manuscript Submissions
1607 Battleground Avenue
Greensboro, NC 27408
(910) 273-9409

Lefthander Magazine
Lefthanders International®

Thank you for your interest in contributing to LEFTHANDER Magazine. We welcome ideas and articles from both new and established freelance writers.

LEFTHANDER Magazine is an international publication with a readership of 35,000 in all 50 states and 12 foreign countries. The one thing they all have in common is a genuine pride and interest in lefthandedness as a way of life, as a personal asset and as a common bond with other readers.

Since our readers are in other ways a general audience, we print articles on a wide variety of topics, but always keying into lefthandedness as it relates to the topic. This is a very important point. We do not print articles that have no relationship to the specialized theme of our magazine.

We accept articles on famous people who are lefthanded, famous people who have achieved something interesting as a lefty, research articles on handedness and brain laterality, "how-to" articles on performing a specific craft or sport as a southpaw, articles on teaching lefthanded children and helpful tips to parents with lefthanded children. First person accounts involving the problems or rewards of being a lefty are published in our Perspective Department.

We will review all manuscripts received, but strongly suggest writers to consult us first with a query letter concerning the proposed topic. Payment for an assigned or accepted piece is due upon publication and LEFTHANDER Magazine purchases all publication rights unless otherwise agreed. If an article is accepted for publication and is not used, a 25 percent kill fee will be paid to the writer. Cover stories are generally paid at a rate of $100.00 per piece. Second features are reimbursed at $85.00 and Perspective pieces receive $25.00. Good quality color photos are needed to illustrate features. Some telephone expenses may be reimbursable if requested at the time of an assignment.

Please let us know if we can answer any other questions you may have. We are always looking for steady, consistently good writers and we welcome your contributions.

Contact Information:
Kim Kipers, Editor
P.O. Box 8249
Topeka, KS 66608
(913) 234-2177

Libido
Magazine

Dear Contributor:

To paraphrase Oscar Wilde, LIBIDO is a literary answer to a horizontal urge. It is a journal of the erotic arts and uses fiction, wordplay, photography, poetry, fine arts, essays, interviews and reviews dealing in sex and sensibility.

LIBIDO's guidelines are purposely simple and loose. All sexual orientations are appreciated. The only taboos are exploitative and violent sex.

Stories should be in the range of 1,000 to 3,000 words, with a maximum of 5,000 words. We accept submissions on disks compatible with Macintosh and Microsoft Word.

Poetry of all styles. (You should know, however, that LIBIDO uses very little poetry.)

Essays should be 1,000 to 2,000 words.

Reviews of current books, films, and music should be 400 to 800 words.

Black and white photos. We prefer 8"x10", B&W prints, but 5"x7"s are OK. We will look at slides, contact sheets, and portfolios. All photos taken after July 5, 1995 require a photo ID as well as model release, per federal requirements.

So send us your work! We'll use your name or we'll let you use a pseudonym. In return, we'll promote you, shower you with untold honor and glory, and send you two copies of your issue—along with lunch money.

Sincerely,
Marianna Beck & Jack Hafferkamp
Co-Publishers/Editors

Contact Information:
P.O. Box 146721
Chicago, IL 60614
(312) 275-0842 • FAX: (312) 275-0752

Light and Life Magazine

As the official publication of the Free Methodist Church of North America, *Light and Life* exists to serve the spiritual and temporal needs of the entire denomination by providing wholesome reading material that will inform, instruct, and inspire. It also serves as an outreach publication to help draw unbelievers toward Christ and the church.

The Free Methodist Church is an evangelical denomination of Wesleyan-Armenian persuasion. It originated in 1860 when the parent denomination failed to take a strong stand against slavery, make the gospel freely available to the poor, allow for freedom in worship, and preach and teach holiness of life. Today the Free Methodist Church reaches around the world with ministries in many countries. In North America seven colleges, twelve hundred local congregations, and a variety of social service agencies represent the ongoing efforts of the denomination to earnestly serve Christ and human need.

Though a denominational magazine, *Light and Life* welcomes articles from the broader evangelical community. Approximately 40 percent of each issue is provided by freelance writers. Every manuscript is evaluated carefully. We are able to use about twelve of every one hundred unsolicited articles we receive.

READERSHIP

One word describes this audience: diversity. Extremes exist in education, age, environment, vocation, interest, attitude, need, spiritual sensitivity, reading ability, and church background. In ministering to this wide range of readers, *Light and Life* must maintain a delicate balance of content. We want each reader to find something of value. We work to ensure that each article is easy to read, attractive, compelling, and crystal clear.

ARTICLES

We are looking for several types of articles.

1. First-person stories of God's help in times of crisis. Articles should be warm, dramatic, and should offer clear evidence of God's response to prayer and faith. 1,000-1,200 words.

2. Christian living articles. Fresh, lively, upbeat pieces about practical Christian living.

First-person, with touches of humor when appropriate. Show relevance of the gospel to everyday life. 500-600 words.

3. Christian growth articles. In-depth articles on subjects helpful to the maturing Christian. May include doctrine, Christian experience, relationships, human need, social issues, and the church. 1,000-1,200 words.

4. How-to articles. Practical pieces on various facets of Christian discipleship. Things like prayer, witnessing, Bible study, worship, the deeper life, and service opportunities. 500-600 words or 1,000-1,200 words.

5. Devotional articles. Brief pieces wrapped around an interesting anecdote and tie together with a poignant application. Use Scripture artfully. 500-600 words.

6. Christian perspective articles. Sound treatments offering a Christian perspective on key issues facing the Evangelical in contemporary society. Fresh treatments of topics such as family values, Christian social action, Christians and politics, and the sanctity of life should offer no pat answers but deal intelligently with each issue. 1,000-1,200 words.

7. Personal opinion essays. Skillfully written, expressing an opinion on a current topic. A good assignment for new writers. Past subjects have included prayer in public school, contemporary worship, and a Christian's response to secular rock music. 500-600 words.

We are interested in other articles as well. Study the magazine to see the kind of material and the type of writing we want. Be sensitive to our theological slant. Avoid preachy writing. Use lots of anecdotes and vivid expressions. We aim at an eighth-grade reading level. Be sure to thoroughly document every quotation, including Scripture versions. Any footnote-type annotations should be included within the body of the article rather than footnoted at the end.

SUBMISSIONS

On the first page place your name, address, and phone number in the upper left-hand corner. Place the number of words in the upper right-hand corner. One-third of the way down the page, give your manuscript title and your name. Include your name and consecutive page numbers at the top of each succeeding page. Include a cover letter to introduce yourself and the article. Allow six weeks for response. Send seasonal material at least six months in advance.

PAYMENT

Rate of pay is four cents per word. Your check and a complimentary copy are sent on publication.

PHOTOGRAPHS

Good quality black-and-white or color photos related to article are welcome. Include photo credit.

POETRY

We will consider short pieces only. Must be fresh, unique, and thought-provoking. Minimum payment $10.00.

RIGHTS

Light and Life is a copyrighted periodical. We copyright the "work as a whole" and not the individual articles. However, the inclusion of your article in *Light and Life* does satisfy the notice requirements of the copyright office in Washington, D.C. To quote a government guidebook about the copyright law of 1976: "the rights in an individual contribution to a collective work generally would not be affected by the lack of a separate notice as long as the collective work as a whole bears a notice."

We do not encourage submission of "second rights" or reprint articles. Such articles are very rarely used.

Light and Life buys one-time rights. We prefer first-time rights. Inquiries regarding reprinting articles that have appeared in Light and Life are always referred to the author for permission and payment arrangements. Reprints of our articles in other publications should carry a credit line indicating that the article first appeared in *Light and Life*.

SAMPLE ISSUE

Sample issue of *Light and Life*: $1.50.

Contact Information:
Doug Newton, Editor
P.O. Box 535002
Indianapolis, IN 46253-5002
(317) 244-3660

Ligourian

STATEMENT OF PURPOSE

LIGOURIAN is a leading Catholic magazine written and edited for Catholics of all ages. Our purpose is to lead our readers to a fuller Christian life by helping them to better understand the teachings of the gospel and the Church, and by illustrating how these teachings apply to life and the problems confronting them as members of families, the Church, and society.

AUTHOR'S GUIDELINES

1. Articles and stories should not exceed 2,000 words. Style and vocabulary should be popular and readable. Use an interest-grabbing opening, state why the subject is important to readers, use examples, quotes, anecdotes, make practical applications, and end strongly.
2. LIGOURIAN does not consider simultaneous submissions or articles previously accepted or published.
3. Topical articles should be submitted six months in advance.
4. Manuscripts should include name, address, and social security number. (No check may be issued without a SS#.)
5. Please allow six to eight weeks for our response.
6. We pay 10 to 12 cents a published word on acceptance.
7. Authors are advised to read and study several issues of LIGOURIAN before submitting articles.
8. LIGOURIAN receives over 200 manuscripts each month. Your manuscript stands a better chance of acceptance if it is carefully polished, and on a topic of special interest to our readers.

Good luck and we hope to be hearing from you soon.

Contact Information:
Editor
Ligouri, MO 63057

The Lion Magazine

THE LION Magazine welcomes freelance article and photo submissions that depict the service goals and projects of Lions clubs on the local, national and international level.

Contributors may also submit general interest articles that reflect the humanitarian, community betterment and service activism ideals of the worldwide association.

Lions Clubs International is the world's largest service club organization, with a membership composed of more than 1.4 million men and women in 178 countries and geographical areas. Lions are recognized globally for their commitment to projects that benefit the blind, visually handicapped and people in need.

The Headquarters Edition of THE LION Magazine, produced in Oak Brook, Illinois, is published 10 times yearly; December/January and July/August are combined issues. The circulation of the Headquarters Edition reaches approximately 600,000 readers.

Article length should not exceed 2,000 words, and is subject to editing. No gags, fillers, quizzes or poems are accepted. Photos should be at least 5 x 7 glossies; color prints are preferred. THE LION Magazine pays upon acceptance of material.

Advance queries save your time and ours.

Contact Information:
Robert Kleinfelder, Senior Editor
300 22nd Street
Oak Brook, IL 60521-8842
• FAX: (708) 571-8890

Listen Magazine
Drug-Free Possibilities For Teens

LISTEN is a magazine primarily aimed at teenagers, but some younger and many older readers are subscribers as well. It encourages development of good habits and high ideals of physical, social, and mental health. It bases its editorial philosophy of primary drug prevention on total abstinence from alcohol and other drugs. Because it is used extensively in public high school classes, it does not accept articles and stories with overt religious emphasis.

Published monthly, 32 pages, four-color. Circulation: 65,000. Reports in six weeks. Pays on acceptance. LISTEN buys rights to publish in LISTEN, in subsequent reprints and advertising excerpts. All material is copyrighted on publication. All submissions should include the author's social security number; submissions on disk are encouraged.

LISTEN regularly seeks professionally-written, teen-oriented articles and stories running 1,000 to 1,200 words, with a standard payment rate of 5 to 10 cents per word.

Five basic kinds of articles appear in each issue of LISTEN:

Narratives. These should be true-to-life fictional stories on basic conflicts and concerns that teen-agers face each day. They may or may not be related directly to drug use. Such issues as friendship, peer pressure, decision-making, family conflict, self-discipline, suicide have also been addressed.

Factuals. These articles should present current, accurate information on the nature and effects of alcohol, tobacco, and other drugs. A variety of reliable sources should be quoted; style and diction should be such as to communicate effectively with teenage readers. Recent subjects have been LSD, cocaine, designer drugs, alcohol advertising, smokeless tobacco, and the war against drugs.

Positive Alternatives. These articles should offer their readers activities that increase one's sense of self-worth through achievement and/or involvement in helping others. They are often categorized by three kinds of focus:

1. Hobbies - Recent subjects have been model railroading, bread baking, remote-control aircraft, amateur radio, baseball cards.

2. Recreation - LISTEN has recently featured articles on canoeing, orienteering, sky-diving, windsurfing, horseback riding, ice-boating.

Personalities and Organizations. These articles focus on teenagers and adults who, because of their achievements as well as their wholesome, upbeat drug-free lifestyles, may serve as positive role models for LISTEN's teenage readers. Subjects may come from everyday life as well as professional or amateur sports, the entertainment world, or public life. This kind of article also sometimes features organizations that are making positive contributions to drug-prevention efforts in their communities.

Self-Help and Social Skills. With this kind of article, LISTEN offers positive, practical ways in which teenagers may cope with everyday conflicts and develop self-esteem. Subjects may or may not have a direct connection to drug use. Recent topics have been handling spare time, learning ten ways to say no, coping with depression, handling stress, overcoming self-centeredness, getting along with a stepparent, etc.

Contact Information:
Lincoln Steed, Editor
55 West Oak Ridge Drive
Hagerstown, MD 21740
(301) 745-3888 • FAX: (301) 790-9734

The Literary Review
An International Quarterly

MAJOR INTERESTS:

TLR has an international focus and welcomes works in translation.

CONTENT:

Original Poetry, fiction, work in translation, essays, review essays on contemporary writers and literary issues. Review-essays should include a group of works of common interest rather than a single title.

LENGTH:

We have no length restrictions for fiction or poetry; however, long works must meet an exceptionally high standard of excellence. In general, essays should be under 5,000 words and reviews from 1,500 to 2,500 words.

STYLE:

We accept work in any format or style, ranging from traditional to experimental. We expect our contributors to have a strong understanding of technique and a wide familiarity of contemporary writing, but editorial decisions are based on quality alone.

NUMBER:

We read only one story, essay, or review-essay by an author at one time, and no more than six poems. A self-addressed, stamped envelope must be included for return of the editorial decision.

PRESENTATION:

Clear photocopies and dot matrix printouts are permissible.

TIME:

We try to advise of our decision within 8 to 12 weeks of receiving a manuscript. Accepted manuscripts usually appear within 18 - 24 months, often sooner, depending upon our commitment to special issues.

COMPENSATION:

Contributors receive two copies of the issue in which their work appears and are eligible to compete in our annual Charles Angoff cash award.

COPYRIGHT:

All material appearing in *TLR* is copyrighted. Authors are granted reprint rights as *TLR* only holds one-time rights to their work.

SAMPLES:

Sample copies are available for $5.00 U.S., $6.00 foreign, prepaid.

Contact Information:
Walter Cummins, Editor-in-Chief
Fairleigh Dickinson University
285 Madison Avenue
Madison, NJ 07940
(201) 443-8564
E-mail: TLR@fdu.edu

Live

ABOUT LIVE:

LIVE is a take-home story paper distributed weekly in young adult and adult Sunday School classes. It is freelance and has a circulation of about 160,000. The audience is Christian adults. We seek to encourage Christians in living for God through stories which apply biblical principles to everyday problems. Solutions to life's problems can be found in the Scriptures.

LIVE publishes fiction and true stories (indicate they are true). Poems, first-person anecdotes, and short humor are used as fillers. LIVE presents realistic characters who utilize biblical principles to resolve their problems scripturally.

WRITING TIPS:

We do not accept science or Bible fiction. The stories should be encouraging, challenging, humorous. Even problem-centered stories should be upbeat. Stories should not be preachy, pat, critical, or moralizing.

We accept first and second rights and reprints. Manuscripts are published about 1 year after acceptance. Payment is made upon acceptance but does not guarantee publication. Manuscripts may be edited slightly for clarification.

Plot: Stories should consist of action, not just thought-life; interaction, not just insight. Heroes and heroines should rise above failures, take risks for God, prove that scriptural principles meet their needs. Conflict and suspense should increase to a climax! Avoid pious conclusions.

Characters: Characters should be interesting, believable, and realistic. Avoid stereotypes. Characters should be active, not just pawns to move the plot along. They should confront conflict and change in believable ways. Describe the character's looks and reveal his personality through his actions to such an extent that the reader feels he has met that person. Readers should care about the character enough to finish the story. Feature racial, ethnic, and regional characters in rural and urban settings.

Style: Use precise, active, vivid verbs. Avoid overworked adjectives and phrases. Keep a consistent perspective (voice) on both time (past or present) and point of view (first person, second person, etc.). Avoid flashbacks.

PREPARATION OF COPY:

1. Type your name and complete address in the upper left corner of page 1.
2. Type the approximate number of words in the upper right corner of page 1. Indicate first or second rights. Indicate if it is a simultaneous submission.
3. Number each page and include the title and your name on each page.

WORD LENGTHS:

Stories: 800 to 1,600
Fillers: 200 to 700
Poetry: 12 to 25 lines

SEASONAL MATERIAL:

All seasonal materials should be submitted more than 12 months in advance.

PAYMENT:

First rights: 5 cents per word.
Second rights/reprint rights: 3 cents per word.
Poetry: $10 to $15

You will be notified within 6 weeks of receipt if your manuscript was accepted for publication.

Contact Information:
Paul W. Smith, Adult Editor
1445 Boonville
Springfield, MO 65802
(417) 862-2781, x4355

Live Steam
Celebrating 25 Years of Enlightenment for the Serious Model Maker

LIVE STEAM Magazine is a multifaceted publication that covers virtually all aspects of steam power. Its primary function is to serve the hobby aspect, however, and most feature article material is directed toward the hobbyist who is involved in scale model building.

Our readers are about 80% into large scale model railroading (mainly live steam powered, but often diesel and electric, too), so the content of the magazine reflects that percentage in its balance of content. Other interests, in a descending order of importance, are: stationary steam engines, steamboats, steam traction engines, Automotive steam, and miscellaneous other steam powered engines.

We often publish articles about prototypical steam engines (e.g. restoration and preservation projects, scenic railways, experimental projects, new technology, currently operating steam railways in other countries, historically important engines of all sorts). Our readers are extremely knowledgeable about these things, though, and any articles of this type must be written at a very sophisticated level. If you don't know a great deal about steam power, I would discourage you from writing about the subject without consulting with someone who you (or we) consider to be somewhat of an expert. QUERY FIRST is the best policy here.

We are not terribly interested in "people" features: we get more than we need, all unsolicited. There are lots of people in the hobby who may be particularly outstanding as modelers—at least to you, or people in your region—but there are truly superior modelers the world over who may very well be ten times the modeler that your subject may be. We know about them and most have already been featured. If you think you have found a modeler who is truly "world class," query us first and describe in some detail what this person's qualifications are that he should be featured in LIVE STEAM.

We are most interested in articles that describe how to fabricate something related to the Live Steam hobby. Length is of no concern in this sort of article. The important thing, of course, is to say it clearly, with enough detail that a modeler has no difficulty understanding all the steps involved. Following are some general guides for writing such articles.

COPY

The important thing is that your copy be written in the most logical and sequential manner possible. It should be detailed enough that a novice machinist/hobbyist can accomplish the task, given the proper tools. Use complete sentences. If you're describing a process or use of materials, please avoid idiomatic expressions or abbreviations that are not universally used and accepted. A bill of materials is highly recommended for any fabrication project at whatever level of sophistication. You may also want to list your favorite source for the materials you list. Owning a Machinery's Handbook may be the best investment you ever made as an author or as a machinist. It will aid you in many ways. We have both IBM and Macintosh computers here, so if you want to send your copy on disc, we can handle it. Be sure to send a hard copy with the disc, however.

PHOTOGRAPHS

Your photos can make or break an article. We strongly prefer black and white glossy prints. We can, however, work with color pints that have good contrast and a clear image. We would prefer not to have to deal with color slides at all, except for possible use on the cover. Cover photos are almost always slides. We do return all slides and prints that are used in the magazine. If you must use slides only, send them to us; we'll shoot the ones we want to use and return them to you. Avoid writing on the back of prints more than an identifying number. Do a separate sheet with captions and photo credits or attach a typewritten caption by clear tape to the bottom of each photo. Best of all, number the photo and refer to it in your text by its number. The size of the photo does not matter so much as the clarity of the image. When you are shooting your photo, stay back far enough from your subject so everything you want is in focus. Too close and your depth of field (focus) is very shallow. Also remember that you can never use too much light on your subject, though it is best to diffuse the light somehow to reduce glare off the shiny metal surfaces.

DRAWINGS

We are extremely picky about drawings! Most authors will simply send us sketches or blueprints of their working drawings and we have our draftsman redraw them to our size and line weight specs. Most important is that you double check for errors, whether they be in dimensioning or important omission of lines.

Make your drawings as clear and detailed as you possibly can. Even if we want to use your article, we may have to send the drawings back to you for more work before proceeding with publication. A construction article without drawings is virtually useless, so I would encourage you to include them whenever possible.

We do pay more per page when you furnish us with finished, inked, drawings that we can use without having to pay a draftsman to redraw them. You are welcome to try it, but don't be disappointed if we decide to have them redone after all your work. Take a careful look at the style of drawings already published in LIVE STEAM. Let them be your guide. Unless you can do your lettering with a Leroy template, just use a light blue pencil for dimensions and written information, and we will have it set in type here. You might attach a tissue (transparent) overlay and indicate the lettering and dimensioning there rather than writing on the original. All drawings you see published were reduced to half their original size. Whatever you draw would also be reduced 50%, so you need to scale your drawing so it fits on a published page comfortably. Basically, we stick to the ANSI drafting standards as a guide. You can get a set of those standards by writing to the American Society of Mechanical Engineers (ASME), United Engineering Center, 345 east 47th Street, New York, NY 10017.

We can also work with certain computer generated drawings directly off the disk. If you have that capability, and plan to send them on disc, we ask that you save your drawings to a TIFF file. Again, ANSI standards are the rule. Object lines should be twice or three times as heavy as hidden or dimension lines. Hard copies must accompany any disc, just in case we cannot read your computer language.

WORD PROCESSORS

We also encourage you to send us computer/word processor text both on disc and in hard copy. There are many benefits to doing this. It saves us having to have the text keystroked again. Also, your computer spell checker will clean up most typos.

OTHER THOUGHTS

When you're putting your article together, keep your drawing and photo numbering system simple; just begin with Number 1 and follow consecutively, whether it is a photo, figure, or table (e.g. Photo 1 . . . Figure 2 . . . Photo 3 . . . Table 4, etc.). Figures refer to drawings, charts, or other visuals not a part of regular text or photos. In most cases it makes more sense and less confusion than when there is Photos 1, 2, 3, etc., Figures 1, 2, 3, etc., and Tables 1, 2, 3, etc.

Regarding titles, you are welcome to suggest one for your article, but we do reserve the right to change and use our own instead.

You must use your real name, or an established pen name. We cannot use nicknames such as "Steamin' Sam," or "The Antique Amateur" (how would you ever be able to cash your check?).

LIVE STEAM buys First North American Serial Rights on articles published. We copyright all material except articles that are previously copyrighted by an author. Then that copyright is noted with the article. If you wish to have it published (reprinted) in another publication at a later date, it will be necessary for you or the other publisher to obtain written permission from LIVE STEAM before proceeding. We do not accept simultaneous submissions (where you have submitted your article to two magazines at the same time), and do not recommend the practice for any reason (at least to hobby magazines). We may, at some point, wish to republish your article again in book form, and we reserve the right to do so without further permission.

We do pay for articles published (see below). I appreciate your interest in sharing your knowledge and expertise with our readers. I am available by phone or mail to assist you. Thank you for your interest!

AUTHORS' PAYMENT RATES   Effective 1/1/93

Minimum per full published page	$30.00
Published photos with feature articles (each)$ 8.00	
Cover Photo*	$40.00
Published pages with finished drawings (not requiring redrawing by our draftsman)	$50.00
Short columns or articles less than a full page	$20.00
Filler items	$15.00
Book or video review	$25.00

Letters to the editor that get published are considered to be gratis.

Payment is made upon publication. The editor reserves the right to make payment upon acceptance in unusual cases, however.

* LIVE STEAM magazine rarely accepts cover photo submissions unaccompanied by feature article material, but will give them consideration.

Pay rates subject to change without notice.

***Contact Information:* Joe Rice, Editor**
P.O. Box 1810
Traverse City, MI 49685
(616) 946-3712

LIVING WITH *Teenagers*

Living With Teenagers

Living With Teenagers is a Christian monthly magazine for parents of teenagers. It focuses on the practical aspects of parenting, as well as informs, educates, and inspires parents to be aware of issues and understand their teenagers as they grow into responsible young adults.

Content: The editorial staff will evaluate articles dealing with any subject of interest to parents of teenagers.

Preparation: Cover page should include suggested title and blurb, byline, author's full name, address, social security number, and rights offered (all, first, one-time reprint).

Submit manuscripts 600-1,220 words in length.

Queries with writing sample are preferred.

Disk submissions must be accompanied by a hard copy. Prefer disk on a Macintosh word processing program, but can convert most IBM programs.

Writing Tips: Quoted material must be properly documented (publisher, location, date, and page numbers), along with permission verification.

Include Bible references and thoughts when appropriate.

Remember readers are parents of teenagers.

Use brief, clear sentences.

Construct paragraphs logically.

Sidebars helpful.

Payment: Payment is negotiable and on acceptance.

Publication: Writers will receive, without cost, 3 advance copies of the issue in which their manuscripts are published. Extra copies can be ordered from the Customer Service Center (MSN 113 at address below, or (800) 458-BSSB).

- For a sample copy, send a 9x12 manila envelope with your address and return postage.

Contact Information:
Michelle Hicks, Managing Editor
127 Ninth Avenue, North
Nashville, TN 37234-0140
(615) 251-2229

Log Home Living

Description

Log Home Living magazine is published 10 times a year for people who own or are planning to build contemporary log homes. It is devoted almost exclusively to modern manufactured and hand crafted log homes. Our interest in historical or nostalgic stories of very old log cabins, reconstructed log homes, or one-of-a-kind owner-built homes is secondary and should be queried first.

Readership

Our audience comprises primarily married couples between 30 and 45 years old. They are generally well-educated and very individualistic do-it-yourselfers.

Specifications

Log Home Living welcomes new talent and tries to develop long-term relationships with those contributors who consistently deliver quality work. We buy two to four bylined feature articles of 1,000 to 2,000 words per issue. These articles should reflect readers' lifestyles and interest in log homes as follows:

- Log Home Owner Profiles. Articles about people who have built modern log homes from manufactured or hand-crafted kits. In a conversational tone, describe the home as it is and tell how it came to be. Emphasize the elements that make this home special—intent, design, solutions to unique problems, features, furnishings, interior design and landscaping. Every story must include feature photos. Floor plans of the contemplated home, construction costs and schedules are a plus.
- Design & Decor Features. Photo stories on various architectural features of log homes. Stories can focus on a particular home or the same architectural feature on different homes.
- Historical Features. Articles about historical log structures in North America or abroad and restorations of same.
- Technical Articles. How-to advice about specific aspects of log home construction or pre-construction. Examples are scheduling a construction project, selecting wood preservatives, installing flooring, decorating log homes, dealing with subcontractors and innovative financing programs. Writers of these articles should be experts or able to interview experts and convey the information for a lay audience.

Submissions

Computer printouts are acceptable, but we prefer they be unjustified (ragged right) and letter quality. We will read unsolicited manuscripts but prefer an outline or a detailed query letter first.

Photos

Stories must be accompanied by extensive professional-quality color photographs of log home interiors, exteriors or construction shots as appropriate. See our Photographers Guidelines for specific requirements. If you are not a professional photographer, advise us in your query. Also tell us if you know a professional photographer who can work with you on an assignment; otherwise, we will locate one to accompany you.

Payment

Payment for features ranges from $250 to $500 (without and with photos), depending on their length, the nature of the work and the amount of editing required. We acknowledge receipt of submissions and try to provide an editor's response within thirty days. Payment is made within thirty days of acceptance.

Cancellations

If we determine that a submitted article requires substantial rewriting, we will pay a $100 research fee for the information supplied. If we decide not to use an assigned accepted article, we will pay a $100 kill fee.

Rights & Conditions

Log Home Living buys first North American rights and nonexclusive reprint rights. Upon publication, authors will receive two complimentary copies of the issue with their work.

We cannot accept responsibility for the personal safety or property of any freelancer while on assignment for the magazine. Writers and photographers are urged to have their own insurance in place while on assignment.

We assume that all contributed manuscripts are original and that all facts and quotes have been verified. Articles that have been published or submitted elsewhere must be so identified; in such cases the author is responsible for obtaining permission to reprint previously published materials prior to submission to *Log Home Living*.

Expenses

Reasonable expenses will be covered, provided that travel plans and all anticipated costs are discussed beforehand with the editor. A complete expense report, including receipts for all claims, should accompany the contributor's work. Expense reimbursement is made with payment for an accepted article.

Sample Copy

If you would like a sample copy of *Log Home Living* magazine, please send your check or money order for $4.00 to HBPI, Attn: Sample Copy, P.O. Box 220039, Chantilly, VA 20153.

Contact Information:
Janice Brewster, Executive Editor
4200-T Lafayette Center Drive
Chantilly, VA 20151
(800) 826-3893 or (703) 222-9411 • FAX: (703) 222-3209

The Long Term View

Editorial Philosophy

The *Long Term View* is a public policy journal which devotes each issue to a balanced discussion of a single topic or question. We provide a forum where academics, professionals, and other knowledgeable persons can make their information available to lay persons in a direct and readable manner.

To achieve this objective, we welcome submissions in many forms, including essays and analytical articles. Whatever the format, we want unambiguous, economical prose. We discourage the extensive use of footnotes: main points should be made in the text. Authors are responsible for the accuracy of all citations and data.

Manuscripts will be edited for clarity, brevity, and style. Topics for future issues of *LTV* are printed at the end of each issue.

Manuscripts Guidelines

Authors are asked to include a disk copy of their manuscript (along with the name and version umber of the software package).

Any footnotes should appear at the end of the manuscript.

Except where content and style suggest otherwise, *The Long Term View f*ollows guidelines set forth in the *Chicago Manual of Style* (14th ed., 1993).

Please include a separate cover page with your name, affiliation, title of manuscript, and a brief biographical note.

Direct all queries regarding topics, submission guidelines, and deadlines to:

Contact Information:
Lawrence R. Velvel, Editor-in-Chief
Douglas Velvel, Editor
Dermot Whittaker, Editor
Woodland Park
500 Federal Street
Andover, MA 01810
(508) 681-0800

The Lookout
For Today's Growing Christian

Our Magazine

THE LOOKOUT is a 16-page, full-color weekly magazine from Standard Publishing with a circulation of more than 105,000.

THE LOOKOUT is written and designed to provide Christian adults with true-to-the-Bible teaching and current information that will help them fulfill their desire to mature as individual believers, develop godly homes, and live in the world as faithful witnesses of Christ. In short, we want to help our readers understand and respond to the world from a biblically-based viewpoint.

THE LOOKOUT publishes from a theologically conservative, nondenominational, and non-charismatic perspective. It is a member of the Evangelical Press Association.

Our Readers

We have a diverse audience, but our main readership can be readily described:

• We have readers in every adult age group, but we aim primarily for those aged 35 to 55.

• Most readers are married and have older elementary to young adult children. But a large number come from other home situations as well.

• Our emphasis is on the needs of ordinary Christians who want to grow in their faith, rather than on trained theologians or church leaders.

Our Needs

As a Christian general-interest magazine, we cover a wide variety of topics—from individual discipleship to family concerns to social involvement. We value well-informed articles that offer lively and clear writing as well as strong application. We often address tough issues and seek to explore fresh ideas or recent developments affecting today's Christians.

A list of major upcoming themes is available on request (send a self-addressed, stamped envelope). Please query for theme-related articles. You may send complete manuscripts for non-theme articles and fiction.

Nonfiction. We usually publish four kinds of articles:

• Teaching articles (500-1,800 words): Help readers practically apply Scripture to present-day needs or show them fresh ways to grow in their Christian walk. Your article should provide either solid principles to help readers better understand your subject or skills to help them effectively respond.

• Informational and journalistic articles (500-1,800 words): We are looking for timely, well-researched articles, interviews, profiles, or essays dealing with topics of current concern. (List sources when applicable.)

• Human-interest stories (400-1,800 words): Let your unique experiences and observations help our readers see God at work in the world. Better yet, show us the experiences of others. Become a reporter and tell our readers about Christian individuals or families with extraordinary stories. We want to tell the stories of real people involved in meaningful service. Humor and brief inspirational articles are welcome.

• "Outlook" (350-800 words): Many weeks we publish a reader-written opinion essay addressing a current issue that concerns Christians. Address your submission to "Outlook."

Fiction. We print about 15 short stories per year. Fiction is usually 1,000 to 1,800 words long. Make your story wholesome, but true to life. Convey a message through the story, but don't preach. Plots should be about present-day situations. Humorous fiction is also welcome.

Your Submission

• Please query for theme-related articles. You may send complete manuscripts for non-theme articles and fiction.

• FAX transmissions are acceptable, but remember we cannot guarantee a reply.

• Please contact our office regarding electronic submissions (diskettes, e-mail).

• With your submission, please provide your name, address, daytime telephone number, social security number, and approximate word count.

• Allow up to 10 weeks for reply.

• Submit seasonal material six months in advance.

• THE LOOKOUT pays up to nine cents per word for first rights on unsolicited articles; up to fifteen cents per word on assigned articles (first rights); up to six cents per word for one-time or second (reprint) rights. We pay on acceptance.

• Simultaneous submissions are acceptable.

• THE LOOKOUT does not accept unsolicited poetry.

• To receive a theme list, send a self-addressed, stamped envelope with your request.

• To receive a sample issue, please send 75¢ and your mailing address with your request.

• Send all correspondence and submissions to:

Contact Information:
8121 Hamilton Avenue
Cincinnati, OH 45231
(513) 931-4050 • FAX: (513) 931-0904

LottoWorld Magazine
America's Lottery Magazine

I. EDITORIAL MISSION

Our mission is to be the nation's #1 authority on lotto playing. We will accomplish this through the pages of our magazine by providing our readers with the most original, thoughtful, entertaining and informative news and analysis of lottery games everywhere in the U.S. We will strive to provide our shareholders with a fair return on their investment, while maintaining the highest ethical standards. At all times we will treat our readers, suppliers, colleagues and shareholders professionally and with respect.

II. READER PROFILE

LottoWorld magazine is written for the 100 million lottery players in the United States, 42 million of whom play the lottery weekly. The magazine is distributed nationally and is designed for readers over 18 years of age. Every month we reach readers who play, or are contemplating playing, three, four, five, six or more numbered lotteries, including Powerball, Keno and instant scratch-off games. The wide-range of readers' interests in a diversified field of lottery play, dictate the versatile and wide-ranging contents of the magazine.

III. EDITORIAL GUIDELINES

We welcome insightful and unique approaches to lottery play—as long as they are plausible, playable and not plagiarized.

Prospective freelance writers should study the magazine as well as other literature currently available on playing the various lotteries (a bibliographical index is attached).

Articles should be typewritten with left and right margins of 1.5 inches. We encourage submissions via our on-line service (see address below). Articles may be submitted on a 3½ inch or 5¼ inch disk saved either in an ASCII format or WordPerfect.

We do not encourage blind submissions, rather we would prefer FAXed, mailed, or phone-in story idea queries directed to the assistant managing editor. All unsolicited articles are presented by the writer on speculation. Writers should expect to hear about the acceptance or rejection of their work as soon as possible. (Patience is a virtue.)

Rights: *LottoWorld* magazine purchases a contributor's right, title and interest in the article, including, but not limited to, the right, in any medium whether now existing or hereafter developed, to copy, print, reproduce, publish, sell, distribute, transmit, market, advertise and promote the article and the right to license the preceding rights. The rights granted to *LottoWorld* shall extend to all contracts to license or sell the article in all territories, in all languages and in all media throughout the world. Contributor agrees that it is within the sole discretion of *LottoWorld* to publish or not publish the article, change the text or combine the text with materials created by other authors.

Payment Rates: Payment is based on word count, complexity of topic, amount of background research necessary, number of interviews necessary and other criteria unique to each story assignment. Rates will be discussed when assignment is made.

Contracts: Once an assignment is made *LottoWorld*'s assistant managing editor will mail a contract to the contributor outlining the assignment, issue planned, deadline, word count and compensation rate. The contributor will sign, retain their portion and mail back the original copy to *LottoWorld*'s assistant managing editor.

Each issue is devoted to:

35% — playing systems, tips, strategies, techniques and research on how to improve the odds and chances for winning prizes and jackpots.

25% — technical system such as frequency (hot and cold number) analysis sum total analysis, ball set analysis, odd-even analysis, winning number prognostication and forecasts, wheels, etc.

25% — human interest stories about millionaires and general interest articles that advance the knowledge of the lottery player.

15% — lottery questions and answers, lottery software, astrology and lottery ticket sweepstakes.

Suggested Topics

1.) Human Interest - We want our stories to be compelling, original, exciting, informative, tragic, joyous (you get the picture) about lottery players winners and losers alike.

- Why people do or don't play the lottery.
- Interesting lottery history and trivia.
- Profiles on new millionaires — if they are of celebrity status or high profile — that's terrific.
- Know someone who wins consistently? Find out who, what, where, when, why and

most importantly, how they do it.

2.) Winning Systems - Strategies and systems to help the lottery player get an edge on the odds.

- Proof that lottery playing is not purely random number selection!
- Using hot number and other techniques for predicting numbers.
  Ways to increase your odds and chances of winning.
- Systems using astrology, numerology, bio-rhythms, horary astrology of combinations.

3.) Technical Systems - Frequency analysis, sum total analysis, ball set analysis, wheels, etc.

4.) Computer Systems - Software discussions/comparisons, track records, successes, etc.

5.) Lottery Clubs and Pools - Descriptions, advantages, success stories!

6.) State Lottery Stories - Successes, failures, interesting anecdotes, controversies, major personnel changes, unique new games and lottery trends at the state and national level.

Getting Started

You are our eyes and our ears! If you hear about any new and exciting lottery news — please call 1-800-223-6814 and ask for the assistant managing editor or FAX/mail a story idea query.

1.) If your query turns out to be newsworthy — we will make a story assignment.

2.) There are at least four levels where you can make an editorial contribution:

a.) Feature story of national significance (approx. 800-1,200)

b.) Feature story of state significance (approx. 200-400 words)

c.) News briefs (for our "Lottery News Roundup) approx. 75-150 words

d.) Scanning newspapers and periodicals for interesting stories about the lottery. Clip and send via FAX or mail.

Please take time to study *LottoWorld* so that your query will be appropriate to the content and format of the magazine. A sample issue of *LottoWorld* may be obtained for study by interested writers. Sample issue requests should be accompanied by a 9" x 7" envelope with five (5) first class postage stamps enclosed.

Contact Information:
Lynne Groth, Assistant Managing Editor
2150 Goodlette Road, Suite 200
Naples, FL 33940
(800) 223-6814 or (941) 643-1677 • FAX: (941) 263-0809
E-mail: vpyn24b@Prodigy.com

Maine In Print
Maine Writers & Publishers Alliance

We generally run two full-length feature articles. Word limits range from 900-1,600 words. We pay approximately $50-$75 upon publication; $25 for reprints. We cannot accept fiction, poetry, etc.

I prefer to see a one or two paragraph proposal, but if you prefer to send the entire manuscript, that is also acceptable. Our readers include writers, publishers, booksellers, editors, librarians, illustrators, and more. We print profiles, interviews, articles on the craft of writing (all genres), the business of publishing, issues facing booksellers, trends in publishing, small press news, and more. (Trends are of special interest to me.)

If you have any questions about *Maine In Print*, or these guidelines, please do not hesitate to write or call.

Thank you for your interest in Maine Writers and Publishers Alliance. If you are not already a member, please consider joining us.

Sincerely,
Lisa Holbrook, Editor-in-Chief

Contact Information:
12 Pleasant Street
Brunswick, ME 04011-2201
(207) 729-6333 • FAX: (207) 725-1014

Mânoa
A Pacific Journal of International Writing

Thank you for inquiring about *Mânoa*'s guidelines/requirements.

Mânoa publishes fiction, poetry, and translations; natural-history essays; occasional articles of current literary or cultural interest; and short reviews.

Fiction, poetry, and essays need not be related to Asia, the Pacific or Hawai'i in particular, nor be by writers from the region. We're as interested in Tennessee or Toronto as a locale for a story as we are in Tonga. Ordinarily, we are not interested in genre or formalist writing for its own sake, or Pacific exotica and picturesque impressions of the region. We also prefer to see five or six poems at a time, depending upon the length.

Translations are usually commissioned by a guest editor who is responsible for a portion of the issue; and that portion of the issue usually features writings from one country. The rest of the issue is usually reserved for North American writings. We may occasionally run translations other than the guest editor's, but you might want to query us first.

We do not have specific length, subject matter, or style requirements; like most literary magazines, we suggest reading a copy of the magazine to get an idea of what we like to publish. A sample copy is $10 (including postage); to order one, please mail a check with your name and return address information to the address below.

We value the reviews section of our magazine very highly and appreciate the effort that goes into a well-crafted essay. Reviews are on recent books in the arts, humanities, or natural sciences; usually, these books are related to Asia, the Pacific, or Hawai'i, or are published in these places. As you write your review, please keep in mind the following guidelines:

- Though we are university-based, *Mânoa* is not an academic journal; our readers are generalists. We encourage reviewers to find their own style and to clearly state their point of view, but we prefer to avoid academic language, theoretical criticism, and terminology that belongs to a particular field or profession. Our goal is to bring contemporary writing to the attention of our readers, particularly writing that is neglected by the major review media, such as the *New York Times*, and to do it in a stimulating and informed way.
- Please keep your review within a range of four to six double-spaced typescript pages. Manuscripts should be submitted with your full name and address on the first page. Please be sure to proofread carefully any direct quotations from the book. Using the format of the sample below, please list at the beginning of your review the book's full title, subtitle, author, place of publication, publisher, date of publication, number of pages, and price for paper and/or cloth editions.

PALM-OF-THE-HAND-STORIES, by Yasunari Kawabata, translated from the Japanese by Lane Dunlop and J. Martin Holman. Berkeley: North Point Press, 1988. 238 pages, cloth $19.95.

• Occasionally we may find it necessary to edit reviews for length, and we copy edit all manuscripts for clarity and consistency with house style. So that you may answer any queries our editor has and review suggested editing changes, we will send you galleys.

Please contact our office if you have any questions. We look forward to receiving your review.

Mânoa is published twice a year, summer and winter, and accepts submissions throughout the year. Submissions should be originals or good photocopies. Please allow about four weeks for reply on poetry manuscripts, essays, and reviews, and about eight weeks for reply on fiction manuscripts.

If you have any questions, we'll be glad to answer them. Just drop us a note. We try to reply promptly.

Contact Information:
Poetry, Essays: Frank Stewart, Editor
Fiction: Jan Macmillan, Fiction Editor
Reviews: Charlene Gilmore, Reviews Editor
University of Hawaii
Department of English
Honolulu, HI
(808) 956-3070

Marine Corps Gazette

The *Marine Corps Gazette* is the professional journal of Marines. It is a monthly that averages 88 pages per issue with a circulation near 40,000. Marine officers are the principal subscribers, but there is readership among members of other armed services, enlisted Marines, and retirees. The Marine Corps Association, a private not-for-profit organization, is the publisher.

The *Gazette* welcomes submissions from all military and civilian authors. Most of the publication's content is Marine Corps specific; articles on Marine policies, tactics, techniques, equipment, and leadership. Some material of a broader scope is published. There is no payment offered for unsolicited articles.

Submissions should be well organized and clearly written. Feature articles are 2,500 to 5,000 words and are approved for publication by the magazine's editorial board. Shorter articles for the magazine's "Ideas and Issues" section normally are 500 to 1,500 words, and are approved for publication by the editor. Letters to the Editor should be limited to 300 words or less. Book reviews should be 300 to 750 words. Many book reviews are solicited by the editor; cold submissions run the risk of addressing works that do not interest the magazine. The *Gazette* also accepts submissions for a tactical game section (interested authors should contact the magazine for information).

Material should be original and unpublished elsewhere. Authors who are accepted for publication in the *Gazette* are asked to sign a copyright form giving the magazine control of the material. As a matter of policy, however, the *Gazette* allows authors to make any subsequent use of their articles as they see fit. Because of space considerations, not all accepted material is published.

Authors are expected to guard against the use of classified material, though responsibility for security review rests with the editorial board and staff. If there is any doubt, your material will be submitted to the appropriate agency for a determination and deletion of any classified content.

Contact Information:
Col. John Greenwood, Editor
Box 1775
Quantico, VA 22134
(703) 640-6161

Marion Zimmer Bradley's Fantasy Magazine

Marion Zimmer Bradley's Fantasy Magazine buys well-plotted short stories, up to 5,500 words (yes, this is a firm limit). We prefer 3,500 to 4,000 wds, but we also buy short stories (under 1,000 wds). Stories longer than 5,500 words are bought by commission only.

We buy original fantasy with no particular objection to modern settings, but we do want action and adventure. The primary purpose of your story should be to entertain the reader; and although any good story has a central point behind the plot, the reader should be able to deduce it rather than have it thrust upon him. Fantasy content should start on the first page and must appear within the first five pages. We prefer strong female characters, and will reject out of hand stories in which we find objectionable sexism. We do not favor strong language because, although we ARE NOT a magazine aimed at children or young adults, we do have many young readers. Nonfiction should be queried; it is done on commission only.

Please read a few issues before submitting so that you can see the kind of thing that we do buy. For a sample copy, send $4.00 and a 9" x 12" self-addressed envelope.

PLEASE DO NOT SUBMIT:

Poetry, serials, children's stories, shared world stories, science fiction, hard technology, occult, horror, re-written fairy tales, radical feminism, romances (in which love, romance and marriage are the main motivations), surrealism, or avant-garde stories, or stories about God, the Devil, or "hearth-witches."

Beware of: "dime-a-dozen" subjects such as dragons, elves, unicorns, wizards, sea creatures, brute warriors, ghosts, adventuring sorcerers/sorceresses, thieves/assassins, or final exams for wizards. We get dozens of these kinds of stories every week, and we reject all but the truly unusual and well-written ones.

GENERAL INFORMATION:

- We do not accept simultaneous submissions or reprints (no matter how obscure the original).
- Do not resubmit a story unless we specifically request it. This applies also to stories submitted to *MZB* for any other market, such as SWORD AND SORCERESS. Since *MZB* reads everything herself, each story is considered for all the projects she's working on unless the author requests otherwise.
- *MZB* can not read small, dim or dot matrix printing, and if she can't read it, she can't buy it. Type must be at least 12 point, and we prefer Courier 12 typeface. Do not justify the right margin. Please underline any phrases in the manuscript which should appear in italics; do not actually use italics.
- If you need to know we received your story, enclose a self-addressed stamped postal card. If your manuscript is rejected, it will be returned as soon as possible. If we do not return

it within three months, we are probably holding it for possible use and will write to you as soon as we can.

• DON'T use Certified, Express or Registered mail; we haven't time to stand in line and sign for them.

• We buy only first magazine rights. Rates are professionally competitive, and we pay on acceptance. Send all manuscripts to:

Contact Information:
Mrs. Marion Zimmer Bradley, Editor
PO Box 249
Berkeley, CA 94701
(510) 644-9222

Martial Arts Training

Dear Writer,

Thank you for your interest in M. A. TRAINING, the leading magazine covering physical and mental training in the martial arts. About 90% of the magazine is written by freelancers, so your innovative ideas and dazzling prose are much needed and appreciated.

Before sending a complete article to M. A. TRAINING, however, it is advisable to send a query letter, outlining your proposed topic. If the subject fits our format, and has not been covered too recently, you may then be asked to send the complete manuscript with photos.

What is the magazine's format? MAT does not deal with self defense techniques. Instead, we focus on the conditioning that allows a martial artist to execute those techniques to their fullest. This includes training drills, exercise tips, workouts with new or home-built training tools and advice on injury prevention, etc.

Articles focusing on drills for increased speed, strength, agility, power, etc., are the most likely to be accepted right now. The content ratio should be 4/5 (or more) drill how-to and no more than 1/5 telling the importance of the drills, physiological explanations or quotes. Do not include self-defense techniques except if necessary to briefly explain how the exercises are applicable. Also, do not identify the exercises as being from, or for, a specific martial art. M. A. TRAINING's articles are meant to be for martial artists of all styles.

Articles should be about 2,000 words long or slightly shorter if many photos accompany the piece. Because our manuscripts are scanned electronically, do not send dot-matrix submissions. Articles should not be written in first person ("I train this way. This happened to me," etc.). Do, however, include a short "about the author" to run after the article.

Though you may initially send a manuscript without photos for consideration, photos must be provided for final acceptance. (Usually, photos are not purchased without a manuscript.) The photos, which may be black and white or color, should be clear, well-lit and in focus. The subject should contrast with the background. Photos should illustrate the training techniques in the story and should include a general lead shot. Model release forms should accompany the photos. We will gladly send a copy of our model release form if requested.

Payment for an article and accompanying photos is approximately $125 - $175 for all rights. If you have further questions about M. A. TRAINING, please feel welcome to write or call.

Sincerely,
Doug Jeffrey, Executive Editor

Contact Information:
24715 Avenue Rockefeller
Valencia, CA 91355
(800) 423-2874 or (805) 257-4066 • FAX: (805) 257-3028

May Trends

MAY TRENDS is a free-subscription publication edited specifically for executives involved in the management of medium and small-sized business. Its purpose is to help identify economic, marketing and technological trends that have an impact on small companies and to present the ideas and viewpoints of individuals familiar with small business challenges. Publication dates are kept flexible to accommodate the bust schedules of the nationally-known leaders and authors who often contribute articles.

We also accept articles by business and technical writers, if the material is particularly germane to the interests of owners and managers of medium and small-sized businesses.

Articles submitted for consideration should be 2,000 to 3,000 words, targeted toward small business interests, and submitted on speculation. We pay $150 to $500 on publication, and with this buy publishing rights and release for use in the management consulting field.

TRENDS does not accept or publish articles in areas concerning legal matters, taxes or regulations relating to banks or savings and loan associations. We do not use cartoons, serialized reports, informational/opinion columns or news releases, nor do we review books. Occasional filler pieces (500 to 750 words) are accepted at the rate of $75 on publication.

Send submissions on business subjects related to the interests of owners and managers of small/medium sized businesses to:

Contact Information:
Rosalind J. Angell, Editor
303 South Northwest Highway
Park Ridge, IL 60068-4255
(708) 825-8806

McCall's

Thank you for your inquiry. All manuscripts are submitted on speculation at the author's risk. Manuscripts are usually read and processed within 6 to 8 weeks. Study recent back issues carefully before submitting work. Articles dealing with food, fashion, beauty and home decorating are staff-produced. *McCall's* purchases material in the following categories:

ARTICLES: *McCall's* is in the market for first person, as-told-to human interest narratives, self-help and popular psychology articles, and articles about social issues or trends. These articles usually run 1,200 to 2,000 words. We also need consumer-oriented pieces of approximately 750 words, and work-related pieces of approximately 1,400 words. In addition, our "Love Lessons" column publishes first person essays of approximately 1,400 words describing true stories that convey a useful maxim about love. Finally, in our "Families" column, we publish "how-to" articles of approximately 1400 words on topics of interest to parents.

HEALTH: "Health Sense" publishes short, newsy items. "Better Health" is a one-page column publishing stories of approximately 600 words on health/medical topics. In "Medical Report," we are looking for topics that will sustain lengthier articles (approximately 1200 words, and sometimes more). For both columns, we are interested in recent research and useful information of interest to a large number of women.

EXTRA: This special section of *McCall's* will appear six times a year and go only to subscribers in the 50 to 64 age bracket. We are offering these "prime of life" readers upbeat, interesting articles on health, finance, self-help, beauty and travel. We also consider personal essays. Overall, our focus will not be on aging but on living life to its fullest. Articles and essays should run between 800 and 1000 words. Send a query letter first. Pay varies. Address queries to EXTRA Edition Editor.

Contact Information:
General Articles: Jane Farrell, Senior Editor
Health: Ann Ranard, Health Editor
Parenting, Travel: Laura Manske, Contributing Editor
110 Fifth Avenue
New York, NY 10011
(212) 463-1000

Message Magazine

Thank you for your interest in MESSAGE Magazine. MESSAGE is the oldest and most widely circulated religious journal addressing ethnic issues in the USA. We work hard to preserve our unique role interpreting current events through a Black, Christian perspective. We're happy you want to be a part of this powerful ministry.

GET TO KNOW MESSAGE

- Published: Bimonthly, in a 32-page format, by The Review and Herald® Publishing Association. Sponsored by the Seventh-Day Adventist Church.
- Audience: Predominantly Black and Seventh-Day Adventist. *Message* is, however, a missionary journal geared for the unchurched.
- Lead time: When submitting seasonal material, remember our production schedule requires us to work four to six months ahead.
- Payments: *Message* pays upon acceptance.
- Rights: *Message* purchases first rights to all articles. Each article should carry a credit line for *Message* when reprinted elsewhere.

WHAT TO WRITE

- *Message* publishes: informational, devotional, inspirational, doctrinal, profile, interview and self-help articles that have wide appeal to people of many backgrounds.
- *Message* does not accept: sermons, outlines, poetry, reprints, or anything that is not in an article format.
- Topics include: biblical exposition, celebrity and humanitarian profiles, family, health, education, worship, news and current events, religious freedom and racial reconciliation. Often our writers query us by phone about article ideas. Feel free to call and bounce an idea off the editors.

Departments

Message also accepts freelance material for the following departments:

- Healthspan—This 700 word column covers a variety of health topics of interest to our audience. It is typically accompanied by a sidebar or chart.
- Message Jr—Our column reserved for children, ages 5 to 8, is no longer than 500 words. We prefer biblical stories, but stories with a clear-cut moral are also accepted.

HOW TO GET PUBLISHED

Nine ways to woo our editors:

- Make sure your article is biblically sound and offers spiritual perspective and insight.
- Support your material with facts, statistics and quotes from experts.
- Invite the reader to reads your whole story by writing an interesting lead.

- Sharpen your focus. Sometimes writing a title, subtitles and subheadings helps.
- Use interesting, fresh, insightful angles to old topics. Say something new.
- Take a position, make a point, stick to the point, then cut to the chase.
- Write about timely topics and events.
- Answer the underlying, heartfelt questions a reader may have about your topic.
- Be a good storyteller. Make people and places come alive by expressing details.

How to submit a manuscript

- Submit articles no longer than five pages.
- Enclose your name, address, and social security number.
- Enclose a line about yourself.
- We greatly appreciate manuscripts on computer disk with a WordPerfect (PC) format, along with the hard copy.
- You will be notified by postcard that we have received your manuscript. If your article is accepted, you will be notified within six to eight weeks.

Contact Information:
Stephen P. Ruff, Editor
55 West Oak Ridge Drive
Hagerstown, MD 21740
(301) 791-7000, x2565 • FAX: (301) 714-1753

MetroSports Magazine

So you want to write for *MetroSports* Magazine. We're flattered, and we encourage you to submit your work. To help make your efforts successful, we offer the following guidelines.

1. Think regional. Our coverage consists primarily of sports, activities, and personalities in the Northeast, although we will consider travel pieces. Of course, many topics are not bound by geographic restraints. Such topics include fitness, health, and nutrition issues, technological pieces, and trends in sports and lifestyles.

2. If you would like to be considered to write a piece, please submit writing samples and a brief summary of how you plan to cover your topic. Remember that you're writing for a knowledgeable, fit, and upscale consumer audience. Feel free to submit your story ideas.

3. Sign on the dotted line. If *MetroSports* decides to contract you on a freelance basis, you may be asked to work closely with the editors throughout the planning, writing, and revision process. *MetroSports* reserves the right to kill a story at any time. We ask that the story be submitted on paper and on disk (call ahead for format) via Priority Mail 2-day from the Post office. *MetroSport*'s pay scale for freelancers varies and should be discussed with the publisher prior to submission.

Good luck. We hope to work with you in the future. Call me anytime if you would like to come down to *MetroSports* and discuss story ideas.

Sincerely,

Dave Levine, Editor

Contact Information:
27 West 24th Street, Suite 10B
New York, NY 10010
(212) 627-7040 • FAX: (212) 627-7446

MidWest Outdoors

DEADLINE SCHEDULE Remember: THE EARLIER THE BETTER!

Main Section: 35 Days Preceding Publication. Example: April 25th for the June issue. Subscribers receive the issue the 28th and newsstand sales start the 1st.

Iowa, Michigan, Minnesota, Wisconsin and Indiana Sections: 1st of the Month Preceding Publication. Example: May 1st for the June issue.

Northern and Southern Illinois Section: 5th of the Month Preceding Publication. Example: May 5th for the June issue.

Writing for state sections would be the best way for first time writers to break into *MidWest Outdoors*.

EDITORIAL REQUIREMENTS

MidWest Outdoors is interested in where to go and how to do it stories on outdoor recreation in the Midwest—an area encompassing a 10 to 15 hour drive from Chicago. Material should provide information the outdoorsman can use in his immediate vicinity and in areas he can travel to on weekends or a short vacation.

The accent in *MidWest Outdoors* is on •FISHING •HUNTING •CAMPING

Related subjects are hunting dogs, archery, boats, snowmobiling, trap shooting, skeet shooting and canoeing.

Keep in mind that you are writing for publication two to three months in the future, and your subject matter should reflect that time lapse. Spring fishing articles should be submitted in January, February and march; fall hunting articles in July and August. Illinois turkey hunting, for example, is in April, but turkey stories should be printed as early as February because that's when hunters must apply for permits. We never want to lose sight of our primary goal which is to provide useful information for the reader.

Any material accepted is subject to such revision as is necessary to meet the requirements of this publication.

Some materials may be held over several months or years before being published.

Please include a title of the article on each page. Also include an overline or subtitle (example: Walleye Hotspot - Fox River Spring Madness). Include a byline and page number on each page and please include your social security number. If you submit a timely item, please indicate the month for suggested use.

MAIN VS. STATE SECTION REQUIREMENTS

MAIN SECTION EDITORIAL should be general in tone. The Main section is seen and read by people throughout the Midwest. Please keep facts such as fishing regulations or opening dates out of your material or specify the areas such rules are intended for. Example: readers in Iowa or Illinois would be confused by length requirements for Wisconsin northern pike.

STATE SECTION EDITORIAL should focus on one state exclusively or be written for one particular region.

Example for a good state story: bass fishing on the Illinois River for the Illinois section.

Example for a good regional story: fishing Wisconsin's southern lakes for the Wisconsin and Illinois sections.

THE MIDWEST OUTDOORS PHILOSOPHY

MidWest Outdoors is in business to help people enjoy the outdoors, so keep your writing positive. The outdoors is a great experience. *MidWest Outdoors* does not dwell on pollution, poaching, bad manners, etc. Please do not be critical of lakes, products or services. If you do mention a product, service or resort, please give us a contact name for possible advertising.

Never write two or three part stories or refer to previous articles. When you do this, we get swamped with requests for back issues. Do not promise readers that you will cover an event next month.

SPECIAL EDITIONS

EDITION	SUBJECT	DEADLINE
IceBreakers	The most comprehensive ice fishing manual in the Midwest	Oct. 1st
Canada Fever	The only two months *MidWest Outdoors* features Canadian editorial.	Dec.1st and Jan. 1st
Great Lakes	An in-depth look at the lakes which make the Midwest so rich in opportunity for the outdoorsman.	Feb. 1st

THE MIDWEST OUTDOORS DIFFERENCE

The difference between *MidWest Outdoors* and the rest of the magazine pack is helpful, practical information about the area you live in. You will never read about African lion hunts or blue marlin fishing in the Caribbean. *MidWest Outdoors* covers the information our readers can use, so they can enjoy the outdoors without wasting a lot of time or money.

The reason *MidWest Outdoors* has continued to grow for the past 29 years is simple. We have over 200 top-notch writers who know their areas and their sport better than any group of men in the Midwest. Our staff writers, recognized as the best in the business, love to help other outdoorsmen catch more fish and bag more game.

MidWest Outdoors covers the area where readers live with a tremendous amount of information. *MidWest Outdoors* is the one magazine that gives the information a Midwest outdoorsman can use. We want *MidWest Outdoors* to be a great value for our readers.

SPECIFIC REQUIREMENTS FOR *MIDWEST OUTDOORS*

STORIES . . .

- should be accompanied by black and white or color photos or slides
- should be between 600 and 1,500 words - with shorter stories preferred. The story's focus should be where to and how to. Stories should impart information in an entertaining fashion, and not in a text book or preachy tone.
- should be prepared with the top sheet as illustrated below.

- IF YOU PRODUCE YOUR MATERIAL ON A MACINTOSH, IBM OR IBM COMPATIBLE COMPUTER, WE WILL ACCEPT 3½" DISKS. PLEASE SEND HARD COPY WITH THE DISK SO MIDWEST OUTDOORS CAN BE SURE YOUR WORK IS COMPATIBLE WITH OUR SYSTEM REQUIREMENTS.

PHOTOS . . .

- *MidWest Outdoors* can accept color or black and white photos or color slides. A good photo is usually one that catches the action of some outdoor pursuit.
- Please send no more than 3 to 4 photos per story.
- YOU MUST PLACE YOUR RETURN ADDRESS ON THE BACK OF THE PHOTO IF YOU WANT IT RETURNED. Caption sheet, with the title of the story it accompanies should be taped to the back of the photo. There is no better way to ensure that your photo will not be used with another writer's story.

MAPS . . .

- are a great way to visually tell where the lake, pond or river is located and where the fish are located in the body of water. DEFINITELY A PLUS FOR FIRST TIME WRITERS.

TOP SHEET ILLUSTRATION

Joe Writer		Submitted January, 1995
123 Main Street	Approx. 900 words-(4) pages	For use in March, 1995
Anytown, IL 60000	One (1) 8x10 B/W: Walleye on line	
SS#450-59-8943	One (1) 8x10 B/W: Man holding walleye	
	See back of photo and/or page 4 for captions	
	THE SOUTHERN ILLINOIS SCENE	

IMPORTANT CHECKLIST BEFORE SENDING IN MATERIAL

- Your name is on all pages and photos.
- You have included your social security number.
- You have indicated what month the material is for.
- You have written a headline and subline.
- You have written a caption for each photo.

PLEASE REMEMBER: If we do not plan on using your material, it will be returned to you within 10 days of receipt. The best check to have for knowing if we have used your material is if you receive a check from *MidWest Outdoors*.

Contact Information:
Gene Laulunen, Publisher
Carolyn Figge, Assistant Editor
111 Shore Drive
Burr Ridge, IL 60521-5885
(708) 887-7722

Military History

(Please refer to Cowles History Group.)

Miniature Quilts

(Please refer to Chitra Publications.)

Minority Engineer

(Please refer to Equal Opportunity Publications.)

The Missouri Review

The editors invite submissions of poetry, fiction and essays of general interest (no literary criticism). Please clearly mark the outer envelope as fiction, poetry or essay. Do not mix genres within the same submission.

Previously unpublished material only. Standard response time is from 10-12 weeks. Manuscripts are read year round. Sample copies are available for $7.00.

POETRY

MR publishes poetry features only—6 to 12 pages of poems by each of 3 to 5 poets per issue. Please keep in mind the length of features when submitting poems. No multiple submissions.

The McAfee Discovery Feature in poetry is an ongoing series, awarded at least once a year at the discretion of the editors, to showcase the work of an outstanding new poet who has not yet published a book. This award is chosen from among regular submissions. There are no deadlines and no application process. This feature carries an additional cash award beyond the regular payment schedule and has been funded by the family and friends of Tom McAfee.

FICTION

While there are no length restrictions, "flash fictions" are rarely accepted. We recommend that writers familiarize themselves with fiction from previous issues before submitting.

The William Peden Prize is a $1,000 prize awarded annually to the best piece of fiction to have appeared in the previous volume year. The winner is chosen by an outside judge from stories published in *MR*. There is no separate application process.

ESSAYS

Essays of general interest only. There are no restrictions on length or topic, but we suggest that writers familiarize themselves with essays from previous issues. Queries are welcome. Excerpts from book-length creative nonfiction manuscripts will be considered.

EDITORS' PRIZE

MR sponsors an annual Editors' Prize Contest in fiction, essay and poetry, with a winner and 3 finalists named in each category. Length restrictions are 25 pages for fiction and essay, 10 pages for poetry. Winners receive $1,000 plus publication in fiction and essay; $500 in poetry. Postmark deadline is October 15. A $15 fee per submission includes a one-year subscription to *MR*. Query for details beginning in late summer.

Contact Information:
Fiction Editor/Poetry Editor/Essay Editor
1507 Hillcrest Hall
University of Missouri
Columbia, MO 65211
(573) 882-4474

Modern Dad
For a New Generation of Fathers

Thank you for your interest in writing for *Modern Dad*. As we are a new publication, the majority of the articles will be written by people like yourself who are interested in men and their roles as fathers. We encourage you to familiarize yourself with *Modern Dad* and its goals. The more informed you are as a writer, the better prepared you will be to produce an appropriate article.

Modern Dad addresses the aspects of being Modern man and a Dad in today's information age. We publish articles that aid, educate and inform our readership on subjects that might be of interest to them. *Modern Dad*, a bimonthly publication, has the following sections:

FEATURE articles in *Modern Dad* value fathering *and* the family and explore all the possibilities of fatherhood in the '90s. Men want to be independent role models for their children and to feel that they are an important part of the family. The FEATURES section provides them with informative and entertaining articles designed to strengthen their fathering skills and keep dads in-the-loop.

OCCUPATION: DAD contains the tools and guidance necessary to enhance their fathering skills. This section spotlights the concerns and interests of fathers in their desire to raise happy, healthy children. Within this section, there are a number of rotating departments, which include:

FIELD TRIPS gives fathers the tools to guide their families creatively, but carefully, toward a successful and enjoyable trip.

COMPUTER KIDS reviews appropriate educational and entertainment software for children. Safe sites for kids on the Internet, like on-line "Sesame Street," are also covered as a regular feature.

CONSCIENTIOUS CONSUMER reviews new products that are relevant to family life and makes spending money a more enjoyable, less risky adventure.

IN THE KITCHEN guarantees 20 minute dinners to gourmet feasts that are nutritious, easy to prepare and don't require exotic ingredients.

EMERGENCY CARE gives fathers quick lessons in dealing with emergency situations that kids get into everyday and equips fathers with the basic know-how to immediately care for their child while waiting for professional help.

HEALTH focuses on the health and fitness of children. It features a Physician's Advice (Q&A) column in which a doctor on our advisory board will respond with complete and understandable answers to readers' questions.

KIDS FASHION keeps fathers in touch with today's style conscious kids and explains where to find it, how much it costs and whether their kids really need it.

MEDIA provides fathers with valuable information on what's out there for kids—what to look for and what to avoid. Reviews on controversial and entertaining media subjects enable fathers to make the best choices.

FEATURED FATHERS profiles dads who want to share their personal and fatherhood experiences with other readers.

RAINY DAY DAD gives dads a pull-out activity for those rainy days with restless kids, including needed household supplies, required time, and easy-to-follow instructions.

SPORTS simplifies the rules of the games so that men can teach the basics to their children. This section also includes details such as jargon, game plays, and tips from professionals.

STAYING TOGETHER provides advice for separated fathers on how to make the most of the time with their children, including ideas for activities, outings, and quiet time, and advice on children's emotional troubles that may accompany a divorce or separation.

STORY TIME features short stories that dads can read to younger children and gives tips on how to invent their own stories.

BITS & PIECES keeps dads up-to-date on a wide range of news relevant to fatherhood. It provides concise reviews of issues, facts, and events that impact their lives.

The GROWING ON YOU section gives fathers an easy reference guide to understanding the physical, intellectual, and psychological changes that accompany their children's development and covers eight distinct age groups ranging from 0 through the teen years.

EVERYMAN is the section which provides men with insight into their lives, meeting their intellectual needs and interests in a rapidly changing world. It should enlarge their sphere of knowledge on which to base their own personal and parenting decisions. Within this section, there are a number of rotating departments, which include:

DRIVER'S ED is for every type of driver. Automobile reviews from sports cars to minivans, an ongoing car care guide and a used car quality index fill this department.

CAREER's goal is to sort and condense the Wall Street Journal on a monthly basis to give our readers information on trends that may affect their professional lives.

COMPUTER reviews the latest in software, hardware, and services, including the Internet, and suggests the best options based on price, usage, customer service and quality.

TO YOUR HEALTH provides information pertinent to a healthy lifestyle, including good nutrition and a better sex life.

HOME OFFICE organizes dads that work at home by reporting the latest in tax laws, new products, and how to stay connected with the rest of the business world.

WEEKEND WORKSHOP provides quick tips such as fixing a leaky faucet, to ongoing, larger scale projects such as designing and building a nursery. This department will appeal to both the beginner and the professional.

FAMILY FINANCE is for dads who recognize that their paychecks need to go further than their savings accounts.

RELATIONSHIPS are tough when you have kids. Married, divorced and separated dads will benefit from our expert advisory group on relationships.

SPORTS & RECREATION explains the rules and necessary equipment allowing dads to try something new or just improve their swing.

WHEN I WAS A KID . . . challenges our readers to write an original, true story from their childhood.

The following are GUIDELINES for freelance submissions. If, after reading these guidelines, you still have questions, please feel free to call us. We want to work with you to produce the best possible article for *Modern Dad*.

The TONE of these articles should be fairly light. We want to inform and entertain. Our readers want to develop their fathering skills through positive content. Each article should offer readers information that they can apply to their lives.

We do award ASSIGNMENTS to freelance writers who seek to build a lasting relationship. Our magazine is growing and we welcome newcomers who want to grow with us.

LENGTH is not a significant consideration since smaller articles can be placed in departments and larger articles can be placed as feature stories. We think that it is important for you to say what you need to say, after which we can work together for the most effective presentation. Common sense guidelines range from 200 to 4,000 words.

A conventional FORMAT makes it easy for us to review and cooperatively edit your work. Articles should be submitted both in hard copy and on disk (PC or Mac) in text format. Special formatting (italics, bold . . .) should be noted on the hard copy.

In order for *Modern Dad* to be a useful REFERENCE guide for fathers, please include as many phone numbers, addresses, books on the subject, places, organizations, etc. that apply to your article. Fathers should enjoy the reading and then have summary information to reference.

Accompanying ART can be submitted with your article. Photos and illustrations are certainly welcome and add to your intended quality of the article. Both color and B/W photos are accepted. Slide or 4x5 film should be used. Illustrations should be camera ready.

Please include a brief BIOGRAPHICAL SKETCH at the end of your submission so that we can print it if your article is used. On a separate sheet, please give us your PERSONAL INFORMATION. Please include your name, address, phone numbers, FAX, e-mail and the best times to reach you (EST) by phone.

We will accept PREVIOUSLY PUBLISHED material for consideration. Please include all details and a copy in its published form.

MONEY is important to all of us. We are a start-up and our first, full-sized issue hasn't yet been published at the time these guidelines were written. We ask all writers to consider submitting their FIRST ARTICLE GRATIS allowing us time to build our magazine. A compensation package will be designed for those writers willing to build with us.

Contact Information:
Elisha R. Kronish, Editor
7628 North Rogers Avenue
Chicago, IL 60626
(312) 465-8088 • FAX: (312) 465-8299
E-mail: Moderndad@aol.com or www.moderndad.com

Modern Drummer

Modern Drummer is dedicated to helping drummers in all areas of music, and at every level of ability. It is important to understand the *MD* is not a "fan magazine" for people who like drummers; it is a professional magazine for the drummers themselves. In fact, many of our columns are written by top professional drummers and drum teachers. While it is not crucial that all of our writers actually be drummers, it is necessary that they know enough about drums and drumming to be able to write about such topics as technique, equipment, style, and musical philosophies. A certain amount of biographical information is good, as long as it serves to provide background or put things in perspective. But remember: There are any number of magazines providing biographical and life-style information; *MD* is read by people who want information about drumming, so do not get too far away from our main focus.

Additionally, *MD* is looking for music journalists rather than music critics. Our aim is to provide information, not to make value judgments. Therefore, keep all articles as objective as possible. We are interested in how and why a drummer plays a certain way; the readers can make their own decisions about whether or not they like it.

Before you attempt to write an article for *Modern Drummer*, make sure you are very familiar with the magazine. You should have read at least three recent issues to acquaint yourself with our general style and tone. (Sample copies are available on request at $2.50 apiece.) In addition, when considering an article, you might ask yourself the following questions: Will this article help a substantial group of drummers improve their abilities? Will it enlighten them on a particular phase of drumming? Will it save the reader time, money, or effort? Is the topic interesting enough to attract a large number of readers? Will the article help the reader arrive at a decision or draw a conclusion? Will the article help drummers do their jobs better? Not every article will do all of those things, but if the article does not do any of them, then *MD* will probably not be interested in it.

Please query us on lengthy material before you begin writing. This helps us avoid receiving articles we cannot use, and it will help you avoid having your article returned. Send us a brief outline on the subject matter and your angle on the story. The editors will then be able to guide you in tailoring the material to the exact needs of the magazine. Also, if your idea has already been assigned or covered, we can notify you before you begin working. If you are writing for *MD* for the first time, or if your idea is somewhat out of the ordinary, you will be asked to submit your piece on speculation.

The above information should guide you in submitting material to *Modern Drummer*. If you need any further information, please write to us. We are always interested in acquiring good editorial material. And in finding talented, competent writers.

PAYMENT

Modern Drummer pays upon publication. Rates vary depending on the length of the story after editing, whether the article will be used as a feature article or column, and, to some extent, the length of the writer's association with *Modern Drummer*.

General Rates

Feature article:	$200 - $500. Buys all rights.
Column:	$25 - $150. Buys all rights.

(Receipt of payment generally occurs three to six weeks after publication.)

COPY LENGTHS

Feature material should range from 5,000 to 8,000 words.
Column material should range from 500 to 2,500 words.

OPEN COLUMNS

Music Columns—Column material can be technical, conceptual, or philosophical in nature. Topics should be very specific, and we encourage the use of musical examples, where appropriate, as well as photos or illustrations. (If using music, request our Music Guidelines.)

Rock Perspectives: Mainstream or commercial rock
Rock 'n' Jazz Clinic: Progressive rock and fusion
Jazz Drummers Workshop: Mainstream, bebop, or avant-garde jazz
Driver's Seat: Big band
Strictly Technique: Technical studies which could be applied to any area of drumming
Shop Talk: How-to's concerning maintaining, customizing and restoring drums
South Of The Border: Latin and reggae rhythms as applied to drumset
Teacher's Forum: Articles dealing with teaching and education
Jobbing Drummer: Freelance drumming—casuals, weddings, etc.
In The Studio: All facets of recording
Show Drummer's Seminar: Broadway, Vegas, theater, resorts, circus, ice shows, etc.

Profile Columns—These columns are similar to feature interviews, but shorter in length (2,500 -3,000 words).

Portraits: Drummers from all areas of music
Up & Coming: Drummers who have recently come to national attention
From The Past: Historical drummers from all areas of music.

EDITORIAL POLICY

Manuscripts are edited to conform with style policies, as well as for consistency and readability. This may involve condensing, rearranging, retitling, and, to some extent, rewording the article. Final decisions regarding style, grammar, and presentation are the right of the editorial staff of *Modern Drummer*.

Contact Information:
Ron Spagnardi, Editor
William Miller, Features Editor
Rick Van Horn, Managing Editor
12 Old Bridge Road
Cedar Grove, NJ 07009
(201) 239-4140

Moment Magazine
The Jewish Magazine For The '90s

Moment is an independent Jewish bimonthly magazine. We print cultural, political, historical, religious and "lifestyle" articles relating to the North American Jewish community and Israel. Our departments include "Responsa," providing rabbinic answers to contemporary dilemmas; "Holiday," concise essays on an aspect of a Jewish holiday or ritual; "Books," reviews of contemporary fiction and nonfiction of Jewish interest; and "Guest Columns" on any topic of Jewish interest.

The unsolicited manuscripts we select for publication are distinguished by one or more of the following: 1.) a fresh perspective on an on-going community issue; 2.) an in-depth journalistic treatment of an individual, institution or phenomenon; 3.) first-person writing that reveals universal themes in individual experiences; 4.) a national or global perspective on otherwise local affairs; 5.) a demonstrated familiarity with other work being done in the same field or topic; 6.) superior writing.

Moment rarely publishes fiction or poetry; also be aware that we receive many more articles on the following topics than we are able to publish: analysis of current events, Holocaust memoirs, immigrant stories, a parent's thoughts on a child's life-cycle event, "Jewish traveler" how-to's, and sermons. Prospective writers are also requested to familiarize themselves with *Moment*'s style and content.

Major articles are from 2,500 to 4,000 words in length; "Responsa" and "Guest Columns" are 800 to 1,200 words; book reviews are 400 words. Writers of lengthy articles are strongly urged to send a detailed query letter rather than a completed manuscript.

Contact Information:
Suzanne Singer, Managing Editor
4710 41st Street NW
Washington, D.C. 20016
(202) 364-3300

Mosaica Digest

Mosaica uses about 85% reprints of previously published articles for its 25-30 stories per bimonthly issue. Articles may be used on either first rights, second rights (reprints) or one-time basis. Please indicate if you are interested in allowing free access to material, as many other publications ask us for free material.

- Byline will be given, as well as source magazine (if any).
- Payment is based on a variety of factors, but runs from $10—$200 plus copies.
- Lead time is 4 months, so please submit seasonal articles at least 5 months in advance.
- If photos or artwork are available, be sure to state this, and send either photos or photocopies of material.
- Preferred length can be anywhere from 500—3,000 words.
- Articles need not be Jewish, but must be of interest to Jewish families.
- Humor, health, parenting, etc., are all welcome, but everything must be very clean. No scatological or sexual humor or stories.

Contact Information:
Submissions Editor
242 Fourth Street
Lakewood, NJ 08701-3227
(908) 901-8880

MOTHERJONES

Mother Jones

WHO WE ARE

Mother Jones, with a paid circulation of 120,000 is one of the largest progressive publications in the country. The national bimonthly magazine is known for its investigative journalism and exposés, and its coverage of social issues, public affairs and popular culture. Most of the articles we print are written by freelancers.

WHAT WE'RE LOOKING FOR

- Hard-hitting, investigative reports exposing government cover-ups, corporate malfeasance, scientific myopia, institutional fraud or hypocrisy, etc.
- Thoughtful, provocative articles which challenge the conventional wisdom (on the right or the left) concerning issues of national importance.
- Timely, people-oriented stories on issues such as the environment, labor, the media, health care, consumer protection, and cultural trends.

HOW TO QUERY US

Send us a letter proposing your story idea(s). Explain what you plan to cover and how you will proceed with the reporting. The query should convey your approach, tone, and style, and should answer the following: What are your specific qualifications to write on this topic? What "ins" do you have with your sources? Can you provide full documentation so that your story can be fact-checked?

Keep in mind that our lead time is three months and submissions should not be so time-bound that they will appear dated. If we, or another publication, have run a similar story in the last few years, explain how your story will differ.

If you have not contributed to *Mother Jones* before, please send two or three photocopies of previously published articles along with your query. We do not accept unsolicited manuscripts or fiction. Please do not query us by phone or FAX.

Back issues are $6.00 and can be ordered through Reader Services at the address below.

Contact Information:
Feminism, Environmental: Sarah Pollock, Senior Editor
Politics: Christopher Orr, Senior Editor
Culture, Multi-cultural: Kerry Lauerman, Associate Editor
731 Market Street, Suite 600
San Francisco, CA 94103
(415) 665-6637 • FAX: (415) 665-6696
E-mail: last name@motherjones.com

Mountain Living

1. SUBJECT

Subject will be determined following discussion with editor, who will provide resource materials, contact names and suggestions for research when possible. Editor prefers written queries.

2. LENGTH

Department articles usually run 300-1,500 words. Feature articles run 1,200-2,000 words.

3. DEADLINES.

All assignments are due on the morning of the date assigned. If an agreed-upon deadline can't be met, please contact the editor a minimum of two weeks beforehand to renegotiate an appropriate date.

4. SIDEBARS

As discussed with editor. Department articles may require a sidebar with information such as reference-book listing, ingredients, facts and figures, and addresses.

5. PHOTOGRAPHS

For all department articles and some features, we ask that you speak with your sources about obtaining photographs. Slides or transparencies are preferable. When possible, mail the photos with your completed article. Otherwise, include a list of photo resources. We will return all artwork after the issue has been published.

6. RESOURCE LIST

Each home feature must be accompanied by a list of interior designers, architects, landscape planners, contractors, builders, etc., who have contributed to the project, as well as their company names, addresses and phone numbers. Each feature must also be accompanied by a list of design resources, for ALL furnishings, fabrics and materials (available retail or wholesale) used in the project. Only antiques are excluded—custom pieces should be identified as such, with credit to the designer and manufacturer. The interior designer or other professionals who contributed to the project are usually willing to help put together this list.

7. COMPLIMENTARY COPIES

Include a list of photo, research and interview resources, their addresses and phone numbers, so we can send a complimentary copy of the magazine.

8. DELIVERY

Printed submissions should be accompanied by a disk. Speak with the editor about sending articles on-line.

9. PAYMENT

As discussed with the editor and stipulated in the contract. Checks are usually mailed two to three weeks after the material is accepted. A 15 percent kill fee is paid for unacceptable material.

Contact Information:
Robyn Griggs, Editor
7009 South Potomac Street
Englewood, CO 80112
(800) 945-0973 or (303) 397-7600 • FAX: (303) 397-7619

Mushing
The Magazine of Dog-Powered Sports

Mushing works with experienced freelance writers and photojournalists as well as first-time authors and photographers. These guidelines are intended to provide an idea of the kinds of submissions we are looking for as well as how our submission process works. Please feel free to contact us if you have any questions or if you would like to discuss an idea for submission.

EDITORIAL PROFILE

Mushing is an international bimonthly magazine that covers all aspects of dog-powered sports. *Mushing* was founded in 1987 and strives to inform, educate and entertain readers by publishing articles on all aspects of the growing sports of dogsledding, skijoring, carting, dog packing and weight pulling. *Mushing* promotes responsible dog care through feature articles and updates on working animal health care, safety, nutrition and training.

Available by subscriptions and in retail outlets, *Mushing* is distributed in 49 states and 25 countries. Readers include both recreational and competitive mushers with a wide range of experience, from beginners to veterans. In addition, some readers are "armchair mushers," those who enjoy reading about or watching the sport but who are not mushers themselves.

We urge contributors to study the magazine before submitting material. Samples are $5 in the United States, $6 U.S. to Canada and $8 U.S. to other countries.

SUBMISSIONS

We prefer detailed query letters but also consider unsolicited manuscripts. Please make proposal letters informative yet to the point and succinct. Spell out your qualifications for handling the topic. We like to see clips of previously published material, but we are eager to work with new and unpublished authors too.

Submissions should include your telephone number, social security number (for tax purposes), name(s), address and the article's approximate word count. Queries (not manuscripts) may be sent by FAX or by e-mail, but these may be responded to by mail, so please include complete contact information.

Please number all pages after the first. Also include an author's biography of three to four sentences. Include a cover letter with the manuscript. Submissions on 3½" Macintosh or IBM-format computer disks are encouraged, but please include a complete hard copy to protect against disk errors. Please specify the type of computer hardware and software the document was created on.

ARTICLE CONTENT

Each issue of *Mushing* includes a mix of information, features and columns. We consider articles on canine health and nutrition, sled dog behavior and training, musher profiles and interviews, equipment how-to's, trail tips, expedition and race accounts, innovations, sled dog history, current issues, personal experiences and humor. We use primarily nonfiction but will consider well-written and relevant or timely fiction. We also consider cartoons and junior puzzles. See editorial calendar below for current special issue focuses.

All articles should be well researched, logically organized and readable. Appropriate photo support and/or illustrations are welcomed. (See "Images" below.)

STYLE AND LENGTH

We prefer clear, concise, straightforward writing. We generally follow Associated Press style, although we also have our own style guide and consult the *Chicago Manual of Style* on occasion. We reserve the right to edit all submissions.

Features generally run between 1,000 and 2,500 words. Longer articles are considered if well written and of particular interest. Columns and departments usually run from 500 to 1,000 words. Short news pieces run from 150 to 500 words.

PHOTOGRAPHS

Mushing uses both color and black-and-white photographs. All photos and slides to be considered must be clean, sharp and accurately exposed. Potential subjects include dogs working, playing and resting as well as expedition and racing events, recreational mushing, skijoring, winter camping, freighting, mushing equipment and mushing personalities. We use a variety of horizontals and verticals.

We work at least three months ahead of each publication date, so we need summer photos beginning in February and winter photos in July. We are always looking for good cover photographs. These should be strong, sharp vertical photographs with enough open area at the top for the *Mushing* banner.

Submitted black-and-white photos should ideally be 8" by 10" glossy prints or negatives accompanied by a contact sheet. High quality 8" by 10" prints on semi-matte paper are acceptable but not preferred.

We prefer color photos in 35mm or 120mm Kodachrome transparencies but will consider other formats. Slides must be submitted in plastic slide sheets and accompanied by a detailed caption sheet. Every slide or print must be clearly marked with the photographer's name and address. You may submit duplicate slides so long as the originals are available for final printing. Please identify any duplicate slides.

Black-and-white photographs account for about 50 to 80 percent of the art in any given issue, so we welcome good black-and-white submissions. However, color submissions are often published as black-and-white images as well. Contributors of color images agree to have their images published in the black-and-white format unless a specific written agreement is made with *Mushing* in advance of submission.

ARTWORK

Mushing uses black-and-white illustrations and drawings on occasion. Mostly we use simple images of sled dogs doing something—running, howling, sleeping, eating, playing, etc.—although we are always open to other possibilities. We also occasionally use color artwork on the cover.

In addition, sled dog-related cartoons are considered. Some artists submit work (or good photocopies) that *Mushing* can keep on file and use as the need arises.

All photographs, slides and original artwork are returned after consideration or use unless other arrangements are specified.

RATES, RIGHTS AND PAYMENT

We purchase first serial rights and second (reprint) rights. Article rates average $.07 per published word. Photograph and artwork payment rates average as follows:

Black and white:	$10 to $ 40
Color:	up to $ 50
Back cover:	up to $ 80
Front cover:	up to $175

We send payment within 60 days of publication. Unless a written agreement is made between *Mushing* and a writer or photographer, exact rate of payment for articles or photographs will be determined by the editorial staff of *Mushing*.

Unless otherwise notified in writing, all contributions are considered to be submitted on a speculation basis. An affirmative response to a query proposal does not necessarily mean the resulting article will be accepted.

All slides with a copyright notice on the slide cover should be accompanied by a signed release that gives *Mushing* the right to duplicate images for processing (i.e., to make a black-and-white interneg and print or color separation and proof).

EDITORIAL SCHEDULE

The following are submission deadlines for the six bimonthly issues of *Mushing*. We welcome early submissions to allow ample time for questions and clarifications. Issue focuses are subject to change.

Issue	Focus	Deadline
Jan./Feb.	Iditarod Issue	Oct. 15
Mar./Apr.	Expedition/Peak of the Season	Dec. 15
May/Jun.	Health & Nutrition	Feb. 15
Jul./Aug.	Meet the Mushers	Apr. 15
Sep./Oct.	Equipment Issue	Jun. 15
Nov./Dec.	Races & Places	Aug. 15

Contact Information:
Managing Editor
P.O. Box 149
Ester, AK 99725-0149
(907) 479-0454
E-mail: mushing@polarnet.com

The Nation

Thank you for your interest in writing for *The Nation*. We are a journal of left/liberal political opinion—130 years old this summer—covering national and international affairs. We publish weekly (summer bi-weekly).

We are looking both for reporting and for fresh analysis. On the domestic front, we are particularly interested in civil liberties; civil rights; labor, economics, environmental and feminist issues and the role and future of the Democratic Party. Because we have readers all over the country, it's important that stories with a local focus have real national significance. In our foreign affairs coverage we prefer pieces on international political, economic and social developments. As the magazine which published Ralph Nader's first piece (and there is a long list of Nation "firsts"), we are seeking new writers.

While detailed queries (a page or two) are preferred, we're happy to consider finished pieces on timely issues. FAXed manuscripts will only be acknowledged if accepted. Our full-length pieces run 1,500 to 2,000 words and (signed) editorials 500 to 750. Calvin Trillin has made us famous for paying in the high two or very low three figures—that is, from $75 for an editorial to $225-300 for a full-length piece. Deadlines are 10 days before the magazine goes to print for stories, 4 days for editorials. The magazine goes to print on Wednesdays.

Queries and submissions on books and the arts should be addressed to our literary editors, Sue and John Leonard. Also, *The Nation* publishes poems of outstanding aesthetic quality, by poets such as Emily Dickinson, William Butler Yeats, D.H. Lawrence, Marianne Moore, William Carlos Williams, Robert Lowell, Randall Jarrell, W.S. Merwin, Derek Walcott, Pablo Neruda, Mona Van Duyn, Joseph Brodsky. Send poems to Grace Schulman, Poetry Editor. Payment: $1 a line not to exceed $35. For details about Discovery—The Nation, a contest for poets whose work has not yet been published in book form, write to Grace Schulman, with SASE. Let us hear from you.

Contact Information:
The Editor
72 Fifth Avenue
New York, NY 10011
(212) 242-8400 • FAX: (212) 463-9712

Natural Health
The Guide to Well-Being

It is the policy of *Natural Health* to read all unsolicited queries and manuscripts. We do not have specific "writer's guidelines" per se; we expect that writers interested in having their work published in *Natural Health* have a familiarity with the magazine and submit their work accordingly. We do request that writers send a resume or include their credentials in a letter which accompanies their detailed query or manuscript. Writing samples should also be included. Thank you for your interest in *Natural Health*.

Sincerely,
Elizabeth Cameron, Editorial Assistant

Contact Information:
17 Station Street
P.O. Box 1200
Brookline Village, MA 02147
(617) 232-1000 • FAX: (617) 232-1572

NATURAL HISTORY

Natural History

1. *Natural History* is a magazine of nature, science and culture, published monthly by the American Museum of Natural History, Central Park West at 79th Street, New York, NY 10024.

2. Articles for *Natural History* must be written with a depth of knowledge and understanding of the subject matter. We are not only interested in a description of what happens, but most importantly, why it happens.

3. Stories can range from natural phenomena to human biology and cultural events, plants, animals, geology, astronomy. Nothing natural is beyond the scope of an article for *Natural History* magazine.

4. We accept articles by both scientists and writers. Scientists may write about their own research and writers may consolidate the writings of work of other scientists.

5. The most important thing to do before submitting a proposal to *Natural History* is to look carefully at the magazine. Articles vary in length; shorter articles are easier to pace than longer articles.

6. Writers should submit a short proposal demonstrating their understanding of the subject matter about which they want to write. Scientists may send a published version of their work in other journals or a description of their work if it has not yet been published but is new and ongoing.

7. We are interested in accounts of scientists' work in the field, we are interested in studies of individual animals and plants, places, and studies that have worked on entire ecosystems.

8. There are several columns that writers might consider writing for. A partial list includes: Journal, a short piece of reporting from somewhere in the field or scientific conference or from events that have occurred recently; Naturalist At Large is a column about a scientist

working in the field. We are interested in essays on both human and natural history, commentary on current events on science and nature. And always on stories concerning evolution; Discovery is a piece that takes the reader to some place and describes a natural history visit to some site. Everything from a place to dig fossils to a place to observe birds. Though usually places where the scientist has been doing long term fieldwork.

9. Feature articles run anywhere from 1,500 to 3,500 words. They are often accompanied by photographs, but there is no expectation that scientists or writers will submit photographs with articles. If the article warrants, photographers will frequently be sent to the story location in order to get the appropriate pictures to accompany the story.

10. In the proposal, please suggest a length for the story and if it is proposed for one of the columns or as a feature. It is best to submit a proposal and not a finished article.

11. Unless arranged beforehand, we do not accept proposals or submissions via FAX. Articles that are submitted must be accompanied by a computer disk in any format.

12. All submissions will be reviewed by experts in the field and subjected to rigorous fact-checking procedures.

13. *Natural History* is a unique venue for scientists and writers and we look forward to your ideas and stories.

Contact Information:
Bruce Stutz, Editor
Central Park West @ 79th Street
New York, NY 10024
(212) 769-5500 • FAX: (212) 769-5511

Naturally

OVERVIEW:

NATURALLY magazine's focus is on clothes-free vacation resorts, nude beaches, and wholesome nude family recreation. Our objective is to market the desirability of nude recreation to mainstream America. We give preference to articles that include quality photography and/or other visual support. Materials selected for publication are generally informative, upbeat, and present a positive nudist, naturist, or nude-recreation image. Emphasis is on travel and upscale nudist resorts.

PHOTOGRAPHY:

NATURALLY's photo policy is liberal. We encourage photography at all clothes-free events by courteous and considerate photographers. Although NATURALLY publishes only the work of nudist and naturist (amateur and professional) photographers, we believe that all who are interested in taking pictures at nude events should be free to do so and not be restricted for purposes of protecting some nudists' anonymity. Unreasonable photo restrictions sabotage the depiction of genuine, open and sincere nude recreation. Of course, we do respect the rights of nudist and naturist clubs to set the rules as hosts. NATURALLY will honor imposed publishing restrictions placed upon some photos by a host.

Photographs taken on public land or in establishments open to the public, do not require photo releases unless intended for commercial use (e.g., in an advertisement, to sell something). However, common courtesy and consideration prevails. Photographs acquired by insensitive methods are not accepted for publication.

Photographs taken in closed private areas, not generally thought of as public, should have releases from all recognizable persons when the photo is not of a newsworthy situation.

For a legitimate newsworthy photograph, NATURALLY magazine does not require photo releases, even when the picture is taken on private property. Again, common courtesy and consideration prevails, and photographs acquired by insensitive methods are not accepted for publication. Photo releases are the responsibility of the photographer.

Photographs may be submitted in color or b & w, as prints, negatives, or slides. Slides or negatives yield the highest reproduction quality.

Payments for published photographs include the value of the photo print or transparency. Prints or transparencies that are requested returned, a deduction of $10 per photo is made from payments, otherwise selected photos for publication are retained as file copies for possible future use. Unpublished photos are returned as a matter of procedure, unless there is a good chance for future publication in NATURALLY magazine or other books and magazines published by Events Unlimited.

ORGANIZATIONS:

We support most naturist and nudist groups and organizations in their endeavor to educate the mainstream about nude recreation. Toward this endeavor, we have chosen a less political and more lighthearted approach. However, articles and/or photos submitted by nudist/naturist organizations, to inform, to promote an event or political agenda, are accepted and appreciated.

Fund-raising appeals are accepted for publication from naturist/nudist organizations. Brevity is requested.

We accept event schedules for publication if open to all-comers and dated sufficiently ahead (preferably 5-6 months) to be useful to our readers for at least up to one month after publication.

PAID PARTICIPATION (at time of publication):

All contributors receive copies of NATURALLY magazine in which their material appears.

NATURALLY pays $50 per published page (text and/or visuals). Fractional pages or fillers are pro-rated.

Frequent contributors and regular columnists who develop a following through NATURALLY, such as Paul LeValley and Richard West, are paid from the Frequent Features Budget. Payments increase on the basis of frequency of participation, and the budget is adjusted quarterly as NATURALLY grows.

We purchase news items that are creatively combined and submitted as one major news article. Blurbs or short news write-ups are graciously accepted as contributions to the cause (see unpaid participation).

UNPAID PARTICIPATION & CONTRIBUTIONS:

Published materials, submitted with a commercial agenda, such as product releases, news releases, resort news, etc. are not paid for.

Published articles intended to promote a commercial entity, resort or nudist park, organization, group, etc. are not paid. It is generally understood that NATURALLY publishes this material as free promotional/publicity support.

Short news (current events) items and clippings are also appreciated as contributions to the cause of promoting the benefits of clothes-optional freedom.

Opinion pieces are accepted as contributions only when adequately researched.

EXCLUSIVITY:

We accept articles and photos that have been previously published elsewhere, when submitted by the original authors or photographers. However, the value of the material is diminished as a non-exclusive submission. We deduct 30% from previously published submissions if accepted for publication.

ASSIGNMENTS:

All-expense-paid assignments are occasionally awarded. NATURALLY magazine will provide paid travel arrangements and accommodations. Food and other routine daily living expenses are not paid for. Additional payments are made for the published article(s) and/or photo(s), based upon the above-stated criteria. Articles and photos resulting from assignments are for NATURALLY magazine's exclusive use.

Contact Information:
Bernard J. Loibl, Editor
P.O. Box 317
Newfoundland, NJ 07435
(210) 697-8313

Nature Photographer

"The Magazine for People Who Love to Photograph Our Natural World"

NATURE PHOTOGRAPHER is an international photography magazine published six (6) times a year. The focus of NATURE PHOTOGRAPHER is photographing in the wilderness throughout the world. We are looking for two to five articles per issue that discuss how to improve technique (e.g., submit thorough, well-planned "how-to" articles) for all aspects of nature photography in the wild, including macro subjects, wild flowers, wildlife, landscapes, underwater, and nature abstracts. Looking for travel destination articles and unique photo location pieces which include how-to information. Please, no pets, images of wild animals that have been obtained by feeding the animals (birds at backyard feeders are acceptable for publication), wildlife "setup" shots, zoo shots, or shots of animals confined in any way (this includes insects, reptiles, and amphibians). No game farm "rent an animal" images accepted. Due to the wilderness focus of NATURE PHOTOGRAPHER, we do not accept computer manipulated or enhanced images. NATURE PHOTOGRAPHER's regular departments are staff-written and include interviews, field notes, wildlife images, wild lore, conservation articles, and equipment reviews. The one exception to regular departments being staff written is Photo Techniques and Gear which is written by various experts in the field of photographic techniques and those who are well familiar with photographic gear. We welcome queries for this department.

QUERY BY LETTER FIRST! Please, no phone queries. NATURE PHOTOGRAPHER maintains high editorial standards. Upon our acceptance of a queried idea, the manuscript will range from 750 to 2,000 words.

We review 35mm, 2¼" x 2¼", 6"x7", and 4"x5" transparencies. (NO GLASS MOUNTS ACCEPTED.) We only review or accept color prints for publication which were taken by young people between the ages of 5 yrs. and 18 yrs. All submissions made by adults must be made on slides/transparency film. All submissions must include the photographer's name, address, and subject identification on the slide mount or on the back of the black and white print. Transparencies should be presented in clear slide saver sheets. We do not review slides packed in their yellow Kodak boxes or wrapped in tissue. Please limit your submissions to 40 or less. Quality is better than quantity. IMAGES FOR COVER CONSIDERATION MUST BE VERTICAL, SHOT IN THE WILD, AND DRAMATIC. Black backgrounds or excessively dark backgrounds DO NOT WORK for our covers.

Our review schedule for slides is as follows—please DO NOT send slides at other times of the year:

Review for Mar./Apr., May/June and July/Aug. issues (Spring & Summer Images)—11/1 (submit in late October)

Review for Sept./Oct., Nov./Dec., and Jan./Feb. issues (Fall and Winter images, including tropical scenes and wading birds photographed in southern destinations during winter) - 5/1 (submit in late April)

PLEASE DO NOT SEND SLIDES EARLY.

When submitting query letters, please do not include slides with the query letters.

We do not pay holding fees. We cannot return shipping memos and postcards included with submissions.

If we accept your idea, we will either have color separations made from the slides selected for publication or convert the slides to black and white prints if the article or a portion of it is to be printed in black and white. Slides must be publication-quality duplicate 70mm transparencies or original 35mm, 2¼" x 2¼", 4"x5", or 6"x7" transparencies. NATURE PHOTOGRAPHER reserves the right to reject prints or slides of unacceptable quality.

NATURE PHOTOGRAPHER will take first rights on all material accepted for publication. However, we do review previously published material, as long as six months have elapsed since its publication.

NATURE PHOTOGRAPHER and Nature Photographer Publishing Co., Inc. do not accept the premise that any transparencies, prints, or negatives are worth a minimum of $1,500. NATURE PHOTOGRAPHER is not responsible for submissions in transit. Furthermore, NATURE PHOTOGRAPHER is not responsible for submissions in our possession beyond their material cost (material cost limited to $5.00 for each transparency, $3.00 for 5"x7" prints, and $6.00 for 8"x10" prints). NATURE PHOTOGRAPHER does not pay holding fees or research fees. Unless approved in writing before the arrival of the photographs, NATURE PHOTOGRAPHER and Nature Photographer Publishing Co., Inc. cannot, and NATURE PHOTOGRAPHER does not acknowledge the terms and stipulations on delivery memos and other paperwork accompanying the submission of photographs. Packages of slides delivered with conflicting delivery memos are returned unexamined. If any slide or slides receive damage during color separation, the color separator's liability is limited to $250 per slide.

Payment rates: $75 - $150 for package, text and photographs. Single photo rate $15 to $30. Front cover $100. Magazine printed in 4-color and B&W. You can expect to receive your payment after publication during the first month of issue date in which your work is published. Payment for reprints is 75% of article rate.

Office hours are Eastern Standard Time 8:00 am to 4:00 pm Mon. through Fri. Call only if absolutely necessary, please. Voice mail available 24 hrs. a day. We are unable to respond to submissions. If your submission is not returned within four months, it most likely means that we are holding it for possible publication at a future date.

Contact Information:

Article/Slides Comb.: Evamarie Mathaey, Editor/Publisher
Slides: Helen Longest-Slaughter, Photo Editor
P.O. Box 2037
West Palm Beach, FL 33402-2037
(407) 622-5223

Navy Times

Thank you for your interest in *Navy Times*.

We publish an independent newspaper for Navy, Marine Corps and Coast Guard personnel, retirees and their families. [See also Times News Service.]

Our newspaper has a circulation of about 90,000 and an estimated readership of about a half million. We are part of the privately owned Army Times Publishing Co., which also publishes the *Army Times*, *Air Force Times*, *Federal Times*, *Defense News* and *Space News*.

WHAT TYPE OF ARTICLES WE WANT: Navy Times is interested in well-written freelance articles that are informative, entertaining or stimulating and deal with sea service life. We do not publish fiction or poetry. We do accept opinion and commentary pieces to a maximum of 800 words. We typically pay $75 for commentaries.

We are interested in good, colorful stories. They can highlight how some unit or ship in the Navy, Marine Corps or Coast Guard functions; what life is like on an installation in the United States or overseas; or how some regulation directly affects a service member or his or her family. The stories also can describe special military events; outstanding individual performance; inter- or intraservice sports; interesting characters or trends in sea service lifestyles. Stories should be written "off the news" —that is, they should have a timely reason for being written and reported.

Stories can range in length from 500 to 1,500 words. Payment varies from $125 to about $250. When you send us a query, we'll give you guidance concerning length.

PHOTOS: We are interested in good color photographs or slides, or B&W photographs, to illustrate story submissions. We do want identification of people and objects in the photographs and slides. We prefer to receive a selection to choose from and will pay up to $50 apiece for slides or photographs published.

We prefer to receive both a hard copy and an IBM-compatible 3½" floppy disk on which your submission has been saved in MS Word or "text only" format. It is better to query us in advance.

If you want to buy a copy of the newspaper to see the kinds of material we use, please call our single copy sales department (800) 424-9335, ext. 7400. Feel free to write or call us at the number below to discuss your ideas.

Contact Information:
Editor
6883 Commercial Drive
Springfield, VA 22159
(703) 750-8636

The New Era

GENERAL INFORMATION: *The New Era* is published for youth of the Church of Jesus Christ of Latter-day Saints (the Mormons), their church leaders, parents, and teachers. Established in 1971, it is a 51-page monthly magazine. A sample copy will be sent for $1.50. It is best to query before submitting a manuscript. *The New Era* buys about 100 manuscripts a year and purchases all rights, but rights may be reassigned to the author after publication. Seasonal material should be submitted six months to one year in advance. We report back in 6-8 weeks. Payment is on acceptance.

NONFICTION: We're after material that shows how the Church of Jesus Christ of Latter-day Saints is relevant in the lives of young people today. It should capture the excitement of being a young Latter-day Saint. We have a special interest in personal experiences; inspirational conversion and missionary stories; stories about families; personality profiles; activities involving LDS youth; and in the experience of young Latter-day Saints in other countries. Please don't send library research or formula pieces without the New Era slant. LENGTH: 150 to 2,000 words. We also use short, humorous anecdotes about Mormon life, ideas for Mormonads (refer to magazine for format), and material for the FYI ("For Your

Information") section, which features news of young Latter-day Saints from around the world.

FICTION: All varieties of wholesome fiction are used, but they must relate to a young Mormon audience.

POETRY: We accept traditional forms, free verse, and all other forms. Again, however, it must relate to our editorial viewpoint. Short poems are preferred.

PHOTOS: With stories, we use color slides, and/or color or black-and-white photos. Some photos are used for the "Photo of the Month" feature on the inside back cover.

ILLUSTRATIONS: We use both color and black-and-white illustrations of all types, but assignments are made exclusively to artists who have shown their portfolio to our designers. Send slides or make an appointment and let them see your work.

HOW TO BREAK IN: Study the magazine. Then query by letter, showing an example of your proposed writing style. See "So You Want to Write for *The New Era*," by Adrian Gostick, in the August 1991 issue.

Contact Information:
Richard M. Romney, Managing Editor
50 East North Temple Street
Salt lake City, UT 84150
(801) 240-2951

New Humor Magazine

The mail comes in and gets piled on the table where the entire staff rips the envelopes open looking for checks. Not finding any, most of the staff gets laid off until the next day and the process repeats itself. Near the publication deadline some of the material is actually read and the writers and cartoonists that take the least money get into the magazine. Now you know.

What really happens is the mail gets carefully separated, the death threats in one pile, the refund requests in another pile. Okay, what really, really happens is we read all the mail and look for material that says funny. Speaking as the editor now, I like Dave Barry, the great satirist of our time. I automatically buy anything with the name Barry on it. If your name is just Dave, it doesn't count as much. If your first and last initials are D and B, respectively, then you have a pretty good chance. Although, some stories that we print don't even look like Dave's work. Hey, go figure. Also, please keep your stories to around 1,000 words or less.

As far as poems go, well, Dave Barry doesn't write poetry. I like poems that are on the shorter side. I'm surprised by the range of humor offered by poets that contribute. How can one say what to write about in a poem? There are so many subjects that lend themselves to humor. One note, don't forget this is a humor magazine. The sad stuff I get makes the whole staff cry. Very bad for morale.

Cartoons are a favorite here at the *New Humor Magazine*. Cartoonists think they are in a privileged class all by themselves. Well, that's true, they are. I can draw as well as Rembrandt could after he died. If I could sell cartoons for a living I would move to some place warm and doodle on the beach. All I can currently pay for cartoons are $25 and they can be reprints if that's all you'll sell me.

Pay for stories range from $35 to a high of $100. I want to pay more but we are a small magazine and the only person making more money is the printer. Jokes and short poems pay from $5 to $15 and fillers pay a little bit more. You always get a few copies of the magazine when you're published.

The best advice I can give is to send in $4.50 for a copy of the magazine (although, we have a subscription sale right now and $9.68 gets you a full year. Note: You don't have to be a subscriber to contribute; the editorial side never knows the difference—unless you tell them! No, forget I said that.) The sample copy includes postage and we supply the envelope. And, no, we don't use clipping services, sorry.

Thanks for writing,
Edward Savaria Jr., Editor

Contact Information:
P.O. Box 216
Lafayette Hill, PA 19444
• FAX: (215) 487-2640
E-mail: Newhumor@aol.com

New Woman

Thank you for your query concerning our writer's guidelines.

New Woman is interested in considering articles on relationships and psychology. The categories which make up our magazine are good guidelines to what we're looking for: e.g. Self-Discovery, Relationships, Successful Living, Love and Sex, and Career and Money. We're also interested in travel articles with a self-discovery angle.

We like articles that are based on solid research, as well as more personal essay-like pieces. In terms of style, we like a friendly, accessible, intimate approach. Our articles run anywhere from 800 to 2,500 words, depending on the subject matter and the category.

We pay on acceptance; between $500 and $2,500, depending on the length and "weight" of the article—and how long the writer has been working with us.

It's not necessary for you to have an agent to represent your work. You may submit either a query or a finished manuscript.

Please address your submission to *New Woman*, Manuscripts and Proposals, at the address below.

We look forward to considering your work.

Please note that the magazine no longer accepts fiction or poetry submissions.

Contact Information:
Ms. Sharlene Breakey, Managing Editor
Ms. Susan Kane, Executive Editor
215 Lexington Avenue, 3rd Floor
New York, NY 10016
(212) 251-1500

New Writer's Magazine
Publishing Since 1986

NEW WRITER'S MAGAZINE (NW) is a bimonthly publication for aspiring writers and professional ones as well. NW serves as a "Meeting Place" where all writers are free to exchange thoughts, ideas, backgrounds and samples of their work. We are always seeking new and innovative writers with imagination and promise. And we are always looking for 'how-to' articles with a different slant. New trends in the publishing field and freelance writing is always welcomed.

Nonfiction: An "Up Close and Personal" interview of a recognized or new author, preferably with photos, and all major "in depth" articles on writing and the writing life. All such articles must be original and previously unpublished. 700-1,000 words. Payment on publication: $10 up to $50.

FICTION: Will publish a good fiction piece that has some sort of tie-in with the world of the new writer. Open to all styles/forms of expression. 700-800 words. Payment on publication: $20-$40.00.

POETRY: Humorous slant on writing life especially welcomed. Free verse, light verse and traditional. Submit maximum 3 poems. Length 8-20 lines. Payment on publication: $5.00 each poem.

CARTOONS: Black & white line drawings. Humorous slant on writing life. Submit copies or originals. Payment on publication: $10.00 each.

FILLERS: Anecdotes, facts, and short humor. Length: 20-100 words. Payment on publication: $5 maximum.

AMERICA ONLINE (AOL): NW is an information provider to AOL. Visit NW in the Writers Club section under Articles/Columns, and then to New Writers Market News, updated monthly.

Sample copy is $3.00: Send check payable to Sarasota Bay Publishing/New Writer's Magazine.

Guidelines information effective: May 1, 1996

SUBSCRIPTION INFORMATION:

One year (six issues)	$15.00
Two years (twelve issues)	$25.00
Canadian one year	$20.00 (U.S. funds)
International one year	$35.00 (U.S. funds)

Contact Information:
George J. Haborak, Editor and Publisher
P.O. Box 5976
Sarasota, FL 34277
(941) 953-7903 E-mail: Newriters@aol.com

Newsday

Dear Contributor:

Thank you for your interest in writing for Newsday.

We require that all manuscripts be submitted on spec providing that no trip has been subsidized in any way. Proof of payment will be required if story is accepted for publication.

If you have original slides, please do not include them with the manuscript. Duplicate slides or glossies are acceptable. Or indicate that photos are available.

Stories generally run about 1,200 words, plus 300 words for an If You Go box. Payment runs between $75 and $350, depending on usage. We pay extra for use of your photographs.

Looking forward to your manuscript,

Contact Information:
Marjorie Robins, Travel Editor
Travel Section
235 Pinelawn Road
Melville, NY 11747-4250

Nocturnal Ecstasy Vampire Coven

If you have a question or uncertainty about a submission, send a sample or inquiry. The best guideline is to simply send it in. All submissions should be vampire related, or related to the vampire lifestyle (gloomy types of work, as well as twisted or evil material, body piercing, music, suicide, S&M, torture, cults, death, religion, fetishes, anything of a gothic nature, fashion, other obsessions, castles, cemeteries, tattoos. . . you get the idea!)

I prefer submissions to be typed or on 3½" IBM compatible disk. If you are hand writing a submission, please print.

At the present time we are unable to compensate contributors with payment. Our profits are a negative amount. However, the journal is distributed worldwide, and is seen by most of the other vampire publications as well as other editors and staffs of major publications. It is sent out to various record label employees as well as bands around the world.

We encourage our readers to send in comments on items published and will pass on any reviews that your material receives.

Nocturnal Ecstasy is a great place to get your work seen by others. Exposure is what we offer at the present time. Should you care to order an issue in which your work appears, we do offer sample copies at $6 each.

POETRY: All forms of poetry accepted (including free verse, haiku, cinquain).

SHORT STORIES: All fiction accepted, providing that characters are original. (No previously copyrighted characters, unless the character is a creation of your own. We want your version of a vampire not Bram Stoker or Anne Rice's.) Erotica, power vampires, any twisted or unusual vampires, etc. Use your creativity. The more original, the better your chances of being published with Nocturnal Ecstasy. Keep in mind that we like stories that deal with sex. (All vampires have nympho tendencies.) Stories that are 3,000 words or less are preferred; although we have been known to accept stories that were up to 5,000 words. Like I said, it's best to send it in.

Nonfiction: All nonfiction accepted. Your own research, authors, artists, self proclaimed vampires and blood fetishists, as well as your own letters, observations, essays or debate.

REVIEWS: All reviews should include title, year and publisher or movie/record label. If you have something of your own creation that you would like to see reviewed in NE, send it to Reviews, c/o *NEVC*. (books) All fiction and nonfiction reviews accepted, including children's stories, magazines, and comic books. (movies) all movie reviews accepted, including TV series, made for television, and cartoons. (music) all music reviews accepted. Vampire bands, as well as gothic, doom, industrial and punk encouraged. Full length recordings as well as one song reviews are accepted.

PHOTOGRAPHY: All photos are accepted, including member photos, people dressed up like vampires, gothic & bondage images, etc.

VAMPIRE NEWS: Anything vampire related that you think may be of interest to members.

INTERVIEWS: Interviews with bands, artists, vampire researchers, writers, zine editors, music industry people, etc. are encouraged. We prefer article format rather that Q&A, but both are accepted.

No rights are required for submissions, as all rights revert back to the respective contributors upon publication. By sending in a submission, you agree to our one time publishing rights.

Contact Information:
Darlene Daniels, Editor
P.O. Box 147
Palos Heights, IL 60463-0147
E-mail: VAMPIR4@aol.com

The North American *Review*

The North American Review

The *NAR* is the oldest literary magazine in America (founded in 1815) and one of the most respected; though we have no prejudices about the subject matter of material sent to us, our first concern is quality.

The *NAR* pays fifty cents a line for poems (minimum payment is $20) and approximately $12 a published page for prose. Do NOT submit book reviews. We try to report on manuscripts within three months, but we have a very small staff to read some 4,000 submissions annually. If you haven't had a response within three months, you should ask us what the status of your work is. If we purchase work from you, note that we buy First North American Serial Rights only; copyright reverts to the author after publication.

Please note that we read fiction ONLY between January 1st and April 1st. We read poetry and nonfiction year-round. Fiction received between April 1st and January 1st will be returned unread.

We do NOT consider material that is being submitted simultaneously to other markets, nor do we consider material that has been previously published, even if earlier publication is of small circulation.

Some trivia: Please don't mail your work to us in a Tyvek envelope; it defies letter-openers. Otherwise, our mechanical requirements are the usual ones. Please don't send diskettes; if we buy the work, we'll ask if it's available on diskette, or if it can be directly uploaded from your computer to ours.

And DO send us work you're proud of.

We hope you're already a reader, but if not, we invite you to subscribe at the special authors' rate of $16 for six issues, or send us $4 for the current issue of THE NORTH AMERICAN REVIEW.

Contact Information:
Poetry: Peter Cooley
All Prose: The Editor
University of Northern Iowa
Cedar Falls, IA 50614-0516
(319) 273-6455

Northeast Outdoors
The Publication for Camping & Recreation

Thanks for asking about contributing to NORTHEAST OUTDOORS, the publication for recreation vehicle (RV) owners and campers in the Northeast states.

Our readers are family campers looking for information about:

- specific campgrounds and areas in which to camp in the Northeast (including recreation/touring opportunities and campground facilities),
- RV and camping tips (including RV maintenance, safety, and how to make camping more enjoyable), and
- camp cooking (featuring RV and campfire recipes/

First person articles are preferred, which share family camping and traveling experiences. The average feature length is 800 to 1,000 words, and most articles are purchased with photos (see below).

You may query with an article idea or send a completed (typed) manuscript. We reply within two weeks.

We purchase one-time rights. Please tell whether the story has been previously published, and don't submit a story to us that is being simultaneously submitted to another RV/ camping publication. Payment is upon publication, ranging from $40 (for a manuscript alone) to $80 (for a manuscript with photos we publish).

Photos are published only to illustrate accompanying stories. Black and white, medium-tone (not high contrast) glossies are preferred. Cartoons are often published about RV and camping situations (no Western or Florida settings); payment is $20 per cartoon upon acceptance.

Best regards,

Contact Information:
John Florian, Editorial Director
P.O. Box 2180
Waterbury, CT 06722-2180
(800) 325-6745 or (203) 755-0158 • FAX: (203) 755-3480

Nor'westing

Mission

Nor'westing aims to be the definitive journal of Pacific Northwest cruising. Our goal is to reflect the boater's experience afloat, and to describe the many reasons Pacific Northwest residents chose to ply our local waters. Our articles include experiences from the Oregon Coast to the Alaskan shores. Since our topics deal with cruising destinations and local boating characters, we serve both a power and sailboat audience.

We also enjoy delving into our area's rich maritime history, our boating artisans, and the local industry. We keep an eye on state and federal issues that affect boaters — including tax concerns and environmental action. We watch clubs for happenings, and highlight newsworthy action both on the water and in the clubhouse. Columnists cover galley tips, fishing, trailerboating, and boating electronics.

Because we are a subscriber-based magazine, we listen to our most important critic — the reader. *Nor'westing* is like a trusty ol' boat — constantly evolving (with the owner's love and care) to make the cruising experience as pleasurable as possible, while serving the one initial purpose — to get all enthusiasts out on the water.

In GENERAL:

• All queries and submitted material will be read and responded to. As we have a small editorial staff, this process sometimes takes up to eight weeks.

• Please allow us at least six weeks lead time; a summer cruising piece received in August has far less chance than the same article in April.

• Please send photos! These greatly enhance the story and increase its chances of being considered.

In SPECIFIC:

Cover Photos:

We want high quality, high action, and high resolution photos in sharp focus, with varying contrast. Simple compositions work best, and vertical shots most easily fit the 8½" x 11" format.

We look for photos that tell a story — or, as some of our photographers refer to as "slice of (boating) life" photography. We prefer slidework to be duplicates and clearly identified with photographer's name, and a brief description of the image. Please send SASE with all submissions, we'll add insurance to the mailing cost.

Editorial Photos:

We work most often with story/photo/graphics combinations. Feature work should be taken with black and white film (35mm or larger), close to subject matter, and uncluttered. Glossy prints are preferred, but contact sheets with negatives are accepted. Color prints are accepted in lieu of black and white. We encourage graphics and graphics ideas in any form.

Rights:

Nor'westing generally buys first-time rights and onetime rights to all stories and photographs. We will consider reworked stories from non-competing publications. Information and a copy of the story or photo must be provided upon submission.

Queries:

Mail a manuscript or query letter, rather than call. We appreciate the inclusion of published writing samples along with your letter. All queries will be responded to within eight weeks time.

Editing:

All accepted stories are subject to editing. It's easier for us if your story comes to us on an IBM-formatted disk (along with the hard-copy), on any common word-processing software.

Fees:

Fees vary. Typically, a feature story will earn $100; a longer story with artwork, however, can earn $150. Columnists earn between $50-$75, depending on research put into the piece and the length of the article.

Length:

Features should be 1,500-3,000 words. Columns should be 700-900 words.

Contact Information:
Gloria Kruzner, Editor
6044 Seaview Avenue N.W.
Seattle, WA 98107
(206) 783-8939 • FAX: (206) 783-9011

Nutrition Health Review

Nutrition Health Review, also known as "The Consumer's Medical Journal," is published quarterly. The page size is 10" by 17", the equivalent of four 8½" by 11" pages, double spaced.

The publication is vegetarian-oriented, meaning we do not deal with subjects that favor animal testing, animal foods, cruelty to animals or recipes that contain animal products.

We seek manuscripts dealing with medical progress, information relating to nutritional therapy, genetics, psychiatry, behavior therapy, surgery, pharmacology, animal health, and vignettes relating to health and nutrition.

Humor is welcomed; so are pertinent cartoons and topical llustrations.

Payment is made upon publication.

Unless your manuscript is already finished and meets the outline above, do not write an article before conferring with us.

If you have an outline of facts and prefer to have the material composed by our professionals, please contact us for further instructions.

Our editorial policy is not anti-medical establishment, although we do not hesitate to publish well-documented material critical of current medical errors.

Please communicate with us about whatever ideas you may have.

Contact Information:
P.O. Box 406
Haverford, PA 19041
(610) 896-1853

Oatmeal & Poetry; Wholesome Nutrition From The Heart

(Please refer to Voyager Publishing)

Old West

(Please refer to Western Publications.)

On the Issues
The Progressive Woman's Quarterly

On the Issues is a quarterly magazine for "thinking feminists" – women and men interested in progressive social change, advances in feminist thought, and coverage of politics, society, economics, medicine, relationships, the media and the arts from a range of feminist viewpoints.

Each issue contains news, investigative reports, analytical articles, opinion pieces, personal essays, profiles, interviews, and book reviews. We do not publish fiction or poetry. Rates of pay are modest. We pay upon acceptance.

On the Issues is supported by Choices, a women's medical center in Forest Hills, NY.

Subscriptions are $14.95 per year.

Queries and Writing Samples

The editors welcome ideas from American and international writers, reporters, and thinkers. The best approach is to write us a query letter describing your approach and how you would implement it. We will also consider unsolicited manuscripts. Please let us know if you are submitting the same idea or manuscript elsewhere, or have published on a similar subject within the past two years.

Please include samples of previous publications with your query. We know that many writers are "typecast" by editors, so don't worry if your samples are far afield from the subject matter you want to write about. The editors try to give writers the opportunity to publish pieces too daring, challenging, innovative, or pungent to be published elsewhere. So bring us your best ideas, the ones you feel most the passionate about.

Computer-ease

Please check with the editor about submitting your article electronically, via modem, E-mail, or on disk. We can convert files from most of the popular word processing programs if you send a disk; simply identify what program and which generation of that program your file is in. We can accept either 3.5" or 5.25" disks.

Back-up materials

We will need photocopies of sources for all statistics and hard facts. Also, please include the names and phone numbers of people you have interviewed. We will preserve anonymity, if your sources insist on it, but we will still need to check the quotes.

Revisions

The editors reserve the right to ask for needed improvements in reporting and writing. All articles go through an editing process. Authors who wish to review the final edited copy of their articles should provide a FAX number to which it can be sent.

Photographs and Illustrations

We would appreciate a list of recommendations and sources for photographs and illustrations relevant to your article.

Expenses

We will reimburse for long distance telephone calls, FAX, and overnight delivery if approved by the editor. Any additional expenses must be pre-approved.

Contact Information:
Merle Hoffman, Editor-in-Chief
Ronni Sandroff, Editor
John Stoltenberg, Executive Editor
97-77 Queens Boulevard
Forest Hills, NY 11374-3317
(718) 459-1888

Opera News
Metropolitan Opera Guild, Inc.

Editor: Patrick J. Smith
Managing Editor: Brian Kellow

75% freelance written. Monthly magazine (May-November, biweekly December-April), for people interested in opera; the opera professional as well as the opera audience. Estab. 1936. Circ. 130,000. Pays on publication. Publishes ms an average of 4 months after acceptance. Byline given. Buys first serial rights only. Query for electronic submissions. Sample copy for $4.

Nonfiction: Most articles are commissioned in advance. Monthly issues feature articles on various aspects of opera worldwide; biweekly issues contain articles related to the broadcasts from the Metropolitan Opera. Emphasis is on high quality writing and an intellectual interest to the opera-oriented public. Informational, personal experience, interview, profile, historical, think pieces, personal opinion, opera reviews. Also willing to consider quality fiction and poetry on opera-related themes though acceptance is rare. Written query to Kitty March. No telephone or FAX inquiries. Length: 1,500-2,500 words. Pays $450-$1,000. Sometimes pays the expenses of writers on assignment.

Photos: State availability of photos with submission. Buys one-time rights.

Columns/Departments: Buys 24 mss/year.

Contact Information:
Kitty March, Associate Editor
70 Lincoln Center Plaza, 6th Floor
New York, NY 10023-6593
(212) 769-7080 • FAX: (212) 769-7007

Paddler Magazine
World's No. 1 Canoeing, Kayaking and Rafting Magazine

Paddler Magazine is published six times per year and is written by and for those knowledgeable about river running, canoeing and sea kayaking. Our core audience is the intermediate to advanced paddler, yet we strive to cover the entire range from beginners to experts.

Paddler represents a perfect opportunity for writers and photographers to bolster their portfolios with an established publication. Our editorial coverage is divided between whitewater rafting, kayaking, canoeing and sea kayaking. We strive for a balance between the eastern and western U.S. paddling scene and regularly cover international expeditions. Since one of the publications merged to form *Paddler* was *Canadian Paddler*, we also try to integrate the Canadian paddling scene into each publication.

WRITER'S GUIDELINES

We prefer to receive manuscripts on 3.5-inch, Macintosh-compatible disks under Microsoft Word or Works programs. Please submit material on double-density disks instead of high density. Include typed hard copy with each submission. Dot matrix printouts are acceptable; letter-quality is preferred. Please include name, address, telephone number and social security number in upper left-hand corner of title page. Place name and page number in upper left of each succeeding page.

We prefer queries, but will look at manuscripts on speculation. Most positive responses to queries are on spec, but based on experience, we will occasionally make assignments. Please allow six to eight weeks for a response.

Features and Departments:

Features: *Paddler* publishes at least three features per issue, trying to give equal representation to whitewater rafting, kayaking, sea kayaking and canoeing. One feature per issue is of general interest to all paddlers (i.e. Riverborn Businesses, Top 10 Paddle Towns, etc.). Surprise us with unique ideas. We see entirely too many overwritten, "Me and Joe" destination manuscripts. Unless it's special, save destination-type stories for our destination section. All features should be between 2,000 and 3,000 words and accompanied by high quality transparencies.

Departments: *Paddler* has seven sections per issue. Each submission should include transparencies or black and white photographs.

- "Profiles" is about unique people involved in the sport. We include three profiles per issue: one canoeist, one sea kayaker and one whitewater rafter or kayaker. Each profile should be no longer than 600 words.
- "Destinations" is designed to inform paddlers of unique places to take their crafts. Submissions should include map and photo (800 words).
- "Hotline" concerns itself with timely news relating to the paddling industry. Ideas should be newsworthy (250-750 words).
- "Gear" is about equipment paddlers use, from boats and paddles to collapsible chairs and other accessories (250-800 words).
- "Paddle Tales" are short, humorous anecdotes from trips past, giving the reader a way to get involved with the magazine (75-250 words).
- "Skills" presents a forum for experts to share their tricks of the trade, from techniques to cooking in the backcountry (250-1,000 words).
- "Environment" covers issues related to the paddling environment, from dam updates to access issues and profiles (250-1,000 words).

Manuscript Payment:

Paddler pays 10 cents per word upon publication, based upon the published column inch. This averages out to about $5 per column inch. To encourage brevity, we pay a maximum of $300 for features. Contributors to "Paddle Tales" will receive a subscription to *Paddler*. Letters to the Editor and press releases are unpaid. *Paddler* buys first North American serial rights. All subsequent rights revert back to the author.

PHOTOGRAPHY:

Photo submissions should be 35mm transparencies (Kodachrome or Fujichrome preferred) and/or black-and-white glossy prints. Dupes are acceptable if so marked and if originals are available for publication. Place name, address and phone number on each image. We give one photo credit per image and pay on publication. Photos for "Frames" tend to be scenic; photos for "Ender" are more off-the-wall. Payment is as follows:

Color:

- $150 for cover; $50 for cover inset
- $75 for full page
- $50 for half page to full page
- $25 for a quarter page to half page
- $20 for less than a quarter page

Black and White:

- $50 full page
- $25 half to full page
- $20 quarter to half page
- $15 less than quarter page

Contact Information:
Eugene Buchanan, Editor
P.O. Box 5450
Steamboat Springs, CO 80477
(970) 879-1450

Painting Magazine

Don't be timid...We'd love to hear from you!

Painting Magazine welcomes all types of articles related to painting:

- instructional how-to's
- general interest features
- tips and hints
- techniques

Instructional how-to's include Quick Paint, 1 • 2 • 3 designs, other designs, and the Educational Series.

1 • 2 • 3 designs are extremely popular because they appeal to a wider audience. They let readers choose the amount of detail to be added and show how skills can be improved. The same medium is used to show three paintings in a progressive format. (See recent issues for style/format.)

POLICIES

Final Acceptance

• When your design has been accepted for publication, you will be given a deadline to send the completed design and materials. We deserve the right to ask that you rework your design or the right to return it if we feel it does not meet our necessary standard for publication.

Contracts

• Contracts are sent after the material's due date, provided the completed design and instructions are in our office (see Deadlines).

• Payment is sent within 30 days after the due date stated in the contract. Otherwise, payment is sent within 30 days after receipt of the contract.

• Materials may be sent prior to the deadline; however, the contract will not be sent prior to the materials due date.

Fees

• Fees are based on quality, originality, craftsmanship, complexity, and appeal of the design. We also consider the accuracy and completeness of the instructions.

• Fees are for all rights to the design (see Rights).

• Six complimentary copies (three to "Wise Ideas" contributors and columnists) of the issue in which your design appears are sent shortly after the on-sale date. Depending on the quantity, additional copies are available on request to the editor.

Rights

• Fees are for all rights, meaning you grant us all rights to the design/article, including the right to use it in printed form, video productions, and other derivative works. (The painted piece is returned to you.)

• If you wish to print your original article in another publication after we have paid for all rights, please let us know the publication title and date; we will be happy to grant permission whenever possible.

- You must warrant that you are the sole owner of the design/article, that it is original and does not infringe upon the copyrights or rights of others, and that it has never been published in any form.
- First rights are negotiable.

Issue of Publication

- When a design/article is accepted, we will notify you of the issue in which publication is scheduled. If we move your design/article to another issue before or after (contract is signed and payment processed) the materials deadline, we will notify you.

Manufacturer/Product Names

- To assist our readers, make sure you include:

All information related to products/brushes used to complete the design (manufacturer name, product line name, size, color[s], quantity, etc.) Example: brush manufacturer, brush line name, type (flat, round, etc.), series number, sizes.

Surface source, with address and phone. Make sure the source accepts retail orders.

Completed Designs

- We prefer that you send the completed design so that we can photograph it in our studio. The completed design also helps us edit instructions accurately.
- We will keep your design until the magazine is published and return it shortly after the on-sale date.
- If you need your design returned earlier, let us know in advance and we will do our best to comply.
- Unless return is requested in advance, original instructions, line art, worksheet, etc. are filed at our office.

Pattern, Worksheet

- For worksheets, use a flexible surface that can be wrapped around the color scanner drum.
- Our readers prefer patterns that do not require reduction or enlargement (see Artwork for maximum sizes).

GUIDELINES

1. Submissions

Send a photo or transparency of your original painted piece, your address and phone number where you can be reached during the day. Include a brief description of the surface, medium, size, etc. DO NOT send the painted item until the article has been accepted and a deadline given to you.

2. Acknowledgment/Acceptance

We will send a postcard acknowledging receipt of your submission or materials. You will be notified if the piece is accepted or if it is not accepted.

Postcards are also sent when materials are returned.

3. Artwork

- Use a flexible surface for all line drawings (patterns) and worksheets.
- Use black permanent ink for line drawings, not a felt-tip pen. Penciled and shaded items require special reproduction. Blue pencil does not photograph.
- Include a step-by-step color worksheet as a visual guide for our readers. DO NOT include any wording on the worksheet. Place tracing paper over the worksheet and write information in the correct position. We will typeset the information later. Use the same procedure for line art.

- Oversized patterns will be reduced to fit our format. Magazine trim size is 8" x 10½", including ½" margins on all sides. Maximum pattern sizes without reduction: 7½ " x 10" or 15½" x 10".
- Original instructions, worksheets, and line art are not returned unless requested.
- Include your surface size and source (company name, address, phone). Make sure the company accepts consumer queries/orders.

4. Format

Use the following order when preparing your article.

Refer to recent issues of the magazine. (Some may not apply to your article.)

Title

Byline (your name)

Opening/Introduction

A brief, informal paragraph that is funny or serious, like: why this piece was painted, an interesting story, suggestions for uses, etc.

Palette

List ALL colors under company brand name. (Example: DecoArt Americana). If abbreviations are used in instructions, include them here. List conversions. Include mixes.

Brushes

List ALL under the company brand name. Include type, series (if given), and size.

Supplies

List ALL other needed. (Company name, product name; then size, color, quantity.)

Surface Source

Make sure surface is available and if retail orders are accepted. If surface is not readily available to readers, give alternatives. Include name, address, phone number. Note: If wood surfaces can be cut, include measurements/instructions.

Preparation

Give step-by-step information.

Tips for Success

Give suggestions or reminders that will help readers as they are painting.

Terms or Techniques

Give descriptions that clarify your methods. Include necessary artwork/line art.

Painting Instructions

Include instructions under each element of the design (example: leaves). List color mixes under palette.

Make sure to identify which brush is used when, and how it is loaded. (Past articles have included a long list of brushes, but little or no instruction on which brush is used during painting.)

Include line art or photos if needed and indicate placement.

Antiquing

Finishing

Give the final details (example: varnishing, trim, fabric care, etc.).

Closing

Include appropriate comments.

Short Bio

Give brief information in four to five sentences.

Referral

Include "Write to…first name and address."

5. Shipping

Once scheduled, we send a reminder postcard a month prior to the materials deadline for each issue.

Deadlines

Issue:	Photo Submission/Description Due:	Materials Due (Once accepted):
February	June 1	August 1
April	August 1	October 1
June	October 1	December 1
August	December 1	February 1
October	February 1	April 1
December	April 1	June 1

To assist with seasonal designs: Each issue is mailed to subscribers approximately four-and-one-half months after the materials due date and is on-sale (newsstand) two weeks later. Example: February mails around December 12; is on sale around December 26.

Note: Christmas designs are published throughout the year.

1 • 2 • 3 Articles

Refer to recent issues for the progressive format. Progressive means that the articles are similar to building blocks—the design can be completed as instructed in 1• Basic or with additional instructions/details included under 2 • Added details and 3 • Add more details.

Please call or write if more explanation is needed.

Addendum

Due to a continuing paper shortage and rising costs we will be keeping tighter control on the editorial pages, resulting in rescheduling some articles. This means that, except for 1-2-3 and educational series articles, the 1996 issues are booked.

Because our readers prefer full-size patterns (hopefully without having to piece them together) and our pattern pages are either eight or twelve pages, we will be looking closer at pattern sizes when considering submissions. Like most magazines, the trim size is not 8-½" x 11". Ours is 8" x 10-½"—to avoid piecing, the maximum pattern sizes are 7-½" x 10" or 15-½" x 10". (This doesn't mean that articles with oversize patterns will automatically be declined.

Our readers have also requested that more information be included about ordering the surface used. Having to write for prices and shipping charges, or not having a number to call, delays ordering—critical for holiday pieces. I've explained that price changes could cause problems for the supplier, especially if they are painting from a back issue. Their request was that at least a phone number be included. It is also important that you contact the surface source to assure that retail mail orders are accepted (if not, provide an alternative). If you sell the surface, it's OK with us—just be sure to include shipping. Information re cutting their own wood is also OK, but remember that many painters do not have access to a wood cutter.

Another reader request: Tell them which brushes are used when. The supply list often includes a long list of brushes, but little or no information in the instructions.

I welcome 1-2-3 articles anytime—they are the most difficult to obtain, yet are the most popular with our readers. The educational series are 2-3 brief articles that build information on a particular subject or technique.

I hope this helps in preparing articles and submissions.

Contact Information:

Beth Browning, Editor
2400 Devon, Suite 375
Des Plaines, IL 60018-4618
(800) CRAFTS-1 or (847) 635-5800

Parabola

The Magazine of Myth and Tradition

PARABOLA is a quarterly journal devoted to the exploration of the quest for meaning as it is expressed in the myths, symbols, and tales of the world's religious traditions. Particular emphasis is focused in the journal on the relationship between this vast store of wisdom and life in the contemporary world.

Each issue of PARABOLA is organized around a theme. Examples of themes we have explored in the past include Rites of Passage, Sacred Space, The Child, Ceremonies, Addiction, The Sense of Humor, Hospitality, The Hunter, and The Call.

TYPES OF SUBMISSIONS

Articles and Translations

PARABOLA welcomes original essays and translations. We look for lively, penetrating material unencumbered by jargon or academic argument. All articles must be directly related to the theme of an issue.

Tangents

PARABOLA occasionally publishes extended reviews of books, movies, videos, performances, art exhibitions, and other current programs or events in a section called "Tangents." These reviews are intended as a bridge between the theme-related front half of the magazine and the reviews at the rear. "Tangents" should bear some connection to the theme of the issue, although it does not have to be as direct as an article.

Poetry and Short Fiction

We will occasionally consider poetry and short fiction, but only if directly related to the theme of an issue. If you have poems or stories for more than one issue, please make a separate submission for each one.

Book Reviews and Epicycles

Separate guidelines for book, video, and audio reviews and retellings of traditional stories are available on request.

SUBMISSION GUIDELINES

1. Length

Articles and Tangents run 2,000-4,000 words.
Book reviews run 500 words.
Retellings of traditional stories run 500-1,500 words.
Poetry runs 70 lines maximum.

2. Query letter

Please send us a one-page letter describing what you propose to write about and how it relates to a given theme. We will let you know if we are interested, or we may suggest a different approach or subject. If the idea fits into our editorial plans, you will be given a deadline to submit a finished manuscript. Assignment of a deadline does not guarantee acceptance or publication of an article; it only means that we are interested in your idea and would like to pursue it.

Brief queries may be sent via e-mail.

3. Preparation of copy

In the upper left-hand corner of the first page of your article, please type the following information:

1. Your name
2. Your address and telephone number
3. Your social security number
4. Word Count

If endnotes are used, they should be as complete as possible: include the author's name, book or article title, translator or editor (if applicable), city of publication, name of publisher, date, and page numbers.

4. Electronic submissions

All articles should be submitted as hard copy. Please state in your cover letter if you will be able to provide us with electronic copy on disk or by e-mail. We can accept 3.5" or 5.25" diskettes in most Macintosh and IBM-compatible applications; 3.5" is preferable.

Upon acceptance we will request your disk or transmission. PARABOLA will not accept any articles via e-mail without a prior query.

If you are sending us a disk copy, please try to keep the formatting as simple as possible. In particular, we prefer manual endnotes to automatic footers.

5. Biographical information

On a separate page, include a brief (2-3 sentence) biographical description of yourself. Fit the description to the subject matter of the article, e.g., for an article on Tibetan Buddhism, "Smith spent three years raveling in Tibet." Or, a publication credit "Smith is the author of *Pilgrimage in Tibet* (W. W. Norton, 1987)." Least interesting, though acceptable, "Smith is a freelance writer and student of Tibetan Buddhism." Be brief and specific. Rather than "Smith is a novelist," say "Smith's most recent book is *Tibetan Myths and Masters* (E. P. Dutton, 1989)." Always include your publisher.

6. Rights

PARABOLA purchases the right to use an article in all substantially complete versions (including non-print versions) of a single issue of our journal. We also request the right to use the piece in the promotion of PARABOLA, and to authorize single-copy reproductions for academic purposes. All other rights are retained by the author.

7. Payment

Payment is made upon publication. Publication is not guaranteed.

Contact Information:
The Editors
656 Broadway
New York, NY 10012
(212) 505-9037
E-mail: parabola@panix.com

Parade Publications, Inc.

Thank you for your interest in *Parade*. The following guidelines should help prospective writers tailor and present article ideas for editorial consideration.

Give us a unique perspective on the news.

Parade covers topics as diverse as the 81 million readers we reach each Sunday. Many stories involve news, social issues, common health concerns, sports, community problem-solving or extraordinary achievements of ordinary people. We seek unique angles on all topics—this is especially important for subjects that have already received national attention in newspapers and other media.

Topics must appeal to a broad audience.

- Your subject must have national scope or implications. For example, a story about first-year interns at a Dubuque hospital might have limited appeal, but the subject of job opportunities or working conditions in hospitals across the nation would be of widespread concern.
- Reporting must be authoritative and original, based on interviews that you conduct yourself. Health articles, for example, should quote medical experts rather than simply relate a personal tale.
- Choose a topic that you care about deeply. If your story does not make you happy or sad, angry or elated, excited or curious, chances are that *Parade* readers won't care that much either.

Do not propose spot news, fiction or poetry, cartoons, regular columns, nostalgia or history, quizzes, puzzles, or compilations of quotes or trivia. We almost never assign unsolicited technical-science queries or unsolicited queries for interviews with entertainment celebrities, politicians or sports figures.

You should be able to write your article concisely.

Parade has room to publish only the most tightly focused story. Topics that will be compelling and complete at 1,200 to 1,500 words are the only ones worth proposing.

How to submit your proposal to *Parade*.

Assignments are based on query letters of one page—three or four paragraphs should be sufficient. Propose only one topic per query. The query should include:

- Your central theme or point in no more than a few sentences. If you cannot state the theme in this way, the article surely lacks focus.
- Your sources on all sides of the issue. Whom will you interview?
- The story's general trajectory. How will you organize it?
- A summary of your most important writing credits.

Attach one or two writing samples and send to the address below.

Though many queries have merit, because of great volume we can only assign those few that can precisely meet our needs and standards. Again, thank you for your interest, and best of luck in your efforts.

Contact Information:
Articles Correspondent
711 Third Avenue
New York, NY 10017
(212) 450-7000

Paramour Magazine

All submissions should have erotic, sexual or sensual content; it need not be explicit. We publish a wide range of work from subtle/sensual to graphic/explicit. All styles of sexuality (gay, straight, bi, mono; leather, lace, appliance, vegetable...) are acceptable. If you have not seen the magazine and would like to see it, sample copies are available for $4.95 US ($6 overseas) by check or money order payable to *Paramour*.

All work should have your name, address and phone number on every page. All work submitted should be for publication; don't send samples of work which you don't intend for us to publish. If you must send work that has been published before or has been multiple-submitted, please tell us where (we're extremely peevish about this)! Also, please include a two or three sentence biography, suitable for use in our Contributors Notes. If we've already published your work, let us know if it needs to be updated. If your work is accepted we may want to use it on our (Internet) Web site. If you don't want your work on the net, please let us know.

WRITING SUBMISSIONS:

Paramour accepts unsolicited fiction and poetry. We're also interested in essays, interviews, reviews (film, video, performance, book, comic, and many other products) and column ideas, but strongly suggest you discuss your concept with us first. If we encourage you to pursue your concept, this does not guarantee your piece will be accepted. Interviews and reviews should be accompanied by imagery of the subject whenever possible.

Please submit your work in hard copy. If possible, also submit it on a Mac disk, in Microsoft Word or ASCII file format. Or, you may e-mail submissions to us – please place the text within the e-mail message, unencoded.

Fiction: We generally print one or two stories per issue of up to 4,000 words. We print a great many more stories of 1,000 - 2,000 words or even shorter.

Poetry: Please do not send more than ten poems per quarter.

Writing submissions will not be returned.

ARTWORK SUBMISSIONS:

Paramour accepts photographs, illustrations, cartoons, collages and reproductions of larger media.

Photos: Slides are acceptable (please number them!), but we prefer prints, 4 x 6" or larger if possible (black and white are best; color work that has a lot of contrast is fine). Photos must be accompanied by copies of your model releases AND COPIES OF MODELS' DRIVER'S LICENSES OR BIRTH CERTIFICATES (YES, THIS IS NEW).

Drawings, Paintings, Cartoons, etc.: Please do not send your originals! If you get half-tones, use a 150 line screen. If the reproductions you send are not adequate print quality, we'll contact you.

Artwork will be returned only if you send a SASE with correct postage. Don't meter the return envelope!

PAYMENT:

Payment is 3 copies of the issue in which your work appears plus a one-year subscription to the magazine.

Please allow up to four months response time.

Deadlines: March 1 for Spring/Summer Issue; release date May 1
June 1 for Summer/Fall Issue; release date August 1
September 1 for Fall/Winter; release date November 1
December 1 for Winter/Spring; release date February 1

Please call or e-mail us if you have questions. Thank you for your interest.

Contact Information:
P.O. Box 949
Cambridge, MA 02140-0008
(617)-499-0069
E-mail: paramour@xensei.com

ParentGuide

Thank you for your interest in PARENTGUIDE, the New York Metropolitan area's largest oldest parenting publication. We are a monthly, tabloid-sized newspaper catering to the needs and interests of parents who have children under the age of 12. Our total circulation is 210,000. PARENTGUIDE's monthly column and feature articles health, education, child-rearing, current events, parenting issues, recreational activities and social events. We also run a complete calendar of local events. We welcome articles from professional authors as well as never-before-published writers. Share your personal experiences, advice, humorous anecdotes, parental concerns, professional knowledge or newsworthy observations with us. Manuscripts can be written in either third or first person format. You are invited to send a query letter or finished manuscript. Allow for a three month lead time. All manuscripts should be between 750 and 1,500 words in length. A brief bio should be included and, if possible, photos or any other artwork. We do NOT offer financial payment to any of our freelance writers, but all contributors do receive masthead credit, a byline and a brief bio. We appreciate your interest and look forward to working with you.

Thank you,
Jenine DeLuca, Editor

Contact Information:
419 Park Avenue South, 13th Floor
New York, NY 10016
(212) 213-8840

ParentLife

ParentLife

ParentLife is a Christian monthly magazine for parents of children birth to twelve. It focuses on the practical aspects of parenting, as well as informs, educates, and inspires parents to be aware of issues and understand their children at each stage of development.

Content: The editorial staff will evaluate articles dealing with any subject of interest to parents of preschoolers and children.

Preparation: Cover page should include suggested title and blurb, byline, author's full name, address, social security number, and rights offered (all, first, one-time reprint).

Submit manuscripts 600-1,220 words in length.

Queries with writing sample are preferred.

Disk submissions must be accompanied by a hard copy. Prefer disk on a Macintosh word processing program, but can convert most IBM programs.

Writing Tips: Quoted material must be properly documented (publisher, location, date, and page numbers), along with permission verification.

Include Bible references and thoughts when appropriate.

Remember readers are parents of preschoolers and children.

Use brief, clear sentences.

Construct paragraphs logically.

Sidebars helpful.

Payment: Payment is negotiable and on acceptance.

Publication: Writers will receive, without cost, 3 advance copies of the issue in which their manuscripts are published. Extra copies can be ordered from the Customer Service Center (MSN 113 at address below, or (800) 458-BSSB).

• For a sample copy, send a 9"x12" manila envelope with your address and return postage.

Contact Information:
Michelle Hicks, Managing Editor
127 Ninth Avenue, North
Nashville, TN 37234-0140
(615) 251-2229

Peace

PEACE, the magazine of the 60s is published quarterly (March, June, September and December). We are 98% subscriber written. The preferred material is nonfiction, but fiction is acceptable. Virtually any subject matter is acceptable, however; the 60s must be integral to the story. General length is wide open, preferably under 3,000 words, although longer works will also be considered.

Some features of PEACE include:

• Life on the Road: Touring the US in the ever popular VW bus, hitchhiking through Europe, trekking across Marakesh, Backpacking in Nepal.

• War: Stories from the men and women in Vietnam, stories from the survivors of those who did not come back. The good stories, as well as the bad. Articles from the antiwar protests, the draft resistors, conscientious objectors, draft card burners. Stories from those who did not go to Vietnam, for whatever reason.

• Interviews: People, writers, artists. The influential, famous, infamous, and the not so famous.

• Politics: Civil rights movement, women's movement, gay rights, Watergate, 1968 Democratic convention, ecology, and the environment.

• Life in the 60s: top singles, albums, music and television trivia.

• Photo Gallery: vehicles, fashion, body painting, poster art, album covers, movie posters.

• Classified: Here is where you can find your long lost buddies, find your 60s memorabilia, or sell that lava lamp.

• Generation Gap II: A new perspective on the 60s by the generation raised in the late 60s/early 70s. Today's college students and their rising concern over the same issues as their parents.

• Artwork: All artwork considered. Psychedelic, black & white photos, line drawings, pen and ink.

As a new magazine our pay rate is admittedly low, but with your support, as we grow, our fees shall increase. Payment rate for one time publishing rights: $0.05 per word up to a maximum of $100.00 (temporarily suspended).

Send your queries, essays, article ideas, artwork, photos, poetry, fiction (hard copy or MS Word for Mac 3½" diskette). For a sample of PEACE, please enclose a check for $4.50 to see what we've been doing.

Contact Information:
Linda James, Editor
2753 East Broadway, Suite #101-1969
Mesa, AZ 85204
(602) 817-0124

Penthouse Variations

Thank you for expressing interest in contributing to *Penthouse Variations* magazine. Your unique lifestyles and liberated erotic experiences make up our entire publication.

Contributions to *Variations* should reflect good grammar and the kind of language you would be proud to use with a good friend.

Variations is proud of its reader-generated sections and less experienced writers should feel free to make submissions to the editor on this basis. Although we do not make payments for letter material, the staff makes necessary editorial corrections and letters are published supporting most of the featured stories. Unfortunately, we cannot reply to each letter personally with sexual advice or the date of publication.

You may feel your material is good enough to qualify to compete with other professional writers. If you are making a professional freelance submission to be published as one of our featured stories, be sure to clearly indicate this in a cover letter to the editor. We pay up to $400 for an accepted, fully-revised manuscript. We publish 3,000-word first person narratives of erotic experience, squarely focused within one of the pleasure categories, described as an earnest contribution to a couple's sexual lifestyle.

Manuscripts take six to eight weeks to be read. They are rejected usually because of the quality of the writing or because the category described is unsuitable or oversold to us. Thorough perusal of several issues will show you categories most often used, as well as our style and vocabulary.

We guarantee confidentiality of all material, both letters and articles, Your name will never appear in print. In fact, we choose pseudonyms in order to avoid any inclination toward the writers libeling themselves in choosing their own.

Good luck with your writing.

The Editors

Contact Information:
277 Park Avenue, 4th Floor
New York, NY 10172
(212) 702-6000

Perceptions Magazine

SUBJECT

Perceptions magazine editorial staff works with writers to develop themes. A list of requested articles is available. To prevent duplication of efforts, call or write to advise us of your article's subject matter.

FORMAT

Writer's name, address and phone number and a word count must appear on the upper right corner of the first or cover page. Articles may be up to 2,500 words. This length has proven effective in our presentation and allows us to keep a variety of subjects in each issue.

Submit two copies (2) of the article.

Submissions must include an electronic format. If you cannot submit an electronic format, please call us to make alternate arrangements. This is likely to delay the publishing of the article.

We accept IBM, Macintosh, or Apple IIe disks, or text via modem. When submitting an IBM disk, use Rich Text Format (RTF) on a 3.5 inch disk. If your word processing program does not have this feature, please submit in ASCII.

ELECTRONIC MAIL

Contact us at either address shown below.

SUBMISSION TIMES

We must receive a first draft no less than two months prior to layout. Nevertheless, since we work up to two issues in advance, your article may not be published for several months. This has no reflection on the quality of your work. If you have sent an article and have not received a reply within 30 days, call our office.

An editor will contact you for clarification or for rewrites. Photographs, slides, negatives and graphics that accompany the article are encouraged. Any ideas for graphics should also be noted.

Send two copies of your article to the address below. Call if further clarification is needed. All requests for publication of articles submitted after deadline will be denied; please do not request an exception.

REVIEW PROCEDURE

Two editors review all articles submitted.

If your article is published, we will retain it per the terms of the Work-For-Hire agreement. All articles are subject to editing for clarity and length. If extensive editing is required, it will be returned to you for a rewrite. Any major changes will be reviewed with the writer prior to publication.

PAYMENT

Perceptions pays $5.00 per published article as a gesture of gratitude along with three magazines of each issue in which it is published. All articles published become the property of the Publisher, all rights reserved. A Work-For-Hire Contract sent at the time of the article's proposal or acceptance must be returned before publication.

WORK-FOR-HIRE-CONTRACT

This contract is standard in the industry. It is used by *Perceptions* magazine as an agreement for any article that you submit that we accept for publication. Our interest applies to the amount of time *Perceptions* takes to work with writers and articles: editing, reworking, formatting, layout, etc.

TO REPRINT – you will be issued a "no fee" license to reprint your *Perception*'s article in another publication with the stipulation that the following appears with it: "Reprinted from *Perceptions* magazine (issue and date) – 6 issues $25, call for international rates (800)276-4448." If another publication offers *Perceptions* remuneration for the article, *Perceptions* will pay you 50%.

If you change your article substantially after we have published it by expanding the ideas presented, changing the angle or shortening the article, you remove it from the Work-For-Hire category.

The Work-For-Hire Contract in essence makes the writer and *Perceptions* magazine partners in the publishing venture, since we supply the layout, publishing costs, and broad market exposure for the writer.

STYLE/CONTENT

Our goal is to ensure personal freedom by educating the public. We seek succinct, vital articles that address poignant issues with a balance of realism and optimism. Heavy-handed approaches are best avoided; the intensity of most topics speaks for itself. Promotional articles are treated as advertisements; space must be purchased at the same rate as any display ad.

When presenting controversial material, quote references and/or use footnotes. Writers' personal views should be stated as such. If controversial or provocative claims cannot be substantiated, this must also be clarified. Writers are encouraged to read their article to friends for feedback prior to submission. Please familiarize yourself with our "Tips on Libel."

RECOMMENDED READING

William Zinsser's *On Writing Well*, and *Elements of Style* by William Strunk and E. B. White. We use Associated Press Guidelines.

Contact Information:
Judi V. Brewer, Editor-in-Chief
c/o 10736 Jefferson Boulevard, Suite 502
Culver City, CA 90230
(310) 313-5185
E-mail: perceptions@primenet.com or perceptmag@aol.com

Persimmon Hill

Persimmon Hill

Persimmon Hill magazine is published quarterly by the National Cowboy Hall of Fame and Western Heritage Center (address below), for an audience interested in Western art, history, ranching and rodeo. Circulation approximately 15,000. Buys first North American rights; byline given. Accepts no reprints. Pays upon publication. Query with clips. No phone queries are accepted. Allow a minimum of six weeks for a response from the editor and editorial board. Sample copy $8.00, including postage and handling.

Nonfiction: Historical and contemporary articles on notable persons connected with pioneering the American West; Western art, rodeo, cowboys; Western flora and animal life; or other phenomena of the West of today or yesterday. Only thoroughly researched and historically authentic material is considered. We require lively, top-notch writing for a popular audience. Length: 1,500 words. Pay ranges from $150 to $250, including illustrations.

Photos: Black and white glossy prints or color transparencies, submitted and purchased with the manuscript. Captions required.

Format for Submissions: We accept only typed or letter quality computer submissions. Computer discs accompanied by letter quality print-out may be submitted. Discs must be in a software program that is compatible with WordPerfect 6.0. Software program information must be provided with the manuscript. The discs will not be returned.

Tips: Send us a story that captures the spirit of adventure and individualism that typifies the Old West or reveals a facet of the Western lifestyle in contemporary society. The availability of superior illustrations or photographs will strongly influence the sale of an article to us.

Contact Information:
M.J. Van Deventer, Director of Publications
1700 N.E. 63rd Street
Oklahoma City, OK 73111
(405) 478-6404

Petersen's PHOTOgraphic

EDITORIAL CONCEPT: *Petersen's PHOTOgraphic* magazine is edited for the beginner through advanced amateur to cover all aspects of still and video photography. Emphasis is on "how-to" articles that explain how to create the aesthetic and interesting photographs we showcase. Articles are clearly written and well illustrated, in color and black-and-white. No fiction, cartoons or poetry. Contributions are on speculation, subject to final editorial approval. Assignments are rarely given.

FEATURE REQUIREMENTS: We run articles that help our readers improve their photographic skills. Therefore, we only run photographic portfolios with an accompanying text that explains how the images were made. Articles should cover a photographic specialty (such as fashion photography, wildlife photography), a photographic topic (darkroom, film, filters, lighting techniques, video), a photographic technique (fill-flash, special effects, high-key lighting) or any other type of how-to article that will help our readers improve their photographic skills or expand their photographic horizons.

MONTHLY PHOTO CONTEST SECTION: The Monthly Photo Contest has its own, unique rules and is not subject to the guidelines or pay rates listed here. Please follow the rules found in each issue of the magazine.

GENERAL COPY REQUIREMENTS: Since the concept of our magazine is photography, photographs must be reviewed before an article is accepted. A selection of the photographs appropriate to the article must accompany article queries and manuscripts.

MAC or IBM PC-created manuscripts are preferred. (If you send a disk, always include a paper printout of the manuscript.) Save text as Microsoft Word or ASCII, if possible. Typed manuscripts should have a maximum of 60 characters per line. Manuscripts must be submitted in final draft form, with captions on a separate sheet. *Petersen's PHOTOgraphic* reserves the right to edit or condense all or part of the manuscript to meet our editorial needs.

GENERAL PHOTO REQUIREMENTS: Because *PHOTOgraphic* magazine is devoted to photography, all photographic submissions must be of the finest quality—they must be aesthetically pleasing and technically superb. The following are general rules of thumb for contributors:

1. Color images may be submitted as transparencies or prints, although transparencies are preferred. Black-and-white images should be printed on 8"x10" or 11"x14" glossy paper and sent to us unmounted.
2. We require model releases for all recognizable people in photographs.
3. Before/After pictures are especially needed, because they illustrate the benefits of using a particular technique, composition, etc.

4. If a technique or process is the theme of the article, try to show every step. We can edit out pictures if we don't have the space to run them; however, we cannot add pictures if we don't have them.

5. If mechanical drawings, plans, cutaways, charts, etc. would be helpful in showing what is to be achieved, please include a rough sketch, properly identified with dimensions and all other information.

6. Captions must be provided for all photographs on a separate sheet of paper.

7. We reserve the right to publish color images in black-and-white, depending upon our editorial needs.

SUBMISSION REQUIREMENTS: Glass-mounted slides are unacceptable. If you require proof of receipt, please do not call the magazine; rather, send your submission via certified mail, return receipt requested.

PAY RATES: EDITORIAL: Rates vary, based upon usage. Full articles (photos and text) average $300-$400. We purchase one-time usage of photographs. COVERS: Payment for cover usage will be negotiated separately with the photographer.

ACCEPTANCE: Manuscripts submitted to *PHOTOgraphic* are considered "accepted" upon publication. All material held on a "tentatively scheduled" basis is subject to change or rejection up to the time of printing. It is understood that material submitted to *PHOTOgraphic* is original, free and clear of all copyrights and in no way infringes upon previously published works. Upon publication, the material is copyrighted by *Petersen's PHOTOgraphic* magazine, and permission to reprint any of the material must be obtained from the publisher.

SCHEDULING: Generally, the editorial staff of *Petersen's PHOTOgraphic* magazine plans issues six to 12 months in advance.

Contact Information:
Geoff Engel, Editor
6420 Wilshire Boulevard
Los Angeles, CA 90048
(213) 782-2200

Phi Delta Kappa Educational Foundation

The Special Publications department of Phi Delta Kappa is an activity of the Phi Delta Kappa Educational Foundation.

When Dr. George H. Reavis made possible the establishment of the Foundation, he articulated a vision of the Foundation's work:

The purpose of the Phi Delta Kappa Educational Foundation is to contribute to a better understanding of 1.) the nature of the educative process, and 2.) the relation of education to human welfare.

Dr. Reavis viewed this purpose in a larger sense as shaping public policy through understanding:

In our democracy public policy is determined by popular will, and popular will is based upon popular understanding. Our governmental (and educational) policy can be no better in the long run than our popular understanding.

This statement of purpose and its rationale laid a foundation for the role of Special

Publications within the Foundation. Since the establishment of the Foundation in 1966, Special Publications has acquired and published a variety of works designed to enhance the professional literature of education. Those works are brought to print either as Foundation monographs, which are books of various lengths, or as Fastbacks.

Following are guidelines for writers who wish to develop a manuscript for one of these forms.

Fastbacks®

The *PDK* fastbacks were initiated in 1972 as a continuing series of short, authoritative publications for educators at all levels. Since the series was created, more than 7 million copies of the fastbacks have been disseminated. Today, the fastbacks are published in two annual sets of eight titles. These sets are released in the fall and spring.

The fastbacks often have been described as "sophisticated primers." Each one focuses on a specific, often fairly narrow topic. Many, if not most, are oriented to the practitioner, such as an elementary classroom teacher, an instructional specialist, a principal, a school superintendent, or a university professor. A few are more theoretical. Several focus on exemplary programs or Profile specific schools.

In short, the topic range is as broad as the profession. Indeed, this is specifically done in order to mirror the broad membership base of Phi Delta Kappa.

Manuscript length: 10,000 words

Honorarium: $500

Short Monographs

Like the fastbacks, *PDK*'s short monographs are narrowly focused and practical in character. Good examples in this range are titles such as Planning for Disaster, Responding to Adolescent Suicide, and the nine volumes of the Elementary Principal series.

Manuscript length: 20,000 - 30,000 words Honorarium: $1,000 - $2,000

Books

Books published by the *PDK* Educational Foundation, like the fastbacks and short monographs, reflect a broad range of professional interests and topics. Some are sweeping in scope; a good example is John I. Goodlad's classic What Schools Are For. Others focus more narrowly, such as Kenneth Chuska's Improving Classroom Questions and Carol Hillman's Before the School Bell Rings. Some concentrate on current issues, such a John F. Jennings' four-volume series, National Issues in Education. Still others are basic resources, an example being the third edition of A Digest of Supreme Court Decisions Affecting Education.

Manuscript length: 40,000 - 70,000 words. Honorarium: $3,000 - $5,000

Of course, the best way to understand the scope and character of *PDK* Special Publications is to per use the product catalogue and to read a few of the books, monographs, and fastbacks.

Guidelines for Submissions

1. Initially, a query letter is preferred. This letter should succinctly state the purpose and audience for the publication, a proposed manuscript length, and a suggested writing timeline. The editor responds to queries usually within two weeks.

2. A prospective author should be prepared to submit a well-developed, annotated outline. For longer works, the editor may request a sample chapter. The editor responds to such proposals usually within two months, often sooner.

3. In most instances, an author-publisher agreement (contract) is issued on the basis of a proposal. In some cases, however, submission of the full manuscript will be required prior to the issuance of a contract to publish.

4. The editor will assist the author in developing a successful manuscript. However, despite the best intentions of both author and editor, sometimes a manuscript will be judged

unacceptable. Authors should be aware that *PDK* editors reserve the right to edit extensively and, on occasion, to rewrite poorly written materials. But substantive changes are not made without the author's permission.

5. Authors are advised to avoid education jargon. Simple, straightforward prose that makes ample use of examples, anecdotes, and case studies is preferred. Any citations must be complete and the *PDK* style is based on the *Chicago Manual of Style*.

6. Tables, charts, and graphs should be used only when they are necessary to understand the text. Large figures are discouraged, particularly for the fastbacks which are printed in a small format.

7. Photographs may be submitted with a manuscript. Clear, 5x7-inch (or larger) black-and-white prints are preferred. All photos must include captions. A model release must be provided for all persons who can be identified in a photograph.

8. Manuscripts must be submitted on standard size paper using a type that can be electronically scanned. Authors may submit their work on computer disk; however, a hard copy also must be provided.

9. *PDK* purchases all rights by contract. Payment is made in the form of a one-time honorarium, which is paid about one month prior to publication. Special Publications does not pay royalties.

10. The editor reserves the right to select the manner of publication - for example, whether to bring out a book in a paperback or hardback form - and how the work will be promoted. Costs of production, promotion, and dissemination are borne by *PDK*.

Queries, proposals, and other correspondence should be directed to:

Contact Information:
Donovan R. Walling, Editor of Special Publications
P.O. Box 789
Bloomington, IN 47402-0789
(812) 339-1156 • FAX: (812) 339-0018

The Phoenix

Recovery • Renewal • Growth

Story Topics: Query or submit manuscript. Articles that address one of our themes (editorial calendar available) or fit the Bodywise, Family Skills, or Personal Story departments have the best chance of being accepted. Study sample issues (free with 9"x12" SASE with 4 first class stamps) and be sure you understand our mission (on page 4 of every issue). In general our readers are interested in articles that help them explore how to improve their physical, emotional, mental and spiritual well-being. Some of the articles we publish deal specifically with recovery related to addictions and Twelve Step programs.

Story Length: 500-1,500 words. Shorter pieces are easier to place.

Deadlines: We'll discuss the deadline when the story is assigned, but in general, we need to have copy and a disk by the first of the month two months before publication. If you can't send a disk copy, please give us another ten days.

Publication: There is no guarantee of publication in nay specific issue, even if planned for that issue. If we've assigned an article and you've delivered a satisfactory piece on time, we will make every effort to publish it promptly. In the rare event that it becomes necessary, we will pay a kill fee of 1¢ per word (we determine the appropriate word count).

Payment: We pay within 30 days of publication. We pay between 3 - 5¢ per word or, for those who want name recognition in the community, with an extended byline. Extended bylines should be 3 - 5 sentences. We reserve the right to edit. Your phone number will be printed in the byline if you wish, but we do not include addresses or dates of events. Don't include adjectives or adverbs—just the facts. "Best-selling" is okay if true; phrases like "the best" are not. We will mention the title and publisher's name for a book, but nothing else.

Copyright: We buy first rights. Occasionally we buy reprints. We also reserve the right to reprint the piece in anthologies or other work by the publisher, for which we will pay the writer an all-inclusive royalty of 25% of the original fee for the piece, or 1¢ per word, whichever is greater, for each second and subsequent use of the piece. Writers retain all other rights.

Submission standards: If possible, send both a printed copy and a disk. (Never send only the disk.) We can read just about any Macintosh or IBM-compatible disk (3.5") except Apple II. We prefer DSDD or higher density disks. Label the disk with your name, title of the piece, and word processor used.

Indicate estimated word count in upper left hand corner of a printed copy. Include your name and page number on each of the printed pages, but don't include page headers on the disk copy. Use em-dashes to separate tangential or supplemental phrases—phrases that add information to the text or emphasize a point—rather than parentheses. If your word processor can't make one—use a double hyphen. Use italics for emphasis. Do not use ALL CAPS for anything! Do not underline for any reason! Put subheads in boldface. Include your byline in boldface: By Pat Samples. Put publication titles in italics, except The PHOENIX, which should be bold and italics.

On the path of recovery and growth, every issue is a gift.

Contact Information:
Pat Samples, Editor
7152 Unity Avenue, North
Brooklyn Center, MN 55429
(800) 983-9887 or (612) 560-5199 • FAX: (612) 291-0533
E-mail: phoenix1@winternet.com or http://www.gartland.com/phoenix

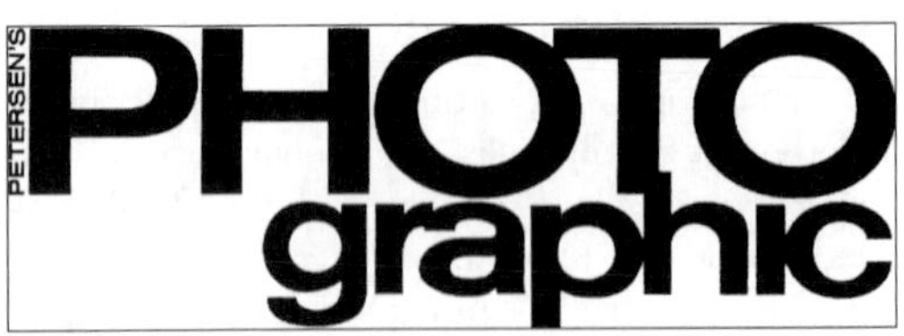

Photo Techniques

First principle: Be easy on yourself. Our acceptance ratio is low. Unless you really don't mind doing a lot of work—quite possibly for nothing—query us first with an idea or outline before you go to the trouble of writing up an entire article on speculation. When sending work as illustrations, don't put your self out unnecessarily. Send dupe slides or repro prints you can afford to live without for a while. If you need your pictures returned to you while an article is being held for possible publication, by all means let us know.

Second principle: Be easy on us. We do everything on Macintosh computers. All submissions should include: cover letter, hard copy, the text file of the article on a 3.5" disc; and illustrations 8.5" x 11" or less in size unless a larger size is unavoidable. Slides must be good dupes in slide pages. With prints, for both reproduction purposes and for organizational convenience, we much prefer 8 x 10s to any other size.

Formatting [bold, italic, etc.] disc files: Use a minimum of formatting unless you are using WriteNow version 4.0 for Macintosh. We can convert PC files, but we need 3.5" floppies. With Mac discs, save your files as WriteNow (first choice), Microsoft Word (second choice), or ASCII a.k.a. "text" (third choice). Note to frequent contributors: WriteNow is not an expensive program…hint…hint…

Charts and graphs should be sent as hard copy.

If you don't have access to a computer, typewritten copy, 40 characters per line, will serve. If accepted, it will be scanned into our computer.

Style Guidelines:

1. We are a magazine aimed at an audience which has two main distinguishing features: they have already made a commitment to photography, and they are already actively involved in photography. For many contributors, this means you will be writing for an audience of your peers. Therefore, don't talk down to your readers and don't address them as you would students or beginners. (Playing guru never goes over big.) You can explain basic things, but do so succinctly and assume reasonably high levels of intelligence and experience in the reader. (Actually, you can reasonably assume that some readers will exceed you in one or both of those attributes. Writing a PT article is a little like what a Leica lens designer once said of the process of designing a lens: It's like walking across a room full of tigers; i.e., you're doing fine if you make it to the far side without getting bitten on the ass too many times.)

2. Remember that when you make a submission, you are a writer. Take the writing challenges seriously. Use at least good, solid college-level composition skills, and be sure to proofread your work carefully! If you're not used to writing regularly, get someone else to proofread and check your copy for you before you send it to us. NO AMOUNT OF EDITING CAN COMPENSATE FOR DEEPLY FLAWED WRITING!! A discouraging percentage of first-time manuscripts submitted to us are not written to the standard of an average high-school English composition. This—ah, now how shall I put this kindly?—predisposes the editor against them.

On the other hand, if you really have something to say….

Content guidelines:

1. The preferred article is one that devoted photographer/darkroom workers will find impossible not to keep indefinitely for future reference. In fact, a large percentage of our subscribers do not discard their back issues. A well-crafted article about a topic that is useful to practicing photographers is of the greatest interest to us.

2. Do your own research, and back up what you claim. It is imperative in a nonscholarly field like photography that you not try to generalize or universalize beyond what you know to be the case. If you are testing a film dryer that dries roll film on reels, don't try it with one film and then claim that it doesn't curl film; just say it doesn't curl that particular film. You will get into trouble with our audience if your premises are not well-conceived or your conclusions are insufficiently rigorous. Especially, do not repeat uncritically what you have read from one or two sources. Contrary to popular belief, there is a great deal of creativity inherent in conceiving an article and a great deal of cleverness inherent in devising ways to test and explore your hypotheses and conclusions.

3. Try to choose a topic that will be of interest to some sizable subset of our readership! Note that this DOESN'T mean picking a broad, bland, general topic. A recently accepted article idea concerns the history of PermaWash (of all things), simply because the author managed to convince us that it's a fascinating story; a recently published article is a somewhat whimsical one (but dead true) about using vitamin C as a component of print developer. Broad subjects like how to choose a zoom lens—or overly specialized ones like a how-to on something too arcane to be of use to more than a few people—are both problematic.

4. If you can't be useful or present definitive research, BE ENTERTAINING! Presumably, you are a person who loves photography yourself: so ask yourself, what kinds of things do you love to read? Write to satisfy people who share your passions and enthusiasms about all things photographic. If you'd really like to read it, chances are our audience would, too.

Offbeat or controversial premises can be interesting if handled well. However, personal attacks, vituperation and the like are not appropriate. If you hate modern art, slide film, or photographers who don't use tripods, vent to your spouse—not our readers.

If you're on the right track, we'll work with you. In the past, PT has taken as long as three years working with an author on a piece in order to get it right.

We pay a minimum of $100 per page on publication and respond within two months, usually much sooner.

Thanks!

Contact Information:
Mike Johnston, Editor
P.O. Box 48312
Niles, IL 60714

Picture Perfect Magazine

Deadline:

60 days before publication date.

Payment:

Upon publication. $0.05 per word for articles, plus 3 copies of the issue in which article appears.

$10 each for each photo or illustration.

Photos:

35mm color slides or 8" x 10" black and white prints preferred. Up to 8" x 10" if used as part of article.

All black and white photos must have enough contrast for screening. Captions, subject identifications and model releases required for all photos with identifiable people.

Seasonal Material:

Submit 3 months in advance.

Article Length:

150 to 1,000 words.

Sample Copies:

Copies of each magazine available for $4 each.

Format Accepted.

3½" high density computer diskettes, PC compatible: txt files, WordPerfect, Word for

Windows or PageMaker, e-mail.

Special Conditions:

1. All material subject to editing.
2. All information must be verified and is subject to revision.
3. All articles for which Aquino International pays will be copyrighted by those publications, First North American Serial Rights only, when agreed to in writing by the publisher. Otherwise, all articles will be the exclusive property of Aquino International.
4. Photographers may retain copyrights to their photos. First North American Serial Rights apply to all photos.
5. Signed model release must accompany any photo submission in which people are identifiable. Articles and/or photos showing models without release forms will be rejected.
6. Captions and identification of subjects required for all photos.
7. Aquino International reserves the right not to publish an article it has purchased and/or to publish it or republish it at a later date.

Tips:

1.) We welcome material for our regular departments as well as for special editorials.

2.) All nonfiction material must be factual and easy to read.

3.) Familiarize yourself with our magazine. Send $4 for a sample copy. It will be sent to you by first class mail.

SUBJECTS:

Photographers. Description: In-depth interviews accompanied by photographs with famous or up and coming photographers. May be fashion, nature, technical or other photographers. Discussions about their backgrounds, creative ideas, innovative techniques, future projects. Positive, factual, constructive information. Sample of work must be included. Release must accompany photos or illustrations for editorial purposes. No monetary compensation will be provided to the subject of the coverage or for the use of his/her photos; only to you as a writer. Photographer release must accompany photos.

Photography. Creative, useful information. Unique use of photography by art directors or corporations. Business opportunities for photographers. Where to sell photos.

Travel destinations. Exotic locales around the world. Anecdotes accompanied by off-the-beaten track photos, nontypical tourist spots of interest to photographers.

Illustrations & Humor Spot Fillers now eelcome. $10.

READERS:

PICTURE PERFECT is targeted at advanced amateurs and professionals in the photography field. We prefer information which will help our readers better themselves or their businesses photographically. No gossip.

Contact Information:

Mr. Andres Aquino, Publisher
AQUINO INTERNATIONAL
P.O. Box 15760
Stamford, CT 06901-0760
(203) 967-9952 • FAX: (203) 353-9661
E-mail: aaquinoint@aol.com or aaquino@ix.netcom.com

Pipeline & Utilities Construction

OILDOM PUBLISHING'S WRITERS GUIDELINES:

• Article rate includes basic telephone work. However, extensive long distance phone work and/or FAXes, along with other relevant expenses may be paid by Oildom Publishing. Significant expenses (generally defined as over $25 per story) should be pre-approved. Payment upon final article approval by the magazines' editors. Always submit invoice with final story draft/disk.

• We prefer stories submitted on disk. Oildom Publishing is PC based. Sometimes stories written on a Mac can be imported via special programs we have; often times they can't. The word processing software we support for a PC is WordPerfect Windows 6.0a, Microsoft Word for Windows 6.0, XyWrite III+, or generally any program in ASCII or ANSI formats. To circumvent any software incompatibilities, a clean, clear hard copy should accompany all submissions. We can then scan the story into our system. For specific questions on formats and compatibility issues, contact Michael Speer, in the Houston Office, (713) 558-6930, ext. 11.

• Whenever possible, all stories should be accompanied by artwork: slides, color photographs, and/or graphics. For specific graphic formats and compatibility inquiries, contact Sherrie Anderson for PUC, (713) 558-6930, ext. 16, or Sheri Biscardi, ext. 14 for PGJ.

• We like to break out all significant manufacturers, vendors and/or contractors with reader service numbers so interested readers can easily obtain information. Please include contact names, address, phone and FAX numbers whenever possible.

• We buy exclusive rights. We prefer story queries, but cold submissions are considered. We generally will respond within 30 days.

• As a rule, we follow the *Associated Press Stylebook*. Exceptions include certain industry-accepted terms and abbreviations, and two-letter state abbreviations.

• Our readers tend to be management personnel from both contractors and owning companies. Technical material is acceptable only to a moderate level. Our readers are responsible for dollars. Always try to include economic considerations when applicable and practical.

• Kill fees are addressed on a case-by-case basis.

Contact Information:
Underground Construction: Robert Carpenter, Editor
P.O. Box 219368
Houston, TX 77218-9368
(713) 558-6930 • FAX: (713) 558-7029

Pizza Today

Pizza Today is a monthly four-color trade publication for owners and managers of pizza-based restaurant businesses. Our approximately 46,000 readers range from single-store neighborhood parlors to national and international chains. We are also read by over 2,000 suppliers of products and services for the pizza industry.

Articles for submission to *Pizza Today* should provide readers with bottom-line operational and management advice applicable to the foodservice industry. Authors should offer insights into innovations leading to future money-making ideas for pizza restaurant owners. The magazine bills itself as "the monthly professional guide to pizza profits." Articles should reflect this theme.

Authors should write in an entertaining, conversational style; just as importantly, they should offer solid information and creative solutions to specific management problems. We strive to present an "insider's view." Every story published in *Pizza Today* should be crammed with tips for operating a better business. Complex or technical concepts should be presented in a manner that's clear to the lay reader contemplating entry into the pizza foodservice industry, but not so basic that experienced veterans are turned off. Style: We encourage the author's voice and style to show. However, we prefer articles presented in the present tense, using active verbs and personal nouns and pronouns. Fully identify principals in first-mentions, then refer to last names.

Pizza Today is 75 percent staff- and contributor-written, 25 percent freelance-written. Articles are due at least 90 days before date of publication. We seek stories in the following subject areas: staff training and management; food preparation and presentation; foodservice marketing and promotion; foodservice delivery; pizza ingredients: cheeses, sauces, dough, toppings, etc.; complementary beverages; safety, security, cleaning and maintenance applicable to the pizza foodservice industry. Additionally, Pizza Pacesetters, featuring companies that set regional or national trends; Profiles in Pizza, featuring profitably-managed companies; Tips of the Month, highlighting prize-winning hints to improve operations, prize-winning Recipes; and Cutting Edge, focusing on innovative products and business concepts, are part of the monthly editorial fare.

Payment upon acceptance ranges from $250-$500 for most features. Buys all rights—photos and illustrations included. Some expenses reimbursed with prior approval. Reports in 90 days. Queries only to:

Contact Information:
Kevin Nickols, Managing Editor
P.O. Box 1347
New Albany, IN 47151
(812) 949-0909

Planetary Connections
International Forum for Solution-Oriented News

Planetary Connections is an international newspaper. It features news about people and organizations that have a positive impact on the world.

Planetary Connections is a quarterly tabloid-size newspaper, printed in soy ink on recycled newsprint. There are four editions released during the year: Winter Issue (January), Spring Issue (April), Summer Issue (July), and Autumn Issue (October).

Circulation and distribution: This widely-respected publication is found in over 80 countries and in every state in the USA. Annual subscriptions are only $18. Individual issues are sold at bookstores, health food stores, churches, and various international meetings. They are also distributed through environmental and other organizations, as well as health practitioners.

Readers are self-motivated networkers. They are interested in personal health and well-being, the arts, spiritual unfoldment, and social and environmental issues. *Planetary Connections* provides a link that creates a supportive, wide-spread community of lightworkers.

Join the team—60,000 readers from 80 countries are waiting for news from you!

Planetary Connections is looking for both correspondents and writers.

Regional correspondents agree to submit quarterly news from their city, region, or nation. This includes original articles and clippings from other publications. Regional correspondents are recognized as volunteer staff members of the paper.

Writers submit single or occasional articles.

Please label all material with your name, address and phone number.

Submissions

We welcome contributions that are:

- news of positive planetary transformation
- reports on major conferences, meetings, and organizations around the globe
- interviews with people living with heart and purpose
- profiles of organizations making a social or environmental difference
- letters from readers

Clippings from other publications (with source and date) and photos are welcome. Submission does not guarantee publication. We reserve the right to edit all materials.

How to submit

Send submissions as text only (synonymous with ASCII or DOS file) or rich text files (indicate file type and name) on 3.5" floppy disk with printed copy. We also accept typed, and occasionally handwritten submissions.

Selection process: our criteria

- Does the article tell about people using positive, solutions-oriented approaches to solving problems?
- Is the topic about current, contemporary events which affect many people?
- Is the story complete, including participant's names, as well as locations and dates?
- Does the topic have broad enough appeal for our global audience?
- Is a good quality photo included?
- Is the content non-promotional in nature?
- Is the article the right length (500-1,000 words)?

Other considerations

Planetary Connections is a newspaper rather than a magazine. We print concise, objective and timely articles. With rare exceptions, we do not use self-help or how-to articles. We will consider analysis or commentary on issues of wide-spread concern.

We do not use press releases and articles that obviously promote products and services. Instead, we encourage you to purchase our reasonably priced and highly effective advertising space for such promotions. Contact Advertising Director Earle Belle at the number below.

Deadlines (livelines?)

Issue	*Submit by*
Winter	October 1
Spring	January 1
Summer	April 1
Autumn	July 1

Articles not used in a particular issue may be used in a subsequent one.

Photographs

Good black & white or color photos that show activity in progress, or individuals engaged in problem-solving discussions are welcome.

Please include the following:

- names and addresses of people in photo
- details of subject and date when picture was taken
- your name, address and phone number
- photographer's name, address and phone number (if known)

Payment

Planetary Connections does not currently offer payment for news or photos. However, a biographical sketch (three lines or less) is printed at the end of the article. Please include a brief statement about your profession, education, residence, or other networking information.

Exceptions: In some cases a small honorarium is awarded to authors of exceptional articles that originate in Eastern Europe, the Middle East, Africa, South America, or Asia.

Contact Information:
Nancie Belle, Editor
305 West Magnolia Street, Suite 348
Fort Collins, CO 80521
(800) 873-1620 or (970) 282-1797 • FAX: (800) 889-7372
or (970) 282-0091
E-mail: planetnews@aol.com

Planning

Planning is published monthly by the American Planning Association. It offers news and analyses of events in planning (including suburban, rural, and small town planning, environmental planning, neighborhood revitalization, economic development, social planning, and urban design).

Query First

If you have an idea for a story, don't send a completed manuscript. Instead, send a letter briefly describing what you have in mind, why the topic is important, and how it is relevant to our audience.

Say something about the sources of your information (personal involvement? interviews?) and about your present position and background.

If you are a planner, say something about your writing experience. If you are primarily a writer, tell us if you have had exposure to planning.

Tell us what types of photographs and graphics are available to illustrate your story.

Be sure to include an address and a daytime phone number.

Types of Stories

Planning runs full-length feature articles (including case studies and trends), short stories about newsworthy events, book reviews, news about APA activities, viewpoint essays, letters, and news of projects that are in the works.

Longer, academic articles based on original research should be sent to the Journal of the American Planning Association (Virginia Commonwealth University, 816 W Franklin St., Box 842504, Richmond, VA 23284).

News Stories

News of events in the field (including news about planning programs) is reported each month in *Planning*'s news section. Some news stories are contributed; however, most are staff-written, based on interviews and material supplied by planners. A timely news angle is most important, news stories typically are under 500 words.

Feature Articles

Articles for *Planning* should be on a topic of significant interest to the field. Although features also may have a news angle, their greater length allows more in-depth exploration of the issues raised by a particular event.

Features include case studies of particular places or planning programs, stories analyzing trends, profiles of notable planners, evaluations of planning programs, and descriptions of planning practice and techniques. Stories comparing two or more techniques or programs are encouraged. A typical feature story is 2,500 words.

Book Reviews

Books chosen for review in *Planning* include new works by major figures in the profession, how-to books, and case studies. Unsolicited reviews are almost never used. Individual reviews run from 500 to 700 words; several reviews appear each month.

Writing Guidelines

Planning tries to maintain a straightforward, nontechnical style. Every story should make clear, near the beginning, why the topic is of interest at this time. The facts of the case should be presented with a minimum of elaboration. Only essential background details should be included. (An exception is the "Planning Practice" feature in each issue, where details of a noteworthy case study or planning technique are discussed at length.) The primary focus should be on how a program has worked, special techniques used, and solutions to problems encountered. Stories about planning achievements should include information about their political and economic context.

Accuracy is vital. All facts should be double-checked before a manuscript is submitted. Each manuscript should be accompanied by a list of resources on the topic at hand: relevant books and reports, conferences, and contact people and their phone numbers.

To settle points of style, *Planning*'s editors use *The Chicago Manual of Style* (University of Chicago Press). A good, basic writing guide is *The Elements of Style*, by William Strunk, Jr., and E.B. White.

Illustrations

Planning uses black-and-white photographs on inside pages and color photos on the front cover.

Photographs: 5-by-7-inch or 8-by-10-inch glossy prints are preferred for black-and-white photos, and 35mm or 4-by-5-inch transparencies for color. Color prints are acceptable but not our first choice. All photographs should include credit and caption information.

Line art: We are always on the lookout for pertinent and well-drawn cartoons and drawings. Suggestions for reprints from magazines and newspapers are welcomed.

Charts, graphs, and maps: Simple, uncluttered material works best. Graphic material should be black and white, preferably camera ready.

Payment

Planning generally does not pay for articles by practicing planners, attorneys, or university faculty members. For others, fees are worked out individually; they usually range from $100 to $900 for articles, depending on length, and $50 to $300 for photographs and drawings.

Contact Information:

Sylvia Lewis, Editor and Associate Publisher
American Planning Association
122 South Michigan Avenue, Suite 1600
Chicago, IL 60603
(312) 431-9100

Playgirl Magazine

PLAYGIRL addresses the needs, interests and desires of women 18 years of age and older. We provide something no other American women's magazine can: an uninhibited approach to exploring sexuality and fantasy that empowers, enlightens, and entertains.

We publish feature articles of all sorts: interviews with top celebrities; essays and humor pieces on sexually related topics; first-person accounts of sensual adventures; articles on the latest trends in sex, love, romance and dating; and how-to stories that give readers sexy news they can use. We also publish erotic fiction—from a women's perspective or from an empathetic, sex-positive male point of view—and reader fantasies. The common thread—besides, of course, good, lively writing and scrupulous research—is a fresh, open-minded, inquisitive attitude.

Prospective writers should read a few issues before submitting ideas. Query letters with published clips are preferred, but completed, unsolicited manuscripts will be considered. Payment rates vary.

NONFICTION FEATURES: These run 1,800 to 2,500 words. Send an outline of your idea and tell how you would approach the topic. Include proposed sources of information.

CELEBRITY FEATURES: Mostly assigned in-house, but we'll consider pitches from reputable freelancers. 2,500-3,500 words. Must supply contacts you are working with, interview transcript and interview tape.

PLAYGIRL PUNCH LINE: A humorous look at a wide range of sexually related topics—from offbeat experiences to kinky explorations. 1,000 words.

GUEST ROOM: First person essays on sex-positive, fun experiences from both male and female perspectives. 2,000-2,500 words.

GIRL TALK: Q&A and features of fabulously engaging women who in some way empower the evolution of female sensuality and pleasure. 2,000-3,000 words.

FANTASY FORUM: Our readers are major contributors to this creative column devoted to female pleasures of the flesh. This is the best place for new writers to break into the magazine. Fantasy of the Month pays $100, while others are $25. Submissions should be sent to fantasy Forum, c/o PLAYGIRL.

EROTIC FICTION: We consider ourselves the country's premier magazine outlet for erotica from a woman's perspective and encourage writers to submit complete manuscripts only. We look for well-written, well-structured prose of 3,000-4,000 words that includes sizzling sex scenes and storylines related to female sexual self-expression. Send submissions to the Managing Editor.

All other submissions should be directed to the Editor-in-Chief.

Contact Information:

Judy Cole, Editor-in-Chief
Patrice Baldwin, Managing Editor
801 2nd Avenue, Suite 1600
New York, NY 10017
(212) 661-7878 • FAX: (212) 697-6343

Ploughshares

Ploughshares welcomes unsolicited submissions of fiction and poetry. We consider manuscripts postmarked between August 1 and March 31. All submissions received between April and July are returned unread. We adhere very strictly to the postmark restrictions. Since we operate on a first-received, first-read basis, we cannot make exceptions or hold work.

Ploughshares is published three times a year: usually mixed issues of poetry and fiction in the Spring and Winter and a fiction issue in the Fall, with each guest-edited by a different writer.

In the past, guest editors often announced specific themes for issues, but we have revised our editorial policies and no longer restrict submissions to thematic topics. In general, if you believe your work is in keeping with our standards of literary quality and value, submit it at any time during our reading period.

We do not recommend trying to target specific guest editors unless you have a legitimate acquaintance with them. Our backlog is unpredictable, and staff editors ultimately have the responsibility of determining for which editor a work is most appropriate. If a manuscript is not suitable or timely for one issue, it will be considered for another. For your information, however, Yusef Komunyakaa will be reading fiction and poetry for the Spring 1997 issue.

Please send only one short story and/or one to three poems at a time (mail fiction and poetry separately). Poems should be individually typed either single- or double-spaced on one side. Prose should be no longer than 25 double-spaced pages. Although we look primarily for short stories, we occasionally publish personal essays and memoirs. Novel excerpts are acceptable if they are self-contained. We do not accept unsolicited book reviews or criticism, nor do we consider book-length manuscripts of any sort.

Please do not send multiple submissions of the same genre for different issues/editors, and do not send another manuscript until you hear about the first. Additional submissions will be returned unread. Unsolicited work sent directly to a guest editor's home or office will be discarded. We suggest you include a SASE with one ounce postage for a reply only, with the manuscript to be recycled if unaccepted (photocopying is usually cheaper than return postage).

Expect three to five months for a decision (sometimes faster, depending on the backlog). We have a small staff and receive quite a number of submissions, but we are committed to considering each manuscript carefully. Simultaneous submissions are amenable to us as long as they are indicated as such and we are notified immediately upon acceptance elsewhere. Please do not query us until five months have passed, and f you do, please write to us, indicating the postmark date of submission, instead of calling. We cannot accommodate revisions, changes of return address, or forgotten SASE.'s after the fact. We do not print previously published work. Translations are welcome if permission has been granted. Payment is upon publication: $25 a printed page, with a $50 minimum per title and a $250 maximum per issue, plus two copies of the issue and a one-year subscription.

More information about *Ploughshares* is available on the World Wide Web at the address below.

Thank you for your interest in *Ploughshares*.

Contact Information:
Fiction Editor or Poetry Editor
100 Beacon Street, Emerson College
Boston, MA 02116
(617) 824-8753
E-mail: www.emerson.edu/ploughshares/

Pockets

You can write for the Upper Room.

The meditations in each issue are written by people just like you, people who are listening to God and trying to live by what they hear. The Upper Room is built on a worldwide community of Christians who share their faith with one another.

The Upper Room is meant for an international, interdenominational audience. We want to encourage Christians in their personal life of prayer and discipleship. We seek to build on what unites us as believers and to link believers in prayer around the world.

Literally millions of people use the magazine each day. Your meditation will be sent around the world, to be translated into more than 40 languages and printed in over 60 editions. Those who read the day's meditation and pray the prayer join with others in over 80 countries around the world, reading the same passage of scripture and bringing the same concerns before God.

Have God's care and presence become real for you in your interactions with others? Has the Bible given you guidance and helped you see God at work? Has the meaning of scripture become personal for you as you reflected on it? Then you have something to share in a meditation.

Where do I begin?

You begin in your own relationship with God. Christians believe that God speaks to us and guides us as we study the Bible and pray. Good meditations are closely tied to scripture and show how it has shed light on a specific situation. Good meditations make the message of the Bible come alive.

Good devotional writing is first of all authentic. It connects real events of daily life with the ongoing activity of God. It comes across as the direct, honest statement of personal faith in Christ and how that faith grows. It is one believer sharing with another an insight or struggle about what it means to live faithfully.

Second, good devotional writing uses many sensory details—what color it was, how high it bounced, what it smelled like. The more sensory details the writing includes, the better. Though the events of daily life may seem too mundane to be the subject of devotional writing, actually they provide the richest store of sensory details. And when we connect God's activity to common objects and activities, each encounter with them can serve as a reminder of God's work.

Finally, good devotional writing is exploratory. It searches and considers and asks questions. It examines the faith without knowing in advance what all the answers will be. It is open to God's continuing self-revelation through scripture, people, and events. Good writing chronicles growth and change, seeing God behind both.

What goes in a meditation?

Each day's meditation includes a title, a suggested Bible reading, a scripture text, a personal witness or reflection on scripture, a prayer, a "thought for the day" (a pithy, summarizing statement), and a suggested subject for prayer during the day (usually tied to the content of the story). Including all of these elements, the meditation should be about 250 words long. Indicate what version of the Bible is quoted in the text, and give references for any scripture passages mentioned.

Use clear, simple words and develop one idea only. Think about how you can deepen the Christian commitment of readers and nurture their spiritual growth. Encourage readers to deeper engagement with the Bible.

Include your name, address, and social security number on each page you submit. Always give the original source of any materials you quote. Meditations containing quotes or other secondary material which cannot be verified will not be used.

What should not go in a meditation?

Previously published material cannot be used.

Hymns, poems, and word plays such as acrostics or homonyms make meditations unusable because the material in The Upper Room is translated into many languages. Translations cannot do justice to these forms.

Also, very familiar illustrations ("The Touch of the Master's Hand," stories like George Washington cutting down the cherry tree) have little impact and should not be used. Remember that your personal experience provides unique material—no one is exactly like you.

How do I get started writing a meditation?

When you find yourself in the middle of some situation thinking, "Why—that's how God is, too!" or, "That's like that story in the Bible . . .," that can become a meditation. Excellent ideas come from reading and meditating in scripture, looking for connections between it and daily life. When you see such a helpful connection, here's a simple formula for getting it to paper:

1. Retell the Bible teaching or summarize the passage briefly.
2. Describe the situation you link to the Bible passage, using a specific incident. Write down as many details of the real-life situation as you can. For example, if you write about an incident when people were talking, write down what each person said.
3. Tell how you can apply this spiritual truth in days to come.

After a few days, look carefully at what you have written. Decide which details best convey your message, and delete the others. Ask yourself whether this insight will be helpful to believers in other countries and other situations. If you feel that it will, add any elements that are necessary to The Upper Room's format. Then you are ready to submit your meditation for consideration for possible use in The Upper Room.

When are the deadlines?

We continually need meditations, and you can submit a meditation at any time. However, seasonal material should reach us fifteen months before use date. Below are due dates and special emphases for the various issues.

Issue	Due Date	Special Emphases
January-February	August 1 of second year preceeding. (For example, 1997 should reach us by Aug. 1, 1996)	New Year, Epiphany, Ash Wednesday
March-April	Oct. 1 of second year preceeding.	Lent, Palm Sunday, Maundy Thursday, Good Friday; Easter; World Day of Prayer
May-June	Dec. 1 of second year preceeding.	Festival of the Christian home, Ascension Day,Pentecost, Trinity Sunday.
July-August	Feb. 1 of preceding year.	Creative uses of leisure.
September-October	April 1 of preceding year.	World Communion Sunday; God and our daily work.
November-December	June 1 of preceding year.	*Bible* Sunday, All Saints' Day, Thanksgiving, Advent, Christmas

When will I know if my meditation is going to be used?

If your work is being considered for use, we will send you a postcard, usually within six weeks after receiving your work. Later, if your meditation is chosen for publication, you will receive a copyright release card to sign and return to us. It may be as much as a year before a final decision is made; seasonal material may be held even longer. We are unable to give updates on the status of individual meditations. All published meditations are edited. We buy the right to translate your meditation for one-time use in our editions around the world, including electronic and software-driven formats. We pay $15 for each meditation, on publication.

Please send no more than three meditations at a time.

Contact Information:
Lynn W. Gilliam, Associate Editor
P.O. Box 189
Nashville, TN 37202
(615) 340-7333

Police Times & The Chief of Police Magazine

POLICE TIMES (tabloid) is the official journal of the American Federation of Police. We seek articles on speculation regarding all areas of law enforcement, with a special emphasis on stories involving smaller police departments or individuals who have made a special place in law enforcement… past or present. The magazine is published bimonthly as is THE CHIEF OF POLICE, the official journal of the National Association of Chiefs of Police. For THE CHIEF OF POLICE, we seek articles that would be of particular interest to command-rank American law enforcement personnel. If accepted we may elect to publish a particularly interesting piece in both publications. Allow 90-180 days for publication, which is at the editor's discretion.

We pay one cent per word, $5 per photo or cartoon and $25 for photos used in the color mode. Photos, however, may be submitted in b&w or color. Fillers and short articles are also considered and paid at the same rate. Length of articles may vary, but usually range up to 3,500 words for POLICE TIMES; 5,000 words for THE CHIEF OF POLICE. Payment is made upon acceptance. One comp copy of the issue in which the article appears is provided to the writer.

SAMPLE COPIES: For POLICE TIMES $2.50, for THE CHIEF OF POLICE $3.00. Include SASE with al submissions.

ASSIGNED ARTICLES: Articles specifically assigned by the editor are paid at double scale. These are reserved for writers who have already had material published in our publications.

FAXED PROPOSALS: Accepted by FAXing short proposal to number below. Allow ample time for reply.

Contact Information:
Jim Gordon, Executive Editor
3801 Biscayne Boulevard
Miami, FL 33137
(305) 573-0070 • FAX: (305) 573-9819

Popular Electronics

AN OPEN LETTER TO AUTHORS WHO WISH TO BE PUBLISHED IN POPULAR ELECTRONICS

Dear Author:

If you have a story or a story idea centered around electronics, I'd like to have the chance to read it, and consider it for purchase and use in *Popular Electronics*. To improve the probability of your story being published, I have placed some suggestions in this guide to help you prepare your article.

What types of articles is *Popular Electronics* seeking? I've always sought first-rate stories covering communications, computers, test equipment, audio, video and virtually every other electronics subject. Good construction, tutorial, informational, and how-to articles are always in demand. If they are timely, their appeal and chances of acceptance are further enhanced.

Articles about new technology or the theory behind new devices are particularly valuable and make for interesting reading. The key to writing such an article with authority is thorough research and accuracy. A poorly researched article can lose its author some respect among the editors as well as the sale. Make sure of your facts, and make them complete. The editors should not have to do your research job. If you aren't in a position to research thoroughly and document the facts, you shouldn't write the story in the first place.

How-to-do-it features are among the most interesting types of articles that you can write. Show a reader ten new ways to use his oscilloscope or sweep generator, an easy way to make printed circuit boards, etc., and your story will be enjoyed by our readers.

Troubleshooting and service manuscripts, on the other hand, require an experienced author. Nothing falls apart as thoroughly as a troubleshooting article written by someone who knows little about the subject. Technical inaccuracies in the manuscript quickly ruin its chances for acceptance.

Construction articles show readers how to build electronic projects. The devices discussed must be of practical use in the field of electronics, in hobby pursuits, or around the house or in the car. The cost of parts is important; the cost of assembling a project should be justified by what it does. I seek construction stories at different levels—some for neophytes and some for those who have the training to carry out complex building instructions. In general, easier projects take preference, although a premium goes to the story that tells how to build some advanced project easily.

Construction manuscripts need special care. Schematics must be complete and detailed. Show all IC pinouts, power connections, bypass capacitors, parts designations and values, etc. If a printed circuit board is used, a clear, reproducible, full-size foil pattern must be included. Parts-placement diagrams should be shown from the component side of the board and the parts should be identified by part number, not values. Completely describe all construction methods and techniques that are not common knowledge.

Include calibration and adjustment instructions in all construction articles that require them. Include debugging information: How long did it take to get the device working? To build it? The reader may experience some of the same difficulties. Place critical voltages on schematic diagrams; those help the project builder check the operation of the finished project.

Include a complete list of parts, manufacturers, type numbers, and electrical/electronic specifications and ratings where appropriate. Make sure that the list agrees with the information presented in the text and on schematic diagrams. Accuracy is absolutely necessary! Avoid hard-to-get items or those that are one-of-kind. If you must use an uncommon part you must give two sources for that part. Where values are not critical, say so and give approximate tolerances. Where special parts are required, be precise in the Parts List by including all the specifications. Do not merely say "5,000-ohm relay" if contact spacing or armature tension is critical. Tell us (in the text) why a particular part is chosen over others like it. Failure to make the Parts List complete may mean some reader can't make the project work and will blame the magazine or author.

Check and double check your work. Be sure that the schematic agrees with the Parts List, the parts-placement diagram, other illustrations, and the text. Our editors review every manuscript for accuracy, but it is impossible to catch all errors. Your reputation as an author, as well as the reputation of this magazine, can be damaged by inaccurate or sloppy work.

Commonly used abbreviations such as AC, DC, IC, Hz, etc., may be used freely. However, the use of less common abbreviations should be limited except when their use promotes clarity. All such abbreviations must be defined in the article the first time they are used.

Do not dismantle your equipment or change it after sending us your manuscript. If the article is accepted, the editors must compare it to its description to check for accuracy.

Finish the job! Don't send half-done manuscripts. "Photos to come" or "material to be added here" are flags of incompleteness. I can't judge the manuscript without seeing all of it. Incomplete articles will be rejected as they cannot be properly evaluated.

MECHANICS:

There are some things you should consider when writing any article; let's explore those things next. The best-written articles are useless if they can't be published. An article on high-voltage sources might be perfect; but if it requires five TV-receiver schematic diagrams, it will not be printed because the drawings alone would take up too much space in the magazine. Stories with no illustrations, or those without enough text to hold the illustrations together, show poor preparation and are not acceptable.

You must type your name and address in the top left corner of the first page.; some authors use a rubber stamp to put their name and address on the back of each succeeding page. Also include a telephone number where you can be reached during the day in case my editors have a question that requires immediate attention.

If you are working on a computer, submit your story with text pages printed on a letter-quality or dot-matrix printer and include a 5-¼ inch floppy disk of the manuscript, in ASCII, readable by an IBM or compatible computer. Tell us what DOS version and word-processor program you use. A disk of your article will save input time and eliminate typing errors at this end. Do not send photocopies of the manuscript or the illustrations. Send the original.

ILLUSTRATIONS:

If any of your illustrations are smaller than 8 by 10 inches, fasten them to a standard-size sheet of paper.

Photographs should be 5 by 7 inches or larger black-and-white glossy prints, and in good focus all over. Avoid using color prints. All details should be easy to see—not hidden in dark areas or "washed out" in overexposed or too bright areas. Don't mark or write on prints; you simply spoil them for reproduction. If you need to identify sections of a photograph, put a piece of tracing paper over the print and make the identification on that, or send an extra print.

Put an asterisk or the figure number in the margin of your text when you refer to an illustration or figure. Try to scatter illustrations throughout the story so they're not all bunched.

Diagrams must be clearly drawn in pencil or ink, but need not be finished artwork, as all art is redrawn here in *Popular Electronics* style. To enhance accuracy, we request that you adopt *Popular Electronics* parts designations and symbol conventions where possible. Contact us for a sample issue if needed.

Draw each diagram on a separate page. Use standard-size paper or sheets that can be folded to standard size. Drawings must be accurate. Check each one carefully—it is almost impossible for the editors to catch all errors.

RATE OF PAYMENT:

My payment calculations are more complex than a simple page rate, since I consider such variables as reader interest, illustrations, text, photography, how much editing my staff will have to do, accuracy of research, and originality of approach.

The payment rate currently ranges from $100 to $500. Manuscripts that need practically no editing, are complete, that hit precisely the slant we want, that are written in the easy-reading style of *Popular Electronics*, and that are thoughtfully and imaginatively illustrated will command the highest payment rate.

The staff members are trained in writing, researching, and editing. As you are developing your story, I will gladly work with you. After I buy your manuscript, your help is often needed to fill gaps in your story, check a doubtful connection on a schematic diagram, etc. The editors take every possible step and precaution to make sure that your article is authoritative, easy-to-read, and interesting, but much of the responsibility must, of course, rest with the author.

I'll look forward to receiving your manuscripts.

Sincerely, Carl Laron, Editor

Contact Information:
500-B Bi-County Boulevard
Farmingdale, NY 11735
(516) 293-3000 • FAX: (516) 293-3115

Popular Science

Popular Science covers new and emerging technology in the areas of science, automobiles, the environment, recreation, electronics, the home, photography, aviation and space, and computers and software. Our mission is to provide service to our readers by reporting on how these technologies work and what difference they will make in our readers' lives. Our readers are well-educated professionals who are vitally interested in the technologies we cover.

We seek stories that are up-to-the-minute in information and accuracy. We expect the writer to interview all sources who are essential to the story, as well as experts who can provide analysis and perspective. If a hands-on approach is called for, the writer should visit critical sites to see the technology first-hand—including trying it out when appropriate.

We publish stories ranging from hands-on product reviews to investigative feature stories, on everything from black holes to black-budget airplanes. We expect submissions to be, above all else, well-written: that is, distinguished by good story-telling, human interest, anecdotes, analogies, and humor, among other traits of good writing. Stories should be free of jargon, vague statements, and unconfirmed facts and figures.

We seek publishable stories written to an agreed-upon length, with text for agreed-upon components such as sidebars or how-to boxes. The writer is responsible for the factual content of the story and is expected to have made a systematic checking of facts. We require that the writer file with his story contact numbers for all important sources and subjects in the story.

We expect our authors to deliver a complete package. The *Popular Science* art dept. requires illustrations, photographs, and diagrams/sketches pertaining to stories submitted. These may be in the form of copies, but we prefer camera-ready artwork. We accept the following formats: four-color or black and white photography, illustration and digital files (TIFF or EPS). We track and log all artwork and, if indicated on the original, we will return artwork. We also require more than one piece of reference material. This allows for more accurate and original artistic interpretations.

A story should come with a headline for each story element and captions for photos. The complete package will include background material and documentation used by the author.

Freelance contributions to *Popular Science* range from feature-length stories to shorter "newsfront pieces" and shorter-yet stories to accompany What's New products.

We respond promptly to queries, which should be a single page or less. The writer should submit a tight summary of the proposed article and provide some indication of the plan of execution. Samples of the writer's past work and clips concerning the emerging story are helpful.

Contact Information:
2 Park Avenue
New York, NY 10016
(212) 779-5000

Popular Woodworking

Popular Woodworking is a bimonthly magazine that invites the woodworker into a community of experts who share their hard-won shop experience through in-depth projects and technique articles, which helps the readers hone their existing skills and develop new ones. Related stories increase the readers' understanding and enjoyment of their craft. Any project submitted must be aesthetically pleasing, of sound construction and offer a challenge to readers.

FEATURES

On the average, we use six to nine features per issue. Our primary needs are "how-to" articles on woodworking projects and instructional features dealing with woodworking tools and techniques. Our secondary need is for articles that will inspire discussion concerning woodworking. Tone of articles should be conversational and informal, as if the writer is speaking directly to the reader. Word length ranges from 1,200 to 2,500. Payment for features starts at $125 per published page, depending on the total package submitted, including its quality, and the writer's level of woodworking and writing experience.

COLUMNS

- Tricks of the Trade. This section shares one- to two-paragraph "tips" on how to make woodworking easier or safer. We pay $35 per printed submission.
- Out of the Woodwork. This one-page article, averaging about 500 words, reflects on the writer's thoughts about woodworking as a profession or hobby. The article can be either humorous or serious. Payment is $100.
- Business End. This column focuses on woodworking's professional side to offer helpful tips and insight.

QUERIES

All submissions, except Tricks of the Trade, need to be preceded by a query. We will accept unsolicited manuscripts and artwork.

Queries must include:

- A brief outline of the proposed article.
- A summary of the techniques used to complete the project. Include step-by-step illustrations.
- A short biographical sketch, including both your woodworking and writing experience and accomplishments. Also provide your address and daytime telephone number.
- A color photo or transparency of the project.
- A list of all material needed (it's best to use materials that are easily available).

MANUSCRIPT SUBMISSIONS

Your manuscript must be, whenever possible, on 3½" computer disc (save all manuscripts generically, preferably in ASCII). We also accept submissions through e-mail.

For project articles, include the following:

1. Introduction: Describe an important point about your project or subject. What made you develop or design it? Also note any unusual qualities.
2. Preparation: Explain any work needed to be done before starting the project.
3. Instructions: Go step-by-step through the process, explaining each point clearly and concisely. Include all pertinent details, and write in a conversational style. When writing, keep in mind that there may be multiple ways to do any one step. Offering these options to the reader makes your manuscript more flexible and appealing. Clarify any technical words. NOTE: Brand names should only be included when they are critical to the construction or finishing process.
4. Finishing: Give complete instructions on how to finish the project.
5. Closing: Close your article with a brief paragraph that ties everything together.
6. Materials: Please provide the list of all materials used in the project, including types and sizes (thickness, width & length). Also, if materials are hard to find, include the supplier's address and telephone number (with the price of the product and shipping, if available).
7. About the Writer: Provide a brief biography on your experience and interests.

MISCELLANEOUS

- Visual aids are an important part of instruction, and essential to both projects and articles. Remember to submit well-lit photographs (clearly labeled color transparencies are preferred). Place any copy describing the process or technique on a piece of paper attached to the back of the illustration. Keep plenty of blank space around each step. We often have to crop illustrations for design purposes.
- If a complex technique is necessary for the project, make a suggestion for a special "sidebar" demonstrating it. Sidebars can also be used as an important source of additional information, such as suggesting alternative methods or tools.
- All artwork, photographs and drawings will be returned upon request.

ORIGINALITY AND RIGHTS

All material submitted must be original and unpublished. *Popular Woodworking* purchases first North American serial rights for one-time use in the magazine, and all rights for use of the article (both text and illustrations) in any F&W publications, Inc. promotional material/product or reprint. You always retain the copyright to your work, and are free to use it in any way after it appears in the magazine. We request, however, that you do not publish the same material for at least six months from the time it appears in our publication.

POPULAR WOODWORKING'S GUIDE TO WRITING AND STYLE

- Writing should be concise and straightforward.
- Watch redundancies and get rid of unnecessary words, such as that, all , rather, in order, very, etc.
- Avoid repeating the same word within the sentence or in the following one. For example: The board should be sanded on the board's right side. Include a pronoun instead: The board should be sanded on its right side. Don't be afraid to use pronouns, unless they hinder comprehension.
- Replace passive voice with active voice to avoid redundancies and increase clarity. Hint: Watch for words like was, were, is, and are—they usually indicate passive voice. Passive: The project was a success. Active: The project succeeded.
- Possessive apostrophes also can cut back on your word count. For example, the side of the board can become the board's side. As a side note, remember that it's is a contraction of

it is, while its shows possession.

• For measurements, *Popular Woodworking*'s style is: 7" x 8", 7", 7"-thick board. Take note of the difference between measurements: The 7"-thick board should be cut 2" wide. The hyphenated version is used as an adjective of an object, while no hyphen denotes a measurement itself.

• Commas, as a general rule, should be placed where the reader would pause naturally.

• Generally, a comma does not separate the last series member from a verb. For example: You will need shellac, sandpaper and wood. However, if the omission of commas becomes too confusing, leave them in: You will need shellac and stain, sandpaper and steel, and pine and maple wood.

• When using and, so, nor, or, remember the comma always precedes them. Also never use the phrase and then. Only then is necessary.

• Parentheses should be used sparingly and only for information that needs understatement. For example, note the distinction between the use of dashes and parentheses in this sentence: For ten hours—but only ten hours—let the glue dry (yellow carpenter's glue works best) so your project will not come apart while you are working.

• Always have punctuation follow parentheses, unless a complete sentence is within it:

This book is excellent for beginners (zero to one year experience), but only a handy guide for more advanced levels.

I cut the wood according to size. (I later found out I had used the wrong materials.)

FINAL CHECKLIST

Although the following reminders are simple, they've been neglected by writers in the past. So make sure your manuscripts meets these requirements when you read it over a final time:

• Sentences must have both a subject and a verb to be complete.

• If you have any doubts on a word's spelling, don't hesitate to look it up.

• make sure you're getting your point across to the readers. Look at the article through their eyes—not your own experienced ones.

• Double check all measurements and facts to make sure they're correct. We don't want any unsuccessful projects!

• Watch the overuse of you and I. It does make the piece more personable, but use sparingly. Often you can get the same point across after omitting them.

• Make sure all punctuation is used correctly.

Contact Information:
Cristine Antolik, Managing Editor
1507 Dana Avenue
Cincinnati, OH 45207
(513) 531-2690 • FAX: (513) 531-1843
E-mail: Wudworker@aol.com

Potpourri

POTPOURRI, a magazine of the literary arts, is a quarterly, small press publication of short stories, poetry, essays, and travel. Subscriptions are mailed to home or office and are supplemented by community and national distribution.

OBJECTIVES

a.) To encourage the art of reading
b.) To further the skill of writing
c.) To promote the works of authors
d.) To advance social awareness of literary classics
e.) To foster appreciation of our culturally diverse society

GENRE

POTPOURRI accepts a broad genre. Both fiction and nonfiction will be published.

No religious, confessional, racial, political, erotic, abusive, or sexual preference material will be accepted unless fictional and necessary to plot or characterization.

PAYMENT

Payment is one copy when published. Writers also benefit from publication in POTPOURRI and from readership response. Authors may order at professional discount copies of issue containing their work. POTPOURRI offers annual prizes poetry and fiction for best of volume and also the National Literature Award for the poem or short story (alternating years) which best expresses our multicultural diversity or historical background. Write for CNLA guidelines.

SUBMISSIONS

POTPOURRI is copyrighted but not registered. The writer's work is protected by copyright of this publication. All prior rights and all rights to new material revert to the contributor after publication. Contributors must obtain and supply copyright permissions for any previously published material.

a.) Submit your best original material but no more than three (3) poems and one work of prose with a maximum of 3,500 words.

b.) For prose, type your name, address, and telephone number at the upper left margin of your first page and the total number of words in your manuscript in the upper right hand corner. Type your last name and page number on each consecutive page. When prose is accepted, editors will request a copy on Macintosh or IBM 3½ inch disk in Word, WordPerfect, Quark Express, or PageMaker. We prefer that computer documents be sent in ASCII or text format, particularly if using word processing programs with a version number higher than 5 (e.g. Word 6, WordPerfect 6).

c.) For poetry, submit as in (b) except that poetry may be single spaced. Submit no more than one poem on a page with your name and address on each poem, length to 75 lines, — approximately 30 lines preferred.

d.) For illustrations, submit black and white line art work for cover and interior illustrations. Theme and tone should be appropriate for a literary magazine.

e.) Submit seasonal themes nine months in advance.

f.) For sample copy, send 9 x 12 envelope and $4.95, shipping and handling included. For overseas, add $2.25 surface mail.

g.) E-mail address is for correspondence only. Submissions must be sent via conventional mail.

Contact Information:
Nonfiction, Fiction: Polly Swafford, Senior Editor
Poetry: Terry Hoyland, Poetry editor
Haiku: Robert Duchouquette, Haiku Editor
P.O. Box 8278
Prairie Village, KS 66208
(913) 642-1503 • FAX: (913) 642-3128
E-mail: Potpourpub@aol.com

POWER &MOTORYACHT

Power & Motoryacht

EDITORIAL PROFILE

Power & Motoryacht is edited and designed to meet the needs and pleasures of owners of powerboats 24 feet and larger, with special emphasis on the 35-foot-plus market. Launched in 1985, the magazine gives readers accurate advice on how to choose, operate, and maintain their boats as well as what electronics and gear will help them pursue their favorite pastime. In addition, since powerboating is truly a lifestyle and not just a hobby for these experienced readers, *PMY* reports on a host of other topics that affect their enjoyment of the water: chartering, cruising (day, weekend, and extended trips), sportfishing, and the environment.

Some of the regular features are:

SEAMANSHIP — Rules of the Road and boating protocol techniques
CRUISING — places readers can take their own boats for a few days' enjoyment
MAINTENANCE — tips on upkeep and repair
MAKING A DIFFERENCE — profiles of individuals working to improve the marine environment
SPORTFISHING DIGEST — fishing news and travel pieces

WRITING STYLE

Since *PMY* readers have an average of 28 years' experience boating, articles must be clear, concise, and authoritative; knowledge of the marine industry is mandatory. Include personal experience and information from marine industry experts where appropriate. Also include a list of the people and organizations (with phone numbers) contacted during your research.

All manuscripts must be sent on disk (WordPerfect, Microsoft Word, or another DOS-compatible format) and in hard-copy form. Articles should run between 1,000 and 2,000 words. If a travel story is being submitted, 35mm color slides must accompany the manuscript.

PAYMENT POLICY

Depending on article length, compensation is between $500 and $1,000; this fee includes photography if it is part of an assignment. Payment is upon acceptance; if an assigned article does not meet with our guidelines, a one-third kill fee will be given.

SUBMISSIONS

Query first; unsolicited manuscripts and photography are not accepted and will not be returned.

Send a one-page query to:

Contact Information:
Diane M. Byrne, Managing Editor
249 W. 17th Street, 4th Floor
New York, NY 10011
(212)463-6427 • FAX: (212) 463-6435

The Preacher's Magazine

". . . speaking the truth in love. . . "

Memo to: Freelance Writers
From: *The Preacher*'s magazine Editorial Staff

The Preacher's Magazine is a quarterly publication for Christian ministers. It is Wesleyan-Armenian in theological persuasion, and it seeks to provide insights and resources for lifelong ministerial development. Endeavoring to apply Biblical theological truths to modern day ministry, *The Preacher's Magazine* uses both scholarly and practical articles.

The magazine has two parts. The first part is divided into departments made up of articles on major sections such as: Church Administration, Church Growth, Pastoral Care, Evangelism, Theology, Multiple Staff Ministries, The Minister's Mate, Pastor's Personal Growth, Pastor's Professional growth, Holiness Heritage, Preaching, Biblical Studies, Church Music, and Finance.

Articles should be 700 to 2,500 words in length. When thinking of manuscript length, please keep in mind, "less is better." Payment is $.035 per published word upon publication. Payment will notify the writer of his acceptance.

All scripture quotations must be identified, including the version quoted. For example: (James 5:16, KJV). Only the New International Version need not be identified because it is covered throughout the magazine. The NIV example would be: (James 5:16).

Quotations should be identified by footnotes to give the source: author's name, title of book, city of publisher, publisher, date of publication, and page(s) quoted. For example: Randal E. Denny, In Jesus' Strong Hands (Kansas City, MO: Beacon Hill Press, 1989), p.2. The writer must obtain permission to use copyrighted material of more than 120 words. Permission letter should accompany the submitted manuscript.

Due to limited number of magazines printed, we are unable to send sample copies.

Contact Information:
Randal E. Denny, Editor
10814 East Broadway
Spokane, WA 99206
(509) 226-3464

Presbyterians Today

Presbyterians Today

Presbyterians Today is a magazine for members of the Presbyterian Church (U.S.A.). It is published 10 times a year, with combined January/February and July/August issues. Circulation is more than 90,000.

The target audience for *Presbyterians Today* is laypeople. Readers are quite diverse in age, sex, education, theological viewpoints, and involvement in the life of the church.

Presbyterians Today seeks to

1. Stimulate interest in and provide a more complete awareness and support of the mission of the Presbyterian Church (U.S.A.).

2. Report in a balanced way the news and activities of the denomination as it performs its mission through its designated agencies, governing bodies and congregations.

3. Enhance and celebrate the common bonds of heritage and faith that bind the Presbyterian Church (U.S.A.) together as a community of believers, and to provide for an expression of the rich diversity within the denomination.

4. Provide information, inspiration and guidance for readers as they seek to live as Christians in all aspects of life.

5. Confess that Jesus Christ is Lord, to lead readers to strengthen their understanding of the meaning of Christ and commitment to him, and to reflect the resources available through the Christian community.

6. Portray in an informative and stimulating manner the interaction of the Presbyterian Church (U.S.A.) with other Christian bodies and to interpret theologically the world in which and for which it performs its mission.

7. Foster understanding of the oneness of the Christian Church.

FEATURE ARTICLES

Presbyterians Today welcomes contributions from freelance writers. Stories vary in length (800 - 2,000 words; preferred, 1,000 - 1,500). Appropriate subjects: profiles of interesting Presbyterians and of Presbyterian programs and activities; issues of current concern to the church; ways in which individuals and Christian families express their Christian faith in significant ways or relate their faith to the problems of society. Most articles have some direct relevance to a Presbyterian audience; however, *Presbyterians Today* also seeks well informed articles written for a general audience that can help individuals and families cope with the stresses of daily living from a Christian perspective.

Presbyterians Today almost never uses fiction or short fillers, and poetry only occasionally. Original manuscripts are preferred. Reprints are occasionally used, but submission of reprints and multiple submissions are not encouraged.

Authors are asked to submit only one article at a time. Manuscripts are read by at least two editors, and a reply given normally within one month of receipt.

Presbyterians Today pays for articles upon acceptance. With the author's permission, the magazine may hold a manuscript for future consideration (which does not preclude the author from submitting the article elsewhere), and payment will be offered at the time the article is scheduled for publication—if publication rights are available to *Presbyterians Today* at that time. Authors receive complimentary copies of issues in which their articles appear.

SHORT FEATURES

Presbyterians Today also accepts short features (250-600 words) about interesting people, programs, events and congregations related to the Presbyterian Church (U.S.A.), for the "Spotlight" department. The editors may suggest that a full-length feature article, because of timeliness, space limitations or content, would be more appropriate as a "Spotlight" feature.

HUMOR

Presbyterians Today uses jokes or short humorous stories for the "LaughLines" department. Credit will be given to contributors, but the material should be in the public domain, not copyrighted. A minimal payment is given for original stories. Preferred length: 150 words or less.

QUERIES

Queries are not required, but may save effort and postage if a subject proposed is clearly inappropriate or if similar articles have been fairly recently used or are currently in the works.

Manuscripts are received on speculation.

SUBMISSIONS

The author's name, address and social security number should be typed on the manuscript as well as the cover letter. Manuscripts may be submitted by e-mail.

Photos accompanying a manuscript should be of good quality for reproduction. Black-and-white or color prints, transparencies, or contact sheets are acceptable. They should be identified as to content and credit line. Photos may be sent after an article is accepted, but it is helpful to know whether or not they are or could be available.

Presbyterians Today normally uses the New Revised Standard Version for Biblical quotations; if another version of scripture is used, this should be indicated. If copyrighted material is quoted, the author should secure permission in writing from the copyright holder and cite the work, author, publisher and date of copyright.

RULES FOR WRITING

Writer's Digest has suggested 20 rules for good writing:

1. Prefer the plain word to the fancy.
2. Prefer the familiar word to the unfamiliar.
3. Prefer the Saxon word to the Romance.
4. Prefer nouns and verbs to adjectives and adverbs.
5. Prefer picture nouns and action verbs.
6. Never use a long word when a short one will do as well.
7. Master the simple declarative sentence.
8. Prefer the simple sentence to the complicated.
9. Vary the sentence length.
10. Put the word you want to emphasize at the beginning or end of your sentence.
11. Use the active voice.
12. Put the statements in a positive form.
13. Use short paragraphs.
14. Cut needless words, sentences and paragraphs.
15. Use plain, conversational language.
16. Avoid imitation. Write in your natural style.
17. Write clearly.
18. Avoid gobbledygook and jargon.
19. Write to be understood, not to impress.
20. Revise and rewrite. Improvement is always possible.

To these *Presbyterians Today* adds one more:

Reporting is preferred to reflection. Your chances of having your article accepted for publication increase to the extent that you write in the third person, not the first person. Most stories can be told better without the use of "I."

Before you begin to write, ask yourself: "What do I want to say?" "Why?" "To whom?" "How do I plan to say it?" If your article is geared to a Presbyterian audience, make sure it is clear how and why the subject relates to that audience. Assemble and organize your material. An outline may help. After you have written your first draft, it is good practice to leave it for a time. When you return to it, read it aloud, making sure its language flows freely and comfortably.

Contact Information:
Catherine Cottingham, Managing Editor
100 Witherspoon Street
Louisville, KY 40202
(502) 569-5634
E-mail: today@pcusa.org or PresbyNet (in-box: today)

Pure-Bred Dogs/American Kennel Gazette

Editorial Profile: The GAZETTE is the official publication of the American Kennel Club. It is read by breeders and exhibitors of pure-bred dogs, by dog show judges, by individuals who compete in obedience and field trials, hunting and tracking tests and other events, and by other individuals with a serious interest in the sport of dogs. The GAZETTE publishes articles on a wide range of subjects, including veterinary medicine, nutrition and health, care and training and living with dogs: their behavior and temperament, exhibition, handling and conditioning. The common denominator in all GAZETTE editorial is that it acknowledges the reader's sophistication and seriousness about the subject matter and is never condescending.

The GAZETTE gives highest priority to the breeds that are recognized by the American Kennel Club and to activities that are sanctioned by the AKC. A smaller amount of space is devoted to non-AKC activities that nevertheless are of interest to fanciers. The magazine strives to keep readers informed on issues affecting dogs and dog owners in society today.

Freelance Opportunities: We are looking for authoritative pieces that explore a subject of general interest or that report on specific events or activities. Because of its affiliation with the American Kennel Club, the GAZETTE cannot accept stories that appear to promote individual dogs, judges, handlers, breeders or kennels; nor that appear to rate or endorse specific products. (Exceptions are when a story has news value.)

Articles should be factual rather than opinion, except for monthly Point of View essays (see below). Whatever the subject, writers should be knowledgeable and credible and should be able to quote several expert sources. Veterinary articles are written by or with a veterinarian. Most unsolicited material rejected by the editors consists of "true life" accounts, in memorium pieces, or other related material pertaining to one's own pet. Unless a work contains a timely, topical or newsworthy story of general interest to the dog fancy, the GAZETTE generally can't use it.

Fiction: Except for an annual short fiction contest (rules are published June through September, or are available on request with an SASE), the GAZETTE doesn't publish fiction.

Poetry, Puzzles, Cartoons: The GAZETTE does not publish poetry or puzzles. Cartoons are commissioned by the art director, and freelancers should not submit unsolicited cartoons.

Profiles: Profiles of individuals are published regularly, but should always be queried first in writing to the editor.

Clippings: These are never used.

Photography: The GAZETTE sponsors an annual photography contest (rules published September through December, or are available on request with an SASE). In addition, it welcomes candid photos of show-quality dogs in either color or black and white, and event-specific or relevant photography to accompany feature articles.

Illustrations: Professional illustrators interested in working with the GAZETTE should contact the art director. All art is commissioned. Illustrators should be able to accurately depict pure-bred dogs.

Point of View: The monthly Point of View column invites 800 word essays on important subjects facing the sport or the fancy. These are first-person opinion pieces and are published with a photograph of the author.

Specifications: Length: 1,000-3,000 words; payment: $200-$400. High-quality photos in either color or black and white are a definite plus; payment for photos is separate and is based on number and size used in magazine, ranging from $25 to $100 apiece.

Simultaneous submissions or previously published material will be considered, but author must advise in query letter.

Send query letter, proposal or complete manuscript. Reports in three weeks. Payment on acceptance for manuscripts; on publication for photography. Buys first North American serial rights, onetime use. All contributors retain copyright and reprint requests will be forwarded to them.

Contact Information:
Mary Witherell, Managing Editor
Mark Roland, Features Editor
Josh Adams, New Products Editor
51 Madison Avenue
New York, NY 10010

Quilting Today

(Please refer to Chitra Publications.)

Racquet/The Golfer

These departments are open to freelance contributions:

Courtside: These are short pieces (usually 500 to 1,500 words), usually telling a first person account of a tennis related experience. This section is also the place for obits, quirky player stories that are not big enough to be features and other odds and ends. The tone is generally light. Make sure to include both a title and a deck.

Sports Fitness: Written with an authority on some aspect of fitness. These stories are usually written with the "we" voice (i.e. We should avoid dehydration.), mixed with references to "players" or "athletes" and maybe the very occasional "you." The goal of this section is to inform, hopefully about something "cutting edge" while trying to avoid making things sound dry and scientific. Usually about 1,400 words.

Postcards: An occasional department containing first person experiences from all over the world. Tennis does not have to be the only thing in the story, but it should play an important part. Avoid taking on the tone of a reviewer, and remember both a title and a deck.

Chip Shots: The golf version of Courtside. Personal experiences are great, but beware the fact that at one time or another most golf writers believe that they have written the first story about someone who has a real passion for the game. Look for the offbeat.

Destinations: First-person travel stories. Approximately 1,000 to 2,000 words. See Postcards.

Contact Information:
Tennis: Allison Roarty, Associate Editor
Golf: Evan Rothman, Features Editor
21 East 40th Street
New York, NY 10018
(212) 768-8360

R-A-D-A-R

8121 Hamilton Avenue • Cincinnati, Ohio • 45231

R-A-D-A-R

R-A-D-A-R is a weekly Sunday school take-home paper for children in grades three through six. Our goal is to reach these children with the truth with God's word and to help them make it the guide of their lives.

Most of R-A-D-A-R's features correlate with Standard Publishing's Middle and Junior Sunday school curriculum; therefore, we buy submissions to fit in with specific themes. A quarterly theme list is available on request.

Preparing Your Submission

- Use a 60-character line.
- Place your name, address, social security number, and approximate number of words in your manuscript on the first page.

Payment and Perks

- Fiction/nonfiction—3 - 7 cents a word.
- Puzzles—$15.00 - $17.50
- Poetry—50 cents per line
- Cartoons—$15.00 - $20.00
- R-A-D-A-R pays on acceptance.
- Contributors receive two copies of the issue in which their work appears.
- We purchase first rights and reprint rights.

Materials Accepted for Publication

Fiction—The hero of the story should be an eleven- or twelve-year-old in a situation involving one or more of the following: mystery, animals, sports, adventure, school, travel, relationships (with parents, friends, and others). Stories should have believable plots. They should be wholesome and teach Christian values. Make prayer, church attendance, and Bible reading a natural part of the story. Brief references to such actions throughout the story will do more than tacking a moral onto the end of the story.

Word length should be 900-1,000 words. Occasionally we use a two-part story of 2,000 words complete length. Please allow 3-4 weeks for consideration of submissions not written for a specific topic. Allow 1-2 weeks after the due date for consideration of materials submitted for a specific theme. (The due date is on the quarterly theme list.)

Nonfiction—We purchase articles of 400-500 words on hobbies, animals, nature, life in other lands, sports, science, etc. Articles should have a religious emphasis. Document your article with the sources you have used. Please allow 1-2 weeks after the due date for consideration of nonfiction submissions. (The due date is on the quarterly theme list.)

Puzzles—Correlate with the quarterly theme list or with holidays and special occasions. We use word searches, acrostics, crosswords, fill-in-the-blanks, and matching puzzles. Our official translation for puzzles is the New International Version of the Bible. Answers to all puzzles should be given. Puzzles should be challenging, but not too difficult, and they should not be longer than one printed page of R-A-D-A-R.

Cartoons—
Appeal to 8-12 year old children.
Do not correlate with themes.

Poetry—
Biblical, or about nature.
Does not correlate with themes.

Final Thoughts

Keep in mind that children of today are different from the way they were when you were a child. Get to know children before you begin to write for them. Many manuscripts are rejected simply because the plot or vocabulary is outdated for modern children.

Before you submit, get to know R-A-D-A-R. Sample issues are available on request (enclose SASE, please). We are always looking for great ideas and fresh manuscripts. We hope to see your work soon!

Contact Information:
Elaina Meyers, Editor
8121 Hamilton Avenue
Cincinnati, OH 45231
(513) 931-4050

Radiance
The Magazine for Large Women

RADIANCE: The Magazine for Large Women, is a quarterly magazine now celebrating our eleventh year in print with more than 50,000 readers worldwide. Our target audience is the one woman in four who wears a size 16 or over—an estimated 30 million women in the United States alone. RADIANCE brings a fresh, vital new voice to women all sizes of large with our positive images, profiles of dynamic large women from all walks of life, and our compelling articles on health, media, fashion, and politics. We urge women to feel good about themselves now—whatever their body size or shape. RADIANCE, one of the leading resources in the "Size Acceptance Movement," links large women to the network of products, services, and information just for them.

DEPARTMENTS

Up Front & Personal: Interviews or first-person accounts of living life as a large woman. We like strong, intimate, in-depth profiles about a person's life and philosophy.

Health & Well-Being: Articles on health, fitness, and emotional well-being related to women in general and large women in particular. Also, profiles of healthcare professionals sensitive to the needs of large women.

Perspectives: Cultural, historical, and social views on body size and female beauty.

Expressions: Interviews with artists who are either large themselves, or whose work features large women.

Getaways: Articles on vacation spots around the world. Prefer if article includes ideas or tips for women of size.

On the Move: Articles about full-bodied women and sports and physical activities. Fitness video reviews.

Images: Interviews with designers or manufacturers of large and supersize clothing and accessories. Also welcome—articles on color, style, wardrobe planning.

Children and Young Adults: Articles on issues of children, weight, and self-esteem.

Inner Journeys: Articles on personal growth and inner-directed approaches to feeling better about oneself.

Book Reviews: Books relating to women, body image, health, spirituality, eating and food, cooking, career, psychology, politics, media, fashion, cultural attitudes, self-esteem and acceptance, travel, hobbies, leisure activities.

Short Stories & Poetry: Stories and poetry on body image, health, well-being, food and eating, work, politics, fashion, cultural attitudes, self-esteem and acceptance.

Home, Cooking, Gardening, Dining Out: Articles on any of these.

Women and Mid-Life, Aging: Articles on all aspects of these passages in a woman's life.

DEADLINES

Winter: June 15; Spring: September 15; Summer: December 15; Fall: March 15

TO WRITERS

We recommend that you read at least one issue of RADIANCE prior to writing for us. A sample copy for writers costs $3.50. Query us far in advance of the deadline if you want assurance that your article(s) will be considered for a particular issue. Our usual response time is about four to six months. We have a small staff and are committed to reading each submission carefully. Include your name, address, and phone number(s) on the title page and type your name and page number on subsequent pages. Remember to indicate availability of photos, artwork or illustrations (or ideas for them) in your query or with your article. Pertinent, high quality photos or art can greatly enhance an article's desirability. If you do send photos, please make sure that they are marked with a caption and the photographer's name, phone number and address.

At this time, payment is made upon publication. We intend to pay upon acceptance in the near future. As we grow, we will increase payments to writers, photographers and illustrators. We appreciate and value your interest in contributing to RADIANCE.

PAYMENT

Book Reviews	$35 to $75
Features/Profiles	$50 to $100
Poetry/Short Stories	$10 to $50
Color Cover Photos	$50 to $200
B & W Inside Photos	$15 to $25
Illustration/Artwork	$25 to $100

Once we develop a good working relationship with the writer, artist or photographer and we can count on your professionalism, service, quality and reliability, payment can increase. We will always send the contributor a copy of the magazine she/he is in. The contributor needs to send us an invoice after the work is completed with details of the service.

Contact Information:

EDITORIAL STAFF
Catherine Taylor - Senior Editor
Carol Squires - Editorial Assistant
Katherine L. Kaiser - Copy Editor/Proofreader
Alice Ansfield, Publisher/Editor
P.O. Box 30246
Oakland, CA 94604
(510) 482-0680

Ranger Rick

SUBJECT SELECTION

• Our audience ranges from ages six to twelve, though we aim the reading level of most materials at nine-year-olds or fourth graders.

• Fiction and nonfiction articles may be written on any aspect of wildlife, nature, outdoor adventure and discovery, domestic animals with a "wild" connection (such as domestic pigs and wild boars), science, conservation, or related subjects. To find out what subjects have been covered recently, consult our annual indexes or the *Children's Magazine Guide*. These are available in many libraries.

• The National Wildlife Federation (NWF) discourages the keeping of wildlife as pets, so the keeping of such pets should not be featured in your copy. We also do not accept pieces on wildlife rehabilitation, except for the rehabilitation of threatened or endangered species.

• Except in rare cases, human qualities are attributed to animals only in our regular feature, "Adventures of Ranger Rick," which is staff written.

• Avoid the stereotyping of any group. For instance, girls can enjoy nature and the outdoors as much as boys can, and mothers can be just as knowledgeable as fathers. Stories should reflect the ethnic and cultural diversity of our society.

• The only way you can write successfully for *Ranger Rick* is to know the kinds of subjects and approaches we like. And the only way you can do that is to read the magazine. Recent issues can be found in most libraries or are available from our office. To obtain a copy from our office, please send $2.15 plus a 9x12 self-addressed, stamped envelope.

SUBMITTING MATERIALS

• Send a query describing your intended subject, along with a lead or sample paragraph. Any special qualifications you may have to write on that subject would be worth mentioning. If you are not an expert on the subject, please list your main references and names of experts you will contact. **Please do not query by phone or FAX.**

• Unless you are an expert in the field you are covering, or unless your information is clearly anecdotal or from personal experience, all facts within your copy must be supported by up-to-date, authoritative references.

NEW POLICY: An index number must follow each fact and must refer to a footnote listed on a separate sheet. (See example below.) Any manuscript not footnoted in this manner may be rejected, and any agreement on a kill fee may be canceled.

We strongly recommend that you consult with experts in the field when developing material and that one of them read the finished manuscript for accuracy before you submit it.

Footnoting Style:

... the spitting cobra rears up and sprays venom into the face of any intruder [6]...

(Separate sheet)

6. *Living Snakes of the World*, by J.M. Mehrtens
   (Sterling Press, 1987), page 254.

• All submissions are made on speculation unless other arrangements have been made. Manuscripts are considered carefully and will be returned or accepted within one to two months. Our planning schedule is 10 months prior to cover date. Please do not submit your manuscript to other magazines simultaneously.

• Except for letters on our "Dear Ranger Rick" pages, we do not publish material written directly by children. Articles with children's bylines have in fact been written "as told to" an adult, by an adult.

PAYMENTS

• Payments range up to $575 for a full-length feature (about 900 words), depending on quality of writing and research.

• Upon acceptance of a manuscript, a transfer of rights form will be sent to you. NWF purchases exclusive first-time worldwide rights and non-exclusive worldwide rights thereafter. Payment checks will be processed after we receive the signed transfer of rights form. (To receive a sample form send a self-addressed, stamped envelope.)

• It is not necessary that illustrations or photographs accompany your materials. If we do use photographs you've included with your copy, these will be paid for separately at current market rates.

The NWF makes every effort to return submission materials if accompanied by a self-addressed, stamped envelope.

GUIDELINES - ADDENDUM

• Fiction: Science fiction, mystery, fantasy, straightforward fiction, plays, and fables (but no myths, please). Particularly interested in stories with minority or multicultural characters and stories that don't take place in the suburbs. Present-day stories need to be about today's kids (with working and/or single parents, day care, etc.). Stories must treat children respectfully (no wise old grandfather teaches dumb kid, please). All nature and environmental subjects OK, but no anthropomorphizing of wildlife. We publish fiction about four times per year; plays or fables every two years. About 900 words maximum.

• Poetry: We are currently overloaded with poetry and not accepting new submissions.

• Puzzles: No word searches, instantly visible dot-to-dots, or crossword puzzles. A puzzle should be nature-related, challenging, fun, creative, unlike schoolwork, and something an 8- to 10-year-old can finish without help. It should also offer the possibility of an attractive illustration. Please cite your source for each fact in the puzzle, unless the fact is very well known. Sending a photocopy of the source is especially helpful. We buy one or two freelance puzzles a year, but would like to buy more with fresh ideas.

• Riddles: We aren't buying any these days. We're asking readers to send in their favorites and may occasionally get permission from a publisher to use a group of riddles from a book.

Direct all correspondence to our editorial offices:

Contact Information:
Gerald Bishop, Editor
National Wildlife Federation
8925 Leesburg Pike
Vienna, VA 22184
(703) 790-4000
E-mail: http://www.nwf.org/nwf

Real People

Dear Friend:

Thank you for expressing an interest in writing for REAL PEOPLE Magazine.
We are interested in queries about articles that deal with men and women of signifi-

cance.

Her are some tips for writers:

1. Length should be 500-1,500 words maximum unless otherwise requested.

2. We are mainly interested in articles/interviews with celebrities of national prominence (i.e. instantly recognizable personalities from television, film, society pages, some sports, etc.). Profiles of celebrities must be based on personal interviews. As a rule, profiles should be tough, revealing, exciting and entertaining. Please, no secondhand bios from sources already published in books, magazines, etc.

3. Q&A formats are not encouraged. Please check with editors before undertaking such a project.

4. All unsolicited and assigned manuscripts are on speculation only unless prior arrangement is made.

5. We only consider original unpublished material.

6. We do not consider simultaneous submissions.

7. Please, no fiction, poetry or cartoons.

8. Fees range from $100-$300. Payment is on publication.

9. If you own an IBM compatible PC, we would appreciate receiving both a print-out of the manuscript and a 5¼" diskette. Our system prefers WordPerfect 4.2 but can translate most other programs. Please specify.

Sample copies of the magazine are available for $4.00 per issue plus postage. Send check or money order to the address below.

Thank you for thinking of us at REAL PEOPLE.

Contact Information:
Features: Alex Polner, Editor
Short Fillers: Brad Hamilton, Editor
950 3rd Avenue, 16th Floor
New York, NY 10022
(212) 371-4932 • FAX: (212) 838-8420

Recreation News

About 80% of the feature articles in *Recreation News* come from freelance writers or outside contractors. Although we have many fine writers whose work consistently appears on our pages, you can increase your chances of breaking into the lineup if your story meets certain criteria. We offer the following guidelines to help you tilt the odds in your favor.

Your article must fit the publication. Our target readership is the more than 250,000 federal employees working in the Washington, D.C., metropolitan area. They want to know about relaxing or stimulating—but always interesting—ways to spend their leisure time. Your story must address that need. Most articles we flatly reject are turned down because they have nothing to do with recreation, fail to provide a logical Washington connection, or they offer little of interest to the typical government worker. We strongly suggest you browse several recent issues, if possible. If not, we will be glad to mail you a sample copy if you send us a self-addressed 9x12 envelope bearing $1.05 postage.

It's not essential that your story deal with a place or activity near Washington, D.C., but it helps. Most of our features cover subjects within a weekend drive of the capital area. Yes, our readers do travel out of the region, which is why we have a "Great Escape" column, a feature spotlighting more distant locales across the country. But most of our readers' leisure time is spent near home. We therefore don't cover foreign travel, except for an occasional story about

Canada, Mexico or nearby islands.

Approach and style. For the most part, *Recreation News* strives for a lively, informal style. That doesn't mean wordiness or endless tangents. It does mean a conversational tone that's lean and brisk. Try to give your article a fresh point of view and, if at all possible, cover some out-of-the-ordinary subject matter. Your article must go beyond the self-serving listing of information doled out by visitors' bureaus, travel agencies and PR firms. Work in quotes from visitors to the sites, or the participants in a particular activity, and let them express their thoughts about how they feel about a particular place or activity. If they happen to be federal employees and/or from around Washington—hooray! And particularly with destination pieces, comments from colorful locals also spice up a story. Remember, you'll catch our eye faster with a piece about a little-known location or activity rather than with one about a subject everyone already knows about. We basically follow the *Associated Press Stylebook* and *Webster's New World Dictionary, Second College Edition*.

If you're planning to submit a piece solely on a favorite resort, hotel, inn, lodge or restaurant . . . please don't. You'll stand a much better chance of scoring with us by expanding your coverage to a wider scope. It's helpful to give passing mention to lodging and dining facilities available, but only as sidebar material. And remember, no blatant puffery, please.

How long should an article be? *Recreation News* stories are relatively short. Our longest pieces—those featured on our cover—seldom exceed 2,200 words. In addition to "Great Escape," cover stories are culled from our "Pursuits" column (sports or activities around the Washington, D.C. area) or "Weekend Away" (destinations within a three-hour drive of Washington, D.C.). Stories intended for the "Day Off" column (activities or destinations around the Washington area) should run about 900 words. Pieces aimed at our "Sporting Life" column (usually light, first-person articles about a personal experience involving some sort of recreational activity) should also be around 900 words. And except for "Sporting Life" pieces, all stories should be accompanied by a sidebar, or information box, listing pertinent contact information, hours, rates, etc. *Recreation News* does not carry poetry or "reflection" type articles.

Our editorial calendar. We plan and assign articles anywhere from six months to a year in advance, so writers should plan accordingly. In other words, don't wait until the snow falls to query us about a skiing or ice-fishing piece.

Because of an unusually heavy upsurge in unsolicited manuscripts during the past year or so, our editorial cupboard is heavily stocked, especially with "Great Escape" vacation-site stories outside the Washington area. Some manuscripts have been on hold for more than six months waiting for a spot to open, so be prepared for a wait. Stories aimed at "Day Off," "Pursuits," and "Weekend Away" are currently more in demand.

Acceptance and payment. If we accept your article, you will be sent an agreement spelling out your rights and the rights you sell to us. Specific questions you may have about the agreement should be directed to the editor at the address or phone number on the agreement.

Recreation News pays upon publication, with checks being mailed within a day or two of the 15th of the month of publication. Rates vary, depending on length, placement, previous publication and other factors negotiated between the author and the editors. As a general rule, rates range from $50 to a ceiling of $300. All articles are submitted on speculation.

Photography. *Recreation News* welcomes photographs that illustrate your story. Photos must be of good quality and composition and should, as a rule of thumb, include people enjoying the location. Black-and-white prints are preferred, however, good sharp color prints are acceptable. Color slides are only used as cover illustrations and are not acceptable for conversions to black and white. Rates for original photographs are $25 for each published black-and-white print and $120 for a color slide used on the cover. We do not pay for photos supplied by PR firms and visitors' bureaus, although they are certainly welcome with your article. A well-written article, accompanied by good photography, has the best chance of being published in *Recreation News*.

Thanks for thinking of *Recreation News* and good luck on your submissions to us.

Contact Information:
Rebecca Heaton, Editor
P.O. Box 32335, Calvert Station
Washington, D.C. 20007-0635
(202) 965-6960

Red Herring Mystery Magazine

RED HERRING MYSTERY MAGAZINE is a quarterly publication published by Potpourri Publications Company, a not for profit corporation. It is sold by subscription and at bookstores.

RED HERRING accepts only short mystery fiction. Submit your best original material up to 6,000 words. No gratuitous sex or violence. No true crime. One story per submission. Advise if the story is a simultaneous submission.

Authors and artists will be paid for First North American serial rights with one contributor's copy plus a flat fee of $5.00 or more, depending upon grants received. In addition, authors and artists may purchase five additional copies at reduced cost.

Editors will report in three months or sooner. Stories will be published three to twelve months after acceptance. Three months after publication in RED HERRING, you are free to sell reprint rights.

RED HERRING MYSTERY MAGAZINE is copyrighted, but not registered. The writer's and artist's work is protected by copyright of this publication.

Type your name, address, and telephone number at the upper left margin of your first page and the total number of words in your manuscript in the upper right hand corner. Type your name and page number on each consecutive page. Submit seasonal stories at least six months in advance.

When your story is accepted, we will request a copy on Macintosh or IBM 3½ inch disk in WordPerfect, Word, Quark Express, or PageMaker.

Artists: Please submit two color (black and red), clean line art work for cover and interior illustrations. Theme and tone should be appropriate for mystery, intrigue and suspense. Prefer 7½" x 6¼" format.

Authors and artists: please include a brief biographical sketch with a cover letter.

Sample copy available for $4.95 including postage.

Contact Information:
Donna Trombla, Editor
Kitty Mendenhall, Editor
Juliet Kincaid, Editor
P.O. Box 8278
Prairie Village, KS 66208
(913) 642-1503 • FAX: (913) 642-3128

Reptile & Amphibian Magazine

Original articles from freelance authors are welcome. *Reptile & Amphibian Magazine* is directed to the devoted, advanced amateur herpetologist. Generally, our readers are college educated and familiar with the basics of herpetology. They enjoy articles on life cycles of various reptiles and amphibians; special behavioral characteristics of common species dealing with reproduction, feeding, adaptation to environmental changes, etc.; interrelationships with other species, including man; and captive care and breeding. Many of our articles are written from an ecological perspective, but we do not actively promote any special causes.

Manuscripts: Feature articles should be about 1,500-2,500 words in length, book reviews approximately 750 words. Submit tables and diagrams if they help clarify text. (They must be self-explanatory and neatly presented; our graphic department can convert them to final form for printing.) The use of generic names is preferred. A trade name, when necessary, must be verified as complete and accurate (correct spelling, capitalization, hyphenation). If not well-known, include the full name and address of the manufacturer. Authors should adopt a journalistic/textbook style, and avoid first-person narratives. If data is given in metric measurements it must be accompanied by English conversions. Submission on disk is encouraged (3.5", any popular word processing format can be translated), and should be accompanied by a hard copy as well.

Editorial Review: Controversial or unfamiliar subjects may be clarified by editorial commentary, and the Editor reserves the right to make revisions when appropriate. Likewise, the cropping of photos and illustrations is at the editor's discretion.

Payment: We purchase first-time, one-time North American publishing rights, and pay upon acceptance. Feature articles are paid $75-$100 each, depending on length and content. Book reviews are paid $50 each. All authors receive a byline; authors, photographers, and artists also receive credit on the masthead. Complimentary issues are provided to contributors.

Before submitting a manuscript, the author is encouraged to consult the editor to ensure that the topic has not been covered by another writer. For a sample copy, send $4. To see what articles have been published, an Index is available (send a SASE). The U.S. subscription rate is $16 per year (6 issues) or $28 for two years (12 issues).

PHOTOGRAPHER'S GUIDELINES

Submission of Photographs: *Reptile & Amphibian Magazine* publishes approximately 300 photographs per year. About 80% of these are full-color reproductions of 35mm slides submitted by freelance photographers. Each transparency received is examined on a light table. If it is considered to be a likely purchase, an internegative and a print are produced. Immediately following this procedure, all originals are returned to the photographer, or agency, of origin. Final selections are made from the prints, based on both technical quality and editorial needs. We also accept artwork, medium format color transparencies, color prints, black and white prints, and 35mm color or B&W negatives. The above procedure is adapted to accommodate these other formats; in all cases the originals are returned within 60-90 days and final selection is made from the reproductions.

Payment: *Reptile & Amphibian Magazine* pays $25 per color photo or artwork, and $10 per black & white photo or artwork. If photos are included as part of a manuscript, or if they fill an immediate need, payment may be made upon selection. In all other cases, payment is upon publication. Payment is made each time a photo is used (i.e.—if a picture, or a part of that picture is used in three issues, the photographer is paid three times). It is not our intention to purchase exclusive, or first-time rights to any photograph. Photographers may submit previously published material and likewise sell material to other markets after the originals are returned, even before publication in *Reptile & Amphibian Magazine*. Also, it is not our intention to purchase copyright privileges, which remain with the author.

Credit & Editorial Review: Controversial or unfamiliar subjects may be qualified by editorial commentary, and the Editor reserves the right to crop photos and illustrations. Photographers and artists are credited on the masthead and also receive complimentary copies of any issue in which their work appears. All species must be identified on the mount with common and scientific name.

A clearly worded statement indicating that photos being submitted are intended for use in *Reptile & Amphibian Magazine* must accompany all photographs. The photographer may also state any special conditions which affect publication of his/her pictures. A standard permission form (below) is included for this purpose, or photographers may write their own.

PHOTOGRAPHER'S STATEMENT

I hereby give Ramus Publishing, Inc. and *Reptile & Amphibian Magazine* permission to copy my imprinted and/or copyrighted photographic material for use in *Reptile & Amphibian Magazine*/HERP NEWS TODAY.

Signed ____________________ Copyright or imprint sample as it appears on

Studio Name ________________ photographic material ________________

Contact Information:

Erica Ramus, Editor and Publisher
RD #3, Box 3709-A
Pottsville, PA 17901
(717) 622-6050 • FAX: (717) 622-5858
E-mail: ERamus@ricnet.pottsville.com

The Retired Officer Magazine
A Tradition of Service . . . Since 1929

General

Publisher: The Retired Officer Association, a nonprofit organization.

Editor: Col. Charles D. Cooper, USAF-Ret.

Audience: Commissioned and warrant officers, families, surviving spouses of the seven uniformed services: Army, Navy, Air Force, Marine Corps, Coast Guard, Public Health Service, and National Oceanic and Atmospheric Administration.

Circulation: 400,000 monthly. Sample magazine on request with 9x12 SASE.

Editorial Requirements

Format: Original material. No footnotes. No fiction, poetry, or fillers.

Topics: Current military/political affairs; recent military history, especially Vietnam and Korea; travel; money; hobbies; health and fitness; second career job opportunities; military family and retirement lifestyles.

Queries: Submit detailed query before sending manuscript, and enclose copies of published clips and resume. Unsolicited manuscripts rarely accepted.

Style: Active voice, nontechnical with quotes. Optimistic, upbeat theme. Use the *Associated Press Stylebook*.

Length: 800 to 2,000 words.

Terms: First rights. No simultaneous submissions or reprints.

Payment: Up to $1,000. Payment on acceptance.

Submit to: Articles editor at address below. Submit holiday features at least 12 months in advance.

Notification: By letter within eight weeks. No phone calls, please.

Photographs

Supporting: Supporting photos purchased with manuscript. Original color slides or transparencies suitable for color separation preferred. Up to $125 for each slide or transparency used. 5"x7" or 8"x10" black and white glossies acceptable sometimes. $20 for each black and white photo used. Prefer caption and credit line on separate sheet.

Cover: Original color slides or transparencies, up to $200. Prefer captions and credit line on separate sheet.

Contact Information:
Articles Editor
201 North Washington Street
Alexandria, VA 22314-2539
(800) 245-8762 or (703) 549-2311

ROCK & ICE
AMERICA'S #1 CLIMBING MAGAZINE

Rock & Ice

Rock & Ice is published six times a year; issues appear in January, March, May, July, September and November. Issue line-ups are finalized three months before the publication date. Please be aware of this scheduling if you are submitting seasonal material. A guide to a summer rock climbing area, for example, would have to be suggested by March 10; it would be due April 10 for inclusion in our July issue.

We encourage you to query first with your idea. Please include published writing samples with your query. Full manuscripts are also considered. In either case, please mention the availability of professional-quality transparencies or prints to illustrate your article. If the query/manuscript is accepted, we will expect you to provide the work on disk and to carefully fact-check all your material. Please include your name, address, telephone number and social security number on every submission.

Rock & Ice pays $200 per page; pages unbroken by decorative elements (photos, headlines, pull quotes) contain about 1,000 words.

FEATURES

Features run from 1,500 to 5,000 words and generally fall into one of the following categories: profiles, issues, climbing adventure travel, surveys or guides to foreign and domestic climbing locations, humor and fiction.

We're looking for profiles of articulate, interesting personalities—cutting-edge climbers, historical figures, people who have combined climbing with careers (expedition doctors, climbing rangers) are examples. Profiles should deal with the climber as a whole person—the emphasis should be on his or her climbing, but the personality must be rounded out for a fuller portrait. Quotes from people who know the climber well add an important perspective to profiles.

Issues deal with the more serious side of climbing. In one article, for example, we looked at mountain-guide certification and the politics behind guide concessions in Denali. Issues must be thoroughly researched and fact-checked with extreme care.

We receive the most submissions for our climbing adventure travel category. We're looking for one of the following hooks: the place must either be unusual or relatively unknown; something of particular interest or drama must have occurred during the trip; a well-known area must be looked at from a special angle (best intermediate routes; European sport tour). Climbing travel should be accompanied by top-notch photography and be extremely well written (first-person, humor and/or drama are always good). Since this is our most competitive category, we are quite choosy.

Humor/fiction articles are free-form. *Rock & Ice* is known for not shying away from the irreverent or the weird, and we don't plan to change that.

Guides should either be to areas that have not been covered by guidebooks or to ones that have a number of new routes that have not been previously covered. Please see separate "Guidelines for Guides" sheet.

DEPARTMENTS

All departments except "Reviews" and "Competitions" should be 1,500 to 2,500 words. Write tightly and don't leave anything out.

Performance: Clear, step-by-step instructions on how to do anything related to climbing, from building an indoor gym to climbing steep terrain.

Body Logic: This section covers anything to do with staying alive and healthy: nutrition, sports medicine, wilderness first aid are some examples. All articles must have a climbing angle.

Enviro: How climbing impacts the environment, and how environmental problems can be mitigated or prevented.

History: An historical look at the people, places and equipment that makes up the fabric of our climbing culture.

Rap Station: We're looking for excellent writing for this one-page section. Express a point of view, or just wax lyrical. Please limit to 1,000 words.

Reviews: Critical reviews of guidebooks, fiction, adventure, medicine, how-tos—any books or videos that apply to climbing and climbers. 300-600 words.

Competitions: Competition reports should be 300-500 words on events of national importance; focus more on human-interest elements that occurred during the comp than on the traditional and-then-he-lunged-for-the-next-jug reporting. Query (phone or write) before submitting a comp report.

You should get feedback from us within six weeks of your submission. Good luck, and thank you for thinking of *Rock & Ice*.

Contact Information:
Marjorie McCloy, Editor
603A South Broadway
Boulder, CO 80303
(303) 499-8410

Roofer Magazine

Exclusivity—We require all contributors to inform the editorial staff if the potential article has appeared in, or is being reviewed by, another publication serving the roofing industry. Our primary competitors are *RSI*, *Professional Roofing*, *Contractor's Guide*, *Metal Construction News*, and *Western Roofing*. Our secondary competitors are: *Construction Specifier*, *Canadian Roofing Contractor*, *Building Design and Construction*, *Buildings Magazine*, *Rural Builder*, *ENR*, *Journal of Light Construction*, and *American School & University*.

Content - All submitted articles must be generic, unless otherwise specified. Any self-serving statements must serve the article and not the author. Articles should be 1000-1500 words, with photo captions if applicable.

Readability - Ninety percent of our readership is roofing contractors, but we also serve many architects, specifiers, building owners and manufacturers. This imperfect industry has shown the amount of diversity in opinions, so it is necessary to consider all points of view with any article. It is also imperative that "real world" circumstances be acknowledged. Please make technical information as readable and as interesting as possible. We have always felt that roofing can be interesting if given half a chance. Humor is acceptable only if it is appropriate and does not detract from the subject matter.

Documentation —Please use quotes, survey results, and diverse sources whenever possible. All comparison charts must be qualified from a reputable source. Except for freelance material, all articles submitted must be accompanied with author's credentials.

Controversy—We will print controversial material so long as it is truthful, properly documented, and all sides of the argument are presented fairly. However, this is not the place for vendettas or personal biases. Any disparaging remarks about proprietary items must be proven through reliable means.

Artwork—Please submit any artwork that is applicable to the subject matter. Color prints are our preferable medium. PMT's of charts and/or graphs are welcome. If desired, please provide captions and credit lines. If none are available, please suggest any artwork to accompany the material. Note that any photos showing improper or unsafe working habits (unless to show an example) will NOT be used.

Deadlines—Meeting deadlines is extremely important to ensure the proper presentation of your material. Please make sure that your material arrives in sufficient time for editing and proofing.

Contact Information:
Angela Williamson, Editor
12734 Kenwood Lane, Building 73
Fort Myers, FL 33907
(941) 489-2929 • FAX: (941) 489-1747
E-mail: roofmag.com

Rosebud
For People Who Enjoy Writing

Dear Writer:

Thank you for your interest in *Rosebud.*™ It is a magazine for people who enjoy writing, and I encourage you to submit material for consideration in our upcoming issues. We review material throughout the year.

Something has to "happen" in the pieces we choose, but what happens inside characters is much more interesting to us than plot manipulation. We like good storytelling, real emotion, and authentic voice. We are seeking stories, articles, profiles, and poems that fit the tone of these rotating departments (the editor will make the final designation):

1. City and Shadow (urban settings)
2. Songs of Suburbia (suburban themes)
3. These Green Hills (nature and nostalgia)
4. En Route (any type of travel)
5. Mothers, Daughters, Wives (relationships)
6. Ulysses' Bow (manhood)
7. Paper, Scissors, Rock (childhood, middle age, old age)
8. The Jeweled Prize (concerning love)
9. Lost and Found (loss and discovery)
10. The Way It Was (the past)
11. Voices in Other Rooms (historic or of other culture)

12. Overtime (involving work)
13. Anything Goes (humor)
14. I Hear Music (music)
15. Season to Taste (food)
16. Word Jazz (word play)
17. Apples to Oranges (miscellanea, excerpts, profiles)
18. Sneak Preview (excerpts from longer pieces about to be published)

An ideal length for most pieces is between 1,200 and 1,800 words. *Rosebud* will pay $45 plus two extra copies (upon publication) for complete pieces that are accepted. The short excerpts in Apples to Oranges and Word Jazz will earn $15. At the time of the Summer Issue, three awards of $150 will also be made for the top three selections of the previous year.

Submissions must include the writer's name at the top of each page. We use *The Chicago Manual of Style* and *Webster's Collegiate Dictionary (10th Edition)* as editorial guides.

In order to further assist writers (and still allow the editor or publisher to personally read each piece) we depart from the procedures of most traditional magazines in five additional ways. We believe they are essential to our publication's and our contributors' future efficiency and success:

1. We encourage simultaneous submissions. *Rosebud* buys both first and secondary rights. In the case of a "new voice," it does not matter if the piece has been published in a small publication or regionally; we are interested in giving it national exposure.

2. We prefer to respond with an individualized letter (send an SASE for this) and recycle submitted manuscripts. In this age of laser printers and copiers it is wasteful and time consuming to shuffle paper which will be unusable.

3. We can only give detailed editorial feedback on pieces we are going to buy. As much as we would like to oblige (and encourage) new writers, our manpower and money has to be directed toward producing a magazine.

4. Please send hardcopy initially. Eventually we will require all manuscripts we choose to publish to be transmitted electronically by disk or modem after selection. As much as possible we try to have writers who are accepted do this now—the time keyboarding, scanning, and proofing hardcopy for errors is costly.

5. *Rosebud* purchases one time rights of original and previously published pieces. All other rights belong to the writer. If the idea of writing is to reach an audience, "exclusivity" unnecessarily restricts this, especially since small press magazines, national magazines, books, and anthologies each have their own audiences.

Rosebud is distributed nationally (50 states), in Canada, and in Europe with subscribers in many other parts of the world. It is available through all major bookstore chains. As writers, we're dependent upon magazines which publish our work. And these magazines depend upon us. If we don't buy, read, and promote them, they cease to exist. This is particularly true of periodicals that are open to submissions from new voices, like *Rosebud*. We are a non-profit organization with no outside affiliation.

A one year subscription (4 issues) is $19; a 2-year subscription (8 issues) is $33. Sample copies are $5.50 each. For subscriptions, renewals, and sample copies contact Beth Swan, Circulation Manager, 4218 Barnett Street, Madison, WI 53704. (608) 249-9511

Send in your manuscript; send in your subscription. Let us, together, create a new kind of writing-publishing success.

Sincerely,
Roderick Clark, Editor

Contact Information:
P.O. Box 459
Cambridge, WI 53523
(608) 423-9780 • FAX: (608) 423-9690

The Rotarian Magazine

EDITORIAL PROFILE

THE ROTARIAN is the official magazine of Rotary International, a nonprofit world fellowship of more than one million business and professional leaders united in the ideal of "Service Above Self"; that is, betterment of business and professional ethics, community life, and international understanding and goodwill. THE ROTARIAN's editorial content reflects these aims.

CIRCULATION

More than 520,000 readers in some 150 countries subscribe to THE ROTARIAN. Therefore, our articles must be of interest to an international audience.

EDITORIAL PURPOSE

The chief aim of THE ROTARIAN is to report rotary organizational news. Most of this information comes through Rotary channels and is staff-written or edited.

The best field for freelance articles is the general-interest category. These run the gamut from humor pieces and "how-to" stories to articles about such significant concerns as business management, world health, and the environment.

Generally, THE ROTARIAN publishes articles of 1,500 words or less. We look for topical 800-word articles for our Manager's Memo, Executive Health, Executive Lifestyle, Trends, and Earth Diary columns.

EDITORIAL EMPHASIS

Since THE ROTARIAN's establishment in 1911, the bylines of the likes of Albert Einstein, Thomas Mann, Helen Keller, Winston Churchill, Mahatma Gandhi, Betty Friedan, Luigi Barzini, Bill Moyers, Jacque Cousteau, and Jimmy Carter have appeared in our pages. Most of the work of this international array of authors has covered four major areas which complement Rotary's ideal of service.

1.) Advancement of international understanding, goodwill, and peace, and discussion of global issues.

The United Nations, European unity, Pan-American relations, international assistance programs, world trade . . . all are topics THE ROTARIAN covers occasionally, such as "The Land Mine Crisis," by Boutros Boutros-Ghali, and "Global Television," by John M. Dunn. We have devoted the editorial content of special issues to topics such as AIDS, drug abuse, world literacy, and endangered species.

2.) Better vocational relationships.

Articles in this category encourage high standards in business and the professions, and explore new ideas in management and business technology. Our award-winning article "Strung Out on the Job" took a hard look at employees who abuse drugs and alcohol at work—and at what employers can do to help those workers. Other features have dealt with career counseling for young people, vocational education for high-school dropouts, and business and professional ethics.

3.) Better community life.

Such articles make readers aware of community concerns and problems and suggest solutions. In "Too Much Trash," THE ROTARIAN examined options for effective waste management, a problem that confronts industrialized and developing nations alike. We also run articles on urban affairs, crime prevention, alternative energy sources, and new educational methods.

4.) Better human relationships

Rotary is interested in improving the human condition and promoting goodwill among all of the world's people. THE ROTARIAN has presented special issues that focused on mental health, illness, and old age. We tell about institutions that help the physically, mentally, and socially disabled. Since Rotary activities furnish us with a wealth of such material, we have little need for freelance submissions on these subjects. When we do accept freelance articles about community projects, we like them to have some Rotary connection—either with a Rotary club or an individual Rotarian.

Also, culture- and travel-related articles, particularly about the site of annual Rotary conventions, are very popular. General interest articles frequently appear in our pages, such as "Communities of the Mind" (exploring the Internet) and "Crossword Puzzles."

THE ROTARIAN IS NOT INTERESTED IN

- criticism and exposés, or articles with direct political and religious slants (except for ethical discussions). The magazine's rationale, mirroring that of the organization it serves, is one of hope and encouragement.
- articles that are solely "U.S." in subject matter and viewpoint.
- We do not buy fiction or poetry.

PAYMENT TERMS

We pay on acceptance, and our rates depend on the value of the material to us.

PHOTOGRAPHY AND ILLUSTRATIONS

Because photos and artwork accompany our articles, we encourage authors to include photos (slides preferred) with their manuscripts, or indicate sources of good images.

Both black-and-white and color images and illustrations are used in the body of the magazine, while our cover is always four-color. Cover illustrations are always photos or conceptual art, and we are particularly interested in easily identifiable landscapes (This is Japan . . . This is Brazil . . .) and lively shots of people.

CONTACT

We prefer written queries, though the editors do consider all submissions. Please furnish final manuscripts on 3.5" diskettes, preferably in a Word for Windows format.

We look forward to hearing from you.

Contact Information:
One Rotary Center
1560 Sherman Avenue
Evanston, IL 60201
(847) 866-3000

RURAL HERITAGE™

Rural Heritage

RURAL HERITAGE was established in 1975 as a link with the past, not for nostalgic reasons, but to help preserve a way of life for future generations. Our readers are common-sense country folks who enjoy doing things for themselves. Many of them have always farmed with horses, mules, or oxen; others are returning to the practice for economic and/or environmental reasons. Our editorial policy is guided by the philosophy that the past holds the key to the future.

Subjects: We publish hands-on how-to stories covering the broad spectrum of rural skills and creative problem solving, with emphasis on draft animals used in the field or woodlot. We are especially seeking technical details on specific pieces of horse-drawn equipment, how it was obtained/restored, how much it cost, how it's put together, how it works, problems encountered, and how they were solved. We do not publish religious material or non-relevant political or social topics.

Submission: If you are unknown to us, please either submit your material on speculation or else query (outline what you intend to cover and how you'll handle it) and if possible include clips of three previously published pieces. Be sure you know your subject—our savvy readers are quick to notice errors in terminology, breed identification, and similar details.

Format: We prefer submissions in standard manuscript format, accompanied by a diskette (either size and density) in WordPerfect 5.1 or ASCII. Please include a two or three sentence bionote describing your non-writing interests and qualifications for your subject.

Length: Minimum is 650 words with at least one illustration (850 words without illustration); features run 1,200 to 1,500 words; special subjects occasionally run longer.

Illustrations: Illustrations are not required, but we do feel the author is best qualified to provide appropriate photos or artwork. We will look at black and white glossy prints or color prints with good contrast (no snapshots). Please include detailed captions identifying breed(s), equipment, and visible people, and indicate the name of the photographer or artist to whom we should give credit. Put your name and address on the back of each piece and send a self-addressed stamped envelope for the return of your material.

Payment: Payment for first English language rights is 5 cents per published word and $10 per illustration, paid on publication, and two copies of the issue bearing your work.

Sample copy: If you are not familiar with RURAL HERITAGE and would like a sample issue, please send $6.00 (US$6.50 to Canada or overseas). Subscriptions to the bimonthly are $19.00 per year (US$23.20 to Canada, US$24.00 overseas).

Contact Information:
Gail Damerow, Editor
281 Dean Ridge Lane
Gainesboro, TN 38562-5039
(615) 268-0655

Safari Magazine

SAFARI Magazine was founded in 1971 as the official publication of Safari Club International. *SAFARI Magazine* is bimonthly; is focused on big game and includes editorials, feature stories and standing columns about SCI chapter activities, affiliated organizations and members 'hunting reports from around the world. Circulation is 20,000-22,000, mailed nationally/internationally to the SCI membership list and selected other individuals and organizations.

EDITORIAL CONTENT

The magazine scope of interest is:

- outdoor recreation with special emphasis on big game hunting around the world
- current or historical hunting and conservation
- background on a particular species
- ethnic and traditional hunts of particular regions around the world
- philosophy and heritage of hunting
- conservation and environmental affairs relevant to big game or hunters

Queries prior to story or photo submissions are encouraged. No fiction or poetry is used. Avoid sending simple hunting narratives that lack new approaches. Features run 2,000-2,500 words. Stories should be informative, accurate and designed to appeal to sportsmen and women as wells as others who enjoy the out-of-doors. Rate for a full-length story with illustrations submitted by a professional writer is $200 paid upon publication. Shorter stories or non-pro contributions by SCI members rate an honorarium of $25. (Professional photographers will be paid up to $100 for color photos used, depending on size, and up to $45 for B&W, all on an if published/when published basis).

News briefs are welcomed and will include bylines, but are not bought by *SAFARI*.

MANUSCRIPT PREPARATION

Submitted manuscripts should fit these specifications in order to be reviewed.

- Original: typed or laser jet printout, no photocopies.
- Computer disks: ASCII language, accepted with hard copy (Mac @ 3½" or IBM @ 5¼")
- All pages: 1½" left margin, 1" right and base
- Title page (first page): Author name, address, telephone in upper right corner, title halfway down first page, followed by text. Author-name on all pages following
- Consecutive number all manuscript pages
- Pica-size type preferred
- Spell-check for proper names, animals, places
- Do not staple manuscript
- We have prepared an editorial style sheet for information and use on any manuscript

PHOTOGRAPHY SUBMISSION

We are interested only in huntable big game subjects of trophy quality in a natural setting.

Color photographs, slides or transparencies are preferred. (Prints accepted for color or black-and-white uses. In all cases, use will depend on the reproduction quality of submitted materials.)

All photos must be captioned. Type caption information on a separate sheet of paper and number to match slide or print being described. We prefer to receive more photos than we may be able to use, in order to have a choice. All photos will be returned following publication unless otherwise directed.

- Color Slides: use plastic sheets to hold slides or transparencies; do not ship unprotected. Label each slide with your name stamp or ink.
- Slides or transparencies preferred for color and should be sharp and well-exposed. (Prints are OK, glossy preferred. If 35mm: double-sized, or @ 5"x7" or larger.)
- Black-and-White: 35mm contacts, glossy or semi-gloss prints; added minimum of ½" white border on four sides preferred.
- Print sizes @ 5"x7", 8"x10" preferred; others considered based on quality and story needs.
- Do not write on prints. Attach label with pre-typed information or use grease-pencil only.

Contact Information:

Elaine Cummings, Manuscript Editor
William R. Quimby, Director of Publications
4800 West Gates Pass Road
Tucson, AZ 85745
(520) 620-1220

SageWoman
Celebrating the Goddess in Every Woman

SageWoman is a quarterly magazine of women's spirituality. Our readers are people (primarily but not exclusively women) who identify positively with the term 'Goddess'. This does not mean that they are necessarily self-identified Goddess worshippers, Pagans, or Wiccans, although a majority of our readers would probably be comfortable with those terms. Our readers include women of a variety of religious faiths, ranging from Roman Catholic to Lesbian Separatist Witch and everywhere in between.

What our readers have in common is summed up in the statement 'Celebrating the Goddess in every woman'. If you feel a connection with our subject matter, we welcome your contributions to our pages. The majority of every issue is created from the contributions of our readers, so your creativity and willingness to share is vital to *SageWoman*'s existence! We welcome material from women of all races, ages, sexual orientations, and socioeconomic backgrounds. Due to our readership and distribution, we ask that written contributions and letters to us be submitted in English, but we encourage submissions from non-American women and women for whom English may be a second language. We also strongly encourage contributions from women of color.

SageWoman offers the following guidelines to help you in submitting your work to us.

1. Subject matter:

a. All submissions should focus on issues of concern to pagan and other spiritually minded women. We accept nonfiction prose related to women's spiritual experience. We accept very modest amounts of poetry, and receive far more poetry than we can publish. We also accept photographs and graphic artwork (drawings, painting, prints, etc.) suitable for publishing in a magazine format. We do not accept fiction, screenplays, or long narrative poems due to space limitations.

b. *SageWoman* is dedicated to helping women explore their spiritual, emotional, and mundane lives in a way which respects all persons, creatures, and the Earth. We encourage women of all spiritual paths to send writings and artwork, but our focus is on material which expresses an Earth-centered spirituality. Personal experience, scholarly research, Goddess lore, ritual material, interviews, humor, reviews—all are welcome. Please, don't limit yourself because you aren't a "professional" writer or artist—most of our published material is not from professionals. We depend on the contributions of our readers to survive—*SageWoman* is you! If you haven't seen a copy of *SageWoman*, please send for a sample copy ($7) before submitting material; this will enable you to understand the kind of material we publish, and will save both you and us a lot of time!

c. *SageWoman* accepts material created by women only. (Male contributors are encouraged to contact our brother publication, *The Green Man*, at the same address.) The concerns of our sisters, of women, form the core of our editorial and design, and is, in fact, the reason that we gather in the Circle of *SageWoman*.

SageWoman is not a separatist magazine; you may write or portray any person or subject, male or female, in material you submit to us. However, contributors should be aware that some of our readers strongly oppose any mention or portrayal of men in our pages. Others thank us for allowing them the freedom to discuss the whole of their lives and experience, including the men that they love, hate, or interact with. We continue to balance the need for women-only space, and the need for openness and a lack of self-censorship about topics for sharing and discussion as an ongoing dance in the creation of *SageWoman*. We invite you to join in this creative process.

2. Written Submissions

a. All written submissions should be the original work of the author. We prefer receiving material on computer disk if possible (it saves us valuable typing time) accompanied by a paper manuscript. (Please don't just send the disk - sometimes compatibility problems prevent us from reading disks which are submitted to us, and without a manuscript, we won't be able to evaluate your submission!) We are PC-based and prefer 3½" floppy disks, ASCII compatible, but we may be able to translate Macintosh based disks as well. If computer-based submission is not possible, typed manuscripts are also acceptable, as well as neatly handwritten pieces if no other method is possible. (Short pieces, such as Weaving the Web, The Rattle, and A Circle is Cast, as well as poetry, are best sent simply as typed manuscripts.)

b. Articles should be between 200 and 5,000 words in length, and contain the author's name, pen name (if appropriate), address and phone number on each page. We can sometimes publish longer material, but if your article exceeds these limits, we may ask you to edit it for length. Please be clear under what name you wish us to publish your material if we decide to use it.

c. We are aware that you have worked hard on your writing, it is personal and special to you, and contains your unique voice. Nonetheless, we often find it necessary to edit for length, clarity and grammar, sometimes at the last minute before publication. We make every effort to keep such editing to a minimum, in order to accurately represent your vision to our readers; however, we CANNOT guarantee that your article will appear precisely as you submitted it. If you do not want your material edited in any way, please do not submit your writing to us. Our ability to edit if necessary is an important tool in our creation of the magazine. We thank you for understanding and working with us on these issues. (Also, please inform us of deliberate uses of nontraditional spelling so the tone of your work will not be accidentally altered.)

3. Graphic Art

a. All graphic art submissions should be the original work of the artist. Clear, black and white drawings are best, but penciled or colored works may be acceptable in some cases. Please be aware that all artwork will be reproduced in black and white only except for pieces used on our outside covers. Our covers are usually commissioned works, but you may feel free to submit color photocopies or slides of your color work for possible use on the cover. Please send us clean copies of your artwork only—we cannot be responsible for your original artwork! We encourage the submission of artwork which celebrates the Goddess and women in all of our many guises; different skin colors, cultures, ages, sexual orientations, body types, sizes, and shapes, and levels of ableness.

b. We are always looking for new artists to share their creativity in our pages. If you have a portfolio of your work, feel free to send it; when sending a body of work, please inform us if any of the pieces have been previously published or are not available for publication. We do commission special pieces of artwork for the magazine; however, the majority of artwork we publish has been sent by artists on spec. We keep files of artwork, by artist, and when an issue is in production we find the pieces of artwork on file that fit each article, and then inform the artist in question that we have decided to publish their work. For this reason, your artwork may be on file for months, or years, without being used—if this is a problem for you, please inform us so we can work out other arrangements with you.

4. Photography

a. All photographic submissions should be the original work of the photographer. If persons other than the photographer are shown, a signed release from said person(s) must be included in order for us to publish the photo. Please send standard black and white or color prints—we cannot publish from negatives or slides. All photographs will be reproduced in black and white only. Our use of photography is similar to that of graphic art; please see guidelines above.

5. General Information

a. If you do not wish for your submission to be returned, please write 'Do not return' on it, and simply send us a SASE or stamped postcard for us to respond to your submission. Please put your name, address and phone number on each page of your manuscript.

b. Your submission will be acknowledged when we receive your material; we cannot guarantee exact publishing dates but will attempt to keep you up-to-date on the status of your work. We prefer to accept material which has not been previously seen or published—please inform us of multiple submissions or previous publishings.

c. *SageWoman* publishes quarterly. All material should be sent to the attention of the Editor at the address given below. Upcoming issue themes and deadlines are listed at the end of this letter.

5. Compensation and Rights

a. *SageWoman* offers modest cash payments for unsolicited artwork, photography, or articles. Articles are compensated at approximately $.03 per word for unsolicited material, with a minimum of $10. (No payment is made for Rattle letters or networking information printed in Weaving the Web.) Artwork and photography are compensated on a piece-by-piece basis, depending on the size, complexity and usefulness of the piece. Artists and photographers are paid a minimum of $15 per piece for their work. We are often able to pay more in cases where the article, artwork, illustration or photograph is commissioned especially for *SageWoman*; please contact us if you are interested in working with us on commission.

We realize how very modest these payments are; we offer them not as full compensation for your creativity, but as a 'thank you' for sharing your gifts with us. Our ability to pay is limited by the nature of our publication; we operate primarily as a gift from and to the Goddess, not as a money-making venture, and our budget reflects this fact. If you are a business or craftsperson who would benefit from advertising in our pages, please inform us that you are interested in trading advertising for your contributions; we are able to be substantially more generous in trading for advertising space than we can be in our cash payments!

b. If your material is accepted, you will also receive a free copy of the issue in which your work appears; if you are a subscriber this will be in addition to the copy you receive as part of your subscription. Payment will be sent to you within 30 days of your return of our contributor's form, which is sent out to all contributors shortly after an issue goes to press. *SageWoman* prefers to acquire first North American serial rights, all rights for one year, and the right to reprint in future *SageWoman* collections. All remaining rights will revert to you. When you submit work to us, we will assume your work is available for the purchase of these rights at the compensation level specified above, unless you state otherwise.

If there are any questions which these guidelines do not answer, please feel free to call or write to us for more information, or simply to try out your ideas on us! Our staffing is quite variable, so if you call you may reach only our answering machine; please don't let that bother you, just leave a message and we will return your call!

Upcoming topics for *SageWoman*

Every issue, we list some ideas for upcoming topics in the first few pages of each issue. These ideas are not meant to limit you, only as starting points! Articles on general Goddess spirituality and seasonal topics are always welcome, although articles not written to theme will be less likely to be accepted for publication due to space limitations.

Issue Name and Date	*Theme*	*Submission deadline (in our hands)*
Autumn 1997 (issue 39)	'Naming Ourselves'	due May 1, 1997
Winter 1997 (issue 40)	'Angels and Guardians'	due August 1, 1997

Our advertising deadlines are generally about 6 weeks later than our submission deadlines. Please contact us for a rate card and details if you are interested advertising.

Thanks again for your interest in *SageWoman*. I look forward to hearing from you soon.

Blessed Be,

Anne Niven, Publisher and Editor

Contact Information:
PO Box 641
Point Arena, CA 95468
(707) 882-2052 • FAX: (707) 882-2793

SAIL

SAIL Magazine is written and edited for everyone who sails—aboard a one-design boat or an offshore racer, a daysailer or an auxiliary cruiser. The articles in the front and the back concentrate on the technique of sailing and on technical aspects of hull and rig design and construction, while the feature section emphasizes the joys and rewards of sailing—often in a practical and instructive way. In short, we are a special-interest magazine in a field where our readers are hungry for more knowledge of their chosen sport.

ARTICLES

Length: 1,500 - 3,500 words

Form: Author's name and address should be on each page.

Payment: Variable, paid on publication.

Subject: We look for unique ways of viewing sailing. Skim old issues of SAIL for ideas about the types of articles we publish. Always remember that SAIL is a sailing magazine. Stay away from gloomy articles detailing all the things that went wrong on your boat. Think constructively and write about how to avoid certain problems. Here are some specific hints for different sections of the magazine.

Features: You should focus on a theme or choose some aspect of sailing and discuss a personal attitude or new philosophical approach to the subject. Notice that we have certain issues devoted to special themes—for example, chartering, electronics, commissioning, and the like.

Stay away from pieces that chronicle your journey in the day-by-day style of a logbook. These are generally dull and uninteresting. Select specific actions or events (preferably sailing events, not shorebound activities), and build your articles around them. Emphasize the sailing.

How-to, Technical—These should be clear, concise articles to the intelligent layman. Discuss systems or techniques for navigation, sail trim, or seamanship that have worked well for you. Technical articles should describe the successful methods of approaching projects or concepts of sailing, but not bemoan unsuccessful ways. Deal with one subject in detail, rather than cover a wide range of topics superficially.

Short Features—These short articles (1,000 to 1,500 words max.) run the gamut from vignettes of daysailing, cruising, and racing life, at home or abroad, straight or humorous, to accounts of maritime history, astronomy, marine life, cooking aboard, nautical lore, fishing, etc., to miscellaneous how-to pieces about boat owning, building, and outfitting. How-to pieces should be specific and instructive. These short features must sharply focus on a single theme of broad interest to sailors and, if appropriate, should be illustrated by anecdotes from your personal experience.

News—We usually assign news reporting in advance. Query SAIL at least one month prior to the event you are interested in covering. News reporting must be accurate and clear. Regatta reports should include a copy of the official score sheet and the names, home cities, and final scores of the top ten finishers. Be sure to describe the number and type of boats competing, the weather, and general racing action. Advance queries about nonracing events are always welcome.

Queries: We strongly suggest that potential writers query SAIL about specific ideas. Although we cannot make a final decision without seeing the piece, we can tell you whether or not your idea is appropriate for SAIL.

Time: Remember SAIL operates on a long time lead. For instance, we need to see a Christmas article by late summer for it to meet our schedule. We attempt to read, consider, and reply to your article within 60 days.

PHOTOGRAPHS INSIDE THE MAGAZINE

Form: All photographs and slides should have the photographer's name and address on them.

Color: Original 35mm (Kodachrome K-25 or K-64) or larger slide transparencies. Negatives with prints are acceptable but not recommended.

General Requirements: Sharp focus, good variety of close-up and overall shots (depending on the subject).

Color—Evenly lit, good saturation in warm colors

Black and White—Good contrast, full range of grays, good blacks

Subject: Generally, SAIL does not publish photographic essays without accompanying articles. Photos should parallel the writing and tell a visual story. Photos can depict people and boats, boat sailing, or illustrate design and mechanism features.

Time: Photographs for inside the magazine are considered with their accompanying manuscripts. We attempt to reply within 60 days.

COVER PHOTOGRAPHS

Form: All photographs and slides

General Requirements: Vertical in format. Good-quality color. Sharp focus. Strong composition.

Subject: SAIL covers feature people and boats acting together. They should be conceptually clear, so the reader can discern the mood and context immediately. Good SAIL covers are usually, but not always, action shots. Good cruising shots are always desirable.

Time: We attempt to reply within 60 days after considering a photograph and its suitability for the cover of SAIL.

SAIL reserves the right to reproduce its existing covers and layouts (including photography and art) for incidental magazine promotional uses, i.e., circulation and advertising sales.

Contact Information:
Amy Ullrich, Managing Editor
84 State Street
Boston, MA 02109-2202
(617) 720-8600 • FAX: (617) 964-8948

Salt Water Sportsman

Salt Water Sportsman buys fact-feature articles, short fillers, and color transparencies (slides) dealing with marine sport fishing along the coast of the United States and Canada, the Caribbean, Central America, Bermuda, and occasionally South America and other overseas locations.

IMPORTANT!!

In all cases, we suggest that you query us first with your story ideas. This will prevent wasted effort on your part. Contact the editor in writing (no phone calls, please) and briefly outline the article you have in mind. Tell us what the story is about, what you intend to cover, when the peak season is for that type of fishing, and what you have available for photos and illustrations. We will get back to you within a week or two. This gives us the opportunity to cross-check your proposal against material we're currently holding in inventory or have out on assignment, and we're thus able to give you a better answer as to whether we think we can use your story.

We do not buy "blood and thunder," and we do not want overly romantic "remember when." We buy no poetry, fiction, or cartoons. Editorial advertising is strictly taboo. A popular lure or tackle item should be described if possible; however, a brand name and/or model number may be given if it's pertinent to the story and if it is the most concise way of describing the item to the reader.

Example:

Unacceptable: "We skimmed out into the bay in our soft-riding Whizzer Craft model 1802 powered by a reliable, smooth-running Gale 25-hp motor."

Acceptable: "In seven days of fishing, we found that red-headed, four-inch darting plugs, such as the MirrOlure 99-M, produced the most snook for us that area of the river."

There is no taboo about naming charter skippers, lodges, airlines, guides, people, etc. However, we are not interested in celebrities per se—our celebrity is the marine angler. Above all, avoid promotion simply for the sake of promotion!

Emphasis should be on the how-to, where-to, when-to of salt water fishing, not straight "Me & Joe" adventures. We need specific semi-technical information that our average reader will understand. Articles dealing with fishing at a specific time of the year should be submitted about six months ahead of the optimum publication date and no less than four months. We rarely hold material for more than six months ahead of acceptance, except for the straight how-to piece that isn't road-blocked by a time element.

Preferred copy length for feature material is 800 to 1,200 words. We frown on manuscripts much over 1,500 words and we do not publish "Continued Next Month" serials.

Rates we pay vary, depending on the overall quality of the photo/manuscript package. The average rate tends to run from $300 to $500, but may be more if copy is clean and photos are above average. Similarly, less will be paid if we must extensively rewrite and/or provide photos for your story. *Salt Water Sportsman* buys First American Rights, and strives to report back within 30 days. We pay on acceptance. We try to work with our writers, and articles submitted on speculation are carefully considered. If they cannot be used, we attempt to tell the writer why.

Each submission should be accompanied by a stamped, self-addressed, envelope unless the writer has previously sold material to this magazine. All manuscripts and photos that are returned for any reason, including photos returned after an article has been published, will be sent via First-Class U.S. Mail. Contributors who would prefer a different method of return shipping must provide that means to *Salt Water Sportsman*.

No FAXes or photocopies of manuscripts will be considered. The manuscript should be paper clipped together, not stapled, and mailed in an envelope stout enough to defeat the U.S. mail service. If a story has been written on a computer, a floppy disk (either size 5.25" or 3.5") with the story on it and a note describing the software program it was written in (i.e. WordPerfect, Microsoft Word) and the version of the program (i.e. WordPerfect 5.1) should be submitted as part of the manuscript package. Disks will be returned with photos. When in doubt as to which computer programs are compatible with our system, don't hesitate to call.

The first page of your manuscript should include your name, address, and social security number at the top left. At top right, give us an estimate of wordage. Space down at least three or four inches and give us the title of your choice. Beneath the title, center your byline as you wish to see it in print. Be advised that we may not use your title.

Submissions should be sent to Barry Gibson, Editor, at the address below.

Fillers and Short Features

SWS is currently seeking short feature articles ranging from 500 to 1,000 words. Subject can focus on regional hot spots, species, special rigs, fishing methods, etc. Payment will range from $200 to $500, depending on the quality of writing and accompanying photos. Please query first.

SWS also welcomes "over-the-transom" (no query necessary) submissions for our "Sportsman's Workbench" department. We're looking for 100- to 300-word articles dealing with all phases of salt water fishing, tackle, boats, and related equipment. Emphasis is on building, repairing, or reconditioning specific items or gear. Rough or finished art work, samples, and/or black-and-white photos should accompany copy. All "Workbench" and short feature submissions should be sent to the attention of Tom Richardson, Managing Editor.

Photo and Illustration Guidelines

Salt Water Sportsman is asking that 35mm color transparencies be used to illustrate feature and department articles and for cover shot submissions.

Subject: Photos provided to illustrate an article should, first of all, tell a story. Try to include scenic shots with human interest, shots of the boat, water conditions, the lodge, close-ups of rods and reels used, lures, baits, flies, equipment, structure, fish being landed and released, and general how-to. Action is most important, and it should be right there at the scene, not back at the dock. Try to tell the story with the camera. Shoot early and late in the day for best light. Have your subject take off his or her hat, or use fill-flash to illuminate the face. Try shots of releasing fish or removing hooks. Leave lures or flies in fish's mouth to show what it was caught on. Watch out for shadows, crooked horizons, and rods, hands, or other distracting objects intruding into the frame.

By all means, include a picture of yourself in action if you want, but do not send us a great many photos of yourself or the same fishing companions. This is especially important if you are a fairly regular contributor—readers want to see new faces, and we want to give credit to a host of fine skippers, guides, and sportsmen out there, not just a select few.

We do not want photos of piles of dead fish. Large numbers of dead fish are unimportant and they offend conservation-minded readers. Stress quality in sport, not quantity.

Transparencies: Color transparencies should be 35mm slides. Give us a good selection of horizontals and verticals. All slides should be sent in a transparency sleeve, never loose in an envelope or box. Make sure your name, address, and phone number is labeled on every slide, and that each slide is numbered to correspond to the caption sheet (see below).

Captions: Caption information must accompany all photos. We prefer that photos be numbered and submitted with a separate caption sheet. Give us as much information as possible in the captions, such as model names, dates, places, fish species, sizes of fish, lures or baits used, boat names, and so forth. Even if these things aren't evident in the photo we'd rather have too much info than not enough.

Covers: We pay $1,000 for one-time use of cover transparencies. We're looking for 35mm vertical-format slides (or 2.25" x 2.25") that are colorful, sharp, and show fishing action or mood. Be sure there is enough room (dead space) at the top for our logo. Think scenery, human interest, boats on the grounds, story-telling close-ups of anglers in action, and so forth. Make it "come alive"—and don't bother us with obviously posed "dead fish with fisherman" shots taken back at the dock.

We cannot use: snapshots, black & whites, Polaroids, color prints or matte prints of any kind. We will not accept negatives for any reason. Do not send contact sheets and negatives, asking us to indicate what we want to see and requesting that we return them to you for processing. You pick the shots you think are best and have them processed into prints before sending the package to us.

Computer-Altered or Enhanced Images: *Salt Water Sportsman* requires that any computer-manipulated image be identified as such.

Illustrations: Drawings, particularly those which depict a specific rig, tackle item, or how-to procedure are always welcome. These may be rough sketches, and should include appropriate labels so that we can produce the finished art work. Similarly, nautical chart segments and/or maps of fishing areas are very valuable in illustrating a story. We can use black-and-white photos or Polaroids as guidance for illustrations. Also, if appropriate, send us the actual lure, fly, rig or materials used to build it so we can use them as reference.

Payment: We pay between $50 and $400 for inside photos, depending on size used. We pay $1,000 for cover shots. Payment is made after publication of image.

Return of Photos: Rejected photos will be returned via the method provided for by the photographer. Otherwise they will be sent via U.S. Mail. Most photos used in the magazine will be returned via UPS 3-day service within a month after publication, unless special arrangements are made.

Contact Information:
77 Franklin Street
Boston, MA 02110
(617) 338-2300 • FAX: (617) 338-2309

San Diego Parent

(Please refer to L.A. Parent Magazine.)

Scouting

This magazine is published by the Boy Scouts of America six times a year. Issues are: January-February, March-April, May-June, September, October, and November-December. It is mailed to about one million volunteer and professional adult Scout leaders. Subscription is included as part of the Scouter's annual registration fee.

We consider *Scouting* a family magazine because it contains material that we feet aids parents in strengthening families. We write mostly about Cub Scout packs, Boy Scout troops, and Explorer posts succeeding in getting the BSA program to youth. We talk about how leaders can improve their Scouting performance. We often provide hints for parents to do their family jobs better. We also feature entertaining general-interest articles geared to our adult audience.

Most stories are written by staff members or professional writers assigned by us. We seldom publish unsolicited manuscripts. But our best articles come from ideas sent to us by volunteer and professional Scouters.

A query with a synopsis or outline of a proposed story is essential.

We buy short features of 500+/-words; some longer features, 1,500+/-words, usually the result of a definite assignment to a professional writer. We do not buy fiction or poetry.

We purchase first rights unless otherwise specified. A purchase does not guarantee publication. We pay on acceptance, additional for photos. But photos are usually bought as the result of a specific assignment. Story rates depend on how professionally the article is written. We pay front $125 tip for a short feature, up to $600 for a long piece.

We respond to all contributors or potential contributors within three weeks of receipt of the query.

A writer or photographer wishing to be published in this magazine should be familiar with the Scouting program and *Scouting* magazine. A sample copy will be sent if you provide a stamped, self-addressed 9 3/4" x 12 5/8" envelope and 60 cents.

INFORMATION FOR PHOTOGRAPHERS

The Magazine Division BSA publishes three magazines: BOYS' LIFE, SCOUTING, and EXPLORING.

BOYS' LIFE Is a national monthly periodical, circulation 1.4 million, read by boys ages 8 to 14. It covers a broad range of interests including sports, hobbies, careers, crafts, and special Interests of cub Scouts, Boy Scouts and Explorers (the latter are 14 and older).

SCOUTING, with a circulation of one million, is written for adults in our organization. It Is published seven times a year. It contains articles helpful to leaders In *Scouting* and Includes general Interest articles.

EXPLORING is published four times a year with an audience of young men and women ages 14 to 20.

We demand quality action, dramatic- photos, and our rates are competitive with those paid by other major magazines. We buy first rights only to all photography submitted on assignment.

Almost all of our photography is assigned to help illustrate a particular article. We buy almost no photos on speculation. Please query us regarding a particular photo idea. Suggestions should be as specific as possible.

We do not encourage sending unsolicited photos—in fact, we discourage this.

Contact Information:
Jon C. Halter, Editor
1325 West Walnut Hill Lane
P.O. Box 152079
Irving, TX 75015-2079
(972) 580-2000 • FAX: (972) 580-2079

Sea Kayaker

Sea Kayaker is devoted solely to sea kayaks, their use, design, and history. Our feature articles, written by both amateur and professional writers, explore subjects in depth. Because we seek to inform, as well as entertain, we prefer contributions from experienced kayakers. Our ideal manuscript conveys interesting and useful information in clear, vivid terms.

Proposals and queries

If you have a story idea you think might interest us, phone us to get our immediate feedback. After we've had a chance to establish the story's suitability, we may ask you to follow up with a more detailed outline and samples of your work. If you have slides, photos or drawings that might help us in our evaluation, send those along. You are welcome to submit finished manuscripts, but you can often save a lot of work by consulting with us before you write.

Get familiar with the magazine

To gain a better understanding of the types of articles we tend to publish, look at a few back issues. We'll gladly sell those to you if they aren't available in your area. To order back issues give us a call at (206) 789-9536. Keep in mind, however, that we welcome new ideas and approaches. Our emphasis is on touring, though we occasionally look at other aspects of the sport such as surf kayaking, ocean kayak racing, or surf skiing.

Article topics

To submit a Health, Safety, Navigation, or Equipment article, you must have some expertise on the subject about which you are writing. Similar guidelines apply to History pieces (traditional equipment and technique, journeys from long ago, ethnographic research, legends, etc.). We occasionally accept stories or poems about sea kayaking under our Fiction or Poetry headings. For our Journey section, we look for well-crafted stories that convey a strong sense of place and adventure. Destination articles are straightforward descriptions of the paddling potential of areas that can accommodate lots of trips without becoming crowded. We look for familiarity with the area (local knowledge); one trip is not enough. Under our Technique heading, we've published articles on bracing, surf entry and exit, and various Eskimo rolls. Kayaking with kids, military use of kayaks, and kite sailing are some of the topics we've covered in the Alternatives section. In Pursuits, we've looked at beachcombing, fishing, beach hiking, expedition planning, and team kayaking. Directions for a homemade spray skirt, Greenland paddle, kite, and kayak building projects have appeared in our Do-It-Yourself pages. We've run a few articles on kayak design, a subject that interests us a great deal. We have a significant Environment section in which we've published a series on marine invertebrates, a series on birds, and articles about pollution, geology, and bears. We also do Essays, and evocative Impression pieces, occasional profiles and book excerpts, and book reviews.

Submission requirements

Articles usually run from 1,000 to 4,000 words, depending on the subject. If you write on a word processor, please send a diskette with your hard copy. Mark your diskette with your name, the file name, and the program used. We prefer 3.5" micro-diskettes, but we can have 5.25" diskettes converted. Enter plain text; any fancy formatting makes conversion to our system difficult.

When submitting a story with illustrations or photographs, include a list of captions or descriptions. Maps, if they are appropriate, should accompany your submission. Mark locations as they relate to the text.

We will acknowledge receipt of your submission as soon as possible, but it may take us some time to evaluate it. Once we have accepted an article it will be at least three months before it is published.

Photographs

We work most often from color slides. If you send either black-and-white or color prints we may ask for negatives so we can make prints to meet our requirements. We publish most of our photos in black and white, but in each issue we have limited space for color photos. Our choice of color photos depends on the appeal of the image and the space available. We prefer to work with original slides instead of duplicates.

Unusual, humorous, or spectacular photos suitable for our Document section (a "parting shot" photo) or for our cover artists pay around $45.

Mark all prints and slides with your name and address. Include a list of descriptions. If you mark your slides for copyright ©, please send us a signed letter authorizing us to make prints of them.

Artwork

We use color (cover) artwork (oil, acrylic, watercolor). We sometimes use other mediums, such as serigraphs, etchings, or stained glass, for cover art. We often use photographs for inspiration and departure points for our artists, and we will consider especially artistic photographs for the cover. Contact us for details. We also commission artwork for inside pages.

Return of Materials

Discs and reference materials (maps, sketches, etc.) will be returned by first-class mail.

Irreplaceable photographs and artwork should be sent via registered mail. We will return such materials by the same means (certified, registered, insured, etc.) in which we received them.

Rates

Text: We pay about $100 per 1,000 words. Excellent writing and special projects may pay more.

Artwork: We pay $250 for cover art, more for commissioned works. For other drawings and illustrations we pay between $25 and $250, depending upon size, colors and complexity.

Photographs:	*Color*	*B&W*
Full page	$100	$75
¾ page	$75	$60
½ page	$65	$45
¼ page	$45	$30
Spot	$25	$15

We buy First North American Rights, and occasionally consider Second Rights. You are welcome to submit your material on speculation. Simultaneous submissions or inquiries must be clearly identified as such. Freelance contributions are paid upon publication. We will send you a copy of the issue in which your contribution appears when it is available.

Thank you, and we hope to hear from you.

Contact Information:
Karen Reed, Editor
P.O. Box 17170
Seattle, WA 98107-0870
(206) 789-1326

The Secret Place

The Secret Place was begun over fifty years ago by a woman who wanted to provide a way to draw Christians closer to Christ and one another. It's now a quarterly devotional magazine with a worldwide readership of over 150,000 and editions in regular print, large print, Braille, and cassette. Produced primarily by Educational Ministries of the American Baptist Churches in the U.S.A., *The Secret Place* is published jointly by the American Baptist Churches in the U.S.A. and the Christian Church (Disciples of Christ), Christian Board of Publication.

The Secret Place is written by freelance writers, and anyone may submit original meditations. Each submission should be typed, if possible, and contain:

• your name, address, phone number, and social security number in the upper left corner.

• a title.

• a suggested Scripture reading of five to ten verses.

• a "Thought For Today," which is usually a Scripture quote (be sure to cite chapter, verses, and Bible version) but may also be a pertinent thought. We will use the New Revised Standard Version unless you specify otherwise.

• an original meditation of 100 to 175 words that relates to the suggested Scripture reading and "Thought For Today." (Do not quote another source unless you have obtained written permission and attached it to your submission.)

• a brief concluding prayer.

We are especially interested in devotional meditations that:

- are original, creative, and spiritually insightful.
- explore less familiar biblical passages.
- address urban/suburban as well as rural/nature experiences.
- appeal to young adults as well as older adults.
- encourage outreach, mission, and service.
- are concise and focused on one theme.
- are inclusive in their use of language.
- are racially and culturally diverse.

We retain the right to edit submissions for clarity, brevity, and inclusivity of language. Original one-page poems and clear, high-quality photographs (eight-by-ten-inch color prints for the cover, four-by-six-inch or larger black/white or color prints for inside) are also welcome. We pay $15 for each submission published and buy first rights to published materials. We work nine to twelve months ahead of schedule, so please plan your submissions accordingly and allow up to six months for response. Published material will not be returned.

SAMPLE

Your Name
Your Street Address
Your City, State, and ZIP Code
Your Telephone Number
Your Social Security Number

Philippians 4:4-8 Saying Thanks

THOUGHT FOR TODAY: It is good to give thanks to the Lord. Psalm 92:1

Kristen's birthday party was over. Her many gifts were on the table, along with plates of partially eaten cake and ice cream. As her last friend left, Kristen remarked, "It was a nice party, but where's my puppy? I though I was going to get what I wanted on my birthday!" I saw her mother's disappointed expression; she had spent days and considerable money to make this a happy day for Kristen. She needed some appreciation and thanks.

God must feel like that. God gives us so many blessings, both in our physical world and in our individual lives. We think those are fine, but "I want" statements still prevail in our thoughts and prayers. The Bible speaks about the importance of being thankful. We can trust the One who knows everything about us, loves us, and cares for our every need. We deprive ourselves as well as God when we forget to be thankful.

PRAYER: Dear God, you are generous to me in so many ways. Forgive my shortsightedness and lack of appreciation. Today I simply give you thanks; in Jesus' name. Amen.

Your Name—City, State

Thank you for contributing to this ministry through your support, submissions, and prayers.

Send your meditations, poems, and photographs to:

Contact Information:
Kathleen Hayes, Editor
P.O. Box 851
Valley Forge, PA 19482-0851

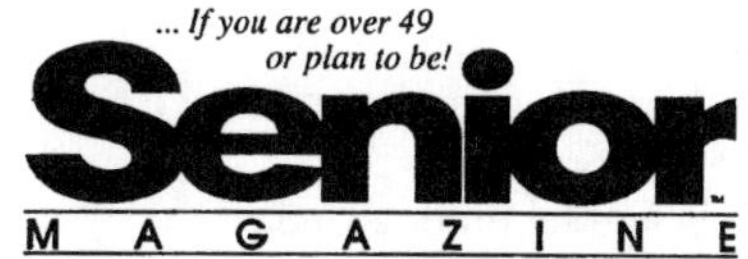

Senior Magazine
. . . If you're over 49 or plan to be!

The editors of *Senior Magazine* are happy to consider freelance material for publication.

Simultaneous submissions are okay. We might hold an article for several months before publishing it. You might want to submit your material to other markets during this time.

We prefer upbeat rather than gloomy articles. We prefer short rather than long; 600-1,200 words is ideal.

We consider personality profiles, health-oriented articles, travel, nostalgia, unique experiences, and humor (subtle, not heavy-handed) are appropriate themes. We also consider book reviews. These could include outstanding books of the past which warrant re-reading.

Keep in mind that while *Senior* is aimed at the 50 years and older crowd, its real target is the young at heart.

Be sure to put your name, address, and telephone number in the upper left-hand corner of the first page of your manuscript.

Standard payment is $1.50 a column inch unless other arrangements are made with the editor.

We accept black and white photos to accompany articles. Payment for photos is $15.00-$25.00.

Queries are welcome.

For a sample copy of the magazine send $1.50 in postage and a large self-addressed envelope.

Contact Information:
George Brams, Managing Editor
3565 South Higuera Street
San Luis Obispo, CA 93401
(805) 544-8711 • FAX: (805) 544-4450

Seventeen

Fiction Guidelines:

Seventeen publishes one 1,000- to 4,000-word story each month and pays writers on acceptance for first-time rights. We welcome stories that are relevant to young women (and young men) and their experience, fiction that somehow touches contemporary young adult life. We are looking for submissions that will be accessible and appealing to our readers (ages 13-21), as well as challenging and inspiring. In essence, we want stories that possess the quality and integrity of today's best literary short fiction.

Winner of the 1984 National Magazine Award for outstanding editorial achievement in fiction, *Seventeen* has published such distinguished writers as Anne Tyler, Lorrie Moore, Michael Dorris, Joyce Carol Oates, Joy Williams, Amy Tan, and Margaret Atwood.

We read all submissions and try to respond within twelve weeks. We regret that we cannot offer individual comments or criticism.

We also run an annual fiction contest for writers between 13 and 21 years old. Rules for the contest are published each year in our November issue.

We strongly recommend reading the magazine before submitting your work.

Nonfiction Guidelines:

Seventeen accepts articles on subjects of interest to teenagers. Writers who are not familiar with the magazine or who have not read it frequently are advised to go through a year of back issues (most libraries carry *Seventeen*) to, learn more about what the magazine publishes. Desired length varies from 800 words for short features to 2,500 words for a major article.

Seventeen gives assignments and guarantees a fee only to writers who have been published in the magazine or whose professional work is known to the editors. Thus, writers whose work has not appeared in *Seventeen* should include a list of their credits and tear sheets of published articles. Writers who have had no articles, or only a few articles published, may be asked to write on speculation with no guarantee of payment.

Allow at least six weeks for consideration of a query or manuscript. Seasonal material should be submitted at least six months in advance. Work that is purchased is paid for on acceptance. Rates vary, depending on quality, length, and placement in the magazine.

Send article ideas and manuscripts to the appropriate editor named below. No follow-up phone calls, please.

We regret that it is not our policy to give complimentary issues.

VOICE GUIDELINES:

Do you have an opinion, an idea, or an experience you'd like to share? Tell us what you're thinking. VOICE is the section of the magazine devoted to young writers, and we welcome all original contributions. We are looking for interesting events and true stories, opinion essays, reflective essays focusing on personal decisions and relationships, and light or funny pieces about unusual situations or new perspectives on an old topic.

The VOICE section really does encompass everything. Recent pieces have included first-person narratives about volunteering at a refugee camp in Croatia, protesting sexist T-shirts, and making the transition from high school to college. Other essays have included a defense of New Jersey, a description of living with eccentric parents, and a reflection on being overweight. Basically, VOICE is your section—a chance for you to speak about what matters to you in your own individual style—so we encourage you to be as creative as you'd like.

Your article should be no longer than six pages. Be sure to include your name, address, birth date, and telephone number. Submit to VOICE at the address below.

Contact Information:
Nonfiction: Susan Brenna, Features Editor
Fiction: Ben Shrank, Fiction Editor
850 3rd Avenue
New York, NY 10022
(212) 407-9700

Sierra
The Magazine of the Sierra Club

Sierra is a bimonthly national magazine publishing writing, photography and art about the natural world. Our readers are environmentally concerned and politically diverse; most are active in the outdoors. We are looking for fine writing that will provoke, entertain, and enlighten this readership.

Though open to new writers, we find ourselves most often working with writers we have sought out or who have worked with us for some time. We ask writers who would like to publish in *Sierra* to submit written queries; phone calls are strongly discouraged. Queries should be accompanied by clips of previously published work. Prospective *Sierra* writers should familiarize themselves with recent issues of the magazine; for a sample copy, send a self-addressed envelope and a check for $3 payable to *Sierra*.

Please be patient: Though the editors meet weekly to discuss recently received queries, a response time of from six to eight weeks is usual.

Feature Articles

Sierra is looking for strong, well-researched, literate writing on significant environmental and conservation issues. Features often focus on aspects of the Sierra Club's national conservation work. For more information, contact our Information Center. Writers should look for ways to cast new light on well-established issues. We look for stories of national or international significance; local issues, while sometimes useful as examples of broader trends, are seldom of interest in themselves. We are always looking for adventure travel pieces that weave events, discoveries and environmental insights into the narrative.

We do not want descriptive wildlife articles, unless larger conservation issues figure strongly in the story. We are not interested in editorials, general essays about environmentalism, or in highly technical writing. We do not publish unsolicited poetry or fiction; please do not submit works in either genre.

Nonfiction essays on the natural world are welcome, especially in our annual nature-writing contest. We announce the contest in our November/December issue; winners are published in the following year's July/August issue.

Recent feature articles that display the special qualities we look for are "The Limits of Paradise" by John Daniel (March/April 1994), "Pandora's Poison" by Eric F. Coppolino (September/October 1994), and "Improving on Nature" by Paul Rauber (March/April 1995). Feature length ranges from 1,000 to 3,000 words; payment is from $800 to $2500, plus negotiated reimbursement for expenses.

Departments

Much of the material in *Sierra*'s departments is written by staff editors and contributing writers. The following sections of the magazine, however, are open to freelancers. Articles range from 750 to 1,000 words in length; payment is $500 unless otherwise noted. Expenses up to $50 may be paid in some cases.

"Food for Thought" is concerned with what we eat and its connection to the environment. Topics range from drying food for backpacking to bovine growth hormones to the consequences of buying Southern Hemisphere produce. The column is oriented toward cooking and eating; submissions should include an appropriate recipe.

"Good Going" tells of an adventure journey or destination. We are not looking for descriptive itineraries, but rather for travel writing at its traditional best, with thoughtful observation of place and personality.

"Hearth & Home" offers information with advice on how we can live our environmental principles in our own homes; topics have ranged from composting with worms to building with straw to cooking with insects. Articles for this department should be accurate, lively, and helpful.

"Way to Go" travels to wild areas the Sierra Club is working to protect or has recently preserved, tells how to get there and how to help.

"Priorities" focuses on environmental issues of national or international concern. Regional issues are considered when they have national implications. At 700 to 1,200 words,

"Priorities" articles are not sweeping surveys, but tightly focused, provocative, well-researched investigations of environmental issues. Payment varies according to length.

"In Print" offers short (200-to-300 word) reviews of books on environmentalism and natural history. Payment is $50 per review.

Payment for all articles is on acceptance, which is contingent on a favorable review of the manuscript by our editorial staff, and by knowledgeable outside reviewers, where appropriate. Kill fees are negotiated when a story is assigned.

Contact Information:
Marc LeCard, Managing Editor
85 Second Street, 2nd Floor
San Francisco, CA 94105-3441
(415) 977-5500 • FAX: (415) 776-4868

Skeptical Inquirer
The Magazine for Science and Reason

The SKEPTICAL INQUIRER critically examines claims of paranormal, fringe-science, and pseudoscientific phenomena from a responsible, scientific point of view and provides a forum for informed discussion of all relevant issues. We encourage science and scientific inquiry, critical thinking, and the use of reason and the methods of science in examining important issues. The readership includes scholars and researchers in many fields and lay readers of diverse backgrounds. Write clearly, interestingly, and simply. Avoid unnecessary technical terms. Maintain a factual, professional, and restrained tone. All submissions are judged on the basis of interest, clarity, significance, relevance, authority, and topicality.

Direct critiques toward ideas and issues, not individuals. Be prepared to provide documentation of all factual assertions. A useful set of guidelines for those who seek to evaluate paranormal claims, titled "Proper Criticism" and written by Professor Rav Hyman, is available from the editor. Among the guidelines: clarify your objectives, let the facts speak for themselves, be precise and careful with language, and avoid loaded words and sensationalism.

State others' positions in a fair, objective, and nonemotional manner.

CATEGORIES OF CONTRIBUTIONS

Categories of contributions include: Articles, Book Reviews, News and Comment, Forum, Follow-Up, and Letters to the Editor.

Articles: Articles may be evaluative, investigative, or explanatory. They may examine specific claims or broader questions. Well-focused discussions on scientific, educational, or social issues of wide common interest are welcome. We especially seek articles that provide new information or bring fresh perspective to familiar subjects. Articles that help people find natural explanations of unusual personal experiences are useful. So are articles that portray the vigor and excitement of a particular scientific topic and help readers distinguish between scientific and 1.)pseudoscientific approaches.

Well-balanced articles that report on and evaluate controversial scientific claims within science itself are also needed. The SKEPTICAL INQUIRER must be a source of authoritative, responsible scientific information and perspective. The editor will usually send manuscripts dealing with technical or controversial matters to reviewers. The authors, however, are responsible for the accuracy of fact and perspective. It is good practice to have knowledgeable colleagues review drafts before submission. Reports of original research, especially highly technical experimental or statistical studies, are best submitted to a formal scientific journal; a nontechnical summary may be submitted to the SKEPTICAL INQUIRER. Studies based on small-scale tests or surveys of students will be considered only if they establish something new, provide a needed replication of some important earlier study, or test some new theoretical position. Space is at a premium; there are always many accepted articles awaiting publication, and many submitted articles cannot be published. Articles are typically 2,000 to 3,500 words (about 8 to 12 double-spaced typewritten pages). We cannot publish treatises. Articles should be organized around one central point or theme. Be succinct. Remember, Watson and Crick's paper reporting the discovery of the structure of DNA took just over one page in Nature.

Articles should have a title page. Begin with a succinct, inviting title followed by a concise, 20- to 30-word statement of the article's main point or theme. This "abstract" will be published in display type on the first page of the printed article and used as a summary on the contents page. The title page should also give the name of the author(s), full addresses, and the lead author's office and home telephone numbers, fax number, and e-mail address. At the end of the manuscript include a suggested author note of one to three sentences that gives relevant affiliations and credentials and an address for correspondence. If you do not want your address included in the author note, please say so. The manuscript should be accompanied by a brief cover letter stating that the article has not been submitted elsewhere and providing any other essential background for the Editor.

Reviews: Most book reviews are about 600 to 1,200 words. Both solicited and unsolicited reviews are used. Include publication data at the top of the review in this order: Title. Author. Publisher, city, year. ISBN. Number of pages. Hardcover or paperback (or both), price. Include a suggested author note. If possible, include the cover of the book for illustration.

News and Comment: News articles from 250 to 1,000 words are welcome. They should involve timely events and issues and be written in interpretative journalistic style. Use third person. The news sections of Nature, Science, New Scientist, and Science News are excellent models. Balance, fairness, and perspective are important. In reporting on controversies, seek and include comment and perspective from the various opposing parties.

Forum: The Forum column consists of brief, lively, well-written columns of comment and opinion generally no more than 1,000 words. Space allows only one or two per issue.

Follow-Up: The Follow-Up column is for response from persons whose work or claims have been the subject of previous articles. The original authors may respond in the same or a later issue.

Letters to the Editor: Letters to the Editor are for views on matters raised in previous issues. Letters should be no more than 250 words. Due to the volume of letters received, they cannot be acknowledged, and not all can be published. Those selected may be edited for space and clarity. Authors whose articles are criticized in the letters column may be given the opportunity to respond in the same issue.

MECHANICAL REQUIREMENTS

Text: All manuscripts should be printed out double-spaced, including notes and references. Number all pages in sequence, including those for references, figures, and captions. For Articles, submit an original and two photocopies (for reviewers); for other categories, an original and one photocopy. In either case, we will also need the document on a computer disk, which may he submitted at the same time or upon acceptance (see below).

References and Notes: SKEPTICAL INQUIRER uses the author-date system of documentation as found in *The Chicago Manual of Style*. Sources are cited in the text, usually in parentheses, by author's last name and year of publication: (Smith 1994). These text citations are amplified in a list of References (alphabetized by last name of author), which gives full bibliographic information.

Sample book entry: Smith, John. 1994. *A Skeptical Book*. New York: Jones Press. Sample journal-article entry: Smith, John, and Jane Jones. 1994. A skeptical article. *The Journal* 5(1): 7-12. Use endnotes (not footnotes) for explaining or amplifying discussions in the text.

Illustrations: Figures and graphs should be in high-quality camera-ready form. Photos can be glossy or matte black-and-white. Color photos are also acceptable. Assign each illustration a Figure number and supply captions on a separate sheet. Suggestions for obtaining other illustrations are welcome.

Disks: For all contributions except letters and short items, we will need a 3-½" computer disk. Preferably, it should be submitted to the editor with the manuscript (to save time). Otherwise, it should be sent to our editorial production office once the manuscript is accepted. In the latter case, send it to:

Gwen A. Burda, Managing Editor
SKEPTICAL INQUIRER
P.O. Box 703
Amherst, N.Y. 14226, U.S.A.

Any Macintosh or PC word-processing format is acceptable, although a Macintosh format is preferred.

Proofs: Once the manuscript of an article, review, or column has been tentatively scheduled, copyedited, and typeset, we send proofs to the author. The proofs should be returned corrected within 72 hours.

Copyright: Unless otherwise agreed, copyright will be transferred to CSICOP (Committee for the Scientific Investigation of Claims of the Paranormal) upon publication. Authors are sent several complimentary copies of the issue, plus a form for ordering reprints.

The fax number shown below may be used for important messages and inquiries. It is generally not for submission of manuscripts, with the exception of short editorial items from abroad or other brief contributions known to be urgent.

Do not send manuscripts to CSICOP's headquarters in Amherst, N.Y. Do not use Certified mail; that only delays delivery. If you use overnight express (generally not necessary), please initial the signature-waiver requirement. All manuscripts should be mailed to:

Contact Information:
Kendrick Frazier, Editor
SKEPTICAL INQUIRER
944 Deer Dr. NE
Albuquerque, NM 87122 U.S.A.
FAX: (505) 828-2080

Small Farm Today

Small Farm Today magazine is dedicated to preserving and promoting small farming, rural living, community and agripreneurship. We use a "can-do," upbeat, positive approach and all articles submitted should reflect this attitude.

We need "how-to" articles (how to grow, raise, market, build, etc.), as well as articles about small farmers who are experiencing success through diversification, specialty/alternative crops and livestock, and direct marketing. *Small Farm Today* is especially interested in articles that explain how to do something from start to finish citing specific examples involved in the process or operation being discussed. Please include data on production costs, budgets, potential profits, etc. See the list of topics at the end of theses guidelines for ideas. We do not usually use fiction, poetry or political pieces.

REPRINTS: If your manuscript has been printed in another publication, please list the publications and the dates published. We prefer to publish original articles.

MANUSCRIPTS

We welcome both completed manuscripts and queries, but recommend you query your idea before sending in a manuscript.

Manuscripts submitted for consideration become the property of Missouri Farm Publishing, Inc. We also accept articles on disks compatible with a Macintosh computer. Length, depending on subject, should probably be between 600 and 3,000 words (we usually prefer 1,000-1,800 words.

Because we use an image scanner to transfer most hard copies of manuscripts onto the computer, we would prefer an original copy of your manuscript or a very clean photocopy.

Include the addresses and phone numbers of your primary sources/interviewees. We usually include this information at the end of the article so the readers can contact them for more information. Please specify if the source or interviewee does not wish to have their phone number or address listed at the end of the article.

If you have charts, diagrams or sources for additional information on your subject matter, we will try to use them as sidebars with the article.

OUR PLACE

Small Farm Today features a special section called Our Place. This section is written by farmers/landowners about their own property. We prefer it to be written in first person form (I, we, our). It should include a description of your farm and what you raise. Some "how-to" tips on what you have learned from dealing with your crops/livestock would be appreciated. Other things that can be mentioned are: how you got started, plans for the future, what makes your property unique, and marketing strategies you employ.

Several people have expressed concern about their writing abilities—don't worry. The story will be edited for publication, but will still contain your own unique voice.

Payment for Our Place is a box of magazines of the issue featuring your story. You can pass it out to family, friends, and customers.

ON THE FARM

Another special section is On The Farm. This features farmers/landowners writing about their own on-farm research—methods that have worked for you. The article should explain what you raise, how you raise it, and how well it works. Costs of production would be appreciated.

Topics in the past have included growing garlic, seaweed powder to reduce livestock stress, and combining forage, corn and sheep.

Payment is the standard rate, listed below.

HOLDING POLICY

After the article is received, it is submitted to the editor for review. If approved, it will be slated for production. If we do not have a specific issue in mind, we will place the article in our "on-hold" stack. If we have not published the issue in one year, we will return the story to you (if you have included an SASE). If you would prefer not to have your story held, please send notification of this with your manuscript.

EDITORIAL CALENDAR AND DEADLINES FOR ARTICLES

Deadlines for manuscripts are as follows:

ISSUE	EMPHASIS	DEADLINES
February issue	Wool & Fiber	December 5

April issue	Equipment	February 10
June issue	Livestock	April 10
August issue	Alternative & Rare Breeds	June 10
October issue	Draft Animals	August 10
December issue	Greenhouses & Gardening	October 10

PAYMENT

Unless otherwise arranged with the publisher, Missouri Farm Publishing, Inc. buys first serial rights and nonexclusive reprint rights (the right to reprint the article in an anthology) for both manuscripts and photos. Missouri Farm Publishing, Inc. reserves the right to edit the story for publication. Rate of pay for reprints may be less than our standard rate of pay.

Payment for articles:
- 3.5¢ per word for each word published (see above paragraph) for fist serial rights
- 2¢ per word for each word published for reprinted articles
- We do not pay for book reviews

Payment for photos:
- $6.00 each for b&w or color prints
- $10.00 for photo used on cover
- $4.00 each for negatives or slides

Payment for line art, graphs, charts, and cartoons:
- $5.00 each

Payment is made 30-60 days after publication. Sorry, no exceptions.

PHOTOS, LINE ART, GRAPHS, CHARTS & CARTOONS

Please send color or black and white prints of photos and include information about each photo for use in captions. Only color photos can be used on the cover. If you do not have prints, we can use negatives or slides. All photos sent to us will be returned if you include a return address on the back of EACH photo.

Cartoons, line art, graphs and charts are also welcome.

SUBJECT MATTER

Here is a list if some of the topics we cover regularly:
- Money-making alternatives for the small farm
- Exotic animals (ostriches, buffalo and elk are some we have covered)
- Minor breeds (Jacob sheep, Dexter cattle and red wattle hogs are some we have covered)
- Draft horses (using them on a small farm; also other draft animals)
- Small stock (sheep, goats, rabbits, poultry)
- Direct marketing (farmers markets, subscription marketing, roadside stands, U-pick)
- Gardening
- Specialty crops
- New uses for traditional crops (ethanol and plastic from corn, for example)
- New sustainable farming methods
- Rural living (particularly how-to)
- Small fruits (grapes, berries, exotic new fruits)
- Tree fruits
- Sustainable agriculture (organic, reduced input, agroecology)
- Horticulture (herbs, ornamentals, wild flowers, vegetables, other opportunities)
- Aquaculture (catfish, crawfish, fee fishing, tropical fish)
- Home-based business (crafts, food processing)

• Small-scale production of livestock (cattle, hogs, poultry)

Be warned that stories may have a long lead time—as of this writing, we have 80 stories in stock. We do not limit ourselves to the topics on this list. If you have an idea for a story, drop us a note outlining your idea. If you are not familiar with *Small Farm Today*, we can send you a sample copy for $3.00.

Thank you for showing an interest in *Small Farm Today*! If you have any other questions, please write or call:

Contact Information:
Paul Berg, Managing Editor
3903 West Ridge Trail Road
Clark, MO 65243-9525
(573) 687-3525

Smithsonian Magazine

Thank you for inquiring about submitting articles to SMITHSONIAN magazine. We prefer a written proposal of one or two pages as a preliminary query. The proposal should convince us that we should cover the subject, offer descriptive information on how you, the writer, would treat the subject and offer us an opportunity to judge your writing ability. Background information on writing credentials and samples are helpful.

All unsolicited proposals are sent to us on speculation and you should receive a reply within eight weeks. We also accept proposals via electronic mail. If we decide to commission an article, the writer receives full payment on acceptance of the manuscript. If the article is found unsuitable, one third of the payment serves as a kill fee.

SMITHSONIAN is buying First North American Serial Rights only. Our article length ranges from a 1,000 word humor column to a 4,000 word full-length feature. We consider focused subjects that fall within the general range of Smithsonian Institution interests, such as cultural history, physical science, art and natural history. We are always looking for offbeat subjects and profiles. We do not consider fiction, poetry, travel features, political and news events, or previously published articles. We have a two-month lead time.

Illustrations are not the responsibility of authors, but if you do have photographs or illustration materials, please include a selection of them with your submission. In general, 35mm color transparencies or black-and-white prints are perfectly acceptable. Photographs published in the magazine are usually obtained through assignments, stock agencies or specialized sources. No photo library is maintained and photographs should be submitted only to accompany a specific article proposal.

Copies of the magazine may be obtained by sending your request and a check for $3.00 per copy for the current issue ($5.00 per copy for back issues) to the subscription office at the address below.

We publish only 12 issues a year, so it is difficult to place an article in SMITHSONIAN Magazine, but please be assured that all proposals are considered.

"Back Page" Humor Column

The "Back Page" is a monthly column which aims at humor and is mostly written by freelancers. Its length runs between 900 and 1,000 words. Because of the difficulty in judging humor by proposal, we require submission of a completed manuscript. Payment for the column is $1,000 and there is no kill fee.

The article should be amusing and genial; a mini-essay rather than a one-joke list of anecdotes. The best columns deal with an aspect of society that strikes the author as odd, funny, or worth musing about. Although the essay is often personal in tone, and frequently relates to a writer's own experience, it should have some universal application that might appeal to a general audience.

We buy First North American Serial Rights only. All unsolicited contributions are sent on speculation. New contributions are welcome and we appreciate your interest in SMITHSONIAN.

Contact Information:
Marlane A. Liddell, Articles Editor
900 Jefferson Drive, SW
Washington, D.C. 20560
(202) 786-2900
E-mail: siarticles@aol.com

Snow Country
The Year-Round Magazine of Mountain Sports and Living

What is *Snow Country*?

Snow Country is subtitled "The Year-Round Magazine of Mountain Sports and Living," and the phrase perfectly describes our magazine. As more and more people move to the mountains or vacation there, *Snow Country* reflects both the reality and fantasy of life in the high country. Ours is a regional magazine based on geography: We cover those places defined by mountains and lofty elevations or cold climates, places where outdoor recreation is a way of life. *Snow Country* stretches from the Sierra Nevadas of California and the Coast Mountains of British Columbia to the Adirondacks and the White Mountains of the East. It includes remote rural communities as cosmopolitan resort towns.

In six winter issues, we cover all of the snow sports: alpine skiing at resorts and in the backcountry; snowboarding, whether alpine carving or freestyle; nordic skiing, from skating to telemarking to touring. In two warm-weather issues, we cover the things people do in the mountains once the snow melts: mountain biking, hiking, whitewater rafting, camping, in-line skating, fly-fishing and more. And all year long, our editorial mix includes a wide range of lifestyle articles: profiles of people who live in the mountains or recently have moved there, analysis of important issues confronting the high country, tales of adventure and intriguing events.

Snow Country also covers the recreational equipment people use in the mountains, from skis and snowboards to bikes and hiking boots, and offers helpful instruction articles and fitness tips for skiing and other sports.

Recent issues, for example, have included articles on topics as varied as heli-skiing in British Columbia, the snowmobiling scene in Yellowstone, "bikepacking" on wilderness trails, adventure-sport summer schools, the death of two young rangers on Washington's Mount Rainier, how to use a skidded turn to improve your skiing, and efforts to control growth and development in Montana's Flathead County.

What kind of stories does *Snow Country* look for?

Snow Country looks for articles that educate, inform or entertain our readers. And if a single word can describe the writing style we hope to achieve, it's "lively." Whether in a first-person feature or a straightforward service article, we're interested in colorful quotes, unexpected anecdotes and engaging material that not only imparts information but also paints a colorful picture for readers.

In addition, it's critical that the article be carefully researched and accurate. We do not have a fact-checker to catch mistakes. With that in mind, we insist that writers verify their own work before submitting it. Our readers rely on us for accurate information, and writers who can't meet that standard will not work with us again.

Beyond that, it's difficult to describe the perfect *Snow Country* article. Often, we simply know it when we see it. So the best way to understand our magazine is to read it.

What kind of articles does *Snow Country* reject?

Every week, we receive dozens of queries that are variations on the same tired theme: "My Excellent Ski Trip to Fill-In-The-Blank Resort." Although there's nothing better than a great day on the slopes, these articles are the ski-magazine version of your great-aunt's slide show from her trip to Texas. Other common and cliched themes: How I Learned to Ski or Snowboard, How I Learned to Ski or Snowboard (And I'm Over 40!), Senior Citizens Who Ski, Teaching Your Kids to Ski, Why I Don't Like Snowboarders, and How I Recovered from a Painful Knee Injury. If your story idea is along any of these lines, you're likely to get a rejection letter.

What areas of the magazine are open to freelancers?

A few sections of the magazine are developed by our staff and contributing editors, and generally are not written by freelancers. These include our annual equipment reviews skis and boots, snowboards, hiking boots and cars), our fashion coverage (outdoor apparel and accessories) and two departments: Real Estate and Travel Watch. That said, we occasionally publish articles on these topics by outside writers. So if you think you have a good idea, send it.

In other areas, we rely heavily on freelance writers. Here's the editorial line-up:

Mountain Living is a magazine within a magazine. As the title suggests, the five-page department offers a wide-ranging slice of high-country life: news and gossip, people and points of view, anecdotes, trends and issues. Stories range in length from 100 to 700 words. In general, the short takes tend to be offbeat, pithy and lighthearted. The longer stories often deal with more serious topics. Recent issues have included pieces on a Steamboat rancher fighting to save his valley from real estate development and a proposed Montana gold mine that could threaten Yellowstone National park. Suggesting a good Mountain Living item is the best way for freelance writers to "break in" to *Snow Country*.

Datebook lets readers know about "can't-miss" events in the mountains. World Cup races and athletic competitions, guided trips and outdoor adventures, ski clinics and outdoor sports camps, festivals and concerts and street fairs. In every issue, we select 12 events. Each item runs no longer than 120 words. Freelancers occasionally contribute to Datebook, and we also pay a nominal fee for great Datebook ideas.

Portfolio is a six-page photo essay. Normally, these essays focus on the work of one outstanding mountain photographer, and center around an unusual theme or central point in his work. The text is almost always written by our editors.

Featurettes are stories that aren't long enough to qualify for the feature well. These articles run in the front of the book, range from 1,000 to 2,000 words and usually fall into one of several broad categories: first-person adventure articles (dogsledding in Minnesota, toboggan racing in Maine, skiing the new alpine terrain parks); short travel articles (spending the holidays in Santa Fe, skiing the Swiss resorts of Klosters and Davos); service-oriented stories (best ski-town bars, great ridgeline hikes); profiles of interesting snow country residents (Gerald Hines of Aspen Highlands, a paraplegic ski patroller at Washington's Crystal Mountain); and investigative or issue-oriented articles (ski-area liability laws, turmoil in the U.S. Skiing boardroom).

Features cover the same topics as featurettes, but deserve more space. Features generally occupy four or six ad-free pages, and can run as long as 4,000 words. The feature well is also where you'll find *Snow Country*'s annual Top 50 Resorts package (September), our major equipment reviews (October through December), and major-destination resort profiles.

Follow Me is an instruction department that offers one easy-to-understand tip on each page. In winter, the tips cover alpine skiing, snowboarding, nordic skiing, snowshoeing and other snow sports. In summer, we turn to mountain biking, hiking, in-line skating and the like. Follow me is always written or ghost-written by highly qualified experts, such as members of the PSIA demonstration team or pro mountain-bike racers. High-quality photography is critical to the department and must be assigned and overseen by the *Snow Country* staff.

Architecture is a topic we try to cover as often as possible. Past articles have included a story on a house built atop Telluride Mountain, a two-page illustration by a leading architect who designed the ultimate ski house, and a piece on Janet's Cabin, a solar-powered backcountry lodge on Colorado's Tenth Mountain Trail.

Does it Work offers capsule reviews of new gear that people use in the mountains, excluding the equipment we cover in our annual packages (skis, boots, bindings and snowboards, hiking boots). Recent examples include an oversized ski bag, replacement liners for Sorel boots, a deluxe headlamp and an innovative water purifier.

Armchair Mountaineer reviews the latest books, videos, software and CD-ROMs that might be of interest to our readers. Each review runs no longer than 200 words.

Money and other details

Snow Country's basic pay rate is 80 cents per word, although it can vary, depending on circumstances. In general, rates reflect how much time and effort the story will take. Fees are negotiable in advance with the story editor, as are expenses. We generally reimburse writers for phone calls, and usually pay mileage, lodging, meals and other predetermined costs. The fee includes any rewrites and any additional reporting that may be required.

We pay on acceptance, which means when the editors agree that the article is ready to go. *Snow Country* buys first-time-allworld rights, which includes the right to publish the article on our World Wide Web online site.

If we haven't worked with you before, your query must be accompanied by clips and a resume. We try to respond to all queries promptly. If the answer is "no," you'll probably hear from us within two weeks. If we're interested in your idea or your writing style, you'll be contacted by an editor, but it may take a bit longer. On rare occasions, if you're new to *Snow Country*, you may be asked to write the article on spec.

Thanks for your interest in *Snow Country*.

Contact Information:
Kathleen James Ring, Senior Editor
5520 Park Avenue
Trumbull, CT 06611
(203) 373-7000
E-mail: sceditors@aol.com

Soccer Now

Departments/Features

DEPARTMENTS

- Prez Says—AYSO National President Harvey Lightstone. (Regular Department)
- Ask The Experts—Q&A on soccer issues, both on and off the field. Topic determined by editorial staff and kids who write in. (Regular Department)
- Tips From Fergie—Hints on better soccer playing. (Regular Department)

- Throw-Ins—Letters and Drawings and Stuff (Oh My!) (Regular Department)
- The AYSO Bunch—Cartoon content determined by editorial staff and Cartoonist Mike Browne. (Regular Department)
- Hotshots—Profiles of AYSO players who excel in other activities. (Occasional Department)
- Coach's Corner—Article from a coach. (Occasional Department)
- Tweet! You Make The Call—A reader's chance to play referee. May be substituted for any feature involving a ref. (Occasional Department)
- Touch Lines—National Sponsors supporting AYSO at tournaments, special events, etc. (Occasional Department)
- Friends of AYSO—Professional team players (sometimes AYSO grads) on the move.
- Soccer News—What's happening in the world of U.S. Soccer. (Occasional Department)
- Corner Kicks—Games & Puzzles. (Occasional Department)
- AYSO Information—Featuring a meeting, bylaw changes, round-ups, etc. (Occasional Department)
- Calendar of Events—A listing of upcoming soccer events, tournaments, and national games. Can be AYSO or other affiliation. (Occasional Department)
- Joy Jams on Stuff That Counts—U.S. National team player Joy Fawcett promotes Character Counts! Program in her column. (Regular Department)

FEATURES

- On The Spot—Former AYSO player or coach talks about national championships, the national team, etc. (Regular Feature)
- Your Stories—AYSO players answer questions from Soccer Now staff. Topic determined by editorial staff. (Regular Feature)
- Game Break—Feature on upcoming conference, championship, etc. (Occasional Feature)
- VIP—Soccer program for kids with special needs. (Occasional Feature)

Note: Departments and features subject to change.

Article Format

Preferences:

1. Include a slug (2-3 word description of article), name of author, and date at the upper left-hand corner.
2. Saved in Microsoft Word for Windows (PC), Version 6.0.
3. Spell-checked.
4. Send a 5.25 or 3.5" disk and a hard copy.

Realities:

Send article on either a Mac or PC-formatted disk in either size, using any major word processing program, but saved as a text file. Mail along with hard copy.

Audience/Demographics

1. Most are between 6 and 12 years of age.
2. 64 percent male, 36 percent female (subject to change).
3. Most active AYSO players are in Southern California, New York, Midwest, Hawaii, etc. Southern California sections: 1, 10, 11.
4. Readers really like playing tips.
5. Readers will interact with magazine and write in their comments and suggestions for articles.
6. The secondary market (parents) is just as important as the kids, for they make the purchase decisions based on advertising.
7. Circulation: 420,000, 1.5 million pass-along.

Writing Style

Keeping in mind our audience's level of comprehension, writers for *Soccer Now* should take care not to write over the readers' heads. Upbeat, fun stories that help the kids interact with the subject matter seem to work best. Inspirational stories of AYSO kids who go above and beyond, parents who "do it all," and coaches and referees who educate while maintaining friendly competition comprise much of our story content. Aside from *Soccer Now*, writers may want to pick up *Sports Illustrated for Kids* and/or *Soccer Jr.* For other style examples.

As with any other publication, the editors of *Soccer Now* reserve the right to edit copy. If a story is bumped from the production schedule, we will make every effort to notify you of its status.

A story can only be enhanced by artwork, such as a photo, chart, clip art or other art. If you see an opportunity to get a photo of the subject you're writing about, by all means do so!

Compensation

At this time, *Soccer Now* writers receive a byline and copies of their work for portfolio use.

InPlay

AYSO coaches and referees also have the opportunity to contribute to *InPlay*, the official AYSO newsletter for coaches and referees. Please send submissions (using the same formatting as above).

Contact Information:
Sean Hilferty, Editor/Art Director
Maura Hudson Pomije, Senior Editor
Lolly Keys, Editor-in-Chief
5403 West 138th Street
Hawthorne, CA 90250
(310) 643-6455

Soldier of Fortune
The Journal of Professional Adventurers

SOLDIER OF FORTUNE MAGAZINE is a military/adventure publication written for an active audience interested in going and doing. We specialize in first-person reporting from battlegrounds around the world, with emphasis on current military developments, special units, weapons, tactics, politics and history. Our most successful writers are experienced professionals, more often than not ex-military and frequent *SOF* readers. We take a unique, active and up-close approach to our subjects and are not looking for academic theses, book-length manuscripts, fiction or poetry. The latter are not read and get immediately rejected.

We're not an impossible market, however, and accept between 30 and 60 freelance manuscripts each year. Below are details of what we expect from our contributors and what you can expect from us.

YOUR END:

QUERIES & OUTLINES These are important if you're concerned with saving yourself a lot of time and effort. Before embarking on a lengthy project, do yourself a favor and send us a query letter with an outline. This will tell us whether you're on the right track and give us some indication of your ability to communicate via the written word. We will get back in touch with you and let you know our thoughts on your query. A good query letter includes the following elements: subject matter you will be covering (and source material from which you'll draw your information, i.e., firsthand experience, interviews, etc.), projected length (in double-spaced typed pages), brief description of artwork available, deadline when you can have the article finished, any special conditions of purchase and rights you are selling, and whether your article has been previously published and where. Also include some clips of your published work, if available.

PHOTOS & ILLUSTRATIONS Photographs and line drawings are collectively termed "art." *SOF* is a newsstand magazine and therefore must be illustrated. Magazine buyers like pictures. Your story has a much better chance of being accepted if you can provide art to go along with what you are describing in your text. Lacking that, let us know where we can find such art. If we're absolutely dazzled by your manuscript, but your camera was in two feet of mud at the time of your story, we will commission an artist to draw appropriate illustrations. This is expensive—hence we really have to like your article before we'll do this. We prefer 35mm color slides and glossy 5x7 b&w prints, but will try to work with whatever you can provide, be it a daguerreotype or a rough terrain sketch.

SIMULTANEOUS SUBMISSIONS This is the practice of sending essentially the same story to more than one publication at the same time. If you are engaging in this practice, please make a note to that effect in your cover letter. Our contracts require exclusive rights among competing magazines, so we frown upon authors who sell similar stories to our competitors. For these purposes, newspapers and newsletters are not considered competition; other magazines are! Failure to head this rule will result in all future submissions being returned unread.

EDITING Granted, many of our authors will go on to become the future Hemingways and Sinclairs of their generation, but until that time expect your material to be edited if necessary. Our capable editorial staff will go over your copy and make it conform to our style and standards of English expression. If questions arise concerning content and we feel changes are required, we will do our best to contact you and work the problems out. We try to furnish you with an edited version of your story before publication, but that's sometimes impossible due to our tight production schedule.

JUST THE FACTS We accept manuscripts either typewritten or on any-size/any-density IBM-compatible disk. Label all your photographs with name and address and provide captions. Also write a few paragraphs detailing your background and any relevant experience. Columns are generally 1,200 words or less, while feature articles rarely exceed 4,000 words. We buy all or one-time rights to an editorial package (text and photos). Payment is made on publication for first-time contributors and on acceptance for our regular hands. Article submissions should be sent to the address below. Colonel Robert K. Brown is Publisher of *SOF* and does not deal with freelance manuscripts. Since he's usually chasing down a story himself, mail addressed to him suffers a considerable delay in processing.

OUR END:

ASSIGNMENTS If you've never written for us before or are not personally known to us, chances of obtaining an assignment are slim. We may help you with a letter of introduction your first time out and agree to look at your story, but money up front is out of the question. Story assignment and commission transactions can be done over the phone, but should also be documented by a follow-up letter or • FAX. Stories which are OK'd by us in writing before being submitted are considered "solicited" articles. Articles which are sent to us on speculation or that arrive "over the transom" are "unsolicited" articles.

RETURNING MATERIAL We will keep your editorial package until we publish your article. Photo selection cannot be made until that time. On publication we will return your artwork, but not your original manuscript. We keep these on file in case questions pertaining to content arise after publication. The Friday following the publication date, authors are sent a package containing their art, full payment as per our contract, and an advance copy of the issue in which the author's story appears.

DAMAGED MATERIAL Solicited material is our responsibility while in *SOF*'s possession and restitution will be made for any lost or damaged art. We pay $10 for each lost image, up to a maximum of $250. These rates are low, so do not send us originals. We do not pay for lost manuscripts.

YOUR FRIEND THE SASE If your article arrives without an SASE and we do not accept it for publication, it is destroyed. The number of manuscripts we receive precludes us from paying to ship your material back to you. Foreign contributors should not send foreign stamps, as the U.S. Postal Service is very particular about what it accepts.

KILL FEES This does not refer to body count. A kill fee is paid to authors whose work is rejected after gaining an assignment or is not published due to no fault of the author. In these cases the author receives 25% of the previously agreed-upon amount and all rights to his article are returned to him, effective immediately.

CREDITS We always give our authors full credit for their work and pseudonyms and pen names are perfectly acceptable. If you're submitting someone else's photographs, note the photographer's name on the back; if unknown, write "unknown."

THE BIG BUCKS Payment for feature stories is made per editorial package and varies from article to article. On average we pay $100 per magazine page for history (e.g., anything over five years old) and $150 per page for current topics. If you dodged a few live ones getting your story and have pictures to prove it, we'll pay you more. A cover photo gets you an extra $300-$500. Columns pay $200 flat rate, and the I Was There column pays $150. Bulletin Board pieces and book reviews (99% done on assignment) pay $50. Letters to the editor are unpaid.

WE WANT YOU TO WRITE FOR *SOF* We're professionals and we'll work only with writers and photographers who conduct themselves professionally. Be sure your submitted manuscript is accurate (we check everything) and, like the U.S. Army, the best it can be; we don't like to waste our time on substandard drivel, racist tirades or anything that starts out, "I'd tell you about my fifth 'Nam tour but it's still classified." Don't call our office daily inquiring on the status of your story. We'll be in touch and let you know. Often manuscripts are sent to our contributing editors for evaluation, so time delays are involved. If we're taking longer than you can wait, let us know and we'll return your article. We depend on freelancers like yourself for some of our best material, and actively invite your submissions. Best of luck.

Contact Information:

Dwight Swift, Managing Editor
P.O. Box 693
Boulder, CO 80306
(303) 449-3750 • FAX: (303) 444-5617

SouthwestArt

Southwest Art is edited for art collectors and art appreciators interested in the artists, events and market trends in the representational and figural arts West of the Mississippi River. We profile artists, art dealers, collectors and museum professionals, as well as reporting on major museum and gallery exhibitions. Article types include profiles, critical reviews, interviews, essay/commentary and scholarly research.

Editorial Review Package

Article proposals may be submitted by artists, writers or dealers. The recommended procedure is to submit a review package consisting, at a minimum, of the following:

1.) 20 selected reproductions of the artist's work. Representative 35mm slides or color glossies are acceptable. Snapshots, Polaroids and video tapes will not be considered.

2.) A full outline-form resume, listing education, major public and private collections, exhibition record, awards, publications, gallery affiliations, etc.

3.) A statement of philosophy and intent.

4.) Copies of articles, reviews, gallery brochures, museum catalogs, etc.

Notice of receipt is issued upon arrival of the editorial review package in our Houston offices. Processing of materials may take up to a year. Inclusion in *Southwest Art* magazine is at the discretion of the editors.

Article Submission/Ready for Publication

Southwest Art will review manuscripts on speculation. Articles should be submitted as follows:

Length—approximately 1,600 words (may submit WP 5.1 disk).

Illustrations—a minimum of ten (10) 4-by-5-inch or 2-¼-inch color transparencies with color bar and gray scales. Artwork should be identified by title, medium, dimensions (height by width) and caption information (optional).

Bio photo—35mm slide or black-and-white glossy of artist.

Southwest Art reserves the right to edit material to comply with publication format and specifications. Payment is made after contractual acceptance. All photographic materials are returned approximately one-month following publication.

Contact Information:
Susan H. McGarry, Editor in Chief
P.O. Box 460535
Houston, TX 77056
(713) 850-0990 • FAX: (713) 850-1314

Stained Glass
Quarterly of the Stained Glass Association of America

General:

1. Queries accepted. Article outlines or abstracts preferred.

2. Electronic media in IBM or Mac ASCII format accepted. Some software programs can be accepted without conversion to ASCII. Please inquire about our capacity to translate a word processing program prior to submittal. Modem transmission by arrangement.

3. All manuscripts must contain author's name, address, and telephone number. No anonymous material accepted. Upon author's written request, name may be deleted or a pseudonym considered for published manuscript.

4. Preferred edited length of final manuscript is approximately 2,500 words. Exceptions may be made for scholarly or unusual works.

Copyright:

Author releases and/or assigns all rights under U.S. copyright law currently in effect at the time of publication to the publisher of *Stained Glass* magazine, unless prior agreement has been made.

Style:

The *Associated Press Stylebook* with exceptions. *Webster's New World Dictionary, Second College Edition* for footnote and bibliography form.

Editorial Focus:

Manuscripts directly related to the historical, contemporary, architectural, technical, artistic or aspects of the stained and decorative glass craft given first consideration. However, manuscripts of general or peripheral interest may be considered.

Copy Deadlines:

January 15, Spring Issue
April 15, Summer Issue
July 15, Fall Issue
October 15, Winter Issue

Notification of Acceptance:

Within 60 days of receipt.

Returns:

Materials returned within 60 days of publication or upon notification if accompanied by a self-addressed, stamped envelope.

Photographs:

Photographs or intended illustrations should accompany manuscript. See photographic guidelines. Disclaimer: Although exceptional care of author's materials is exercised, *Stained Glass* magazine, its owners, publishers, editors, or staff shall not be responsible for the loss or destruction of, or damage to, any solicited or unsolicited material.

Photographic Guidelines

Color:

Original, high-resolution, reproduction grade, parallax corrected, large format transparencies are preferred for publication. Duplicate transparencies may accompany initial query. 35mm mounted slides acceptable for publication in some instances, Kodachrome 64ASA or 25ASA speed film preferred. Color prints are generally unacceptable.

Black & White:

Glossy prints preferred. Negatives accompanied by proof of contact sheet acceptable.

Legend:

All photographic submissions must be individually numbered on sleeves and accompanied by a separate and correspondingly numbered legend sheet. All information contained on the legend sheet must be completed. Important! Each photograph should be marked with the photographer's name to avoid possible misplacement or confusion. All photographs should also be clearly marked to indicate "top" on viewed side of image. A colored dot affixed to the upper right corner of the side to be viewed is suggested. Photographs should be numbered on the upper right corner of the mount or sleeve. Corresponding photo legend sheets, which must accompany the photographs, are available from *Stained Glass*.

Notification of Acceptance:

Within 60 days of receipt.

Copyright:

Photographer releases and/or assigns all rights under U.S. copyright law currently in effect at the time of publication to the publisher of *Stained Glass* magazine, unless prior agreement has been made.

Photographic Credit:

Photographs where photographers are known will carry proper credit printed alongside the published image.

Returns:

Materials returned within 30 days of publication or upon notification if accompanied by a self-addressed, stamped envelope.

Disclaimer:

Although exceptional care of author's materials is exercised, *Stained Glass* magazine, its owners, publishers, editors, or staff shall not be responsible for the loss or destruction of, or damage to, any solicited or unsolicited material.

Contact Information:
Stained Glass **Architectural Only: Richard Gross, Editor**
6 SW Second Street, #7
Lee's Summit, MO 64063
(800) 438-9581 or (816) 524-4518 • FAX: (816) 524-9405

Stand *Magazine*

Dear Prospective Contributor,

Thank you for requesting submission guidelines to *Stand*.

If you are not familiar with *Stand*, we strongly recommend that you read one or two issues to ascertain whether or not we are the right kind of market for your work. (Back issues can be obtained from us for five dollars; please make your check out to Amanda Kay. Checks for subscriptions should be made out to *Stand*.) There are no rigid stipulations on the kind of poetry and short fiction we publish, but we do avoid writing which is in a specific genre: science fiction, travel, detective stories, etc. We DO NOT publish complete collections of poetry, full-length novels or plays. As a rough guide we ask to see not more than 6 poems and 2-3 short stories, with a maximum number of 5,000 words for prose.

If accepted, contributors will be notified and will receive a copy of the magazine and payment upon publication. The current rates are approximately £30.00 per poem (or equivalent in U.S. dollars) and £30.00 per 1,000 words of prose. Such is the quantity of work presently awaiting publication that there may be a delay of as much as 18 months between the day we notify acceptance and the date of publication in the magazine.

As U.S. editors we review submissions and send on for further consideration whatever we think appropriate for the magazine. The final publication decision is made by the senior editors in England. You should hear from us within three months of the time of submission.

Thank you once again for your interest.

Yours sincerely,
Short fiction: Daniel Schenker, U.S. Editor
Poetry: Amanda Kay, U.S. Editor

Contact Information:
122 Morris Road
Lacey's Spring, AL 35754
(205) 883-7453

Standard

Thank you for considering *Standard* for your freelance submission.

Standard is published 52 times a year by Beacon Hill Press of Kansas City and has a circulation of more than 150,000. Based on biblical truth and the Wesleyan-Armenian tradition, *Standard* seeks to present quality Christian material for adults to read. *Standard* uses over 200 manuscripts and 100 poems per year.

Standard is read by a diversity of adults: college age through retirement age, single or married, widowed or divorced, parents and grandparents.

Standard publishes a variety of material, including:

- Short stories (fiction or true experience)
- Christian poetry
- Puzzles
- Cartoons

In *Standard* we want to show Christianity in action, and we prefer to do that through stories. We do not use Bible expositions, sermons, devotionals, or how-to articles, which are all published in other areas of WordAction Publishing. Our main interest is short stories which demonstrate Christians dealing with life's issues in ways that result in spiritual growth.

Standard purchases one-time rights, either first or reprint, and will respond within 90 days. Payment is made on acceptance as follows:

- First Rights: 3½ cents per word
- Reprint and simultaneous submissions: 2 cents per word
- Poetry: 25 cents per line

Material accepted for publication will appear in *Standard* approximately 18 months after acceptance. Contributors will also receive five complimentary copies at time of publication.

Please send manuscripts for review to the address shown below.

To save on rising costs of postage, please send a manuscript we do not need to return. Then your return envelope will only need one first-class stamp. Be sure to write the manuscript title on the return envelope, so you will know what manuscript is being referenced when it comes back. Or you can request that the first page of the manuscript be returned in your envelope.

Even though postage is getting higher, we still need a self-addressed, stamped envelope—not a postcard. If your manuscript is accepted, we need the envelope to correspond with you.

RIGHTS

Selling Your Rights

Your manuscript is your property. You own it and simply sell the publication the right to print it. These are the most common rights sold:

First Rights (Formerly, North America Serial Rights)

When you sell first rights, you give the magazine the opportunity to be the first publication to print your articles.

Reprint Rights (Second Rights)

When you've sold an article to one publication, you're free to sell it elsewhere. That's what Reprint Rights means—you're giving a publication the opportunity to reprint this article. You still maintain ownership.

Simultaneous Submissions

This is sending the same article, story, or poem to several publishers at the same time.

Always indicate on the manuscript if you are doing this. *Standard* does not purchase first rights on simultaneous submissions. Due to our lead time, we assume that the story will appear elsewhere before *Standard* goes to press.

Above information courtesy of: From Dreams to Dividends ©
1992 by Jeanette D. Gardner. For more information contact:
Jeanette D. Gardner Publication Services
4708 Delmar
Roeland Park, KS 66205-1344
(913) 722-4601
For *Standard* subscription information write:
Subscription Department
Beacon Hill Press of Kansas City
P.O. Box 419527
Kansas City, MO 64141
Or call, 1-800-877-0700

STYLE TIPS

- Stories should express biblical principles and a holiness lifestyle through action and dialogue. Avoid moralizing.
- Keep in mind the international audience of *Standard* with regard to scenarios, references, and holidays. We cannot use stories about cultural, national, or secular holidays.
- Do not mention specific church affiliations. *Standard* is read in a variety of denominations.
- Keep your writing crisp and entertaining by using action verbs, avoiding passive voice, and keeping sentences concise. Vary sentence length. Make the dialogue and characters believable. Always keep in mind the rules of good fiction writing.
- Avoid clichés—both secular and religious.
- Be conscientious in your use of Scripture. Don't overload your story with Scripture quotations. When you do quote Scripture, quote it exactly and cite your reference. (*Standard* will handle copyrights.)
- Except for quotations from the Bible, written permission for the use of any other copyrighted material is the responsibility of the writer.
- Do not send query letters. Since we accept unsolicited manuscripts, query letters are unnecessary. Submit only complete manuscripts.
- Articles should be no longer than 1,700 words.

MANUSCRIPT PREPARATION

Tear sheets are acceptable, if photocopied to 8 ½" X 11" size. Seasonal material will be considered at any time. Do not submit any manuscript which has been submitted to or published in any of the following: *Vista, Wesleyan Advocate, Herald of Holiness, Preacher's Magazine, World Mission*, or various teen and children's publications produced by WordAction Publishing Company. These are overlapping markets.

Please include the information shown below at the top of the first sheet when submitting manuscripts to *Standard* for consideration.

Your Name
Approximate Number of Words
Mailing Address
Simultaneous Submission?
City, State/Province, Zip
Fiction or True Experience?
Telephone Number

Rights Offered?
Social Security Number
If Reprint, Where Published?

Type and double-space your text. Do not staple the pages of the manuscript together. Please use paper clips. Please repeat your last name, the story title, and the page number in one line on page two and following. (Sometimes pages get separated.)

Proofread your manuscript. Check your grammar and punctuation. Neatness counts, too! Always include a SASE (a self-addressed, stamped envelope).

May God bless you as you write!

Contact Information:
Rev. Everett Leadingham, Editor
6401 The Paseo
Kansas City, KS 64131
(816) 333-7000

St. Anthony Messenger

GENERAL INFORMATION FOR ALL FREELANCE WRITERS

St. Anthony Messenger is a general-interest, family-oriented Catholic magazine. It is written and edited largely for people living in families or the family-like situation of church and community. We want to help our readers better understand the teachings of the gospel and Catholic Church, and how they apply to life and the full range of problems confronting us as members of families, the Church and society.

Types and examples of the kinds of articles we publish:

1. Church and Religion: "The Church Against the Mafia," "Which Scripture Translation is Best," "Lessons from the Book of Genesis: An Interview With Dianne Bergant," "Images of Jesus From Around the World," "I'd Like to Say: Wake Me Up When Mass is Over."
2. Marriage, Family and Parenting: "Toughing Out the Tough Times Together," "Long Distance Grandparenting," " Holy Families Aren't Always Perfect Families," "Stay At Home Dads."
3. Social: "The Death Penalty and the Catholic's Conscience," " Sister Mary Howard Johnstone: Compassionate Attorney for Kids Who Need Protection," "A Job-Training Program That Works," "HOPE House: A Place of New Beginnings."
4. Inspiration: "Prayers for Caregivers," "Veronica Wipes the Face of the World," "The Eucharist: Life, Love & Communion," "Eight Gifts of Motherhood."
5. Psychology: "Codependency: Killing Yourself With Kindness—to Others," "Forgiving Doesn't Mean Forgetting," "Making Retirement the Time of Your Life," "The Death of a Lie."
6. Profiles and Interviews: "Tim Russert: Feisty Host of Meet The Press," "Skater Bonnie Blair and Her Gold-Medal Attitude," "Chicago Remembers Mother Cabrini," "Father Solanus Casey: Saintliness of a 'Slow' Priest," "Pope John Paul II at 75."
7. Fiction: "The Bridge," "The Calling Card," "Legerdemain," "Paper Prayers."

THE BEST WAY TO KNOW WHAT WE PUBLISH IS TO READ AND STUDY SEVERAL RECENT ISSUES OF ST. ANTHONY MESSENGER.

WRITING, PREPARING AND SUBMITTING AN ARTICLE

1. Query in advance. State proposed topic, sources, authorities and your qualifications

to do the article. Library research does not suffice. Fresh sources and interviews with experts or people in the field will be necessary. Reporting articles are more needed than opinion pieces. Seasonal material (Mother's Day, Lent, Christmas, etc.) should be submitted six or more months in advance.

2. We do not publish filler material—anecdotes, jokes, thoughts to ponder.

3. We do not publish articles or stories in installment or serial form. And we very rarely reprint from other sources.

4. We do not use essays or personal reminiscences. Articles about historical events or people no longer living need a current peg.

5. We do not consider articles submitted simultaneously to other magazines.

6. Mark your submission fact or fiction. Place your name, address, phone number and Social Security number on the first page. Number the pages.

7. Articles should not exceed 3,000 words. Oversize articles invite automatic rejection.

8. Keep the vocabulary simple. Avoid jargon, technical and theological language. Keep sentences short. Ask, "Would my grandmother understand this?"

9. An attention-getting introduction is important! Use anecdotes, examples, quotes from real people. Make practical applications. End strongly.

10. Please allow up to eight weeks for return or purchase of publication rights. Hardly any manuscript is published without review by eight or more staff members. Phoning the editor for a progress report invites aborting review process and returning the manuscript immediately to avoid more phone calls.

11. Payment for articles and fiction is 14 cents a published word—upon acceptance and return of signed author-publisher agreement form.

12. Payment for photos accompanying an article is $25 for each photo used. Photos should be documented with any necessary releases from photographers or persons in the photos. Payment for photos is made after photos have been selected and the issue laid out and printed.

13. Articles sent after a positive response to a query are received on a speculation basis.

14. If no article is received within two months after a positive response to a query, we feel free to consider a query on the same subject from another author.

FICTION AUTHORS

Besides these guidelines, freelance authors submitting fiction pieces should read the general information section (above) for all freelance writers. Note the audience for whom we publish and the purpose of *St. Anthony Messenger*. Most of our readers live in families. The greater part are women between 40 and 70 years old.

1. Preferred word length for short stories is 2,500 to 3,000 words.

2. Please do not phone to ask if your manuscript has been received. Allow six to eight weeks for a response or return of your manuscript. Any story that is accepted will have had at least six or eight readers. And many that are returned may also have had as many readers.

3. We receive over 1,000 short story submissions a year. We publish 12 at the most—one an issue. Many stories must be returned—even stories that may be well-written and have merit.

4. In submitting a short story please clearly label it as fiction. Number the pages. Include your social security number (information we must supply the IRS when issuing a purchase check).

5. We pay 14 cents a word on acceptance for First North American Serial Rights and do not consider stories submitted to other publications at the same time or reprints.

6. We are interested in stories about family relationships, people struggling and coping with the same problems of life our readers face. Stories that show people triumphing in adversity, persevering in faith, overcoming doubt or despair, coming to spiritual insights. Stories about people that offer hope. Characters and resolutions must be real and believable. Sudden

realizations, instant conversions and miracle solutions won't do.

7. Stories that sound more like essays or monologues, stories that are straight narratives with no dialogue or interaction on the part of characters will not succeed.

8. Dialogue should contribute to moving the story forward. It should sound real—the way people talk to each other in real life. Conversation should not be artificial or sound stilted.

9. We are not interested in retold Bible stories or stories overly sentimental or pietistic.

10. Seasonal stories (Christmas, Easter, etc.) should be submitted at least six months in advance.

POETRY WRITERS

The poetry we publish attempts to reflect the philosophy stated in the opening paragraph of the general information section above. Poetry is subjective, for the most part, but we do require that the poems we publish have most or all of these characteristics: 1.) originality, 2.) creativity in word choice, images and overall thought/idea, 3.) each section of the poem fitting together well with other sections, 4.) subject matter somewhat universal in nature, 5.) a religious (in a broad sense, not theological) or family dimension.

Both rhyming and non-rhyming material are considered. We do not consider previously published poetry, or poetry submitted at the same time to other publications.

Each poetry submission should be typed, double-spaced on a separate piece of paper. Your name, address and social security number should be typed at the top.

PLEASE DO NOT SUBMIT POEMS LONGER THAN 20-25 LINES—the shorter, the better. Due to space limitations, the poetry section does not appear every month. When space is available for it, there is room for only one page of poetry (four to five poems at the most). Therefore, OUR POETRY NEEDS ARE VERY LIMITED.

As we like to give as many people as possible the chance to be published poets, we do not buy "collections" of poems for publication (that is the role of a poetry book publisher), nor do we usually buy more than a few works from each poet per year. And while we pay on acceptance, publication may not follow for a considerable length of time. When a poem is published, the poet receives two complimentary copies of the issue it appears in.

WE PAY $2 (two dollars) PER LINE for each poem purchased. We try to return poems not accepted within FOUR TO SIX WEEKS. Please do not write or phone to ask if your poem has been received until that amount of time has passed.

Due to the poetry editor's time constraints, poetry critiques will not be given. Thank you very much for your interest!

Contact Information:
The Editor
1615 Republic Street
Cincinnati, OH 45210
(513) 241-5615

Stone Soup
The Magazine by Young Writers and Artists

Strict Requirement: Unfortunately, we cannot send any response at all to contributors whose work is not accompanied by a self-addressed stamped envelope. (Foreign contributors need not include return postage.)

Reporting Time: If you have enclosed an SASE, you will hear from us within four weeks of the date we receive your submission. We usually publish work three months to a year after notification of acceptance.

General Information: *Stone Soup* is made up of stories, poems, book reviews, and art by children through age 13. We encourage you to send us your work! To get an idea of the kind of work we like, the best thing you can do is to read a couple of issues of *Stone Soup*. If it's not in your library, you can order a sample copy for $4.

Send us writing and art about the things you feel most strongly about! Whether your work is about imaginary situations or real ones, use your own experiences and observations to give your work depth and a sense of reality.

Writing need not be typed or copied over. We are happy to consider writing in languages other than English. Include a translation if possible. Art work may be any size, in color or black and white. Please don't send us work that you are also sending to other magazines. Send your work to one magazine at a time.

Illustrators: If you would like to illustrate for us, send us some samples of your art work, along with a letter saying what kind of story you would like to illustrate.

Book Reviewers: If you are interested in reviewing books for *Stone Soup*, write and tell us a little about yourself and what kind of books you like to read. We'll write back with more information.

Payment: All contributors whose work is accepted for publication receive a certificate, two complimentary copies, and discounts on other purchases. In addition, contributors of stories, poems, and art work are paid $10 each, book reviewers are paid $15, illustrators are paid $8 per illustration, and the cover artist is paid $25.

Contact Information:
Ms. Gerry Mandel, Editor
P.O. Box 83
Santa Cruz, CA 95063
(408) 426-5557 • FAX: (408) 426-1161

The Sun
A Magazine of Ideas

We're interested in essays, interviews, fiction, and poetry. While we tend to favor personal writing, we're open to just about anything—even experimental writing, if it doesn't make us feel stupid. Surprise us; we often don't know what we'll like until we read it.

We pay from $50 to $200 for poetry, from $300 to $500 for fiction, and from $300 to $750 for essays and interviews, the amount being determined by length and quality. We may, on occasion, pay more than $750, depending on the scope of the piece, the vagaries of our budget, and the editor's mood. For photographs we pay from $50 to $200, depending on placement. We'll consider photographs of any size, but we can use only black-and-white prints. For drawings and cartoons (which, be forewarned, we rarely publish), we pay up to $75. We also give contributors a complimentary one-year subscription to *The Sun*.

We're willing to read previously published works, though for reprints we pay only half our usual fee. We discourage simultaneous submissions. We rarely run anything longer than seven thousand words. There's no minimum word length, but we halve our fee for short shorts. Don't bother with a query letter, except perhaps on interviews; the subject matter isn't as important to us as what you do with it.

We try to respond within three months. However, with more than seven hundred submissions a month, our backlog of unread manuscripts is often substantial. Don't let a longer wait surprise you.

To save your time and ours, we suggest you take a look at *The Sun* before submitting. Sample issues are $3.50 each.

Thanks for your interest in *The Sun*.

Contact Information:
Sy Safransky, Editor
107 North Roberson Street
Chapel Hill, NC 27604
(919) 942-5282

Swank

EROTIC FICTION

All of the fiction currently used by SWANK is erotic in some sense—that is, both theme and content are sexual. Most of the stories (The Mysterious Stranger, The Bawdy Birthday Present) have been done before, so familiarity with previous tales of this type—in SWANK and elsewhere—is recommended. New angles are always welcome.

*Canadian restrictions: SWANK is distributed in Canada and the censors there practice their own strict standards regarding sexual material. To avoid problems, we generally shy away from material we know they'll object to or edit out any offensive references. Thus, we cannot consider stories about, or containing, the following: 1) S&M (including light bondage and mild humiliation); 2) Sex involving, or between, minors; 3) Unconscious, or dead, participants in sex; 4) Incest; 5) Bestiality.

OTHER FICTION

The magazine's format is currently flexible, and we will consider stories that are not strictly sexual in theme (humor, adventure, detective stories, etc.). However, these types of stories are much more likely to be considered if they portray some sexual element, or scene, within their context.

NONFICTION

1.) Sex-related: Although dealing with sex and sexually related topics, these articles should be serious and well-researched without being overwritten. Examples: "Sexaholics Anonymous," "Dream Programming," and "Voyeurism."

2.) Advice-type articles are also regularly featured. Examples: "How To Pick Up Girls At The Beach," and "How To Make The Man Shortage Work For You."

3.) Action-oriented: We will consider non-sexual articles on topics dealing with action and adventure. The availability of photos to illustrate the articles is crucial to their acceptance—frequently, we will buy a package that includes both the article and transparencies. Recent features include such diverse topics as mercenaries, dangerous occupations and off-road racing. Automotive features run monthly.

4.) Interviews: Although SWANK has not been running interviews lately, we will consider conversations with entertainment, sports and sex-industry celebrities.

PROCEDURE

In most cases, we respond to article queries within three weeks and manuscripts within five weeks. Due to the volume of material we receive, we discourage phone calls.

TERMS

Payment is upon publication. You will be notified of the publication date after acceptance. A sample copy is available for $5.95 postpaid; please make checks or money orders payable to Swank Publications.

Contact Information:
Paul Gambino, Editor
210 Route 4 East, Suite 401
Paramus, NJ 07652-5116
(201) 843-4004 • FAX: (201) 843-8636

T'ai Chi

T'AI CHI is interested in articles on T'ai Chi Ch'uan, other internal martial arts and related topics such as qigong, Chinese traditional medicine and healing practices, Chinese philosophy and culture, as well as news about teachers and their schools.

Generally speaking, an article should take into account the special needs and desires of the readers of T'AI CHI. Many readers are beginners or about to begin. Many are serious students, and have studied and even taught for years.

They are interested in many aspects: self-defense, internal martial arts skills, health, meditation, fitness, self-improvement, ch'i cultivation, meditation, traditional Chinese medicine (acupuncture, herbs, massage, etc.) and spiritual growth.

More specifically, articles may be a feature or interview about a style, self-defense techniques, principles and philosophy, training methods, weapons, case histories of benefits, or new or unusual uses for T'ai Chi Ch'uan. Try to avoid profiles of teachers that focus just on their many skills and accomplishments. Interviews with teachers or personalities should focus on their unique or individual insight into T'ai Chi Ch'uan, internal martial arts, qigong, or traditional Chinese medicine, rather than on their personal achievement or ability, although their background can be woven into the article.

Examples of the uses could be teaching the disabled, teaching of T'ai Chi Ch'uan in a corporate or medical environment, or martial techniques. New approaches to teaching or practice or the basic principles are almost always of interest as long as it doesn't promote a particular teacher. When planning and writing the article, ask yourself: Is the material is new or fresh? Is it useful? Is it interesting?

An examination of past issues is one of your best guides to what we publish.

Present the information clearly, fairly, and objectively. Quotations, anecdotes, examples, and parallel references help make an article more readable and interesting. Writing that is simple and direct is understood best. If organization of the article is a problem, try a question and answer format.

If you want to discuss a story possibility first, please feel free to contact me by phone or with a note or by e-mail. If you are new to the magazine, you can check out our web site: http://www.tai-chi.com.

Please do not send articles that have been published or are simultaneously being sent to other publications, unless it specifies on the first page that it is a news release or that it has been submitted elsewhere, too.

Manuscripts should be typed with a margin not more than 80 characters wide. Put a tentative title on the front page. Put the title abbreviated on each subsequent page with a page number. At the end of the article write "-30-" to indicate it is complete.

Include your name, address, and phone number on the first page and the best times to reach you by phone. Include biographical information.

Articles can be from 500 to 3,500 words long or more. Payment can range from $75.00 to $500.00, depending on the length and quality of the article. This includes payment for photos. Payment is for first North American Serial rights only. Payment is on publication. Publication is usually within 30 days of publication.

If possible, include one or more 4" x 6", 5" x 7" or 8" x 10" glossy black and white prints.

Color photos can be used but may print a little dark, red colors in particular. Indicate if you want them returned. The photos should have identification of the individuals in the photo written on a separate piece of paper sent with the photos or on a post-it on the photo. If the photo is of a posture, the name of the style and posture should be given. Don't write on the back of the photo. Model releases are required. Releases authorizing use of the photos should be dated and witnessed.

We can accept material that has been saved on a disk in Windows WordPerfect or Microsoft Word format. If you have a Mac, we can convert from a Mac Word format into Windows Word.

Editorial deadlines are: February 15, April 15, June 15, August 15, October 15, December 15.

Contact Information:
Marvin Smalheiser, Editor & Publisher
P.O. Box 26156
Los Angeles, CA 90026
(213) 665-7773 • FAX: (213) 665-1627
E-mail: taichi@tai-chi.com or http://www.tai-chi.com

Teaching Tolerance

The biannual magazine *Teaching Tolerance* is dedicated to helping pre-school, elementary, and secondary teachers promote tolerance and understanding between widely diverse groups of students. It includes articles, teaching ideas, and reviews of other resources available to educators. Our interpretation of "tolerance" follows the definition of *American Heritage Dictionary*: The capacity for or the practice of recognizing and respecting the beliefs or practices of others.

In general, we want lively, simple, concise writing. The writing style should be descriptive and reflective. Writers should show the strength of programs dealing successfully with diversity by employing clear descriptions of real scenes and interactions, and by using quotes from teachers and students. We cannot accept articles that employ jargon, rhetoric, or academic analysis. We ask that prospective writers study previous issues of the magazine before sending a query with ideas.

Features: 1,000 - 3,000 words. Should have a strong classroom focus, with national perspective where appropriate. Usually accompanied by sidebars of helpful information such as resources, how-to steps, short profiles. Writers are typically freelance journalists with knowledge of issues in education or educators with experience writing for national non-academic publications. Fees range from $500 to $3,000 depending on length and complexity. The freelance fee is paid on acceptance. If the story is unacceptable as submitted, we will assist in preparing a publishable manuscript, but sometimes, despite the best intentions of both author and editor, a manuscript will be judged unacceptable. In such instances, we will pay the writer's expenses but no freelance fee. A kill fee of $200 will be paid only if the story is accepted for publication and then not used.

Essays: 400-800 words. Personal reflection, description of school program, community-school program, classroom activity, how-to. Writers are typically teachers, parents or other educators. "Between the Lines" essays describe how literature can be used to teach tolerance. Fees range from $300-$800 upon publication.

Idea Exchange: 250-500 words. Brief descriptions of classroom lesson plans, special projects, or other school activities that promote tolerance. These are usually submitted by teachers, administrators or parents who have used the technique or program. Fee: $100 upon publication.

Student Writing: Poems and short essays dealing with diversity, tolerance and justice. Printed when appropriate to magazine content. Fee: $50 upon publication.

Contact Information:
Editor
400 Washington Street
Montgomery, AL 36104
(334) 264-0286 • FAX: (334) 264-3121

Texas Gardener
The magazine for Texas gardeners, by Texas gardeners. ®

TEXAS GARDENER is interested in articles containing practical, how-to information on gardening in Texas. Our readers want to know specific information on how to make gardening succeed in Texas' unique growing conditions. All articles must reflect this slant.

Our bimonthly magazine reaches over 30,000 home gardeners and covers vegetable and fruit production, flowers and ornamentals, landscape and trees, techniques and features on gardeners.

We will accept both technical and feature articles. Technical articles should explain how to do some aspect of gardening (like graft pecans or plant bulbs) in a clear, easy-to-follow manner, and must be accurate. All technical articles should refer to experts in the field. Accompanying artwork such as photographs, illustrations or diagrams are essential.

Feature articles, including interviews or profiles of Texas gardeners, new gardening techniques or photo features should relate specifically to Texas. We will not publish general gardening essays. Personality profiles may be on hobby gardeners or professional horticulturists who are doing something unique.

In-depth articles should run 8-10 double-spaced pages (approximately 1,400 to 1,750 words) though we encourage shorter, concise articles that run 4-6 pages (700 to 1,050 words). All articles are reviewed on speculation. Writers should submit a query and outline of a proposed article first, unless they wish to send a ms. they have already completed. We accept articles on PC disks written in Microsoft Word for Windows or WordPerfect 5.0. Writers should include a list of areas of expertise and a writing sample or copy of published work.

We buy all rights. Payment is made upon publication and includes two copies of the issue in which the author's article appears. We respond to queries within six weeks. Please—no duplicate submissions.

We accept only high-quality color and clear black-and-white photographs. Slides are preferable, but prints, transparencies, and contact sheets may be acceptable. Model releases and identification of subjects are required. We buy all rights.

Contact Information:
Chris Corby, Editor & Publisher
Ashley Blyth, Assistant Editor
P.O. Box 9005
Waco, TX 76714
(817) 772-1270

Times News Service

Thank you for your interest in writing for the Times News Service, which serves *Army Times*, *Navy Times*, and *Air Force Times*, with a combined worldwide circulation of approximately 300,000.

We are always interested in receiving freelance articles that are informative, helpful, entertaining and stimulating to a military audience. We prefer that you first send a query, describing your purpose and goal. If you have an idea with a military angle and aren't sure whether we would be interested, don't hesitate to write us.

WHAT WE WANT: We are looking for articles about military life, its problems and how to handle them, as wells as interesting things people are doing, on the job and in their leisure. Keep in mind that our readers come from all of the military services. For instance, a story can focus on an Army family, but may need to include families or sources from other services as well.

You do not have to be in the military, or part of a military family, to write for us. But the stories we publish reflect a detailed understanding of military life.

WHAT WE DON'T WANT: We don't publish fiction or poetry. We cannot use historical essays or unit histories.

RIGHTS: We purchase only first rights (worldwide). This means that the story, or portions of it, must not have appeared previously in another publication. We will not consider reprinting articles that have been published elsewhere. You may, however, submit an article that has been rewritten extensively.

Payment for articles is made upon acceptance. Remember that once we purchase an article, it might be several months before we publish it. You cannot resell the article to someone else until we have published it. When we do, the article will appear simultaneously on the electronic service Military City Online, a division of Army Times Publishing Co. Your acceptance of payment is acceptance of these conditions.

CATEGORIES OF ARTICLES: Our R&R section appears every week with a variety of features devoted to leisure activities for military people. Many of those features are written by freelancers. They fall into the following categories:

TRAVEL: We look for 700 words on places of distinct interest to military people. We want to give readers stories they can't find in a general-interest newspaper. Rather than an overall piece on the Outer Banks of North Carolina, for instance, we recently published one on scuba diving around sunken warships in the area.

We want our travel stories to focus on a single destination or attraction, but would like you to include a short sidebar covering "other things to see" in the area.

Payment for story and sidebar is $100. (Photos are bought separately; see below.)

PEOPLE: We are looking for members of the military community who have done something unusual. Examples of recent people we have featured are a Navy doctor who took leave to provide free care to the Cheyenne Indians; two civilian colleagues who put together a critical guide to Pentagon eateries; and a retired serviceman and his wife who have made a name for themselves with a newsletter on how to scrimp. These stories should be 600-700 words; we pay $75.

ON THE HOMEFRONT: This feature consists of an essay of about 750 words in which a member of the military community relates a personal experience that would interest other military members or their families. Homefront pieces must be about the writer's own experience. No fiction is accepted. Payment is $100.

PHOTOS: We pay for use of original photographs. Color slides or prints are acceptable. By original, we mean photos that you own either because you took them or because you bought the rights to them. We do not pay for photos bought at a souvenir stand, for example. Generally our payment is $35, but it can be negotiated.

SPECIAL SECTIONS: The Times News Service also publishes regular supplements to *Army Times*, *Navy Times*, and *Air Force Times*. Topics include careers after military service, travel, personal finance and education. Stories generally should include military people. Payment is $150 to $250, on acceptance, for completed articles of 800 to 1,200 words.

Contact Information:
Weekly Features: Maureen Rhea, R&R Editor
Special Supplements/Sections: Margaret Roth
Military News: Kent Miller, Times News Service Editor
6883 Commercial Drive
Springfield, VA 22159
(703) 750-8125 • FAX: (703) 750-8781

The Toastmaster

Circulation

The *Toastmaster* is published monthly by Toastmasters International, a nonprofit educational organization, for 160,000 members in 7,000 clubs worldwide.

Toastmasters are people who recognize a need for self-improvement in communication, especially in their oral presentations, and for developing their leadership potential. Members give at least one speech each month. An average Toastmaster stays with our organization about a year and a half and completes the basic educational projects supplied by our organization. Many members do remain longer to take advantage of more specialized programs, such as advanced speaking programs, listening programs, community involvement and leadership development. Our average reader is 35 years old and has a college degree.

Payment

Toastmasters International will buy all serial rights for $100 to $250; payment is on acceptance. Payment for reprint rights depends on how valuable the material is to us. One-time and/or first serial rights are available on request.

Article Guidelines

Send a query letter first. Article length should be from 1,000 to 2,500. Include a brief author biography.

To speed up publication of your article, we prefer that you send it on a 5¼ inch floppy disk formatted for either the IBM versions of WordPerfect 5.0 or 5.1, or WordStar 3.3. If you do not have access to the above programs, send your article to us on a similar program file and we'll try to convert it. Please include a manuscript hardcopy with your disk.

We need articles related to the fields of communication and leadership, and articles that can be directly applied by our readers in their self-improvement efforts. Anecdotes and examples should be used to present your ideas. We prefer articles written with a "how to" approach, giving our readers practical tips for improving their communication and leadership skills. Appropriate topics include speaking techniques, leadership development and club management principles.

Book reviews, exposes, articles with obvious political and religious slants, poems and speeches will not be accepted for publication.

Contact Information:
Suzanne Frey, Editor
P.O. Box 9052
Mission Viejo, CA 92690-7052
(714) 858-8255

Today's $85,000 Freelance Writer

These guidelines are for both *The Prolific Freelancer* (our current publication) and *Today's $85,000 Freelance Writer* (our new publication due out tentatively in September, 1996).

Today's $85,000 Freelance Writer magazine is seeking material that shows freelance writers how to build a successful writing business and how to earn between $50,000 and $85,000 a year writing for the commercial and entertainment industries.

Our most popular topics that we publish include: Freelance Writing Business Start-ups; Getting Clients; Second Profit Ventures; Commercial and Entertainment Freelance Writing Experiences; Marketing Your Services to Top-Paying Clients; How to Build a Successful Writing Business; How to Self-Promote Yourself and Your business; and many other topics that will help the freelancer establish and operate a successful writing business.

What not to send . . .

We do not publish articles on teaching the craft of writing, how to break into writing markets (such as how to query), or how to get published in magazines.

What to send us . . .

Here is a brief list of topics that we publish and that we need:

- How to start different types of freelance writing businesses, such as copywriting, PR, business writing, newsletter publishing, editorial consulting, and more.
- How to make money freelance writing for the commercial and entertainment industries.
- How to improve your client's copy, such as how to write brochure copy, how to write a press release, how to produce a press kit, how to write a direct mail package, and so on.
- How to work on projects and assignments for clients.
- Internet marketing, such as how to put your own graphic portfolio on the Internet, how to promote your business on-line, and so on.
- How to market your services, such as networking, using direct mail, advertising, and so on.
- How to prepare your own promotional material to get clients.
- How to build a successful business.
- How to get your first clients.
- How to deal with project deadlines.
- How to negotiate with clients for the right price.
- How to create your own contract.
- How to set your own fees.
- How to add extra income to your writing business, such as seminar speaking, selling information through the mail, starting your own newsletter, selling mailing lists, and so on.

- How to break into the commercial and entertainment industries.
- How to make money writing celebrity profiles.
- How to make money selling your ideas to Hollywood.
- How to make money in screen writing or writing documentaries.

We also need articles that help the beginner get started as a commercial freelancer.

Regular Featured Columns

Stealth Selling: shows how to design various types of promotional material to solicit clients.

Creative Copy: how to write various types of copy, such as a brochure, press release, press kit, technical manual, and so on.

Baiting & Tackling Techniques: low cost or no cost marketing and self-promotion techniques for your business.

Tax Tips: how to set up a functioning business.

Better Business Building: how to build a successful business; how to set up your own rules and standards; how to enhance your business's reputation, and so on.

Second Profit Ventures: how to add additional profit to your freelance writing business.

Internet Marketing: how to market your services via the Internet, how to put your portfolio on-line, plus hot web sites, etc.

More Columns to come!

Our current pay for contributions is 0.5 cents per edited word, paid upon publication. We pay regular columnists .10 cents per edited word, paid upon acceptance. Published authors also receive 1-2 contributor's copies.

The magazine's audience includes professional commercial freelance writers, entertainment writers, copywriters, communications consultants, PR pros, direct mail specialists, feature writers, newspaper reporters, and so on.

We publish only nonfiction material, mostly how-to articles, feature articles, tips and professional advice, freelance writing experiences, interviews and profiles. Word length should be no longer than 2,000 words. We love short pieces around 500-1,000 words, as well as in-depth features at 2,000 words. We buy first North American rights and sometimes second reprint rights.

Writers are recommended to send complete manuscript, with 2-3 published clips and a third person biography. Sample copies of *The Prolific Freelancer* are available at $5 a copy (make check/money order payable to BSK Communications). Because we are very specific as to what we publish, we ask that you first read a sample copy.

What we've published in the past . . .

- How to freelance as a copywriter, earning more than $300 writing a single ad.
- How to connect with graphic designers for freelance work.
- How to create your own portfolio to persuade clients to hire you for an upcoming assignment or project.
- How to collect professional samples, testimonials, and contacts before beginning to freelance commercially.
- How to run a writing business legally.
- How to collect late payment from deadbeat clients.
- How to produce the 8-fold, double mailer with reply card to solicit clients.
- How to promote your writing business on the Internet for free.
- How to break into the entertainment industry as a freelance writer.
- 13 laws to protect your writing business.
- Freelance writing for the jewelry and artists industries.
- How to define your market, structure your fees, and get clients.
- How to freelance nationally.
- How to create your own contract or Letter of Agreement.

- How to deal with difficult clients.
- How to sell information through the mail for second profits.
- How to create your own on-line graphical portfolio.
- AND a lot more!

We prefer material on an IBM-compatible 3.5" disk; otherwise material can be submitted on paper.

Contact Information:
Brian S. Konradt, Editor
P.O. Box 554
Oradell, NJ 07649
(201) 262-3277
E-mail: bskcom@internexus.net

Today's Photographer International

The focus of *Today's Photographer International* editorial is to share the success stories that prove you can succeed with your camera. The intent is to encourage a reader's involvement in photography. Inspiration, instruction and information is at the very heart of *Today's Photographer International Magazine*.

What makes a good editorial submission?

It should be an interesting and factual story about your activities as a photographer. We want those step by step experiences, how you make money, operate with clients, find assignments, gain recognition or do anything else successfully. Your story should appeal to photographers and camera enthusiasts who read for pleasure, information or inspiration. It should not be about your subjects—the living conditions of war victims or how a rock group made it—even though you've photographed them. Keep it focused on your activities as a photographer.

How do you turn your activities into an editorial submission? First you should have quality photos to illustrate your story. Then review recent issues of *Today's Photographer International* for editorial content to see if your story "fits." If you are unsure, the following information may be helpful:

Feature articles usually focus on how to make money or gain access to important events. If you have been published or accomplished anything else noteworthy, your story could be a feature.

On Assignment is a forum for you to share your expertise in any aspect of photography and be recognized for your knowledge and business savvy. Frequent topics include how to start or expand a business, protect your rights or copyrights, work with clients, and take advantage of opportunities.

Tech Tips allow you to write about special uses of equipment, supplies or processes. Unusual ideas, practical techniques and "build your own" projects work well here.

Side Trips should include travel photography tips for other photographers. Tell us why it's a Side trip and if you would go again. Do not make it into a travelogue.

Reader Tips is for the "too good to keep" tips on anything that works for you.

Maybe you have a story with a different slant - submit it. You may inspire us to expand our editorial range. Send in submissions as often as you like. Publishing selected submissions is another way for us to reward our readers who share a special bond in their passion for succeeding as photographers ... and making money. Again, our resolution is to support that effort in every issue and to make sure that Today's Photographer International "works" for you.

GENERAL SUBMISSION CHECKLIST:

- Name, 5-Digit Member#, Address and Phone #.
- A photo of YOURSELF (preferably with your camera).
- A typed or clearly handwritten copy of your STORY, ARTICLE, SIDE-TRIP, MAIL BAG or TECH TIP.
- PRINTS or TRANSPARENCIES that illustrate your story (COLOR OR B/W) with captions and proper identification. Be sure to include a separate inventory list of your photos.
- Include information about yourself that you wish to be recognized for such as awards or publishing accomplishments.
- A list of the camera equipment and accessories you use. The kind of film and photo processing services you use.
- Submissions not accompanied by a return envelope will be held on file for future consideration.

Your best chance of being published is when your submission may be kept on file for further consideration in future issues. Submission of your story and photos gives International Photographer Magazine one-time rights to publish your story and photos.

Contact Information:
Editor
P.O. Box 777
Lewisville, NC 27023
(910) 945-9867

tomorrow
Speculative Fiction

We don't really have guidelines—we would rather you surprised us. We take any kind of science fiction, fantasy or horror, provided only that I like it. We publish any story—up to about 20,000 words—if I like it, as I said. We will also look at novels, for serialization, but we encourage you to have a recognizable name; first novels are very difficult to sell us.

We don't take poetry, cartoons, or nonfiction. We have nothing against them—we just don't take them.

We pay at least four cents a word, usually more, with a $75 bottom limit, for most stories. Novels are a flat $2,000. Payment comes on or before publication.

Submit a hard copy first. We'll ask you for a diskette if you have one, after we accept the story.

We normally turn manuscripts around very swiftly; 48 hours, or less. Sometimes I'm out of town. But I'm back in due course. If your manuscript takes as much as six weeks, the reasons are 1.) it got lost in the mail, or 2.) you did not enclose a self-addressed envelope, or a self-addressed envelope and IRC coupons. Category 2.) manuscripts are held for a while, but after three months they get tossed.

Don't enclose a covering letter unless it's to tell me the manuscript is a reprint. Under certain circumstances, we will take reprints. Other covering letters are at best useless. Synopses of the story are totally counterproductive. And don't tell me about other sales, or how much your mother liked the story, or anything like that. Don't enclose a bio. (I know one obsolete listing says the opposite. I didn't write the listing, and it is being changed.) I don't publish authors. I publish stories. If I buy the story, I will, trust me, inquire for particulars of the author.

We never read simultaneous submissions, single-spaced manuscripts, or manuscripts folded over and stuffed into little envelopes.

And that's it. The best of luck to you.

Contact Information:
Algis Budrys, Editor
Box 6038
Evanston, IL 60204
(847) 864-3668

Toward Freedom

Thanks for your interest in *Toward Freedom*. Here's what we're about: *Toward Freedom* provides a progressive perspective on world events, covering political, cultural and environmental issues primarily in the developing countries and Europe. Launched by William Lloyd in 1952, TF emerged as a leading proponent of the non-aligned movement and focused during its early years on African independence movements and UN activities. In 1986, the publication moved its base from Chicago to Vermont and reshaped its editorial mission. It is currently 24 pages per issue and published eight times a year.

MISSION: to publish an international news, analysis and advocacy journal. TF seeks to strengthen and extend human justice and liberties in every sphere. Believing that freedom of the imagination is the basis for a just world, TF opposes all forms of domination that repress human potential to reason, work creatively and dream.

SUBMISSIONS POLICIES: We welcome unsolicited manuscripts and queries, and attempt to report back within 30 days. Many of our writers are correspondents living abroad who write from firsthand experience and incisive knowledge of their subjects. Others may have traveled to a foreign country and/or are erudite on a given topic. We emphasize the following when considering articles for acceptance:

- a clear perspective grounded in firsthand experience or solid research
- passionate defense of a position
- personal experiences
- extended essays on cutting-edge questions
- a constructively critical view of current events in specific regions or countries
- innovations in global management
- stories on grass roots initiatives that promote human liberation, cultural diversity, justice, democracy, and sustainable development.

We are also interested in reviews, travel articles that enlighten readers about another culture or way of life, follow-ups on previously covered stories, and short items/clippings that have been underreported in the mainstream press. We publish occasional stories on the U.S., primarily related to foreign policy or with an international twist. FAX submissions OK once first article has been accepted. Phone story proposals and letters from writers welcomed.

Manuscripts may be submitted on paper or on Macintosh or IBM txt disk. Payment (upon publication) is based on $. 10 per word, and ranges from $50 to $150 for most stories. Major features (2000 words or more) pay more. News stories and columns generally run 600-

900 words.

Art Submissions: TF publishes photographs and illustrations. Though most are based on submitted articles, we consider portfolios and unsolicited materials. Payment is $15-35 per image, more for cover art. Cover-quality photos and graphics are always in demand.

Contact Information:
International (Global) Affairs: Greg Guma, Editor
209 College Street
Burlington, VT 05401
(802) 658-2523. • FAX: (802) 658-3738

Toy Shop
The Indexed Toy Publication

Submissions

Unsolicited manuscripts are welcome.

Content

Toy Shop is published bi-weekly and includes feature stories and columns in alternating issues. Articles are of general interest to toy collectors, focusing mainly (but not exclusively) on toys of the 1940s-present. Stories should focus on the collectibility of specific toys or manufacturers' lines. Features should not be too narrow, but rather hit the highlights of a particular type of toys, such as board games, play sets, farm toys, or construction sets. Smaller features may focus on more specific topics.

Features generally run around 1,500 for a short piece to 2,000-3,500 for a longer feature. All stories are subject to editing for clarity, conciseness, and space considerations.

Current values of toys and other pricing information should be incorporated into features or placed in an accompanying sidebar. Readers want to know not only the historical information about toys, but also what is available and how much it's worth.

Other ideas for stories may include histories of prominent toy companies; interviews with collectors of note; or features on particularly unique, unusual, or large toy collections.

Rights and Payment

Krause Publications purchases perpetual but non-exclusive rights to manuscripts, meaning that after our initial publication, the author is free to sell the work elsewhere, but Krause Publications retains the right to republish the material.

Authors must warrant that each contribution is original work that has not been in the public domain or previously published, unless noted otherwise, and that each is free of unauthorized extractions from other sources, copyrighted or otherwise.

Payment for articles appearing in *Toy Shop* is based on a per-story basis at the editor's discretion. Payment is upon publication, unless other arrangements have been agreed upon. Contact Editor Sharon Korbeck for specific rates.

Manuscript Format

Hard copy submitted must include author's name, address, and phone number at the top. Computer submissions should be on a DS/HD disk in ASCII (text) format with accompanying hard copy.

Style

We follow the basic journalistic style guidelines in The *Associated Press Stylebook*. Consult Strunk & White's *The Elements of Style* for additional considerations.

Photographs

Authors are encouraged to submit color or black-and-white photographs (slides, prints, or transparencies) to accompany their submissions. If desired, photo credits will be given, and photos will be returned upon publication.

Contact Information:
Toy Collecting: Sharon Korbeck, Editor
Krause Publications
700 East State Street
Iola, WI 54990
(715) 445-2214 • FAX: (715) 445-4087

Traditional Quiltworks

(Please refer to Chitra Publications.)

Trafika

Trafika

- Fiction—up to 40 pages.
- Poetry—no more than 10 poems, no less than 5.
- *Trafika* does not publish essays, criticism, or reviews.
- Submitted work must not have been previously published in English. In the case of translated work, publication in the original language, if any, must have been no more than five years previous to submission. Submissions in non-English languages must include an English translation and a copy of the original text. For work from the following languages, a translation is not necessary but will significantly aid the process of consideration: Czech, Danish, French, German, Norwegian, Russian, Slovak, Spanish, Swedish. Please note that we prefer to see a writer's most recent work.
- Please include cover letter with brief bio and all relevant contact information, including e-mail if applicable. For translations, please include translator's bio, previous publication history of text, and permission from author to publish text, if available.
- Writers and translators paid $15 per published page on publication for first international rights.

Subscriptions: $35 US($40 for institutions). Sample copies $10. Payment by check, money order, or credit card (VISA or AMEX). For prices in other currencies, please write.

Contact Information:
Editors
P.O. Box 250413
Columbia Station
New York, NY 10025-1536

Training Magazine
The Human Side of Business

Any manuscript submitted to TRAINING should be tailored specifically to TRAINING's audience. To do that, you have to know what the magazine is about and who reads it.

TRAINING is a monthly, paid-circulation magazine with more than 50,000 subscribers. Subscribers usually receive TRAINING at their offices and route it to coworkers, which means that our total monthly readership is well over 100,000.

We focus on job-related, employer-sponsored training and education in the working world-business, industry, government, service organizations, etc. Our core readers are managers and professionals who specialize in training and human resources development (HRD): corporate training directors, personnel executives, management and organization development specialists, technical trainers in areas as diverse as data processing departments and oil fields, sales trainers, instructional designers, corporate-classroom instructors and so on.

These readers are interested in subjects ranging from broad issues (e.g., how to manage the total employee-training efforts of major multinational corporations) to specific tips (how to design or evaluate a computer-based training course, how to conduct more effective classroom presentations, etc.).

But TRAINING is more than a "how-to" publication for the professional educators of the business world. The ultimate goal of all employer-sponsored training and development activities is to make organizations more effective and productive by making their people more effective and productive. For many of our readers—supervisors, managers and executives of all sorts, in organizations large and small—HRD represents an issue rather than a profession, an issue at the heart of what business organizations are all about. These readers, no less than training professionals, want to know how to motivate employees at all levels of their companies; how to manage, evaluate and develop their subordinates more effectively; how to diagnose and cure performance problems of all sorts.

In other words, TRAINING isn't just about training. It's about human performance—and all the theoretical, practical and organizational factors that affect it.

WRITING FOR TRAINING

We accept and publish only a small fraction of the manuscripts we receive. How can you improve the chances that your submission will be accepted? Remember two things:

1. TRAINING exists for its readers, not for its authors.

2. TRAINING is, as the name suggests, a magazine; it is not an academic or professional "journal." What do those statements mean? The first means that while authors may have many reasons for submitting articles to TRAINING, we do not publish articles in order to publicize authors or to promote or help sell their products or services. Regardless of its form—testimonial, case history or whatever—a manuscript that trumpets the benefits of some product, program or technique without explaining how the reader can achieve those benefits (other than by hiring the author or buying the author's product) will not be accepted. "Tell 'em what

you're going to do for them but don't give 'em the recipe" is a legitimate formula for an advertisement or a client proposal, but not for an article submitted to TRAINING.

The second statement means that we want manuscripts written in the style of magazine articles, not formal "papers." Do not begin with phrases such as "The purpose of this paper is to . . . ." Do not use footnotes; quote sources directly, as newspapers do. Your writing should be clear, crisp, simple, informal and direct. Use active verbs and straightforward language. Do not use passive, stuffy, "impressive" academic language or convoluted "businessese." If you have a Ph.D., let it show in the depth and insight of what you have to say, not in the way you say it.

In short, do not write in the style you would use for a college thesis or a formal proposal. A more effective technique is to write as if you were explaining your subject to a friend or to a small group. Bear in mind that your task is to explain, describe and clarify, not to impress the reader or to complicate the topic.

Our No. I criterion in evaluating manuscripts is the subject matter—what you have to say. But we also place a lot of emphasis on how you say it. Although all accepted articles are edited (and sometimes rewritten) to conform to TRAINING's style, format and readability standards, the closer a manuscript is to being ready for the typesetter, the better its chances of acceptance and early publication.

Before you write, study a few issues of TRAINING. What writing techniques are used? What tone and approach do the articles seem to take? What audience do they appear to be written for?

HOW TO SUBMIT

Manuscripts may vary from one to 15 double-spaced pages. The shorter and more tightly written the article, the better its chance of acceptance.

Submit two copies of each manuscript. Submissions must be accompanied by a cover letter that gives the author's name, address and phone. If available, include a computer disk with text files converted to ASCII. The cover letter also must include a brief identification of the author—title, company, location, etc.

TRAINING insists on exclusive, first-time publication rights to all accepted manuscripts. We do not reprint articles that have appeared in other publications. We do consider original adaptations of material in an author's recent or upcoming book, but we do not print straight excerpts of book chapters or sections.

If you have an article you believe would be useful and/or interesting to our readers, please let us review it Include any photographs, charts or illustrations you think would help readers understand and appreciate the article.

Or, before you write the manuscript, send us a one-page query letter describing the article you intend to write. We'll let you know if the subject and your proposed treatment of it might meet our present or future needs.

All submitted articles are reviewed by our editorial staff. The review process takes approximately six weeks.

TYPES OF ARTICLES

There is a great deal of turnover in the training field, so we're always open to interesting, unpretentious articles that serve as "primers" to novice trainers: "how-to's" on the basics of classroom training, the use of audiovisual support, needs analysis, evaluation and so forth. Unless your article falls into that category, however, the rule of thumb is: Tell us something we haven't heard a thousand times before. That doesn't mean your subject has to be new under the sun, but the manuscript most likely to interest us is one with an unusual premise, a controversial argument, a genuinely new technique or a different slant.

We accept three types of manuscripts:

Features: Feature articles may run anywhere from 800 to 3,000 words (approximately four to 15 double-spaced pages). They may be "how-to's," issue-oriented articles, reportorial-style pieces, case histories, reports on pertinent research or humorous pieces.

Viewpoints: Have a strong opinion on a controversial topic? We accept "guest editorials" for our monthly Viewpoint department. Submissions should be approximately 700 words and written in an essay style—you're a guest columnist. If we accept your Viewpoint, we will request a quality black-and-white photo of you (a "head" shot).

Training Today: Our monthly Training Today section presents an eclectic collection of short (100-700 words) articles ranging from news briefs to specific "how-to" tips to reports on research. You may tailor a submission for the Training Today section (see any issue of TRAINING for format and style). Or, if for some reason we can't use your feature submission as a feature but we think our readers would be interested in some of the points you make, we may ask to adapt part of your manuscript as a Training Today piece. You would receive a letter explaining how that works, and we would not proceed without your signed consent.

WHAT ABOUT PAYMENT?

TRAINING does not pay for articles by people in the HRD business—trainers, consultants, etc. Before you write, decide whether the potential payoff of having an article published in TRAINING—in terms of professional recognition, career advancement, satisfaction or other benefits—will make it worth your time and effort.

TRAINING does pay on acceptance for articles by professional freelance writers. But our acceptance standards are much more strict, and freelance articles almost always must be reportorial-style pieces. Freelancers should always query before proceeding.

To avoid possible confusion, anyone who expects to be paid for an article accepted by TRAINING should say so clearly in a cover letter that accompanies the submission. For more information, call TRAINING's editorial department.

Submit all manuscripts to:

Contact Information:
Editor
50 South Ninth Street
Minneapolis, MN 55402
(612) 333-0471 • FAX: (612) 333-6526.

Transitions Abroad

Tourists are those who bring their homes with them wherever they go, and apply them to whatever they see.... Travelers left home at home, bringing only themselves and a desire to see and hear and feel and take in and grow and learn. —Gary Langer, *Transitions Abroad*, Vol. 1, #1 (1977)

Transitions Abroad, in its 18th year of publication, is the resource magazine for intelligent, active, and responsible travelers of all ages who seek practical information on life-changing international travel that involves learning and enrichment. This means living, studying, working, or vacationing alongside the people of the host country so as to get to know them and their culture as fully as possible. Travel means learning and learning means change. (The title "Transitions" is meant to suggest changes in perception and understanding as well as in place.)

Our readers—most of whom travel on a limited budget to increase their time abroad and their exposure to the culture—are interested in cultural immersion and interaction rather than in passive tourism. Most contributors write from direct experience and supplement their material with sidebars containing contact names, addresses, etc. The emphasis (see quote from Gary Langer above) is on "grow and learn." Our readers are not looking for armchair travelogues but for all the practical details they can use to plan their own adventures—the more usable information presented in a concise manner, the greater the likelihood of publication.

FEATURES AND DEPARTMENTS

What We Are Looking For

Both features (one or two per issue) and departments provide practical information and ideas ("nuts and bolts") on life-enriching travel, work, study, or living in another culture. Since *Transitions Abroad* assumes that all travel abroad involves active engagement and learning, articles should be written with this assumption in mind.

The information and ideas included in articles must be usable to readers who wish to plan a similar experience. As a resource guide, our purpose is to facilitate culturally sensitive, mind-expanding, life-enriching travel—not just to entertain. Information should be fresh, timely, and "unique"—not readily available in guidebooks or from tourist offices. We cannot use descriptions of first-hand experience that merely evoke local color and do not involve direct engagement with the people and culture.

As the editors are unable to check sources, current and accurate information is essential. Writers should be sensitive to the age range of our readers—from high school students to senior citizens. The average age is 40. Most travel abroad at least once a year. Most are college graduates (or students); more than half hold a graduate degree.

What We Do NOT Want in Features or Departments

Sightseeing or "destination" pieces that focus on what to see rather than on the people and culture; personal travelogues or descriptions of unique personal experiences that emphasize the writer's responses rather than usable information; "consumer" articles that objectify the people of other countries or that emphasize what visitors can get from them rather than what they can learn from them.

Length and Format of Feature Articles

Maximum length: 2,000 words. Average length: 1,000-1,500 words. We edit tightly. The author's name and address should appear on at least the first page of the manuscript. If possible, submit manuscripts on diskette or via e-mail (always accompanied by a paper copy). We can use materials submitted on disks formatted for IBM-compatibles (Microsoft Word or ASCII is preferred).

Sidebars

Sidebars include information not in the body of the article: relevant names and addresses, telephone numbers, costs, other options similar to the ones you are describing, etc. Well-researched supporting material in sidebars greatly increases the likelihood of acceptance.

DEPARTMENTS

(Same guidelines and payment rates as features, many more used)

Information Exchange

Readers are encouraged to exchange factual and current practical information on work, study, living, or educational travel abroad. Address letters to "Information Exchange." Be as brief as possible. Material submitted for other departments or as features will sometimes be shortened, with author's permission, for inclusion in Information Exchange. 500 words maximum.

Special Interest Travel: Resources and Program Notes

Department Editor Marian Goldberg welcomes news of publications, services, and other useful information for the learning traveler.

Responsible Travel News

Department Editor Dianne Brause welcomes news, events, or resources on culturally and environmentally responsible travel.

Ecologically Responsible Travel

Department Editor Deborah McLaren welcomes information on how local communities abroad organize and profit from ecotourism, plus ecotourism information sources and details on responsible tour organizers. 1,000 words maximum.

Worldwide Travel Bargains

Current information on good value for money options (not necessarily cheap), usually by travelers just back from a "discovery." Be specific about dates, contacts, etc. in the text. (No sidebars.) Several used each issue. 1,000 words maximum.

The Working Traveler

Editor Susan Griffith, an authority on short-term work abroad, combines her own informative pieces on working around the world with contributions from readers. Several used each issue. 1,000 words maximum.

Activity and Learning Holidays

Ways to combine a vacation abroad with a rewarding activity, from language study to mountain hiking. Several used each issue. 1,000 words maximum.

International Education:

International Career Adviser/Study Abroad Adviser/International Work Adviser/Disability Travel Adviser/Student to Student. . .

All our columnists in the Education Abroad section appreciate your comments, suggestions and contributions on any topic. Write them c/o *Transitions Abroad.*

Program Notes

News of newly organized programs and tours—study, work, or travel—or changes in existing programs. Several used each issue. 250 words maximum.

SUBMISSION PROCEDURES

A query letter is suggested but not essential. Unless otherwise indicated, all material is submitted on speculation. We purchase one-time rights only; rights revert to writers on publication. However, we reserve the right to reprint published articles in part or whole. We will consider reprinted material from publications outside our primary circulation area. Since ours is not the usual travel publication, writers may want to review a recent issue of *Transitions Abroad* for style and content (how to order described below).

- Include black-and-white photographs with your manuscript when available.
- Include a short biographical note at the end of each submission.
- Include your name, address, and telephone numbers (day and evening) on at least the first page of your manuscript and on the back of each photograph.
- Initial response time to manuscripts is usually four weeks or less. We often request permission to hold a submission pending final decision shortly before publication. We record and file each submission and take great care with material "on hold" awaiting the appropriate issue. Unless you need your manuscript or photographs returned immediately, please do not telephone. We cannot provide status reports by phone.
- Payment is on publication, normally \$1.00-\$1.50 per column inch (50-55 words), sometimes more for regular contributors. (For the most part, our contributors are not professional travel writers but travelers with information and ideas to share; we are much more interested in usable first-hand information than in polished prose.) Two copies of the issue in which your story appears will be included with payment. Photos submitted with manuscripts

pay an additional $10 each ($25 each for independent submissions).

PHOTOGRAPHS

We seek black-and-white glossy photographs depicting the people of other countries. While we can sometimes use color prints inside the magazine, we prefer black-and-white prints since we print all photographs in black and white. We seldom consider color slides since converting slides to cibachrome is difficult and costly.

What specifically are we looking for? Our greatest ongoing need is for good cover photos: interesting and engaging close-ups of people of other countries in a "natural" setting. Photographers are encouraged to review a copy of the magazine prior to submission.

We use only people on the cover. For those issues with a geographical focus (see Publication Schedule) our cover photo clearly represents one of the countries of that region. The subjects should be seen in the context of their normal lives, not as interesting curiosities for gawking foreign visitors. They should not appear in pain or distress.

Cover photos also require a particular composition to allow room to overprint the masthead (top two inches) and cover blurbs (left two inches) on a full bleed without interfering with the central image of the photograph.

We encourage photographers to send us not just a stock list but photocopies of selected prints for possible cover use. With these on file, we can contact you and tell you which photographs we would like to receive.

All prints must be identified with a caption as well as the photographer's name and address on the back of the photo. We return all used and unused photos if an SASE is provided.

Payment for photographs used in the text is $25-$50, for cover photos $125-$250, one-time rights only. Photographers are encouraged to submit stock or photocopies of stock for file as potential covers.

EXAMPLE EDITORIAL SCHEDULE (1996)

Transitions Abroad is published bimonthly. Months of publication are January, March, May, July, September, and November. Issues focus on, but are not limited to, the subjects and geographical areas listed for each issue. Writers and photographers should feel free to submit material outside the issue focus.

JANUARY/FEBRUARY

Subject Focus: Short-term jobs around the world, including teaching English
Area Focus: Asia and the Pacific Rim
Special Directory: ESL Training and Placement Programs
Copy Deadline: October 15 previous year.

MARCH/APRIL

Subject Focus: Planning for summer activity vacations
Area Focus: Western Europe
Special Directories: Overseas Student Programs; Key Resources for Study Abroad
Copy Deadline: December 15 previous year.

MAY/JUNE

Subject Focus: Last-minute summer plans; summer and fall study/travel programs
Area Focus: The Americas, the Caribbean, and Africa (south of the Sahara)
Special Directory: Language Schools and Programs
Copy Deadline: February 15

JULY/AUGUST

Subject Focus: Educational Travel Planner: Programs and key resources for alternative travel planning

Area Focus: Worldwide

Special Directories: Adult Study/Travel Programs; Programs for High School Students; Travel and Tours for Families and Seniors; Home Exchange Organizations; Disability Travel Programs; Key Resources for Travel and Family Travel

Copy Deadline: April 15

SEPTEMBER/OCTOBER

Subject Focus: Educational travel in the 1990s: The trends and the trendmakers

Area Focus: Eastern Europe, Russia, and the Newly Independent States

Special Directories: Volunteer Opportunities; Key Resources for Employment and Short-Term Work Abroad

Copy Deadline: June 15

NOVEMBER/DECEMBER

Subject Focus: Off-season travel, out-of-the-way places

Area Focus: The Mediterranean Basin, North Africa, and the Near East

Special Directories: Responsible Travel Programs and Tours; Key Resources for Responsible Travel

Copy Deadline: August 15

HOW TO ORDER A SAMPLE ISSUE/SUBSCRIPTION

Call *Transitions Abroad* at (800) 293-0373 or mail a check ($19.95 for one year subscription; $6.25 for sample issue) to *Transitions Abroad*, P.O. Box 1300, Amherst, MA 01004-1300.

Contact Information:
International Travel: Jason Whitmarsh, Managing Editor
P.O. Box 1300
Amherst, MA 01004-1300
E-mail (for articles or orders): trabroad@aol.com

TriQuarterly
An International Journal of Writing, Art and Cultural Inquiry

Thank you for your inquiry.

TriQuarterly exists for the contemporary writer and the adventurous reader, to nourish the best writing in America and abroad. "Perhaps the preeminent journal for literary fiction" (New York Times), *TriQuarterly* also publishes poetry, translations of both contemporary and classical works, and graphic art. Set apart from the predictable, the established and the familiar, *TriQuarterly* is a magazine of literary exploration and discovery—always lively, intense and varied.

TriQuarterly publishes unsolicited fiction, poetry, artwork and, occasionally, essays of a general and literary nature: memoirs, cultural criticism, unusually literate travel meditations and so on. We do not usually publish scholarly, critical or philosophical essays, or full-length novels. Nor does the magazine often publish excerpts from longer works. Less common forms such as the novella (on the short side), dramatic forms, long poems and others are welcome. Please query regarding essays, but poetry, fiction and artwork—send slides or photos—may be submitted without prior query during our reading period, October 1 to March 31. Manuscripts postmarked between April 1 and September 30 will be returned unread.

All work submitted must be unpublished in the U.S. and elsewhere. This also applies to translations, for which translators must secure permission to publish.

Please send original manuscripts or photocopies rather than carbon copies. We do not like to read manuscripts produced by dot-matrix printers. We try to report on submissions within 8-12 weeks of receipt, but longer works may require more time.

If you are unfamiliar with *TriQuarterly*, please examine a past issue before submitting your work. Sample issues are available from *TriQuarterly* for $5.

Contact Information:
Fiction, Poetry, Essays: Reginald Gibbons, Editor
Northwestern University
2020 Ridge Avenue
Evanston, IL 60208
(847) 491-7614

Troika

Dear freelance writer,

It was a pleasure receiving your enquiry regarding editorial matter for our award-winning* magazine, TROIKA.

TROIKA is a magazine for men and women seeking a balanced lifestyle: personal achievement, family commitment, and community involvement. Our readership is highly educated, achievement-oriented, and upscale, in the 30's-50's age bracket. The magazine focuses on issues such as the arts, health, science, human interest, international, pro bono, business, leisure, ethics and personal finance.

We are currently seeking professional, freelance writers interested in writing, with creativity and humor, for this target audience.

We are always open to reviewing manuscripts and proposals for story ideas. Please be aware that we only purchase finished manuscripts.

We are especially interested in writers looking to develop a long term relationship with a magazine named by Hearst Magazine Enterprises as "one of the top launches of 1994". Our standard fees are $250 for a one page column (750 -1200 words), up to $1000 for feature length articles (approx. 2500 words), payable 30 days after publication.

We purchase first North American rights; accepted manuscripts should be submitted in hard copy and on 3½" diskette, ASCII format (if IBM compatible) or MacWord (Macintosh); or forwarded via e-mail.

*Top 50 Launches of 1994; Samir Husni, Guide to New Magazines (Hearst) Ozzie Silver; Best New Magazine Design- Consumer; over 100,000 circulation. Ozzie Silver; Best Cover Design- Summer '94-Consumer; over I 00,000 circ.; Print Magazine Regional Design Annual; Best Cover Design: Spring '94, Fall '94, Winter 94/ 95. Folio: 1996 Annual Editorial Excellence Awards; Nominee- Winter 95/96.

Please feel free to send manuscripts or call me.
Sincerely,
Celia Meadow, Editor

Contact Information:
125 Main Street, Suite 360
Westport, CT 06880
(203) 227-5377
E-mail: Troikamag@aol.com.

True West

(Please refer to Western Publications.)

Turtle

(Please refer to Children's Better Health Institute.)

Twins Magazine

WE WILL CONSIDER . . .

Articles which offer professional and/or personal insights into family life with multiples and marriage relationships between multiples, and a multiple and a singleton.

Articles that help women to cope with our rapidly changing world as individuals, mothers, professionals and other roles.

Well-documented articles on the problems and success of toddler, preschool, school age, and adolescent multiples, their siblings, and their families.

Practical supportive guides to routines of caring for infant multiples.

Reports of new trends and significant research findings in education and in mental and physical health. Explain how those topics relate to multiples.

First-person reports about being a multiple and/or living with multiples—lessons learned therein.

Articles encouraging informed citizen action on matters of social concern.

Articles should be written with multiples and/or parents of multiples and those who care for them in mind. The word twins or multiples should be used, as well as identical/fraternal and sex-specific information where appropriate.

We prefer a warm, colloquial style of writing, one which avoids the extremes of either slanginess or technical jargon, except where necessary in discussing a particular issue. Relevant viewpoints from both professionals and parents, as well as anecdotes and examples should be used to illustrate points which can then be summed up by straight exposition.

Articles vary in length from 1,000 to 3,000 words. Payment is upon publication and the author assigns all rights to TWINS.

We recommend that writers query us about an article idea before submitting a completed manuscript.

Contact Information:
Susan Alt, Editor
5350 South Rosalyn Street, Suite #400
Englewood, CO 80111-2125

U.S.Art

Circulation: 55,000 nationwide, primarily through a network of 900 galleries

Editorial mission: to reflect current events in the limited-edition print market; to educate collectors and the trade about the market's practices and trends

Frequency: monthly

Writer qualifications: We are open to working with writers whose background is not arts-specific. We generally do not look for art critics but prefer general-assignment reporters who can present factual material with flair in a magazine format. We also are open to opinion pieces from experts (gallery owners, publishers, consultants, show promoters) within the industry.

Freelance submissions: Mss considered but queries preferred. Unsolicited articles not accepted for publication are returned (in SASE only) within four months.

Features: We run an average of six per issue, 1000-2000 words each. These are most often: 1.) roundups of painters whose shared background in limited-edition prints illustrates a point—that is, artists who share a geographical region, heritage or currently popular style; 2.) related to a current news event or art exhibition; 3.) educational on the topic of various print media, buying/selling practices and services available to help collectors make intelligent purchases.

Artist profiles (one per issue) concentrate on current information such as new prints or artistic styles, upcoming shows, anecdotes and future plans.

Feature illustration: Color transparencies are preferred. (U.S.ART keeps these materials for a month or two, then returns them to the source.)

Departments are staff-written. We consider news items and black-and-white photos for the Inside Prints, Showtime, and New Releases columns. Local Color briefly profiles artists whose focus is regional, with a sidebar exploring the region.

Original Graphics (OG) is a 12-page editorial section educating collectors about serigraphy, original lithography and other facets of original printmaking. OG appears in the March, May, August and November issues of U.S.ART.

Writer fee: U.S.ART pays $500 for feature articles within 30 days of acceptance. Publication lead time is three to four months for features, two months for departments. To obtain a sample issue, contact the circulation department at the address, phone or FAX below.

Contact Information:
Sara Gilbert, Managing Editor
220 South 6th Street, Suite 500
Minneapolis, MN 55402
(612) 339-7571 • FAX: (612) 339-5806

Veggie Life

Veggie Life is a full-color food, health and organic gardening magazine for people who are interested in growing and eating a seasonal, low fat, meatless diet for good health. *Veggie Life* focuses on the positive aspects of living a meatless, healthy life without actively condemning opposing views. Our purpose is to encourage and educate our readers in the areas of meatless cuisine, organic gardening and safe and sensible use of natural herbal remedies and nutritional supplements for maintaining good nutrition and health. *Veggie Life* is an international publication, published six times a year primarily in the US and Canada—January,

March, May, July, September, and November.

GENERAL REQUIREMENTS

• All articles must be credible and authoritatively written. We're not interested in personal opinion (product/company bashing), dogma, or religious beliefs. Provide us with clear, concisely written information indicating your expertise in a particular topic, and you'll have our attention.

• All articles must be accompanied by pertinent reference material for fact verification. Reference information must include full names, phone numbers, and any other necessary information. No article will be considered without sufficient fact verification information.

• Queries are preferred to completed manuscripts. If possible, send us a couple of clips or copies of previously published work. Please, no phone queries. Allow six weeks for a response.

• Manuscripts should be submitted in a typed format with proper identification. Include a few sentences about yourself for your "author blurb." For Macintosh or PC users, you may include a digital copy of the manuscript on a 3-½" disk, along with a hard copy of the file. For online writers, our e-mail address is shown below.

• Payment rate is based upon a predetermined scale at the discretion of the publisher. Quality, level of expertise, research complexity, and professional background are major factors that arc considered in the determination of payment (see following features for more information). Payment is made half upon acceptance of the completed manuscript, and half upon publication. EGW Publishing owns all rights to manuscripts and artwork published in *Veggie Life* magazine.

FOOD FEATURES

Food features include a 500 to 700 word article and 6 to 8 recipes with short introductions. Facts about the nutritional benefits of the ingredients are encouraged and information that can be highlighted in a sidebar format is also welcome. Please observe the *Veggie Life* recipe style and write your recipes in the same manner (See below).

We're looking for a wide variety of delicious, lowfat, vegetarian recipes. Regional, ethnic, special occasion, and down-home cooking are our favorites, but we're open to your original ideas. We're always looking for scrumptious lowfat desserts, snack foods, appetizers, kid foods, and new ways to take the fat and meat out of old favorites. Some of our meatless recipes may contain dairy and/or eggs, but vegan options are regularly included, as well as recipes to accommodate special health restrictions (i.e. wheat-free or lacto intolerance).

All recipes accepted for publication will undergo a nutritional analysis. With few exceptions, all of the recipes in *Veggie Life* must have 30% or less calories from fat, and never more than 10 grams of fat per serving; ideally less.

Payment scale and conditions: 25 to 30 cents per published word for feature text and sidebar information, plus 25 to 35 dollars per published recipe. Recipe scale is based on type and complexity of recipe.

FOOD DEPARTMENTS

Meal in Minutes—150 to 200 wd. introduction followed by three recipes for a quick and easy meal. Meals must be ready on the table in 60 minutes or less.

Cooking with Soy—150 to 200 wd. introduction followed by three to four eggless, dairy-free recipes made with a soy product—tofu, tempeh, miso, etc. Remakes of old favorites encouraged.

HEALTH & NUTRITION FEATURES

1,500-2,000 word features on topics related to natural health, nutrition, and fitness as they relate to a meatless diet. Gender specific and age specific (i.e., children, adolescents, seniors) topics are encouraged. We look for author expertise and credibility. Solid authority and reference information is crucial. Pays 35 cents per word (or more for professional credentialed authors).

HEALTH DEPARTMENTS

Preventive/Healing Foods—1000 wd. article followed by four or five recipes focusing on eating to improve health and prevent disease.

To Your Health—200-500 wd. shorts on the latest-breaking news in the area of natural health and nutrition.

GARDENING FEATURES

1500 word gardening features clearly related to growing vegetables, fruits, herbs, or other edible plants organically. Example topics would be: focus on growing a particular type of edible plant, basic gardening techniques, chemical-free pest control, space-saving and container gardening. Photographs are a strong plus in considering gardening submissions. Although we do illustrate some features, professional-quality photos are preferred. Payment: 25-30 cents per word.

GARDENING DEPARTMENTS

Featured Herb—800-1000 words with two to three recipes focusing on a particular herb covering: historic origins; locality; folklore; medicinal and culinary uses; how to grow, harvest and store the herb.

Blooming Garden—800-1000 word feature on growing organic ornamentals. Photos helpful.

The Tool Shed—500 wds. about purchasing and using a featured gardening tool or product.

***Veggie Life* Recipe Guide**

RECIPE TITLE:

The recipe title should be descriptive and creative. Avoid personalizing the recipe like "Aunt Betty's Marmalade."

INTRO:

Give two to three descriptive phrases about the recipe's taste, nutrition, and/or compatibility with other foods, etc. Our editors will take it from there.

INGREDIENTS:

The ingredients should be listed in the order in which the steps refer to them.

Any preparation (i.e. slicing, chopping, draining) should follow the ingredient (1 large onion, chopped), except in the case of precooked ingredients (½ cup cooked kidney beans).

Spell out measurements (i.e., tablespoon, ounce, quart).

Our definition of a low fat recipe is one that derives 30% or less of its total calories from fat and no more than 10 grams of fat per serving. All of our recipes undergo a nutritional analysis and will be tested for this criteria before they are accepted.

- Low fat cooking tips: Cut back on nuts, oils, butters, and eggs. Sauté vegetables in wine or vegetable stock instead of oil. Use pan sprays instead of oils or margarines.
- In most recipes, substitute 2 egg-whites for one whole egg.
- Use non or low fat dairy products. List ingredients in the easiest unit of measure (i.e. ¼ cup, not 4 tablespoons)

When possible, use the entire unit (can, package, carrot, or apple) in the recipe.

Provide can and package sizes—(1 15-½ ounce can kidney beans).

If an ingredient is optional, follow the ingredient with the word "optional" in parenthesis.

INSTRUCTIONS:

Keep the steps simple. Be sure to note the size and type of mixing bowls, cookware, and bakewear used (in a large skillet; 9xl3-inch baking pan).

Use phrases that create a picture of the procedure or result in the reader's mind (Chill until syrupy; beat until frothy; mixture thickens to the consistency of sour cream).

Name each ingredient as they are to be combined rather than saying "Add remaining ingredients" or "Add spices."

Try to foresee questions, problems, or doubts. For example, if you have developed a cake recipe and the batter is unusually thin, say so.

Instructions for preheating the oven generally should be the first step.

Give specific and descriptive cooking or baking times. For example, Bake 20 minutes or until puffed and golden.

Number of Servings:

List how many cups, cookies, slices, etc. equal one serving.

State how many servings per recipe; most of our recipes serve 6.

SAMPLE RECIPE

Pasta Fagioli Soup

"Fagioli" is the Italian word for "bean"—and there's plenty more good things to be found in this hearty meal in a pot.

1 large onion, chopped
6 cups vegetable stock or water
2 cloves garlic, chopped
1 cup diced carrots
1 cup sliced celery
1 28-ounce can crushed tomatoes
1 teaspoon each, dried oregano and basil
1 15-ounce can cannelloni or navy beans, drained
4 ounces ziti or penne pasta
6 ounces prepared veggie or soy burgers, crumbled
Salt and pepper
Chopped parsley (optional)
Parmesan cheese (optional)

1. In a large pot over medium heat, cook onion in ½ cup vegetable stock or water until softened, about 4 minutes. Add garlic, carrots, celery, tomatoes, oregano, basil, beans, and remaining vegetable stock or water. Bring to a boil, reduce heat to low, and simmer, partially covered, until vegetables are tender, about 15 minutes.

2. Add ziti and cook until almost tender, 7 to 10 minutes. Stir in crumbled burgers, and salt and pepper to taste. Cook until heated through, about 3 minutes. Garnish with chopped parsley and Parmesan cheese, if desired.

Makes 6 servings.

Contact Information:

Sharon Mikkelson, Editor
1041 Shary Circle
Concord, CA 94518
(510) 671-9852 • FAX: (510) 671-0692
E-mail: VeggieEd@aol.com

VFW Magazine

VFW Magazine is published by the Veterans of Foreign Wars at national headquarters in Kansas City, Mo. VFW is the nation's 29th largest magazine in circulation. It is published monthly (the June and July issues are combined), and has a readership of some two million.

Subscription is largely through VFW membership, which is restricted to honorably discharged veterans who received an officially recognized campaign medal. Founded in 1899, the VFW is the oldest major veterans organization in America.

TOPICS

Recognition of veterans and military service is paramount at the VFW. Articles related to current foreign policy and defense along with all veterans issues are of prime interest. Topics pertaining to American armed forces abroad and international events affecting U.S. national security are particularly in demand.

Some national political and social issues also qualify for inclusion in the magazine, especially if covered by VFW resolutions. New resolutions are passed each August at the VFW national convention and priority goals are subsequently established, based on these formal issue positions. Lists of standing resolutions are published annually in the October issue of the Communicator.

And, of course, we are always looking for up-to-date stories on veterans concerns. Insight into how recent legislation affects the average veteran is always welcome. Anything that contributes to a better understanding of how the Department of Veterans Affairs operates is useful to fellow veterans. Positive, upbeat stories on successful veterans who have made significant contributions to their communities make for good reading, too.

Also, interviews with prominent figures are of interest if professionally done.

We do not use poetry or fiction.

We do not review books.

No first-person accounts or personality profiles accepted.

MANUSCRIPTS

Manuscripts should be no longer than five double-spaced typewritten pages (or about 1,000 words), depending on the subject. Simultaneous submissions and reprints are not considered. Changes are often required to make copy conform to editorial requirements. Absolute accuracy is a must. If little-known facts or statistics and quotes are used, please cite a reference.

Quotes from relevant individuals are a must. Bibliographies are useful if the subject required extensive research and/or is open to dispute. If you work on a word processor, please use a 40 column format and letter-quality print. Submit manuscripts on 3 ½" diskette, and please include a hard copy. Most word processing software is translatable, however, it is advised to also send in ASCII format.

STYLE

Clarity and simplicity are the two cardinal virtues of good writing. Originality, concrete detail, short paragraphs and strong words are essential. Write in the active voice, and avoid flowery prose and military jargon. Please feel free to suggest descriptive decks (subtitles) and use sub-heads in the body of the copy. Consult The *Associated Press Stylebook* for correct grammar and punctuation.

PHOTOGRAPHS

Photos of exceptional interest are considered for publication. Payment is arranged in advance. Captions must accompany photos, including a separate Caption sheet. Pictures accompanying manuscripts are generally for one-time use only. Please send along all relevant sketches, maps, charts and photos. Sources of additional artwork are also most helpful. Color transparencies (35mm slides or 2 ¼" x 2 ¼") are preferred. But we can always use color as well as black and white prints (5"x7" or 8"xlO").

PAYMENT

Payment generally ranges up to $500 per article, depending on length and writing quality. Commissioned articles are negotiable. Payment is made upon acceptance, and entitles *VFW Magazine* to First North American Serial Rights. Kill fees are paid if the writer is working on assignment and the article is not published.

QUERIES

Do not query over the telephone. A one-page outline (theme, scope, organization) of the proposed article will save the author and editor valuable time and effort in determining the suitability of a piece for *VFW Magazine*. Articles are submitted on a speculative basis for first-time contributors unless commissioned. Topics that coincide with an anniversary should be submitted at least four months in advance.

Use the query letter to demonstrate your knowledge and writing ability. Send along published examples of your work. Familiarize yourself with *VFW Magazine* before writing full-length features.

BIOGRAPHIES

Finally, please enclose a brief biography describing your military service and expertise in the field in which you are writing. Three sentences is generally sufficient. If you are a VFW member, let us know.

VFW Magazine looks forward to receiving submissions from members and freelancers alike.

Contact Information:
406 West 34th Street, Suite 523
Kansas City, MO 64111
(816) 756-3390 • FAX: (816) 968-1169

Videomaker

Editorial Purpose

Videomaker provides comprehensive coverage of analog and digital consumer-level video production tools. It gives tips and techniques appropriate for anyone involved with videomaking as a hobby, in business, or education.

Readership

Videomaker has a circulation of over 80,000. The average *Videomaker* reader is male, 45-84 years old and a professional in a field other than video production. Most of our readers consider themselves intermediate-level videomakers.

Thus, *Videomaker* encourages its writers to use a conversational, "user friendly" style of writing. All articles—no matter how technically complicated—should be accessible to the beginning videomaker; explain all technical concepts in layman's language and avoid the use of jargon.

General Policies

Videomaker welcomes freelance queries and submissions. We prefer queries; a query guideline sheet is available. We suggest you request this before querying us with an article idea.

If you've already written an article suitable for our readership, you can forward it to us on speculation. In general, our feature stories run about 2000 words in length; however, we regularly schedule shorter articles as "filler" features. Note: all columns are written on assignment only. We do not accept column submissions.

If we buy your manuscript, it will become the property of *Videomaker* with all rights reserved. With rare exceptions, *Videomaker* will not accept copy published or submitted for publication elsewhere.

Payment for manuscripts occurs upon publication. The amount depends on a work's uniqueness, timeliness, research requirements and length, as well as the amount of editorial preparation it requires. Writers of accepted submissions receive contracts outlining publication terms and payment procedures.

Writers for *Videomaker* are not authorized to represent themselves as agents of the magazine; contacts must originate from your status as a "freelance writer," independent of *Videomaker* affiliation. As a policy, the *Videomaker* editorial and advertising departments generally account for all the manufacturer solicitations and inquiries—including product loans. Please heed this policy.

Videomaker Style

The best guide for *Videomaker* style is a current copy of the magazine. For style consistency, *Videomaker* editors refer to The *Associated Press Stylebook*. Here's a short list of some of our style guidelines:

Readability

Write in the active, not passive, voice. For example, instead of writing "A cutaway can be used to help tell a story,,, write "Use cutaways to help tell a story." For those of you with computer grammar checkers, reduce passive voice constructions to 3 percent or less.

Write in a clear, concise and logical style. One way we measure writing clarity is with the Gunning Fog Index, which formally rates writing complexity. Microsoft Word for Windows and Mac measures the Gunning Fog Index as part of the grammar checker. Writing for *Videomaker* must have a Gunning Fog Index of 12.0 or less. If your grammar checker has a Bormuth Grade level checker, shoot for a Bormuth rating of 11 or lower.

Punctuation

Do not use the Harvard comma. In a series of three or more words or phrases, do not place a comma before "and" or "or.'[(e.g., The unit features an 8:1 power zoom, flying erase head and f/1.4 lens.)

Use a comma in numerical expressions only with numbers of more than five digits. ($1000, not $1,000).

Contractions

Use contractions whenever possible; this fosters a conversational tone of writing ("it's" instead of "it is")

Numbers

Spell out "zero" through "nine"; use numerals thereafter.

Use numerals when referencing identifications (pin 4 or Fig. 6) or electrical units (9-volt output) .

Spell out fractions less than one (three-quarter-inch); use numerals for fractions greater than one (4 ¼).

Dimensions, Weights, Degrees

In text, use numerals for amounts, but spell out dimension units. (The VCR, measuring 15 inches wide by 4 inches high by 13 inches deep, comes with a 5-foot remote.) In charts and diagrams, abbreviate all units of measurement.

Use numerals for amounts and spell out weight units, as well as the word "degree." (The camera weighs 5 pounds, 1 ounce; camera in hand, he panned 180 degrees.)

Percentages

Spell out the word "percent" in text. Use decimals instead of fractions when appropriate. For amounts less than 1 percent, precede the decimal with a zero. (The price of tripods rose 0.8 percent.) Use the percent sign (%) in charts and graphs only.

Titles

Italicize titles of movies, periodicals and book titles.

Emphasis

To emphasize a word or phrase, place it in italics. *Videomaker* does not use underscored text.

Abbreviations

States: CA, NY, IL, etc. (Postal Service style: Toledo, OH) SP, EP (standard/extended-play on first reference)

SEG (special-effects generator on first reference)

TBC (time-base corrector on first reference)

mike, not mic, for microphone

Artwork

Videomaker encourages its writers to make suggestions regarding the presentation of copy. This includes ideas for page layout, support photography, charts and illustrations.

Photo submissions can be either color (preferred) or black-and-white. Prints should be as sharp as possible, with contrast appropriate for publication. *Videomaker* prefers color slides or transparencies to prints.

Take the time to write complete, descriptive captions for all diagrams, tables, listings and photos. Write lightly on the back of photos and other artwork to identify their origins and specify corresponding copy.

Be sure to identify the sources of all submissions and the individuals or organizations to credit in print, if necessary.

Manuscript Preparation

Include your name, address, phone number and social security number on the first page of your manuscript.

Include headline proposals for the main text as well as sidebars.

Limit (or break down) paragraphs to six lines maximum, assuming standard 12-point characters with 1-inch margins.

Write subheadings (breakheads) to "headline,' each new section of your article. Subheadings should serve as transitions marking the natural flow of the story, from lead to middle sections to conclusion.

Submit diagrams on separate sheets of paper—not within text. In lieu of footnoting, include a bibliography for references. For the benefit of *Videomaker* readers, we encourage you to cite additional reading sources at the end of your manuscript.

Please include a brief paragraph of biographical information suitable for publication. Refer to bios found in previous issues of *Videomaker* for style examples.

Manuscript Submission

Videomaker encourages submissions on computer disk. We prefer files saved in Rich Text Format (RTF) or Microsoft Word for Windows format. (As a last resort, you can submit your document as a "text-only" file. Do not use line breaks.) A hard copy of the manuscript should accompany the disk.

In addition, you may e-mail your manuscript to us in one of three ways:

1.) Internet users may attach a binary file (RTF or Word format preferred) to a standard message. E-mail address is shown below.

2.) CompuServe users may attach a binary file to a standard message; address it to CompuServe user# 71161.1722. Please send a message to the e-mail address below, alerting us to the upload.

3.) AOL users may attach an RTF file only to a standard message to Internet (e-mail) address below.

Communication

Submit all queries in writing; please do not call. Keep queries as brief as possible. Send your resume and clips of previously published work with your query.

Send materials unfolded in a 9- by 12-inch envelope to:

Contact Information:
Query Editor
P.O. Box 4591
Chico, CA 95927
920 Main Street (For UPS; Zip 95928)
(916) 891-8410 • FAX: (916) 891-8443.
E-mail: editor@videomaker.com.

Vietnam

(Please refer to Cowles History Group.)

The Virginia Quarterly Review

1. For results only, include a #10 SASE. You will not be notified otherwise.
2. No simultaneous submissions are accepted.
3. Submissions per envelope are limited to two stories or five poems.
4. Articles, essays, memoirs, and short stories are usually reviewed within three weeks, but, due to the large number of poems we receive, results for these may be delayed three months or longer.

The Emily Clark Balch awards for fiction and poetry are made annually for the best short story and best poem published in the *Virginia Quarterly Review* during the calendar year. There are no specific guidelines except that submissions be of reasonable length (fiction: 2,000-7,000 words; no length restrictions on poetry).

Contact Information:
Articles, Short Stories: Staige D. Blackford, Editor
Poetry: Gregory Orr, Poetry Editor
One West Range
Charlottesville, VA 22903
(804) 924-3124

Visions

(Please refer to Communications Publishing Group.)

Visions-International

How to Send & Submit Poems to Magazines

As an editor and active poet I've learned a lot about the mistakes you can make in submitting poems. It's important to know the simple courtesies that make an editor not feel like trashing your work or returning it unread. It pays to check what the requirements are. The most comprehensive source for this information is the *International Directory of Little Magazines and Small Presses*. Among the things it will tell you are: 1. If they accept unsolicited m's. 2. Are copies acceptable. 3. Are there certain times when they don't read m's. 4. What are the length and number limits. 5. Usually it will also tell the kind of work they're looking for, how long the response time is, and if there's any payment (some don't even give copies, a questionable policy in this editor's opinion).

Most editors appreciate a brief Vita (½ a page or less) and don't want to see another submission from a rejected author within a year (unless asked).

Before selecting poems try to review a sample of the magazine to see what they like (a sample of VISIONS-International is only $4.00). Here are some of our own policies: 1. We like to see 3-6 poems (rarely more than three double-spaced pages each). 2. We don't accept old fashioned, sentimental stuff. On the other hand we don't like the obscure, ultra-modern, often emotionless pap published by some well known academic type journals. (We don't mind rhyme but it's hard to do well.) 3. We like to see Vita but don't let it influence our judgement and a "big name" means nothing to us. 4. If you don't want us to make editorial comments on your poems tell us ahead of time. If we do it's a compliment (means it was worth the bother).

Also don't forget that if you're going to get published the magazines have to survive (believe it or not most editors are poor and their magazines don't make money), so subscribe to at least a couple (VISIONS-International is only $15.00 per year for 3 issues). Sample issues are available for $4.00. Good luck!

Contact Information:
Poetry, Queries: Bradley R. Strahan, Editor/Publisher
Illustrative Art: Kathleen Oettinger, Art Editor
Black Buzzard Press
1110 Seaton Lane
Falls Church, VA 22046
(703) 241-8626

Voyager Publishing

Oatmeal & Poetry, Wholesome Nutrition From The Heart

STATEMENT OF PURPOSE

OATMEAL & POETRY, Wholesome Nutrition From The heart, is the product of a dream; to keep alive the integrity and beauty of traditional, metric poetry as an art form. Along with poetry, we welcome stories and articles which allow one to see with the mind's eye—the picture of life's creation—the human spirit.

Voyager Publishing is homed in the plush St. Croix River Valley, the birth place of Minnesota—Stillwater. We offer OATMEAL & POETRY as a forum for new as well as established poets and writers. Each submission is considered for publication based on its own merit.

Authors do not "compete for the privilege of publication." We will not consider any work which is excessively violent, sexually explicit, or strewn with profanity. This is a family digest. Poems and stories by children as well as adults are encouraged.

About Our Journal

Now entering our second year of publication, OATMEAL & POETRY is a full-size (8.5"x11") literary journal, formatted on an IBM compatible computer, using Microsoft Publisher for Windows. "OPIE" is printed on 20 lb. white stock with a 60 lb. colored cardstock cover, and saddle stapled.

WHAT WE PUBLISH

Haiku, Senryu, Tanka, Ballads, Limericks, Sonnets, Pastorals, etc. Form poetry is always welcomed. We do publish free and blank verse, but they must be exceptional and meet our high standards of excellence. What most important is that you send us your best work!

We want stories about country life, love and family. Stories should stir the imagination and have a positive message. Stories can be romantic, life-changing, spiritual, mysterious, humorous, adventurous . . . again—send us your best!

In addition, our "Network Muse Market" section can get you in touch with other fine publications and informs you of nationwide contests offering top cash prizes.

SUBMISSION GUIDELINES

POETRY: Max 30 lines. Rhymed verse preferred. Free verse must be exceptional to be published. $1.00 reading fee for each poem.

SHORT STORIES: 1200 wd max. $2.00 reading fee per story.

ARTICLES: 500 wd max. $2.00 reading fee per article.

NOTE: As of 1/1/96, an Editor's Choice cash prize of $15.00 is awarded in each issue. (Editor's choice may be poetry or prose.)

Fees under $5.00, please send cash to avoid bank service charges. SUBSCRIBERS never pay a reading fee to have their submissions considered for publication.

CONTESTS: Cash prize contests held quarterly. Guidelines for contests available free of charge for a #10 SASE.

CHAPBOOK REVIEWS: Submit complimentary copy of your published chapbook along with $3.00 reading fee and it will be reviewed in OATMEAL & POETRY.

PAYMENT: Current payment for publication is in 1 copy wherein your work(s) appear. We request one-time rights. Copyright reverts to author upon publication.

Let's Get personal

We encourage all contributors to send us a personal biography about themselves, their family and their literary accomplishments, to share with readers, along with a photo if possible. Bios published as space permits.

The best way to see what we like and what we publish is to send for a sample copy—only $4.50 post paid. Subscription rates are as follows: $18.00 for one year (U.S.); $26.00 for one year (Canada & Overseas). Check or money order IN U.S. FUNDS ONLY should be made payable to Voyager Publishing.

Contact Information:
Poems, Short Stories, Articles: Demitra Flanagan, Editor
Artwork, Photography: Nadia Giordana, Associate Editor
P.O. Box 2215
Stillwater, MN 55082
(612) 578-9589

The War Cry

The War Cry is the national publication of The Salvation Army in the United States. The Salvation Army, an international movement, is an evangelical part of the universal Christian church. Its message is based on the Bible. Its ministry is motivated by the love of God. Its mission is to preach the gospel of Jesus Christ and to meet human needs in His name without discrimination.

Circulation:

The War Cry is published biweekly. On average, circulation for a regular issue is more than 300,000 copies. For the annual Christmas issue, it is about 4 million copies, for the annual Easter issue, it is about 1.5 million copies.

Principal Needs:

Nonfiction articles related to modern life that offer inspiration, information, or evangelization. Our readership encompasses people from all walks of life. We especially like essays that provide insightful perspectives on living the Christian life or practical advice for putting faith in action. Length should be 700 to 1,500 words. Sample copies of *The War Cry* are available upon request.

Ongoing series for which we need articles are:

- Focus on Issues (Biblical perspectives on modern issues)
- Christ and Culture (media portrayals of the Gospel)
- Evangelism page (450-word articles that lead readers to seek Christ. Each of these should tell a brief story without being preachy. The stories usually illustrate general concepts rather than relate purely personal experiences.)
- Religious News (reports of what is currently taking place in the religious community-especially within The Salvation Army)
- Trophies of Grace (stories of people whom God's grace has touched in a remarkable way)
- Triumph Through Tears (stories of how God has enabled people to triumph over adversity)

Also Will Consider:

- Christmas, Easter and other special day themes.
- Photos (5"x7" or 8"xl0" color prints and transparencies)

Rates:

Sliding scale depending on the material and its use. For articles, the rate is generally 20 cents per word. For photos, the usual rate is $100-$150 per photo.

Rights:

First rights and reprints

Response:

Manuscripts with SASEs will be returned within 30 days. Payment is upon acceptance.

Contact Information:
The War Cry
615 Slaters Lane
P.O. Box 269
Alexandria, Virginia 22313
(703) 684-5500

WaterSki Magazine
The World's Leading Water Skiing Magazine

WaterSki is the superior vehicle for informing, entertaining and motivating water skiers of all levels and disciplines. The magazine focuses special attention on reaching the core audience of intermediate-level skiers and boaters. Each issue includes departments on instruction, boating, travel, equipment and competition. Features run the gamut from personality pieces to travel stories to new product analysis.

FORMAT:

Both solicited and unsolicited articles should be submitted on an IBM-compatible disc (either 3.5 or 5.25 inch) in the following formats: WordPerfect 5.1, Microsoft Word for Windows through 6.0, Quark Express, Pagemaker or any ASCII text format. We can also receive articles (text only) via Internet (see address below). Hard copy is also accepted, but not recommended. Please include a clean hard copy with each disc.

TERMS:

Payment for all published material is made 30 days after publication. Most feature articles are paid 30 days after acceptance.

FEATURES:

Feature articles pay $200-$500 and are 1,250 to 2,000 words in length, including sidebars. Travel features and personality profiles are paid based on specific assignment.

INSTRUCTIONAL FEATURES AND TIPS:

How-to articles pay $175 each and are approximately 1,350 words in length, including sidebars. Short instructional tips pay $35 and run no longer than 350 words.

COLUMNS:

Columns pay $150, run about 750 words and are made by assignment only.

WaterSki Magazine and its parent company, World publications, consider for publication only those manuscripts that are previously unpublished and checked for factual accuracy. All submissions must be clearly labeled and addressed to:

Contact Information:
Richard P. Brunelli, Editor-in-Chief
330 West Canton Avenue
Winter Park, FL 32789
(407) 628-4802
Internet: waterski@worldzine.com

WD—Workforce Diversity

(Please refer to Equal Opportunity Publications.)

Western Angler

We want broadly applicable, how-to articles about reservoir, river and alpine methods. Technical articles about boats, motors, electronics, tackle and other equipment are also needed.

We'll reward articles which also include interviews with recognized expert anglers from multiple western states. Interviews with manufacturers and biologists are also encouraged. With your manuscript, send a list of relevant photos you may have.

EDITORIAL REQUIREMENTS

- WESTERN focus
- Content including reservoir, river, Pacific coast or alpine fishery
- An educational theme with theoretical background and practical suggestions—whys and hows
- Focuses on trout, bass, walleye, striper, salmon or steelhead
- Multi-species and/or multi-state applicability
- Complex concepts simplified and discussed in laymen's terms
- Interviews with experts, manufacturers and scientists
- Seasonal concepts relative to Northwest, Southwest and Intermountain regions

RATES

- Articles—750 to 2500 words—$150 to $450.
- Destinations West articles—800 to 1100 words—$100 to $150.
- Photos—$25 to $75.
- Cover photos—$200 to $400. We prefer scenic shots including angler and live fish.

Payment for articles and photographs payable 30 to 45 days after publication.

Season-specific submissions should reach us a minimum of four months in advance.

Contact Information:
350 East Center Street, Suite 201
Provo, UT 84606
(801) 377-7111

Western Publications
"Publishers of Western Americana Since 1953"

TRUE WEST and OLD WEST magazines publish nonfiction articles on the history of the American West from prehistory to 1930. More recent topics may be used if they have a historical angle or retain the Old West flavor of trail dust and saddle leather.

Our readers are predominantly male, forty-five years of age or older, from rural areas and small towns. Nearly all have graduated from high school, and slightly more than half have attended college. They are knowledgeable about western history and ranching and want articles to be informative and entertaining.

We cover al states west of the Mississippi and all areas of western history—Native Americans, trappers, miners, cowboys, ranchers, farmers, pioneers, the military, ghost towns, lost mines, women, and minorities. Current, travel-oriented stories work well if they have a historical angle. We especially need good western humor and stories on lesser-known people and events. If widely-known topics are used, the article should include newly discovered information or take a fresh approach to the subject. We cannot use anything on western movies, television, or fiction.

Historical accuracy and strict adherence to the facts are essential. We much prefer material based on primary sources (archives, court records, documents, contemporary newspapers, and first person accounts) to those that rely mainly on secondary sources (published books, magazines, and journals). We occasionally use first person reminiscences, but proper names and dates must be accurate and double-checked by the author. We do not want dialogue unless it can be documented, and we do not use fictionalized treatments of historical subjects. Manuscripts other than first person recollections should be accompanied by a bibliographic list of sources.

We usually need from four to eight photos for each story, and we rely on writers to provide them. It is best to send photocopies of available photos with your manuscript. Let us know from whom the photos are available, the cost of prints, use fees, etc. When we accept your manuscript, we will let you know which photos we want to use. We will reimburse you for your photo expenses. If photos are unavailable for an especially good article, we will have it illustrated by an artist. Appropriate maps enhance our articles, and we appreciate receiving sketches for our artists to work from.

Nearly all our articles are written by freelance writers on speculation. A byline is always given, and photos and illustrations are credited. Writers are given an opportunity to proofread galleys before their articles go to press. We will consider unsolicited manuscripts, but it is best to query us in writing first. Manuscripts are processed in the order received, usually within six to eight weeks. We pay from three to five cents per word, on acceptance. Rate of pay depends entirely on the quality of the writing and the depth of the research. On publication of your article, we will return your photos and send two complimentary copies of the issue.

Your name, address, telephone number, social security number, and an approximate word count should appear on the first page of your manuscript, along with your byline exactly as you want it to appear. Maximum length is 4,500 words; ideal length to break in is about 2,500 words. We also take shorter pieces, especially humor, ranging from 300 to 1,500 words.

To judge our needs, consult our back issues; a 1953-1980 index is available for purchase. "Writing the Short Western Article," by John Joerschke, in *The Western Writer's Handbook*, James L. Collins, editor (Boulder, Colorado: Johnson Books, 1987), explains our approach in detail.

Contact Information:

History of American West to 1920: John Joerschke, Editor
P.O. Box 2107
Stillwater, OK 74074
(405) 743-3370 • FAX: (405) 743-3374

Wild West

(Please refer to Cowles History Group.)

Wired

Submit 150 words or less with a really great story idea (not a topic idea). E-mail submissions only.

Contact Information:

520 3rd Street, 4th Floor
San Francisco, CA 94107-1815
E-mail: submit@wired.com

Woman Engineer

(Please refer to Equal Opportunity Publications.)

Woman's Touch
An Inspirational Magazine for Women

ABOUT *Woman's Touch*

Woman's Touch is a bimonthly inspirational magazine for women published by the Women's Ministries Department, Division of Church Ministries, Assemblies of God. We are committed to providing help and inspiration for Christian women, strengthening family life, and reaching out in witness to others. *Woman's Touch* is the voice of Women's Ministries across the nation.

The editors of *Woman's Touch* would like strong, original articles written from the Christian's perspective and geared specifically for women. Our greatest demand is for practical articles on women's relationships with various family members and peers, personal/spiritual growth, health and beauty, current issues in society, women and careers, crafts and humor. We would also like to see feature articles written about women's Ministries groups or individuals. We are not currently accepting articles on abortion, Mary and Martha, Christmas' loss of meaning, or personal life stories.

In planning the magazine, the editorial staff follows these general themes:

JANUARY/FEBRUARY

MAIN THEME: Personal Growth

SECONDARY THEME: couple relationships and friendships, Valentine's Day, new year (starting over, becoming a better person, goal-setting, etc.), singleness, careers, health and beauty.

MARCH/APRIL

MAIN THEME-. Personal Relationship with God—building character, daily walk, understanding God

SECONDARY THEMES: Easter, church, home, parent care/relationships, local evangelism

MAY/JUNE

MAIN THEME: Family—relationship with husband and children, Mother's Day

SECONDARY THEMES: working mothers; singleness and single parenting; stepparenting, parents dealing with loss of a child, teenagers, adoption

JULY/AUGUST

MAIN THEME: Country-patriotism; current issues facing women in America

SECONDARY THEMES: helping others (outreach), relationships with peers (friends, siblings, coworkers, etc.), prayer, vacations/moving

SEPTEMBER/OCTOBER

MAIN THEME: Education and Careers

SECONDARY THEMES: raising children-traditionally, as a working mother, as a single mother, home organization, personal friendships, school, the workplace, dealing with divorce

NOVEMBER/DECEMBER

MAIN THEME: Holidays-seasonal articles for Thanksgiving and Christmas

SECONDARY THEMES: relationships with extended family and in-laws, family evangelism, elderly, dealing with loss

ABOUT WRITING YOUR MANUSCRIPT

- We will consider manuscripts Up to 1,000 words. Longer manuscripts would probably not be usable due to our limited space.
- Study our style and content to find what type of articles we use. For a sample copy of *Woman's Touch*, send a self-addressed manila envelope (9 by 12 inches) with 75¢ postage, or subscribe to the magazine.
- Give the version of the Bible you are using when you quote Scripture. Verify and identify other sources you have used. Confirm all illustrations and references to Scripture, history, nature, animal life, science, etc.
- *Woman's Touch* does not accept fiction. We very rarely use poetry.

ABOUT SUBMITTING YOUR MANUSCRIPT

- In the upper left-hand corner of your manuscript, place your name, mailing address, city, state, ZIP code, telephone number and area code, and social security number, which we will need if we purchase your manuscript. In the upper right-hand corner place the approximate number of words of your manuscript, and printing rights offered (first rights, second rights, reprinted from . . .). Also indicate if you have submitted the manuscript simultaneously to other publications.
- We would also like to know if your manuscript is on computer disk so we may request the disk if we do purchase your manuscript. A 3.5-inch DOS or MAC disk with your article in a Microsoft Word for Windows format is best. Our second preference is Word Perfect 5.0 or 5. 1. Please indicate at the bottom of your cover letter if your article is available on disk and in what format, even if it is not one mentioned above. You do not need to send the disk with your initial submission.

ABOUT YOUR MANUSCRIPTS EVALUATION

- All manuscripts will be evaluated. We prefer not to receive query letters.
- We will endeavor to respond within 90 days of your submission.
- Payment will be made on publication of the manuscript. When the manuscript is printed, you will receive two complimentary copies of the issue in which it appears.
- Seasonal manuscripts to be evaluated should reach us I to 2 months prior to the holiday or season described. If your manuscript is chosen, it will be scheduled for the following year.
- The editors of *Woman's Touch* reserve the right to edit your manuscript for clarity and space.

Thank you for considering *Woman's Touch* for your manuscripts. God bless your writing ministry!

Address your manuscript to:

Contact Information:
1445 Boonville Avenue
Springfield, MO 65802-1894
(417) 862-2781

Woman's Way
A quarterly publication for self-discovery and self-expression

We will accept legible handwritten material, if you do not have access to a typewriter or word processor. If your material is accepted for publication, we will request that you send us the material on a computer disk. If you want to include the disk, we accept both PC and Mac (3 ½" disks).

Please put your name and address on the top of each page to insure proper identification of material.

Include a brief (1-3 sentences) biography to be included at the end of your material.

We are more likely to publish shorter articles (800 words) and short poems, etc. We are also interested in columns and in serializing longer pieces.

We are particularly interested in personal experiences. Some possible subjects for articles or columns are: women's psychology; the body, health, and nutrition; issues of older women, women of color, and gay women; women and work; ritual; issues of creativity; biographies of women you find inspiring; book, tape, or movie reviews; journal excerpts; poems; short stories.

As *WW* is a forum, we want to hear about what you are inspired by. If you have an idea for a column, please write a brief outline and/or call.

Themes:

Spring - Aging & Eldering
Summer - Earth & Ecofeminism

Submission of black and white artwork:

We are interested in photographs, B&W artwork, or cartoons

Please put your name, address, phone number on each page of submission.

If we choose to publish your work we will call or write and request that you send us the original material.

To all Contributors:

Please be patient. If you do not hear back as quickly as you'd like, feel free to call or write. Reviewing submissions is only one task among many in producing *Woman's Way*. Unfortunately, I frequently have to file them until I have time to read them with the attention they all deserve. If your submission does not appear in the next issue, I may choose to hold onto it for consideration for a later issue. If you prefer that I return it to you sooner, let me know.

Although we are not in a position to pay contributors at this time, this does not reflect a lack of value and respect for your work. As soon as we are in a more solid financial position, we will begin to support your creative endeavors with an honorarium. In the meantime, we hope that contributing to *Woman's Way* supports you in other ways.

Contributions by men are also appreciated. Shortly, we hope to start a section entitled "A Man's Perspective." Submissions by children are also welcome.

Thank you very much for your Interest and support of *Woman's Way* and good luck with all your creative endeavors.

All the Best,
Lynn Marlow, Editor & Publisher

Contact Information:
P.O. Box 19614
Boulder, CO 80308-2614
(303) 530-7617

Women Alive!

We are especially interested in articles which encourage spiritual growth such as those on prayer, praise, and Bible reading. Other topics of interest to our readers:

Living as a Christian in the workplace
Mothering—helps in discipline and in rearing spiritual children
Improving marriage
Discouragement—especially in ministry
Self-consciousness/shyness—relating to new people
Improve communication in family and marriage
Help with handling finances
Do retired women still have a place of service?
Temptations known only to the singles
Reinforcement techniques for single mothers
How can I reach the unsaved?

We are interested in articles which show Scripture applied to daily living. Most Christian women understand what they should do but need godly role models, so we prefer that you use examples of your obedience rather than your failures.

To receive a sample magazine please send $1.25 or a 9 x 12 envelope with four first-class stamps.

Editors of *Women Alive* evaluate a manuscript using the following criteria:

1. Can the focus of the article be supported by Scripture?
2. Does it meet our purpose of helping women who are intent on spiritual growth?
3. Is the focus maintained throughout the article?
4. Is it well developed and illustrated?
5. Does it have a unique approach to the subject?
6. Is it written in a natural style (avoiding triteness and clichés)?
7. Will it have impact?
8. Will the reader's interest be maintained throughout the article?

Women Alive pays from $15 to $30 for each article depending on length and quality of article. *Women Alive* purchases either first rights or reprints but with payment we purchase the right to allow the articles to be translated into other languages by nonprofit missionary organizations.

We look forward to receiving your articles!

Contact Information:
Aletha Hinthorn, Editor
P.O. Box 4683
Overland Park, KS 66204

Woodall Publications

Woodall Publications publishes six monthly and one bimonthly regional tabloids for RVers, prospective RV owners and others interested in the RV lifestyle. Our regional publications are:

WOODALL'S California RV Traveler, The RV Lifestyle Source for the Golden State

- California (excluding northern California)
- 12 issues per year
- Minimum monthly circulation: 25,000

WOODALL'S Camperways, The Middle Atlantic RV Lifestyle Source

- Delaware, Maryland, New Jersey, New York, eastern Pennsylvania and Virginia
- 12 issues per year
- Minimum monthly circulation: 30,000-36,000

WOODALL'S Camp-orama, The RVers Guide to Florida

- Florida
- 12 issues per year
- Minimum monthly circulation: 30,000 -35,000

WOODALL'S RV Traveler*, (formerly *Trails-a-Way*): *The RVers Guide to the Midwest

- Illinois, Wisconsin, Indiana, Michigan, Ohio and western Pennsylvania
- 11 issues per year (November and December are combined)
- Minimum monthly circulation 35,000

WOODALL'S Southern RV, The RV Lifestyle Source for the Southeast

- Georgia, South Carolina, North Carolina, Tennessee and Kentucky
- 12 issues per year
- Minimum monthly circulation: 20,000-24,000

WOODALL'S Texas RV, The RVers Guide to Family Camping in Texas

- Texas
- 6 issues per year (bimonthly)
- Minimum monthly circulation 25,000-30,000

WOODALL'S Carolina RV Traveler: The RV Lifestyle Source for the Carolinas

- North and South Carolina
- 10 issues per year
- Minimum monthly circulation 10,000

READERSHIP

Our readers are owners or prospective owners of RVs. They are primarily interested in nonfiction articles about places to go and things to see and do in the respective geographic regions of each publication. We will review articles on the following topics-.

- Specific destinations within the regions
- Regional activities such as fishing, festivals or special events
- Profiles of RV owners
- RV hints or technical information on RVing or camping
- Humorous or insightful camping trips
- Interesting or unusual campgrounds
- Opinion pieces on the RVing lifestyle
- RVing lifestyle pieces from the RV Man or RV Woman's perspective

SUBMISSIONS

Please send query letters. Queries by phone are not accepted. FAX and unsolicited manuscripts are not encouraged.

The author's name, address, telephone number and social security number, word count, and rights offered should appear on the first page of any manuscript. If a submitted article has been previously published, the publication and date must be noted. The author's name and story title should appear on subsequent pages, along with page numbers.

Each article should include a sidebar listing any sources, contacts or destinations mentioned, noting exact addresses, phone numbers, directions, admission prices, hours of operation and restrictions. Photos (prints, not slides) and/or illustrations should accompany stories (Destination stories need accompanying photos). Each photograph must include the author's name and the story name on the back.

We have the capability to copy manuscripts from 3 ½-inch computer floppy disks. We use Macintosh Microsoft Word software, and can read all versions up to and including MacWrite and Word Perfect for the Macintosh.

The publisher reserves the right to edit all copy. Payment will be made on the published word count.

For sample copies, send a 10 x 13 SASE (four first class stamps) for each publication requested.

PAYMENT

Some flat rate fees are offered. Standard payment is $.05 per published word, $5 per published photo, for First North American Rights, made upon publication. In the rare case that an article (not a query) be accepted for publication and then not used, we offer a kill fee of 50%.

We reserve reprint rights for accepted material with multi-regional applications for 6 months. Payment for reprints of original material in each of Woodall's monthly publications is $25 per publication and $5 per published photo. Generally, manuscripts previously published in non-RV/camping-related publications will be considered for one-time rights.

Payment for first rights to a column with possible reprint rights in other publications will be determined by the editor.

Payment, return of materials and a writer's copy are sent at the end of the month in which the article is published. Materials and tearsheets are returned under separate cover.

Contact Information:

All: Debbie Harmsen, Editor
13975 W. Polo Trail Dr.
P.O. Box 5000
Lake Forest IL 60045-5000
(800) 323-9076 or (847) 362-6700 • FAX: (847) 362-6844

Working Mother

Thank you for your interest in WORKING MOTHER. The magazine is looking for articles (about 1,500 to 2,000 words in length) that help women in their task of juggling job, home and family. We like humorous pieces and articles which sensibly solve or illuminate a problem unique to our readers. Topics that particularly interest us include: time, home and money management, health, family relationships, humorous essays and personal narratives and job-related issues. Pieces dealing with food, beauty and fashion are usually staff-written.

Manuscripts must be submitted on speculation at the author's risk. We prefer receiving proposals for pieces, rather than completed work. Then, if we find the subject suitable, we can discuss the best way to handle the material.

All manuscripts and queries should be addressed to the appropriate editor, as shown below.

Contact Information:
Education, Child Rearing: Mary McLaughlin, Executive Editor
Work, Family Issues: Deborah Wilburn, Senior Editor
Health, Travel: Linda Hamilton, Articles Editor
230 Park Avenue
New York, NY 10169
(212) 551-9500

World
The Journal of the Unitarian Universalist Association

The *World* is the bimonthly denominational magazine of the Unitarian Universalist Association of Congregations. Its purpose is to articulate Unitarian Universalist and other liberal religious values, purposes, aesthetics, and spirituality and to publicize UU activities, personalities, and history.

To be considered for publication in the *World*, an article must be directly relevant to Unitarian Universalism. In addition, many issues of the *World* have themes. Topics we plan to cover in the near future include diversity; theology; leadership; and money and charitable giving. It's a good idea to read a few issues and become familiar with the *World* before submitting your work. To order an issue, send $4.00 to the address below.

We publish unsolicited manuscripts most often as "op ed" Commentaries, Among Ourselves news notes about UU activities, or letters to the editor. Occasionally, we publish unsolicited book reviews. Writers of these articles receive two copies of the issue in which they appear; there is no payment.

Materials or story ideas submitted by readers have served as the basis for feature articles, sidebars, and profiles; however, these kinds of articles are usually solicited from freelancers well in advance. If you would like to be considered for *World* feature assignments, send us your resume and one or two writing samples. Payment for features is negotiated when the article is assigned.

We receive many manuscripts; send us your best work. Manuscripts should be succinct, well-though-out final drafts. We do not accept previously published material, fiction, or unsolicited poetry.

You may send your article or query by e-mail to the address below.

Or you may submit your work on 3½" high-density disks. Most word processing programs are acceptable; limited formatting is preferable—do not insert carriage returns at the end of each line. Include a hard copy, and let us know what program you used.

Thank you for considering the *World*. Every submission increases our understanding of Unitarian Universalism and thus represents a real contribution to our efforts.

Contact Information:
25 Beacon Street
Boston, MA 02108
(617) 742-2100 • FAX: (617) 367-3237
E-mail: worldmag@uua.org

World War II

(Please refer to Cowles History Group.)

Writer's Digest

General Focus

Writer's Digest is a monthly handbook for writers who want to write better and sell more. Every word we publish must inform, instruct or inspire the freelancer. Our readers want specific ideas and tips that will help them succeed - and success to our readers means getting into print.

Yet, that doesn't mean that we don't have a little fun in WD. Our style is informal and personal. We try to entertain as well as instruct. We try to speak with the voice of a compassionate colleague, a friend as well as a teacher. And though we don't shy away from explaining the difficulties of getting published today, all of our articles share a certain optimism. WD is infused with a belief in anyone's potential to succeed as a writer.

You can best understand our philosophy by being intimately familiar with *Writer's Digest*. We are a monthly publication with a circulation of more than 200,000. Our readers are of all ages and are scattered throughout the US, Canada and several other countries. Each year we buy about 60-90 major articles and scores of shorter items; our annual *Writer's Yearbook* and associated publications use an additional 15-30 manuscripts.

To obtain sample issues of *Writer's Digest*, send $3.50 per copy ($3.70 in Ohio) to the Circulation Secretary, *Writer's Digest*, 1507 Dana Ave., Cincinnati, Ohio 45207. An index of each year's contents is published in the December issue.

How to Submit

Writer's Digest editors prefer queries over unsolicited manuscripts. Queries allow us to review your article ideas and to suggest how to tailor them for our audience before you begin writing. Queries also save you time and energy should we reject your idea.

Queries should include a thorough outline that introduces your article proposal and highlights each of the points you intend to make. Your query should discuss how the article will benefit our readers and why you are the appropriate writer to discuss the topic. Although we welcome the work of new writers, we respect success and believe the selling writer can instruct our reader better and establish more credibility than the writer with a good idea but no sales.

Please submit only one query at a time, and allow us 4-8 weeks to review your proposal; ideas that spark our interest are routed among the magazine's editors for review. Queries to *Writer's Digest* are also considered for *Writer's Yearbook* and associated publications. There is no need to query these publications separately.

If we like your proposal, we may either assign you to do the article or ask to see it on speculation ("on spec"). We often work on spec with authors who are new to us or whose article ideas are not as clearly developed as we would like. It's also possible that we'll ask to see a more detailed query before we make a decision.

In certain cases, we do prefer complete manuscripts. These include short items and poetry for The Writing Life department, Tip Sheet items, and Chronicle articles. We'll look at good-quality dot-matrix printed manuscripts, but we prefer letter quality. Each submission must include your name, address and daytime telephone number.

No simultaneous submissions, please.

Also, we do not use fiction or scripts; we do not buy newspaper clippings; and we handle book and software reviews in-house.

In your query, tell us if you can submit assigned work on disk or via modem. We do accept unsolicited electronic submissions.

Finally, we expect writers to double-check all facts included in their stories and to submit documentation to support the information included in their stories.

Photos and Artwork

Whenever possible, we want to show our readers how writers work, and we encourage you to suggest how your article can be enhanced with graphics. Past issues have included marked-up manuscript pages (to show how Joe Gores revises his work), photos of Hong Kong by Robert Ludlum (to show how he keeps a sense of his novels' settings), character sketches used by Clive Cussler, timesheets, book promotional materials, correspondence with editors, submission logs, and similar materials related to writing and the business of freelancing.

We use cartoons, but they must be well drawn to merit consideration here. A clever gagline alone won't do. Send finished cartoons only, in batches of ten or more. We prefer single panels, either with or without gaglines. The theme is the writing life -we want cartoons that deal with writers and the trials of writing and selling their work. Also, cartoons about writing from a historical standpoint (past works), language use, and other literary themes. Original artwork is returned after publication.

We do not accept unsolicited illustrations.

Payment and General Terms

For manuscripts, we usually pay 10-30¢ per word, on acceptance, for first North American serial rights, one-time use only. Poetry earns $25-$50, depending on length. Cartoons bring $50-$100. Contributor copies are sent to writers and artists whose work appears in that issue. (Should we want to reprint anything we've purchased from you, we will pay you 25% of the original purchase price for reprint rights for each use.)

What We Want—Long Stuff

Freelance submissions are accepted for all sections of the magazine, with the exception of our regular columns and bylined department sections.

How-to Articles are our mainstay: how to write better, market successfully, recycle and resell manuscripts, maintain records ... and more. These articles present a common problem or goal, offer the appropriate solution, and give an example of how that solution has worked. Articles generally run 2,000-3,000 words, though cover stories often run longer. We also took for pieces that can cover a topic completely in 1,000 words or fewer. Actual length will be discussed when the article is assigned.

Topics for features vary widely. Categories that we seek material for include writers' opportunities and money-making ideas; the business of writing; reference sources; writers' tools, equipment and supplies (however, we are not interested in material on word processing, which is covered by one of our columnists and seldom appears elsewhere in the magazine);

writing discipline; language use; quizzes; personal experiences (but only if they teach a lesson or prove a point); marketing mechanics; and three types that will be covered more fully below: writing techniques, profiles/interviews and market reports.

In general, don't shy away from the word I in your articles. The first-person perspective is important to establishing your credibility. But don't overdo it. We want instructive articles, not "and then I wrote" essays. Round out your experiences with those of other writers and with information from editors, when appropriate.

We use a friendly, informal—but not lackadaisical or cutesy—style. We demand lively writing. Use anecdotes, examples, samples and quotes to strengthen the message of the article. We like lively headlines, and our articles are sprinkled with subheads at appropriate places to help readers locate particular sections when returning to the article. Writers who use lively headlines and subheads in their manuscripts demonstrate their familiarity with our style.

Writing Technique Articles. This brand of how-to article is most important to Writers Digest. These pieces highlight an often misunderstood or poorly utilized writing method and detail how to use it precisely, appropriately and successfully. We are always hungry for these articles. Examples include how to write an effective lead, how to use dialogue to establish character, how to brighten your prose, how to use suspense effectively.

Articles may cover fiction, nonfiction, poetry or scriptwriting techniques, but must be accessible to all writers and offer advice that can be applied directly or indirectly to all forms of writing. How a particular piece is structured depends on the complexity of the subject, but every piece will need to:

• Define the technique and its importance. Draw broad lines of application to other forms of writing.

• Outline how to use the technique. The best explanations break the technique down into distinct parts and deal with each part individually. When appropriate, use a step-by-step explanation.

• Give examples of its usage. A vital part of your article; give us more than you think necessary—and then add two more. Illustrate every point with examples—either from your own writing or from well-known works. On major points, readers can benefit from "right" and "wrong" or "before" and "after" examples, showing writing before the technique is applied or when it is used inappropriately, followed by the corrected version.

• If appropriate, give readers tips on incorporating the technique into their writing. For example, an article on using anecdotes gave tips on how to collect anecdotes to use.

As with all how-to articles, instruction is the key to making the article work. Analyze your own writing to determine what gives it power, what makes it successful. Then give our readers a thorough guide to using that technique powerfully and successfully, too.

Interviews and Profiles. Major interviews, using the Q&A format, should be with authors of stature—those currently in the news or on the bestseller lists. Length ranges from 2,500 to 4,000 words; we occasionally use longer pieces as the subject warrants. Narrative-style profiles of major writers usually run 2,500-3,000 words. We also use short profiles (about 1,000 words or fewer) of lesser-known authors who can inspire and give advice to our readers.

Lively quotes, anecdotes and solid information are as essential for profiles and interviews as they are for other WD articles.

Even more essential is an understanding of the major elements of a WD interview or profile. These articles must be directed at the working writer; pieces rewritten from general interest magazines or book-review tabloids are not acceptable. For that reason, we require a detailed query for all interviews.

These are the major elements of a WD interview or profile (in order of importance):

• The writer's product. What the writer produces and why it is different and noteworthy; why it succeeds. (Writing samples often help, but they cannot tell the full story.) How the writer developed this trait and refined it. What the writer thinks of his work. What needs the writer thinks he is fulfilling. What brings power to his work. The conscious process of putting words on paper.

- Advice to other writers. What can other writers learn from the author and his work, his career? What problems can the writer steer readers around? What techniques can he instruct them in? What shortcuts can the writer suggest? What solutions to common problems can the writer recommend?
- The road to success. Failures and handicaps the writer has overcome, and how they were overcome. When the writer first realized he could succeed at the typewriter. The first break, and where it led. The rewards and the costs of success.
- How the writer works. Work habits, including number of hours per day and his or her timetable. The physical act of writing-does the writer use pencil, pen, typewriter or word processor? Where does the writer work? How does the writer discipline himself?

Photos and graphics are essential to the interview/profile, Photos should concentrate on the subject's face and upper body. We like a good selection of shots that show gestures and capture the character of the subject. We prefer shots in which the subject is looking directly into the camera-though not awkwardly so. We also like to see a few middle-distance shots that show the subject in his/her work area, at the typewriter, or interacting with others who are pertinent to the story. If there's something special about the writer's environment, give, us a long shot of the writer in this atmosphere. Natural lighting is best—avoid shadows, etc. If you cannot provide these photos yourself, provide us with a source for them. Other graphics for profiles and features should give our readers a glimpse of the writer's work. Original drafts, revised manuscript pages, notes, outlines, journal pages and other materials help demonstrate the universality of the writing experience. For more information, see "Photos and Artwork" on page 2.

Market Reports highlight general article or book styles and offer instruction on how any writer might break into this lucrative area. Examples might be writing the true-life drama, or the as-told-to article or book. A market report may also identify a particular market, such as writing for trade publications or writing a cookbook, but the market most be large and diverse, we aren't interested in pieces that spotlight highly specialized markets that can embrace only a few writers. Paint with a large brush in market reports—we're more likely to publish an article on writing expertly about health and fitness than an article on writing for the health and fitness market. There's a difference. If you don't understand that difference, don't attempt to write market reports.

In writing the market report, you'll want to cover several essential elements. This isn't a formula—only a checklist. Remember, anecdotes, specific examples and quotes are important here, too.

- Establish the market. It must be current and have a growing need for manuscripts. Quote editors. Emphasize specific sales and payments, either your own or other writers'.
- Describe the market. Detail the differences from and similarities to other markets and types of writing. Give an idea of who's interested in these types of articles so readers will know if this is a market that appeals to them.
- Explain how to find ideas for the market. What kinds of topics and treatments does the market use most? Point out how writers can generate ideas that are salable. Provide tips on matching ideas to publications.
- Explain how to write for the market. Detail the process of turning ideas into salable stories. What are the special requirements of writing for this market or writing this type of article or book? Point out common pitfalls and how to avoid them.

What We Want—Short Stuff

The Writing Life. This section uses brief, lively items that are offbeat or on-the-mark glimpses of the traits, transgressions and follies peculiar to writers and their life. This section is always fun and light, but instructional tips that also entertain are welcome. Length is 50-500 words—and here, shorter is better. We don't buy jokes, but we do buy short bits of humor (anecdotes, ironies, quotes and puns). Submit items on separate sheets of paper, please.

Poetry. We seldom use more than two poems an issue, so competition is severe. And we have very definite needs. Poetry is used only in The Writing Life department, so short, light verse is preferred. Serious verse is acceptable, but stands less chance of acceptance. Whether it's light or serious, all poetry must focus on writers—their joys, despairs, strategies and relationships to the world. Length rarely exceeds 20 lines.

Tip Sheet. This department offers short (1,000 words, tops), instructional bits of information that help writers live, write and market more successfully. Topics include advice on manuscript problems, business concerns, language stumbling blocks and tax questions; suggestions on new ways to make money as a writer; useful "tricks of the trade"; reports on legal and business developments that affect writers; and explanations of more efficient office procedures.

Chronicle. These are first-person accounts of writing successes, failures, incidents, problems and insights.

They should be, as the name suggests, open, honest accounts—told either humorously or dramatically—as if you were sharing a few pages of your journal. A narrative style and a message that all readers can share are musts. Length is 1,500 words maximum.

Contact Information:
Submissions Editor
1507 Dana Avenue
Cincinnati, OH 45207
(513) 531-2222

---

ym
Young & Modern

Thank you for your interest in *YM*.

We are a national magazine for young women ages 15 to 24. Our readers are bright, enthusiastic and inquisitive. Our goal is to guide them—in effect, to be a second "best friend" through the many exciting, yet often rough, aspects of young adulthood.

Writers who are not familiar with the magazine or who have not read it recently are advised to go through back issues—your local library might have a selection, or send us a check ($2.50 per issue) and we'll send them to you—to learn more about how we are changing and what we publish. While most of *YM*'s columns and all of our fashion, beauty and lifestyle are staff written, we buy articles (up to 2,500 words for a major piece) on topics of interest to young women. In the past year, for example, we have tackled everything from interracial dating to sexual abuse to eating disorders.

All articles should be lively and informative (but not academic in tone), and any "expert" opinions (psychologists, authors and teachers) should be included as a supplement to the feelings and experiences of young women. Writers whose work has not appeared in *YM* should include tearsheets of published articles.

Payment varies according to the length and type of article, but writers who have few or no published articles will be asked to write on speculation (no guarantee of payment). Please query us in writing; we prefer that to telephone calls, FAXes and unsolicited manuscripts (mark "Query" on the envelope). Allow four weeks for consideration. Seasonal material should be submitted at least eight weeks in advance. Work that is accepted is paid for upon approval.

We do not publish fiction or poetry.

Contact Information:
685 Third Avenue
New York, NY 10017

Yoga Journal
For Health and Conscious Living

We cover a variety of fields and disciplines devoted to enhancing human health and consciousness, while maintaining our emphasis on the practice and philosophy of yoga. We define yoga broadly to encompass practices that aspire to union or communion with some higher power, greater truth, or deeper source of wisdom, as well as practices that tend to increase harmony of body, mind, and spirit.

In particular we welcome articles on the following themes:

1. Leaders, spokespersons, and visionaries who teach and exemplify a conscious, holistic lifestyle;
2. Spiritual disciplines, teachings, and leading practitioners and teachers, both Eastern and Western;
3. The practice of hatha yoga;
4. Applications of yoga to everyday life (e.g., relationships, social issues, livelihood, environment, etc.);
5. Hatha yoga anatomy and kinesiology and therapeutic yoga;
6. Transpersonal philosophy and psychology and their application to everyday life situations and problems;
7. Natural healing, massage and bodywork, the martial arts, and exercise that is consonant with the practice of yoga.
8. Nutrition and diet, cooking, and natural skin and body care.
9. Relevant ideas, people, and events that broaden and deepen our understanding of ourselves, each other, and the world.

If you have an idea that does not fall into one of these categories, feel free to suggest it to us. We encourage a well-written query letter outlining your subject and describing its appeal. Query before submitting an article.

We encourage you to read an issue of *Yoga Journal* carefully before submitting a query. Please keep in mind our editorial department's three E's: Articles should be enlightening, educational, and entertaining. Please avoid new age jargon and in-house buzz-words as much as possible. Features run approximately 3,000 to 5,000 words. Departments run 1,000 to 2,500 words. Centering runs about 750 words. We do not print unsolicited poetry. We consider everything except a direct assignment to be submitted on a speculative basis. If an article has been assigned, we will send you a contract specifying terms, kill fee, and deadline.

Remember to indicate the availability of photos or artwork in your query letter or with your article. (Pertinent, high quality photos or illustrations can greatly enhance an article's desirability.)

Payment varies, depending on length, depth of research, etc. We pay within 90 days of final acceptance: $1200 for cover stories, $600 to $1000 for features, $250 to $500 for departments, and $75 to $100 for book reviews.

Include your name, address, and phone number on your title page, and write your name and page number on each subsequent page. Also include a concise, two-sentence tagline identifying your self to our readers.

Make sure all photos are marked with a brief descriptive caption and the photographer's name and address.

Contact Information:
Book Reviews: Holly Hammond, Associate Editor
Food, Health: Linda Sparrowe, Managing Editor
General queries: Anne Cushman, Senior Editor
General queries: Rick Fields, Editor-in-Chief
2054 University Avenue
Berkeley, CA 94704
(510) 841-9200 • FAX: (510) 644-3101

Your Church

Our Readers

Our readers are the decision makers in the church—pastors, board members, church administrators, treasurers. Our slant is that pastors and key lay leaders are good at what they do; they are dedicated Christians wanting to be good stewards of their church-business responsibilities, and they are eager for cutting-edge, down-to-earth advice from people who know what they're talking about. We don't patronize them or scold them. Instead, we provide for them the best of current thinking—material far beyond first-consideration thoughts almost anybody could produce after a little thought.

Our Subject Matter

The purpose of YOUR CHURCH magazine is to provide pastors and other church leaders the insight, information, and action initiatives they need to be effective Christian stewards of the church resources entrusted to them. YOUR CHURCH focuses particularly on the fields of church business administration, purchasing, and facilities management.

We've given YOUR CHURCH a narrow focus on the business administration side of church life. The articles are brief, factual, bare bones. We would never be accused of being too literary or artsy. Instead, we want to be a bottom-line, here's-the-facts kind of magazine. How-to articles form our editorial backbone—articles coming from real life, not just theory, from experience, not just what ought to be.

Whatever YOUR CHURCH prints needs to be information church leaders can put right to work. Brief examples help, as do checklists, points to consider, rules of thumb, short illustrations, and key ideas.

Our Writing Style

Content makes an article worthwhile; style makes it readable and interesting. While our businesslike style is hardly lyrical, it has to be clear, compelling, and concise. We must get the most use out of every column inch we devote to editorial copy.

We place many "road signs" in the text to give the reader the ability to scan and spot the essential information. Road signs are words such as: Example, Reason, Key, First Step, Next, Problem, Advice, Impact, Opportunity, and Options. Rather than writing "The reason for this is ...", we write "Reason: ..."

We know that many pastors place administration near the bottom of their interest lists. Therefore, YOUR CHURCH must bend over backwards to provide lucid and compelling writing that draws readers into the subject matter. We want to produce such a well-written and useful magazine that readers will approach it with a sense of anticipation, considering it indispensable.

Have you read *The Elements of Style* by Strunk and White? We recommend this widely read little paperback as a guide for style.

• Use action verbs. Forms of the verb "to be"—is, was, were, etc.—make for dead writing. In every possible case, choose forceful verbs.

• Use short sentences whenever possible. Variety of length, of course, contributes to good style, but writers err more often with too many long sentences than short ones.

• Always define your jargon. Some technical terms simply have to be used, but assume your reader isn't among the initiated. Give the definition to necessary but obscure words. And avoid long words whenever possible.

Assume your reader bores easily. Keep asking yourself, "What grabs my attention? An illustration? A fresh insight? A well-turned phrase? A solution to a difficult problem?" Keep the reader with you by introducing a constant stream of interesting material.

After writing your manuscript, go through it and see how many action verbs you have. Mark each noun you can taste, hear, see, smell, or feel. Good writers fill their prose with objects you can see in your mind's eye. Be as specific as possible. For instance, "crashing cymbal" is better than "a loud noise" for conjuring up an image.

Rewording and simplifying sentences always improves copy. Dig for fresh ideas and then polish your work. Find all unnecessary words and slash them out. Scores of phrases and words just sit there without contributing force to the sentence. The discipline of our kind of writing demands a readable, commanding, and fluent style.

YOUR CHURCH solicits most of its manuscripts. It does, however, receive unsolicited manuscripts. The full name, address, and phone number of the author should appear on the first page of the manuscript, with the last name appearing near the page number on each succeeding page. We prefer material on floppy disk in ASCII format, but please enclose an accompanying printout.

Contact Information:
465 Gundersen Drive
Carol Stream, IL 60188
(708) 260-6200 • FAX: (708) 260-0114

Your Health

Dear Health Writer:

YOUR HEALTH magazine invites professional health and medical writers to contribute both original and previously published material for consideration. Our editorial focus: consumer-oriented general health, fitness and medical stories and service articles (how-to's), targeting any adult age group, but with am emphasis on women over 35. We've recently added more articles on natural health and healing.

The most important requirement in writing for YOUR HEALTH is to provide well-researched stories. Writers must include up-to-date statistics, cite from the latest studies conducted at respected research institutions and include quotes from recognized experts in the filed both pro and con.

Examples of department topics are: Natural health and Healing, Skin, Nutrition, Dieting, Fitness, In The Kitchen (cooking & recipes), Behavior, Controversies, Women's Health, Men's Health, Trends, Environment, New Products, Consumer Watch, Aging, Lifestyle,

Parenting, First Person (personal experience with a health problem and its solution – must include well-researched advice from experts), Diseases (Heart Disease, Cancer, Diabetes, Arthritis, etc.), Safety . . . the list is endless.

Articles for departments should be 1,000-1,500 words; longer feature articles, up to 2,500 words. If available, black and white glossy photos or color transparencies are appreciated.

Payment is upon publication and depends on length of article and whether photos are included. Please keep in mind that even though we are nationally distributed, our circulation is about 50,000.

Sincerely,
Susan Gregg, Editor

Contact Information:
5401 N.W. Broken Sound Boulevard
Boca Raton, FL 33487
(407) 997-7733 • FAX: (407) 997-9210

Section Two
Book Publishers

Alyson Publications, Inc.

We are happy to consider new book manuscripts for possible publication. Please note the following before submitting material:

INQUIRY: Please send a one-page synopsis before submitting a complete manuscript. This will save you the effort and expense of sending the whole manuscript if it seems clearly not suitable for us.

CONTENT: We publish both fiction and nonfiction (but not poetry) aimed at a gay and/or lesbian audience. We do not have any prescribed formulas regarding length, content, etc. Nonfiction should be written in a popular (i.e., non-academic) style.

MANUSCRIPT: Manuscripts should be accompanied by the synopsis.

DECISION-TIME: We try to give serious consideration to each manuscript we receive. Our goal is to get a decision to you within three to twelve weeks of receiving your manuscript. If you cannot wait this long, please say so in the letter accompanying the manuscript.

Contact information:
Julie K. Trevelyan, Editorial Assistant
6922 Hollywood Boulevard, Suite 1000
Los Angeles, CA 90028
(213) 871-1225 • FAX: (213) 467-6805

Avalon Books

(Please refer to Thomas Bouregy & Company, Inc.)

Avery Publishing Group

Avery is a publisher of nonfiction adult oriented books. We do not publish fiction, poetry or children's books.

When submitting a manuscript proposal for the first time, we ask that you send us the following items:

- Cover letter explaining the type of book you intend to write, its market, the need for such a book, and some background about yourself.
- Table of contents outlining what material will be covered in your book.
- Preface which explains your overall approach.

We ask that you not send us a manuscript without a specific request from us. If you send a manuscript without a request, we are, in fact, less likely to review your work.

Contact information
Managing Editor
120 Old Broadway
Garden City Park, NY 11040
(516) 741-2155 • FAX: (516) 742-1892

Avon Books
The Hearst Book Group

BOOKS FOR YOUNG READERS

AVON FLARE

Books for young adults. For ages 12 and up. Manuscript length should run between 35,000 and 45,000 words. General fiction (coming of age, family, peer stories), historical fiction, horror, suspense. Romance can be a plot element, but we are not interested in formula romance. No poetry, story collections, science fiction/fantasy, or nonfiction.

CAMELOT

Books for middle readers. For ages 8-12. Manuscript length should run between 20,000 and 35,000 words. General fiction (family, peer, school related stories), historical fiction, mystery/adventure, humor. Limited interest in science fiction/fantasy, or nonfiction.

PLEASE NOTE: WE DO NOT PUBLISH PICTURE BOOKS, POETRY OR SHORT STORIES.

We prefer to see complete manuscripts or sample chapters plus an outline. We are interested in writing style as well as plot, so it is difficult for us to evaluate from a query letter.

For a copy of our catalogue, please send an 8x11 SASE

Contact information:
BOOKS FOR YOUNG READERS or AVON BOOKS
1350 Avenue of the Americas
New York, NY 10019
(212) 261-6800 • FAX: (212) 261-6895

Baen Books

Dear Author:

We publish only science fiction and fantasy. Writers familiar with what we have published in the past will know what sort of material we are most likely to publish in the future: powerful plots with solid scientific and philosophical underpinnings are the sine qua non for consideration for science fiction submissions. As for fantasy, any magical system must be both rigorously coherent and integral to the plot, and overall the work must at least strive for originality.

Those manuscripts which survive the “first cut” as outlined above are then judged primarily on plot and characterization. Style: Simple is generally better; in our opinion good style, like good breeding, never calls attention to itself.

Payment rates: very competitive.

Preferred length: 80,000 - 110,000 words.

Standard manuscript format only, including 1 ½" margins on all four sides of the page. We will consider photocopies if they are dark and clear. Letter quality dot matrix is acceptable. Manuscripts that are difficult to read probably won’t be.

Submission procedures: Query letters are not necessary. We prefer to see complete manuscripts accompanied by a synopsis. We prefer not to see simultaneous submissions. We do not accept electronic submissions.

Reporting time: usually within 90 days.
Thank you for thinking of Baen Books.

Contact information:
The Editors
P.O. Box 1403
Riverdale, NY 10471
(718) 548-3100 • FAX: (718) 548-3102

Baker Book House Co.
Baker, Revell, and Chosen Books

Preparing a Proposal

Book proposals are always welcomed by the editors of Baker, Revell, and Chosen Books. Indeed, we editors insist on seeing a proposal before examining a manuscript. So whether you wish to submit an idea for a manuscript or a finished manuscript, you must supply us first with a proposal.

There are good reasons for you to develop a proposal before writing most of the manuscript. This enables you to obtain from us guidelines for the project, which increases the likelihood that we will accept it for publication.

Should your book be intended, not for a more general Christian readership, but more specifically for pastors and others in Christian ministry, please request the brochure "Preparing a Proposal: Professional Books" and follow its guidelines, not those that follow in this brochure. Should your book be designed as a text for use in Christian colleges or evangelical seminaries, ask for the brochure "Preparing a Proposal: Academic Books."

Proposals for "trade books" consist of answers to several key questions, along with some supporting materials. First some questions for you to answer briefly.

Questions

1. What has motivated you to pursue this project?
2. What primary point(s) do you seek to make in this work?
3. For what specific audience(s) are you writing?
4. Have you presented this material in any other media or public forums? If so, describe the medium or forum and characterize audience response.
5. What additional evidence do you have that a readership exists for this material in book form?
6. If you have not already made this clear, explain the impact you want this book to have on the reader.
7. What title (and subtitle) do you now favor for this book? (Include several possibilities if no one title has yet risen to the top.)
8. What evangelical books now in print would your book compete with? What uniqueness and strengths set your book apart from the competition? If no competition exists, does this say anything, positive or negative, about the market for your book?
9. Is the manuscript complete? If not, when do you plan to finish it?

Other Material

1. An outline of the book (the table of contents), with paragraph summaries or brief outlines of each chapter.
2. An estimate of the length of each chapter and of the entire work (see table 1 below). Most trade books have a total of 125-225 printed pages.

3. An explanation of the kinds and quantity of illustrative material (such as photographs, line drawings, maps, charts, and tables) that need to be included. If you plan to provide any original artwork, please include a sample or two.

4. Preferably one or two chapters. This chapter should be drawn from the part of your book that represents its most important contribution. At least one sample chapter is essential if this is your first book.

5. Your resumé, which should include, in addition to standard items, the following:

a) a complete bibliography of your published articles and books,

b) a description of any public speaking that you do on a reasonably regular basis,

c) your ecclesiastical connections, including any parachurch organizations in which you have been active, and

d) any information that will demonstrate your qualifications to write the proposed volume.

6. For a first-time author: the names of any published writers with whom you are personally acquainted. You might want to include a letter of recommendation from one of them.

Pointers

Put your proposal in the most refined form you can. We will judge your ability to craft a well-written manuscript by the quality of your proposal.

If you prepare your proposal on a word-processor, do not send the proposal in electronic form; supply hard-copy only.

We naturally prefer that you submit your proposal to our company first. If you choose to submit it simultaneously to other publishers as well, we ask only that you say as much in your cover letter.

After evaluating your proposal, we will: (1) advise you to send it elsewhere, (2) suggest ways to revise it, (3) encourage you to proceed with the project, or (4) offer you a contract (if you are an experienced author and if we are totally committed to your book-idea.)

When we encourage you to complete the manuscript but offer no contract (option 3), this means that we accept the basic concept for your book as a valid one, find evidence in the proposal that you can write an acceptable manuscript, and will very likely publish the completed manuscript if it meets our standards.

Estimating Length

When estimating the length of a project, use table 1. This table is based on these specifications: a typewritten page of 65 characters per line (on average) and 26 lines per page; and a typeset page of 11-point type, 23 picas per line, and 37 lines per page. As you count characters, include the notes and ignore the fact that, when typeset, they will appear in smaller type than regular text.

Table 1	Characters	Words	Typed Pages	Printed Pages
	180,000	30,000	107	104
	240,000	40,000	142	139
	300,000	50,000	178	174
	360,000	60,000	213	208
	420,000	70,000	248	243

Contact information:

Ms. Jane Schrier, Assistant to Director of Publications
Baker Books or Fleming H. Revell
P.O. Box 6287
Grand Rapids, MI 49516-6287
or Chosen Books
3985 Bradwater Street
Fairfax, VA 22031

Barbour & Company, Inc.

Barbour Books

The Basics: All manuscripts considered for Barbour Books should present overall a conservative, evangelical Christian world view. (Editor's Note: See also Heartsong Presents page 447) Manuscripts that are not grounded as such will be returned to the author(s).

Specifics: Barbour Books, a bargain book publisher, aims for the broadest segment of the Christian evangelical market and not one particular audience. Therefore rigorous Bible studies or theological works are shunned, while lighter subject matter with great mass appeal may be accepted.

Things To Consider: The need for a personal commitment to and relationship with Jesus Christ should be readily apparent. Our readers consider themselves born again Christians and rely on Barbour Books to confirm their values and beliefs.

Things To Avoid: Avoid such controversial topics as the following, should they present themselves in the story line:

1. Spirit baptism (and time of, at conversion vs. second experience of grace)
2. Water baptism (meaning of and time of, children or adults)
3. Gifts of the Spirit (e.g., are tongues still around?)
4. End times (setting dates)
5. Lord's Supper (ordinance vs. sacrament)
6. Women's ordination
7. Christian perfection
8. Transferring qualities of Jesus—or passages in the Bible that refer to Jesus—to heroes in books. This also applies to Mary, Jesus' earthly mother.

Avoid strictly any language that could be considered foul and use or mention of alcohol or drugs. Euphemisms such as heck, darn, and so on should not be used. To many of our readers these words are substitutes for curses. Although the main characters should be Christians, they need not be saints. Their actions should be consistent with Christian teaching.

One Final Point: One particular biblical message should be threaded throughout if possible. This message can be presented from many different characters, through symbols, and so on.

To Submit: If you believe you have a manuscript that would fit Barbour Books guidelines, please send us a cover letter in which you introduce yourself and your writing/publishing experience and a typewritten summary of the story and three to four randomly selected chapters. All inquiries and materials should be sent to the following:

Contact information:
General: Susan Johnson, Managing Editor
Inspirational Romance: Becky Germany, Managing Editor
P.O. Box 719
Uhrichsville, OH 44683
(614) 922 6045

Barron's Educational Series, Inc.

1) For initial consideration of your project a brief outline is acceptable. The outline should include a table of contents or headings for the material that you plan to include; the market you are trying to reach with the book (i.e., children, ages 2-4, secondary school teachers, etc.); and a brief summary of the project.

2) Manuscripts for children's story books should be sent in their entirety.

3) It is not necessary to submit illustrations for a children's story book to be considered for publication.

4) If you will be providing the illustrations please include a sample.

5) When submitting a work of nonfiction please include a Table of Contents, two sample chapters, an overview of the project and author's credentials.

6) We will contact you if additional information or material is needed in order to properly evaluate your project. DO NOT SEND ADDITIONAL MATERIAL UNLESS SPECIFICALLY REQUESTED TO DO SO! IT WILL BE DISCARDED!

7) Complete evaluation of your project may take as long as ten months. We accept simultaneous submissions.

8) If you would like a catalog please submit a 9"x12" SASE

9) Due to the large number of submissions we receive we can no longer track the status of individual projects.

Thank you for your adherence to the above guidelines.

Contact information:
Ms. Grace Freedson, Managing Editor/Director of Acquisitions
250 Wireless Boulevard
Hauppauge, NY 11788-3917
(516) 434-3311 • FAX: (516) 434-3723

Baywood Publishing Company, Incorporated

Baywood publishing invites authors to forward proposals for publications in counseling, death & bereavement, psychology, and gerontology, health policy, and technical communication. We welcome submissions in these areas from authors who desire to publish with a scholarly professional press. These guidelines are provided to expedite the submission process.

The Proposal Package

1. *Cover letter* introducing yourself, the title of your proposed publication, a concise description of the purpose and scope of the book, and an indication of whom the audience will be.

2. *Curriculum vita(e)* for each author(s)/editor(s) involved. This should include: Names, titles, addresses, and phone/fax numbers.

3. *List of contributors*, if applicable. Please indicate the total number of contributors and provide their names, titles, addresses, and phone/fax numbers.

4. *Table of Contents*, to include chapter titles and paragraphs describing those chapters.

5. *Introduction or Preface*, and at least one chapter for the proposed publication.

6. *The primary specialty* and any areas of subspecialization for the author/editor.

7. *Status* of the manuscript: Is it in the idea stage? Is it less than 50% complete? More than 50% complete? Has any of the material been previously published?

8. *Probable date* that the manuscript will be completed.

9. *Mechanical dimensions* including: number of typed double-spaced pages; number of charts; number of tables.

10. *Potential markets.* Describe the primary and any secondary professional and/or student markets for which the book is intended and the level of readership at which it is aimed.

11. *Timeliness.* Please try to estimate how long, in years, the content of the book will remain current and useful.

12. *List of competing titles.* Please include the author, title, publisher, year, pages, price of each competing publication.

13. *Uniqueness.* How does this book differ from competing titles? List any special or unique features your work contains.

Contact information:
Stuart Cohen, Managing Editor
26 Austin Avenue
P.O. Box 337
Amityville, NY 11701
(516) 691-1270 • FAX: (516) 691-1770
E-mail: baywood@baywood.com Web site: http://baywood.com

Beacon Hill Press of Kansas City

Thanks for your interest in Beacon Hill Press of Kansas City. Below are answers to commonly asked questions about our submission and publication requirements.

Does Beacon Hill Press of Kansas City accept freelance material?

Beacon Hill Press will consider every unsolicited submission. Because we are a denominational publisher of holiness literature, our books reflect an evangelical Wesleyan in accord with the Church of the Nazarene. We seek practical as well as serious treatments of issues of faith consistent with the Wesleyan tradition. We publish Christian fiction, but no juvenile fiction, books of poetry, or children's books.

What should I include in my proposal?

The query or cover letter should answer four important questions:

- What is your subject matter and approach? (two or three specific paragraphs are usually sufficient.)
- For whom is it written? (It is helpful to have an idea of the market niche you envision.)
- What distinguishes your material from what is currently available on the subject? (It is wise to check your local Christian bookstore.)
- What are your qualifications to write on this subject? (Please include a vita.)

In what form should I submit my proposal In

Electronic or hard copy submissions are acceptable. We prefer a 3.5" disk with the software clearly marked on the label. (A 5.25 inch disk is also workable.)

When can I expect an answer?

We try to update you on the status of your submission within eight weeks of its arrival. If your submission passes the initial screening, the complete reviewing process often takes several months as your manuscript is circulated for further evaluation.

What are the financial arrangements if Beacon Hill publishes my manuscript?

Most of our publishing is on a royalty basis: the author receives a percentage of the net receipts. In some instances authors are paid a flat fee for their work. We publish and market the book at our expense for as long as its sales warrant keeping it in print. One-time fees for permissions and rights to photographs are the author's responsibility. These arrangements are detailed in the legal contract we make with the author.

Can I obtain editorial advice from you about my manuscript?

The volume of manuscripts we receive makes it impossible for us to report on unpublished manuscripts. Our evaluation takes into account the amount of editing required.

We trust this information is helpful as you seek the right publisher for your manuscript. If you require additional information, do not hesitate to contact us. Thank you for your confidence in Beacon Hill Press of Kansas City.

Contact information:
Shona Fisher, Editorial Coordinator
6401 The Paseo
Kansas City, MO 64131
(816) 333-7000

Beacon Press

Thank you for your inquiry. Beacon Press is a non-profit publisher of general and scholarly nonfiction. We publish 50 to 60 titles a year, and specialize in women's studies; religion; Asian-American, African-American, Native American and Jewish studies; gay and lesbian issues; philosophy; environmental concerns; and current affairs. We are not currently considering original fiction, poetry, children's literature, inspirational literature, memoirs, or books of aphorisms or personal philosophy.

We are happy to consider nonfiction manuscripts and suggest that you submit a brief proposal describing the planned project, a table of contents, two sample chapters, and a copy of your curriculum vitae to the attention of the editorial department. You should receive a response within six to eight weeks of submitting the proposal.

Please also understand that due to the small size of our editorial staff and the large number of submissions we receive, we are unable to comment in detail on the manuscripts we decline.

Again, thank you for your interest in Beacon. We look forward to hearing from you.

Contact information:
Editorial Department
25 Beacon Street
Boston, MA 02108-2892
(617) 742-2110 • FAX: (617) 723-3097/742-2290

Blue Dolphin
Publishing, Inc.
FINE BOOKS FOR ALL AGES

Blue Dolphin Publishing

FROM THE PUBLISHER

Dear Friends,

Greetings to all of you who read and support our publications. Blue Dolphin Publishing is now ten years old, an outgrowth of Blue Dolphin Press, a printing company which we began in 1976.

Many people ask, "Why 'Blue Dolphin'?" At first, we were protesting dolphins being caught in tuna nets. We also knew that the first printer in Italy, Aldus, used a dolphin coiled around an anchor for his logo, and that from early days, dolphins were known as "saviors" by rescuing drowning mariners in the Mediterranean. In addition, dolphins roam all the oceans of the world and represent for us, symbolically, a melding of the world's cultures.

When we began publishing, we wanted to produce books that would help ourselves and other people delve more deeply into who we are and what our life is for. Over the last ten years we have published some seventy books . . . but to be fair, we always say, "We don't publish books; we publish *authors*"—authors who are living, growing, and changing. Publishers are "purveyors of messages," and each author represents for us the privilege of getting to know a new friend, a special and exciting person who has taught us valuable lessons—and who may open new doorways for *you*.

Trying to be in step with the collective consciousness for our reading public and the next turn of the evolutionary spiral is a big challenge! We feel many of our authors have important messages for our entire society. Corbin Harney (*The way It Is*), for example, has been working internationally to stop nuclear testing and its effects. Dr. Thomas *Collins (Comprehensive Health Care for Everyone)* has presented a revolutionary approach to modern health care that will benefit everyone. And Master Cheng Yen (*Master of Love and Mercy*)—the "Mother Teresa of Asia"—has been nominated for a Nobel Peace Prize. These are serious authors with important and compelling messages, and we feel *everyone* should be aware of what they are saying and contributing to our well-being.

As the many letters to our authors reveal, Blue Dolphin books and tapes really do inspire and help people. We appreciate your support and encouragement and welcome your suggestions.

We have many exciting New Releases sprinkled throughout [our] catalog which complement and expand some of our earlier titles. In this day of multimedia adventures, may we all still retain the privacy and coziness of settling in with a good book!

Wishing you all Peace, Health, and Happiness,

Paul and Nancy Clemens

Manuscript Submission Guidelines

Because we receive nearly 400 book submissions and queries per month, we ask you to review our statement of purpose [reproduced above] to determine if your submission is suitable to our publishing efforts. To help us review your manuscript, please include the following information:

Cover Letter: Include your submission title, total number of double-spaced pages, and your reason for writing the book.

Synopsis: (one page) Discuss the main topics, viewpoints, overall organization, and conclusions.

Table of Contents: Chapter by chapter—annotated outlines of each chapter are optional.

Sample chapters: Approximately 50 to 100 pages, or the entire manuscript.

Author resume: (one page) Professional and personal credentials—photo optional. Include your ideas about how to market your manuscript.

Time: Allow at least 3-6 months for a reply.

Please . . . no phone calls. Simultaneous submissions to other publishers are acceptable.

All of our best wishes to you.

Contact information:

Nonfiction: Paul Clemens, Publisher

Self-Help: Chris Comins, Marketing Director

Fiction: Lisa Horrell, Promotions Manager

P.O. Box 8

Nevada City, CA 95959

(916) 265-6925 • FAX: (916) 265-0787

Bonus Books, Inc.

We publish primarily nonfiction trade books.

If you would like to submit a manuscript or proposal for our review, please follow these guidelines:

1. If you are submitting a proposal, please include an outline or summary of your book and a few sample chapters.
2. Allow six to eight weeks for a response.

Thank you for the opportunity to consider your work.

Contact information:
Assistant Editor
160 East Illinois Street
Chicago, IL 60611
(312) 467-0580

Brassey's, Inc.

Leading Publishers in National & International Affairs, Military History, Foreign Affairs & Defense

Please note that our editorial advisory board prefers to review proposals first before seeing entire manuscripts. A proposal should consist of a half-page synopsis, a one- or two-page outline that provides an idea of the book's structure, one or two sample chapters that provide an idea of the book's style and the author's writing ability, photocopies of representative photos (if any), a biographical sketch of the author (including titles of previously published works), and the total word count. Evaluation normally takes two to six weeks. At that point the board would decide whether to ask for the entire manuscript or decline.

Also, you should know that our policy is no longer to evaluate fiction by unpublished authors.

We look forward to seeing your proposal on a topic in our subject areas. Thanks for your interest in Brassey's.

EDITOR'S NOTE: Brassey's includes a lengthy manuscript preparation and style guide along with the general guidelines shown above. We have not included it for space reasons, and also because it deals with submission procedures and form factor requirements for *final submissions*. Should you submit a proposal to Brassey's, request a copy of their MANUSCRIPT PREPARATION AND STYLE GUIDE. You will need it if your proposal results in your being asked to submit a manuscript.

Contact information:
Don McKeon, Editorial Director
1313 Dolly Madison Boulevard, Suite 401
McLean, VA 22101
(703) 442-4545

Bucknell University Press

Bucknell University Press publishes scholarly books in the humanities and social sciences for a scholarly audience. Our primary criteria are the originality and importance of the scholarship and the clarity of its presentation.

Please do not send us your manuscript unless we have asked for it. Send us a proposal explaining clearly what you have done. With it, send us a copy of your current *curriculum vitae*. We will then respond to your proposal.

We expect that each scholarly work we publish will have an appropriate scholarly bibliography. We expect it to be included with the manuscript at the time of submission.

Associated University Presses, our publishers, use the latest edition of the University of Chicago ***Manual of Style*** in copyediting all manuscripts. *Manuscripts may be submitted to us in any recognized format, but once we have accepted a manuscript its author or editor must make whatever changes in it may be necessary to bring it into conformity with the* **Manual of Style.**

All manuscripts submitted to **Bucknell University Press** must be typewritten or printed by laser printer or other printer producing text of similar quality; we will accept clear photocopies of such originals. **We will not print out manuscripts from diskettes.**

Contact information:
Mills F. Edgerton, Jr., Director
Bucknell University Press
Lewisburg, PA 17837
(717) 524-3674

Carolrhoda Books, Inc.

Carolrhoda Books publishes high-quality fiction and nonfiction for children ages 4 to 12. We specialize in **nonfiction:** biographies, photo essays, nature and science books, beginning readers, and books published in series. We look for nonfiction that is interesting and entertaining as well as informative.

We publish only a few **picture books** each year. We like to see unique, honest stories that stay away from preachy moralizing, unoriginal plots, religious themes, and anthropomorphic antagonists. We also publish some **fiction** for ages 7 to 10 and some **historical fiction** for ages 8 to 12.

In both fiction and nonfiction, we are especially interested in new ideas and fresh topics. We like to see multicultural themes. Make sure your **writing avoids racial and sexual stereotypes. We do not publish** alphabet books, textbooks, workbooks, songbooks, puzzles, plays, or religious material. The best way to familiarize yourself with our list is to study our catalog or find our books in the library. For a **catalog**, send a self-addressed 9x12 envelope with three first class stamps.

We prefer to see a completed manuscript, but we will accept an outline and sample chapters for longer biographies or fiction. Please include a cover letter outlining your project and listing any previous publications.

You do not need to send art with your submission as we generally commission our own artists, but if you are sending art samples, **do not send originals**.

We will notify you of our decision regarding your manuscript at the earliest possible time. Our response time is generally three months. Please do not expect a personal response from an editor, as time does not permit this.

Thank you for your interest in Carolrhoda Books. We'll look forward to hearing from you.

Contact information:
Rebecca Poole, Submissions Editor
241 1st Avenue North
Minneapolis, MN 55401
(612) 332-3344

Chatelaine Press

Chatelaine Press primarily publishes works in the field of public administration; this is where we have already built up a list of contacts and know the market. In addition, we also publish education books for the college market, but this is a smaller facet of our business. Guidelines for submission:

- MS can be in any media
- Includes disk, FTP [Author Note: Internet; see address below], or hard copy.
- Disk can be either Mac, PC, or iomega zip drive
- Author should keep in mind that MS should be directed toward a college-level audience, though the MS will not necessarily be marketed solely toward college students.

We will consider any manuscript related to public administration. A sample of the PA books we have published in the past have dealt with the decision-making process concerning the debate over DNA research in the 70's, a three part "Best Of " series from a PA journal, works on organizational theory, the proceedings of a citizen and government representative discussion on improving the operations of government at all levels, and a theoretical work on the American character. In education, our books have dealt with American educational history and the application of personality theory (Myers-Briggs) to educational practice.

Contact information:
Sean Forbes, Senior Editor
6454 Honey Tree Court
Burke, VA 22015-3901
(703) 569-2062
Web site: http://www.chatpress.com

Chicago Plays, Inc.

To be considered for representation by Chicago Plays, original work must meet the following criteria:

- Submissions must have received a professional production in the Chicago area. Professional production is defined as:

- Production reviewed by one or more daily newspapers.
- Production received more than twenty-four performances within a three month period.
- Royalties or like compensation were paid to the playwright.
- Submissions should have a proof of, or notice of application for copyright.
- Manuscripts should be accompanied by publicity material, reviews, programs, etc.
- Manuscripts should be typed in a standard script format in a clear, legible fashion. Manuscripts should be properly bound (no paper clips). Always include your name, address, and telephone number on the title page.
- Of course, there are always exceptions to the rules.

Contact information:
Jill Murray, President
2632 North Lincoln
Chicago, IL 60614
(312) 348-4658 • FAX: (312) 348-5561

Coffee House Press

Who Coffee House Press Publishes

Coffee House Press (CHP) publishes emerging and mid-career authors. All CHP authors have had works published in literary magazines or other publications. A résumé including a list of prior publications can strengthen your submission. We regard it as an important part of our mission to present first novels. Recent titles have included Through the Arc of the Rain Forest by Karen Tei Yamashita, A place Where the Sea Remembers by Sandra Benítez, and Losing Absalom by Alexs Pate. We look forward to new visions by new writers.

What Coffee House Press Publishes

Coffee House Press publishes literary novels, full-length short story collections, poetry, and essays. CHP does not accept submissions for our anthologies. CHP also does not publish genre fiction such as mysteries, Gothic romances, Westerns, science fiction, or books for children.

Since Coffee House press produces relatively few titles each year, CHP books reflect the individual tastes of its small staff. CHP looks for writing that instructs, inspires, and/or entertains the reader, and that does so with a unique voice. CHP currently publishes 12 to 15 trade titles annually, eight of which are fiction.

Coffee House press highly recommends that you familiarize yourself with CHP books to see if your work and CHP's list are compatible. Most independent bookstores and many libraries carry our titles.

How to submit a manuscript

Coffee House Press does not accept simultaneous submissions, fax queries, or electronic/disk submission. We prefer to see samples (20-30 pages) with outlines before reviewing entire manuscripts. Our response time on samples is 6-8 weeks. The review process for full length manuscripts currently takes 6-8 months. Manuscripts that seem appropriate for CHP are given several careful readings, and the final decision to publish rests with CHP's publisher, Allan Kornblum. We empathize with your anticipation and appreciate your patience when submitting your manuscript. Phone calls or letters of inquiry will not hasten the process.

Contact information:
Christopher Fischbach
27 North 4th Street, Suite 400
Minneapolis, MN 55401
(612) 338-0125 • FAX: (612) 338-4004

Cornell Maritime Press, Inc.

Thank you for thinking of us as a prospective publisher. In response to your request for our submission procedures or manuscript guidelines, we would like you to know something about our publishing venue.

The topic of your book must fall within our current areas of interest. As specialized publishers, we undertake only three kinds of projects: pragmatic works for the merchant marine, a few books for serious boaters (also of a practical nature), and regional works mostly confined to Maryland, the Delmarva Peninsula, and the Chesapeake Bay. Our very particular publishing focus excludes personal narratives, adult fiction, and poetry.

We publish only two children's books per year, and they also must have a regional element.

Submission Procedure

I. A proposal

To inquire about our possible interest in a work that has not yet been written, we would like you to send us:

a) A proposal letter that describes the work in prospect. This proposal should include the answers to such questions as:

(1) What is the book about?

(2) Who is its audience?

(3) How large is the audience?

(4) In what ways are you qualified to write such a work? What are your "credentials"?

(5) How does the proposed work differ from other books, if any, that are already available?

(6) How extensive a work is contemplated? How many pages of manuscript?

(7) What additional elements are to be included, such as illustrations (drawings, photographs, or other), appendices, bibliography, index, and so forth?

(8) What sort of schedule have you in mind? When might the manuscript be ready for submission?

b) An outline or a proposed table of contents, in as much detail as possible, to indicate the breadth and depth of the work.

c) A sample chapter or two, or a previously written piece of comparable character. This is to reveal, of course, the basic qualities of your written work.

In this regard, please be sure that the sample you submit is something with which you are comfortable. Do not send something that is incomplete, needs "polishing," or is not, in your view, putting your best foot forward. It need not be perfectly typed, but it should be completely legible. (Please note the instructions below that describe the form submissions should take.)

II. A manuscript

In general it is preferred that you first write a descriptive letter, giving us a chance to confirm that your manuscript is one that is appropriate to our list and that we would like to consider for publication. We might choose to decline the opportunity to consider a given manuscript at a particular time for any one of a number of reasons. We might, for example, have a manuscript on the same topic already under way, or the work might be fiction (which we don not publish at all), or it could be in a field that falls outside our publishing purview. Writing a letter first could save you the trouble and expense of an inappropriate submission.

III. The form that submissions should take

The pages should be consecutively numbered, but need not be bound or fastened in any way.

Word-processed copy is acceptable, of course, but we would prefer near-letter-quality. Photocopies are acceptable also.

It is best not to send unique documents. In the preliminary stages, even relatively rough copies or photocopies of photographs or sketches will convey your intention quite adequately.

Contact information:
Charlotte Kurst, Managing Editor
P.O. Box 456
Centreville, MD 21617
(410) 758-1075

DAW Books, Inc.
Publishers of Science Fiction, Fantasy and Horror
Since 1971

Dear Writer:

Thank you for your inquiry concerning our requirements. We hope the following information will answer your questions.

We publish science fiction and fantasy novels. We do not want short stories, short story collections, novellas, or poetry. The average length of the novels we publish varies but is almost never less than 60,000 words. (To estimate the length of your manuscript, you may want to use the technique explained later in this letter.)

Please number your pages consecutively, and put the title of your novel at the top of each page.

Very important: Please type your name, address and phone number on the upper right hand corner of the first page of your manuscript. Right under this, please put the length of your manuscript in number of words.

We publish first novels if they are of professional quality. A literary agent is not required for submission. We will not consider manuscripts that are currently on submission to another publisher.

It may require up to three months or more for our editors to review a submission and come to a decision.

It is not necessary for you to register or copyright your work before publication—it is protected by law as long as it has not been published. When published, we will copyright the book in the author's name and register that copyright with the Library of Congress.

ADDITIONAL INFORMATION FOR NEW WRITERS:
HOW TO GET THE WORD COUNT OF A MANUSCRIPT

1. Count the words in 10 lines and divide the total number of words by 10.
2. Count the lines on an average page.
3. Multiply the total number of lines for the sample full page by the approximate word count for one line. This gives you the word count for one page.
4. The multiply this total count for the words on one page by the total number of pages in your manuscript. This is the total length of your manuscript in words. Please put this number on page one of your manuscript, right under your name and address.
5. To check the accuracy of your count, please repeat this process twice.

To receive our free catalog, please write to us and we would be happy to send you our DAW catalog.

Cordially, Peter Stampfel

Contact information:
Peter Stampfel, Submission Editor
375 Hudson Street, 3rd Floor
New York, NY 10014-3658
(212) 366-2096 • FAX: (212) 366-2090

Dial Books for Young Readers

Due to the enormously heavy load of unsolicited manuscripts we receive, we are no longer sending out manuscript guidelines, and we no longer read unsolicited manuscripts. If you send in a manuscript with a SASE, it will be returned to you unread. We regret having to draw this line, but unfortunately we do not have the staff to handle the large numbers of submissions we are getting. To find representation for your manuscript, we suggest looking under "Agents" in a large book called THE LITERARY MARKETPLACE, available at most public libraries. An agent can usually tell whether your material is marketable.

Thank you for your interest in Dial, and best of luck with future endeavors.

The Editors

Children's (QUERIES ONLY): Victoria Wells, Assistant Editor
375 Hudson Street
New York, NY 10014

Dorchester Publishing Co., Inc.

THE FOLLOWING ARE THE ONLY CATEGORIES OF ORIGINAL FICTION WE ARE CURRENTLY ACQUIRING.

EDITORIAL GUIDELINES FOR LEISURE BOOKS AND LOVE SPELL.

HISTORICAL ROMANCE – Sensual romances with strong plots and carefully thought-out characterizations. Spunky heroine whose love for the hero never wavers; he's the only one she makes love with, and she's as passionate as he, although he may have to instruct her in the ways of love, since she's almost invariably untouched before she falls in love with the hero. Hero is often arrogant, overbearing; heroine often can't stand him at first, but discovers that beneath the surface lies a tender, virile, and experienced lover. It helps if both the hero and heroine have a sense of humor – a certain amount of wit leavens the heavy-breathing passion. Hero and heroine are separated by emotional conflict or the twists and turns of the plot, but in the end they overcome the barriers between them and live happily ever after.

We don't want a heroine who sleeps around, or a hero who's sadistic, although if there's a villain or villainess, he or she can be as nasty as possible.

Historical background, details of costume, etc., should be accurate; however, we don't want endless descriptions of battles, the political climate of the period, or a treatise on contemporary social history. Our readers are much more interested in the trials, tribulations, and love life of the heroine than in how many men Napoleon lost at the Battle of Waterloo.

Historical Romances should be approximately 120,000 words.

FUTURISTIC ROMANCE – Futuristic Romances contain all the elements of Historical Romances – beautiful heroine, dashing hero, some conflict that separates them, a happy ending, etc. – but they are set in lavish lands in distant worlds.

Avoid science-fiction-type hardware, technology, etc.

Finished manuscripts should be 120,000 words.

TIME-TRAVEL ROMANCE – A modern-day hero or heroine goes back in time and falls in love. Traditional guidelines for Historical Romances apply. The challenge here is to maintain credibility during the transition between the present and the past. The fun is seeing history and another way of life through the eyes of someone from our own time. The conflict and resolution of the romance arise from the fact that the hero and the heroine are from different eras.

Beware of a lot of philosophizing about fate, the meaning of time, and how the past affects the present. No time machines please.

Finished manuscripts should be 120,000 words.

PARANORMAL ROMANCE – Either historical or contemporary romance with magic, witches, ghosts, vampires, etc., as a subsidiary element. Must have a happy ending.

Finished manuscripts should be 120,000 words.

ANGEL ROMANCE – Historical, time-travel or contemporary romance in which a guardian angel lends a hand in bringing the lovers together.

Finished manuscripts should be 120,000 words.

GUIDELINES FOR SUBMITTING MATERIAL TO LEISURE BOOKS AND LOVE SPELL

Please query or submit synopsis and first three chapters only – no complete manuscripts unless specifically requested.

Synopsis, sample chapters (and manuscript if requested) must be typed. Word processors are okay, but letter quality only.

For a free catalogue of Leisure Books, please send a self-addressed, stamped envelope (#10) to the address below.

The best way to learn to write a Leisure or Love Spell romance is
to read a Leisure or Love Spell romance.

Contact information:
Romance: Jennifer Eaton, Editorial Assistant
Westerns, Horror: Don D'Auria, Editor
276 5th Avenue
New York, NY 10001
(212) 725-8811 (212) 532-1054

Dutton Children's Books

GUIDELINES FOR MANUSCRIPT PREPARATION AND EVALUATION

1. A covering letter should accompany all manuscripts, giving titles and publishers of any published children's books – as well as names of magazines and newspapers in which the author's work has appeared. We would also like to know if the manuscript is a simultaneous submission: this will not disqualify submissions.

2. We will read manuscripts printed in high-quality dot matrix format.

3. Picture books may be sent in their entirety. Please send synopsis and only the first three chapters of longer manuscripts.

4. The author's full name and address must appear on the title page of the manuscript, and the last name should be typed on each page.

5. Publishers as a rule select suitable illustrators for manuscripts chosen for publication, unless the author is also the illustrator. We do not require or encourage authors to seek out illustrators for materials they plan to submit.

6. Authors may enclose a self-addressed, stamped business envelope for a reply only.

7. We believe it is best that authors send their materials either via first class mail or fourth class manuscript rate. Costly overnight letters draw no attention to manuscripts.

8. Authors who wish to confirm that we have received their materials should either mail them "return receipt requested" from the post office – or should enclose a self-addressed, stamped post card with the work's title on it – we will stamp the date received on the post card and mail it.

9. Manuscripts are read as soon as possible – usually within eight weeks. Some manu-

scripts may be held for further consideration.

10.Unfortunately, the volume of manuscripts makes it impossible for us to write a critique of every submission. We do, however, give all materials a fair and extensive reading.

11. We discourage the submission of costly or irreplaceable items.

Contact information:
Children's/Young Adults only: Lucia Monfried, Editor-in-Chief
375 Hudson Street
New York, NY 10014
(212) 366-2604 • FAX (212) 366-2011

Eakin Press
An Imprint of Sunbelt Media, Inc.

DEAR AUTHOR:

The categories Eakin Press can consider are as follows:

CHILDREN'S BOOKS

Our top priority is dealing with the history, culture, geography, etc. of Texas and the Southwest.

1) Picture books and chapter books for preschool-grade 3
2) Middle reader books: nonfiction a priority, 25 to 35 thousand words, grades 4-7
3) Young adult fiction and nonfiction, up to 40-50 thousand words

Books which include glossaries and indexes along with a TEACHER'S GUIDE will have great appeal to the school market. One of the most important things to remember is that an active and enthusiastic author can sell more books than any expensive advertising campaign bought by a publisher.

ADULT'S BOOKS

Texana—Nonfiction
Regional Cookbooks
World War II, Military
Mexico and the Southwest
African American Studies
Regional Studies
Sports
We no longer publish adult Fiction.

REQUIREMENTS FOR AUTHORS

Before we can consider either a solicited or unsolicited manuscript, the following format must be followed:

- Queries preferred over unsolicited manuscript.
- Review of manuscript requires from one week to three months. Send card for notification of receipt.
- When submitting a manuscript please include the following: Upfront material, especially the contents, and detailed vita of author with publication credits. A brief synopsis would be helpful. Number all manuscript pages, not just by chapter. Place number of words and age of readership on title page.
- Dot matrix copy accepted if print is dark enough for easy reading.
- If we accept it for publication, we must receive either a copy that can be scanned by

our optical scanner, or a word processor diskette, IBM compatible, in DOS or ASCII file format.

- MANUSCRIPTS MUST INCLUDE:

Title page, table of contents, preface or introduction, manuscript numbered consecutively with all back copy (appendix, bibliography, glossary, etc.) that you propose, category (nonfiction, fiction, cookbook, etc.), age written for (adult, young adult, jr. high, etc.).

- Brief vita of the author.
- If illustrated, include copies of some of the illustrations and brief vita of illustrator.

Sincerely, Edwin M. Eakin

Contact information:
Edwin M. Eakin, President and Acquisitions Editor
P.O. Drawer 90159
Austin, TX 78709-0159
(512) 288-1771 • FAX: (512) 288-1813

ETC Publications

Textbooks/Travel/Education: Our guidelines are the *Chicago Manual of Style* (the book).

Contact information:
Richard W. Holstrop, Ph.D., Publisher
700 East Vereda del Sur
Palm Springs, CA 92262
(619) 325-5352

Farrar, Straus & Giroux
Books For Young Readers

Especially in the case of longer manuscripts, it is a good idea to send a letter of inquiry before submitting the entire manuscript.

Include a cover letter containing any pertinent information about yourself, your writing, your manuscript, etc.

Be sure that your name and address are on the manuscript itself, as well as on the cover letter.

If you have illustrations, please send only two or three samples. Do NOT send original artwork.

The length of the story depends on the age of the reader for whom it is intended; there are no fixed lengths.

Do not expect an editor to give you specific comments. We receive far too many manuscripts for this to be possible.

We suggest familiarizing yourself with various children's publishers to get a sense of which company would be most receptive to your type of work. Most publishers will send their catalogue if you write a letter requesting it and provide a self-addressed, stamped manila envelope for it.

THE LITERARY MARKETPLACE, published by R.R. Bowker, contains a list of all publishers; a list of children's book publishers can be obtained from the Children's Book Council, 568 Broadway, New York, NY 10012.

** Please note: Response time for queries is generally within six weeks; for manuscripts, between one and three months. **

Contact information:
Books For Young Readers: Margaret Ferguson, Editor-in-Chief
19 Union Square West
New York, NY 10003
(212) 741-6900

The Graduate Group

We look for manuscripts that will be helpful to high school, college and graduate students in their attempt to establish themselves in a career, manuscripts which alert students to opportunities and ways to become more effective.

Graduate Group books are distributed exclusively to career planning offices and libraries in the U.S. and abroad.

Authors are provided a liberal royalty.

Contact information:
Mara Whitman, President
P.O. Box 370351
West Hartford, CT 06137-0351
(860) 233-2330

Great Quotations

Great Quotations seeks original material for the following general categories:
- Humor
- Inspiration
- Motivation
- Success
- Romance
- Tributes to mom/dad/grandma/grandpa, etc.

Generally speaking we do not currently publish:
- Children's books and others requiring multi-color illustration on the inside
- Novels and other such fiction
- Manuscripts substantially consisting of poetry
- Highly controversial subject matter

Our books are often purchased on impulse. Therefore the material must be simple, concise, and a light read. They are also physically small and short in length, and comprise five different formats:

Paperback Books	6 x 4 ½	168 pp.	Retail $5.95
Comb Bound Books	4 ½ x 6	78 pp.	Retail $7.95
Mini-Perpetual Calendars	4 x 3 ¾	365 pp.	Retail $6.50
Large Perpetual Calendars	5 ½ x 4 ½	365 pp.	Retail $8.95
Hard Cover Books	4 x 5 ½	64 pp.	Retail $6.50

The ideal submission consists of a cover letter explaining the idea and a few sample pages of text sent to the attention of Acquisitions. We do not respond initially by phone.

We publish new books twice a year, in January and July. Submissions are usually reviewed approximately six months prior to publishing deadlines.

As an aside, we do not hire freelance readers/editors.

Thank you, and Good Luck!

Contact information:
The New Product Team at Great Quotations
Editor
1967 Quincy Court
Glendale Heights, IL 60139
(708) 582-2800

Group Publishing

Group Publishing's mission is: To encourage Christian growth in children, youth and adults. To that end, Group publishes more than 50 titles each year under the following imprints:

Group Books

Resources for Christian education in local churches, including youth and children's ministry. Both single-author royalty books and multiple author compilations assigned on a works-for-hire basis.

Active Bible Curriculum

Four-week, topical curriculum that uses active learning techniques. For junior and senior high and adult classes.

Hands-On Bible Curriculum

Innovative, interactive Bible lessons for preschool through sixth grade. Each quarter includes a Teachers Guide containing reproducible handouts and a Learning Lab.

Writing Curriculum

We're always looking for good writers who know kids, who understand active learning and who have the ability to write lessons that help kids apply the Bible to their lives.

Our editors have set up a trial assignment system to allow potential writers to try their hand at writing curriculum. Check out our various curriculum lines at your local Christian bookstore. Then write and request a trial assignment specifying the age level and curriculum line that interests you. For quick processing, write "Trial Assignment Request" on the outside of the envelope.

In addition to trial assignment, we'll ask you to fill out an author information sheet that gives us a quick overview of your skills, background and writing interests.

You can expect to hear from us within three weeks after you mail in your trial assignment and author information sheet.

Writing Group Books

Group Publishing receives hundreds of book proposals each year. These questions are designed to help you evaluate your own manuscript the way our editors would.

- Is it original? How is your book different from other books on a similar topic?
- Is it practical? Group publishes books that our readers—youth workers, parents, Sunday school teachers and Christian education directors—can pull off the shelf and use immediately.
- Is it need-oriented? People buy books that meet their needs. What needs does your book address? Why would people feel compelled to buy and read it?
- Does it reflect Biblical principles? Group is an interdenominational Christian publisher and everything we produce reflects that perspective.
- Is it clear and easy to use? Does it make its point concisely? Are instructions easy to follow?

Submitting a Book Proposal

If you have a manuscript that meets the criteria just listed, we'd like to know about it. You're welcome to submit a book proposal that includes:

- A one-page description of the book's focus, purpose, audience, and estimated manuscript length.
- A description of what qualifies you to write the book—experience with children or teenagers, education and previous writing experience.
- A sample chapter.
- An outline and synopsis of the remainder of the book.
- Samples of materials you've previously published.

Contact information:
Adult Acquisitions Editor
Youth Acquisitions Editor
Children's Acquisitions Editor
Box 481
Loveland, CO 80539
(970) 669-3836

Hambleton-Hill Publishing, Inc.
Ideals Children's Books

Ideals Children's Books accepts submissions only from agented authors and members of the Society of Children's Books Writers and Illustrators (SCBWI). Authors who have previously published may also submit with a list of writing credits.

Please become familiar with our publications and with the children's market in general before you submit material. We recommend that you look at the following sample titles:

See the Ocean by Estelle Condra; illustrated by Linda Crockett-Blassingame

What Do Animals Do In Winter? by Melvin and Gilda Berger; illustrated by Susan Harrison

Nobiah's Well by Donna Guthrie; illustrated by Rob Roth

ACCEPTED MATERIAL

We publish fiction and nonfiction picture books for preschool and beginning readers. Book lengths are generally 24, 32, or 48 pages and vary from 600-2,000 words. We prefer to see the entire manuscript rather than a query. The reply time is three to six months.

PREPARING YOUR MANUSCRIPT

1. Good photocopies are acceptable.
2. Document all quotes, statistical information, and unusual facts. Provide photocopies of sources, if possible.
3. Simultaneous submissions of book-length manuscripts are acceptable, but please identify them as such in your cover letter.
4. Send manuscripts to the attention of the Copy Editor at the address given below.
5. Please allow 3-6 months for a response.

Payments and copyrights are determined by contract. If your manuscript is accepted, Ideals Children's Books retains the right to edit your material as we deem necessary.

Contact information:
Copy Editor
1501 County Hospital Road
Nashville, TN 37218
(615) 254-2480

Hancock House

Preliminary

Hancock House requires the following for reviewing prospective manuscripts:

A brief (one or two page) synopsis of the proposed manuscript.

An account of any miscellaneous support information, such as the writer's expertise, or any marketing advantage inherent to the manuscript.

A sample of the writer's work, such as a chapter from the work in question.

Enclose your phone number as well as address.

Hancock House Titles

Our titles are predominantly as follows:

Pacific Northwest history and biography, nature guides, and native culture; and international natural history, biological science, and conservation biology including aviculture and animal husbandry.

Manuscript Format

We require both a computer disc, DOS format, and a hard copy.

Contact information:
1431 Harrison Avenue
Blaine, WA 98230
(800) 938-1114 • FAX: (604) 538-2262

Harvest House Publishers

Thank you for your interest in Harvest House Publishers. We are pleased to send you information regarding our publishing objectives and marketing philosophy. Read over this material carefully before you submit your material. If your manuscript is not within our guidelines, then we suggest you contact other publishers for possible use.

Harvest House Publishers-
"Books That Help the Hurts of People"

Harvest House Publishers is a strong evangelical Christian publishing company which is progressive and eager to proclaim the Gospel of Jesus Christ, even though sometimes in only parts of the book. Our goal is to publish books which will encourage the faith of our readers and turn their attention to Jesus Christ as the answer to the problems and questions of life. The foundation of our publishing program is to publish books that "help the hurts of people" and nurture spiritual growth.

Harvest House also publishes study books, Bible-related material, topical, contemporary, and fiction works which have a message to promote the gospel.

We seek exceptional manuscripts which are original, relevant, well-written, and grounded in the teachings of Scripture.

Guidelines for Manuscript Submission

Many publishing houses are quite general in their line of publication, but we have specialty books that "help the hurts of people" and help men, women, and children grow spiritually strong. We publish books with a Biblical emphasis and fiction with a Christian theme or message consistent with Scripture.

Harvest House Book Subjects

Adult fiction	Counseling	Leadership
Biblical study	Cults	Marriage
Bible study aids	Devotions	Prayer
Bible study methods	Discipling	Stewardship
Bible teaching	Ethics	Theology
Christian education	Evangelism	Witnessing
Christian Living	Family life	Women
Contemporary issues		

Harvest House does not publish poetry or short stories, cookbooks, sheet music, theses or dissertations, biographies, autobiographies, sermon collections, or booklets. We have also discontinued our Rhapsody Romance (contemporary romance) line.

Instruction for submitting a manuscript to Harvest House Publishers:

1. Pages should be numbered consecutively throughout the manuscript-not by chapters.

2. All Scripture references in the manuscript must state the translation or paraphrase from which they were taken.

3. Footnotes must be complete with the author, name of the book, publisher, state where published, copyright date, and page number of quote. The author is responsible for obtaining permissions for copyrighted material which goes beyond the guidelines of "fair use."

4. We prefer that a query letter be sent-that is, one page telling what the manuscript is about, why you wrote it, who it is for (projected audience), and what the benefit will be for the reader. The table of contents and the first two or three chapters can also be sent at this stage.

Please include an information sheet about yourself-your spiritual experience, qualifications for writing, educational background, and previously published works, if any.

5. If after receiving this material we are still interested, we will request the remainder of the manuscript for further review.

6. At this point a decision will be made. Once a manuscript satisfies our editorial requirements, we assume all costs of production and distribution. The author receives a royalty on each book sold, the rates being comparable with those paid by other publishers in the industry.

We normally respond within two to eight weeks. While each submission is given individual attention, we are unable to critique manuscripts. If you have not heard from us after eight weeks, feel free to write and inquire about the status of your submission. Send all manuscripts to:

Contact information:
Pat Smith, Manuscript Coordinator
1075 Arrowsmith
Eugene, OR 97487
(541) 343-0123

Hay House, Inc.

Thank you for your request.

Hay House publishes hardcover and trade paperback originals, and trade paperback reprints. Firm averages 12 titles a year. Receives approximately 1,200 submissions/tear. 5% of books are from first-time authors. 25% from unagented writers. Pays standard royalty. Publishes books an average of 8 - 15 months after acceptance. Simultaneous submissions OK. Reports in 4 weeks on queries; 2 months on manuscripts. Free book catalog.

NONFICTION: Self-Help, New Age, Sociology, Philosophy, Psychology, and Astrology. Subjects include social issues, current events, ecology, business and economics, foods and nutrition, education/environment, health/medicine, money/finance, nature, recreation, religion, and women's issues/studies. "Hay House is interested in a variety of subjects as long as they have a positive self-help slant to them. No poetry, quotation books, children's books, or negative concepts that are not conducive to helping/healing ourselves, or our planet. Query, or submit outline/synopsis and sample chapters.

BESTSELLING NONFICTION TITLES: You Can Heal Your Life, by Louise L. Hay (metaphysics/self-help). Losing Your Pounds of Pain, by Doreen Virtue, Ph.D.; As Someone Dies, by Elizabeth A. Johnson.

TIPS: "Our audience is concerned with our planet, the healing properties of love, and self-help principles. Hay House has noticed that our readers are interested in taking more control of their lives. If I were a writer trying to market a book today, I would research the market thoroughly to make sure that there weren't already too many books on the subject I was interested in writing about. Then I would make sure that I had a unique slant on my idea."

Contact information:
Jill Kramer, Editorial Director
P.O. Box 5100
Carlsbad, CA 92018-5100
(619) 431-7695

Heartsong Presents
An Imprint of Barbour Books, Inc.

The Basics: All manuscripts in the Heartsong Presents inspirational line should present a conservative, evangelical Christian world view. Manuscripts that do not reflect this position will be returned to the author(s).

Specifics: Heartsong Presents will consider contemporary and historical manuscripts between 50,000-55,000 words. An historical manuscript, for our purposes, is any time period covering the years prior to and during World War II. A contemporary manuscript would be any time period after or post-World War II, although, strictly speaking, we would probably not consider a manuscript set in the 1950s as contemporary. Since all of the contemporaries we have published thus far have been set in the 1990s, your best bet for acceptance is the present time period.

Things to consider: The underlying theme in all of our romances is the belief that a true and honest faith in God is the foundation for any romantic relationship. Although we are not looking for "sermons in novel form," the importance and need for a personal relationship with Jesus Christ should be apparent.

Our readers are primarily women who consider themselves born again Christians. One of the reasons they choose Heartsong Presents books over other reading material is because our books confirm their values and beliefs. As a writer/editor, you must take this into consideration.

Things to avoid: Avoid the truly controversial. Although conflict is important for any story line, certain matters should be avoided at all costs. Stay away from any language that could be considered foul. Avoid euphemisms like heck or darn. To many of our readers these words are substitutes for curses, and in their minds as bad, or worse. Main characters should be Christians (or Christians by the end of the book) and should act accordingly. They need not be "saints," but their actions should be consistent with Christian teaching.

The hero and heroine should not be divorced. This is acceptable for secondary and non-Christian characters. The idea of divorce and remarriage for a Christian is a problem for most of our readers.

Most of our readers also find a woman as a pastor, or even an assistant pastor, unbiblical. If your heroine is a woman who is a pastor or youth pastor, etc., we will not consider your manuscript.

The use of alcohol is offensive and incompatible with Christian teaching, according to many of our readers. While drinking is unacceptable for the Christian characters, however, for non-Christians this conflict can be explored. In handling drinking in your novel, it is important that the reader understand that this behavior is not acceptable. Exceptions such as may be found in historical novels will be evaluated individually. The same is true for dancing, another activity that is offensive to most of our readers. Dancing in historical novels, however, is not as offensive as it might be in a contemporary novel. In contemporaries it is usually the setting that is more offensive than the dancing, for example, a bar/club.

Avoid controversial doctrinal issues. We will not list these (there are too many); however, if you keep in mind that we are appealing to a broad range of Christian evangelical readers, we believe you will be on the right track.

Physical tension between characters should not be overdone. Do not be overly descriptive when describing how characters feel in a particular romantic moment, for example, kissing, embracing, and so on.

Characters, especially women characters, should be modestly dressed. They should never appear outside their bedrooms in nightgowns, underwear, and other private garments. No matter how innocent some of this may seem to you, we will edit questionable scenes out of manuscripts.

Controversial Items to Steer Clear of:

1. Spirit baptism
2. Water baptism (meaning of)
3. Time of Spirit baptism (at conversion vs. second experience of grace)
4. Time of water baptism (children or adults)
5. Gifts of the Spirit (e.g., are tongues still around?)
6. End times (setting dates)
7. Lord's Supper (ordinance vs. sacrament)
8. Women's ordination
9. Christian perfection
10. Transferring qualities of Jesus—or passages in the Bible that refer to Jesus—to heroes in books. This also applies to Mary, Jesus' earthly mother.

Summary: One particular biblical message or inspirational theme should be threaded throughout if possible. This can be presented from many different characters, through symbols, and so on. The main element of books is the *romance* and to that end characters must be perceived as appealing and capable of finding each other attractive. Conflict within the relationship will draw hero and heroine closer and involve the readers more personally.

Few would doubt the breathless appeal of a love story. But a Christian love story combines the elements of enchantment and inspiration to produce a tale that is unforgettable.

To Submit: If you believe you have an inspirational romance that would fit Heartsong Presents guidelines, please send a summary of the story along with three to four randomly selected chapters to:

Contact information:
Heartsong Presents
Editorial Department
P.O. Box 719
Uhrichsville, OH 44683

Herald Press

Herald Press . . .

A division of Mennonite Publishing House, Inc. (owned by the Mennonite Church), each year releases a wide variety of new books for adults, young people, and children (primarily for ages 9 and up).

We Invite . . .

Book proposals from Christian authors in the areas of (1) current issues, (2) peace and justice, (3) missions and evangelism, (4) family life, (5) personal experience, (6) juvenile fiction, (7) adult fiction, (8) Bible study, (9) inspiration, (10) devotional, (11) church history, and (12) Christian ethics and theology.

Our Purpose . . .

To publish books which are consistent with Scripture as interpreted in the Anabaptist/Mennonite tradition. Books that are honest in presentation, clear in thought, stimulating in content, appropriate in appearance, superior in printing and binding, and conducive to the spiritual growth and welfare of the reader.

Our Royalty Terms . . .

Usually 10% of the retail price of each book sold up to 25,000 copies, going to 11% for the next 25,000, and 12% thereafter.

Recommended Procedure . . .

Send to address below the following: (1) a one-page summary of your book; (2) a one-

or two-sentence summary of each chapter; (3) the first chapter and one other, with numbered and detached pages, and name of Bible version used (we recommend NRSV); (4) a brief statement of your educational, publishing, religious, professional, and community involvements; and (5) the information listed below, stating the significance of the book and describing your target audience. You may expect a reply in about two months. If your proposal appears to have potential for Herald Press, a finished manuscript will be requested. Herald Press depends on capable and dedicated authors to continue publishing high-quality Christian literature.

Information to include:

Title of Manuscript
Author's name
Home and business addresses
Home and business phones
E-mail and Fax
Brief description of contents of this book
Brief explanation of how this book differs from other books on the same subject.
Your interpretation of the significance of this book
Brief description of the basic audience you feel will buy this book
Other comments

Contact information:
S. David Garber, Book Editor
616 Walnut Avenue
Scottdale, PA 15683
(412) 887-8500

Heritage Books, Inc.

SO YOU WANT TO PUBLISH A BOOK?

As a prospective author you probably find yourself in one of several situations: 1) you have a desire to compile a book, but don't know just what to write about or how to go about it; 2) you have a specific topic in mind, and may have done some work on it, but have not yet completed it; 3) you have finished compiling a book and are looking for a publisher, or 4) you published a book in the past that is now out of print, and you are looking for a publisher to reprint it. In any case this packet of information will help you decide how to proceed with Heritage Books, Inc.

There are three essential requirements you need to keep in mind to be successful: 1) pick a topic for which there is a significant market, 2) pick a publisher who can effectively reach that market, and 3) start working with that publisher as early in the process as possible in order to maximize the success of your book. Please read the following sections, Heritage Books in a NutShell and A Matter of interest. The later sections, Acceptance and Rejection, Acceptable Formats, and Test Marketing give an overview of our policies and the book production process.

HERITAGE BOOKS IN A NUTSHELL

Heritage Books, Inc. is one of the leading publishers of books on local history and genealogy in the United States. We publish about twenty new titles each month; some are completely new compilations, while others are historical reprints - often with added name indexes or other improvements.

Our publications are predominantly paper bound editions in 5.5"x8.5" or 8.5"x11" formats. They are printed on pH neutral paper with multi-color, plastic film laminated covers. We favor the 5.5"x8.5" size because it fits bookshelves better, is less subject to damage in the mail, and is usually less expensive to produce. However, the larger format is sometimes necessary to accommodate charts, maps, etc. We concentrate on paper bound editions because they are less expensive than cloth bound, and we can produce them in print runs of as few as 100 copies; that makes it possible for us to publish, and keep in print, books which it would be impractical to publish in cloth bindings,

The primary audiences for our publications are history and genealogy buffs, and the institutions that serve those groups, such as libraries, and historical and genealogical societies. We reach that market primarily through our monthly newsletter/catalog (500,000 mailed per year), as well as through classified and space ads in various publications, through book reviews (about 10% of the print-run is allotted for this), and via listings in Books in Print and other such bibliographies. Our authors are encouraged to participate in the marketing of their books via special flyers, radio talk shows, book signings, etc., and should discuss their ideas with our marketer as early as possible.

A MATTER OF INTEREST

The subject matter of interest to us is naturally determined by the market we serve. In general terms, we are interested in materials on American history and genealogy, including nonfiction narrative works and compilations of source records from the earliest time period available through the Civil War. Since the market for such materials tends to increase geometrically as one moves back in time, the older the material the better in most cases. We have little market for material pertaining to the period after the Civil War, and rarely publish anything pertaining to the present century,

Material with some genealogical character frequently does better for us than outright history. Among possible genealogical topics, early source records tend to be best, followed by genealogical dictionaries covering many early settlers in a given area, single surname genealogies, multiple surname genealogies, and lineages, in that order. A biography of a single person would have poor prospects in most cases.

When it comes to historical and genealogical source record compilations, the availability of the source is a key factor. For example, newspaper abstracts are in much more demand than census records because the latter are readily available on microfilm and easily searched in comparison with newspapers.

SUBMISSION FORMATS

Please consider your situation in the light of the four general cases discussed below and respond accordingly:

CASE 1 - If you do not have any definite plans as to what you want to write about, please write to us expressing your interest and describing your experience and training. We will work with you to help you select a topic of interest to you which is also one we feel we could effectively publish and market.

CASE 2 - If you have a specific topic in mind, but have not finished the work, please send us an outline, sample chapters, table of contents, and any introductory material you may have. Please describe your plans for completing the book so we may have a clear idea of the finished product. Your estimates of the final size of the work and its potential market should also be included, as well as your resume of experience and training relating to the subject matter. We will respond with our evaluation of your project.

CASE 3 - If you have completed an early draft of the whole work, please respond as per CASE 2 above. If we like your proposal, we will respond with a request to see a final draft.

CASE 4 - If you have published a book that is now out of print, and which you think we should reprint, please send us a copy of the book and a synopsis of its printing history.

If you have any questions regarding your submission, please call our Editorial Director at the number listed below. In any case, do not send us originals of text, photographs, or art work unless we specifically request them.

We attempt to respond promptly to all submissions. If you have not heard from us within thirty days, please contact us.

ACCEPTANCE AND REJECTION

Naturally, we would like to accept all the book proposals which we receive, but that is not economically feasible, and it is not in the author's best interest for us to accept books which we cannot effectively market. However, it is our policy to accept, in some way, proposals which meet our standards regarding content, and where we can justify a print run of at least 100 copies.

All acceptances are, of course, tentative until a publishing agreement has been signed. We do not sign publishing contracts until we have the finished work in hand, and, if it is a conditional acceptance contingent on a marketing test, until the test has been successfully passed.

Our response to your specific submission will take one of the following forms:

REJECTION - We must reject outright some proposals we receive simply because they are clearly outside the range of subject matter or time frame that we can effectively market. We cannot offer any editorial critique on rejected proposals.

CONDITIONAL ACCEPTANCE - Book proposals that are narrow in scope and have a limited market we accept on a conditional basis when possible. The usual conditions are: a) that the author provide acceptable camera-ready copy for the book, and b) that we test market the book in order to determine its potential market, and to verify that at least a minimum print run is feasible.

TENTATIVE ACCEPTANCE - We will tentatively accept a proposal when we feel certain that we can effectively market the book, but the book is not yet completed. A final evaluation by our selection committee is made after the work is finished.

OUTRIGHT ACCEPTANCE - If your book is complete and acceptable to us, then we will send you a publishing agreement for your immediate signature.

Our publishing contract is quite standard. In exchange for the publishing rights to the work, we pay a royalty (typically 10%) based on the retail price of the book. It is paid on all the copies we sell, either wholesale or retail. The royalties are paid at six month intervals. We do not offer advances against future royalties. In addition, the author receives five complimentary copies of the book and the right to purchase additional copies for personal sales or other purposes at a 45% discount off the retail price; author purchases also earn royalties. The contract also contains a sunset clause whereby all rights to the work revert to the author automatically if at some point we let the work remain out of print for more than three years.

ACCEPTABLE FORMATS

Once your proposal has been accepted you will need to provide us with copy for your book in one of four forms depending on your facilities and the terms of our agreement: 1) a typescript; 2) on electronic media; 3) as camera-ready copy; or 4) in the form of an existing book in the case of a reprint.

TYPESCRIPT - A satisfactory typescript can be prepared with most electric typewriters or computer driven, letter quality printers. The type must be clear and unbroken, and of uniform darkness on each page. Each page should be numbered.

ELECTRONIC MEDIA - Copy submitted on electronic media is acceptable if your hardware and software are compatible with ours. We use IBM compatible computers, and can accept copy on MS DOS diskettes in either 5.25" or 3.25" sizes, or in Word 6.Oa for Windows 3.1. In addition, we can translate and work with a variety of the more common word processing software packages. **Please contact us early on to discuss compatibility.**

If you can provide the copy for your book in electronic form, it may be possible to produce typeset copy with little formatting and editing on our part which can greatly accelerate the production process.

Once we look at your sample pages, we can decide on a layout which would be most suitable for your book, and we will give you the specific instructions for arranging the text. When submitting a manuscript on electronic media, include a complete listing of the contents so that we can check that the computer copy is complete.

CAMERA-READY COPY - Camera-ready copy is copy that is completely finished and ready for photographing to make the printing plates. (We typeset the title page, copyright page, and the cover, unless you would like to do these also.) Since this can be a complex process, it is essential that we see and approve the format you plan to use before you set up your book.

Once we look at your sample pages, we can decide on a layout which will be most suitable for your book, and we will give you the specific instructions for arranging the text.

If, as is commonly the case, the copy is produced oversize, and is to be photo-reduced in the printing process, all the copy must be set up for the same reduction. Thus, any tables, charts, maps, photographs, or other illustrations must be prepared in the proper size so that they can be reproduced at the same reduction as the rest of the text. Line art such as tables, charts, maps and other line drawings present no special problems because they reproduce just like typed text.. Photographs or drawings which require shading do present special problems and they **must** be replaced positive by half-tones. (A half-tone is basically a photograph taken through a screen which converts the continuous shades of the photo into black dots of varying density on the half-tone.) Many photo-finishing stores offer this service; you should be able to find one locally. At the same time as the half-tones are being made, you should have the photographs scaled to fit the page dimensions that we decide upon.

Any line art in your camera-ready copy must be present in the proper positions on the pages where it belongs, in the proper size with captions in place. Likewise any photographs should be present as positive half-tones pasted onto the pages where they belong with the captions in place. Be sure to write identifying information on the back of each photograph or illustration, such as your name, the title of the book, and the illustration's location. **Please, do not send us original photographs, maps etc. that cannot be replaced!**

Page Size and Appearance - It is important that all pages are aligned within the same margins and that the ink coverage is uniform on all pages throughout the book.

Page Numbering - Each page should be appropriately numbered. All of the front matter (table of contents, dedication, preface, introduction etc.) should be numbered with lowercase Roman numerals; the remainder of the book should be numbered with Arabic numerals. Each new section should begin on an odd-numbered page; blank pages must be inserted when necessary to accomplish this. Each blank page is counted as if it were a regular numbered page. See The Chicago Manual of Style for sample page numbering.

Number of Pages - The minimum number of pages per book is 100. The maximum number of pages per book is 640; however, we recommend that you actually have no more than 500 pages. A book larger than 640 pages may be split into two volumes for convenience and economy.

EXISTING BOOK - If we are going to reprint your existing book, you will need to provide us with a clean copy of the book to use in the process. We may re-typeset the title and copyright pages, and possibly add an errata page or new index, but the bulk of the book will be a facsimile reprint of the book you provide - possibly with some reduction or enlargement to accommodate our basic page sizes. The book you provide will be completely taken apart in order for us to reprint it, and it is not possible to rebind it. It is only useful for possible later reprintings, and is retained by us for that purpose.

COVER DESIGN

Normally, we use attractive clip-art to design the covers for the books we publish. We do not provide original artwork for the covers or interiors of the books. You are welcome to provide your own artwork for the cover and/or the interior. We can use your artwork and typeset the copy for the front and back covers and the spine, or you may provide us with the camera-ready cover, with the copy typeset around your artwork.

COPYRIGHT

We print the copyright notice on the back of the title page along with other publishing data, but we do not register the copyright with the Library of Congress. If you feel that it may be necessary to legally defend the copyright at some time, then you must officially register the copyright. You may obtain information about the law, registration form, and fee from the Register of Copyrights, Library of Congress, Washington, DC 20559.

TEST MARKETING

Each month we offer all our new publications on a prepublication basis at a substantial discount. We do this for two reasons: 1) to provide our regular customers with the opportunity to buy our publications at a discount; and 2) to test the market for each new title.

If your book is accepted subject to a marketing test, we will offer the book in our usual manner, and make a decision on final acceptance after the initial sales results come in. It does not take long to get meaningful results - we will know by the end of two to four weeks after the book is first offered. Naturally, we only make the marketing test after the book is complete, and we have a publishing agreement in hand signed by the author.

If the book passes the test, we will sign the contracts and return one copy to the author, and proceed to produce and market the book. If the book sales fail to justify a minimum print run, then we will cancel the orders of the few people who have ordered the book, and return the voided contracts to the author along with the copy for the book. There will then be no further obligation on either party.

WE'D LIKE TO HEAR FROM YOU

We wish you success in your efforts to become a published author, and will do all we can to help you bring your project to fruition. Please contact us with specific questions by phone or letter at the address given below.

Contact information:
Editorial Director
1540-E Pointer Ridge Place
Bowie, MD 20716-1859
(301) 390-7708

Highsmith Press

Highsmith Press accepts unsolicited proposals and manuscripts from prospective authors, and we welcome your inquiries. We recommend that you review our online catalog to see the types of materials we publish. Essentially, our primary interests are library reference and professional books, and instructional resources that aid teachers and librarians in serving youth from preschool through high school. Until recently, we also published multicultural picture books for youth, but we are no longer accepting any new manuscripts of that type.

The press has over 120 titles currently in print, and we plan to publish approximately 20 new titles a year for the next several years. We seek to reach a decision on each submission or proposal within 60 days, but in order to achieve this goal we need your cooperation by following these submission guidelines.

For manuscripts which are less than 100 pages, we would like to receive the entire work for review, including illustrations. For longer manuscripts, please send selected sections and illustrations that best describe the project, including the introduction. We also welcome outlines of prospective projects, particularly if they are reference books.

Please include a cover letter summarizing the purpose of the work and its potential market. Identify any other recent books which have been published on a similar topic, and describe how your book differs. In your letter state which computer software you used (or plan to use) to develop your manuscript. We can accept a wide variety of DOS and MAC software programs.

We do not need to receive an electronic version of your manuscript for initial evaluation, but we do require that final manuscripts be in an electronic format. Attach a current resume listing your qualifications.

You may send us a photocopy of your manuscript. We are not troubled by manuscripts which are being simultaneously submitted to other publishers. We do not have any guidelines for photos, although we will consider photos submitted with manuscripts.

You may also check our website on the World Wide Web (URL ttp://www.hpress.highsmith.com) for current information on the types of projects we are most interested in publishing. Prospective authors can also find our entire catalog at that website.

The specific terms we can offer authors and illustrators will vary with the nature of each project.

However, we do provide very competitive royalties and advances, and we emphasize quality design and high production standards. Please call if you have any questions or concerns.

Contact information:
Donald J. Sager, Publisher
PO Box 800
Ft. Atkinson, WI 53538-0800
(414) 563-9571 • FAX: (414) 563-4801 (8 pages or less)
E-mail: hpress@highsmith.com (4 pages or less)

Hunter House Publishers

The guidelines below are in two parts: (a) the subject areas we publish in and the kind of books we do; and (b) the kind of proposals we like to see. They reflect our tag line, which is **Books for health, family and community**, although sometimes it is difficult to keep a clear separation between these three areas.

SUBJECT AREAS

Health and wellness, especially women's health

Our health books focus on emerging or current health issues that may be inadequately covered for the general population. We look for comprehensive, balanced and up-to-date information presented in a clear and accessible manner. The book should describe causes, symptoms, medical theories, current and possible treatments, complementary and alternative therapies, successful strategies for coping, prevention, and so on. Illustrations, sidebars, reading lists, and resource sections that provide additional information or enhance the content are desirable. We specialize in women's health, with sublists on cancer; pregnancy & childbirth; women's health reference, and women's health as a women's issue. We are currently interested in books about aging and complementary therapies. At the top of our health list are *Menopause Without Medicine; Women's Cancers; Running on Empty: The Complete Guide to*

Chronic Fatigue Syndrome (CFIDS); and The Women's Health Products Handbook.

Family: Personal growth, lifestyles, relationships, sexuality

Personal growth topics that we are currently interested in are sexuality; partner and family relationships; and changing, evolutionary lifestyles. Successful titles provide step-by-step aids or a program to help readers understand and approach new perspectives on family issues or dynamics, celebrate their sexuality, and establish healthy, fulfilling lives that incorporate a planetary perspective. Examples include: *Sexual Healing: How Good Loving is Good for You and Your Relationship; Helping Your Child Through Your Divorce; and The Pleasure Prescription —A New Way to well-being.*

Violence prevention and intervention, social justice

We have a small but growing line of books and workbooks, often done in collaboration with nonprofits, which address community issues such as violence prevention, access for people with disabilities, and human rights. They should include clear reviews and explanations, new activities and exercises, provocative insights, and practical theory. Examples are: *Violent No More: Helping Men End Domestic Abuse; Helping Teens Stop Violence: A Practical Guide for Counselors, Educators, and Parents; Computer Resources for People With Disabilities; and The Amnesty International Handbook.*

Resources for counselors and educators

Resources for educators are generally specialized curricula that address violence prevention and social justice issues, including *The Uprooted: Refugees and the United States; Human Rights for Children; and Making the Peace: A Violence Prevention Curriculum for Young People.*

Books for counselors and helping professionals tend to offer information in new and underexplored fields, such as trauma and crisis in children. Titles include *Trauma in the Lives of Children: Crisis and Stress Management Techniques for Counselors and Other Professionals.*

We are also looking for additions to our Growth and Recovery Workbooks series. These materials are for professional or supervised use with young children who have experienced trauma, abuse, or other critical life events. It is important that they have accompanying guides for the professionals who will use them. Titles include *No More Hurt* and *Someone I Love Died.*

Audience

Our health and family books are meant to appeal to both the general reading public and health care and mental health professionals. They should be written clearly to the general reader, but include enough background explanation, theory, and resources so that they are good references for professionals. This comprehensive approach also ensures that readers can trust the authors as authorities on the topic. It is important that authors have credentials and experience within the field. If you do not have this background, it is important that you have a co-author who does. It also helps if a reputable and well-known expert contributes a foreword or the introduction.

Our social issues books should be accessible to lay readers but should speak clearly to the specialized groups involved with the subject on a professional, volunteer, or community basis. Again, we look for credentialed authors with experience and a resource network in their field.

It is crucial that the authors of educational or professional books have credentials and experience within the specific areas they address. We look for a need for information within these areas, and networks through which we can reach the professionals who will use these materials. Endorsements and a preface or foreword from noted individuals within the field are important and helpful.

We do not publish fiction or illustrated books for children.

PREPARING A BOOK PROPOSAL FOR US

A good nonfiction book proposal is made up of the following components: an overview; a chapter-by-chapter outline; about the author(s); and marketing considerations.

The Overview should be a two- to three-page summary of the work: the content, and your presentation and approach. It should include the following:

1. The subject hook, which creates interest in the book, including the title, subtitle, the book's angle on the current market, and approximate length of the book.
2. An anecdote or example that illustrates your theme and its significance.
3. Discussion of the book's other essential ingredients - illustrations, exercises, etc.
4. A foreword, preface, or endorsements for the book written by authorities or celebrities.

The final page of your proposal should discuss the markets for your work, your experience and credibility as an author, and any other information that makes the book unique. Our editors and salespeople must understand why your book should be written. Specify the audience your book will address (women, professionals, tradespeople). Include marketing or promotional ideas you have for getting the book known to your audience. Lastly, list current books that compete with and complement yours.

The Chapter-by-chapter Outline is a 3-6 page outline, including all chapter titles and itemized lists of the major topics or contents of each chapter. Significant illustrations, appendices, and recommended reading should be listed. Work from a table of contents. You should have enough chapters to break up the topic in digestible pieces for the reader, but not so many that the material is scattered. Most books flow from an overall organizing subject or theme - the subject "hook" we ask for in the overview. For example, a book on breast cancer can be organized according to risks and detection, operations and choices involved, and recovery processes. After you complete your table of contents, go on to outline each chapter. Make a brief listing of topics which will be discussed in each chapter, or summarize each chapter in a paragraph.

About the Author: your credentials as evidence you are qualified to write on the subject, and any experience or training that qualifies you especially well for this project. A resume or short biography that includes other publishing experience and media experience is helpful. The more you can tell us about yourself, the more we understand your proposal as a whole.

Marketing and Promotion information: We look for authors who are positive about and have access to publicity. Explain what you will do to help promote the book. Describe your speaking, mass media, TV, radio, or promotional experience and include a plan of how your work can be promoted. Do you lecture, do seminars, tour, or travel for training and business; do you belong to active organizations and have strong networks; do you teach classes or write a newspaper column; are you prepared to market your materials?

The Review Process

If we are interested in pursuing your project further, we will request sample chapters. Please send only two to three sample chapters — not the whole manuscript. Each chapter should have one concept, subject, skill, or technique. Use main headings and subheads so a reader can know at a glance where the chapter is going.

In a chapter that explains a process or teaches a technique, explain the process step-by-step in exactly the order a reader should follow to understand the process. The general and most important concepts come first, while the exceptions and special considerations come last. Any background information can be explained first or in a separate chapter.

To effectively teach an individual step of a process or technique, follow this sequence: state the rule or instruction first. Be clear and to the point. Then give an example of how someone else did this step. Finally, provide an exercise for the reader to perform. This gives the reader three ways to learn the technique: intellectually by precept, emotionally by example, and experientially by doing.

Sending Us Your Manuscript

After you have done your marketing research and written your chapter outlines, consider whether Hunter House is the right publisher for you. We do not publish fiction, autobiography, or general children's books, so those types of works get returned right away. If you do have what we are looking for, then send it on.

We do accept simultaneous submissions and look for computer printouts of good quality, or e-mail. Please inform us if a manuscript is available on computer disk (IBM format is preferable).

Contact information:
Editor
P.O. Box 2914
Alameda, CA 94501-0914
(510) 865-4295 • FAX: (510) 865-4295
E-mail: editorial@hunterhouse.com

Ivan R. Dee, Inc.
Publisher

If you wish to inquire about our interest in a book manuscript you have prepared or are preparing, please send a query letter along with a brief description of the work, if possible a listing of contents or chapters, and at least two sample chapters. If you simply have an idea for a book, write us about it in detail.

Ordinarily you will hear from us within thirty days—sooner if the manuscript is clearly not for us, occasionally later if the work presents a difficult publishing decision.

We are publishers of serious nonfiction, in both hardcover and paperback, in history, politics, literature, biography, and theatre.

Contact information:
Ivan R. Dee, President
1332 North Halsted Street
Chicago, IL 60622
(312) 787-6262 • FAX: (312) 787-6269

Jain Publishing Company, Inc.

We publish in a broad range of subject areas for a variety of audiences including scholars, college courses, libraries and general readers. The following represents a general set of guidelines for submitting proposals and manuscripts.

1. Prior to sending the complete manuscript, send a detailed proposal describing the scope, content, length, and the primary as well as secondary markets for the book. If the book has potential for derivative products such as audio/video cassettes, workbooks, manuals or other sidelines, how this may be accomplished should be described in the proposal.

2. For textbook proposals, include the typical course profile and data (the number of US colleges offering such courses, course levels, frequency, average enrollments, whether such courses are required or electives and whether the work being submitted is intended to be a required text or a supplementary text).

3. Include all available information regarding the competition for the book, i.e., other

similar works currently on the market and aspects of this work that set it apart.

4. Include a chapter-by-chapter outline, including the back matter such as appendices, bibliographies and the like. If there are illustrations, describe their nature and extent. Also indicate who might be willing to read the work and provide Forwards and/or endorsements.

5. Include a resume with special emphasis on prior publications, if any. If possible, the sales data of prior publications should also be included.

6. Direct the material to the Editor-in-Chief at the address below.

7. Complete manuscripts (hard copies only) should be sent upon our request. Unsolicited mss. are acceptable.

8. Once a manuscript is accepted for publication, a disk submission would be required for composition purposes. The inability of the author to provide the entire ms. on a disk may result in the cancellation of the publication agreement.

General

It is strongly advised that as the manuscript is being developed, for correct punctuation, capitalization, organization of material, usage and the like, The Chicago Manual of Style (University of Chicago Press) be followed closely. This will avoid undue copy editing expenses later.

Contact information:
Editor-in-Chief
P.O. Box 3523
Fremont, CA 94539
(510) 659-8272 • FAX: (510) 659-0501
E-mail: jainpub@ix.netcom.com

Johnson Books

Submissions

We suggest a letter with an outline and two or three sample chapters (or some kind of writing sample sufficient for us to evaluate writing style and ability). Please include a brief autobiography relevant to your credentials on the selected topic, along with a publishing history, if applicable. Entire manuscripts should not be sent until requested. Photocopied letters do not make a favorable impression. Telephone queries are welcomed.

Manuscript Preparation

Margins should be 1 ¼ to 1 ½ inches right and left. Please do not bind manuscripts in any way. A good photocopy is acceptable.

Word processor letter-quality printing is acceptable; dot matrix printing is not. Our in-house equipment can read regular and high-density 3 ½ inch disks in Macintosh or IBM format and 5 ¼ inch 360K disks. Please do not send manuscripts on disk until requested.

The first page should contain the author's name, address, telephone number, and the full title of the book. Each succeeding page should be slugged in the upper left-hand corner with the author's last name, short book title, and short chapter title. Successive page numbers, rather than numbering by chapter, is preferred.

A table of contents with full chapter titles should accompany the manuscript. For manuscripts with endnotes, the endnotes should come at the end of the manuscript rather than the end of each chapter. For manuscripts prepared on word processors, please use only one space after a period.

Photographs

Do not send original photographs until requested. Black-and-white photographs must be 5x7 or larger glossy prints. Color prints are usually not acceptable; transparencies are usually required. Each photograph should be labeled with caption, credit line, and the chapter to which it belongs. Permissions fees are the responsibility of the author.

Authorities

Style: *The Chicago Manual of Style*, 14th edition. Chicago: Univ. of Chicago Press, 1993.

Spelling: *The American Heritage Dictionary of the English Language.*

Supplementary: *Words into Type*, 3rd edition. Englewood Cliffs: Prentice-Hall, 1974.

Contact information:
Stephen Topping, Editorial Director
1880 South 57th Court
Boulder, CO 80301
(303) 443-9766 • FAX: (303) 443-1679

Kalmbach Publishing Co.

The Books Department of Kalmbach Publishing Co. publishes quality books about various hobbies including scale model railroading, toy train collecting and operating, prototype railroad history, scale modeling, miniatures, and astronomy.

We sell our books in hobby shops and bookstores, as well as directly to the consumer through mail and phone orders from our catalog. A great many also are sold at the Greenberg Great Train, Toy and Dollhouse Shows held throughout the year. A good way to determine if your subject is suited to either the Greenberg Books or Kalmbach Books imprint is to ask yourself whether a hobby shop or toy train/toy show is the ideal sales outlet for your work.

TERMS OF CONTRACT

We offer the standard arrangement in book publishing: You sell us the right to publish what you have produced (writing, photographs, drawings) in return for a percentage of the net sales (royalty). On a case-by-case basis, we may also be willing to provide the author of an especially promising book with an advance on royalties—usually not more than $1,000. This advance is subtracted from initial royalty payments until it is paid up (usually in the first year). After the advance is repaid, we send you royalty checks twice a year as long as the book remains in print and in stock. You may also negotiate a lump-sum payment for your work in lieu of a royalty.

WHAT TO SUBMIT

Before we issue a contract, we ask that you submit a detailed outline of the content of your proposed book, along with a completed sample chapter. Requiring these items from you is the only way we can gain a full appreciation of your subject knowledge and your ability to write and illustrate a book on it. We also need the outline and chapter to estimate how much work we will have to put into the completed manuscript to produce a finished book.

These estimates, in turn, determine what compensation we will offer in the contract. If a considerable amount of editorial or art effort will be required on our part, we may ask that you accept a lesser royalty or we may choose not to publish the work at all. Do the best possible job of organizing and presenting your material, even if you need to hire an editor to clean up the prose and punctuation. Doing so will assure you the maximum return on your time and talent.

The outline and sample chapter package that we request prior to initiating a contract consists of.

(1) A detailed, chapter-by-chapter outline of the proposed book from beginning to end (see sample outline). Don't rely on generalities: make the outline as specific as possible. Divide each chapter into subtopics, and provide a brief description for each of these topics. Also, provide a brief description of the photos and drawings you propose to use to illustrate each chapter. While this outline requires a fair amount of work, it will be a helpful organizational tool when you're actually writing the book. We have yet to work with an author who did not find the outline valuable.

(2) A sample chapter, preferably from somewhere early in thebook, but not the introductory chapter. This chapter should be a complete and polished package. Include text, captions, photos, and even pencil roughs of other required artwork. Submit this chapter without expecting to rework it at all for use in the book. Like the outline, this involves effort and time on your part, but it is really the only way we can evaluate your work and make reasoned production estimates to calculate our offer to you.

PREPARING HOW-TO BOOKS

Strive for a total presentation—text, photos, captions, and drawings-that stresses the how-to-do-it aspects of your subject. What you submit to us will become the book we produce; if something important is not included in your package, we will not conjure it up. Lack of manuscript completeness is the prime cause of our production delays.

Write for the newcomers to the hobby. Our marketing experts tell us that while experienced hobbyists are the folks the hobbyshop owner knows by name, the novices are the ones to whom the shop owner sells most of the merchandise. To be successful, aim your how-to book at the newcomers. Include some "here's how the experts do it' material, but not at the expense of basic, nuts-and-bolts information.

Writing Style: Feel free to use a conversational tone throughout the text and captions; it will make the book more accessible for newcomers to the hobby. Include lots of detail as you write, because that's what makes a how-to book really helpful. Assume that the reader wants to do everything you mention and that it's up to you to provide the specifics he or she needs to do these things correctly. If you have any doubts about whether you should include some how-to information or leave it out, go ahead and include it! In our kind of hobby book, 'too much information' is rarely a problem. Feel free to provide brand names of products that work well for you. There's no need, however, to give long explanations of procedures that don't work; stick to a discussion of what does.

Photos: Black-and-white prints should be 5" x 7" or larger. Send negatives with the final manuscript; we often need to reprint a photo. We'll return your negatives after the book is published. For how-to books, shoot against a plain, light blue background for indoor pictures—a patterned or wrinkled background is distracting. Bracket your photos, giving us a variety of exposures to choose from. Never write directly on the photos—front or back. If you need to indicate positioning of type or arrows, attach a tracing paper flap, taped to the back of the print with a small piece of Scotch Magic Tape.

In how-to books, use color photos chiefly to show something that can't be properly demonstrated in black and white. We prefer to work with color transparencies, but we can use color prints as long as they don't have a satin (matte) finish. Also, if we accept your proposal for publication, we'll probably ask you to submit color photos for use on the cover.

Type photo captions on individual pieces of paper and tape them to the back of the photo with Scotch Magic Tape. Use complete sentences in the captions, and don't just repeat what you say in the text. Provide the photographer's name for all photos you did not take yourself, and be sure to obtain photo releases for photographs that show individuals or for photographs of a person's collection.

Whenever possible, substitute your own photos for those provided by manufacturers; doing so makes the book look more cohesive and personal, and less like a catalog. We prefer to use photographs, possibly with type overlays, instead of line art in how-to books. Of course, we'll use line art to get the point across clearly where photos simply won't do the job, but artwork is very expensive, and each piece of line art adds to the cover price of the book. When line art is necessary, our artists appreciate having as much reference material as possible to work from.

PREPARING COLLECTOR GUIDES

Our Greenberg collector guides are generally developed by authors who have considerable collecting experience and great knowledge of the specific items on which they are reporting. Often, two or more authors will collaborate on a collector guide when the subject area is so extensive that a single individual is unlikely to have a complete grasp of the topic. This is fine, as long as the two (or more) co-authors are able to work well together and develop a manuscript that reads cohesively as if it were a single, unified effort. The approach you elect to follow is your choice, but be sure that tasks are evenly and fairly divided at the start if you choose a co-author, and be sure that your partner(s) will adhere to strict deadlines in accomplishing his or her work. Keep in mind, too, that co-authors share the royalty (generally with equal shares going to each partner) and that the terms of this distribution are spelled out in the book contract. If, later in the course of completing your manuscript, you discover that your partner has failed to contribute his or her fair share of the work, it's probably too late to make any change in the contract terms.

Item descriptions and value listings are all-important features of our collector guides. The format for these descriptions and listings may vary depending on the product, and first-time authors are advised to refer to previously published Greenberg books to see how this material was presented in other instances. If you have trouble determining how to present your own descriptions and value listings, just give us a call. We'll get you started the right way and avoid much frustration and additional work later on.

Item photography is another very important part of each Greenberg collector guide; our books are highly regarded for their clear, color-correct, and detailed photos. We expect our authors to locate and secure permission to photograph high-quality collections for collector guides. If necessary, our staff photographers will handle the on-site photography, but authors should be aware that this additional expense will affect the royalty they will receive from the book.

OTHER RAILROAD AND NONFICTION BOOKS

While the majority of our published titles are either how-to books or collector guides, we do occasionally publish other nonfiction books outside these categories. The books we publish in the "Other" category are carefully selected on the basis of individual merit, scholarly contribution to their field, and sales potential. Most often these are prototype railroad or rail history books, reference guides for railfans, or specialized reference materials for amateur astronomers and other hobbyists. We must be very selective in contracting for these types of books because they generally serve a specialized and far more limited audience. If you have a topic that you feel is worthy of consideration in this category, we urge you to review the guidelines provided herein (including the Submission Guidelines section) and then contact our Acquisitions team to discuss your idea in depth. Do this before submitting a detailed proposal, because this initial contact with our publishing staff may save you time and avoid misunderstandings or frustration.

REVIEWING YOUR PROPOSAL

Once we've received your outline and sample chapter, your proposal will be reviewed by an editor who is knowledgeable in the topic you've covered. This review will concentrate on the content of your book: the accuracy of the content, the quality of the writing and photographs, the interweaving of text and illustrations, and the organization. Depending on our workload, this may take from four to six weeks-even longer if the manuscript is sent to outside experts for evaluation.

If we agree that you can write the book, the next step is an evaluation of your book's sales potential. We prepare an initial feasibility proposal, and this is then circulated to each department that will contribute to the book's development. If the proposal is approved, we'll offer you a contract for the book. We also assign a project number to your book; this number will follow the manuscript throughout its publishing life. Occasionally we can offer a contract only if you agree to certain restrictions or to make modifications (for example, we might specify that the book be no more than a certain number of pages long). After you have reviewed the contract and returned a signed copy to us, we become full partners in the publishing venture and your book is formally placed into our production schedule.

SUBMISSION GUIDELINES

If you use a computer word-processing program to type your manuscript: We use Macintosh computers with Microsoft Word as our primary word-processing application. We strongly prefer to receive completed manuscripts in electronic form—that is, on a computer disk—so by all means create your manuscript in that way if at all possible. In most parts of the country, you should be able to locate a freelancer who will keyboard your manuscript material for you at a reasonable cost, even if you don't own or have access to a computer yourself.

Even though we are equipped with Macintosh hardware and Microsoft Word word-processing software, we are also able to import (convert) on-disk material created by most other Macintosh word-processing programs and some other PC-based (DOS) word-processing applications. The easiest PC-based conversions for us are from files produced with WordPerfect and PC-Word. If you use other software, we can generally work with files written in ASCII (text file) format. You will need to provide your completed manuscript on 3 1/2" disk(s) rather than 5 1/4" disks. If in doubt, check with us first to assure that the word-processing program you intend to use is one that we can easily 'read' into our system. (Also follow these guidelines for your sample chapter.)

Unless you are sending us a manuscript created with Microsoft Word, do not bother keyboarding your material with complex tab settings. Depending on the program you use, these may be lost or misread in the conversion process. Simply type your manuscript in as straightforward a manner as possible using default tab settings, and avoid using any of the features that allow you to make 'real fractions' or other things that may "look pretty." We'll take care of making everything look right once we have imported your text.

- On the label of any disks you send, always indicate the type of computer you used, the software that produced the tiles, and the file names.
- Identify each page as follows:

  TITLE - Ch. 1 - page 6
- Indicate with a notation in the text (in boldface type) where each photo, drawing, or chart should be placed. Example: **Insert photo 2-1 here.** The first number indicates the chapter, and the second number indicates the sequence of the photo within the chapter. An alternative numbering system for shorter books involves simply numbering all photos consecutively, regardless of chapter. Be as specific as possible regarding placement of these notations so the page designer will be able to correctly position each illustration with the appropriate text.
- Always keep a complete back-up set of your submitted manuscript disk(s), and do not make any changes or additions to this set once you have sent a duplicate set to us. Make

subsequent changes on hard copy (paper); we will then incorporate this material in our disk file.

If you must submit a typewritten manuscript: The only problem with getting a typewritten manuscript from an author is that we have to go through the process of converting it to an electronic form that allows us to eventually set your words in type for the printing presses. This can be a time-consuming and labor-intensive process if someone has to sit at a keyboard and retype your manuscript word by word. We like to think of this as the last (and least attractive/most expensive) alternative.

However, if you are able to provide us with a crisp, clean copy of your typewritten manuscript, there's a good chance that we can electronically scan the pages through an electronic character recognition scanner into our computer system. Experience has shown us that the scanner does best on manuscripts typed or printed in IBM's "Courier' typewriter font with a carbon film ribbon. A new fabric ribbon works almost as well. Manuscripts printed by dot matrix printers scan reasonably well, but again you should be sure to use a new ribbon. Type produced by an old and dirty manual typewriter is nearly impossible to scan.

Remember that this information applies to your final manuscript. For the sample chapter all we require is a hard copy of the material.

If you only have access to a typewriter for your manuscript, please follow these guidelines:

• Set your typewriter for a column 38 characters wide. Don't split words at the end of the line; either stop short or run over.

• Identify each page as follows:

TITLE - Ch. 1 - page 6

• Indent three characters to start a new paragraph. Leave a 1" margin on the left.

• Indicate in the wide right margin where each photo, drawing, or chart should be placed. Be as specific as possible so the page designer will be able to correctly position each illustration with the appropriate text.

• Type or print double-spaced, 25 lines of text per page. This helps us get an accurate line count and estimate how long your book will be.

WHAT HAPPENS NEXT

From the time your proposal is accepted, you and your manuscript will be assigned to a sponsoring editor-we use the title "Acquisitions Editor" because this person's primary function is to work with authors to acquire new and interesting books. The Acquisitions Editor will be your contact person, answering your questions and keeping you updated on the progress of your book. If you submit your manuscript by the deadline stated in the contract, the production of your book will proceed in a timely fashion. If you miss your deadline, we may have to reschedule the book into our production program, where it competes for a slot with numerous other books. This will cause significant delay in its publication—and your royalties!

The Acquisitions Editor assigned to your book will first check the manuscript to ensure that you've submitted all materials contracted for. Next, the editor will perform a substantive edit on your manuscript; that is, he or she will read it thoroughly for structural and content changes. The editor may ask you to make certain changes before turning over the manuscript to the Copy Editor. The Copy Editor will edit the manuscript for grammar and style.

Next, the Acquisitions Editor will send you an edited copy of your manuscript. You will be asked to proofread this carefully and thoroughly. This is your last opportunity to fix information that is incorrect. However, this is not the time for an extensive rewriting of your material. Rewriting at this stage invariably leads to lengthy delays in getting your book into print. You'll usually be given five days to proofread the manuscript, and you'll be expected to abide by this deadline.

When the Acquisitions Editor receives the proof, he or she will make the necessary changes and then send the book to our Book Designers. Several weeks later, your editor will send you a draft copy of the pages of the book, in approximately the form that they will appear in the final printed version. You will have several days to proof and return this material, paying special attention to the positioning of illustrations and to the matching of illustrations and their captions, This is your last opportunity to see the book before it's shipped to the printer. About 6-12 weeks after you return the draft page proofs, you should receive a bound copy of your book.

While we're editing your manuscript, the professional specialists here will also select a title, design the book's cover, and develop marketing plans. Although we do welcome your ideas about these important matters, the final decisions will be made by us. We'll certainly run the final title by you and send you a likeness of the final cover before we print your book. Send your early ideas on any of the above to your Acquisitions Editor, who will pass them on to the appropriate department.

No matter what happens with your proposal, however, we do appreciate the chance to review your work and ideas, and we thank you for considering us as your prospective publisher.

SAMPLE BOOK OUTLINE

I. Introduction
II. Overview of the Market Today—Product Availability in the Various gauges
III. Collecting Toy Trains
  A. Brief History of Manufacturers
  B. What People Collect
  C. Progressions—Stages in the Collecting Hobby
  D. Collecting Specialties
  E. Grading and pricing
  F. Buying Trains
    1. Attic and basement searches
    2. Swap Meets and Hobby Shops
    3. Auctions
    4. Mail Order
  G. Restoring Tin Pieces
  H. Collectors' Organizations
IV. Operating Toy Trains
  A. Planning a Layout
    1. Obtaining the Right of Way (The Art of Domestic Compromise)
    2. Planning for Your Kind of Activity
      a) High Speed Running
      b) Station-Centered Operation
      c) Yard and Industrial Switching
    3. Be realistic about available space
    4. Make scale drawings of available space
    5. Give Yourself Options for Changes
    6. Plan Construction in stages
  B. Building a Layout
    1. Benchwork
      a) Tabletop
      b) Open Grid Framework
      c) "Cookie Cutter" Method
    2. Laying Track
      a) Roadbed
      b) Tinplate With Ties
      c) Gargraves—Type Sections

        d) Bending Curves to Fit
    3. Construction Stages
        a) Don't Try to Do It All at Once
        b) Start Running Trains Early On
        c) Let Layout Grow Naturally
    4. Wiring
        a) Complexity Will Match Operational Activities
        b) Common Ground
        c) Blocks and Feeders
        d) Insulated Sections
        e) Accessories
    5. Scenery
        a) Various Techniques
        b) Terrain
        c) Buildings
        d) Details

V. Concluding Chapter
    A. Summaries
    B. Projections for the Future

VI. Appendices
    A. Selected Bibliography of Books in Print
    B. Selected Bibliography of Magazines and Other Periodicals
    C. List of Dealers and Suppliers

Terry Spohn, Senior Acquisitions Editor
21027 Crossroads Circle
Waukesha, WI 53187
(414) 796-8776 • FAX: (414) 796-1142
E-mail: books@ kalmbach.com

Kregel Publications

OUR MISSION

Kregel Publications exists for the purpose of serving God through the publication and distribution of evangelical Christian literature that will encourage and strengthen believers in their walk by faith, assist Christian workers and lay persons to better understand and proclaim God's Word, and make the Gospel known throughout the world. Books published present a conservative, evangelical faith and uphold the following primary doctrines: the verbal and plenary inspiration of the Bible as God's Word, inerrant in the original writings; One God existing in three persona: Father, Son, and Holy Spirit; the deity of Jesus Christ; His virgin birth, vicarious death, bodily resurrection and personal return; the Holy Spirit who convicts the world of sin, righteousness and judgment, and who regenerates and indwells all believers.

OUR PRIORITIES

Kregel Publications is interested in books that will meet the spiritual needs of readers as well as the professional needs of pastors, missionaries, teachers, and Christian leaders. We publish new material in the area of Christian education and ministry, Bible commentaries and reference, contemporary and family issues, and devotional books. We do not publish school curriculum, poetry, fiction, cartoons, cookbooks, or games. Reading levels should be appropriate for the target audience.

YOUR QUERY LETTER

Rather than sending a complete manuscript, please address a query letter to our Senior Editor at the address shown below. The query letter should contain the following information: a summary of your proposed book, its target audience, and an assessment of its uniqueness in comparison to other books currently available in the same subject area. Please include a brief description of your own qualifications to write on this subject and your educational background when appropriate. Enclose an outline or table of contents of the book and two sample chapters.

YOUR MANUSCRIPT

In response to your query letter, we may request a complete manuscript. Manuscripts may be typed or copied. Originals should be typed in a 12-point courier or roman typeface; material produced on computer should be printed by letter-quality dot matrix or laser printer.

OUR PROCEDURE

Your manuscript will be reviewed by qualified readers and our Senior Editor. Based upon their favorable response, your manuscript will be recommended to our Editorial Committee. They will evaluate your manuscript based upon the reviewers' evaluations, its quality of writing, timeliness, and consistency with the mission of Kregel Publications. Please allow six to eight weeks for us to complete this process. You will be notified of the committee's decision. Should we decide to publish your work, a contract will be sent to you which clearly sets forth the legal agreement to publish, promote, and distribute your book. If we can be of further assistance in preparing your submission, please call or write. We welcome your interest.

Contact information:

Pastoral & Biblical Studies, Devotional: Dennis Hillman, Senior Editor
P.O. Box 2607
Grand Rapids, MI 49501
(616) 451-4775

Lifetime Books, Inc.

Thank you for selecting LIFETIME BOOKS, Inc.

We were established in 1943 in New York City as Fell Publishers, relocating to Hollywood, FL in 1984. We renamed to LIFETIME BOOKS in 1991. Our two imprints are Fell Publishers and Compact Books. In addition to the 20 annual titles published, we distribute books to the trade for 7 publishers. Our books are marketed to the book trade through National Book Network.

We have sales reps, telemarketers and direct mailers in the US, representing us in all fifty states. Our books are sold primarily to bookstores, libraries and special markets. Our international reps force spans across the globe, securing sales and foreign rights for our titles.

We will consider publishing your book or distributing an existing book. We welcome your submission.

In reviewing manuscript proposals we prefer not to receive the entire manuscript right away. It becomes an unnecessary expense on your part. Rather, we would first like to receive an outline of your book. Submit, for example, a list of sample chapters – convince us your book is different or better than the competition in this field. Send us an extensive author biography – tell us how you will be able to push promotions and sales of your book. Lastly, send us a sample chapter and an introduction synopsis of the book.

DO NOT phone us or visit our office to solicit a response to your proposal. Careful consideration of your proposal may take months.

We publish both trade hardcover and paperback, ranging from 200 to 300 pages (45,000 to 65,000 words). If we accept your proposal we will need the manuscript provided to us on a WP 5.1 disk. Our turn-around time from acceptance to publication is approximately six to eight months, with an average first print run of 5,000 - 20,000 books. We generally do not pay an advance - but will consider it in special circumstances.

We accept submissions from best-selling professionals or first-time authors. Some of our more prestigious authors include the best-selling Og Mandino, Irving Wallace, Walter B. Gibson, Robert L. Shook, Alan Truscott, Jane Roberts and Lillian Roth.

The genres or subject matters we prefer are: self-help, business, how-to, current affairs, health, inspirational and spirituality (but not on a specific religion). We especially like books containing information people need to have or find interesting.

Sensational biographies or tabloid-oriented manuscripts will always receive our full attention. We prefer not to consider works of fiction, poetry, children's, games or cookbooks – unless there is something truly unique about the book or your credentials.

Nonfiction books will be given strong consideration. You should consult the library, bookstore or publisher's catalogs and compare your idea with their product. Look at Bowker's BOOKS IN PRINT or FORTHCOMING TITLES. Ask yourself: Is my book really different, better or new and improved? If the answer is "yes" send it to us.

Thank you for considering LIFETIME BOOKS, Inc.

Contact information:

Brian Feinblum, Senior Editor
2131 Hollywood Boulevard
Hollywood, FL 33020-6750
(954) 925-5242, x13 • FAX: (305) 925-5244

Lodestar Books
An Affiliate of Dutton Children's Books

Lodestar Books publishes picture books, photo essays, and fiction and nonfiction for children and young adults ages 8-10, 10-14, and 12 up.

We are no longer accepting unsolicited manuscripts, but if you wish to query us, please send a one-page letter/synopsis only.

Although publishers select a suitable illustrator, you are welcome to send samples of artwork or photographs, but please do not send any originals.

Contact information:

Young Adult/Juvenile Fiction/Nonfiction:
Virginia Buckley, Editorial Director
Photo Essays, Picture Books: Rosemary Brosnan, Executive Editor
375 Hudson Street
New York, NY 10014
(212) 366-2627 • FAX: (212) 366-2011

Lyons & Burford
Publishers

Lyons & Burford welcomes all book proposals that fit our publishing profile—books on outdoor leisure sports, natural history, camping, fishing and the like—whether of a practical or literary nature. Proposals should include a full contents and a representative sample of the text and illustrations. We need to see hard copy rather than electronic submissions.

Bear in mind that our list is expanding all the time and many proposals that may not seem to fit what we have published in the past may in fact be of interest. If you have any question about whether a book is right for us, drop us a note (with SASE please) and we will be glad to respond.

All queries should be directed to:

Contact information:
Editorial Department
31 West 21st Street
New York, NY 10010
(212) 620-9580 • FAX: (212) 929-1836

Meriwether Publishing Ltd.
Contemporary Drama Service

SCHOOL SUBMISSIONS

We are publishers of books, plays, theatre-related books and videotapes. Our primary markets are middle grades, junior highs, high schools and some colleges. We are publishing nothing for the elementary level at present except for Sunday school plays for churches.

DRAMA:

Please include cast list, and (if required) prop list, costume information, set specifications, etc., with all play manuscripts. Following are the types of drama we publish:

- One-act non-royalty plays—originals or adaptations, comedies, parodies, social commentary and novelty drama. Plays with large and small casts and with many parts for women and a few plays for children's theatre.
- Speech contest materials—monologs for women and men duologs, short playlets addressing the high school experience with honest feelings and real situations of current importance.
- Full-length plays—up to three acts, comedy, large casts.
- Adaptations—Shakespeare, the classics, and popular modern works (with original author permission).
- Oral interpretation—folktales and storytelling.
- Prevention plays—drama as a teaching tool about drug abuse, pregnancy, gangs, etc.
- Readers Theatre—adaptations or originals.

BOOKS:

• Our books cover a wide variety of theatre subjects from play anthologies to theatrecraft. We publish books of monologs, duologs, short one-act plays, scenes for students, acting textbooks, how-to speech and theatre textbooks, improvisation and theatre games. We also publish some general humor trade books.

• Send sample chapters or an outline—no complete manuscripts.

QUERY LETTER SPECIFICATIONS:

• Include a synopsis or brief statement of objectives.

• Tell us why you believe your work deserves publication. Define the market you see as the potential audience.

• Please include a list of your publishing credits and/or experience and your payment expectations.

• Allow 4-6 weeks for response from us.

MANUSCRIPT SPECIFICATIONS:

• Include your name on each manuscript page.

• Please inquire about electronic submissions.

PAYMENT TERMS:

• We normally purchase all rights. Sometimes we make an outright purchase of a manuscript, but our usual practice is to offer a royalty contract with payments to an agreed purchase price. Rates vary according to work and credits of author/playwright. Special projects are negotiable.

NOTES:

• To gain a better understanding of the type of materials we publish, write for a book or play catalog. Please include $2 for postage and handling.

• Please obtain permission and give credit for any outside sources used in your work.

CHURCH SUBMISSIONS

Our church customers are of many faiths. Many represent the mainline Protestant denominations. Any church submissions should avoid a denominational slant and instead encompass the Christian truths common to all faiths. Primary emphasis should be themes for mainline church denominations.

DRAMA:

Please include cast list, and (if required) prop list, costume information, set specifications, etc., with all plays and musicals. Following are the types of drama we publish:

• One-act non-royalty plays on religious themes up to 20 pages.

• Christmas and Easter chancel drama or liturgy—length 30 minutes maximum—for children's Sunday school departments and also for adults.

• Collections of short sketches on a central theme—five per collection—humorous, entertaining, Christian.

• Religious musicals for Christmas and Easter—one hour maximum. (Computer-generated musical accompaniment score and set of performance preferred.)

• Readers Theatre script—30 minutes maximum.

• Monologs.

BOOKS:

• Our Christian books cover creative worship on such topics as clown ministry, storytelling, banner-making, drama ministry, children's worship, and more. We also publish anthologies of Christian sketches. We do not publish works of fiction or devotionals.

• Send sample chapters or an outline—no complete manuscripts.

QUERY LETTER SPECIFICATIONS:

- Include a synopsis or brief statement of objectives.
- Tell us why you believe your work deserves publication. Define the market you see as the potential audience.
- Please include a list of your publishing credits and/or experience.
- Let us know your expectation concerning payment for your work.
- Allow 3-5 weeks for response from us.

MANUSCRIPT SPECIFICATIONS:

- Include your name on each manuscript page.
- Please inquire about electronic submissions.

PAYMENT TERMS:

- Contract offers vary according to market potential of the work. We purchase limited or total rights or offer a royalty contract of 10% of sales. We offer some royalty contracts with payment to an agreed purchase price. Rates vary according to script and credits of author/playwright. Special projects are negotiable.

Contact information:
Drama, How-to Theatre Books: Ted Zapel, Associate Editor
885 Elkton Drive
Colorado Springs, CO 80907
(719) 594-4422

M. Evans and Company, Inc.

M. Evans no longer publishes a western line.

We publish very little fiction; however, this doesn't mean we don't want to see your proposal.

We specialize in adult nonfiction books, particularly in the areas of health and self-help.

We do not publish juvenile books.

Please submit a proposal and we will get back to you in a timely manner. Do not submit an entire manuscript.

Contact information:
216 East 49th Street
New York, NY 10017-1502
(212) 688-2810 • FAX: (212) 486-4544

Moon Publications

WHAT KIND OF BOOKS DOES MOON PUBLICATIONS PUBLISH?

Moon Publications publishes insightful, comprehensive guides for independent travelers. Our main areas of interest focus on but are not limited to, the Pacific Basin, Asia, the U.S., Canada, Latin America, and the Caribbean.

Our guides concentrate on the local culture and emphasize low-impact, good value travel. We try to bring out the most interesting, thought-provoking guides in this genre on the market today. They are thoroughly edited, attractively packaged, and contain high-quality illustrations and maps, boxed sidebars, a subject and place-name index, charts, and appendices.

BEFORE YOU SUBMIT YOUR PROPOSAL—THE QUERY

Please do not send unsolicited manuscripts to Moon Publications. If you are interested in writing a travel guide for us, send a brief description of your proposed book.

Tell us:

- The scope and focus of your guide
- The estimated length of your manuscript
- The estimated time needed to complete your manuscript, and how much is already written
- The computer hardware and software you use
- Why you are qualified to write this book
- What articles or works you have published
- Your thoughts on why Moon is the right publisher for your book

We will respond to your initial query within three weeks.

SUBMITTING YOUR PROPOSAL

If we are interested in your book idea and like your writing style, we will send your our proposal guidelines. The proposal's primary purpose is to determine your qualifications and the guide's marketability. We believe the time and effort you put into the book proposal will be well spent, both in convincing us of the merits of your proposed guide, and in helping you focus on the feasibility of your project. Before substantial discussions can be entered into regarding a book contract, you must submit the proposal.

THE CONTRACT

Our royalty rate is within industry standards, based on a percentage of the publisher's net invoice amounts. We offer advances of up to $10,000 against royalties paid in installments. Moon does not pay travel expenses.

With the contract comes a long-term commitment between the publisher and the author. To keep each guide up-to-date and selling well, we publish a new, updated edition every two years. Hence, the author must update and revise the guide on a regular schedule.

THE MANUSCRIPT

From the signing of the contract, we have found that our guides generally take from one to two and a half years to complete, depending on length. We prefer to arrange a chapter-by-chapter schedule for delivery, rather than wait for the completed manuscript and accompanying materials. Once we have the entire manuscript in hand, another five to eight months are required to complete editing, production, and printing.

Moon handbooks are complex and labor-intensive. In addition to the manuscript, the project requires you to collect and/or prepare source maps, slides, and base art from which we can produce finished maps and illustrations. The writer must follow closely our house style, organizational style sheet, and mapping guidelines, which we will send after the contract is signed. We require the author to own or have access to a computer compatible with our system, as the manuscript must be submitted on disk.

WORKING WITH YOUR EDITOR

After you sign a contract, an editor will be assigned to your project. The editor will work with you on organization, content, and style issues, and answer your questions about plans and progress relative to the book.

We look forward to hearing from you.

Contact information:
Taran March, Executive Editor
P.O. Box 3040
Chico, CA 95927-3040
(916) 345-5473 • FAX: (916) 345-5473
E-mail: editor@moon.com

National Textbook Group

(Please refer to NTC Publishing Group.)

Naval Institute Press

Nonfiction

Joint and general military subjects; naval biography; naval history; oceanography; navigation; military law; naval science textbooks; seapower; shipbuilding; professional guides; nautical arts and lore; technical guides.

Submissions require a minimum of two sample chapters, chapter outline, list of sources used, and author's biography.

Fiction

Military fiction only.

Submissions require a synopsis and complete manuscript.

All submissions must be unbound and accompanied by a cover letter. Only photocopies of artwork and photographs should be sent, not originals. Do not send disks with your submission.

Receipt of your manuscript will be acknowledged. Evaluation may take as long as twelve weeks.

Thank you for your interest in Naval Institute Press.

Contact information:
Acquisitions Editor
118 Maryland Avenue
Annapolis, MD 21402-5035
(410) 268-6110 • FAX: (410) 269-7940

New Victoria Publishers
Quality Lesbian Books Since 1976

In 1860 women's rights activist Emily Faithful founded Victoria Press, an all-woman print shop in London, England. Her tradition was revived in New England in 1975 with the establishment of New Victoria Printers and, in 1976, New Victoria Publishers, a non-profit feminist literary and cultural organization publishing the finest in lesbian feminist fiction and nonfiction.

We are primarily interested in well-crafted fiction in all genres featuring lesbians or strong female protagonists. The following ingredients should be present:

- Clear narrative story line.
- Well-drawn, intelligent, introspective characters.
- Accurate background locations or atmosphere.
- Issues pertinent to the lesbian community whether emotional, societal, or political.
- Humor and/or eroticism.

We are especially interested in lesbian or feminist mysteries, ideally with a character or characters who can evolve through a series of books. Mysteries should involve a complex plot, accurate legal/procedural detail, and protagonists with full emotional lives.

We prefer science/speculative fiction or fantasy with amazon adventure themes and/or detailed, well-crafted alternative realities, complete with appropriately original language and culture.

We are also interested in well-researched nonfiction on women, lesbian-feminist herstory, or biography of interest to a general as well as academic audience.

We advise you to look through our catalog to see our past editorial decisions as well as what we are currently marketing. Our books average 80-90,000 words, or 200-250 single-spaced pages.

Please send your enquiry to us with:

- A brief outline or synopsis highlighting key issues in the story, why you wrote it, and any target audience you have in mind.
- Several sample chapters or approximately 50-75 pages.

We prefer single submissions (ms. sent to one publisher only), so please let us know if you have submitted your manuscript to or are under contract with another publisher.

ANTHOLOGIES

New Victoria is seeking submissions for two exciting up-coming anthologies:
LESBIANS CREATING ALTERNATIVES TO MONOGAMY
and
VISIONS OF A FEMINIST TOMORROW
Write or call for detailed guidelines.
A partial List of New Victoria Authors:
Sarah Dreher
The Stoner McTavish Mysteries
Lesléa Newman
Secrets, In Every Laugh a Tear, Saturday is Pattyday, Every Woman's Dream
Kate Allen
Tell Me What You Like, Give My Secrets Back, I Knew You Would Call
J.M. Redmann
Death by the Riverside, Deaths of Jocasta, Chris Anne Wolfe, Shadows of Agar, Fires of Agar
Cris Newport
Sparks Might Fly
Jane Meyerding
Everywhere House
Lesa Luders
Lady God
Morgan Grey & Julia Penelope
Found Goddesses
Claudia McKay
Promise of the Rose Stone, The Kali Connection

ReBecca Béguin
Runway at Eland Springs, In Unlikely Places, Hers Was the Sky

Contact information:
P.O. Box 27
Norwich, VT 05055-0027
(802) 649-5297
e-mail: new.vic@valley.net

Northland Publishing Company

INTRODUCTION

Northland Publishing Company, located in Flagstaff, Arizona, was founded in 1958 as a commercial printing firm and released its first books in 1962. Since 1973 a wholly owned subsidiary of Justin Industries, Fort Worth, Texas, Northland is well regarded in the publishing industry as a publisher of nonfiction books on the natural history, material culture, and indigenous people of the American Southwest. Including fine art, history, natural history, children's books, cookbooks, and journals, Northland's diverse publications are distributed nationally and are directed to a general trade audience with relatively sophisticated and informed tastes.

TO SUBMIT A MANUSCRIPT

It is recommended that authors, illustrators, and photographers research the publisher's background and specific areas of interest before submitting a proposal. We urge anyone who is interested in submitting a proposal to make use of the reference guide Literary Market Place to identify the best publisher for his/her work. Northland will consider nonfiction manuscripts in the areas of natural history; fine art; cookbooks; and Native American culture, myth, art, and crafts. In rare instances we will consider regional fiction. We also will consider unique children's stories, especially Native American folktales (retold by Native Americans), natural history subjects, and stories with a Southwest/West regional themes. All children's stories should be no shorter than 350 words, no longer than 1,500.

A query letter and proposal should be submitted to the editorial department. The proposal should include a detailed outline, a sample chapter, the potential market for the proposed book, and any particular justification the author may feel relevant for publishing the proposed book. For children's books, send a query letter and a copy of the entire manuscript. (It is not necessary to have illustrations made when proposing children's picture books.) Information about the author, illustrator, and/or photographer may also be included. If accepted for publication, manuscripts will be edited according to the guidelines set forth in the Chicago Manual of Style, 13th edition; authors should use this manual as a reference when preparing manuscripts for submission.

When appropriate to the project or when providing art or photography to be kept on file for future consideration, illustrators and photographers should submit samples in the form of printed matter, color photocopies, or duplicate slides—color samples only, please.

Clear computer printouts are acceptable and even encouraged (later, if the manuscript is accepted for publication, it should be turned in on 3.5-inch Macintosh- or IBM-compatible computer floppy disks and in paper form, if possible.) If photographs and/or artwork are integral to the proposal, provide sample 35mm color slides or black-and-white prints. Please do not send "dummy" books. Northland will consider simultaneous submissions, but would like to be told at the outset if this is the case. Please make sure name and address are on the query letter and manuscript.

THE EVALUATION PROCESS

Because publishing any book is a financial risk and requires a major commitment of time and resources, the evaluation process is a critical one. It can take from four to twelve weeks for our editorial board to reach a decision. In the interim, the author may be asked to supply various additional materials. The author will receive an acknowledgment card when the proposal is received. If the evaluation becomes lengthy, an update will be sent; otherwise, the author will be notified upon our decision regarding publication.

The editorial department is the first to handle a proposal. There, it is carefully read and judged on quality and originality of concept, clarity of expression, and potential market competition. If the situation warrants, outside readers will be called upon for further evaluation. The material will be reviewed by the marketing department for analysis of potential sales; by the design and production department for general aesthetic and manufacturing requirements; and finally by the accounting department for evaluation of costs and potential returns on investments.

The proposal is then presented to the publisher along with comments from each department. Here a final decision is reached. If the decision is negative, the author is notified and all materials are returned. If the decision is positive, the author is notified of Northland's intent to publish the work and a rough contract is drafted for the author's review.

Northland Publishing is always willing to review unsolicited manuscripts and to consider serious proposals.

CHILDREN'S BOOK SUBMISSION GUIDELINES

Subject Matter: Unique stories for children ages five to nine, especially stories with Southwest/West regional themes; folktales of Native America (retold by Native American authors) and Mexico (retold by Hispanic authors); and Mexican American and Native American contemporary stories. We are also developing a line of middle readers chapter books (for ages nine to twelve) with similar themes. No "cute" mainstream stories, anthropomorphic animals, science fiction/fantasy, or religion. In general, our picture books are fairly sophisticated and literary, driven by character and message more than plot.

Manuscript Length: Picture books should be no shorter than 350 words, no longer than 1,500, although occasional exception (2,000 words) is made for well-written picture book manuscripts directed to slightly older readers. Middle readers manuscripts should be around 20,000 words, although length varies greatly.

Method of Submission: For help with manuscripts preparation and submission, we suggest you consult the Children's Writer's & Illustrator's Market (Writers Digest Books, Cincinnati, Ohio). To instantly earn a Northland editor's warm feelings toward your manuscript submission, follow these guidelines.

- Include a cover letter.
- Make sure your address is on your cover letter and your manuscript.
- Send a traditionally formatted manuscript instead of a "dummy" book.
- Do not include any covers, folders, or binders; instead, simply clip your manuscript pages together and make sure they are numbered.
- Address the submission to a current member of our editorial staff (see below)
- For picture book manuscripts, submit complete manuscripts instead of query letters or proposals; for middle readers chapter books, submit queries, chapter-by-chapter outlines, and two or three sample chapters.
- Do not send more than one manuscript at a time.
- Be familiar with the types of books we publish. (For a copy of our catalog, send a 9x12 SASE with $1.47 postage.)
- Inform us if your submission is being considered simultaneously by another publisher. (We do not object to simultaneous submissions, but like to know about them; we do,

however, acknowledge that the "shotgun approach" to simultaneous submissions has been a detriment to the evaluation process industry-wide, and cannot encourage authors enough to be familiar with a publishing company before approaching it.)

- Do not query by telephone or fax.

Response Time: Acknowledgment sent upon receipt; eight to twelve weeks for initial evaluation.

Northland publishing receives approximately 4,000 unsolicited manuscripts per year. Approximately two-thirds of our current books came to us as unsolicited manuscripts. Although volume does not allow us to comment on each submission individually, we will when possible send personalized responses to those authors who have put special care into the writing, preparation, and submission of their manuscripts.

Contact information:

Illustrations, Photography Samples: Art Director
Other: Erin Murphy, Editor
P.O. Box 1389
Flagstaff, AZ 86002-1389
(520) 774-5251

NTC Publishing Group

The following are some guidelines for preparing a book proposal for NTC Publishing Group. These guidelines are quite general; you may wish to include other sorts of information or components for the project you have in mind. If you have any questions about preparing the proposal, please call the editor with whom you are working.

Your proposal should include the following elements:

Overview

A brief statement of purpose that includes information about your goals for the project, the specific market you are targeting, and any competing books you are familiar with.

Contents

A breakdown of part and chapter titles. If possible, it is also helpful to have some indication of the topics that will be covered in each chapter.

Writing Sample

One or two sample chapters that demonstrate your writing style and your ability to handle the material.

Biographical Material

A current curriculum vitæ.

Your proposal will be reviewed first by the editorial department, and then, if appropriate, by marketing and management. If your proposal is accepted, your editor will contact you to discuss business arrangements, manuscript deadlines, and publication dates.

Contact information:

English/LA Textbooks: John Nolan, Editorial Group Director
Foreign Language Textbooks: Keith Fry, Executive Editor
Travel books: Dan Spinella, Editor
Career Books: Betsy Lancefield, Editor
NTC Business Books: Rich Hagle, Editor
4255West Touhy Avenue
Lincolnwood, IL 60646-1975
(847) 679-5500 • FAX (708) 679-2494

The Oryx Press

Founded in 1975, The Oryx Press publishes essential information products for libraries and professionals in many subject areas including education, business, government, science and technology, human services, grants and funding sources, health care, and library information science, in print and electronic media.

ACQUISITION ACTIVITIES

We welcome proposals from authors working on or planning projects that fit our publishing program.

To submit your project for publication consideration by The Oryx Press, you must include the following:

1. A statement of purpose and audience.
2. A complete outline of your work.
3. A sample chapter or representative section of your work, or the complete manuscript.

Proposal Review

If your proposal appears to fit our publishing program, we will respond by sending you our author questionnaire, without which we cannot proceed. It will ask for further details about your project. The proposal will then be reviewed in-house and sent out for review by people knowledgeable in the subject field. If reviews are positive, sales estimates are acceptable, the financial picture is good, and no serious competition emerges, the proposal will be sent to the Oryx Press Editorial Board for review, which will vote to accept or reject the project.

A number of reviews may be necessary. The review procedure ensures that your manuscript gets a fair and complete hearing and allows us to help shape your work with you to best fit the needs of the market. The review process takes time, especially when we must get out-of-house comments. Please be prepared to wait from 6-12 weeks for a decision. A few projects may take longer, but you will be informed if that is necessary.

If your proposal is accepted for publication, you will be sent a contract.

Contact Information:
Acquisitions Department
Oryx Press
4041 N. Central Ave.
Phoenix, AZ 85012-3397.

Passport Books

(Please refer to NTC Publishing Group.)

Pelican Publishing Company

Submissions Policy: Pelican Publishing Company does not accept unsolicited manuscripts. All writers should send us a query letter, describing the project briefly and concisely. Multiple (or "simultaneous") submissions are not considered.

A query letter should discuss the following: the book's content, its anticipated length (in double-spaced pages, not in words), its intended audience, the author's writing and professional background, and any promotional ideas and contacts the author may have. If the author has previously been published by another firm, please specify why a change is being sought. A formal synopsis, chapter outline, and/or one or two sample chapters may be sent with a query letter, but these are not required.

Be advised that we have certain expectations in the length of a proposed manuscript. Most young children's books are 32 illustrated pages when published; their manuscripts cover about 7 pages when typed continuously. Proposed books for middle readers (ages 8 and up) should be at least 150 pages. Adult books should be more than this. For cookbooks, we require at least 200 proposed recipes.

If necessary, brief children's books (for readers under nine) may be submitted in their entirety. Photocopies of any accompanying artwork are welcome.

We will respond as promptly as possible (usually one month), letting you know whether or not we feel the project is worth pursuing further. If we feel that it is worthy of consideration, we will request a partial or full manuscript. Following this procedure ensures the most expeditious treatment of all inquiries.

We do not require that writers contacting us have a literary agent representing them.

A phone call to the editor or secretary or an in-person drop off of unrequested material does not automatically imply that a project has been solicited. For this and other obvious reasons, we discourage phone inquiries and in-person drop offs. If an author we have requested additional material from is unclear as to what we're asking for, a phone call to clarify the matter is acceptable.

Solicited manuscripts are carefully scrutinized by the editor(s). On occasion, they may be examined by our sales and/or promotion departments to gauge their marketability. They are then passed on to the publisher for preliminary and final consideration. The submissions are reported on as soon as possible, but this process may take up to three months (12 weeks). If acceptance is recommended, the author(s) will be asked to sign a contract with Pelican Publishing Company.

If the three month period for solicited manuscripts passes without the author being informed of a decision, a polite note of reminder from the author is not out of order. Phone calls on the status of manuscripts are very strongly discouraged. Never badger the editor for an instant decision or make demands or threats; this can only hurt the authors chances of acceptance. Authors who feel unsatisfied with our procedures or the amount of time being taken to reach a decision are free to request the manuscript's return at any time.

Pelican Publishing requires exclusive submission for all solicited manuscripts during the 12-week period mentioned above. This is for obvious reasons. We can only give full attention to those manuscripts which we are likely to be able to publish if accepted by us.

We also ask that authors who have solicited works under consideration please refrain from sending us other works or proposals during this time unless they are specifically requested to do so. Agreement on our part to look at a particular work does not imply blanket authorization to send unrelated materials and doing so could hurt, rather than help, an author. Materials related to the requested submission, such as favorable newspaper clippings, endorsements by qualified professionals in the field the author is writing about, or other amended data may be sent and added to the material already on file. Use careful judgment in selecting these items and be certain that they enhance the material and its chances of being accepted. Sending in later data that refutes or calls into question points made in the earlier submission may cast doubts on the whole project's veracity and damage its chances of acceptance. Always be certain to refer to the work's title, the author name under which it was submitted, and the date the original query was mailed.

Policies regarding SASE's apply to all submissions from foreign countries, including Canada. Return postage must be in stamps, checks on U.S. banks, or international Money

Orders in U.S. Money.

Electronic submissions (discs) are not accepted. These would only be needed once a contract was signed. Never send discs, videotapes, or audio tapes without inquiring beforehand.

Authors should avoid undue "hype-ing" of their work. Material being submitted with author projections of it being a "blockbuster" or "the next *Gone With the Wind*" rarely live up to these pretensions. The publisher and editor(s) are professionals who can make up their own minds on the quality and potential of a proposal without the "self-hype." Comments and/or reviews from professionals or publications, as stated earlier, can be desirable in many cases. Likewise for rejection letters from other publishing companies that acknowledge a project's potential value and which base their rejections on other factors unrelated to quality of author workmanship.

We look for clarity and conciseness of expression and presentation in a synopsis/outline and we ask to see those that will most likely yield proposals fitting our list and that we feel we can market successfully. We turn down thousands of adequate proposals every year just because they have no clear "hooks" or well-defined audiences. The author should present a strong case as to why we should take on the book and who would buy it. Saying that "all children would love it" is very vague, but saying "libraries and schools in Tennessee would like this" is more informative.

All work submitted to us must be in good taste, nonlibelous, and consistent with the level of quality we have established for our company. Although many of our titles are specialized, they are **all** suitable for general readership and are free from gratuitous, off-color words, phrases, or references.

If an author seeking to publish an illustrated work plans to use artwork copyrighted by an author, illustrator, publication, or syndicate, permission must be obtained in writing from that source. Permission in writing must also be obtained by any author seeking to use quotes or other materials from previously copyrighted publications. We will not publish illustrations or portions of another copyrighted work without written authorization to do so.

Authors seeking to have previously published books reprinted must have, in writing from their previous publisher, a signed letter transferring all rights (including copyright) to them. This is required under the 1978 Copyright Law and must be adhered to in all cases.

Under the revisions contained in the 1978 Copyright Law, a work is **automatically** copyrighted at the time of creation. If we agree to accept the work for publication, we will apply for the copyright in the author's name on publication.

TYPES OF BOOKS PUBLISHED: Hardcover and trade paperback originals (90%) and reprints (10%) including hardcover, trade paperback, and mass market. We publish an average of 50 to 60 titles a year and have about 800 currently in print.

Specialties are art/architecture books, cooking/cookbooks, motivational, travel guides, history (especially Louisiana/regional), nonfiction, children's books (illustrated and otherwise), inspirational and religious, humor, social commentary, folklore, and textbooks. A **very limited** number of fictional works are accepted for publication, but we will consider fiction if well written and/or timely.

We seek writers on the cutting edge of ideas who do not write in clichés, or take the old, tired, unimaginative way of foul language and sex scenes to pad a poor writing effort. We strongly encourage writers to be aware of ideas gaining currency. We believe ideas have consequences. One of the consequences is that they lead to best-selling books.

We do publish a limited number of posters, cards, giftware, and similar works of art. Consideration of submission of this type is based on consistency with other motifs we are marketing at the present time.

Finally, we would ask you to study Pelican's books and lists. Our latest catalog is available for free on request, and a look through it will help you understand where our interests lie. We have been called "innovative" by the New York Times. We will consider almost any well-written work by an author who understands promotion.

PAYMENT POLICY: Pelican pays its authors a royalty based on sales. The rate depends on the type of material and the format.

All terms are specified in the contract all authors publishing under our imprint(s) are required to sign. No book will be published by Pelican without a contract signed beforehand.

All guidelines listed above are subject to revision at any time by Pelican Publishing Company and its editorial board.

Contact information:
P.O. Box 3110
Gretna, LA 70054-3110
(504) 368-1175 • FAX: (504) 368-1195

Permeable Press

Permeable Press is an alternative fiction publishing house. What do we mean by "alternative"? Many things, as is reflected by the name of our press, Permeable. We view the big-moneyed "mainstream" media outlets to be Impermeable: they are rigid, formulaic, safe. Permeable Press, a subsidiary of nothing, beholden to no one, is dedicated to the exception, the slip-through-the-cracks, the too-risky-but-too-good. You may not like every thing we publish but you won't be bored.

That being said as a sort of general introduction to our philosophy of fiction publishing, there are a few particulars.

Telephone calls: please don't call us. If you do, we are likely to be extremely brief. Time is short, and there is much to do. More than likely, we won't return your message, either. We're not rude, just busy.

The best way to communicate with us is through the mail. We've got lots of printed material to send you. If you are in on-line kinda person some, but not all, of the printed matter is on our web site.

What do we like?: The best way to get a feel of what we're likely to be interested in is to read some of our books and magazines. You can write for a free catalog-a stamp is appreciated.

NOVELS: We publish several novels and short story collections per year. Please send a query letter with a brief description of the book you are selling, with an even briefer description of your qualifications, plus a page or two of material on why we should publish the work, how it should be marketed, etc. Naturally, you are free to do whatever you want: this is just a guideline.

MAGAZINES: Please note that *Puck Magazine* is on hiatus. It will return in an unexpected form in 1997. Please do not submit to *Puck* in the meantime, but stay tuned to *Permeable Press News* (on-line, or available on paper if you send an SASE every six months or so).

New magazines at Permeable: To fill our obligation to subscribers and keep our periodical hands from idleness, we are doing two zines

Q ZINE is a magazine of books and ideas. Each issue features one or more provocative essays, plus as many book, zine, music, and video reviews as we can squeeze in. Payment for a feature essay is 1/2-cent/word plus copies. Payment for other contributions is copies plus a selection from the Permeable Press catalog.

We are currently seeking essays about: Dreams, Nightmares and Conspiracies; the Future of the Internet; and Alien Abductions.

Reviewers are encouraged to send a brief writing sample, a short list of the types of things they would be interested in reviewing, and a request for an assignment. Or you can simply submit a finished review.

Sample copies of *Q ZINE* are $4; subscriptions are $12/4 issue—subscriptions include a selection from our chapbook catalog.

SHOCK WAVES is a new fiction zine. The next several issues are full. Please watch for news about upcoming issues and editorial needs. Length limits: no longer than 15,000 words. Payment is 1/2-cent/word plus copies, on publication. Sample copies of *SHOCK WAVES* are $4; subscriptions are $12/4 issue—subscriptions include a selection from our chapbook catalog.

CHAPBOOKS: We've been producing about 1 chapbook per month, often with serigraphed covers, or other artbook touches. We've published everything from a small group of poems to novellas. While we welcome unsolicited manuscripts for consideration for the chapbook series, as ever you're better off sending us a query letter to see if we're interested in what you have to offer.

Please feel free to contact us by snail mail or e-mail if you have questions.

Contact Information:
2336 Market Street, #14
San Francisco, CA 94114
(415)255-9765
E-mail: bcclark@igc.org or http://www.armory.com/~jay/permeable.html

PILOT BOOKS

Pilot Books

Subject matter should fit our area of interest.
Book should be a maximum of 80 printed pages. Preferred length 48-64 printed pages.
Submit a brief outline and sample chapter.
You will receive our decision within fourteen days after receipt of proposal.

Contact information:
Anne Small, President
103 Cooper Street
Babylon, NY 11702
(516) 422-2225

Players Press, Inc.

PLAYERS PRESS, Inc. is continually looking for new works to publish. Send a clearly typed copy of your play, musical, or performing arts book to the address below.

Remember to enclose the following:

1. Two stamped, self-addressed envelopes for correspondence.
2. A copy of the flyer and program with production dates on it. **No manuscript will be considered unless it has been produced.** (produced means: one professional production, or two amateur productions, or one award-winning amateur production. A reading is not

considered a production.)

3. A brief biography and/or resume of the writer.
4. Reviews, when available.
5. If accepted for publication, the script must be made available on computer disk. We prefer Macintosh in either Microsoft Word or Pagemaker. Please advise.

Our editors will try to read your work and return it to you within 90 days.

Contact information:
P.O. Box 1132
Studio City, CA 91614-0132

Prima Publishing

GUIDELINES FOR UNSOLICITED, UNAGENTED SUBMISSIONS

PRIMA PUBLISHING, founded in 1984, publishes hardcovers and trade paperbacks in nonfiction categories including popular culture, current affairs and international events, travel, business, careers, legal topics, sports, cooking, health, lifestyle, self-help, and music. Prima also produces a line of computer books geared towards business, professional, and recreational uses, and a line of video/computer game clue books. Prima is among the fastest-growing of the independent publishers and maintains a solid backlist.

Popular Prima titles like the following express the varied interests of the company: *Scout's Honor: Sexual Abuse in America's Most Trusted Institution* by Patrick Boyle, *The Tao of Love* by Ivan Hoffman, *For the Sake of the Children: How to Share Your Children With Your Ex-Spouse- In Spite of Your Anger* by Kris Kline and Stephen Pew, *Links: An Exploration into the Mind, Heart, and Soul of Golf* by Lorne Rubenstein, *Hot & Spicy & Meatless* by Dave DeWitt, Mary Jane Wilan, & Melissa Stock, *The New Palestinians: The Emerging Generation of Leaders* by John Wallach and Janet Wallach, *WordPerfect: How Do I . . . ?* by Cristy Clason, *The Dog Lover's Literary Companion: Great Writers and Artists Celebrate man's Best Friend* by John Richard Stephens, and *The Encyclopedia of Natural Medicine* by Michael T. Murray, N.D. and Joseph Pizzorno, N.D.

Prima does not publish fiction, personal narrative (individual lifestories intended to reveal or instruct), or poetry.

Unsolicited queries are accepted and examined carefully, but certain standards for effective book proposals do exist and would increase the chances of publication for the author.

ADDITIONAL GUIDELINES

- If the author is a first time author, the book should be completed before the proposal is sent. Please do not send a manuscript unless specifically requested.
- If the author has been published before, he or she should include as much information as possible about previous books-titles, dates, publishers, total net sales, etc.
- *Jeff Herman's The Insider's Guide to Book Editors, Publishers, and Literary Agents* and *Write the Perfect Book Proposal: 10 That Sold & Why!* Have detailed sections on how to produce an effective book proposal.
- Please allow four to six weeks for an answer.

PROPOSAL GUIDELINES

Please include the following when sending a proposal to Prima Publishing:

A brief explanation of the book. What is the manuscript about, and why would someone buy it? Like the short text written on the back cover of a book, the explanation should describe the contents of the book while also enticing the reader to know more about it. The overview is also an opportunity for the author to display his or her unique writing style. To prepare for an overview, it may be a worthwhile practice to read the back covers of several books in a local bookstore, noting the way the publisher tries to catch and hold the reader's interest.

A detailed table of contents and chapter outlines. Breaking the manuscript down into individual chapters, write a paragraph discussing the information in each chapter. Chapter outlines and a table of contents convinces the publisher that the author has compiled enough material for a book and is focusing that material in a particular direction.

Anticipated market for the book (this is very important: remember, publishing is a business). Who is the intended audience? Be as specific as possible. Quantify and target the audience: the author of Fantastic Felines may cite the number of cat owners in America. The author may cite another cat book that was recently a best-seller, showing that interest is high in the subject. The author may mention special markets, or areas besides traditional bookstores that could carry the book. For example, the cat book author presents pet stores as a special market. The author must come up with powerful arguments, supported by statistics where applicable, that persuade the publisher to invest time and money in the project. The author must prove that the project will be a profitable venture for all involved.

Competition for the book. Are there other books currently on the market that address the same or similar subjects? Having identified these books, the author then states why his or her book is different; how it fulfills some area the others lacked, etc. The point is not to deny the competition, but to recognize and separate the competition from the author's work. For example, someone who has written a manuscript about arthritis lists several current arthritis books, while adding that none of theses titles has an index of treatment centers and medical specialists as his or her book does.

Author's Qualifications. What makes the author the right person to create this book? Any career experience or educational experience should be noted, as well as teaching or speaking experience.

Contact information:

Trade, Lifestyles: Jennifer Basye Sander, Senior Acquisition Editor
Trade: Georgia Hughes
Computer: Alan Harris
Entertainment, Games: Greg Aaron, Juliana Aldous, Brett Skogen
P.O. Box 1260
Rocklin, CA 95677
(916) 632-4400 • FAX: (916) 632-4405

Publishers Associates

Unsolicited manuscripts will be returned if not preceded with a letter of inquiry containing:

- a cover letter stating that it is not a simultaneous submission
- a synopsis
- a tentative table of contents

All works submitted must be nonfiction.

Footnoting must follow this format:

- author's first, middle, last name(s), Title; subtitle(s), (City, State/Province: Publisher's full nomenclature, date), volume number (if any), pages cited.

Bibliography must include:

• author's first, middle, last name(s), Title; subtitle(s), (City, State/Province: Publisher's full nomenclature, date), volume number (if any), pages cited.

• be in alphabetic order using the author's last name

All content must be gender free of references unless work is about one particular gender. We do not publish sexist materials.

All publications must reflect liberal thinking in all areas.

The publisher has the right to edit grammar, spelling, and syntax. The publisher will not edit or change the author's style.

The presses of Publishers Associates (The Galaxy Group, The Liberal Press, Liberal Arts Press, Minuteman Press, Monument Press, Nichole Graphics, Stardate 2000, Tangelwüld Press) publish only liberal history, liberal politics, gay/lesbian/feminist/minority studies (history, social condition, etc.), and liberation theology. We do not contract for biographies, poetry, autobiographies, conservative or doctrinal works.

Publishers Associates will direct the manuscript to the Press that would be most likely to contract for it. All contracts are issued by the contracting press, not by the consortium Publishers Associates as a whole/unit.

All manuscripts must be sent to:

Contact information:
P.O. Box 140361
Las Colinas, TX 75014-0361

Quill Driver Books/Word Dancer Press, Inc.

We have no formal guidelines. However, we publish nonfiction books only and, if you have one that has a large identifiable and reachable audience, we'd like to hear from you. We do not publish personal narratives (individual lifestories), poetry, children's books, or fiction.

We suggest you read the workshop by Michael Larsen on how to write a nonfiction book proposal in *The Portable Writers' Conference: Your Guide to Getting and Staying Published* available at libraries and bookstores and follow his instructions to the letter. While this isn't absolutely necessary, a properly executed book proposal will increase your chances with us as well as with other publishers. It will also help you think your project through completely.

Recent titles we have published include *The Pediatrician's New Baby Owner's Manual: Your Guide to the Care and Fine-Tuning of Your New Baby* by Horst D. Weinberg, *The American Directory of Writer's Guidelines: What Editors Want, What Editors Buy* compiled by John C. Mutchler, and *Three Strikes and You're Out!: The Chronicle of America's Toughest Anti-Crime Law* by Mike Reynolds & Bill Jones with Dan Evans.

Thanks for your interest.

Stephen Blake Mettee, Publisher

Contact information:
P.O. Box 4638
Fresno, CA 93744-4638
(209) 497-0809 • FAX: (209) 497-9266

The Quilt Digest Press

(Please refer to NTC Publishing Group.)

Rainbow Publishers

Books for Children's Ministries

Our objective:

We publish helpful how-to books, activity books and 'teaching tips" for leaders of children in both the church and home settings. Generally, our children's ministries products are 64-page reproducible books issued in series for various ages and grade levels. All are Bible-based.

We specifically seek:

- Classroom resources for Christian educators, such as crafts, activities and worksheets, bulletin boards and games
- Proposals for our 52 Ways series. Each book contains 52 amplified hints, tips, ideas or lessons on a specific topic for Christian educators
- Manuscripts or queries for other "teacher help" books. All materials must be designed to help Christian educators lead ministries to children
- Additional proposals for books that encourage or teach children about the Christian life

We will not publish:

- Poetry
- Picture books
- Fiction
- Symbolic stories
- Books that require four-color illustrations

The kinds of writers we are looking for:

- Have accepted Jesus as Savior and are dedicated to serving Him and leading others to Him
- Relate well to children and teachers
- Have hands-on experience working with children
- Are active participants in a Bible-believing church
- Write creatively, either published or unpublished

To submit your proposal:

- Send a query, synopsis or the entire manuscript for our evaluation
- Enclose a resume or statement explaining your qualifications for writing the book
- Explain the audience for your book and how your book differs from those already on the market
- We normally respond in two to eight weeks.
- If your proposal includes crafts, be prepared to send the completed crafts if requested.

After evaluating your proposal/manuscript we will do one of the following:

- Suggest you contact another publisher
- Request a contents summary and sample chapters (including, sample crafts, if applicable)
- Ask for revisions and resubmittal
- Seek expanded material from you
- Offer you a contract

Adult Books

Our objective:

We publish growth and development books for evangelical Christians—from a non-denominational viewpoint—that may be marketed primarily through Christian bookstores.

These books may include but are not limited to:

- Devotionals
- Activity ideas for church groups
- Study guides
- Books that encourage or promote Christian values

We will not publish:

- Academic work of a scholarly nature
- Poetry
- Fiction
- Curricula

The kinds of writers we are looking for:

- Have accepted Jesus as Savior and are dedicated to serving Him and leading others to Him
- Relate well to the needs of the evangelical Christian market
- Are active participants in a Bible-believing church
- Write creatively, either published or unpublished

To submit your proposal:

- Send a query, synopsis, or the entire manuscript for our evaluation
- Enclose a resume or statement explaining your qualifications for writing the book
- Explain the audience for your book and how your book differs from those already on the market
- We normally respond in two to eight weeks.

After evaluating your proposal/manuscript we will do one of the following:

- Suggest you contact another publisher
- Request a contents summary and sample chapters
- Ask for revisions and resubmittal
- Seek expanded material from you
- Offer you a contract. We issue both royalty and full-rights contracts, depending on the type of book.

Contact information:
Christy Allen, Editor
P.O. Box 261129
San Diego, CA 92196
(619) 271-7600 • FAX: (619) 578-4795

Schirmer Books
An Imprint of Macmillan, Inc.

GUIDELINES FOR WRITING A MANUSCRIPT PROPOSAL

A. The Book:

1. Brief Description

In one or two paragraphs, describe the work, including its rationale, approach, and pedagogy. "This book is . . . It does . . .Its distinguishing features are . . ."

2. Outline

A detailed outline of the book should be prepared, including the chapters being submitted for review. This gives us an idea of how the material fits together, and how the remaining chapters will be developed. It should include chapter headings and sub-headings, with explanations as necessary.

3. Outstanding features

List briefly what you consider to be the outstanding, distinctive, or unique features of the work.

4. Apparatus

a. Will the book include photographs, line drawings, musical examples, cases, questions, problems, glossaries, bibliography, references, appendices, etc.?

b. If the book is a text, do you plan to provide supplemental material to accompany it? (Teacher's manual, study guide, solutions, answers, workbook, anthology, or other material.)

5. Competition

a. Consider the existing books in this field and discuss specifically their strengths and weaknesses. Spell out how your book will be similar to, as well as different from, competing works.

b. Consider what aspects of topical coverage are similar to or different from the competition. What topics have been left out of competing books and what topics have been left out of yours?

c. Please discuss each competing book in a separate paragraph. The above information will provide the reviewers and the publisher with a frame of reference for evaluating your material. Remember, you are writing for reviewers and not for publication, so be as frank as possible regarding your competition. Give credit where credit is due, and show how you can do it better.

B. Market Considerations:

1. The Primary Market

a. What is the major market for the book? (Text, scholarly/professional, reference, trade?)

b. If this is a text, for what course is the book intended? Is the book a core text or a supplement? What type of student takes this course? What is the level? (Major or non-major; freshman, senior, graduate?) Do you offer this course yourself? If so, how many times have you given it? Is your text class-tested?

c. If the market is scholarly/professional, reference, or trade, how may it best be reached? (Direct mail, relevant journals, professional associations, libraries, book or music stores?) For what type of reader is your book intended?

2. Other Markets

Please list secondary markets where your book may be of interest. (Other course titles, related fields, subsidiary audiences, etc.) If you have done any market research of your own, we would appreciate receiving a brief summary of your findings.

C. Status of the Work:

1. Do you have a timetable for completing the book?
   a. What portion or percentage of the material is now complete?
   b. When do you expect to have a complete manuscript?
2. What do you estimate to be the size of the completed book?

Double-spaced typewritten pages normally reduce about 1/3 when set in type; e.g., 300 typewritten pages make about 200 printed pages. There are about 450 words on a printed page.

a. Approximately how many photographs do you plan to include/

b. Approximately how many line drawings (charts, graphs, diagrams, etc.) will you need?

c. Do you intend to include music examples? If so, how many single lines of music do you estimate will be included? How much of it do you anticipate can be reproduced from existing sources, and how much will need to be newly autographed?

d. Do you plan to include material requiring permission (text, music, lyrics, illustrations)? To what extent? Have you started the permissions request process?

3. Do you plan to class-test the material in your own or other sections of the course? (Any material distributed to students should be protected by copyright notice on the material.)

Sample Chapters

Select one or two chapters of the manuscript that are an integral part of the book. They should be those you consider to be the best-written ones, and do not have to be in sequence. For example, you might submit chapters 3, 7 and 14 of a 20-chapter book, so long as these chapters represent the content and reflect your writing style and pedagogy in the best possible light. It is also advisable to submit any chapter that is innovative or unique.

Sample chapters should contain rough sketches, charts, hand-written musical examples or photocopy reproductions, and descriptions of photographs to be included. The material need not be in final form. In your preparation, emphasis should be on readability.

Reviews

We will, of course, obtain the best available reviewers to consider your work. We would like to include some whose opinions you would consider particularly important. For this purpose, please provide the names, addresses, and phone numbers (if available) of three or four whom you feel would be competent to review your material and whose opinion you would find valuable. We will try to use some of these along with some of our own selection.

Naturally, we do not reveal the names of reviewers without their permission.

Contact information:

Trade: Richard Carlin, Senior Editor
Text, Scholarly: Jill Lectka, Acquisitions Editor
1633 Broadway, 5th Floor
New York, NY 10019-6785
(212) 654-8464

Sierra Club Books

Dear Writer,

This is in regards to your inquiry about guidelines.

The following list describes briefly the items we like to receive with submissions if they apply to your work and if you have them available:

1. Table of contents
2. Précis: overview of the plot, theme, and events of the book in summary
3. Sample chapter
4. Book specifications (if this is a previously published work): number of pages, type size, page format, etc.
5. Outline
6. Samples of any illustrations or photos if appropriate

We appreciate your interest in Sierra Club Books.

Sincerely,

Deborah Gwynn-MacDougall

Editorial Assistant

Contact information:
Editorial Department
85 2nd Street
San Francisco, CA 94105
(415) 291-1600 • FAX: (415) 291-1602

Simon & Schuster
Atheneum Books for Young Readers

Atheneum publishes original hardcover trade books for children from pre-school age through young adult. Our list includes picture books, chapter books, mysteries, science fiction and fantasy, and middle grade young adult fiction and nonfiction. The style and subject matter of the books we publish is almost unlimited. We do not, however, publish textbooks, coloring or activity books, greeting cards, magazines or pamphlets or religious publications. Anne Schwartz Books is a new and highly selective line of books recently added to the Atheneum imprint. The lists of Charles Scribner's Sons Books for Young Readers have been folded into the Atheneum program.

General Submission Guidelines

Atheneum accepts only letters of inquiry describing your work, regardless of length or type (picture books, novels, nonfiction). Should the work seem to be in line with our current publishing needs, we will then request the complete picture book manuscripts or outlines and sample chapters of longer works.

With your submission, you may also wish to include a brief resume of your previous publishing credits.

Each editor evaluates almost all types of books, although science fiction and fantasy and nonfiction submissions should be addressed to Ms. Marshall (see below).

Please allow twelve weeks for your material to be considered. Although it often takes less time, it can take even longer than we would like because of the many thousands of submissions we receive and because every submission is carefully considered.

Picture Book Submissions:

Atheneum publishes 15-20 picture books each year. Do not include illustrations with your manuscript submission since a good book can be turned down because of poor or inappropriate illustrations. It is the prerogative of the publisher to choose illustrators. If you yourself are a professional artist, you might wish to send samples (no larger than 8 ½" x 11") to our art director, Ann Bobco. Should you wish to show your portfolio when you are in the New York area, please contact Ethan Trask at (212) 698-2785. Drop-offs are accepted only on Thursdays at 10 a.m. and will be left at the reception desk for pick up at noon. No manuscripts will be read or considered at this time.

Questions frequently asked:

"What are you looking for?"

The most common answer each editor gives to this question is simply, "Nothing specific—just good writing." Atheneum puts less emphasis on particular trends, fads and gimmicks and more on quality of craftsmanship—fine writing and artwork. This and originality are the most important things we look for in a manuscript.

"Why did you turn my manuscript down?"

Although it is easy to understand a writer's desire for a critique of his work, the constant heavy influx of submissions makes it impossible to offer evaluations of work that has been declined. Form rejection letters are not meant as an insult, but simply are the only way publishers can handle the number of submissions received. A writer can expect feed-back on his work by taking one of the many excellent writing courses offered by local colleges and universities—some of them specifically geared to children's books. Another source of evaluation can be found in joining a local writers group. Such groups commonly critique members' work in progress. THE SUBJECT GUIDE TO BOOKS IN PRINT by R.R. Bowker Company also lists helpful books on writing for children and the Children's Book Council (568 Broadway, New York, NY 10003) has a pamphlet on the subject available on request. But perhaps the simplest and cheapest way of finding out what publishers look for is to go to your local public or school library and read.

Contact information:

Manuscripts may be addressed to:
Jonathan J. Lanman, Editorial Director
Anne Schwartz, Editorial Director (Anne Schwartz Books)
Marcia Marshall, Executive Editor
Sarah Caguiat, Editor
Ana Cerro, Associate Editor
1230 Avenue of the Americas
New York, NY 10020
(212) 698-2721 • FAX: (212) 698-2796

Sourcebooks, Inc.

Dear Author,

Sourcebooks has strong bookstore distribution and provides media support behind each of our titles. Our line specializes in business books—particularly small business, marketing and management, as well as a trade line focusing on more fun, gift-oriented product for mass market.

We are only interested in books that will establish a standard in their domain. We look for books with a well-defined, strong target market. Please do not send complete manuscripts unless a specific request is made for one. Simultaneous submissions are OK.

In order to consider your book for potential publication we will need to see a proposal that includes the following things:

- Title/Author-Co-author
- A bio or resume of the Authors/Co-authors specifying the author's credentials
- A Brief Synopsis in 1-2 paragraphs
- A Complete Table of Contents
- 2-3 Sample Chapters—(not the first)
- A Description of the Target Audience
- A List of Competing or Comparable Titles
- One Page/Paragraph on your book's Unique Advantages
- Length of Manuscript in Words AND Pages
- Information on any Previous Publications by Authors/Co-authors

We return rejections within 4-6 weeks. We may take longer if your book is being considered for publication.

Thank you for thinking of Sourcebooks for your book. We look forward to reviewing your materials shortly and carefully considering your book for publication.

Contact information:
Todd Stocke, Editor
121 North Washington, Suite 2
Naperville, IL 60540
(708) 961-3900 • FAX: (708) 961-2168

Spectrum Press, Inc.

Spectrum Press publishes books on floppy disks, our current list exceeds 250 titles. We publish only on computer disk, but in certain cases we also arrange for print publication by another publisher.

Some bookstores that sell our titles: Tattered Cover - Denver, CO; A Different Light - San Francisco, CA; Lambda Rising - Washington, DC; People Like Us - Chicago, IL.

We're interested in looking at the work of authors with new voices and new attitudes. Of particular interest to us are the following: literary and avant-garde fiction, poetry, drama; criticism in any of the arts (film, drama, fiction, etc.); fiction and poetry translations from other languages; all forms of quality erotica (heterosexual, gay, and lesbian), gay and lesbian fiction and nonfiction; feminist and women's studies nonfiction; African-American fiction and nonfiction; politically left nonfiction.

All nonfiction and fiction, including collections of short stories, should be book-length, which means at least 40,000 words (230K).

We also publish on disks work previously print-published, and some of the contemporary titles on our list are in this category, i.e., we have subsidiary rights contracts with print publishers.

How to submit your work: If the work is nonfiction, query us first with a brief description. If the work is fiction, send the complete work on floppy disk (see below). Please do not send us a complete manuscript on paper unless we ask for it. If a submission does not suit our needs, and there is no return postage, we discard it. Foreign authors: We will not return a package sent to us with International Reply Coupons as return postage (no one seems able to get the coupons stamped correctly).

E-mail queries: If you have an E-mail address, an E-mail query to us is simple and economical. We will usually reply within a day or two. Our E-mail addresses are listed below.

Disk submissions:

1) PC (IBM-compatible) disks: Any size, DD or HD. Will suffice. Our preferred PC format is WordPerfect 5.1. If you cannot convert your files to that format, send plain ASCII text files.

2) Macintosh disks: The Mac disk must be 3.5" HD and formatted at 1.4 Meg. Our preferred Mac format is plain text.

Query us if you need more information about disk submissions.

Contact information:
Daniel Vian, Editor
3023 North Clark Street, #109
Chicago, IL 60657
(312) 281-1419
E-mail: 71022.251@compuserve.com or SPECPRESS (GENIE)

Sterling Publishing Co., Inc.

At present our list is made up primarily of reference and "how-to" books: step-by-step instructions on practical subjects:

woodworking; housebuilding; fiber arts; crafts; lettering; art; sports; business; language; health; gardening; hobbies; pets; tricks; games; herbs; wines; etc.

We also publish books in the following categories:

science; natural history; new age; militaria; puzzles; children's riddles and jokes; and children's science and activities. Our riddle books are substantial collections of 500+ items.

Sterling does not publish any children's picture books, or fiction—children's or adult's.

If you wish to submit an idea or a manuscript:

Please write to us explaining your idea and enclosing, if possible, an outline and a sample chapter. We will contact you in due course, returning your material or asking to see more.

Thank you for your interest in our company.

Contact information:
Sheila Anne Barry, Acquisitions Director
387 Park Avenue South
New York, NY 10016-8810
(212) 532-7160 • FAX: (212) 213-2495

Storey Communications, Inc.

The mission of Storey Communications is to serve our customers by publishing practical information that encourages personal independence in harmony with the environment. We seek to do this in a positive atmosphere that promotes editorial quality, team spirit, and profitability. The books we select to carry out this mission include titles on gardening, small-scale farming, building, cooking, crafts, part-time businesses, home improvement, woodworking, animals, nature, kids, and country living.

We are always pleased to review new proposals, which we try to process expeditiously. We offer both work-for-hire and standard royalty contracts. If you have ideas for a book on any of the subjects in our line, and if you are intrigued by the philosophy expressed in our mission statement, we hope you will think of Storey Communications/Garden Way Publishing.

Book proposal packages should include the following:

- A letter of introduction
- A one-paragraph description of your boo idea
- A brief statement explaining why you think your book is needed and describing the potential readers of your book
- A list of recent books (if any) that are similar to your own, with an explanation of how yours will be different
- A paragraph about yourself and your credentials for writing the book you are proposing (you may also wish to enclose your resume)
- A table of contents, including a brief description of each chapter
- Some of your thoughts about the length, general appearance, and illustrative requirements of the book
- A sample of your writing, if available

Contact information:

Gwen W. Steege, Editorial Director
Schoolhouse Road
Pownal, VT 05261
(802) 823-5200 • FAX: (802) 823-5819

Taylor Publishing Company
Trade Books Division

The editorial department appreciates your interest and requests that you follow these guidelines when submitting your proposal: include a cover letter with a synopsis of the proposed work, biographical information as it pertains to the proposed subject matter (what experience/qualifications you bring to the subject), a brief overview of other similar works on the market and how yours is different, a sample table of contents or outline, and one or two sample chapters (or several articles if the chapters haven't been completed) so that we can assess your writing. Please allow four to six weeks for a response.

Taylor publishes about 25 books a year in the following adult nonfiction categories: gardening, health, sports, how-to/home improvement, biography, pop culture, parenting, and some general nonfiction titles. We do NOT publish fiction, poetry, photography books, Texana, regional (South) books, cookbooks, travel, history, self-help/self-testimonial books, or children's books. If your project does not fit Taylor's list or you would like more information about the publishing industry, consult The Literary Marketplace, a helpful resource which can be found in most local libraries.

Contact information:

Jason Rath, Editorial Assistant
1550 West Mockingbird Lane
Dallas, TX 75235
(214) 819-8560 • FAX: (214) 819-8580

Thomas Bouregy & Company, Inc.
Publishers of Avalon Books

Under its AVALON BOOKS imprint, Thomas Bouregy & Company, Inc., publishes hardcover mysteries, romances and westerns. Our books are wholesome adult fiction, suitable for family reading. There is no graphic sex or profanity in our novels.

We publish 60 books per year. Books range in length from a minimum of 40,000 words to a maximum of 50,000 words (usually about 160 to 210 manuscript pages).

SUBMISSION PROCEDURES

We do accept unagented material and multiple submissions; however, you should indicate that the proposal is a multiple submission. Please include a 2-page synopsis and the first three chapters. We regret that because of the large number of submissions that we receive, we cannot return the submitted material. If we think that your novel might be suitable for our list, we will contact you and request that you submit the entire manuscript.

Contact information:
Marcia Markland, Publisher
401 Lafayette Street
New York, NY 10003
(212) 598-0222

Thoughtful Books
Sta-Kris, Inc.

Sta-Kris, Inc. is an independent publisher who supports the marketing of their books with great energy and knowledge of the market place. Our publicist won the 1993 LMP's Publisher of the Year.

We publish nonfiction gift books that: 1.) portray universal feelings, truths, and values, or 2.) have a special occasion theme, plus small format compilations of statements about professions, issues, attitudes, etc.

Our audiences tend to be women ranging in age from their 20's on up. They generally are well read, in touch with themselves and interested in others. They exhibit a great capacity for listening to and sharing with other people.

Submissions: Query with bio, list of credits, and manuscript.

If you have any questions please contact:

Contact information:
Kathy Wagoner, President
P.O. Box 1131
Marshalltown, IA
(515) 753-4139

Tidewater Publishers

(Please refer to Cornell Maritime Press, Inc.)

The University of Nebraska Press

Mission of the University of Nebraska Press

The University of Nebraska Press, founded in 1941, seeks to encourage, develop, publish, and disseminate research, literature, and the publishing arts. The Press is the largest academic publisher in the Great Plains and a major publisher of books about that region. It is the state's largest repository of the knowledge, arts, and skills of publishing and advises the University and the people of Nebraska about book publishing. Reporting to the Vice-Chancellor for Research and having a faculty advisory board, the Press maintains scholarly standards and fosters innovations guided by refereed evaluations.

What Is the University of Nebraska Press?

The University of Nebraska Press is the second largest state university press in the nation (following only the University of California Press) in terms of titles published, and is among the top ten university presses in the nation in terms of annual sales volume.

The Press is the largest and most diversified university press between Chicago and California, and seeks to serve as the publisher for that enormous region. We proudly publish excellent writers and scholars, including those of our own university system, and foster projects on the culture and history of the state and of the entire West. As the population and influence of the West increase, we intend to keep pace, providing our university, state, and region with a publishing program equal to the energies, needs and intelligence of the area.

We currently have influential programs in Native American studies, the history of the American West, literary and cultural studies, music, and psychology. We are among the leading scholarly publishers of books in translation. We have recently inaugurated successful lists in natural science, photography, sports history, and agricultural policy and planning. Catalogs describing our new books are available, as are specialty catalogs for several of our publishing programs.

We have initiated programs in nonprint publishing, including cassettes, CD-ROM, and on-demand databases, and have an electronic media department that not only produces materials in the current technologies but is actively researching state-of-the-art technological developments to assess their likely opportunities and impact on scholarly publishing.

How to Choose a Publisher

The most important work an aspiring author must do is read. The writer who does not read will seldom become an author. An author must read for two reasons: first, to be sure that what he or she writes is genuinely new; and second, to know which publishers are interested in different kinds of books.

Publishers tend to specialize. Some concentrate on gardening, some on children's books, some on religion, computers, or stamp collecting. Look in a large library and look for recent books like the one you are writing. Write to those publishers that best match your needs. Don't waste time, energy, and postage on publishers that have never shown any interest in the kind of book that interests you. Some guidebooks, available in the reference books section of public and university libraries, that may help in this search are LMP (Literary Market Place), an annual published by R. R. Bowker and Writers Market, an annual published by Writer's Digest Books.

Remember that publishers look upon publishing as a profession. They will want you to behave professionally. Very few amateurs can tolerate the stress and effort required to be a published author.

What does the University of Nebraska Press Publish?

We publish books and scholarly journals only, and have no programs in contemporary fiction or poetry. On occasion, we reprint previously published fiction of established reputation and we have several programs to publish literary works in translation. But we cannot undertake original fiction, regardless of topic, children's books, or the work of living poets. Our mission, defined by the University through the Press Advisory Board of faculty members working in concert with the Press, is to find, evaluate, and publish in the best fashion possible, serious works of nonfiction.

How do I Approach a Publisher

We prefer to see prospectuses prior to inviting completed manuscripts. Such prospectuses should include the following: an outline, with a paragraph describing each chapter; a cover letter describing the length and focus of the manuscript; and a copy of the author's curriculum vitae or resume.

We receive more than 1,000 inquiries each year. Although we are delighted to find so much interest in our press, we can only invite submission of a small fraction of these projects, and then publish an even smaller fraction of the manuscripts actually invited. Literary translations are especially competitive.

When we receive an invited manuscript an acknowledgment of receipt is immediately sent, and we evaluate the work promptly to determine whether it would fit our list. If we think it may be appropriate, we send it to two experts in the field for their comments. If both readers endorse publication, we take the manuscript and readers' reports to our faculty committee and request approval to publish. The entire review process usually takes four to six months, and can be longer if the expert readers counsel significant changes.

We are becoming increasingly adept at using computer disks. Nevertheless, we prefer to see printed pages for any prospectus or invited manuscript. All pages should be prepared in conformity with the *Chicago Manual of Style*, 14th edition.

A guide to manuscript preparation Is available from our receptionist, or by mail upon request.

What If I Write Fiction, Poetry, or Children's Books?

Again, be sure to read dozens if not hundreds of books to understand what other people are reading and writing.

If you want to publish a book of fiction or poetry or a book for children, you must be prepared for a difficult challenge. These are the most competitive areas of publishing, with thousands of authors vying for attention.

Publishers of fiction and poetry prefer authors who have published their work in journals. Most poets and fiction writers have begun publishing in literary magazines. When they have established a reputation they can collect their poems and stories into books.

Spend time in a large library looking at literary journals like *Prairie Schooner*, *Iowa Review*, *Chicago Review*, and *TriQuarterly*. Find a journal that you like and which you believe will like you. Look for its editorial policy and rules for submission.

Where Can I Go for Help?

For addresses of literary journals see *International Directory of Little Magazines and Small Presses*. For addresses of book publishers see *Literary Market Place*.

Should you try to find an agent? Probably not until you have already published several works in different places.

What if the publisher asks for money? Be cautious and learn as much as you can about the publisher and its reputation, as you would in buying any product or service. Be sure you understand what is being offered for the money.

Should I Publish Myself?

Many of the most famous and beloved writers in American literature published their works themselves. These writers include Walt Whitman, Marianne Moore, Ezra Pound, John

Neihardt, Edgar Allan Poe, and Upton Sinclair.

Family stories and family histories are best published by the authors themselves. It is very difficult to sell books you publish yourself, but you can give books to people whose affection and attention matters to you.

To publish yourself you need to find a printer you trust. Look in the phone book to find a list of printers, then call them to see whether they can print and bind books. If they do, visit their offices and see samples of their work. Check different printers to find the best quality at the best price.

There are several guides to publishing books yourself, also, there are professional consultants who offer assistance with the process (see section 64 in LMP). Additionally there are a number of guidebooks to the individual parts of book publishing (production, marketing, publicity, etc.). Large public libraries and writers' workshops may be able to suggest appropriate and useful cities.

Can the University of Nebraska Press Help Me?

Even if we can't publish your book (we, too, must specialize) we can offer some help to citizens of Nebraska. If you receive an offer from a publisher, we will be happy to discuss the offer with you. If you have questions about publishing jargon, we can try to explain it.

If you have a specific question or would like to make an appointment, please call. To place an order for our books, we encourage readers whenever possible to patronize a local bookstore—they are indispensable links in the chain from authors to readers. If necessary, our Customer Service department can be reached at (402) 472-3584.

Preparing Your Manuscript

We at Nebraska want to publish your work as expertly and expeditiously as possible. Because each MS is unique, we cannot present the instructions herein as complete or exhaustive. Keeping in constant contact with your acquisitions editor throughout the MS-writing and -revision process will help eliminate duplicate or unproductive effort on everyone's part and will ensure that we can help and advise you at each step.

The Manuscript

Keep formatting to a minimum, but follow these general guidelines. All parts of the MS, without exception, should be double spaced in 12-point (10-cpi) Courier for ease in copyediting and proofreading. Margins all around should be set to 1 inch, with ragged-right margins and with chapter openings dropped 2 inches from the top of the page. Automatic hyphenation should be turned off. Use underlining instead of italics, and do not set text or heads in full caps. Add extra space between paragraphs only where you wish a space break in the book to indicate a change of subject. Number the pages of the MS straight through from beginning to end (do not start over from 1 in each chapter). The numbering of notes, however, should begin with 1 in each chapter; notes should be collected at the end of text, before the bibliography. Tables, figures, and other illustrations should be on unnumbered pages at the end of the MS. (If yours is a contributed volume, ask your editor about special preparation.) Your editor will supply you with a MS checklist and a review memo to which you should refer before undertaking revision of your MS. Please fill out and sign the checklist and return it with the final version of your Ms.

Since we use your MS disk for typesetting, it is critical that the disk and hard copy you submit be identical. Print the hard copy directly from the floppy disk that you submit with the ms. Complete the Disk Information Sheet and keep it with the disk. The version of your MS submitted should be the original, not a photocopy.

Illustrations

We must have in hand all art-work (illustrations, maps, graphs, tables, etc.), complete captions, and any necessary permissions before we can undertake the copyediting of your MS.

Please read the section on permissions if your MS contains illustrations. Number the illustrations with a gummed label on the back (never write directly on photos, front or back).

Obtaining complete permissions for illustrations remains the responsibility of the author. Start early, since it can take several months to secure permissions.

Photographs

Black-and-white, high-contrast glossies are necessary for sharp reproduction. If at all possible, please provide 8- by 10-inch photographs. All photographs must be accompanied by letters of permission from your source, unless, of course, you took the photograph yourself. Please read the section on Permissions carefully if your MS has photographs.

Drawings and figures

Keep the lines small and light. Extraneous details and great variation in shading and lettering (size, weight) will make the drawing or figure difficult to reproduce. The original should be sharp and legible, on high quality paper, in order to accept the reduction necessary for it to fit within the finished book page area. Please read the Permissions section carefully if your MS has drawings or figures that you have not created yourself for this MS.

Graphs

Although software abounds that enables authors to create their own graphs, at the MS stage no one can know what the design of the final book will be. For that reason, in general we prefer to generate graphs ourselves. This enables our typesetters to generate high quality graphs in a typeface compatible with the text design. Please provide all data points for graphs, whether you or someone else has generated them.

Maps

If you photographically reproduce a map (such as a historical map), follow the quality guidelines for photographs. Treat such maps as photographs in terms of permissions, as well. If you would like to generate your own maps or engage your own freelancer to prepare them, you must send samples to your editor, who will confer with the managing editor and the production manager about usability. Do not place type on your base map; place names should be printed on an overlay. In many cases we can engage a freelance cartographer to provide finished maps for your book. In that case, please provide a double-spaced list of all place names to be included on the map. Use upper- and lowercase as appropriate. This text should also be on your MS disk.

List of illustrations and caption copy

The final version of your MS should be accompanied by two separate lists on unnumbered pages: one list with brief descriptions of all illustrations, and a list of full captions that will accompany the actual illustrations in the finished book. Both the illustrations and captions lists should present the illustrations in the order in which they are to appear in the book.

Captions for images that you do not own yourself should include the credit line as stipulated in the permission letter from the owner (see the section on Permissions).

Permissions

Permissions are probably the least understood aspect of the entire publishing process.

Nonetheless, attention to permissions is essential for the timely publication of your MS. Please identify to your editor any parts of your MS that are not your own words or images or that you have published elsewhere. He or she can then help you determine if your use constitutes fair use or if you should seek permission from the rights holder. We do not recommend that you seek permission without advice from your editor, since unnecessarily requesting permission jeopardizes the concept of fair use and can ultimately defeat it.

Do seek permission as soon as you have established with your editor that you must do so for certain materials. When requesting permission, specify the working title of your MS, the publisher as the University of Nebraska Press (nonprofit), and the estimated season of publication (many permissions expire within 24 months of request). It is most helpful for us if permissions allow for nonexclusive electronic distribution, as well as for printed editions.

Permissions for illustrations must specify by negative number or by description each illustration for which permission is granted. You should request that all letters of permission be sent directly to you: please send us photocopies and retain the originals for your own records. We also need for our files photocopies of any statements defining conditions of use so that we can process stipulations for gratis copies of your book.

Fair and unfair use

Previously published written material requires permission if it is still in copyright (in general, if it was published fewer than 75 years ago) and if your use exceeds fair use. Under Current copyright law, fair use is determined not by word count but by the nature of the copyrighted work, the purpose of its use and the amount used, and the effect of its use on the value of the original work. Most quotation in scholarly books constitutes fair use, although stanzas of poetry, letters, diary entries, and other such items that constitute complete entities in themselves usually require permission.

Note that unpublished documents not your own (e.g., unpublished letters) require permission (see section on Manuscript materials).

Manuscript materials

Fair use does not apply to manuscript materials: permission is always required for unpublished writings. If the material is held by an archives permission is often required from the holder of the literary rights (i.e., the author or the author's heir) as well as from the archives. For letters, the writer rather than the recipient holds the literary rights.

Illustrations

Obtaining permissions for illustrations is time-consuming and can be expensive. Permission for illustrations, like that for manuscript material, is based on two separate and distinct legal theories; ownership of the photo, painting, etc., and ownership of the copyright. In other words, there are two forms of legal protection against unauthorized publication of a photo or piece of art: one is extended to the owner (libraries, archives, or other institutions) of the item, and the other is extended to the holder of the copyright (if there is one), normally the photographer or artist or that person's heir. That a photograph (or other item of visual art) carries no copyright notice does not necessarily mean that it is in the public domain. It is your responsibility to ascertain its status from the Institution holding it. The institution in turn will alert you if further permission is required from an owner of publishing rights. Permission is required for the use of certain materials held by agencies of the federal government such as the National Archives and the Library of Congress. Again, if you are uncertain about whether you need to request permission, check with your editor or the managing editor.

Your own previously published material

If more than a page or two of your MS substantially duplicates material you have published elsewhere, you must obtain permission from the copyright holder (usually the original publisher) for its use. Some scholarly journals specify in their publishing agreements that the author holds all further publishing fights. If that is the case, please send us a photocopy of the agreement or other correspondence indicating that and identify the full bibliographic information on the earlier publication so that we can credit the source appropriately.

Before You Send Us the Final MS

We would like to publish your work in the most expeditious and successful fashion possible. However, the success of our effort depends in large part on your delivery of an accurate, complete, and meticulously prepared MS. Please ensure that we receive in one package everything you want to appear in your book; all text, including acknowledgments and a dedication if appropriate, and all artwork. All necessary letters of permission and conditions-of-use statements should accompany the MS. The computer disk you send should contain the final version of your MS, and you should print the final hard copy from that disk. Before you send in the final draft of your MS, we also urge you to do the following:

Ensure that the title page has your name spelled exactly as you wish it to appear in your book.

Verify the contents page against the chapter titles on the chapter opening pages.

Verify all direct quotations and all source citations and bibliographic entries.

Check credit lines against corresponding letters of permission to ensure that you have met any obligations for specific wording.

Double-check the lists of illustrations, maps, tables, etc., against the caption copy and against the artwork or tables themselves to ensure they correspond.

Final checklist

Along with your final MS draft, we should have on file the following:

- computer disk with all text files (and graphics files as appropriate), preferably in PC/IBM format
- disk Information Sheet
- Previously Published Work form
- University of Nebraska Press Author Checklist
- letters of permission for all artwork, all previously published text, and all MS materials not your own (except those identified by the Press as failing under fair-use definitions)

Contact information:
The University of Nebraska Press
312 North 14th Street
Lincoln NE 68588-0484
(402) 472-3581 • FAX: (402) 472-0308

VGM Career Horizons

(Please refer to NTC Publishing Group.)

William Morrow & Company
Tambourine Books

Thank you for your interest, we would be glad to consider your work.

We ask to see completed manuscripts. If your work is illustrated, we are glad to see a typed text, rough dummy, and a sample finished picture.

Contact information:
Ben Schafer, Editorial Assistant
1350 Avenue of the Americas
New York, NY 10019
(212) 261-6661

WRS Publishing

WRS Publishing, a commercial publisher with eight to twelve new titles a year, invites submissions from both new and experienced authors. We look for well written books for an educated audience that make an important contribution in the fields of character-building, education, family life, and cultural criticism.

We are interested primarily in adult nonfiction, but we publish selected children's books as well.

WRS Publishing

WRS Publishing bought out its first trade book in 1991. Its parent company, WRS Group, Inc., which was founded in 1967, produces health and educational products that are used in schools and hospitals across the country.

As a small press, WRS Publishing offers writers several advantages. We make acquisition decisions promptly, and we work closely with each author to produce a well edited and professionally packaged book quickly and efficiently. Above all, every book we publish is important to us.

The foremost expert on a book is its author. WRS Publishing will therefore work with you to tailor a marketing plan to place your book in the hands of those who need and want it. We solicit reviews and sales of subsidiary rights from scores and even hundreds of sources while aggressively marketing your book to bookstores, libraries, and directly to readers.

HOW TO SUBMIT A PROPOSAL

We invite you to send us a chapter outline or other brief synopsis of your book, a sample chapter if available, and a cover letter describing the book, its intended audience, and its unique and compelling features. Please do not send a complete manuscript. Simultaneous submissions are welcome. We shall try to respond to your inquiry within two weeks, at which point we may ask for further information on which to base our final decision.

Please send your proposal to:

Contact information:

Thomas Spence, Editor-in-Chief
P.O. Box 21207
Waco, TX 76710
(817) 776-6461 • FAX: (817) 757-1454

Young Readers Christian Library

The Basics: All manuscripts considered for the Young Reader's Christian Library (YRCL) series should present overall a conservative, evangelical Christian world view. The heroes and heroines depicted in the series should have led outstanding Christian lives that would serve as worthy examples to young readers. Manuscripts that do not reflect these traits will be returned to the author(s).

Specifics: Manuscripts must total 16,000 words, approximately 147 words per manuscript page. The subject of the manuscript may be contemporary (alive today or post-World War II), a Bible character, or an historical figure. Language should be geared to a sixth-grade reading level. Considering that age group, an action-oriented, fast-paced style is preferred.

Things To Consider: The need for a personal commitment to and relationship with Jesus Christ—the most important decision young people must make—should be readily apparent. Our young readers and their families consider themselves born again Christians. One of the reasons parent and grandparents and other adults choose YRCL books for their children and young friends over other reading material is because our books confirm their values and beliefs.

Things to Avoid: Avoid such controversial topics as the following, should they present themselves in the story line:

1. Spirit baptism (and time of, at conversion vs. second experience of grace)
2. Water baptism (meaning of and time of, children or adults)
3. Gifts of the Spirit (e.g., are tongues still around?)
4. End times (setting dates)
5. Lord's Supper (ordinance vs. sacrament)
6. Women's ordination
7. Christian perfection
8. Transferring qualities of Jesus—or passages in the Bible that refer to Jesus—to heroes in books. This also applies to Mary, Jesus' earthly mother.

Avoid strictly any language that could be considered foul. Euphemisms such as heck, darn, and so on should not be used. To many of our readers and their parents/grandparents these words are substitutes for curses. Although the main characters should be Christians, they need not be saints. Their actions should be consistent with Christian teaching.

One Final Point: One particular biblical message should be threaded throughout if possible. This message can be presented from many different characters, through symbols, and so on.

To Submit: If you believe you have a manuscript that would fit YRCL guidelines, please send us a cover letter in which you introduce yourself and your writing/publishing experience, a summary of the story, and three to four randomly selected chapters. All inquiries and materials should be sent to the following:

Contact information:
Editorial Department
P.O. Box 710
Uhrichsville, OH 44683

A Division of Harper Collins*Publishers*

Zondervan Publishing House

Please provide the following information on 8 1/2" by 11" paper, single-spaced, typed when submitting book proposals and book manuscripts.

Your name.

- Type it exactly as you would like it to appear on the cover and title page.

Information about yourself.

- Prepare a vita, including your:
- address
- telephone number
- present position
- educational background

- biographical information
- previous publications
- Especially emphasize how all of this qualifies you to write the book.

Tentative title of the book. Include:

- subtitle, and
- possible alternative titles

Description of the book (2-4 pages). Here you should describe the book and make a strong case for why the book must be written and published.

- Clarify the focus, purpose, and argument of the book. What is its thesis? What are you advocating, defending, or otherwise trying to achieve in the book?
- Who is the intended readership? What level are you aiming at—(1) average Christian layperson; (2) informed layperson/lower division college; (3) upper division college/introductory seminary; (4) advanced seminary/graduate students/professors; (5) pastors; (6) other professionals in Christian ministries?
- The rationale for writing this book—Why is the book needed?
- Are there other competing titles? If so, what are they and how will your book be superior to or different from them?
- Does the book have realistic potential for textbook adoption or as a required supplemental text? If so, in what courses?
- What will be its unique contribution?

As you write, remember that you are trying to sell us on a book idea. Give a realistic but positive description of what you propose. If you cannot build a good case for why the book should be published, perhaps you should reconsider whether it is worth your time and effort to write it.

Table of contents. At this stage we understand that the table of contents is tentative. Nevertheless,

- give tentative chapter titles
- give a brief outline of the chapter, or
- give a brief paragraph that will explain the focus and development of the chapter

Proposed completion date of the manuscript.

Writing sample. In some circumstances, especially if you have not written for Zondervan before, we would like to have 20-40 sample pages from the proposed book. These should include pages that are:

- typical of the book as a whole
- especially critical to your argument
- potentially controversial, or
- a good overview of the book

We prefer to work with authors in the early stages of new book projects, and the instructions above show you how to put together a good book proposal. However, if you have not followed this procedure and already have a completed manuscript, we are certainly willing to review it.

See instructions below for important mechanical details. If you will follow them, it will make matters much easier for us as we review either your book proposal or book manuscript.

Please observe the following details when submitting book proposals or book manuscripts:

1. Book proposals should be single-spaced, on one side of the page, with one-inch margins on all sides.
2. Number pages consecutively throughout the entire manuscript. Do not have separate pagination for each chapter. Place your "footnotes" after each chapter as endnotes. This makes them easier to edit and easier to insert at the proper place later.
3. Use an ordinary, substantial bond paper that will run through a copy machine. It is

standard practice for us to make one or more photocopies of a manuscript to send to reviewers. The kinds of paper just described will not feed automatically through our photocopy machine. (Copies are made for review purposes only.)

4. Clear photocopies or printouts are acceptable if they are on paper as described in number 3 and if they are of letter quality. We do not accept dot-matrix printouts.

5. **Do not** submit sheets that are stapled, punched with binder holes, torn, crumpled, or folded. If you have made corrections in your manuscript by cutting and taping or pasting, please send us photocopies of these sheets, not the originals. Sheets "abused" in the above ways do not feed through our copy machine and are therefore unacceptable.

6. **Do not** submit your manuscript in a binder of any kind. Loose sheets are preferred.

7. Send your manuscript by First Class Mail. Many authors have found that it is a false economy to send it any other way. If your manuscript is so bulky that it just does not seem feasible to send it First Class, we suggest that you send it by United Parcel Service, Federal Express, or Airborne Express. Above all, **do not** use Book Rate. If you would like to have the manuscript returned to you, please include stamps or a check to cover return postage.

Finally, please send book proposals and manuscripts to:

Contact information:
Stanley N. Gundry, Editor-in-Chief, Book Group
5300 Patterson S.E.
Grand Rapids, MI 49530
(616) 698-6900

Topic Index

-A-

-B-

-C-

-E-

-F-

-G-

-H-

Nonfiction

Nudism

Nursing, cross-cultural

-O-

Occult

Oddities

Online Databases

Outdoors

-Q-

-R-

Rural America

Rural Kentucky

-S-

Satire

Scene Books

Science

Science Fiction

Security

Self Help

Self-Sufficiency

Senior Citizens

Sexuality

Shelter/Homes

Short Stories

Singles

Small Business Issues

Soccer

Society

-T-

-U- -V-

-W-

-X- -Y- -Z-

General Index

A

B

C

D

E

F

G

H

I

J

K

L

M

S

T

U

V

W

Y

Z

Submission Tracking Sheet

Photocopy these two pages together at 98% to fit on an 8½" x 11" sheet.

Title: ______________________________

Notes:

Publisher: ______________________________

Date submitted: ______________________ **Multiple Submission?** ______ **No** ______ **Yes**

Date to follow up: __________ **Date followed up:** __________ **Follow up note:** __________

Date accepted: __________ **Pub date:** __________ **Payment due date:** __________

Payment amount: __________ **Clips received:** __________ **Rejected date:** __________

Publisher: ______________________________

Date submitted: ______________________ **Multiple Submission?** ______ **No** ______ **Yes**

Date to follow up: __________ **Date followed up:** __________ **Follow up note:** __________

Date accepted: __________ **Pub date:** __________ **Payment due date:** __________

Payment amount: __________ **Clips received:** __________ **Rejected date:** __________

Publisher: ______________________________

Date submitted: ______________________ **Multiple Submission?** ______ **No** ______ **Yes**

Date to follow up: __________ **Date followed up:** __________ **Follow up note:** __________

Date accepted: __________ **Pub date:** __________ **Payment due date:** __________

Payment amount: __________ **Clips received:** __________ **Rejected date:** __________

Publisher: ______

Date submitted: ______ **Multiple Submission?** ___ No ___ Yes

Date to follow up: ______ **Date followed up:** ______ **Follow up note:** ______

Date accepted: ______ **Pub date:** ______ **Payment due date:** ______

Payment amount: ______ **Clips received:** ______ **Rejected date:** ______

Publisher: ______

Date submitted: ______ **Multiple Submission?** ___ No ___ Yes

Date to follow up: ______ **Date followed up:** ______ **Follow up note:** ______

Date accepted: ______ **Pub date:** ______ **Payment due date:** ______

Payment amount: ______ **Clips received:** ______ **Rejected date:** ______

Publisher: ______

Date submitted: ______ **Multiple Submission?** ___ No ___ Yes

Date to follow up: ______ **Date followed up:** ______ **Follow up note:** ______

Date accepted: ______ **Pub date:** ______ **Payment due date:** ______

Payment amount: ______ **Clips received:** ______ **Rejected date:** ______

Publisher: ______

Date submitted: ______ **Multiple Submission?** ___ No ___ Yes

Date to follow up: ______ **Date followed up:** ______ **Follow up note:** ______

Date accepted: ______ **Pub date:** ______ **Payment due date:** ______

Payment amount: ______ **Clips received:** ______ **Rejected date:** ______

About The Editor

JOHN MUTCHLER IS A SELF-DESCRIBED MARKETER who claims to hold the world record for time spent chasing writer's guidelines. When not out on a hot and dusty Texas trail in search of the next guideline, he writes and produces promotional material and product user documentation for his day-job boss, writes promotional copy as a freelancer for an occasional commercial client or two, and willingly volunteers to do a lot of work around the house for his night-job boss. His continuing education course titled "Get Published Now!" made its debut at The University of North Texas in the spring of '97—an event that, sad to say, cut into the time he had available to work for his night-job boss.